TRENCHARD

TRENCHARD

by

Andrew Boyle

COLLINS · *St. James's Place, London* · *1962*

Preface

Lord Trenchard asked me to undertake this biography in the early summer of 1955, some ten months before he died. Though he was blind, hard of hearing and enfeebled in body, his mental faculties were as sharp as ever. I had come to his notice because of certain controversial passages in my first book, the life of Group-Captain Leonard Cheshire, v.c. These were read to him, he liked them and sent for me to say that he had always regarded controversy as the very breath of existence and to pay me the still greater compliment of asking me to become his biographer. Subsequently he placed his time unreservedly at my disposal until our last interview which took place on 8th February, 1956.

Thereafter hardly a day passed without my spending several hours alone with him. It was an exciting, invigorating and intensely rewarding experience. The six note-books I filled with his recollections, impressions and judgments of men and events provided me with an important source of information and an insight into his remarkable character.

My first and deepest debt, therefore, is to Trenchard himself; my next to his widow, the late Lady Trenchard, who helped me as much after he died as their surviving son, the present Viscount, did after her death in 1959. I also wish to thank other members of the family for assistance at various stages in my researches. At the end of this book I have added a fuller explanatory note on sources. Here I shall only say that Trenchard accumulated during his public and private life an unusually large number of official and personal papers; and except for the voluminous files of correspondence with the men who, in his own phrase, "either helped or hindered me in my career," these were mostly unclassified and unsorted. To this quarry of fresh material the Trenchard family has given me free access.

Partly because it was in his nature, partly also as a result
of the circumstances of his childhood, Trenchard became a
man who despised and shunned all forms of self-advertisement.
He had an even more pronounced aversion for the techniques
of modern publicity. Since he possessed at the same time an
almost ungovernable knack of exciting public controversy, his
actions were often misunderstood and occasionally misrepresented. It might be said that he thrived on opposition;
but it should be added that his reputation suffered in consequence, and that public appreciation of his achievements
tended to diminish as he grew older and the memory of them
to fade. For the habit acquired in youth of making no concessions whatever to himself, and of answering criticism with
reticence, seemed to grow more stubborn with advancing
years. Is it surprising that to most men of my generation,
born between the two World Wars, the very name of
Trenchard should now convey so little?

It will be shown that he had his temperamental foibles,
that he sometimes misjudged his opponents, and that he made
mistakes. I have not tried to conceal any of them in this book.
My purpose has been to display them side by side with the
more positive qualities of this truly prodigious man of vision.
This volume has been over five years in the making, and my
attempts to unravel both the character and the achievement
have led me far afield. In direct interviews and correspondence, more than 600 witnesses contributed to my knowledge
of the subject; and if, for obvious reasons, I cannot here
mention all of them by name, the reader who perseveres will
be able to assess what I owe them individually and collectively.

But I must acknowledge my particular gratitude to the
late Viscount Weir for permission to examine and use his
private papers; to Lady Reid and others who let me consult
some of the note-books of Maurice Baring; to Lady Henderson, the late Wing-Commander Marson, the late Charles
Evans, the late Lord Quickswood (formerly Lord Hugh
Cecil), the late Lord Templewood (formerly Sir Samuel
Hoare), the late Wing-Commander Gerald Maxwell, and the
late Mr. Colin Brook, literary executor of the first Viscount
Rothermere, for similar aid; and to Professor A. L. Lawrence,
Captain B. H. Liddell Hart and Lord Hankey, each of whom
led me or gave me free access to original information of sub-
stance. I must also thank Sir Winston Churchill, Lord

Beaverbrook and Viscount Davidson for written or oral evidence which enabled me the better to form my own judgment on certain elusive points of importance, as well as Sir Christopher Bullock and Group-Captain Smyth Pigott for their valuable testimony on Trenchard's unexpected return as Chief of the Air Staff in early 1919.

The burden of evaluating several matters in Trenchard's Air Staff and Admiralty documents has been considerably eased for me by the kind advice of many competent witnesses, including Marshals of the R.A.F. Sir John Salmond, Sir Edward Ellington, Lord Newall, Viscount Portal, Lord Tedder, Sir Arthur Harris, Sir John Slessor and Sir Dermot Boyle; Air Chief-Marshals Sir John Steel, Lord Dowding, Sir Edgar Ludlow Hewitt and Sir Ralph Cochrane; Air Marshal Sir John Baldwin, and the late Air Vice-Marshal Sir Charles Langcroft.

As this is primarily a biography, and neither a history of the Royal Air Force nor a study in strategy, I have refused to be drawn into the detailed discussion of large, rambling and endlessly contentious topics which not even qualified historians appear to be always capable of considering with detachment. It will be for future generations to decide Trenchard's exact degree of responsibility for the failings and the virtues of the fighting service which he created; that it saved the British people from virtually certain defeat in 1941, and played a major and possibly decisive part in the conduct of the Second World War after that date, is or should be well known already.

I must thank both authors and publishers for allowing me to quote extracts from the following works: *The World Crisis* by Sir Winston Churchill (Odhams Press); *War in the Air* (vols. 1-6) by N. A. Jones and Sir Walter Raleigh (The Clarendon Press); *Wind, Sand and Stars* by Antoine de Saint-Exupéry (Heinemann); *The Unknown Prime Minister* by Robert Blake (Eyre and Spottiswoode).

My final words of thanks must go to Christina who bore with me so gallantly from the daunting outset to the final draft of the manuscript, and to my friend Wing-Commander A. M. M. Hill whose talents as a historian would have roused Trenchard's admiration.

Putney, London, 1955-61

Contents

Illustrations

ILLUSTRATIONS

Maps

Prologue

The valley was indistinguishable from a thousand others in the Western Transvaal. It was not shown on the maps issued to the troops of Brigadier-General Geoffrey Barton, the commander of the district about the railway loop to Klerksdorp. The Boers had recently been active; and a number of derailments and similar acts of sabotage had caused Barton to leave Krugersdorp at the head of the largest composite formation ever seen in that desolate stretch of veld.

The valley looked deserted. It was a place of little tactical consequence in itself. It had no name, though the owners of the farmhouse on its surprisingly fertile floor called their home Dwarsvlei. The most sedulous student of military affairs will search the history books in vain for any mention, even as an obscure footnote, of the minor action fought there on 9th October, 1900. The Battle of Dwarsvlei was just another incident in a long and inconclusive series of incidents that brought no glory to either side—and only tragedy to individuals.

Tragedy came to several men in the warm and windless dawn of that South African summer's day. It came first to the young officer who had engineered the incident. His name was Hugh Montague Trenchard, a captain in the second battalion of the Royal Scots Fusiliers and the leader of a mixed company of mounted infantry attached to Barton's Brigade. The bullet which thudded into his chest, pitching him flat on his face in the dust a few yards away from the farmhouse door, might have been a lucky ricochet or a perfect bull's-eye scored by a sniper. It was an academic point. Private Donald McDermid was merely certain as he peered into the glazing eyes and wiped away the blood spurting from the wounded man's mouth that Trenchard had picked his last fight. McDermid, his groom, had seen men die violently before.

Two hours earlier, the chase had begun in the half-light, when a Boer commando, one hundred and fifty strong, was surprised in their encampment about ten miles back on the rocky trail from

15

Krugersdorp. Trenchard and his Australian bushmen pursued them
to the rim of this valley. When every obvious escape route had been
sealed, he issued final instructions, chose four men to accompany
him, and slithered down the near slope, under cover.

"Don't start shooting until I give the signal," he said.

There was no signal. The bullet felled him too soon. And the
watchers on the heights could hold their fire no longer. The
Australians charged furiously towards the farmhouse, thirsting for
revenge. When the Ayrshire Yeomanry rode up with a detachment
of the Brigade about an hour later, the action had ended, the farmhouse was in flames. Remembering Roberts's well-known directive
that farms should be burnt only if used by guerillas for warlike
purposes, the Australians had been in no mood for second thoughts.

Half a dozen Boers surrendered. The rest had withdrawn without
loss. One or two Australians had flesh wounds. As the ambulance
wagon rumbled up the slope and away from the farm called
Dwarsvlei, now enveloped in a funeral pyre of smoke, Buxton, the
Australian doctor, was doubtful whether Trenchard would survive
the ride to the railhead.

2

Trenchard did not agree, but he could not speak. He had been
semi-conscious throughout the engagement. He had even noticed
the horror on McDermid's face as the groom knelt by his side; he
had listened to the ticking of the clock on the wall of the farmhouse
kitchen where they had carried him until the sound was submerged
in a flood of unbearable pain. Consciousness returned while the
doctor was openly discussing his slender chances of surviving. It
was the Boer women who asked point-blank: "Will he live?"

The doctor's reply had been inaudible, so Trenchard startled
them all by nodding his head. His groom's voice rose, sharp with
astonishment and delight:

"Christ Almighty, he's got no right to be listening." Buxton had
dressed his wound; and in the jolting wagon the doctor felt his pulse
several times. Now and then, as the wheels bumped over boulders,
Trenchard felt himself transfixed by searing shafts of pain. The
sensation of being pierced through on a red-hot spit would flow over
him in a wave, then he would sink back into a trough of giddy relief,
until the jarring roused him again. He could not even groan when
the dressings worked loose.

It was the eyes of Trenchard, burning with a kind of preternatural brightness, which worried the doctor. They were like live coals in a mask of wax. Nearly half a century afterwards, Buxton heard from the lips of this indestructible being, who had walked into an ambush prepared for his enemies and lived to tell the tale, of the incongruous thought that kept recurring during the lucid intervals of that bumpy ride.

" I was trying to speak with my eyes. It was all I could do. And I envied women the natural gift they have of talking with theirs."

For two days Trenchard lay unconscious in a hospital bed at Krugersdorp. The surgeons confirmed that there seemed no hope of saving him. The bullet had pierced his left lung. And through a tube they removed from the pleura six and a half pints of thickening blood. There had been nothing else to do but wait for him to die, as expected, of shock or blood poisoning. But Trenchard clung to life with a tenacity that confounded everyone.

He dozed away most of his first day of awakening and was roused at night by a cacophony of scurrying feet, excited shouts and heavy objects crashing. It was like a nightmare prolonging itself into feverish semi-consciousness. For the heat and the dull roaring and crackling of flames vaguely recalled the last confused scene at Dwarsvlei. Four orderlies came in; each grabbed a corner of the bed, and lifted him to an open window. The hospital, they explained, had caught fire. They strapped him down, eased him over the ledge, and lowered him from the top-floor window to the ground on a makeshift cradle. Through the flickering red darkness they drove him to an emergency centre for casualties on the danger list.

Three weeks later they moved him again to Johannesburg. There he regained the use of his voice, though the effort of talking was painful. The doctors were pleased. The wound, they said, was healing well. Only when he rose for the first time and tried to put his feet under him did Trenchard momentarily yield to a pang of blind despair. He was half-paralysed from the waist downwards: he had lost the use of his legs.

3

It was not the first blow which fate had so far dealt this young captain; it was incalculably the cruellest. There were moments during his convalescence when he could have wished that his will to live had not been quite so strong, or that the bullet fired by the hidden sniper had killed him outright. A soldier with nothing left to live for, a man of mysterious background with some acquaintances and no real friends, he seemed already to have reached the end of his brief career, an unwanted cripple.

Yet the hour of darkest ordeal became this rare opportunist's hour of self-recognition. There were qualities in him which scorned to acknowledge defeat, or to discuss in afterdays his calculated triumph over infirmity. Dwarsvlei, the place apparently selected by a capricious fate for his inglorious decease, no longer exists. The name would have conveyed nothing to most of the distinguished mourners who thronged Westminster Abbey fifty-six years later for his funeral. Even the memory of that remote valley, where an invincible toughness of mind and body lifted him up and over the threshold of history, remained to the end one of Hugh Montague Trenchard's most jealously guarded secrets. The time has come to unlock the secrets with the memories, and to portray the enigmatic spirit of the extraordinary man behind both as he truly was.

1. A Victorian Child

Trenchard was born on 3rd February, 1873, a day of violent winds that swept across the West Country and most of southern England. There is no record that his father, Henry Montague Trenchard, saw any omen in the torrential rain that lashed the windows of his elegant Victorian mansion on Haines Hill, Taunton, while the child was being delivered upstairs. Omens had no place in his well-appointed world, though a corner was reserved for dreams.

Neither parent had reservations about calling the boy Hugh. The name had appeared on stray branches of the Trenchard tree for four centuries at least; and his father had always taken an inordinate pride in pedigree. Who could tell? Perhaps this son would live to refurbish the splendours of an ancestral past that was wearing thinner than the neighbours knew.

Henry was not particularly thrustful or ambitious. His family, his home, and the solicitor's practice which supported both, filled his conventional horizons. Respected by the town's business-men, acknowledged by the "county," his standing among colleagues in Hammett Street, where most of the lawyers had their offices, was secure. He shared Number Ten with Edgar Watson, a younger man of means from Kidderminster whom he had lately brought into partnership, and was punctilious about routine. He would reflect without vanity that he had done wisely to sell his army commission while still in his thirties and take up law.

Hammett Street had changed little outwardly since Henry's great-grandfather had put up his brass plate on the door of Number Ten towards the end of the eighteenth century. The practice began to thrive, enabling Henry's grandfather to move from the flat above the office to a separate establishment after the death of his first wife, Elizabeth Montague, who had borne him half a dozen children and bequeathed a family name as honourable as his own.

A long lifetime later, and with something more of a flourish, Henry followed his grandfather's example, exchanging the Haines

Hill house for a larger property at Norton FitzWarren, only three miles from the centre of Taunton. His wife, Georgiana, was delighted. Comely, highly strung, and determined, a kinswoman of the Aberdeenshire Gordons and Lumsdens, she cared little for the constraining social atmosphere of provincial town life. The recent arrival of twins, a boy and a girl, had increased her brood to five. A country house within easy reach of Taunton would offer the family more freedom of movement, and widen the circle of her acquaintances among the gentry.

At the time of the move Hugh Trenchard was two, Katharine, the first-born, six, Alex, his elder brother, five; they revelled in the excitement of exploring their new home and its extensive grounds, for Courtlands was half-farm and half-manor. Hugh's earliest memories were of bird-nesting along the hedgerows, of jogging down leafy lanes in the family carriage, of the cold feel of his father's sporting gun which he learnt to handle before he went to school. He developed into a long-legged, sturdy child, with black, unruly hair on a head as notably small as his father's, and with the same penetrating blue-grey eyes. He loved stalking, and gradually acquired an uncanny skill at picking off rabbits with his most treasured toy, a small rifle, a present on his eighth birthday. He was only nine when he brought down a kingfisher on the wing, his intense pleasure being clouded with regret that, of all birds, it had to be his favourite.

The decisive influence in the home was his mother, whose wickerwork crinoline he borrowed once, and never again, as a cage for his budgerigars. Hugh worshipped her at a respectful distance; a sterner disciplinarian than her good-natured husband, Georgiana had masterful ways. Within the stiff conventions of the age, which she religiously obeyed, she enjoyed entertaining, being entertained, and performing good works among the poor of the district. She would drive for miles, in all weathers, to isolated cottages, dispensing clothing and hot soup. Sometimes, as a distraction from lessons, Hugh would accompany her.

The children had a resident tutor, treated her badly, and learnt little. Discipline was lax, incentive to study entirely lacking, for the tutor was neither firm nor subtle enough to break down their mischievous resistance to organised instruction. Dorothy, the sixth and last child, was still in her pram when her elder brothers and sisters began to endure the charade of conversing in French and German for two days a week, whatever they happened to be doing. Unnoticed by parents with few intellectual pretentions, their sense of fun repeatedly burst under the strain. As a result, the linguistic attainments of the Trenchard children were as paltry as their command of the three R's. Hugh's one absorbing interest, which owed more to his father than to his teacher, was family history; and by the age of ten he had become a devout if somewhat indiscriminating ancestor-worshipper.

2

It gave him a thrill of importance to realise, for a start, that the Trenchards claimed descent from Raoul de Trenchant, a knight who had crossed from Normandy to fight on the winning side at Hastings, and whose name is listed to this day on a tablet in the village church of Dives, not far from Caen, among the close companions of William the Conqueror. For five centuries the family were feudal landowners in the Isle of Wight, Hampshire and Dorset. It was from John Trenchard, a sixteenth-century younger son of the house, that the Taunton and Somerset branch directly sprang, and like most of his forebears, John was not distinguished for unswerving allegiance to the Crown.

Of many recorded instances of simple lack of worldly ambition which characterised his breed, one in particular appealed to Hugh Trenchard. In 1505, a fleet of galleons commanded by King Philip of Castille put in at Weymouth. The armada had scarcely left Flanders on a surprise expedition against Aragon when it was driven down-Channel by gales and forced to seek shelter. Sir Thomas Trenchard, the decidedly suspicious High Sheriff of Dorset, rode down to meet his unbidden visitor, dispatched a messenger to inform the king at Windsor, and meanwhile offered the Spanish ruler and his queen hospitality at Wolfeton Hall, the family seat.

According to the family annals, conversation at first was distressingly halting. Sir Thomas knew no Spanish, his guests no English. Then he remembered a ne'er-do-well kinsman who had tried unsuccessfully to make money trading in Spain. John Russell proved an able interpreter. A week went by, then word came that Henry VII would receive Philip at Windsor. Before leaving, the Spanish monarch made his host a gracious offer:

" Name any favour you wish," he said in effect. " I myself will ask your King to grant it."

Such condescension was too much for the prickly self-esteem of a Trenchard, in his own home of all places. " I fear I want for nothing, sire," he said abruptly. " Thank God I am an independent man."

But Philip was not to be denied, and bade Trenchard think again.

" Lands, I have much, money I have enough," Sir Thomas said at length. " Your countrymen do wonderful woodcarving. I should like some for my house. Then there is my kinsman, Russell, who cannot support himself and seems to believe I should. To help him would be most kind."

Russell was duly recommended to the King; a minor position in the Royal Household was found for him; under Henry VIII he became a favourite at court, acquiring Woburn Abbey and nobility after the confiscation of the monasteries. It may be said without exaggeration that the Dukes of Bedford owed the foundation of their dynasty and fortunes to the haughty whim of a Trenchard.

Under the Stuarts, the family resumed the practice of disputing the divine right of rulers to do as they pleased, helping to secure for Cromwell the towns of Dorchester, Weymouth, Portland, Lyme, Wareham and Poole and joining in the siege of Corfe Castle, the chief royalist stronghold in Dorset.

John Trenchard, the Member of Parliament for Wareham, was one of the assessors appointed in 1648 to try Charles I, but absented himself from the hearings and did not sign the death warrant. The family chronicler admits that this was how " he saved himself and his estates."

The sole member of the family to become a Privy Councillor, a Secretary of State and an advisor on foreign affairs was Sir John Trenchard in the reign of William III, whom Bishop Burnet praised for having "a right of understanding of these, being a calm and sedate man," but also reproved for displaying "a great regard for the stars and too little for religion."

None of the later Trenchards achieved distinction as soldiers or lawyers, the professions they commonly followed; some, including an extravagant Regency rake called George and a nineteenth-century daughter of the house who eloped and gave birth to Jack Sheppard, the Stepney cat burglar, achieved a passing notoriety. When the last male representative in the direct line died without issue in 1830, the family traditions, if not its lost treasures and titles, passed to the senior cadet branch in Somerset. Wolfeton Hall was sold; but the sheeted ghost of a seventeenth-century Lady Trenchard, who chose to cut her throat rather than welcome Judge Jeffreys to her table during the Bloody Assize, did not cease to haunt the place. To-day this beautiful house near Dorchester is divided into flats.

It would have been unnatural for a boy of Hugh Trenchard's lively fancy not to put his ancestors on pedestals; it was harder to deceive himself about the prospects of emulating them in a world that laid too much emphasis on education. His parents, possibly misled by the teachers of Allens Preparatory School, near Botley, in Hampshire, where he went to board at the age of ten, thought him clever but lazy. He knew otherwise. Extremely quick at arithmetic, he was slow at every other subject. He disliked the mechanical drudgery. He grudged the hours spent poring over the dead pages of text books as time plundered from life. His father and mother were unmoved by the boy's uninhibited boasting about his limitations. They had long decided on a military career for him. Georgiana favoured the Royal Navy and had her way. In 1884, Hugh entered Hammond's, a select "cramming" establishment near Dover, for entrants to *H.M.S. Britannia* at Dartmouth.

There, it appears, the boy's dislike of being forcibly fed with useless knowledge betrayed itself. Though mathematics presented few difficulties, he had no ear for words and his writing was atrocious. The illogicalities of English spelling endlessly baffled him. When the correct letter arrangements were set beside his own he would ask himself with brooding belligerence: " Why? " Perhaps as an assertion of disbelief, he went on spelling the word "yi? " for many years.

His parents' disappointment when he failed to qualify for Dartmouth astonished him. For their sakes he tried to show contrition. The heaviest crosses of childhood are the crosses of misunderstanding, and the Trenchards seemed unaware of the impression on Hugh's mind of the family past he had heard so much about. Its values were more precious to him than those of the world about him. " Know Thyself," the Trenchard motto, had been a rule of life for many of his ancestors. He had consciously adopted it as the prop of his disconcerting honesty. He longed to be as independent and as true to himself as the best of them had been.

This unusual source of consolation he kept to himself. But on one occasion, in 1884, when the disgrace of failure had lifted slightly, the boy inadvertently shocked his father. They were in London for the summer season, staying at a Kensington hotel near Brompton Road. The first time he went out walking with his father, they happened to pass the site of Harrods' store, which had been gutted by fire the previous winter. The front was boarded up; men in overalls were at work on scaffolding high above the roadway. Hugh remembered the place when it had been a row of two or three unpretentious shops; in a sense it had grown up with him; and its owner, Charles Digby Harrod, had long ago been admitted to Hugh's private gallery of living heroes, alongside his ancestors.

Hugh's father seemed slightly displeased by his intentness as he stood staring up at the scaffolding. Surely, he remonstrated, work-men were common enough even in Taunton.

In an ill-contrived effort to explain his feelings, Hugh blurted out more than he intended. With a last look at the busy constructors across the road, he turned to his father and said: " One day I'll build a Harrods of my own."

There were mild repercussions. To become a tradesman was an unworthy, an unthinkable ambition. Hugh was warned that that dull fate might one day be his unless he applied himself to his books.

They had entered his name at an army crammer's; and during the months he spent at home waiting for admittance the arcadian contentment he had formerly known eluded him. Childhood already lay behind this awkward boy of less than average academic achieve-ment who was none the less gifted with a sensitive insight beyond his years. The burdens which his parents had been carrying, unsuspected, had suddenly become clearer to him.

There was nothing he could say or do to ease the arthritis which seemed to be slowly crippling his mother. She had always been so active that the family, while fussing over her aches and pains, had regarded these as largely imaginary. It was an age which expected exaggerated sensibility of its women folk, and the affectation of being "delicate" seemed little more than a reflection of Georgiana's temperament. That she might really be in poor health had not seriously occurred to any of her children before.

Hugh noticed that his father, too, had become oddly worried and irritable. Tending an invalid wife was possibly only one of his troubles; of the others he could not speak. Then May, the frailer of the twins, to whom Hugh had been devoted, died of diptheria. During her illness an eerie stillness had settled on the house, with white sheets on the bedroom doors and the doctor a regular visitor. The end came one summer morning; and Hugh was not ashamed of his tears as they lowered the tiny flower-covered coffin into the earth at Norton Fitzwarren churchyard.

The paradise of Courtlands could never be the same again. That he knew by instinct. The piercing quality of this earliest sorrow lodged in his memory like a jagged crumb of glass among the anonymous debris of lesser things. When his trunk was packed a few weeks later, and he left for the crammer where his elder brother, Alex, was already a student, Hugh Trenchard felt older and sadder than his thirteen and a half years.

3

For reasons quite unconnected with learning, Hugh Trenchard soon found his feet at Hill Lands, the cramming establishment at Wargrave, in Berkshire. It was easier there than at Hammond's to conceal among 120 boarders, all older than himself, his aversion for assimilating knowledge by rote. Disdain for lessons and teachers was common form; yet the Reverend Albert Pritchard had not earned by accident his reputation as one of the best crammers of backward aspirants for army commissions in the kingdom.

The local people pitied him, feeling perhaps that any cleric who tried to combine the salvation of souls in Wargrave with the instruction of a mob of wayward youths between the ages of fourteen and eighteen deserved condolences. None of Pritchard's charges appeared to work. His staff was small; leisure for all pupils except those in the examination class was abundant; and full advantage was taken of the poor supervision.

Pritchard exerted his authority only when a display of high spirits had gone too far. A shadowy, benign man, with little sense of discipline, he rarely appeared outside of school hours. Hugh Trenchard took an instant dislike to him. The fixed smile of the Principal was worn like a flag of truce, as though he could stand being despised but not ignored. Pritchard lived in the main building, a red brick Victorian house on the brow of the hill, above the High Street and the river. This was Sandhurst House, reserved for the brightest boys. Two separate wings had recently been constructed in the grounds: one for pupils who hoped to qualify for Woolwich, the other for the slow or dull whose best chance of entering the army was through the back door of the militia.

At first Trenchard occupied a bed-sitting-room in the Woolwich wing. He did little work once he discovered that by a happy freak of geography Hill Lands lay only a mile from Holly Lodge, the home of his rich Askew cousins; and during his first year he spent most of his free time with them. To do so he often had to break bounds, a fact that soon came to the notice of Pritchard. Instead of reprimanding him, the Principal diffidently asked Trenchard whether he would

mind introducing him to the Askews, whose acquaintance he was
anxious to cultivate. The incident only increased his disrespect for
Pritchard.

The youngest boy in the school by a long chalk, although his
big, sinewy frame and compact air of assurance belied his fourteen
years, Hugh Trenchard's most enjoyable hours were spent on the
rugby field. He picked up the game quickly; his enthusiasm
benefited from the senior students' tendency to boycott all organised
sport, his skill earned him a place in the first XV. Within two years
he had become captain of the team.

Lessons were a chore which he conscientiously shirked.
Pritchard's assistants, who included a retired army officer living on
the outskirts of Wargrave and two masters with some practical
experience of teaching, were not paid to be original. Competitive
entry to the civil and armed services was still a fairly recent
innovation; crammers big and small, good, bad and indifferent,
thrived on the fear of failure which nagged the vanity of many a
Victorian parent or guardian of the upper and middle classes. Until
the early 1850's public appointments had depended less on what a
candidate knew than on whom he knew: jobbery and nepotism were
the time-honoured means of securing a flying start.

The War Office records are surprisingly bare of information
about army crammers. No control or rights of inspection could be
exercised over them; they were tolerated as a necessary evil.

4

Hugh Trenchard was sixteen years old when his feeling of security
in a crowd was shattered for ever. He had never attempted more
than the bare minimum of work; his promise far outstripped his
slow, unwilling performance; but since he was not in the examination class, nobody appeared to care. One May morning the usual
letter arrived from home. He opened it and read with a sickening
shock that his father was on the verge of bankruptcy.

It had never been Henry's habit to discuss his business affairs
with the family, and the catastrophe was the more overwhelming
for its suddenness. A well-ordered world of ease had come tumbling
down about all their ears without warning; only by piecing together
happenings that had seemed trifling at the time could Hugh detect
its inherent instability. He understood, too late, why his father had
packed two sons off to Pritchard's: a crammer's fees were lower than

those of any public school. He knew, too, why this man whom he idolised had appeared older, gaunter and more withdrawn with each returning holiday. Confiding in himself, bearing the weight of financial worry unaided, his father had struggled to retrieve fortune and self-respect single-handed and failed.

The extent of his failure was measurable by the ordeal that followed. Alex and Hugh were taken away from Pritchard's. They found Courtlands, empty and desolate, already up for sale. Every stick of furniture had gone; even their mother's jewellery had been disposed of; but what finally convinced the younger boy of the fullness of disaster was the disappearance of his own treasure. His rifle and an album of butterflies he had been collecting since the age of five had been auctioned with everything else.

His father was lodging temporarily with friends and Hugh spent part of that unhappy vacation with him. The plight of the Trenchards was common gossip in Taunton, and the boy began to experience the shame of ostracism. Once, when a handsome brougham jingled past them in the roadway, he vowed never to forgive or forget the behaviour of the former neighbour who ignored his father's politely raised hat.

Loyalty was stronger than shame in him. He took the snub mutely to heart. He did not care about the details of his father's debts; the son's faith in his integrity was unquestioning. He was therefore spared the humiliating knowledge that among the largest creditors was Pritchard. The Principal wrote suggesting quite spontaneously that it would be regrettable if Hugh's education had to be cut short, and offering to continue the education of the two boys at reduced terms. It was a gesture of trusting benevolence, coming from a man whose fees had remained unpaid for many months.

Any excuse for not returning to the crammer would have delighted Hugh, who loathed the place and the system. The tricks of cramming were as unsuited to his mind as sugar to the stomach of a diabetic. Yet the headmaster's unsuspected intervention helped to save his future from the wreck of his father's affairs. For several family friends settled the outstanding school bills and the Askews undertook to pay all fees in future.

Hugh was not allowed into the room above the bookshop in Taunton where the creditors gathered one July morning in 1889 to declare his father insolvent. A move to stave off that last indignity and offer him more time to pay was outvoted. The degradation of Henry Montague Trenchard was complete. The sense of having brought dishonour to the name of Trenchard oppressed him far more than the loss of nearly £20,000 or the stigma of bankruptcy.

It was almost with relief that Hugh returned at length to Pritchard's. He needed solitude to readjust his bewildered mind. At sixteen he had reached that most vulnerable age when affronts to pride cut the heart open. Genuine as was his sorrow for both parents he was more deeply hurt than he knew. In his loneliness, he could console himself only with the example of ancestors long dead who lived on in his mind. Had not they endured greater privations without turning a hair?

The upheaval at home was a traumatic experience that left him outwardly unchanged: the hidden scar remained. With the exception of John Robinson, a wealthy boy about his own age, he had no close school companions. Alex, his brother, moved in a different set. Older and more phlegmatic, he seemed quite unaffected by what happened. This led to a gradual estrangement between the brothers. In the work-shy atmosphere of Pritchard's, Hugh fell back more and more on his own resources. An inscrutable youth, reticent about himself, bad at his books and big for his age, he let himself go only at games or in helping to organise elaborate flings at authority.

Everyone agreed, for instance, that Pritchard had been walking about, committing celibacy, for too long and that a bride might improve him. A clandestine committee was formed to marry him off, and Hugh Trenchard joined it. Scores of handbills and gold-edged wedding invitations were printed and distributed locally. When one was sent through the post to Pritchard the whole school was assembled to hear an angry sermon on good manners. Afterwards the Principal called Trenchard aside and rebuked him for his part in an ungentlemanly charade. The rare spectacle of Pritchard's fury instigated the ringleaders to a further outburst of recklessness. As the Principal was undressing the following night he heard half-strangulated noises behind him. Turning back the bed blankets, he found a full-grown donkey lying bound between the sheets, with his nightcap pulled down over its ears and his nightshirt gagging its mouth. There were several suspects; but as each denied the physical possibility of spiriting the beast up his narrow staircase without being heard, Pritchard let them off with a reprimand.

The public houses in Wargrave were freely patronised by older students. Behind the George and Dragon, the more affluent housed the long-handled tandem carriages in which they often drove at night to Henley or Maidenhead. Trenchard avoided these regular revels, first out of financial necessity, then out of choice. The one party he ever attended left him with a terrible hang-over, destroying for all time his taste for gin. Thereafter his reputation for abstemiousness grew. He did not envy fellow-students with money to burn, and despised the few who used it to corrupt others. The hole-and-corner influence of older boys obsessed with sex are sometimes a problem in the best run schools. At Pritchard's, where discipline was lax, viciousness flourished. Trenchard took a stern stand against the vogue of sniggering self-indulgence whenever he encountered it. He felt cleaner and better for it and almost welcomed the unpopularity he earned. On the day they stopped swopping obscenities at his approach, he realised that he had won his first victory outside himself.

In later life Trenchard always spoke of the crammer's as "a hell of vice." Yet religious sentiment played no part in his sense of revulsion. On the contrary, he tended rather naïvely and unfairly to identify Pritchard, the parson, with Pritchard, the Principal, the failings of the latter merely accentuating the emptiness of the creed preached by the former. Attendance at Sunday services in the village church was not compulsory, and Hugh Trenchard was rarely among the worshippers.

For him, God had become an incalculable factor in human destiny. He found it simpler to put the Almighty on one side and cling to the self-reliant values acquired in childhood. At an age when his aggressive individuality might have been systematically moulded out of recognition at a public school, circumstances conspired to make Hugh Trenchard precociously mature. The death of a sister, the disgrace and ruin of his father, the plight of the family and the aimless disorderliness of school developed in him a hard core of responsibility beyond his years.

He was seventeen when his elder brother was expelled for blowing up the ornamental fountain in front of the school's main building. There were no casualties; but the blast shook Pritchard out of his excessive patience. Alex's departure caused Hugh little sorrow or surprise.

Pritchard, for all Hugh Trenchard's scornful dislike, made good his promise to help him. Perhaps the rugged firmness of the young man's character attracted him. Perhaps he simply discerned latent qualities of mind for which a crammer's régime left too little allowance. Whatever his motives, Pritchard persevered with a pupil whose backwardness in class was remarkable. He might well have given him up as a hopeless case after Trenchard ploughed the Woolwich entrance examination twice running; instead, he relegated him to the Militia wing. There, among boys mostly far younger than himself, Hugh Trenchard spent his last two years as a student. The level of knowledge expected of militia applicants for permanent commissions was lower than that for Sandhurst or Woolwich candidates. It proved too steep for Trenchard, who failed in 1891 and again in 1892.

Yet the Principal's trust was at last rewarded. There had been signs of greater interest and keenness on the part of his least responsive pupil since the late summer of 1892, when Trenchard returned to his books after a spell of training in Scotland as a probationary subaltern with the Kincardine and Forfar Artillery. The belated leavening of theory with a little practice seemed to release the boy's brain from its torpor, providing a real incentive that had been missing for six empty years. His name was at once entered a third time for the fateful examination.

Of the 225 militia subalterns who sat in March, 1893, fifty-six were ploughed. To Pritchard's delight, Hugh Trenchard was not among the rejects. The young man was staying with his Askew cousins the following summer when an officially stamped letter arrived with the almost incredible news that he had passed, with 1673 marks out of a possible 2400, just twenty-eight more than the minimum required for success. Trenchard was placed eighth from the bottom of the Infantry list, gazetted as a second-lieutenant in the Second Battalion of the Royal Scots Fusiliers, and posted to India.

2. The Soldier

Two months later, from the deck of the troop-ship *Bothnia*, Trenchard caught his first sight of India. Karachi lay on the horizon, its wharves and buildings shimmering in the early sun. The monotony of the voyage was forgotten. He leaned over the rails, staring at the approaching shore with fascination.

Life was offering him his first chance on nearly equal terms. His relatives, apart from pressing unwanted advice on him, had found the cash necessary for his outfit and kit. A thoughtful uncle had presented him with a good but elderly sporting gun, trusting that he would be soon able to afford the cartridges out of his own pocket. Parting had been easy: this somewhat uncommunicative young man of twenty-one, who stood six feet three inches tall, intended to repay them in deeds, not words.

His battalion was stationed at Sialkot, in the Punjab, and he completed the rail journey across the Sind Desert and the fertile plain beyond unaccompanied.

The hired gharri that took him and his baggage along a dusty, straight road to the depot swayed tipsily from side to side as the driver goaded on his pony. He noticed that the scraggy flanks of the animal were covered with sores and curtly ordered its tormentor to slacken speed. Then he noticed something vaguely familiar in the pattern of the seat-cushions beneath him. It came to him suddenly. This, surely, was the faded, tattered tartan of his new regiment. It heartened him to think that the home and workshop of his army apprenticeship could give fresh life even to a pair of cast-off trousers.

When his duties were explained to him and he was assigned a platoon of his own, he felt a satisfaction deeper than any he had known since childhood. Here was what he had obscurely pined for in the years that lay behind him; he had rediscovered a sense of purpose and with it security in membership not of a crowd, but of a community.

He had enjoyed a foretaste of the life eighteen months before in
Scotland. Nothing very memorable had happened in the militia
training camp at Montrose. Yet he had been supremely happy.

The novelty of parading on the barrack square had soon worn
off. The drill for loading the obsolete guns supplied to artillery units
of the militia had seemed pointless except as an incidental exercise
in discipline. He had learnt at Pritchard's how to mask his thoughts.
It had been less easy to conceal himself from scrutiny on the barrack
square. Height had its disadvantages. Once, during a ceremonial
inspection by the G.O.C. Scottish Command, Trenchard had been
unnerved by the singular interest taken in his headgear.

"Your pill-box," said the great man. "It's not on right." The
general, who was short in stature, instructed Trenchard to stoop
within reach, stood on tiptoes and patted the pill-box into its correct
position, and succeeded only in dislodging a mop of thick, black
hair which flopped down over the subaltern's eyes.

"This won't do," said the general. "Get it cut short."[1] The
rebuke earned him some jocular notoriety and the attentions of a
senior major with the instincts of a martinet. Trenchard, who disliked being bullied, decided that the officer needed a lesson; the
chance to teach one came when the unit went under canvas.
Unfortunately, the scheme misfired. The major, a very light sleeper,
was roused by movements outside, suspected that someone was
loosening the guy ropes and pegs of his tent, jumped out of bed and
groped for the entrance. There Trenchard was waiting. Next day
he had to answer the charge of assaulting a superior officer by
flinging a jugful of cold water in his face, but escaped with a
reprimand.

By careful economics he had spread his small allowance from
generous relatives to cover the hiring of a pony and tandem. The
uniform conferred its own sense of "belonging" and of "being
someone" at last; the independent enjoyment of leisure was the
fruit of his own frugality. The Montrose interlude had also introduced him to a distant relative whose influence for good was far
greater than Trenchard recognised at the time. Irwin Cox was a
rich cousin of his mother's, who sat in the House of Commons for
the Harrow Division of Middlesex and owned two lucrative
periodicals, *The Field* and *The Queen*. A middle-aged bachelor with
expensive tastes and simple ways, who had assumed responsibility
for Trenchard's education, Cox invited him to stay at his Mill Hill
home in the summer of 1892. In the coverts about Moat Mount, he
took his young guest shooting, admiring his dexterity with a gun and

Hugh Trenchard at 14 as a militia cadet

In India, at the age of twenty

learning without surprise that he had inherited the family distaste
for bookishness.

After drawing him out tactfully, and sympathising with his
difficulties at Pritchard's, Cox gave him the run of his library. Its
shelves were lined with hundreds of volumes, old and new, on every
imaginable subject; and Trenchard was encouraged to browse
among them for hours on end. It was to Irwin Cox, the first educated
outsider in his limited experience, that Trenchard owed the
exhilarating discovery of learning to read for pleasure.

He had come far in the eighteen months since, though he talked
little about his past at Sialkot. That in itself excited no comment.
Newcomers to the battalion were better liked for being seen rather
than heard. The mess would hear from Trenchard soon enough;
for, in accordance with tradition, the youngest subaltern was
expected to make a suitable speech on the first guest night. Trenchard
faced this ordeal about a month after his arrival. He knew what
they wanted of him: a solemn recital of regimental history peppered
with dates and names—how glory had come to the Royal Scots
Fusiliers under Marlborough and had been enhanced on dozens of
battle-fields since. He knew it by heart because he had read it up;
but he had no intention of repeating what they knew even better
than he did. His speech was short and sensational. It contained no
frills.

" I am deeply proud to belong to this great regiment," he said
deliberately, staring at the resplendent pipe major behind the top
table. " I hope one day I shall live to command it."

Hoots of incredulous laughter, punctuated by gibes, rose on all
sides. " We'll be dead, thank God. We won't be in it then."[2]

Some but not all appreciated his nerve. The younger officers
admired his talent for transforming his initiation ceremony into a
farce. As he sat down with a disarming grin on his face, not a man
in the room realised that in the nicest possible way Trenchard meant
exactly what he said.

2

Pride in the regiment could never be an abstract sentiment to
Trenchard. It had to be something personally felt, or nothing. His
superiors soon began to see that he had no interest or ambition
beyond it.

The rigorous routine he set himself excluded the dances and

parties and narrow social life of a peace-time station in India. It
was remarked that apart from a single glass of port on guest nights,
he drank only water. Frequently he missed lunch altogether. The
habits of an anchorite seemed oddly inconsistent with a man of his
vitality and robust enthusiasm. He was not ashamed to admit, when
pressed, that unlike others he depended wholly on his army pay.
His brother officers respected him as a strong personality whom it
was more rewarding to tease than to cross-examine. They nicknamed
him the Camel because of the way he carried a small head on a
tall frame, and because of the loud grunting noises he emitted when
anyone addressed him and he had nothing to say. It was equally a
tribute to his abstemiousness.

In the last decade of the Queen Empress's long reign, India was
a paradise for many well-to-do young officers. Outside the messes
lay the cantonments, the clubs and those concentric social circles of
officials and business men who formed an aristocracy more rigid and
exclusive than England had ever known, but one to which officers
of means were welcome. The terrors of the Mutiny were a fading
memory. The periodic disturbances on the North-West Frontier
merely added the spice of danger to a life of gaiety. The frontier
remained a realistic training area and an occasional battlefield,
justifying the administrative costs of the military establishment.
There was a political justification for the expense as well—the
Russian threat to India had been in the minds of politicians since
Disraeli's day.

Every regiment did its turn of duty beyond the Khyber Pass;
and Trenchard's earliest disappointment was to learn that, short of
a major crisis, his battalion would not be ordered forward for many
months to come. No short-cuts to glory were scheduled for this eager,
unmoneyed subaltern of the Royal Scots Fusiliers; but life had its
compensations.

Once his N.C.O.s and men had accustomed themselves to his
demands for punctuality and smartness, they responded to his
frequently expressed resolve to command the best platoon on the
station. He was not content until he had taught them all to become
first-class shots like himself, and the whole battalion shared his
delight when he entered for the All-India Rifle Championship, at
Meerut, early in 1894, and won the Viceroy's gold medal.

On the decisive day his eyes and hands had never been steadier;
it seemed impossible to miss the bull's-eye; his score rose until it
could not be touched. He took his victory calmly.

There was a contretemps, at the presentation, when a magnificently braided major-general handed him the leather case in which the coveted gold medal should have been snugly lying. Unfortunately, Trenchard knew the truth. An A.D.C. had apologetically confided that the new Viceroy, Lord Elgin, had not been long enough in Simla for his image to be stamped on anything. With the impishness of a schoolboy, Trenchard opened the case in full view of the spectators and peered near-sightedly at the invisible prize within. He returned to Sialkot with a reprimand for conduct unbefitting a gentleman. The medal followed at a discreet interval.

It was during his visit to Meerut that his mind turned to an altogether more ambitious pursuit. The commanding officer of the battalion was anything but encouraging when Trenchard asked permission to start forming a polo team. Without positively forbidding it, he reminded him that few officers owned ponies; there were no stables, no suitable ground, no regimental funds available; and he frankly questioned whether anyone could create a polo-playing tradition where none had ever existed.

The colonel underrated Trenchard's immense self-confidence and flair for improvisation. A sympathetic major started him off by offering him the use of a pony for nothing, provided he looked after it. The experiment worked; and in calculating the exact cost of feeding and grooming the animal, Trenchard persuaded several younger officers that they could afford it, too. Slowly he wore down opposition by his reproachful complaint: " Whoever heard of anyone trying to play polo by himself? "

The late Brigadier R. K. Walshe was one of his first recruits. A cautious, rather shy individual who seldom rode and hardly relished the prospect of raising money to buy a mount, Walshe was overborne by Trenchard's persistence. Others joined in when the promoter guaranteed that nobody would be out of pocket.

" He asked for a show of willingness," said Walshe. " The actual work we left to him. It was quite extraordinary. Within six weeks we had the equipment, the ground and our own communal stable of good ponies which Trenchard purchased locally. We learnt by trial and error, our form improved with practice, and within six months we had a team which could hold its own against all-comers."

Trenchard's business methods were uniquely his own. The secret weight of his father's misfortune checked any tendency to recklessness but failed to deter him from backing his own fancy. He prided himself on an uncannily good eye for the finer points of horses and men. His bank manager, fortunately, proved fairly accommodating; but to avoid overstraining his patience, Trenchard occasionally called on bazaar money-lenders, whose interest rates were seldom less than ninety per cent. It was a measure of his faith in his own exalted judgment: to gamble on near-certainties was not to gamble at all.

The colonel's indifference slowly changed to guarded approval; the polo team was now a reality. One fine spring day in 1896 Trenchard led his team in an away match against a strong cavalry side at Ambala. It was a hard, thrilling game with the result open to the last. A short, squarely-built, young man with sandy hair and an excitable temper was foiled of more than one shot at goal by the forceful, spoiling tactics of the visiting captain. One physical clash between them led to a sharp exchange of words. The flushed lieutenant of the 4th Hussars had indulged in a little gamesmanship as he tangled with Trenchard. Using two hands on the reins to balance himself, his uncontrolled stick threshed down suddenly across the neck of Trenchard's pony.

" Play to the rules," Trenchard shouted, " and take that stick out of my eye."

His opponent leaned on all the harder as if determined to unseat both horse and rider. Locked together like centaurs in a three-legged race, they careered along until sheer deadlock brought them straining and sweating to a standstill. Then the hussar glared up at him, and said: " Who the devil were you talking to? If you've a complaint, speak to the umpire."

Trenchard retorted by knocking the loosely held stick out of the other's hand and galloped off.

Later the two men came face to face in the mess. The atmosphere was less tense now; they laughed together over the incident. Observers who saw and heard them then—they included the late Lord Baden-Powell—felt that the pair were well matched, in ruggedness of personality at least. It was Trenchard's first encounter with Winston Churchill; and he had the grace to admit that the man's scowling charm off the field more than compensated for his unimpressive play on it.

3

Before the suffocating heat of summer descended each year, talk frequently turned to Kashmir where, it was said, men could live like lords of creation till their leave and savings ran out. When his first ninety days' leave fell due, Trenchard set off for the hills by dog-cart; and sixty years afterwards he could still recapture the nostalgic excitement of that first trek through a vast unspoilt wilderness: waking refreshed at dawn to the chorus of strange birds, noting how his string of ponies grew livelier as they climbed, feeling as he ate his open-air meals that he had been born again.

For four carefree months he hunted in the hills and roamed from one lakeside resort to another. The stiff, often pompous protocol that ruled behaviour on the plains no longer seemed to apply; social ritual was left behind; and Trenchard could develop his talent as an organising impresario in new fields. Race meetings were his speciality; but parties, picnics and even the occasional gala ball were not outside his range. Most of the men he met seemed content to let someone else arrange their amusements. Such apathy was Trenchard's opportunity; and a succession of hosts and hostesses at Srinagar, Gulmarg and elsewhere came to rely on his resourcefulness. Whether they were men well known or not worth knowing did not matter: the detailed planning of other people's relaxations absorbed him.

Only once did his detachment gain the upper hand, and then under provocation. When the wife of the local brigade major at an outlying hill station invited him to dinner on the strength of his surname, he rashly accepted. She, too, was a Trenchard, she confided; it would be most interesting to compare notes and see how closely they were related. While he was sipping sherry, someone in an adjoining room called, " Trenchard, Trenchard, Trenchard," as if cajoling an unco-operative dog. Perhaps he had wronged his hostess: perhaps, after all, she had a sense of humour. The hope sank within him as the door opened. A small unwilling boy, long past his bedtime, was led in. The discontent on the child's face roused Trenchard's sympathy.

" I'd like to introduce my son," she said. " I had him christened Trenchard, you know, out of feeling for the old name."

Trenchard merely grunted. He did not trust himself to speak, and said little during the meal. Then the table was cleared and the family tree produced. His blood-conscious hostess perched herself like a bird on her favourite bough until he could stand the twittering no longer.

" Madam," he interrupted with gruff solemnity, " I must tell you this before I go. There are only two branches of the family that concern us. There's the main one which I belong to, and there's a second which I've always understood was founded about two hundred years ago by the illegitimate son of an umbrella manufacturer in Manchester."

The calculated insult brought the evening's entertainment to an abrupt close and Trenchard was soon walking away still too jubilant to experience the least twinge of contrition. An official rebuff was awaiting him at Sialkot: the outraged husband had written a bitter letter of complaint to Trenchard's commanding officer.

Women played little part in his self-contained existence. He met a few who attracted him, and could be considerate as an escort; but he was at his best as a matchmaker, contriving wildly improbable attachments between unsuitable partners out of sheer high spirits. Emotional entanglements were for others. Marriage on a lieutenant's pay he regarded as a trap for the weak, the unwary, or the rich. For any hard-up officer of twenty-two, it was inconceivable.

Two companies of the battalion were detached to Amritsar in 1896, and Trenchard went as second-in-command of one. For eighteen months he broadened his social education. It was impossible to escape the clutches of the local hostesses. His tact and skill were often deployed smoothing out petty jealousies. They called him "the man from Cook's," but their patronising graciousness slid off someone so critically aware of their devotion to the finer shades of vanity. It staggered him to reflect that the Raj was ruled by the whims of women, whose sole object was to emulate and impress. Trenchard found that fixing dates that did not clash, and keeping apart the functions of the rich and the not-so-rich, could be a task demanding considerable ingenuity and patience.

He found release in the mountains. One Sunday, on the shores of a remote lake above the Himalayan tree-line, he shot four rare mountain snipe, packed them in salt and sent them home to Irwin Cox. His benefactor was touched and gratified. The birds, he wrote, were valuable specimens, and had received a place of honour in his collection. Trenchard kept up a desultory correspondence with Cox, though he was a poor correspondent whose thoughts did not flow easily on paper. The letters did not mention, for instance, how he spent the long hot afternoons of sweltering heat reading under the flapping punkas, while others slept. Trenchard had begun to redeem the misspent years at Pritchard's, telling nobody.

Biographies were his first choice. The careers of men of action like Warren Hastings, Clive, the Pitts or the Wellesleys proved the most stimulating. It heartened him to trace the rise of these tempestuous spirits, who, despite their innumerable outward differences, had all been fired by a strength of will and singleness of purpose which he longed to cultivate himself.

Reading brought more than inspiration. For his appetite grew by what it fed on. The habit, once formed, was never lost; books became his passport to an ever-deepening knowledge of men, of life and of history. Trenchard managed to educate himself "on the quiet" without destroying the illusion that his interests were confined to outdoor activities. Even his ancestors began to fall into private perspective at last. Nobody realised at Sialkot that steeple-chasing and horse-dealing enabled this inscrutably cheerful young giant both to enjoy polo and still send a regular allowance home.

Sometimes, his colleagues felt, Trenchard pushed his luck too far. In 1896 he narrowly escaped having a foot amputated after being accidentally shot on a leopard hunt. Only his refusal to heed the pessimistic warnings of doctors saved him from the surgeon's knife. The following spring, when he was still limping, his horse threw him during a steeplechase. This time an operation for rupture was judged necessary; but the expense of the voyage to England seemed prohibitive. He cut his losses by sailing on a cargo ship laden with animal bones. It stank to high heaven in the tropical heat. Then, off Algiers, they had to heave to in a gale. As they approached Marseilles bubonic plague broke out among the crew; everything on board, including the clothes of the only three passengers, had to be sterilised. Trenchard reached London a fortnight late for his appointment, sore and shabby, in a shrunken uniform that seemed to have been borrowed from a tramp half his size.

4

The operation for hernia caused Trenchard less distress than his convalescence, part of which he spent with his parents. His joy at seeing them was clouded by bleak recognition of his own inadequacy. He had grown away from them: but in a single night the years of absence rolled away. Privation was their lot. It was etched on their faces, most unmistakably on his mother's. Her tendency to hypochondria had thriven on misfortune.

The painful experience produced its own reaction. Trenchard gradually conceived an active dislike of illness, and of people who lay down under it. The feeling found eventual expression in a phrase that sounded callous. Malingerers and the wounded often heard him say: " I hate sick people," and the ferocity he would put into the words shocked, and was meant to shock. There was no other way of urging men not to make the same tragic error, nor

surrender passively to the misfortunes and manifest injustices of fate
as both his parents had done. Trenchard sought an excuse to cut
short his stay. A better one than could have been invented leaped
to his eye one morning as he scanned a newspaper: fighting had
broken out on the North-West Frontier; reinforcements were
moving up, his own unit among them. Disregarding both medical
and military niceties, Trenchard said his farewells, discharged himself from convalescence and caught the first available ship back.
Before returning home he had applied for, and secured, a transfer
to the First Battalion of his regiment, opting for further service in
India.

At length, after a depressingly slow passage he reached the base
camp at Landkotal in the craggy desolation of the Khyber, only to
learn that the campaign had ended as it had begun, without him.
In the orderly room Trenchard was allotted the unsatisfactory task
of drawing up the campaign medal roll; in the mess, among
strangers, he was soon listening enviously to first-hand impressions
of the latest expedition against turbulent Afridi tribesmen. The
battalion's role in a routine operation resembling in its tactical
features a hundred others before and since had not been decisive;
and individual feats of gallantry that might have been performed
were passed over in well-bred silence.

Yet he could not help being impressed by the air of fulfilment
and quiet authority that characterised every speaker, from the
colonel to the most junior subaltern. These brother officers had
borne the heat of action and been solemnly professed. Trenchard
realised all too well that there would probably be no further call for
punitive action in his time.

His disappointment ran deep and led to petty friction with his
new commanding officer. The colonel of the First Battalion was
cautious in manner, short in stature, and extremely conventional in
outlook. He had a strongly marked sense of the military proprieties.
Having spent his career in the infantry, he saw no reason for
encouraging the ridiculous practice of polo just because a senior
lieutenant happened to be insanely interested in the game. Polo, he
reminded Trenchard, was a cavalry monopoly. The cavalry were
an aristocratic and glamorous élite whom for all sorts of reasons it
would be unwise for the Royal Scots Fusiliers to emulate.

It was after the cease fire, when the battalion moved back to
Peshawar and regimental life slid back into its placid rhythm, that
Trenchard grew weary of trying to convert the colonel by words
alone. The healthy use of leisure, his own and his colleagues', was

being neglected to humour a superior's whim. Like most men of his generation and upbringing, Trenchard believed that sport ranked with cleanliness, above mere godliness, as the ideal expression of the military cult. More than an outlet for manly energies or an aid to morale, it had accumulated through the years of Victorian peace a peculiar mystique of its own. To the British professional soldier at any rate, war spelt more than an instrument of policy used in the last resort. War meant more than dreams of martial glory. War was the supreme occasion for demonstrating that the rules of the playing field could be applied to the battlefield, its grimmer and bloodier extension.

Trenchard had to wait for inspiration. It came one day when the colonel unexpectedly announced at table that he was thinking of selling Australia, a spirited black pony secretly coveted by Trenchard who had disposed of his Sialkot stable to pay for his recent operation. Checking the impulse to offer a firm price there and then, Trenchard raised a substantial overdraft at the bank, called on a dragoon major he knew, and persuaded him to act as middleman. The deal went through without a hitch, and the next day an astonished colonel pulled Trenchard up as he galloped past on Australia. What, he inquired icily, was the idea of borrowing an animal that had only just been sold to someone else? Trenchard retorted that he was the new owner.

The colonel was speechless with anger, but took no action. Time convinced Trenchard that the deception had been thoroughly worthwhile. For though the commanding officer treated him coldly, his interest in the performance of Australia at polo practice became notably more marked; then his presence as a spectator emboldened some who had previously been deterred by his hostility to take the field as players. By the end of 1898 the First Battalion had its communal stable and a well-equipped team; and as if tacitly admitting his error in doubting Trenchard's judgment, the colonel occasionally took the field himself. The bank manager's misgivings had meanwhile been allayed by the incidental profits of horse trading.

The two years immediately following the Queen Empress's Diamond Jubilee were comparatively happy years for Trenchard. The outside world seemed blurred and unreal in the distorting mirror of regimental life. The months flew in a whirl of race meetings, military tournaments, and the customary entertainments that were a wall against tedium: for Trenchard's reputation as an accomplished organiser quickly spread.

Then an incident, trifling in itself, brought Trenchard to the

favourable attention of a very important personage in that confined
and artificial world. Only the unhealthy interest of Sir Edmund
Elles, the District Commander, in the fate of an overambitious rifle-
shooting contest persuaded the harassed members of the organising
committee to "send for the Camel" at the eleventh hour; once co-
opted, Trenchard made them curse and swear more freely than they
cared to remember. But his improvisations worked; missing competitors were enrolled, a fiasco and the general's wrath averted.
Trenchard was singled out by Elles and congratulated. The general
asked him not to hesitate about seeking his personal help or advice
if ever the need should arise.[3]

Whether Sir Edmund had meant what he said, Trenchard did not
pause to inquire. The invitation was as welcome as it was unsolicited; and, with a thrift born of experience, he stored it away
like an expensive umbrella against a rainy day.

3. The Phoenix

An Army mess at Peshawar was hardly the ideal vantage point for a clear understanding of Imperial problems in the last year of the nineteenth century. There was trouble in South Africa, of course, but it caused no concern whatever among officers of the Royal Scots Fusiliers. Rumours of distant unrest were seldom worth discussing. Peace was at its zenith. And of all the domains where the broad writ of the Queen Empress ran, none was happier in its serene indifference to such rumours than India.

Had anyone suggested that before the end of 1899 full-scale fighting would be raging between Boer and Briton on the South African veld, Trenchard for one would have said that the speaker deserved to be instantly certified. Indeed, after returning from convalescence in England, he had considered resigning his commission to try his luck as a gold prospector in the Rand, confiding only in a friendly captain of a similarly restless disposition, whose longing for a change of environment proved, however, much shorter-lived than his own. Two factors had sapped Trenchard's interest. The first was the immediate challenge of a commanding officer who could not abide polo; the second was the gradual discovery from books and articles that South Africa had ceased to be the Eldorado he had originally imagined.

The gold which still lured occasional adventurers from the four corners of the Empire to the high ridges of the Witwatersrand had evidently deepened the ancient discord between Boers and Britons. And Trenchard thought better than to throw up his profession merely to implicate himself willy-nilly in politics on the off-chance of striking it rich. He had no desire for political martyrdom as an "uitlander." The opinions he formed in his course of reading flattered neither oppressors nor oppressed. The Boer pioneers, who had trekked from the Cape into the hinterland nearly half a century before to escape the influences of a civilisation they despised, seemed to have passed on to their descendants a set of values better suited to the age of Moses than to the heyday of British Imperialism.

43

Just as the Boer republics were an obstacle to the prosperous developments of all South Africa, so Joseph Chamberlain and Cecil Rhodes were, for Trenchard, the romantic personifications of Britain's Imperial destiny. The money-making genius of the latter struck him as a happy means to the greater end of bringing half a continent from the Cape to Lake Victoria beneath the Union Jack. The consistency of the former, whose political vision was said to have raised the Colonial Office to a new peak of prestige, was still more appealing. A minister who regarded himself in relation to the Crown's overseas dependencies as a landlord entrusted with a vast estate was a rare phenomenon; and Chamberlain was temporarily admitted to the private gallery of Trenchard's heroes.

The uitlanders, he believed, laboured under genuine grievances. No longer a political minority, they were denied the vote, heavily taxed, and often victimised by corrupt Boer officials. State monopolies in explosives, liquor and transport produced social scandals as well as injustices; yet the only court of appeal open to these second-class citizens was the British Government in London.

The gold dug up by the uitlanders merely strengthened President Kruger's hands, enabling him to place substantial arms orders in Europe, to preserve his country's simple pastoral economy, and to defy London. The uitlanders, seething with discontent, lacked the leaders, the weapons and the training to answer repression with organised violence; and the ill-fated Jameson Raid on New Year's Day, 1896, was calculated not to support a rising but to foment one. This gambler's throw, ending in undignified fiasco, had tarnished the reputation of Rhodes and destroyed his dream of reconciling Boer with Briton by peaceful means.

" A war in South Africa would be . . . in the nature of a civil war," Chamberlain warned Britain, shortly after the Jameson Raid. " It would be a long war, a bitter war and a costly war leaving behind it the embers of a strife which, I believe, generations would hardly be long enough to extinguish. . . ." Opinion in the army and the country dismissed that warning as another excuse for official inaction.

The factor of heedlessness accounted for Trenchard's astonishment and delight when he heard on 11th October, 1899, that the Boer Republics had declared war on Britain. The gathering crisis in South Africa since the spring of that year had not passed unnoticed in India, but its dangers were underrated.

Nobody at Peshawar believed that Kruger would fight, or would last a month if he did. In the summer, when a force of nearly

10,000 men under the command of Sir George White was moved from India to the Cape, Trenchard did not even feel cheated. Troop movements merely showed that British forbearance had begun to fray. They did not, could not, reflect official anxiety about the state of readiness of the token forces stationed on South African soil.

So, after the first sensation of surprise, the declaration of war caused little apprehension. That the struggle would be short and sweet no British officer worthy of the name could doubt. The troops stationed in Natal and the Cape had been reinforced. There seemed no further reason for excitement. Kruger's ultimatum of 9th October, calling for their withdrawal, saved Chamberlain the embarrassment of dispatching an ultimatum of his own.

" They have done it," had been the Minister's first words on being roused from sleep to read Kruger's unequivocal terms.[1] Most of his countrymen shared his incredulity; the few who held that the Boers had right on their side did not imagine that right would prevail against the avenging might of an empire in arms.

2

" I've come here to fight, not to sleep."

Trenchard loaded the words with all the scorn he felt, and could visualise years afterwards their startling impact on the commandant of the Bloemfontein rest camp. Apparently this elderly, overworked major needed an assistant; any likely looking officer in transit would do. It was all the more necessary to convince him that he had misjudged both his moment and his man.

The commandant retorted that the war on the veld was all but finished. One officer replacement left behind would make no difference.

" You're staying," he said finally, " and that's an order."

Trenchard stole out of the camp that night never to return. Escape was imperative; he had not fumed and fretted for eight months to exchange a soft billet in Peshawar for a softer billet behind the front. His plan to rejoin the battalion upcountry was hasty but effective.

As a goods train bound for Johannesburg rumbled slowly across the points outside Bloemfontein station, Trenchard jumped aboard and lay low in a half-empty wagon. He was travelling light; the few essential items of clothing and equipment fitted compactly into a small bag. The rhythmic clatter of the wheels banished sleep and stimulated reflection.

Ever since the troop-ship *Clive* had left Bombay a month earlier, there had been a series of agonising delays. Rough weather had lengthened the voyage; a mild outbreak of plague had caused the vessel to be diverted to East London. Ten days in quarantine had followed. By a strange chance, he had met on shore a ghost from the past: Alex, his elder brother, now a lieutenant in the Cape Mounted Rifles, had stopped him in the street. They had talked of home, and the brief encounter opened a long-locked door on a world which Trenchard had disowned. He banged it shut again while the jolting of the train revived memories of the dismal months he had been obliged to waste in India since the outbreak of war. He could congratulate himself now at a call to arms that might never have sounded had he not seized the bugle himself.

Nobody thought in October, 1899, that the Boers would extend the two divisions of British troops already in the field. A cartoon in *Punch* depicted the enemy as men who fought on foot, a clear enough indication of the British public's ignorance of a foe who virtually lived on horseback. There was less excuse for official complacency; but intelligence was traditionally one of the weaker points of the War Office. The Government had accepted the solemn assurance of Wolseley, the Commander-in-Chief, that the Boers would be checked provided the reinforcements from India arrived in time.

Hence the dismay and incredulity that accompanied reports of the enemy's invasion of Natal and Cape Province. Undoubtedly it affected the soldiers, from Wolseley downwards, more sharply than the civilians. For though White arrived from India in time, and his dispositions for the defence of Natal were orthodox enough, he failed to prevent an astonishingly mobile enemy from turning his flank and rear, and fell back on Ladysmith. Far to the north-west, in Upper Cape Province, another Boer formation meanwhile laid siege to Kimberley. A third troop crossed the western Transvaal border, cut the railway and surrounded Mafeking. The Boers had struck first with an economy of effort and a degree of success which amazed the world without, however, quite demolishing the War Office belief that the British had been merely caught off balance.

These early set-backs were bad enough; but they depressed Trenchard far less than the knowledge that his old battalion formed part of one of the expeditionary corps which embarked for the Cape under General Sir Redvers Buller. At once he applied for permission to rejoin it. His colonel, perhaps misconstruing Trenchard's unrest as a further reflection on himself, opposed the application. Friction broke out between them again. Trenchard submitted fresh requests for transfer with disconcerting regularity; no sooner had one been rejected than another would appear on the commanding officer's desk. Their relations grew no better after Buller's disembarkation: unknown place names like Colenso and Stormberg and Magersfontein suddenly became symbols of unbelievable catastrophe. The flower of an army, as unaccustomed to defeat as its leaders were blind to the demands of a new type of warfare, was unceremoniously cut down during " Black Week " in December. Trenchard's distress matched his frustration. Yet neither then nor in later life would he allow that the army suffered largely because its leaders were incompetent. It would have appalled him had he known that Chamberlain, his political idol, had as little confidence in British Generalship as Lord Chesterfield, who had written at the outset of the American War of Independence:

" I do not know what effect the names of these gentlemen have on the enemy, but I confess they make me tremble."

Volunteers were quickly wanted to replace the killed and wounded; Trenchard's name was among the first submitted. To do the colonel credit, he forwarded it promptly recommending not only his transfer but his promotion to the rank of captain as well. It seemed too good to be anything but suspect. And so it turned out. Confirmation of the promotion came through with an emergency order, signed by the new Viceroy, forbidding the dispatch of further volunteers. Alarmed by the growing shortage of trained leaders, Curzon decreed that no more officers must leave until replaced.

Financially Trenchard was left worse off. Now a captain on the strength of a battalion based in England, he automatically reverted to the lower English rate of pay. The touch of austerity aggravated his restiveness, spurring him on to act with an impetuosity which the colonel found excessive.

By entering into acriminious correspondence with the authorities, civil and military, Trenchard earned repeated reprimands. Correct as ever in discharging his regimental duties, however, he denied his superiors the satisfaction of court-martialling him for neglect or inefficiency. Hunting down gangs of religious fanatics was the only quasi-military distraction for troops in the Peshawar district in the late spring of 1900. The ghazis were Moslem extremists who believed in the shedding of European blood as a passport to salvation. Trenchard, who had little heart for the role of an armed policeman, came within inches of death himself at a gymkhana when the colonel of an English county regiment fell mortally wounded beside him.

The assassination upset Curzon as no reverse in South Africa had yet done. All units were instructed to send detailed reports on incidents, big and small, to Viceroy's House. Trenchard found a way of reducing the order to absurdity. One night, as orderly officer, he rebuked a sergeant who, in a fit of temper, had flung a lump of fat (the first weapon to hand) at a noisy punka coolie. Curzon, he decided, must be informed at once; so he sat down, composed an elaborate description of this tremendous trifle, and insisted on telegraphing it overnight. The colonel was not amused by the cold official reply from the Viceroy.

That was a mischievous wire. There had been one other, drafted in a moment of impulsive desperation, which proved the instrument of his release. The message to Sir Edmund Elles, who had lately left Peshawar for the more exalted post of Military Secretary to Curzon, was terse and self-explanatory. It simply requested that the signatory, Captain Trenchard, should be permitted to rejoin forthwith his own unit overseas.

After two or three weeks of suspense, a movement order reached Peshawar through the proper channels. It bore the Military Secretary's personal commendation. Trenchard was hailed before the colonel, prepared for another snub, only to be told—rather stiffly, he thought—that his last and boldest overture had worked. Evidently the late commander of the Peshawar District not only remembered his promise to help Trenchard, but had not minded being asked point-blank by priority signal whether he proposed to honour it. To Elles, more than anyone else, he owed his escape.

Before dawn, Trenchard dropped off the train, unobserved, as it slowed down for a signal just outside Johannesburg. He felt stiff and tired but immensely relieved to be so near his goal. The battalion was stationed at Krugersdorp, some twenty miles to the west; and when he walked into the mess later that day, his old colleagues fell upon him like a returning prodigal. But several familiar faces were missing; and his joy at being back among men he had known since joining the regiment was tempered by sadness. The Royal Scots Fusiliers, by all accounts, had been in the thick of the fighting almost from the start. Their losses had not been light. At Colenso, in the shambles of Buller's attempt to force the Tugela River, they suffered their first casualties. It was some time before Trenchard grasped from the racy but rather fragmentary impressions of survivors that at Colenso, too, a private of the battalion had earned the first V.C. of the campaign.

While they were out of the line, recovering and reforming, the tide seemed gradually to turn against the enemy. Buller was replaced by Roberts, with Kitchener as Chief of Staff; and new men had meant new tactics. Everyone agreed that the changes were an improvement. Frontal attacks against a well-armed foe with an infallible eye for the arts of concealment and surprise had all but ceased. Outflanking movements by British infantry and cavalry had helped to lift the seige of Kimberley, cut off a large Boer formation at Paardeberg, and enabled the demoted Buller to pass across the Tugela at his fourth attempt and relieve Ladysmith. In February the battalion returned to the line; and at Pieter's Hill Colonel E. E. Carr, the commanding officer, had fallen wounded. The verdict in the mess was that the enemy had not shot his bolt.

Outnumbered the Boers might be, but they resembled the troops of George Washington in having an extra general on their side— the extensive half-wild terrain over which they fought so bravely. Adept in extending their line so that each rifleman was deployed to provide flanking and enveloping fire, the Boers had exposed the failings of an army inelastic in its training, fossilised in its thinking and therefore quite unprepared for the hazards of mobile warfare. A number of reputations had been destroyed in the process. And though Trenchard sometimes argued that Buller was made a scape-goat for the negligence of others, he did not quarrel with the historian of his own regiment that "the ten weeks of the assault on the Tugela bastion had done much to educate Britain in the principles of war, but the lessons had been learnt at a high cost."[2]

The one redeeming feature of the struggle was the dogged gallantry of the British soldier and his junior commanders; watching them from his own eyrie on the Tugela heights, " advancing stolidly to death with unshaken discipline, mishandled and misled," General Botha had rightly surmised that the Boers could not win. . . .[3]

Developments in the first six months of 1900 certainly seemed to support Botha's conclusion. The Boer armies, putting up only token resistance, retired before Roberts could bring them to battle. The Royal Scots Fusiliers were the first British unit to cross into the Transvaal. That had been on 7th May. On the last day of the month Johannesburg fell; and on 5th June Roberts entered Pretoria.

The popular belief that serious fighting was over did not find much backing in the mess at Krugersdorp. True, the power of Kruger appeared to have been broken; the President had fled; his

armed burghers were no longer grouped in field formations;
territories covering nearly 200,000 square miles now lay under
British occupation. At home, the Government and the politicians
rejoiced in the triumph of Roberts's summer campaign; and the
Commander-in-Chief himself, a man not given to light assumptions,
had recently declared that only "police action" would be necessary
to round up Boer leaders still at large.

Yet an undertow of scepticism persisted among these fighting
men for reasons that Trenchard readily accepted. Their respect for
an enemy who despised the canons of conventional warfare was
untinged with heroics. Many questioned whether the Boers were,
in fact, beaten; and the strongest critic of the prevailing mood of
optimism was Major W. A. Young, the acting commanding officer
and a stranger to Trenchard.

Colonel Carr had not yet resumed his command; Young was
striving, against odds, to keep the battalion tuned up for further
operations. Trenchard liked the firmness of his handshake, his
natural air of authority, the simple precision of his views. Very little,
it seemed, escaped the eyes and ears of Major Young whose methods
of testing the worth of newcomers lacked nothing in originality. One
morning, when Trenchard was inured to the monotony of static
garrison duties, he was unexpectedly sent for by Young. The
interview was informal and extremely gratifying.

" I want you to start raising a mounted section in the battalion
at once," said the acting commanding officer.

Young explained the background. The High Command, despite
all the rumours of peace, was uneasy at the shortage of mobile units.
Calls on the cavalry were excessive, and though cavalrymen probably
scorned the only practical alternative, that of putting infantrymen
on horseback, Headquarters took a less prejudiced view. The Boers
could be thanked at least for exploding the unwisdom of the slogan
" Unmounted Men Preferred," which had led at the outset to the
rejection of thousands of natural horsemen from Australia, Canada,
New Zealand and other parts of the Empire. The figures spoke for
themselves: only one soldier out of ten in an army of occupation
nearly a quarter of a million strong was a trained rider.

In Britain the raising of special corps of Imperial Yeomanry was
now a matter of priority; the first drafts were on the way. Meanwhile General Barton, whose 6th (Fusilier) Brigade was responsible
for guarding a tract of desolate country, west of Johannesburg, nearly
two-thirds as big as Wales, was determined to have his own mounted
units without delay. The railway link from Johannesburg to

Klerksdorp cut through his district. It was impossible to protect every mile of it; but with a mobile force at his disposal, Barton would be better able to keep the line open should the Boers restart hostilities.

" There's no reason why this battalion shouldn't be the first in the field with a mounted company," said Young. " From all I've heard you're the man to do it."

Trenchard never forgot those words. The challenge was more acceptable than the compliment, heartening as it was thus to learn that the years in India had not been entirely wasted. Another piece in the puzzle of life fell suddenly into place. The mania for polo, for running stables, for profitable horse-trading was paying an unexpected dividend in the more serious business of training for an unfinished war. Trenchard's reputation had preceded him; its proof lay in the relatively high number of officers and men in the battalion who were passable horsemen already.

Training for battle, with no manuals or set drill to guide him and only the vague checks of general orders to curb his zeal, proved an outlet both dangerous and rewarding for a man of Trenchard's wilful but immature character. Though normally far from loquacious, he was described by a contemporary at Krugersdorp as "an explosive mixture of the choleric and the sanguine" who could "talk anybody under the table"[4] when tactics or military matters cropped up.

Conversation in the mess turned one evening to the disorderliness of the town after dark. It was generally agreed that the Australians were the worst offenders. Trenchard did not appear to be listening until someone suggested that Brigade Headquarters could solve the problem easily by issuing the Australians with horses and letting them work off steam against the Boers. The remark brought him suddenly to life.

It was common knowledge that upcountry depots were still sending colonial volunteers forward while regular units were being withdrawn. The Krugersdorp Australians were a sample of the kind of men whom the overburdened administrative machinery had so far failed to absorb. As such they did not interest Trenchard. Their sole accomplishments appeared to be drinking, gambling and debauchery, their sole contact with the army in repeated scuffles with soldiers or the military police. What Trenchard had not realised until that moment was that these Australians could ride.

At Brigade Headquarters next day he confirmed the fact from the files and inquired whether there would be any objection to incorporating them in his own company. A staff major stared at him in disbelief and hastily gave permission. Trenchard left to round up his new recruits and had to admit, on parading them, that he had never set eyes on "a more slovenly, surly, murderous-looking bunch of ruffians." Contempt for authority was plain in their faces. Reflecting that he would do no good by barking at them, he tried kindness. He was determined to get to the bottom of their grievances. Pointing to a tall, lean, hollow-cheeked man, who was evidently the ringleader, Trenchard invited him to speak for the rest. It seemed that nobody wanted them. They had been left to "rot for a month without boots, breeches, or horses."

All of them claimed to be able to ride and shoot from the saddle, yet none had been allowed *near* a horse since disembarking six weeks before. The familiar tale of muddle and neglect evoked in Trenchard a conspirator's sympathy. He told them not to worry. " Boots and breeches will be provided first."

On discovering that the quartermasters' stores were temporarily short of supplies, Trenchard decided to act alone, especially since he knew that a goods train had been standing unloaded for several days down at the sidings. Choosing a few volunteers and swearing the remainder to secrecy, he led a looting party that very evening to the railway and searched every wagon. The articles they needed, and only those, were removed. The Australians were beside themselves with glee. Here was one imperial officer at least who could pass off as a duty the kind of buccaneering exploit in which they specialised as a matter of course.

Good horses were obtained through orthodox channels. The local remount depot was amply stocked; the Australians, he noticed, chose carefully and well. Presently he was admiring their extraordinary verve and skill in the saddle, for they picked up the rudiments of drill almost without effort. He became fiercely proud of his bushmen. At their head, he intended to give the Boers a taste of their own medicine as soon as Brigade lifted its ridiculous ban on long-range patrolling.

Several times during September, on the edges of the plain that sloped away towards the flat-topped hills west of the town, desultory shots were exchanged with enemy scouts, but orders categorically forbade pursuit. It was no part of Barton's policy to allow half-trained riders to roam at will. Trenchard chafed under the restriction. He was often heard denouncing it, and vainly sought to have it reversed. His colleagues in the mess counselled patience; the time for action would come, they assured him. It could not come soon enough for Trenchard.

Up and down the long, exposed lines of communication in the Orange Free State and the Transvaal, guerilla activities were on the increase. Barton's railway was not spared. During September, a hundred miles down the line, an enemy commando raided Potchefstroom where the Royal Scots Fusiliers had held the enemy in an earlier war. Christian de Wet was thought to have led the attack, removing quantities of dynamite and guns. Since then two supply trains from Klerksdorp had been derailed.

One morning, towards the end of the month, the brigadier ordered Trenchard to lead a strong detachment to a particularly vulnerable section of the line where it passed through a gorge ten miles to the west. A supply train would be going through the following night; as far as possible, every point along the route where an ambush seemed likely must be defended.

His jubilation was unbounded; his first excursion beyond the plain went unimpeded. By dusk the ridges were fully manned on both sides of the track faintly glinting in the shadowy gorge below.

Nothing happened until next morning when the brigade major arrived with an escort to inspect the defence dispositions. Trenchard did not trust himself to speak until the major began to find fault. The pickets, he declared, should be concentrated on the highest points.

" I suggest you put three men on that hill, five on the bigger one next to it, two on the next, and so on according to size," he said, in a would-be helpful tone.

" The general is keen about such details."

" In that case," replied Trenchard, deliberately misunderstanding him, " will you ask the general from me what kind of men he'd like me to put up there, fat men or thin men? "

The major promised to convey the other's insolence to Barton, and galloped off in high dudgeon.

" Jumpy Jeff," as Barton was known to his men, had occasion a few days later to lecture Trenchard on the virtue of restraint in war. On patrol that morning, Trenchard had caused some anxious moments at headquarters by breaking bounds and leading his column of bushmen and Scots at the gallop in pursuit of a Boer party. Thinking of everything but the possible reactions of the garrison lookouts, he yielded to his obsession of trying to outstrip the Boers for once at their own game of hare and hounds without regard to appearances or consequences.

The enemy slackened pace in the long, broken gulleys below the plain and made leisurely for a bluff which was their favourite vantage point. Trenchard beat them to it by riding hard along a parallel track. As the last of his men dismounted on the crest, they could hear from below the clash of hooves on stone and voices arguing in a strange tongue. At last round a bend in the corkscrew path thirty unsuspecting Boers rode slowly into view. Trenchard held his fire until they reached the top. Then a volley of shots echoed from the hills opposite, followed by shouts and groans and the whinnying of fear-stricken horses. A dozen riderless animals bolted. Their owners, presumably wounded, went to earth like ferrets and began to exchange shot for shot from the boulder-strewn shoulder of the ridge. Trenchard had no intention of letting them escape. The Australians were already moving silently down to cut them off when a British courier charged up the slope, disregarding the flying bullets and flinging himself off his horse unharmed a few yards from where Trenchard was crouching. The man bore a message from head-quarters.

" Evacuate the hill at once," it read. " My guns are about to open fire on it."

It was signed " Barton."

There was nothing to do but obey. The lookouts, watching the engagement from afar, had drawn the wrong conclusion. Trenchard reluctantly broke off the action. A puff of smoke in the distance signalled the arrival of the first shell before the column was clear. Shrapnel sprayed about them; they flattened themselves among the rocks; horses fell in untidy heaps of flailing legs; the Boers disappeared, and the column returned without further loss.

The brigadier was complimentary and critical by turns, congratulating Trenchard in one breath for showing initiative and complaining in the next that he had shown too much.

"The Boers must be driven off that ridge," said Barton. "They're up there now in strength. I want you to attack this afternoon. What I don't want are unnecessary casualties."

Trenchard was staggered by his superior's inconsistency.

" I can promise that you'll get the hill, sir. I can't promise there'll be no bloodshed."

Watchers in the town saw the column move off, splitting into small sections and converging at last on the summit. Fortunately, the enemy had gone. But Trenchard brooded long and indignantly over the terms of Barton's order.

" The hardest thing in war," he wrote nearly twenty years later in an oblique reference to this incident, " is to discover commanding officers of sufficient calibre not to mind losing men when the goal is worth the sacrifice."

The patrolling round Krugersdorp increased in intensity, and by early October, it was clear to everyone that a new phase of warfare had begun.

The Boer cities might be occupied; but the Boer spirit of resistance had not been broken. By fighting in guerilla bands recruited from and largely based on their home districts, they could use their mobility and the vastness of veld to harass and confuse the British. The worsening military situation west of Johannesburg and the defensive counter measures adopted there are thus summarised by the historian of the Royal Scots Fusiliers:

> " Barton had a big area to guard, and it had the disadvantage that it was within easy striking distance of the northern Free State where Christian de Wet and his merry men were active. On 5th October, Barton left Krugersdorp with the Scots and the Welsh Fusiliers, 500 mounted troops, a field battery, three pom-poms and a naval gun. He moved slowly south-west along the railway, through the range of low hills known as the Gatsrand.
>
> " On 6th October, at Mulders Drift, there was a brush with a roving commando, when a volunteer company of the Royal Scots Fusiliers acquitted itself well. After that every day brought its skirmish, the bulk of the fighting falling on the Welch Fusiliers and the Scottish Yeomanry."

The term " flying column," currently applied to composite forces of the kind, was a misnomer; for like destroyers screening convoys at sea in later wars, the outriders had to adjust their speed to that of the baggage train. The whole force moved along encumbered with the trappings of a miniature army. Every halt was observed by invisible enemy scouts. The Boers were uncannily ubiquitous, hugging the heights and making occasional forays then scattering before the nearest mounted section reached them. Cursing, and often sniped at, the sweating, overladen soldiers had to push or pull up the precipitous rises and through the narrow defiles heavy ox-drawn gun-carriages that had no place in that wilderness.

Barton's uneasiness grew as he advanced, for he was aware that farms and villages were being reoccupied behind him. By 8th October his men had come fifty miles from Krugersdorp to a point roughly half-way to Klerksdorp. They were now in the heart of difficult country where the dangers of ambush were constant. Once he descended to the plain Barton hoped to tempt the Boers into

attacking him. Only thus could he succeed in crushing them with
superior weight. He therefore ordered the column to rest in the heat
of the day, intending by forced marches to progress faster and with
greater immunity after dark.

The first long night passed without incident. Trenchard's eyes
grew accustomed to the starlit, shadowy veld, his ears to the immense
stillness which caught up and magnified the slightest sound. The
brigade seemed to clatter forward like a blinded giant on tiptoe. Its
clumsiness betrayed it. The mounted troopers, strung out in
sections, had to guard and guide it at every turn. Trenchard seldom

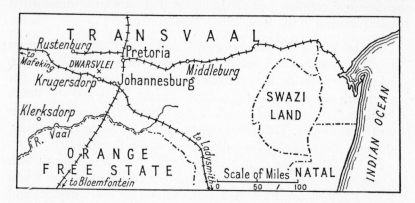

stayed long in one place. He covered many miles trotting from one
section to another; his presence was an insurance against listlessness
or panic. For once he could be thankful that no Boers were astir.

A halt was called at dawn. The infantrymen were relaxing after
the back-breaking monotony of the march when the crackle of rifle-
fire rang out not far ahead. Trenchard, who had fallen behind to
cover the flanks and rear with his Australians, raced forward at once
to investigate. They reached a gully a mile ahead just in time to see
dozens of startled Boers, in varying stages of undress, scrambling to
untether their horses and flee. The Ayrshire Yeomanry, in the van,
had stumbled unawares into an enemy encampment.

The dust thrown up by the retreating hooves of the largest group
of Boers he had yet encountered was the finest sight he could have
asked of fate. This time there would be no mistakes: he would
harry, corner and kill his quarry. There would be no turning back
for Barton. As he came abreast of the Ayrshires, Trenchard bellowed
out a command not to drop behind, but the words were drowned in
a simultaneous outburst of ironical cheers from the Scots as the
Australians drew level and passed them.

According to Trenchard's own estimate he "rode at full blast for ten miles." Unable to shake off their pursuers, the Boers led the way up a steep slope. Behind it lay a large farmhouse nestling two hundred feet below in a rectangular valley as startlingly green as an oasis. So this was their laager; how obliging of them to signpost the way to it. There was no movement in the small plantation of blue gum trees adjoining the farm, none in the fields beyond, but the residents were up. A wisp of smoke curled out of the farmhouse chimney into the blue, windless sky. They might even have been enjoying breakfast when their armed friends descended on them, seeking sanctuary.

The Australians held the heights, an invisible line against escape through the encircling scrub and rocks. Trenchard wished the line were not so thin, and wondered what had become of the Ayrshires. If only they would hurry, he fretted, de Wet himself would scarcely succeed in wriggling free. He knew that he had tracked the Boers down to an important lair. It remained for him to choose his own moment and close the trap.

Half an hour went by. Suddenly the front door opened. A young woman appeared in a long drab dress relieved by a bright apron. For a moment she stood shaking a tablecloth then vanished within. Had she been a British spy she could have given no clearer signal that her guests were expecting no callers.

Private Donald McDermid, the phlegmatic Glaswegian who served as Trenchard's groom, remembered the grim humour of Trenchard's final instructions to the N.C.O.s:

" We'll catch the leaders before they've had time to digest their food," he said. " Four of you will follow me. The rest stay where you are with your eyes open. Wait for my signal, then close in."

The patrol slithered down the slope. With Trenchard went his senior Scots N.C.O., Sergeant Gilbert Lewis, McDermid, and two Australians. As they reached the grassy floor of the valley and broke cover, firing broke out at a dozen points below and bullets whistled about them.

" Take care, sir."

Sergeant Lewis both looked and sounded anxious. Trenchard, seemingly oblivious to fear, ignored him and ran to the sheltering wall of the farmhouse. When Lewis joined him, Trenchard turned and said, with a grin:

" They're so worried they can't even shoot straight."[6]

They were the last words he spoke. Trenchard moved forward

again, withdrawing as a bullet chipped the angle of the wall inches
above his head. The door where the woman had appeared with the
tablecloth was tantalisingly near, too near for him to hesitate more
than an instant. He charged round the corner and was only a few
feet from his goal when he staggered and pitched forward on his face.
He lay twitching in the dust as McDermid knelt down and undid the
bloodstained tunic. The Australians, awaiting a signal that never
came, and seeing their leader fall instead, poured down from the
heights. A fierce, hand-to-hand battle raged about the farmhouse,
called Dwarsvlei, until the few Boers inside who were not killed,
wounded or captured took to their heels and horses. There were no
wanted men with prices on their heads among the prisoners. The
invisible ones lurking elsewhere in the valley, who had encouraged
Trenchard to walk heedlessly into the trap of his own contriving,
disappeared as was their habit without trace.

3

On a wet December morning, two months later, Trenchard hobbled
down the gangplank of a hospital ship at Southampton dragging one
leg painfully behind the other. He could not walk without sticks.
The bullet that felled him should have killed him, the doctors had
said. And there were gloomy moments when he wished it had done
so cleanly.

Had he suspected as he lay in hospital, first at Krugersdorp then
at Johannesburg, what he discovered with certainty on trying to get
out of bed during his convalescence at Maraisburg, in Cape Province,
his determination not to die might well have weakened. The shock
of finding that he was half-paralysed from the waist down filled him
at first with despair, the surmises of the specialists as to what was
actually wrong merely accentuating his mistrust for the medical
profession. The bullet which had left him with only one whole lung
had inexplicably damaged his spine as well on the way out.

His parents were on the damp quayside to welcome him, an
invalid soldier without a future. Their sorrowful concern forced
him to pull himself together until the dark sense of his utter uselessness to anyone closed in again, smothering even the stirrings of self-
reproach for being the author of his own misfortune. Trenchard
was not the best of company in the luxurious Mayfair nursing home
for disabled officers where he spent his first fortnight. It was one of
several centres equipped and maintained for the Red Cross by Lady

Georgiana Dudley, a remarkable woman as distinguished for her philanthropic activities as for her social graces. Trenchard's case came to her notice. She wrote him a personal note promising that no effort or expense would be spared to ensure his recovery. With ungracious haste, he replied curtly that it was not his habit to accept charity from strangers. To his utter confusion Lady Dudley called to see him and did not even mention his letter.

Her gentle insistence nonplussed and shamed him. She had sons of her own in uniform, she said; their treatment in similar circumstances would be no different from his.

" A carriage will take you to my specialist in the morning," she said briskly and departed. Trenchard felt slightly abashed.

The interview with Mr. Douglas Powell the following day was short. After a thorough examination, the specialist told Trenchard that he must go to Switzerland. The mountain air would enable the injured lung to heal; a few months at a resort like St. Moritz would give him a reasonable chance of recovery.

" If you don't go," said Powell, " I can hold out no hope. You may be an invalid for the rest of your days."

It was too difficult to admit that he could not go because he had no money. Nobody on earth outside the family knew how poor he really was; and the generosity of Lady Dudley saved him the humiliation of explaining. Without asking any questions, she presented him with a cheque for the journey. This, she said with meaning, was not the fruit of charity. She had merely drawn on a special fund for cases like his; the money was there, and she had used it.

" She made me feel that I was the one man in the whole army worth looking after," said Trenchard. " It was impossible to refuse."

He arrived at St. Moritz on the last Sunday of December, 1900. He remembered how the cobalt sky and the slanting sunlight dazzled him as he limped out after an early breakfast. The church bells were ringing. A few people were on their way to the service, but he had no inclination to join them. He wanted to spy out the land. The unaccustomed exertion and the thin cold air made him puff and blow and grit his teeth as he leaned harder on his sticks. One bag of his bellows was sound; with practice it might be trained to do the work of two. He sat down to rest on a bench and watch four men skilfully pushing heavy objects like flat-bottomed boulders which twirled and skidded over the glassy surface of the huge lake, round the outer margins of which skaters were racing and pirouetting with enviable speed and grace.

" Curling and skating aren't sports for a man in my condition," he decided.

Half-way up a steep white slope outside the town he had to pause again. An instructor on skis was going through precise turns for the benefit of a group of novices. As he moved pensively on, Trenchard caught a glimpse of something which brought him to a dead stop. Flashing down the sheer flank of the opposite mountainside, like an arrow shot from an invisible bow, skimmed a man on a toboggan. The power and breathtaking ease of the descent was a revelation to Trenchard. In less than a minute the scarred white face of the slope was empty of life and movement. The blurred apparition had vanished round a pine-clad elbow of rock.

" I wonder if I could do that? "

The question sneaked into his mind. It nagged him all that day, and he knew it would go on nagging him unmercifully until he sought the answer himself on the side of the mountain. Lameness was no excuse for holding back. It would be a minor handicap, since gravity would do most of the work. As long as he kept his head, there would be little to fear. Whatever happened, he would have nothing to lose or regret.

Two mornings later, Trenchard was staring down the gleaming, dizzy gradient of the Cresta Run, aware of a faint sinking feeling in the pit of his stomach. He had no right to be there, a beginner with no experience or knowledge of the hazards, an invalid who had unobtrusively dropped his sticks in the snow before lowering himself awkwardly on to his hired toboggan. At eye level the track stretched six feet across from bank to bank, narrowing to the width of a ribbon far beneath him. The first hairpin turn lay a stone's drop below his stiffly outstretched legs. Would he ever get round it?

At least nobody was questioning his right to try. By pretending to be fit and drawing no attention to himself, he had earned that right. There was no going back now. His head and hands were unprotected except for woollen cap and gloves; his boots were without spikes.

As he lay face forward over the steel ribs of his craft, straining to distribute his weight over the sliding board, he remembered the one piece of gratuitous advice that had been tossed at him repeatedly. " Manœuvre yourself at the corners," he had been told. He wondered how the experts did it. A friendly hand pushed him off and the toboggan glided away. The banked ice on either hand seemed to hurtle past him up into the sky. Somehow he negotiated the first bend without slackening speed; he could not have braked had he tried and did not want to brake. He had committed himself as a hostage to gravity; and the exhilaration kept apprehension at bay. He reached the bottom without a spill travelling faster than he had ever travelled in his life before.

On the next three runs his toboggan took him over the edge of the banking, tossing him into space each time like an inert thing. He lay half dazed where he landed in the snow, marvelling that he was still in one piece, bruised and stunned but with no smashed bones as far as he could tell. He waited patiently until rescue came and he was lifted to his feet.

The days went by, and his timing improved. On the whole, however, he relied on luck more than on skill to steer him round corners out of trouble. By leaning his weight outwards as the worst of the bends leaped up as if to throw him, he usually managed to stay on course.

At his hotel he found himself drawn into an amusing circle of chance acquaintances, with an unconventional English family called Hargreaves at the centre. There were three brothers and three sisters, more or less his own age, and all extremely interested in Trenchard's kill-or-cure method of treating his infirmity. They pronounced him mad, but engagingly so; they admired his fearless zest when he went bobsleighing with them; they learnt to emulate him in riding for nothing less than "a win or a spill." When one of them said jokingly: " I suppose you'll be tackling the Cresta Run in earnest now," the taunt echoed in his ears like a challenge: until then Trenchard had not seriously considered the suggestion.

" We'll see," he said philosophically. " If my legs mend, I might."

His legs "mended" in a way which even he could not have visualised. He had taken dozens of hard tumbles already without flinching rather than heed the instructors' constant reproofs that a man of his build must learn to conserve top speed for the downhill stretches between bends. It was too late to start "compensating" as he whizzed one morning into the sharp right-hand turning of Battledore, not far below the junction. As usual, he omitted to dig in his toes. Only by a desperate shift of his body to the side could he hope to prevent the toboggan leaping over the rim of the protective banking.

Somehow he kept the toboggan level. Then it began to run away with him again. Refusing to relax speed, Trenchard realised that he could not negotiate Shuttlecock, the equally sharp left-hand turn in front, unless by some fluke he cut the corner deliberately without losing control. He was too late. He was travelling too fast. The runners soared up and over the banking and a world of white spun convulsively about him like a wobbling top. He parted company with the toboggan in mid-air. His body hit the side of the hill two or three times before coming to rest in a snowdrift nearly thirty feet below.

When he came to his head was throbbing violently. Solicitous hands raised him. He pushed them aside in a sudden fury of excitement and happiness. He could walk again unaided. Whatever other damage he might have done himself as he bounced down the hill-side like a rubber ball, he had recovered the use of his legs. Apart from a dull pain near the base of his spine he felt no after-effects. Something must have clicked back into place; he had cured himself by violence.

The Hargreaves were beside themselves with delight and organised a celebration to commemorate the ceremonial throwing away of Trenchard's sticks. A second noisier party was held soon afterwards to mark a more spectacular triumph still. That morning, to the astonishment of the experts, Trenchard had raced down the Cresta Run to win the Freshman and Novices' Cups for 1901. It was a singular achievement for a man with no previous experience, and for one regarded as a virtual cripple until the week before the event. The trophies were duly stamped with his name. And the official records show that his times for the full course of nearly three-quarters of a mile from the church above the first slope to the finishing line were 227.4 and 224 seconds.

The Hargreaves were sorry when he ignored their pressing pleas to stay. Trenchard felt that he had buried himself long enough in St. Moritz. His damaged lung still troubled him; but he said nothing about that to the local doctor who pronounced him fit to travel. He left without regret, returning to thank Lady Dudley for making possible the miracle of his recovery.

4. The Leader

Re-entering England was as disenchanting as re-entering a cage. The doctors were displeased, the War Office put out, by Trenchard's premature reappearance. The idea of any candidate for a permanent disability pension claiming to be fully fit again and pleading to forgo nine months' sick leave in his eagerness to return to South Africa was most peculiar and quite irregular. They demanded proof of fitness before clearing him for active service. Their rules did not allow for sudden cures; a Lazarus back from the dead could have fared no worse in striving to re-establish his identity.

With no choice but to accept their terms, under protest, Trenchard took up tennis as a comparatively painless method of strengthening his second right lung. The deflated left one was not healing easily. Whenever he coughed, the blood caked inside the pleura seemed to thud against his ribs like a solid little sack of cement. Whenever he climbed stairs or walked too quickly, the extra exertion cost a laborious effort of will, though the following spasms of wheezy breathlessness came fewer in dry weather. Trenchard had played little tennis since childhood. As a boy at home he had been passably competent. Now, he realised, only remarkable improvement in form would convince the War Office that he was no longer an invalid.

Among the best-known doubles players in Britain at the turn of the century were the Allan brothers, identical twins whom tournament umpires found difficult to distinguish on court. Trenchard saw them and explained his predicament. Their coaching fees were discouragingly high, but he was in no mood to haggle and hoped that the expense would justify itself. Besides, he liked the brothers at first sight. They taught him how to save stamina by mixing his strokes and cultivating his exceptionally long reach. Once, during a hard set, Trenchard saw an opening and played his favourite stroke, a forehand volley which sped across court towards the base line. One of the Allans retrieved it almost casually, his return lob leaving Trenchard flat-footed, then flourished his racket, and shouted:

"For God's sake, man, don't play that shot again for a year. I saw it coming before you moved."[1]

It was salutary advice; and the more Trenchard pondered it, the more widely it seemed to apply. To parade his intentions for others to turn to advantage could be a sign of vanity; it was also a weakness which partly explained his present predicament. Life had dealt with him harshly because at a decisive moment he had scorned the use of subtlety.

Early that summer, with the Allans' encouragement, Trenchard entered his name for two knock-out tennis competitions at seaside resorts on the south coast. He had to retire from the semi-finals of both events, unbeaten but near the point of exhaustion.

The spectators embarrassed him with their sympathy. So did reporters from local newspapers who departed happily to exaggerate the quality of his performances in print. Nevertheless, the press cuttings were welcome if unexpected ammunition to silence the sceptical doctors entrenched at the War Office, whose letters summoning him before medical boards had followed him from place to place unanswered. In a covering note enclosed with the newspaper clippings, Trenchard wrote:

"I trust you'll agree that if I'm fit enough for this I'm fit enough to return to the front."

Nor did he bother to await confirmation, the laxity of army procedure enabling him to act on the presumption. When Trenchard embarked on a troop-ship one May morning in 1901, still unexamined by a military doctor, his papers were in order: he had mixed cunning with persuasiveness in passing himself off as a volunteer for a second tour of duty. Nobody challenged him, and he sedulously discouraged friendly inquiries. His history was so strange, the facts of his recent resurrection so incredible, that he had no wish to appear an impostor or a liar.

July was ending when he reached Pretoria, a young man of twenty-eight, frailer than he knew, who had hoodwinked the undertaker and the doctors in turn. He was posted to a company of the 12th Mounted Infantry, whose commanding officer, a Major Thomson of the Seaforth Highlanders, expressed approval of G.H.Q.'s thoughtfulness in sending him an experienced leader. Trenchard could scarcely credit his luck in finding several officers and men seconded from the battalion, and in reclaiming McDermid as his groom. All were astonished to see him again.

"We thought you'd been buried long ago, sir," McDermid greeted him.

Trenchard as a young major in South Africa

Above: the 23rd Mounted Infantry Regiment at Pietermaritzburg. Trenchard is mounted at its head, on the extreme right of the picture. *Below:* Trenchard (*seated, right*) in Nigeria with the Governor, Sir Walter Egerton

There had been some significant changes in his absence. The personality of Kitchener, who had succeeded Roberts as Commander-in-Chief the previous November, was stamped on the tactics of his forces and on the mentality of his officers. Not even generals were safe from his imperious scrutiny; and it was evidently through no lack of thoroughness on his part that the Boers were still in the field.

The heart of Kitchener's plan was concentration. Garrisons had been gradually withdrawn from isolated places. Railways were no longer undefended. Blockhouses of corrugated iron or cement were springing up at measured intervals beside the tracks, and sections of the line between were patrolled by special units. Nearly a quarter of Kitchener's Army of 250,000 men were mounted; nearly half of that quarter were colonial volunteers, trained in a rougher but no less effective school than the finest cavalry regiments.

The enemy were now as ready to abandon guns and supplies when hard pressed as they had once abandoned their towns. From its inaccessible eyrie in the mountains near Lydenburg, the Boer Government retained the allegiance of a self-reliant people in whom the flame of nationalism could not be extinguished by repression or privation. Kitchener's policy of impounding non-combatants, nearly 100,000 of whom suffered the rigours inseparable from confinement in overcrowded, insanitary camps, was as ruthless as his scorched-earth policy of starving out the combatants. Both added immeasurably to the bitterness of the enemy's struggle to avoid complete annihilation.

Trenchard's interest was confined to the obvious success of Kitchener in reorganising and re-equipping his divisions. He heard it said that this God-like, omnicompetent figure took so much on himself that senior commanders as experienced as French and Methuen were denied that wider tactical freedom which might have enabled them to run down the Boers and compel them to surrender piecemeal. The cordon drawn round the enemy could never be pulled tight at the opportune moment; for the multiple problems of controlling a vast army, of relieving the Boers of all responsibility for feeding and clothing their families, of destroying their crops and farms and seizing their cattle, imposed an impossible burden on the Commander-in-Chief. So the war dragged on, a war of endless movement against a foe more implacable and cunning than Kitchener would allow.

Trenchard soon perceived that his men were heartily sick of riding long distances with only the occasional brush at long range to recompense them. The holes in the security net were wide enough for Boers to slip through day or night in all seasons.

" We went north by Potgietersrust to Pietersburg where we were on continual column," he wrote of these marathon rides with mounted formations equivalent in size to brigades. " First I served under Colonel Vandeler, who was killed by the blowing up of the train in which he was travelling, then under Colonel Dawkins. From the railway we would trek out to remote centres like Nylestroom, then back to the railway for a refit and off again."

For three months Trenchard practically lived in the saddle. McDermid, his groom, and Dobby, his batman, were among the few who realised what it cost him. The wound that had deprived him of a lung, leaving a minute scar back and front where the bullet had penetrated, bled easily. Sometimes he felt that the effort of carrying on would kill him.

According to a lieutenant in his own battalion who served under his command at this time:

" Trenchard frequently fainted clean away at the end of a day's trek and had to be lifted bodily off his horse. He never complained just as he never explained. Nor was he ever heard to thank anyone for fussing over him when he recovered. On the contrary:

"'Leave me alone,' he'd growl—and would stagger to his feet as though nothing was wrong. It soon became part of the drill to lift him down and leave him to regain consciousness at his own pace. With the help of a finger or two of whisky, he would usually be himself again within five minutes."

Under the spur of such a will his body dutifully became acclimatised to pain. He denied himself the luxury even of longing for the end of the day, for the unappetising taste of salted beef and biscuits and dried fruit beside the concealed campfire, for the balm of a few hours' rest under a blanket, until he felt surer of himself. His fellow-officers marvelled at his stoic endurance, at his deliberate concern for men and horses after a racking day in the saddle and the customary fainting fit. It was Trenchard's way of gradually disowning the nightmare memory of himself as an invalid.

Thomson called him aside one day at a remount depot in the Transvaal.

" You're wanted at G.H.Q.," he said. " I don't know what's in the wind, but it's urgent."

He left for Pretoria reluctantly, unable wholly to rid himself of the fear that the War Office had found him out. A cavalry staff officer ushered him into an ante-room, said noncommittally that the Commander-in-Chief would be free almost at once, and left him still brooding uncertainly. Was it conceivable that he was about to be confronted with the unanswerable facts of his return as an undischarged invalid?

The uneasy self-questionings ceased as soon as he entered the great man's presence. Kitchener looked "tall and fierce" as he fixed his visitor with a squinting stare of appraisal. He wanted a young officer to inspect and, if necessary, assume temporary command of a recently formed mounted infantry regiment. Trenchard's name had been recommended, among others; he had been looking up his record, and thought he would do as well as anyone.

This regiment had walked into a trap on its first patrol, he explained. The spirit of the survivors was poor. Trenchard must go, judge who or what was to blame, and instil fresh purpose into them. "Remember," said the Commander-in-Chief, "you're acting on my personal authority. Do what's necessary, then report to me."

It was an unconventional assignment, to say the least. Trenchard completed it within a month. The formation mainly needed a few young officers of sufficient experience and worth, a simple discovery came to light during an improvised training exercise. He decided that the acting colonel and two company commanders were total misfits, told them so to their faces, and wired Pretoria urging their instant removal. The reply bore out all he had heard of Kitchener's obsessive interest in details.

"Decision agreed," it said. "But order was—reorganise, not disband."

Trenchard set about fulfilling that order to the letter, driving each company in turn so hard that every officer and man learnt to jump instinctively to obey. When they were ready for action, he notified G.H.Q. and a new commanding officer was sent at once. Puzzled and slightly aggrieved, he returned to find another special task awaiting him at Pretoria.

This time Kitchener ordered him to D'Aar, in Cape Colony, to speed the formation of a corps of mounted infantry which had experienced a series of unaccountable delays in training. Trenchard swept into the camp like a tornado. Several officers objected to his high-handed methods; none obstructed him.

"He was a man in a hurry, but nothing got overlooked," recalled McDermid, his groom. "'What's wrong with now?' he would say if anyone said, 'I'll look into that as soon as I can.' Some of the officers may have hated his guts, but most of the men admired him."

The corps was raised and moulded in record time; Trenchard

led it across the Kalahari Desert himself, escorting a supply convoy
of nearly 8000 laden mules which, in his own words, " never moved
faster than three-quarters of a mile an hour and strayed all over the
place."

A third interview with Kitchener followed in October, 1901,
almost exactly twelve months after the Dwarsvlei ambush. Intelligence sources claimed to have located, not for the first time, the
secret hideout of the Boer Government. The Commander-in-Chief
dwelt on the shattering effect of its capture on the morale of enemy
commandos. In the past he had relied on large contingents but their
approach had always been detected. A surprise swoop by a handful
of men might be more productive. Nine half-caste Kaffirs with an
intimate knowledge of the wild terrain beyond Middleburg were at
Trenchard's disposal.

" If there's anything else you need," Kitchener added, " I'll see
that you get it."

Trenchard's last wish was to rouse the anger of this formidable
man, yet he disliked the plan as it stood. Screwing up his courage, he
said:

" With great respect, sir, could I have a few more men? "

Kitchener frowned at him.

" All right," he replied at last. " Take a column of national
scouts."[2]

A unit of British or Australian riders would have been preferable,
but Trenchard knew that he had said enough. Some so-called
loyalist Boers accompanied him and his escort of British N.C.O.s to
Middleburg, where rumours of his mission had somehow preceded
him.

No incidents marred the forced ride through the darkness on the
first night out, though the behaviour of three officer-interpreters
roused his suspicions. The Kaffir guides, on whom the safety of the
column depended, seemed only too ready to accept guidance from
them; and his ignorance of Afrikaans made it impossible to tell
whether his orders were being trimmed to suit the Boers. Dawn had
broken when a dozen men bringing up the rear suddenly opened
fire with staccato precision as though by a prearranged signal. Then
one of the interpreters pointed out a kloof, barely visible behind a
screen of straggling bushes down the slope they had begun to descend.
There, he said, lay the Boer Government's temporary encampment.
Trenchard crawled forward with McDermid and two N.C.O.s. The
kloof was crammed with well-fed cattle.

" Get mounted and follow me," Trenchard shouted, but few of

the Boers obeyed. Suddenly the slopes of the hill-side seemed to sprout with hidden rifles; bullets began to fly; several men fell wounded and were dragged to cover in a hollow below the crest where Trenchard decided to fight it out. McDermid never forgot the harshness of his voice as he told the survivors:

" Aim to kill and there'll be no dying for us to-day."

The enemy, possibly tiring of a battle which offered no prospect of booty, crippled a few more defenders before making off.

They reached Middleburg next day, a ragged, weary remnant of the column that had started off. The garrison commander stared at Trenchard as though he were a ghost, then blurted out that a Boer scout had ridden in with news that the column had been wiped out in an ambush. At G.H.Q. Kitchener listened impassively to Trenchard's account of the wild goose chase, thanked him briefly and dismissed him. The interlude of working directly to the orders of a general equally capable of using or circumventing his own military machine was over; but the proof that Trenchard had not entirely failed came soon afterwards: he was promoted to acting major and received a glowing mention in dispatches for special services rendered.

His talent for reorganising and leading irregular units was now officially recognised; and possibly his hardest assignment was with the Canadian Scouts at Pretoria, whose extreme antipathy for "smug English officers" he disarmed by the quick understanding he struck up with their leader, Major Charlie Ross, a veteran who had fought as a cavalryman against the Red Indians when Trenchard was at school and more recently won the D.S.O. for gallantry. As second-in-command of the column to which the Canadian Scouts were finally attached, Trenchard had nothing but admiration for these "great-hearted ruffians and natural fighting men."

The Christmas of 1901 passed almost unnoticed on the veld. Patrolling was ceaseless; most of it was devoid of interest and excitement. Weeks would go by without a single clash; then a series of running fights would develop when desperation drove a local Boer commando to replenish its food and supplies by laying ambushes.

Rumours of peace started early in the New Year. Trenchard remembered the period well because it coincided with his appointment as acting commander of the 23rd Mounted Infantry Regiment. Much to his disappointment, he led the regiment in action only once, when Zulu raiders violated the Transvaal border early in 1902 as a reprisal for Boer cattle-thieving.

A report by Colonel T. E. Hickman, one of three or four column leaders under whom he served, illustrates the esteem in which his superiors held him.

" Major Trenchard is the best mounted infantry officer of his rank I have met during this war. . . . His institutions and general arrangements for the comfort of his men are better than those of any other regiment of any arm in the Command. This is due entirely to his personal attention."

Hostilities ceased in May, with the signing of peace terms at Vereeniging. One day Trenchard and his column were patrolling the empty plateau above Pietersburg, the next he was supervising the stacking of arms handed in by hundreds of Boers whom he had never succeeded in drawing to battle. There followed a prolonged anticlimax of waiting, part of which he spent on leave among the reefs of the Low Veld, pegging out five hundred claims at ten shillings each in the reopened workings, staying long enough to assure himself that the first samples of yellow metal unearthed by his hired miners was only "fools' gold", and contenting himself with the hope that his stake in the Transvaal might yield a fortune yet.

Not until July, 1902, was the 23rd Mounted Infantry recalled to Middleburg. On the four-hundred-mile trek south, Trenchard visited one remount depot after another, purchasing good for progressively better horses. None cost him more than twenty pounds; and he arrived well equipped for the polo and the race meetings that were his insurance against boredom. Sir Philip Game, later a close collaborator and then a junior gunner captain, has described the impact of Trenchard's personality on all who encountered him.

" It was amusing but also unusual to find very senior officers deferring to a mere major. Trenchard was extremely self-confident, and with reason. Whatever he arranged came off."

He insisted on backing his own horses exclusively and kept a note of his winnings. His champion mare alone reaped him a profit of £1367 in stake money; and he regretted having to sell her for £250 on his recall to England.

Middleburg put on its military finery when General Lyttleton held a farewell review of his troops. Behind the ranks of marching infantry the 16th Lancers came at the regulation trot, heading column after column of mounted men. Trenchard's regiment rode last, with a widening gap between them and the bobbing heads of the troopers in front; he was anxious to let Lyttleton see "the best cavalrymen anywhere" thundering past at the gallop. The stately beat of the bandsmen's brass fifes and drums was presently drowned in the rhythmic clatter of hooves. The column swept past the saluting base, with Trenchard riding, sword in hand, several paces in front. None of this was in the ceremonial rule book; but the staff heard their general's muttered appreciation before the last gun carriage rumbled out of sight in a pall of red dust.

2

Trenchard still had a month's leave to run in September, 1903, when he spent a long week-end at a country house in Hampshire. It was a long-standing invitation; he had put off the Hargreaves repeatedly for fear of imposing on the hospitality of chance friends who might prove less congenial in their home surroundings than in the cosmopolitan atmosphere of St. Moritz. He was glad in the end that he accepted; for the visit led to another turning point in his life.

The shooting was as excellent as the food, the company diverting. One of the Hargreaves brothers taught him to drive a new "horseless carriage" with a stiff steering-wheel and high seats. Trenchard spent hours roaring along the country lanes, revelling in a new experience. It was less peaceful indoors. Fashionable young women, friends of Violet, seemed to be "all over the house," monopolising the best chairs in the drawing-room and chattering with indefatigable shrillness. The din became a bond between Trenchard and the only other male guest. Presently they discovered deeper interests in common.

Colonel Gilman, who was older than himself, had recently been in West Africa. The War Office had appointed him to look into the recruitment of officers for the South Nigerian Regiment. There was apparently a doleful shortage of good ones; and Gilman dwelt on the reasons with distaste.

" The drinking, gambling and womanising in Calabar and Lagos are past belief," he said. " Only the duds and wasters want to go." The climate, he admitted, did not help; but the main difficulty was the lack of firm handling.

When Trenchard mentioned that he was undecided whether to stay in the army, or settle in the Transvaal on the off-chance of striking gold, Gilman was not exactly complimentary. Why squander a decade of military experience on a mirage? he asked. Trenchard would do better to volunteer for service in Nigeria where there was "real work" to be done, though it was no place for an officer seeking riches or popularity. The phrase stung like a taunt.

" I'm interested in what you say about the risks of unpopularity,"
Trenchard replied at length. " I've found it a sign that you're
working on the right lines when everyone else detests you."

In the end he agreed to give Nigeria a short trial and Gilman
promised to do all in his power to help him. He was as good as his
word. A week later Trenchard was interviewed at the Colonial
Office by Major-General Kemball, the Inspector General of the
West African Frontier Force, who offered him the post of Assistant
Commandant, South Nigerian Regiment, with the right to lead all
expeditions, on condition that he served for at least six months. He
gave the assurance gladly. Only when he reached his destination
towards the end of 1903 did he wonder whether he had done
wisely.

Disembarking at Bonny, in the Gulf of Guinea, he boarded a
small coastwise steamer bound for Calabar. It was early in December
but intensely humid as they left the open sea for the river. The jungle
closed in behind and above them like a vast, overgrown hot-house.
Upstream, primitive landing-stages stood sentinel by palm-thatched
villages with the air of outposts used by travellers who never stayed.
It was easier to understand now why Gilman and Kemball could
not attract enough good officers. Nature was against them. British
rule was hemmed back to the banks of rivers and to the narrow
coastal strip. The hinterland, covering an area larger than France,
was unopened, treacherous and almost entirely unmapped bush.

The traders aboard were disconcertingly candid. Europeans,
they told him, seldom ventured far inland. Even the officials and
soldiers had established few footholds far beyond the river lines:
missionaries sometimes penetrated inland, though God alone knew
what they hoped to gain. Trenchard had a vague, uneasy prejudice
against these zealots as a class. He had never been able to comprehend, far less disentangle, the rival pretentions of Christian churches
claiming to be sole trustees of eternal truth. Here, on the edge of the
immemorial wilderness, their work seemed vain indeed. He doubted
whether it could lighten or dispel the darker mysteries of the
forest, whatever the virtues of missionaries as individuals.

The traders, at least, were clear about their purpose. But what
of the soldiers? As the boat moved through the filtered, eerie sunlight, Trenchard wondered whether they could be as bad as Gilman
had hinted. Next morning, in the regimental mess at Calabar, he
wondered no longer. Punctual to a fault himself, he entered to find
the place unoccupied. Then, one by one, his fellow-officers walked
in. The majority were unshaven and in pyjamas. The commanding

officer, Colonel Montanaro, sat apart, properly dressed, with eyes
riveted to his plate and ears studiously deaf to the buzz of indelicate
conversation.

The drinking, gambling and sexual exploits of which the noisier
of his subordinates were blatantly boasting did not appear to affect
either his appetite or composure. Montanaro, it seemed, had
abandoned the effort of acting as a public keeper of consciences. A
soldier of considerable experience, lean, lined but still active, he was
displeased by Trenchard's unflattering comments on regimental table
manners. Military life on the coast, he said curtly, was not the same
as in England; and he had more important things to do than discuss
morals with a newcomer.

Trenchard held his tongue. As second-in-command to a man
who chose to run a regiment on a very loose rein, he would have to
bide his time before asserting himself. The occasion to do so came
unexpectedly in a way that could hardly have been better calculated
to rouse the colonel's lasting resentment.

The rains were falling again. To judge by the gossip, all Calabar
knew of the regiment's imminent departure into the interior. Inter-
tribal fighting, inspired by ancient and complex superstitions, was
raging again in the Arochuko country. Reports of lootings, burnings,
and ritual murders had been trickling out of the forest during the
summer; the preparations for another expedition to pacify the
district were all but complete when Trenchard arrived, and Montanaro was averse to discussing them, except in vague outline. His
deputy put this down at first to the professional jealousy of an old
campaigner and did not press him. Only the day before the
expedition was due to leave, when Montanaro could no longer keep
the information to himself, did he tell Trenchard that he would
have to stay behind.

"You'd be a liability in the field," said the colonel.

Trenchard's indignation boiled over. He was not without
military experience, he said. Montanaro retorted that experience
did not enter into it; it was a matter of acclimatisation.

Not to be outdone, Trenchard played his one trump card.
General Kemball, he pointed out, had promised him full backing
and had indicated plainly that it would be his function to lead all
expeditions. Wholly unperturbed by what he regarded as a piece
of bluff, Montanaro stated that he could answer for his own decisions
to Kemball. "My orders to you are to take a detachment of forty
men and stand guard at Owerri."

Trenchard complied with reluctance. Before leaving Calabar,

however, he sent a message to Kemball, who was then in the Gold Coast, conveniently near.

" I wired him," Trenchard explained later, " that as I wasn't going to do any good accepting an impossible situation I had no choice but to give up and go home. Kemball got in touch at once with Sir Ralph Moore, the retiring Governor of southern Nigeria, advising him to recall Montanaro and send me up to replace him as leader of the expedition."

When the Governor's message reached Owerri, Trenchard left a lieutenant in charge, returned at once to Calabar, and sailed by launch up the Cross River to the small trading station of Itu, two and a half days behind the expedition. Determined to catch up Montanaro before it was too late, he set off in the clammy noonday heat with carriers, a servant and a hired guide. As they moved away from the water, the invisible roof of the forest suddenly enclosed them in an ominous green twilight. Leathery, vine-like creepers and thorny undergrowth caught at his clothes and scratched his limbs. After the first mile's march his shirt was black with sweat and sticking to his skin, but his eyes grew quickly accustomed to the leafy half-light, his ears to the myriad sounds of strange animal life. Few men, black or white, ever passed that way. By nightfall, he had mastered weariness but prudently called a halt in a clearing beside a clump of cotton trees. Sleep came fitfully on a camp bed laid beneath a makeshift bower of intertwined branches. At daybreak they moved off again.

During the second afternoon the guide, with uncanny prescience, picked up the trail of the column. He gesticulated excitedly and said in broken English that it could not be far ahead. An hour later Trenchard emerged into a treeless open space where the direct glare of the sun half blinded him. Dark-skinned pickets saluted him as he entered the precincts of the makeshift camp. Then he saw Montanaro staring hard at him.

The colonel walked over quickly and said coldly: " What the devil are you doing here? "

" I've been sent to relieve you," Trenchard replied, handing him the crumpled text of the Governor's wire.

The colonel scanned it, his lined, sallow face quite expressionless. Trenchard felt no inclination to gloat; a man who could choke back so well the shock of being overruled commanded pity and respect.

Montanaro looked up, and said evenly: " I'll be leaving in the morning."

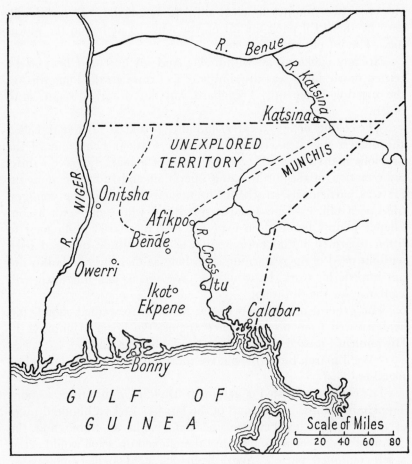

The interior of Southern Nigeria in 1903

Trenchard retired early. The exertions of his first trek had exhausted him. Just as he was dozing off, a hubbub of voices outside the darkened hut roused him. The others had evidently decided not to accept Montanaro's discomfiture passively or without protest.

" Who does this long-legged bastard think he is? " shouted one.

" The whole thing's a bloody disgrace," bawled another.

" If he imagines we can be treated like dirt," cried a third, " then he'd better look out."

They were running short of breath and abuse when Trenchard suddenly towered above them in pyjamas and dressing-gown. " I'll give you two minutes to clear off," he boomed. " If you're still here by then, I'll pack the lot of you off to Calabar in the morning. The lot of you, d'you hear? "

Nobody spoke as he withdrew. And all he could hear as he settled down again was the shuffle of feet through the long grass as the meeting broke up. Trenchard was not disturbed again until dawn.

The colonel departed early, and after breakfast Trenchard called the officers together. He did not refer to their behaviour of the previous night: instead, with the help of a map, he gave a brief appreciation of the forthcoming operation and invited comments. He was particularly struck by the sagacity of one of the youngest officers, a tall, ex-Scots Guards subaltern, who spoke with a confidence plainly founded on experience. Trenchard's willingness to listen disarmed initial apprehensions. His attitude declared itself without need of open warnings. So long as their private habits did not impede his work, he would be prepared to mix tolerance with vigilance for the duration.

The general plan drawn up by Montanaro seemed sound, but he borrowed from his experience against the Boers to improve it. His audience looked somewhat startled when he said:

" We'll march by night, but we must make sure of sticking close together."

The column consisted of 250 men. Dividing it into three sections Trenchard assumed command of the largest. Over a hundred miles of dense jungle lay between the base camp at Ibibio and the disturbed area; for ten days, until they linked up, each would act as a self-contained patrol. Apart from one light artillery company, mainly British in composition, the soldiers were all Yoruba and Hausa volunteers under their own N.C.O.s. Well trained and well disciplined, they adapted themselves to the novelty of resting through the noonday heat with stolid indifference.

Late on the third day's march, the main section came upon the charred debris of a village, deserted but still smouldering. The leading platoon, regardless of orders, suddenly halted beneath a tall cotton tree. Strung up from one of the branches, head downwards, and secured by stakes driven into the ground beside the blackened tree-trunk, hung the naked rotting body of a woman.

She had obviously died by inches in great agony; the arms were outstretched in a frozen gesture of crucifixion; the mouth and private parts, liberally smeared with honey, had been half eaten away by the army of ants still swarming over her putrefying limbs.

At Trenchard's side the political officer accompanying the column studied the gruesome apparition in silence.

" A ritual murder, I'm afraid," he said at length. " Her crime was giving birth to twins."

The practice, he explained, was common in inaccessible parts of the Bende territory above the Niger delta. It increased during periods of unrest.

" They believe that one of the twins is the child of an evil spirit. They can't be sure which twin is which, so they butcher both and make an example of the mother."

Trenchard had overheard people discussing the rite before, but its stark horror filled him with revulsion. The victim was not long dead. The culprits could not be far away. The column moved on.

Darkness had fallen when it stopped again, this time in front of a huge spiked stockade barring the track. Trenchard ordered his men to fan out through the undergrowth and hack a way round on either side. The oppressive silence was broken only by the snapping of roots and branches under the machete blows; for what seemed a small eternity there was no other sound. Then in one frenzied moment the forest awoke. Hordes of screaming Ibo tribesmen leaped up and hurled themselves upon the spreading pincers of the column, brandishing spears, blowpipes and antiquated shotguns. The range was short, the shooting mercifully atrocious. Trenchard drove on his men, inspiring them, as he laid about him, to disregard their fears of poisoned arrows or a charge of powder full in the face. The attackers turned tail when the bodies of twenty or thirty of their number were littering the red, upturned earth by the stockade. Save for half a dozen lightly wounded men, the column was intact.

" Let them run," said Trenchard. " We'll wait in their village till they come back."

He was roused by the guards next morning. The tribesmen, led by the local chief, had indeed come back—to hand in their arms. Six neighbouring chiefs with nearly 10,000 armed men soon followed their example. Tempering standing orders with common sense, Trenchard spared their villages; only those of the stubborn and bellicose were burnt to the ground. The column passed on, living off the territory and taking hostages until the last of the ritual atrocities had been accounted for.

Then Trenchard summoned the Ibo chiefs to the largest village. The district officer interpreted his terms of peace.

" You have been murdering people on Government roads," he said. " That must stop at once. As for what you do to women who

bear you twins, it's the work of the devil. When you do wrong, you
must come before the white man forces you. Your roads are bad,
yet a year ago you promised to make them clean and straight. You
must improve them. I've taken your guns away because guns are
forbidden. You'll be wasting your time and mine buying more."

One of the European officers present that day retains to this an
unaltered impression of Trenchard's simple directness. It moved
the Ibo chiefs far more than the customary banal appeals to their
loyalty, mingled as these so often were with bullying and mild
deception. Trenchard noticed with some suspicion, for instance, that
none of his guides had sustained a scratch during the fighting. The
fact that nearly all of them belonged to the Arochuko tribe, which
exercised a curious domination over the whole thickly peopled
districts between the Niger and Cross Rivers, seemed to him an
incitement to unrest. Their presence in the van of punitive expeditions, he argued, merely added to their local influence by letting
them masquerade as harbingers of the white man's vengeance.
What was to stop them deceiving the British, who relied on them as
guides, and blackmailing their weaker neighbours, who dared not
offend or disobey them? Trenchard had an irrational feeling that
the Aros might well be the instigators of the recent upheaval; his
political officer disagreed.

" Even if your guess is right," he said, " you just can't get rid
of the Aros. Where would you find new guides for the column? "

" The Ibos will do just as well," countered Trenchard. " They
might respond to a little trust."

The experiment was tried; and, somewhat to the surprise of the
political officer, it worked. People were drawn by curiosity from far
and wide to meet the column.

At Bende, a town with an established trade in palm oil, he spent
a week supervising the building of a permanent outpost. The two
other sections rejoined him then a runner arrived bearing fresh
instructions from Government House. At Aba, some sixty miles to
the south, thousands of natives were out of hand: he must go there
and pacify the district at once.

The trail to Aba, running roughly parallel with the Iwo River,
was broader than any Trenchard had yet seen. Progress was rapid
and unimpeded. Outside the village a rather pompous district
commissioner excited Trenchard's easily triggered disrespect by
introducing himself as "the representative of the King" and informing him that though the disorders had died down that the column
should nevertheless stay "for at least a week." Suspects had to be

brought in, cases tried, and the presence of armed troops would speed the process.

" I'm sorry to disappoint you," Trenchard replied, " but since your difficulties have solved themselves I can't stay. Tribesmen are looting and killing still in the district. It's entirely your affair whether you come with me, but I'm leaving first thing in the morning."

The official threatened Trenchard with the consequences of questioning his authority, only to be told bluntly that any king's representative worth his salt should have had more sense than to question the decisions of a military commander.

" He accompanied me next day," Trenchard wrote, " but meanwhile he sent off a hot protest to the new High Commissioner, Mr. (later Sir) Walter Egerton, who had just arrived from the Straits Settlement to govern southern Nigeria. Egerton wired back that I must be regarded as my own political officer in the field and that district commissioners should regard themselves as my assistants. This condition was allowed to continue on all expeditions during the next seven years I was to spend in Nigeria. It worked excellently."

Having consolidated his position, Trenchard had no inhibition about treating the precedents and standard practices of district officials strictly on their merits. When, for instance, he discovered that a batch of Ibo captives had been flogged for refusing to talk, he ordered their instant release, severely reprimanded the officer responsible, and warned all his men that he would not tolerate any maltreatment of prisoners. The paradoxical contrast between Trenchard's overbearing strength of personality and this unexpected manifestation of tenderness towards sullen captives, traditionally held to be incapable of understanding any language but that of physical violence, dumbfounded them. They coined a word for natives, a word redolent of their own half-amused and half-scornful acceptance of an incomprehensible absurdity. " Trenchard's-mustn't-touch-'ems," they called them. And it stuck. Trenchard's attitude, in fact, was inspired by an instinctive contempt for force as an argument anywhere off a battlefield. As a method of emphasising the white man's right to rule, it seemed to him barbaric, inhuman and certain in the long run to defeat its own ends.

On the trail back to Calabar towards the end of March, 1904, another message from the new High Commissioner caused him to press on by forced marches. A tribal revolt in the German Cameroons was spreading like wildfire over the creeks of the upper Cross River into Nigerian territory. Egerton sent for him as soon as Trenchard reached base. The insurrection, he said, had got out of hand. The German authorities had requested him to intervene; and he had promised to do so.

It was the first of many audiences with a colonial Governor whom Trenchard learnt to revere as one of the wisest, noblest and most underrated of British pro-consuls. Egerton put him instantly at ease by referring lightly to the dispute with the district official at Aba. Then he questioned him about the recent expedition.

" You did right," he commented when Trenchard explained why he had banned whipping. " In degrading others we degrade only ourselves."

He had not been long in Nigeria, he admitted, but he knew what the country needed most.

" Give me roads—good, broad, straight roads right through the jungle from one tribal area to the next—then we'll be able to let in the light."

Trenchard never forgot the words or the occasion. Drawing on a lifetime of humane endeavour, Egerton had formulated a policy already beginning to struggle for expression in Trenchard's own mind.

The column was re-equipped and sent ahead by river boat, Trenchard following up the navigable reaches of the Cross River in a missionary launch on hire to a trader. It was heavily laden with a special cargo, the exact nature of which the captain refused to disclose. The mysterious goods, well secured under tarpaulins, restricted the movements of everyone on board and Trenchard was finally induced to pry beneath the shiny, black covers to see what they were. At the sight of a large keg of gunpowder, clearly marked, and a crate of dane guns, he flew into a rage.

The captain shrugged phlegmatically. Bartering guns for yams and vegetable oils was his livelihood, he said. Besides, it was legal. He had been doing it for years.

" Well, this consignment is illegal," said Trenchard.

The guns and ammunition were confiscated at Itu, despite the captain's objections. Egerton was subsequently bombarded with protests from European merchants; but he upheld the decision.

Colonel Muller, the local German commander, and Trenchard then met and agreed to advance down their respective banks of the Upper Cross River. After pacifying Aparabong, the original centre of the revolt, Trenchard had a second meeting with Muller who complained of British leniency towards the rebels. The point of such a policy escaped him; he believed in punishing men who defied the law with the severity they deserved. Trenchard did not argue with him. The thousands of tribesmen who flocked daily to meet the column, surrendering firearms and volunteering information which shortened the mopping-up process, testified to the fact that magnanimity was a mark of strength. Men as rigid as Muller could not be reasoned with. So Trenchard left him to stamp out the large-scale revolt on the far side of the river by Teutonic methods of misplaced thoroughness and led his own column from village to village on the southern bank until the ringleaders came forward. The six chiefs who had joined hands with their repressed blood-brothers over the water, overrunning a German trading station, slaughtering Europeans and ransacking an ammunition depot, owned up to crimes which he would not presume to judge himself. The prisoners were led back to Calabar for trial.

3

In his last despatch to the High Commissioner, Montanaro praised Trenchard's leadership in the field generously.

" The energetic way in which he moved troops through the country enabled him to visit and bring to reason many towns which up to now have been hostile to the Government. I heartily approve his 'rushing' tactics."

Egerton endorsed the commendation in a fuller report to the Colonial Secretary, which, in that late spring of 1904, dispelled fears among backbench critics at Westminster that the British Government might be dealing harshly with rebellious tribesmen in southern Nigeria.

" Major Trenchard carried out the two operations confided to him thoroughly and expeditiously," wrote the High Commissioner. " Most of the fighting took place in thick bush where a man can lie securely concealed within a few yards of the paths along which a column has to move. . . ."

When Montanaro retired that summer, Trenchard served as acting Commandant. His opportunity to "clean up the regiment," as he put it, was now at hand.

It was probably because, like most zealots, Trenchard exaggerated to himself the gross viciousness of their conduct that most of the officers then at Calabar thought of him as a bleak, intolerant puritan. His unpopularity reached its peak during the enervating months of that first summer. He prohibited gambling; he punished men for unpunctuality, slovenliness and drunkenness; he showed no mercy to anyone caught consorting with native women.

The worst offenders were packed off to England in disgrace, and the example he made of these had a salutary effect on the others. By thus enforcing a set of rules, breaches of which were summarily corrected according to the spirit rather than the letter of King's regulations, he succeeded before the next campaigning season started in "separating the wheat from the chaff," to use his own phrase.

The only officer to try conclusions with him was the regimental doctor, a confirmed alcoholic whom Trenchard abruptly dismissed one morning after tripping over the man's black bag on the threshold of the untidiest room he had ever seen anywhere. The contents had spilled out, adding to the dust, soiled clothing and empty whisky bottles on the floor. Trenchard saw that the medical instruments were dirty and rusting through disuse, and decided on the spot that their owner should take them elsewhere. However, the doctor refused to leave without a court-martial, and wrote to the Governor and Kemball urging Trenchard's removal as a certifiable madman.

The dilemma was solved when the doctor burst into the sergeant's mess one day, buttonholed the sergeant-major and invited him to join him as his batman on a dream island in the Mediterranean where the King had been pleased to appoint him Governor. So Trenchard had the doctor certified instead.

By the late summer of 1905, when a new commandant was appointed, plans for the next campaign were virtually complete. Colonel Harry Moorhouse, a stronger and more likeable character than Montanaro, accepted without demur Trenchard's ambitious operational programme for penetrating and bringing under British control an unmapped region the size of Belgium some 200 miles up-country from Calabar.

No previous expedition had trekked into the hinterland between the Cross and Niger Rivers. According to Trenchard's estimates, it would take five months at least to scour the 1200 square miles of forest, plain and swamp in the Bende-Onitsha quadrilateral. And Egerton underlined why the home government attached the utmost importance to the success of this, the most arduous and hazardous military mission so far undertaken in southern Nigeria.

Changes in the political control of the colony were impending. The backward provinces of the southern half of Nigeria were to be merged into a single administrative unit of 1906. If the expedition failed or met with disaster, political progress might be retarded for years. That it did not fail was largely due to the powers of command

and improvisation displayed by Trenchard during the so-called Bende-Onitsha hinterland expedition that winter. The achievement earned him the D.S.O.; yet, at the outset, a mishap which might well have resulted in catastrophe threw his entire plan of action out of gear.

The leading column under Major Mair set off inland from its base camp at Onitsha, on the Niger, to reconnoitre 500 square miles of jungle while Trenchard's main force simultaneously pressed towards it in a westerly direction from Itu on the Cross River. Three days passed, then an exhausted messenger brought disturbing news. Dr. Stewart, one of the medical team who left Calabar late to join the expedition, had been kidnapped by Ibos somewhere along the trail behind. Stewart's fate was unknown; but the tribes were up in arms, a fact which suggested the worst.

" That night we kept marching," Trenchard noted. " Once we fired a star shell in a clearance from the millimetre gun in the hope of a similar answering sign from Mair. We waited, and saw one high above the trees many miles away. . . . The next night I ordered two star shells to be fired in rapid succession—a pre-arranged distress signal which Mair acknowledged. Only then did I tell the others what had been in the original message."

When the two columns met, Trenchard and Mair agreed that they should return in strength to the area where Stewart had vanished. They moved along roughly parallel tracks, in sections, to shorten their excessively long and exposed tail; and towards nightfall Trenchard's central group came to a dead halt in front of an enormous trench, eight feet deep and ten feet wide. Suddenly a hail of bullets, spears and arrows enveloped it; several soldiers fell; the remainder, about fifty, were suddenly locked in hand-to-hand combat with hundreds of milling tribesmen. The entire column, it seemed, and not only its struggling head, was trapped in an ambush from which escape seemed impossible. Then Trenchard remembered the star shells: the artillery officer hesitated on receiving the order to load and fire an experimental salvo into the trees above the trench.

A cluster of vivid red petals hissed and blossomed overhead, and in that instant the hideous noise of battle dwindled to a murmur. Gleaming black faces turned upwards towards the metallic light, their limbs palsied as if by magic. The Ibo warriors, cowering before this manifestation of the white man's awful power, scattered into the forest. The column kept watch all night and moved cautiously into the village beyond the ambush-trench at first light. Only one aged and terror-stricken man emerged, crawling on all-fours, to give himself up. Under cross-examination he confessed that the doctor had been murdered by slow mutilation. The Ibos had borne him, trussed and naked, through ninety villages in the region, dismembering him as they went, leaving a toe here, a finger there, an ear farther on, as ju-ju's, and finally decapitating him in the clearing where Trenchard and Mair were standing. It appeared that the column had returned inopportunely while the elders of the tribe were devouring the doctor's headless trunk.

Trenchard realised that, having once tasted blood, the murderers' superstitious belief in their own indestructibility would quickly conquer the terror induced by star shells. He was astonished in the circumstances that his parlour trick should have deterred them at all. For the Ibos held that the act of eating a white man automatically fortified them with his powers. The pursuit was long and trying; patrols were dispatched by day as well as night for six weeks. The column's supplies were running low when a man crept into the camp one evening with the dispiriting news that five thousand armed Ibos were massed on the edge of a creek less than a mile away. Trenchard deployed half his force against them; and the only action which bore the faintest resemblance to a pitched battle was over in half an hour. The surrounded tribesmen fought with fanatical courage, repeatedly charging the three Maxim gun positions until the swampy grass in front was piled high with the dead and dying. Even then the chiefs' response to Trenchard's terms was slow and unwilling.

" I let it be known that they must hand over the doctor's head and every bone in his body. Otherwise, there would always be fighting because they would say that they had got in them the ju-ju of the white man they'd consumed."

At last a pierced and shattered skull was brought in; the medical officers identified it as the head of a European not long dead. Slowly, piece by piece, all relics of the unfortunate Stewart—"except the hands and the lower part of the left leg"—were retrieved and borne to Calabar for burial. Trenchard remained with the column moving from village to village and pressing thousands of Ibos into service as labourers. Their punishment, he decided, would be for their country's betterment; they would construct the first of the jungle roads.

The maps he had were crudely drawn, the distances at best approximate. Their accuracy varied with the skill and concentration of "the men with the wheel" who measured every step on compass bearings, marking in the features and contours of the land traversed by the column. Two highways were begun, the first from Owerri towards Bende, the second from Owerri to Ikot Ekpene. Hewn out of the bush, forty feet wide, they laid bare to the sun the damp red earth below the tangled undergrowth for the first time in thousands of years. The chiefs were warned of their responsibility, to tend the roads and prevent misdeeds on or near them: he would return in six months to complete the task and judge how well they had obeyed him.

" The chief difficulty met with," Egerton reported to the Colonial Office, "was the country being split up into innumerable independent towns and communities, the chiefs of which are nearly always decrepit old men possessing little authority or control over their tribe, the real power being vested in the young men."

Trenchard took a roundabout way to the Delta, crossing slave trails that led northwards and inspecting fetish groves in country where every turn evoked memories among his men of past skirmishes, cannibalistic orgies, and innumerable ritual crucifixions in the primeval darkness of the forest. The old order would not pass quickly. Yet the highways would help to speed its passage by letting in the light. For wherever the column went the road makers followed.

" For five months," Moorhouse wrote in his dispatch, " Major Trenchard has commanded a column of 800 men in the field and shown energy, resource and powers of organisation far above the average. . . ."

In a bound cash-book, the fading pages of which still bear traces of sweat and damp, Trenchard used to jot down in a scrawling hand the happenings of the day. The detailed diary entries divulged little of his feelings; their matter-of-fact tone reflected a stoic's self-sufficient mind bent on the problems of to-morrow. It recorded the statistics of prisoners or hostages taken, illegal guns surrendered, tribute in yams or eggs levied, and casualties inflicted or sustained. The battles seldom involved more than a few hundred men; yet, as in the conquest of Gaul by the legions of Rome, it was the consolidating of local gains which mattered most. Where the soldiers set foot to-day, the traders, the officials and the missionaries would come to-morrow. Trenchard was probably least in sympathy with the last-named group, not being a very religious man. Their faith in the supernatural passed him by; he was totally uninquisitive about the hereafter. Whether God existed or cared about his alleged creation was scarcely a fit matter for discussion among gentlemen. Trenchard aspired no higher than "to leave my corner of the earth, wherever it might be, a better place than I found it."

He had learned not from books but from life two unbreakable rules for fostering understanding and justice between men, irrespective of colour, creed or degree of civilised development: the first was an "absolute respect for the sacredness of human life"; the second, a "fearless reverence for truth in word and deed." Beyond these bare fundamentals, he could not commit himself. If the missionaries' teaching was true, then the Almighty would have his work cut out in Nigeria where Christ rarely supplanted the grotesque jungle gods but took his place among them.

The only missionary for whom Trenchard conceived respect amounting to veneration was Mary Slessor. By now an old, wrinkled woman, with the iron will and stamina of a man half her age, she twice accompanied his expeditions as his political officer, wearing the long, black skirts and straw bonnet that had been fashionable in her youth. He admired her robust common sense; her opposition, for instance, to the usual missionary practice of clothing female converts in the ridiculous attire of the late Victorians; but not even Mary Slessor could alter his conviction that the missionaries would be better employed at home, or, at a pinch, among unregenerate Europeans at Calabar or Lagos. Only their schools seemed to him of any lasting value.

Once in the Kwa territory, when the first roads were being extended, Trenchard had a strange encounter with a missionary priest that accidentally deepened his scepticism. One of his junior officers had caught a mysterious fever. Trenchard stayed behind after the doctor had declared the patient to be beyond all medical aid, aware of the futility of sitting passively by a death bed in the stifling heat, yet unwilling to leave until the end. About midday the young man stirred, gazed wildly about him, demanded a priest, and sank into a coma.

" I'll see to it," Trenchard said half to himself. The column was in bush country over ten miles from the nearest mission station. He sent an escort which returned towards dusk with an uncommunicative, nondescript man in a Roman collar who ignored Trenchard completely as he prepared to administer the last rites. Stooping over the prone form on the camp bed, droning incomprehensible words, the priest smeared the dying officer with a wisp of oil then wiped it clean. It struck Trenchard as a quaint and meaningless ceremony, until he noticed with a start that the patient had come to and was

trying to lever himself up, his eyes staring at the missionary in
delirious terror.

"God Almighty," he screamed, "it's the devil himself."

And he fell back dead.[3]

Trenchard could find no words to ease the unknown priest's
embarrassment or his own bewilderment. The incident merely
hardened his opinion of the uselessness of missionaries, whose
competitive scrambling for Nigerian souls was no less reprehensible,
to his mind, than the current international scrambling for control of
new African territories.

At the close of the 1906 expedition Trenchard contracted black-
water fever and returned to Calabar on a litter. He had burnt
himself out; and when he recovered Moorhouse sent him home on
sick leave. He had no illusions about his indispensability, but
Nigeria still drew him like a magnet. In his absence the regimental
headquarters was transferred to Lagos, an unhealthy lagoon town
converted into a capital city at the stroke of a Minister's pen, and
one which boasted few amenities.

A young officer called Edward Steele, the brother of a future
Air Chief Marshal, left this description of conditions at this time:

> "I haven't really slept since I arrived. You lie surrounded
> by mosquito nets in a sort of pool of perspiration until from
> sheer weariness you slide into a state of lethargy and welcome
> the dawn to get up and have a bath. ... We've a rotten mess here,
> not a patch on Calabar. If Trenchard had been here, such a
> house would never have been put up. But everyone else is too
> slack to worry."

4

It was March, 1907. Moorhouse's term as commandant had almost
expired. Trenchard stood next in line of succession; indeed, during
his leave in England he had quietly anticipated the day by putting
a perplexing proposition to the managing director of Harrods. He
requested the sole agency to import into southern Nigeria a long list
of goods, including bicycles, tinned food and cloth. When asked
what security he could offer, he replied cheerfully: "None at all.
It's my idea, not the Colonial Secretary's, but I give my word you'll
be put to no loss or inconvenience."

The managing director was noncommittal. He would have to

consult his board, he said. Trenchard's boldness was rewarded when Harrods wrote agreeing to a test period of twelve months; and he sailed with the first consignment of goods on approval stowed in the ship's hold.

Among the merchants at Lagos and Calabar, the rumour that the new commandant intended to corner part of their monopoly was not taken seriously at first. The coast had its quota of commercial lunatics, and one more would make no difference. The mockery ceased as the agency's keen prices forced local merchants to lower theirs. Aggrieved inquiries came from as far away as the Chamber of Commerce in Liverpool and the Colonial Office in London; Egerton was appealed to, but ruled that Trenchard had trespassed on the rights of none.

Even in the mess critics were fewer now. The majority were held by the spellbinding force of his personality. A contemporary wrote to his parents that Trenchard was "only disliked by the worst out here because he makes them work"[4]; and the justice of that verdict grew more apparent during his final period as commandant.

Trenchard had the ramshackle barracks at Lagos pulled down and rebuilt. He laid out playing fields and offered a series of silver cups and trophies for soccer, golf, tennis and polo. He planned and helped to construct a house for his own use, imported *The Oyster*, a small cabin-cruiser, for easier journeys up the local creeks, and shipped from England the first motor cycles ever seen in Nigeria. The caution of Harrods evaporated when the unofficial agency's turnover in its first full year exceeded ten thousand pounds.

His last expedition, from November, 1907, until the following spring, enabled a huge blank area, 8000 miles square, to be filled in on the official maps. Egerton advised Crewe, the Colonial Secretary, that "this addition brings the whole of southern Nigeria under Government control except the small portion in the north-western corner adjoining the northern Nigerian boundary inhabited by Munshi tribes." Egerton was careful not to admit officially that Trenchard had in fact crossed the territory of the Munshi, who for generations had resisted Moslem encroachments as no other tribe had done, acquiring in the process a legendary reputation for ferocity and hostility to strangers.

Legends bored Trenchard, who spent a month up-country before setting off and collected as much authentic information about the Munshi as possible.

" I couldn't discover anyone in authority who claimed to have met a Munshi," he recalled. " Then I had a brainwave. I sent for all my political and intelligence officers, and said: ' Let's find if any of the servants, carriers or local people are married to women not of their own tribe.' After interviewing about twenty, I came across five with Munshi wives. This caused a sensation. Everyone was flabbergasted. Nobody would believe the obvious."

Ignoring the advice of the political officers, Trenchard cut down his force to four officers, an interpreter, twenty-five men, and three machine-guns. The course lay roughly north-east across a seemingly endless grassy plain. Thousands of armed men blocked the track outside the first village they approached, but no attempt was made to molest or stop the small column which eventually penetrated to the Katsina River, on the far bank of which lay an outpost manned by troops of the northern administration, A canoe ferried them across, and the officer in command declared that either Trenchard or his compasses were lying. That so small a patrol could have crossed Munshi territory without expending a single round of ammunition seemed incredible. But Trenchard's only precaution on the way back was to send two messengers ahead with gifts and greetings for the Munshi chiefs. The column followed and was conducted peacefully to a large, well-kept village. " A bloodthirsty-looking gang," was Trenchard's first impression of his hosts who nevertheless seemed pleased with their trinkets and not at all disposed to violence. Four of them accepted his offer of a safe-conduct to Afikpo where they were shown the river steamers, the permanent camp and the trading centre.

" I gave them singlets and looking-glasses, things I always carried on expeditions, and dispatched them to their own land with a guard of honour at the end of a fortnight. All the tales about the Munshi were idle gossip. I knew, and told Egerton, that their country could be opened immediately and without bloodshed."

His only clash with the Munshi occurred while a road was being laid across their plain in the spring of 1909. Thirty-five men in the column led by Captain Eustace Loraine, one of Trenchard's best officers, were killed before their assailants were put to flight.

Trenchard always treasured the sullen remark of their giant leader to his captors :

" Give me one piss-gun (Maxim) and I'll beat you."

The giant had not been easy to apprehend, but was duped by a trick of which Trenchard always remained slightly ashamed. Batches of Munshi prisoners were released and sent back as an inducement to the truculent chief to come and talk peace. At length he relented; but one glance at the visitor's scarred and scowling face con-

vinced Trenchard that such a man would never discuss surrender
terms.

" I therefore collared him and both his sons. They put up a
terrific fight with hands and fists, but eventually were overpowered,
tied to hammocks and sent downstream by launch to Calabar."

There, on Egerton's instructions, the captives were treated as
honoured guests. The chief bore Trenchard no ill-will and invited
him to visit his district again soon. Trenchard did so, and was
welcomed by a huge concourse of dancing tribesmen. He
presented the chief whose trust he had first strained and then
regained with a keepsake, "a smoking-cap made in Birmingham with
a long gilded tassel."

Only six months later, without an escort, Trenchard cycled with
Egerton along the completed highway that now passed through the
lands of this friendly giant. Hospitality was lavished on them, so
that it was all the more distressing to hear soon afterwards of the
Munshi chief's assassination. A jealous rival supplanted him, not,
it appeared, for his lands or wives, his autocratic behaviour or his
new attitude to the white man, but out of covetousness for that cheap
smoking-cap made in Birmingham.

Trenchard was at length able to relax and enjoy himself. For in
1909 the Governor was able to inform Whitehall:

" The annual field operations to extend settled government,
which have taken place during each dry season of the present
century, will no longer be required."

The forest had been mapped and tamed; a policy of firm gentle-
ness had triumphed. In helping to pacify much of South Nigerian
hinterland, Trenchard had incidentally discovered his own powers
as an administrator and an exceptional leader of men. But the fate
which had never spoilt him denied him now the immediate fruits of
that discovery. Early in 1910 he fell dangerously ill. That summer
they shipped him home, still in a parlous condition, with an abscess
on the liver.

5. *Air Apprentice*

Once off the danger list, Trenchard's recovery began to lag. Nor were the doctors surprised. The condition of his blood was appalling; his whole system was poisoned; they implored him to give himself a chance and prescribed a strict régime of rest. The chronic dejection symptomatic of his condition might, they warned, tempt him to overtax his vitality. It did. Trenchard rejected the régime, ignored the warning, doctored himself and so prolonged his unwilling convalescence.

One day seven years earlier at Middleburg, South Africa, a gunner friend had been drawn to a tent near the polo field by an odd smell of burning. Thinking that a fire might have started unnoticed, he entered in haste to find Trenchard stripped to the waist nonchalantly treating a badly sprained wrist with a very hot flat iron. Unfortunately for himself, the flat iron cure was still the cure he favoured.

The mornings were worst. Invariably he would wake up liverish and rise at once, heedless of his tired body's clamorous demands for another hour in bed. He had little appetite and was excessively short of stamina; his limbs would turn to jelly, his heart flutter like a trapped butterfly at the least exertion. He suffered from blinding headaches, and even books afforded no escape. With a defiance engendered partly by his mistrust of medical opinion, partly by the melancholia which consumed him exactly as had been predicted, he ordered the details and discomforts of his slow recovery.

By the late summer of 1910 he was well enough to honour an old pledge and take his parents on holiday to the West Country.

A former colleague who met Trenchard again at this time remarked on his changed appearance: his hair was cropped close, emphasising the unhealthy pallor of his face; he had lost weight and looked much older than his thirty-seven years. He was already resigned to the fact that another door had slammed behind him. One period of full and exhilarating living had abruptly ended, but he made no secret of his resolve to seek another.

In October, when the War Office posted him to the second battalion of his regiment at Londonderry, his contemporaries were soon wondering how long he would stay. Those who knew him well recognised that rank meant as little to Trenchard as medals or titles. The drop from temporary lieutenant-colonel to major aggrieved him far less than the anti-climax of commanding a company after rebuilding and running a regiment. The consensus of opinion was that Londonderry would prove too small to contain him.

Captain James Boyle, a younger son of the Earl of Glasgow, returned to his rented house near Ebrington Barracks a day or two after Trenchard's arrival and told his wife that "a most unusual customer" was creating quite a stir in the mess.

" Why, what's he up to? "

" Well, he's got some of his men taking geranium cuttings and the rest digging the garden because he thinks they haven't enough to do. He wants to start us on polo, and I don't think poor Colonel Stuart yet realises that he's serious."

Mrs. Boyle said: " He sounds quite interesting. What's he like?"

" Oh, big, frightening but harmless. He's been in southern Nigeria and finds the pace here slow. I must say I like him. He's coming to lunch to-morrow."

Trenchard turned out to be much as she had imagined. It was not hard to understand why subalterns were said to scatter like panic-stricken fowl at his approach, yet beneath the exuberant aggressive-ness she detected an element of unspoilt charm. He was curiously well read and observant, talked a lot about polo, less about Nigeria, and laughed heartily at his own jokes. After lunch he accompanied his hosts to the flat meadow behind the house, which Boyle had suggested as a potentially suitable polo ground. Trenchard was delighted; it would be ideal, he said. They could leave him to organise the mowing, the marking and the rest.

The meadow was mowed and marked within a week; the mis-givings of Colonel Stuart, with whom his relations were correct rather than cordial, tended to fade when Trenchard assumed entire responsibility for managing a communal stable. His passionate interest in practical economics extended to bargaining with dealers and chivvying his more extravagant brother officers. " The price of a glass of port is the price of a pony's feed," he would call out whenever someone ordered a drink at the bar. Polo itself was an opiate to him. The more he played the more he wanted to play.

He was never happier than in full cry on horseback. Once after a practice he was taken aback when Mrs. Boyle complimented him equally on the skill of his play and the deafening quality of his voice.

" Perhaps you were just a little too hard on the others in your excitement," she added.

He could only mumble in reply. Such candour, from a woman of all people, was a novel experience. Her stock rose in his estimation. Boyle was lucky indeed in possessing so spirited and beautiful a wife.

McDermid, the taciturn Glaswegian who had pillowed his head in the Dwarsvlei ambush, became Trenchard's groom again and was not without influence as the barrack-room interpreter and advocate of the "finest officer with the biggest heart" he had ever encountered.

" Do you ride, Barton? " asked Trenchard to a second lieutenant, fresh from Sandhurst, who sat down opposite him at breakfast one wintry morning.

" Yes, sir," said Barton who had just been attached to his company.

" Do you like riding? "

" Not very much, sir," said Barton truthfully, recalling the private vow he had sworn on receiving his commission never voluntarily to mount a horse again.

" Good. I'll see you at the stables after lunch."

Barton entered the mess that evening stiff but oddly elated. Thrown by a mettlesome horse at the first gate they reached, he had eventually cleared it under the eye of a surprisingly patient instructor who, in Barton's words, "seemed to know exactly when my mount would grow weary of trifling with me."

Trenchard's first and last church parade at Londonderry was long remembered as the occasion on which he wore his ceremonial busby back to front. From the convulsive sniggers in the ranks and the frantic asides of junior officers, none of whom felt equal to the dangerous task of enlightening him, he realised immediately that something was wrong with his appearance. On a hissed command from Barton, a reluctant company sergeant finally marched forward, saluted, and told him. Trenchard's reaction was resourceful. Removing his head-dress with a flourish, he ordered the parade to stand easy. " Take two minutes' laughter while I fix this thing," he added. " Then let's forget about it."

Several times during the service Trenchard nudged his subaltern in the pew beside him, demanding in a whisper loud enough to distract the less recollected members of the congregation:

" Barton, I want the truth. Did I look a bloody fool? "

Few old soldiers' dodges escaped his sharp, probing scrutiny; he abhorred the mechanical evolutions of barrack square routine as a waste of time, but suspended his distaste and cheerfully conformed. Yet deep inside himself, welling up now and then in a way which forbade articulate expression, was the feeling of being totally out of place. Short questioning the very basis of the British Army's peacetime organisation or entertaining doubts about his soldierly vocation, he had no cause to complain. So he responded by seeking to enlarge the area of his own responsibilities, a course which tended to create jealousy and friction.

He was accused, not altogether unfairly, of "poking in his nose where it wasn't wanted." When, for instance, he "decided one morning to invade the orderly room," Captain Horn, the acting adjutant, objected. Earlier, in an unguarded moment, after listening to a monologue on the vices of form filling, Horn had invited Trenchard, tongue in cheek, to demonstrate the virtues of his simplified system which had halved the paperwork at Calabar and Lagos, never dreaming that the offer would be taken so literally. The quartermaster was no more amenable to interference. As an insurance against any descent on his stores, he lodged a complaint with Colonel Stuart about Trenchard's incessant carping at old-fashioned methods of book-keeping.

" Stuart was a notoriously difficult person to rouse," recalled Horn. " I think it was because he genuinely admired Trenchard that he finally suggested, in so many words, that Londonderry was too small for both of them."

Trenchard, as it happened, had independently reached the same conclusion. Hunting and polo were not enough to compensate for the monotony of regimental life at half-pressure. Torn between loyalty and frustration, conscious as never before that time and opportunity were against him, determined not to degenerate into another mediocrity among majors until the War Office pensioned him off, he cast about for one avenue of escape after another.

" I wonder when you and I will meet again," he wrote to his elder sister, Katharine, in April, 1912, just before she left England to settle as a newly married woman in South Africa.

" I should so like to have come across to see you off, but it's really impossible. I have no cash. I wish I could have sent you more," (the wedding cheque he did send represented half his month's salary) " but I have not got it now. I shall probably come out one day to South Africa to see you if I can only stick out the service for another twelve years."

That final phrase reflected the despondency of a man in his fortieth year whose repeated attempts to secure a wider outlet for his energies had so far failed. Neither the Egyptian Army nor the International Gendarmerie in Macedonia would have him: he was too old, they said. Applications to join the mounted branch of the defence forces in South Africa, Australia and New Zealand were submitted and forwarded; but months passed without an acknowledgment from the War Office. Trenchard even wrote to Richard Burbidge, the ageing managing director of Harrods, recalling their co-operation in the days of the South Nigerian import agency; but Burbidge could promise nothing.

What intervened to change his career—and with it the course of military history—was something uncontrived and almost fortuitous. It was a letter from Captain Eustace Loraine, one of Trenchard's few army colleagues in Nigeria who could call him a friend. The quick brain, the gaiety and the imperturbability of the younger man, both as a member of the headquarters' staff at Lagos and as a section commander during the last expedition into Munshi territory, attracted Trenchard. The trust between them ripened naturally into fellow-feeling; and now Loraine had accomplished a youthful ambition since returning to England by learning to fly.

He had lately taken to stressing, whenever he wrote, that a beneficent War Office was paying him for the privilege of continuing his aviation training, seconding him for that purpose from the Grenadier Guards.

Trenchard could vaguely remember the stifling August evening in 1909 when he and Loraine had discussed the bizarre news reaching Lagos with the latest papers from home. Bleriot's successful flight across the English Channel had certainly not moved him as deeply as it did Loraine, who declared at once:

" This flying business is something I must find out more about."

Trenchard had not discouraged him, but beyond wondering aloud what the Munshi would think of the aeroplane as a manifestation of "white magic," the idea of learning to fly himself had not occured to him. Loraine was a regular correspondent. Yet none of his past letters from Salisbury Plain ever released the spring of desire in his friend's imagination. The final one did, in two artless sentences:

" You've no idea what you're missing," Loraine wrote. " Come and see men like ants crawling."

2

With a contrariness which Trenchard found infuriating Colonel
Stuart began by ridiculing the idea of his turning airman: " You're
far too big," he said. " These contraptions aren't designed for men
with legs as long as yours."

The commanding officer went further. It was a foolish venture
with no military value to commend it. Trenchard would probably
kill himself trying.

" You're far too old," he said.

But Trenchard spurned these objections and systematically wore
down Stuart's resistance until his application for three months paid
leave of absence was endorsed. No query was raised about his
chequered medical history; the fact that he possessed only one whole
lung was either forgotten or conveniently overlooked. War Office
doubts, like the colonel's, were confined to the question of age:
forty was the limit for qualified pilots who wished to join the Royal
Flying Corps; Trenchard was unqualified and thirty-nine.

Beyond the walls of the orderly room and the ears of the few
friends in whom he confided, he let drop no hint of his intention.
Some believed that he was crossing to England on compassionate
leave to visit his father who, by a cruel coincidence, suffered a minor
stroke in June, 1912, shortly before his departure. If he was less
communicative than ever about hopes and plans in the presence of
his parents, this was not altogether due to filial concern. For, by a
still more savage coincidence, one calculated to dismay the stoutest
heart, Trenchard opened a newspaper on arriving in London to read
on an inside page the bare details of a flying accident the previous
day, 5th July, 1912. The Nieuport monoplane which spun down
out of control near Larkhill, on Salisbury Plain, instantly killing the
two men on board, had been piloted by Captain Eustace Loraine,
late of the Grenadier Guards.

Trenchard's grief for this friend and exemplar only steeled his
determination. He took a room in Weybridge, within walking distance of the grassy airfield, its offices and its flimsy-looking hangars.
He had studied the matter of tuition thoroughly; his period of grace
was perilously tight. Indeed if he failed to fly solo and pass the necessary tests within four weeks, he would miss his only chance of being
enrolled as a pupil at the Central Flying School. The list of entrants
for the next course of instruction was already filling up; it had to
be the next course or none.

Beside the broad sweep of grass enclosed by the car-racing circuit were several wooden huts belonging to civilian flying instructors. Trenchard hesitated before deciding which door to knock at, settled for Mr. T. O. M. Sopwith's, and found the owner inside, glad to accommodate another beginner for the usual fee of £75, including insurance for breakages and third-party risks.

" Trenchard impressed me the moment he walked in," recalled Sopwith. " He said that the War Office had given him a fortnight to get his aviator's certificate, and that if for any reason he missed the tests by then he'd be over age. I promised to do my best for him."

About dawn on 18th July, Trenchard was pacing impatiently up and down the strip of road near Sopwith's office. It was shortly after 4 a.m. and misty. Trenchard felt like a caged beast. Then his instructor arrived, a slightly built man in overalls and a leather jacket who introduced himself as Copland Perry, apologising casually for the delay which had been caused by a mechanical fault. He understood Major Trenchard's predicament, he said; he would take him up first; the machine was ready now.

The sun had begun to pierce the veil of mist when Trenchard climbed up and perched himself on the tiny raised passenger seat of the Maurice Farman. A mechanic swung the propeller just behind Trenchard's head, and the engine broke into a stutter of life. Copland Perry manipulated the throttle, leaned round and shouted: " Watch what I do carefully. If you're not sure of anything, sing out."

They bumped over the grass, gathering speed, and when the jarring stopped Trenchard could see the ground falling away beneath the machine's quivering canopy of wire and wood. A panorama of green and grey and gold began to unfold itself. Then Perry banked gently, and belts of tiny trees behind the roofs of toy houses tilted incongruously on their sides. The air had been almost motionless on the ground; but at 1500 feet the wires whistled in the wind of their passage, the noise drowning itself in the louder din of the engine. Trenchard found himself thinking of Loraine's words about " men like ants crawling," and could visualise exactly how Loraine had died. Then he drew heart from the reflection that his breathing was less affected than he feared it might be: the official forms assumed that no intending aviator without the regulation pair of lungs would be insane enough to apply.

It was all over in ten minutes. Perry circled Brooklands twice, gleefully pointing out the sewage farm where pupils sometimes came to grief, and landed as gracefully as he had taken off.

T.   D

There was less grace but no lack of firmness in Trenchard's handling of the same machine when they were airborne over the sleeping town two days later. The instructor crouched over him ready to correct the first false move. Perry, who had until recently been a test pilot at the Royal Aircraft Factory, Farnborough, agreed to give the importunate beginner two lessons in the one day, with results which amply justified the risk.

" Major Trenchard making first rolls on Farman in promising style," the instructor noted in the log that night.

The following week an army staff officer arrived by appointment at Sopwith's early one morning. The only person in sight was an exceptionally tall, spare and disgruntled man who introduced himself as Major Trenchard and loudly cursed the caprices of the weather and the unpunctuality of his instructor. Captain Edward Ellington had been sent by the Director of Military Training, to whom he was temporarily attached, to qualify as a pilot. The queasy feeling in his stomach at the prospect of going up for the first time disappeared in the presence of this formidable stranger, who kept glancing at his watch.

Ellington, who had always thought of flying tutors as members of a superior race apart, said tentatively:

" Perhaps our man's got an explanation."

" It had better be a thundering good one," snapped Trenchard.

When Perry finally appeared, he shrugged contritely as Trenchard rounded on him. Then they walked away together as though nothing had happened, leaving Ellington musing over as one-sided an outburst as he had heard for many a day.[1]

If the instructor found Trenchard's unceremonious brusqueness something of a headache on the ground, he evidently had few doubts about his aptitude or docility in the air. The following extracts from the Sopwith school log underline the rapidity of his progress:

" Friday, 26th July: early morning, Major Trenchard making figures of 8 on school Farman. . . . In evening, on Farman for 10 minutes.

" Saturday, 27th July: early morning. Major Trenchard on Farman.

" Sunday, 28th July. Gales and showers, no flying.

" Monday, 29th July. No flying, hail, wind, rain.

" Tuesday, 30th July. No flying, rain, wind, hail.

" Wednesday, 31st July: morning. Mr. Copland Perry for 10 minutes alone on Burgess-Wright, and afterwards testing school

Farman before handing over to pupils. Major Trenchard then flew for his brevet and passed tests in really excellent style."

He had earned his wings in exactly one hour and four minutes of flying time spread over thirteen days.

" It was no light accomplishment," summed up Sopwith, " but Major Trenchard tackled it with a wonderful spirit. He was out at dawn each morning. He was dead keen to do anything that would expedite tuition. . . . He was a model pupil from whom many younger men should have taken a lead."

A fortnight afterwards, on 13th August, the Royal Aero Club granted him his official "ticket", pilot's certificate No. 270. He had won the first lap of his race against the clock; the second lap would tax other qualities besides his close sense of timing.

" Hugh has gone in for flying and joins the Royal Military Flying Corps on the 16th of this month," his father wrote from his sick bed to Katharine in South Africa during August. " He went to Brooklands to learn, never telling us a word. . . . He is very pleased about it and hopes to get on rapidly. It's much better than plodding on in his regimental duties."

The Royal Flying Corps had come into being almost unnoticed on 13th May, 1912, while Trenchard was still striving to extricate himself from Londonderry. By late August, when he reached Upavon and began sorting his unfavourable first impressions of the new Central Flying School, the Corps was still very much a neglected stepchild. Formally adopted by the State its foster parents, the two fighting services, chose to disregard it. In the view of most army and navy officers, the heavier-than-air machine was just another craze for the shortsighted crank; and, left to themselves, the military leaders would probably have decided against forming a new flying arm, incorporating the old Balloon Company of the Royal Engineers, on the pretext that aerial observation was a futile dream. The politicians were of a different mind, as Lord Haldane, the Secretary of State for War, made clear when addressing a special session of the Committee of Imperial Defence in November, 1911. Its members did not quarrel with his logic. They were unanimous in proposing "the creation of a British aeronautical service to be regarded as one . . . and to consist of a naval wing, a military wing and a Central Flying School."

At this point, a panel of eight technical experts took over. Their guide through the labyrinth of the service departments was a singularly cool and far-sighted man, Brigadier David Henderson, the Director of Military Training at the War Office, who received his brief from the Under-Secretary for War, Colonel J. E. B. Seely, at a meeting in January, 1912.

" All the heads of departments are very anxious to get on with this," said Seely. " But what is the best method to pursue in order to do in a week what is generally done in a year? . . . At the present time we have in this country, as far as I know, of actual flying men in the army about eleven, and of actual flying men in the navy about eight. France has about two hundred and sixty-three, so we are what you might call behind. . . ."[2]

One of the eleven army pilots was Henderson himself, then a veteran of nearly forty-nine; and three of the first eight naval officers whom the Admiralty had released to earn their wings welcomed Trenchard when he reached Upavon. The most senior of them, Captain Godfrey Paine, was a thickset, forthright and energetic man who had accepted the post of Commandant after determined bargaining. The Central Flying School, he argued, being a mixed experimental unit, needed firm direction if conflicting service traditions and customs were not to produce trouble. The authorities thereupon conceded him the right to choose his own staff. Without more ado, Paine selected as his first two instructors Captain E. L. Gerrard of the Royal Marine Light Infantry, and Lieutenant Arthur Longmore, both of whom he had condemned two years previously for compromising their naval careers to train as pilots. Paine had since turned the tables on himself, to the disgust of his superiors, by abandoning destroyers for a pair of wings.

On his second day at Upavon Trenchard was allotted to Longmore's flight. To his annoyance, flying practice was cancelled for the next week owing to bad weather, but the interlude had its providential side. For on the strong recommendation of his "governing committee," the Commandant co-opted Trenchard to the permanent staff before Longmore could test his oldest pupil's proficiency in the air. Flattered but puzzled, Trenchard listened carefully while Paine explained that army entrants outnumbered naval by nearly three to one; the school needed an army adjutant; and Trenchard's service record suggested that his qualifications as a handler of men were excellent.

" Here's a provisional list of duties," said Paine, handing him a sheet of paper. " Most of them are pretty sketchy."

Among the few specific responsibilities laid down in black and white, Trenchard noted, was that of school examiner. The irony of that alone was too rich to admit refusal.

Longmore soon discovered some of Trenchard's deficiencies as a pilot. The seven or eight machines on the hill-top at Upavon were a mixed assortment, including Shorts, Bleriot biplanes, Avros, and a pair of elderly Farman " Longhorns " for beginners. The instructor had the illusion that his Longhorn began to sag a little amidships when his pupil clambered aboard after him for their first flight. The illusion persisted as Trenchard settled his weight on the edge of the petrol tank looking as comfortable as a buzzard in a budgerigar's cage. His bulk seemed to set up considerable head resistance; and, after executing a series of gentle turns, Longmore landed as soon as he decently dared. They changed places; and after one preliminary circuit with the instructor at his elbow, Trenchard insisted on being left to his own rough devices. There followed one of the most peculiar solo exhibitions Longmore had yet witnessed. The Farman seemed to shudder as though every strut were about to come adrift, bumped over the grass at breakneck speed, hovered for one split second of infinite uncertainty, then leaped drunkenly up like a kite in a gale. The instructor's heart stayed in his mouth until Trenchard completed the customary figure of eight, turned slowly and landed rather jerkily a few yards from him. Here was one man, Longmore confided to himself, who would need hours of practice to moderate his over-confidence and acquire finesse.

The entries in his log indicate how conscientiously Trenchard practised. After dawn or about sunset, when the air was thought to be less turbulent, he seldom missed the thrill of taking himself up alone over the rolling plain.

" At best," said Longmore, " he was an indifferent flier. His age told against him, though he showed enviable pluck and per-severence."

On the ground Trenchard's duties grew with his insatiable appetite for discovering exactly what went on in every office, at the workshop benches, and inside the metal sheds beside the landing ground. The school had struggled along so far on a somewhat indefinite rule-of-thumb basis, and Paine was grateful for an assistant familiar with army practices. In drawing up a set of work-able standing orders for a unit as varied in membership as it was unique in purpose, Trenchard had to mix guile and diplomacy with firmness. He adapted what was best in the regulations of army and navy; and, with the set aim of offering the least offence to the greatest number, he jettisoned the rest.

Upavon, in his eyes, was a place for turning novices into specialists. Men came there to master a difficult technique in a new, half-understood element: the challenge itself was a common spur

and a common bond. Whether an officer belonged to cavalry or
infantry, whether he boasted of being a sapper or a gunner, the
prestige attaching to his old unit was forfeited as soon as he entered
the Central Flying School. There could be no room for differences
about drill or dress or custom; everyone had too much to learn.

That Trenchard's rough dexterity proved more than adequate
is borne out by the evidence of Gerrard.

" We had men of every type of the C.F.S., men from nearly every
unit and civilians, too. In time they came from the Indian Army
and farther afield. Trenchard's method stood the test because of
his personality and drive and his really amazing knowledge of
human nature. He didn't believe in standing on ceremony. He
could smell out difficulties as they arose, starting the hunt with
a gambit like this: ' I see they're sending four men from the
Loamshires. I don't have to tell you what damned fellows they
are, so may I suggest we do this . . .' We seldom questioned his
proposals or decisions. He didn't mind criticism and enjoyed a
constructive argument. But we could be sure he'd have those
Loamshires taped from the moment they arrived until they left
the school, disciplined, accomplished airmen with the makings of
a new *esprit de corps*."

Paine's initial gesture of trust was thus handsomely repaid.
The tightening up of routine and discipline was achieved with
surprisingly few casualties; and in October, 1912, Trenchard was
confirmed in office. His grading, to quote the *London Gazette*, was
that of "an instructor (Squadron Commander) *vice* Captain E. B.
Loraine, deceased." The wheel of fate had come full circle.

Trenchard had much to give; he had also much to learn, not
only about flying as an art but about the past efforts of pioneer
aviators and designers to move the twin mountains of popular
scepticism and official inertia. The general knowledge he picked up
from articles, books and conversations, was sharpened and refined
by personal impressions which helped to explain why in 1912, nine
years after the historic flight of the Wright brothers, a British
Government was not yet prepared to invest more than £320,000
in its new Flying Corps.

Early one day, for instance, when an experimental machine made
a forced landing at Upavon in thick mist, Trenchard came face to
face with Alliot Verdon-Roe, the pilot, designer and constructor.
The meeting was an education in itself. Verdon-Roe clearly
belonged to a select company of men still ready to back their vision

with limited capital and unlimited courage. If the barriers of disbelief were beginning to tumble, the credit for that was largely theirs. While Trenchard had been buried in Nigeria, this enterprising engineer had narrowly escaped arrest for daring to fly and land his own machine; the law was not in sympathy with adventurers who endangered other people's lives as well as their own by seeking to defy the laws of nature. When Verdon-Roe later wrote to *The Times* predicting that air travel would one day be as safe as any other form, the engineering editor dismissed his claim as nonsensical. Trenchard had sometimes encountered similar obscurantism among his own superiors and he was proud to share the capacity of the Sopwiths, the Shorts, the Verdon-Roes, the Codys, the Handley-Pages and others like them, for peering beyond the clouded horizons of the present.

3

What opened his eyes wider to the military possibilities of flying was his experience as an air observer during the army manœuvres of September, 1912. Longmore and five other pilots were chosen to "spot" for the northern force under General Grierson; and Trenchard accompanied his instructor. They flew from Thetford, Suffolk, on the first day of the exercise, with orders to locate General Haig's advancing southern force. As they passed over a town in East Anglia, Trenchard's voice suddenly roared out above the din of the engine. Columns of men were streaming down a road like the ants once described by Loraine, their weapons and equipment glittering at every step. The enemy line of advance was reported to an incredulous Grierson within an hour of take-off.

The general and his staff were put out by the information. The cavalry, it seemed, had already been dispatched in another direction and there was no quick way of recalling them. Trenchard thought it was time to intervene. Could not Longmore and himself pass on fresh instructions from the air? Grierson looked dubious only for a moment.

" It's worth a trial," he said. His staff bustled round him. Orders were written and handed to Trenchard for personal delivery to Briggs, the cavalry commander; and five minutes later the aircraft was aloft again.

They eventually sighted horse-drawn transport and the flashing points of cavalry lances by the hedges of the Newmarket road. Heads turned up in curiosity, hands waved in mock-greeting, as the Farman circled above. Trenchard's eyes raked the area for a glimpse of braid and red tabs: " How vulnerable they are," he said to Longmore. " And how far off course! "

The roof had been suddenly removed from the mock-battlefield. No commander, he knew, could ever depend entirely again on luck or strength or skill; a regiment of cavalry was no substitute for a single reconnaissance aircraft.

Longmore banked steeply and landed in a meadow. Trenchard handed the sealed message to General Briggs who acted on it at once. Afterwards it was admitted officially that the manœuvres had been largely influenced by the "intervention of aircraft" which secured the initiative for Grierson. The pilots on Haig's side were no less active, but the advantage of surprise, once lost, was hard to recover.

" In the course of a few days," commented Sir Walter Raleigh, the air historian, " the aeroplanes rose into such esteem that they were asked to verify information which had been brought in by the cavalry."

Improvisation was the order of the exercise for the two or three dozen Flying Corps representatives attached to the rival forces. A second-hand Daimler, privately owned, followed Longmore and Trenchard wherever they went, loaded with mechanics, tools and spares.

They were never far behind when needed; and not once did the machine for which they were responsible fail to take off. It brought home to Trenchard as no amount of theorising could have done the value of the Central Flying School and the importance of his own place in it. Arguments between specialists about the superior merits of the monoplane over the slower, stabler biplane seemed of small significance compared with the elaborate human problem of producing first-class pilots and technicians for a Military Wing which hardly existed yet except on paper.

Before 1912 ended, Trenchard set written tests in map-reading, signalling, the rudiments of the internal combustion engine and the theory of aerial reconnaissance; sat the examination with the rest; marked the answers himself in accordance with his official duties; and was among the thirty-two candidates out of thirty-four who passed. From 1913 onwards Upavon men graduated to the Military Wing at an average rate of thirty every quarter. Among them were dozens destined to become great air leaders, men like John and Geoffrey Salmond, Brancker, Dowding, Ludlow Hewitt, Ellington

and Barratt. The majority of the pupils were young enough to be
Trenchard's sons; all were adventurous and high spirited; few
gained more than a nodding acquaintance with the bristling surface
of his character because the courses were so short; yet none who met
him forgot or underrated him.

The image of Trenchard, the disciplinarian, etched itself more
sharply on the minds of newcomers than the image of Trenchard
the administrator. Yet seldom did any of them leave Upavon
nursing the unkindly impression that Paine's right-hand man was
"all boom and no brains." A hint of personal grief, misfortune or
distress from any individual, and Trenchard's compassion was
easily engaged. His human understanding was of the warm spontaneous variety; his insight into temperamental quirks, like his
intuitive judgment of motives, needed time not words to prove its
accuracy in nine cases out of ten.

" It was generally felt that the fate of an officer on the course
almost entirely depended on whether he came up to Major Trenchard's standards," one of his pupils told this writer. " During the
second course three officers were sent down. I have no doubt the
decision was a right one but at the time it seemed harsh. He was
accordingly feared and disliked by many officers still under instruction. Perhaps our opinion of him may best be described by Kipling's
phrase—a just beast."[3]

One January morning, a naval sub-lieutenant who had recently
learnt to fly crashed shortly after taking off. Within minutes a
stretcher party reached the splintered wreckage. The pilot, J. R. W.
Smyth Pigott, was unconscious in the smashed cockpit; his legs,
bent back under him, had been horribly injured by the impact.

A telegram was automatically dispatched from the orderly room
to the next-of-kin. Smyth Pigott's mother, a somewhat militant
Roman Catholic, wired back by return demanding that a priest be
called to her son's bedside. As a matter of course, but without
Trenchard's knowledge, this was done. The priest eventually came
only to be asked his business on the steps of the mess by a testy
major who treated him like a trespasser and absolutely forbade
him to visit Smyth Pigott.

" He's unconscious and can't see anyone," said Trenchard. " If
you care to waste your time waiting, you can wait in the mess."

The priest remonstrated politely. There must be some misunderstanding, he said; the matter was one of life and death;
nevertheless, if Trenchard insisted on barring his entry to the sick-
quarters, he would like to wait somewhere else.

" I'm carrying the viaticum," said the priest. " I'd prefer a room by myself."

Trenchard replied that this was out of the question. Every room and office was occupied. In that case, suggested the priest hesitantly, perhaps there might be a Catholic on the station who was fasting?

" Of course there isn't. They've had their breakfast ages ago. What's all this nonsense about fasting, anyway? "

Choosing his words with care, the priest was trying to explain when Trenchard interrupted.

" If that's what's troubling you, let me have this bread. I'll eat it myself."

The unaffected spontaneity of the offer softened the overtone of blasphemy. The priest was so dumbfounded that he left without seeing Smyth Pigott. The patient gradually recovered, and during convalescence Trenchard used to look in regularly for a chat. Once, in a burst of confidence, he related with relish his brush with the priest on the day of the accident.

" I'm rather glad I didn't die, sir," commented the sub-lieutenant.

" Why do you say that? "

" Well, there'd have been a lot of explaining to do to my mother. She's a strong-minded character herself."

Piqued by unsatisfied curiosity, Smyth Pigott mustered courage enough to ask: " Why didn't you let him visit me, sir? "

" It's a rather long story," said Trenchard. " It began in Nigeria some years ago. We were in the bush and one of my junior officers was at death's door. Like you, he was a Catholic. Like you, he also wanted a priest. . . ."

Then he recounted the macabre anecdote at length, dwelling on the weird and fatal reaction of the stricken officer who emerged from a coma to find himself peering into the face of someone bent low over the campbed anointing him.

" He thought he saw the devil," said Trenchard.

"Yes, sir," said Smyth Pigott. "But I still don't see the connection?"

" The connection should be plain. The young man died, didn't he? Well, this time, I wanted no repetition."[4]

4

About the middle of August, 1913, Sir David Henderson, by now
the Director of Military Aeronautics, appointed Trenchard as
second-in-command to Captain Godfrey Paine, R.N., with the
temporary rank of lieutenant-colonel, thus fixing an official seal of
approval on what was an accomplished fact: for, in all but name,
Trenchard " had been virtually running the school for months," to
quote a member of Henderson's War Office staff.[5] The recognition
brought fresh responsibilities as well as added status; and in the next
twelve months Trenchard saw a good deal of the men who controlled
the uncertain workings of military aviation and acquired in the
process a knowledge of its precarious position.

It had been due to Haldane's initiative that the R.F.C. was
directly answerable not to the professional heads of the army
but to the Secretary of State himself; but such independence proved
nominal in practice. When Seely succeeded Haldane, probably the
wisest and ablest Minister ever to hold the War Office, the R.F.C.
was already in being; but the Royal Navy, under the impetus of
Winston Churchill, had already begun to show symptoms of what
has been aptly called its inherent "centrifugal tendency." During
1913, at Upavon and elsewhere, Trenchard met the First Lord of
the Admiralty several times. These encounters convinced him that
Seely would always be at a natural disadvantage in competing with
such a rival for public funds.

Churchill was then taking flying lessons with Gerrard as his
instructor; and though the First Lord went more often to Eastchurch,
the naval equivalent of Upavon, Trenchard watched him
"wallowing about the sky" several times and reserved judgment on
his proficiency.

" He seemed altogether too impatient for a good pupil, and I
could sympathise. He would arrive unexpectedly, usually without
pyjamas or even a handkerchief, see what he wanted to see, and stay
the night—or what was left of it when he'd finished talking," said
Trenchard. " Everything, including flying, was subordinated in his
mind to a single purpose: getting the fleet ready for a war in which
Germany would be the enemy. If the Admiralty had grasped his
view of what aviation could do to help, the history of air-power might
have taken a different turning."

Personal relations between Churchill and Seely were happily

very good. Moreover, through a small, informal committee of principals known as the " High-Level Bridge " some measure of inter-departmental co-operation was ensured. The tardy growth of military as opposed to naval aviation from 1912 until the outbreak of the First World War can be attributed partly to Seely's uncertainty, partly to the conservatism of the General Staff, partly to public apathy, but chiefly to the acquisitiveness and foresight of Churchill as First Lord.

" Before the war," he wrote, " the War Office claimed, on behalf of the Royal Flying Corps, complete and sole responsibility for the aerial defence of Great Britain. But owing to the difficulties of getting money they were unable to make any provision for this responsibility, every aeroplane they had being earmarked for the Expeditionary Force. Seeing this and finding myself able to procure funds by various shifts and devices, I began in 1912 to form under the Royal Naval Air Service flights of aeroplanes as well as of seaplanes. . . .

" The War Office viewed this development with disfavour, and . . . adhered to the principle . . ."

The appropriations for the R.F.C. in 1912 and 1913 amounted to barely half a million pounds sterling. This paltry sum debarred Henderson from carrying out any research and development, quite apart from denying him the new machines he needed. Private manufacturers languished from lack of orders; some turned to the Admiralty which had far more cash to spare for the purpose. By the spring of 1913, the Military Wing had barely sufficient aeroplanes to equip a single squadron on an immediate war footing; and when Seely rashly declared during the Army Estimates debate that the R.F.C. had, in all, 101 serviceable machines at its disposal, he was challenged to produce them.

" We had to rake the depots and dumps for aeroplanes in every condition," recorded Sir Bertie Fisher, then on Henderson's staff. " Ordinary work was more or less disrupted while the mustering went on to substantiate the Minister's arithmetic for the benefit of parliamentary visitors to Upavon and Netheravon."

By the end of 1913 the Naval Wing gave notice of its semi-independent status by assuming the significant title of the Royal Naval Air Service. In Captain Murray Sueter it had an untiring and competent director, whose plan to build seaplane and airship stations along Britain's east coastline was wholly admirable of its kind. If the Military Wing's function in war, as conceived by Henderson, was to scout for Haldane's six divisions, Churchill ensured that the Naval Wing should be detached for the complementary role of safeguarding the installations of the fleet at home. Neither scheme prospered, however, for not even the drive and ingenuity of a Churchill could short-circuit the system of subdivided responsibility under which the Admiralty's Parliamentary Secretary remained the arbiter of finance, the Civil Lords of contracts and dockyard business, the Sea Lords of plans and all service affairs. Just as Henderson was starved of funds, so Sueter became the victim of too many masters.

So, by the spring of 1914, two separate and sickly branches of the original Royal Flying Corps were in being, a development which was bound to produce a struggle for the control of air resources between army and navy, under the stresses of war conditions. Only at the Central Flying School was the original concept of a single unified air service honoured and preserved; and Trenchard's contribution to that result by sheer force of character and a massive indifference to his pupils' parent services or arms of service was acknowledged by Henderson and his staff at the War Office.

Indeed, the only officer of consequence in the Flying Corps who underrated him was Lieutenant-Colonel Frederick Sykes, the commander of the Military Wing. Sykes had been Henderson's assistant when the constitution of the R.F.C. was being drafted; and there can be no doubt that this ex-cavalry officer, Staff College graduate and qualified aviator earned and held the confidence of his chief.

There can equally be no doubt that Henderson's esteem of Sykes was not widely shared. Paine and the staff at the Military Aeronautics Directorate disliked him as "an intriguer" with too fine a conceit of himself; and he tended to be unpopular with his subordinates at Netheravon, most of whom thought him "a cold fish." The antipathy between Sykes and Trenchard was immediate and most marked. It surprised none who knew them. For, temperamentally, the pair stood poles apart, a fact which Henderson, a person of equanimity, tolerance and rare detachment, invariably took into account when minor differences of opinion between them were reported to him.

By and large, however, the twelve months preceding the outbreak of the First World War were richly satisfying months for Trenchard. His Londonderry friends, the Boyles, had moved to Salisbury (Captain James Boyle having been appointed to the staff of Lieutenant-General Smith-Dorrien), and their house in St. Anne's Street, near the cathedral, became a home from home for members of the Flying School staff.

Mrs. Boyle noticed how greatly Trenchard had changed.

" He obviously lived for flying now and talked of little else. My husband was interested in the subject. Alan Boyle, his brother, had been the first amateur pilot in Britain to make a cross-country flight in his own Avis monoplane. There were frequent arguments about the uses of aircraft in warfare and here Hugh Trenchard held extremely advanced views. He used to assert that the aeroplane would one day transform the battlefield, and did so one evening at table in the hearing of General Smith-Dorrien. His words were coldly received."

The majority of instructors and pupils at the Central Flying School regarded him as a very indifferent pilot, yet his log-book shows that he flew almost every day, usually for practice, occasionally to transport himself to the scene of a crash on the plain. His accident reports were welcomed at the War Office for leaving nothing to conjecture; and his own luck deserted him only once when he decided to test a newly delivered Bristol experimental machine. It was a wet spring morning. A light breeze whipped the misty drizzle into his face as Trenchard left the ground with Henri Biard, a new pupil but a natural airman who would later achieve fame as a test pilot.

" The wind was worse upstairs than on the ground," Biard recalled, " but Trenchard completed the tests and had turned the machine homewards, when an unusually severe gust flung us completely over on our side. He took the one slender chance there was of saving us from disaster.

" Twisting round and round, we dropped like a comet towards the earth. I for one thought we were both booked. As we fell headlong into the opaque mist, Trenchard straightened out the machine. Almost simultaneously it hit the ground. Even with my slight knowledge of flying I knew that an almost perfect landing had been made under merciless conditions."

After inspecting the remains of the machine, Trenchard strode off "fierce-faced and without a word," compiled a faithfully accurate report on the accident but never spoke of it to Biard again.[6]

Flying was a dangerous business. Hence Trenchard's insistence on discipline and strict training schedules for everyone. These trainee pilots, he believed, would one day have to fight in the air alone, with nothing but their own morale, their stamina, and their acquired skill to sustain them. Hence also his ruthlessness in judging aptitude and character. He preened himself, not without reason, on being able to read people like books. None disputed his ability to shut them up even more easily. His mind worked like the fixed blade of a guillotine, slicing people down to size. Yet, by and large, his verdicts on men, arbitrary and intuitive as they mostly were, proved accurate.

They called him "Umph" as much as "Boom," the phonetic equivalent of his response to juniors who bade him "good morning" too early. *The Times* was invariably propped up in front of him; rarely did he lower it to reveal his face. At the end of one of the early training courses, the pupils gave a dinner to the staff. The examinations were over; none yet knew his fate, but there was a general sense of unwinding as the champagne flowed. The atmosphere grew hilarious so that even the dullest of after-dinner speeches was received with hazy attentiveness. Paine was verbose; they feared he would never sit down. Then Trenchard rose slowly, gazing about him with the stern air of a sober Roundhead about to censure a gathering of roistering Cavaliers.

" There was a pause as he stared round the room," said a young officer who was present. " In the sudden silence that followed he simply said ' Umph ' and sat down. A storm of applause followed. With a single sound he had transformed himself for us from an ogre into a man of understanding. Our fate might still be in his hands, but in an instant we were content that it should be so."[7]

5

It cannot be said that the departure of Seely from the War Office on 30th March, 1914, caused undue sorrow to Trenchard or any other officer with first-hand knowledge of the Flying Corps' material handicaps; yet the political circumstances of his going were so extraordinary, even by the turbulent standards of the day, that they must be considered if only in outline.

Seely's crime was the unpardonable one of compromising the Liberal Government's policy of giving Home Rule to Ireland.[8] Whether he was guilty of blundering or inadvertence remains a moot point; but no Minister responsible for mishandling a delicate situation which incited extreme disaffection among Anglo-Irish and Ulster-born officers in the army could expect to hold office afterwards. Irrelevant as the so-called "Curragh Mutiny" may seem to the story of Trenchard, who from first to last was only a scandalised and half-comprehending onlooker, its future effects on the morale of the army and the standing of its leaders were so profound that the affair cannot be passed over in silence.

Shortly before he left Londonderry in the late spring of 1912, a Home Rule Bill, designed to surrender control of Irish internal affairs to a Parliament in Dublin, was introduced at Westminster. It provoked an immediate, impassioned reaction from Protestant Ulster. Trenchard understood the dilemma in general terms: he had listened, without approval, enjoyment or sympathy, to colleagues in the battalion hotly disputing the pros and cons.

By the time the controversial Bill came up for its second reading in March, 1914, with every prospect of its becoming law shortly, the situation had become explosive. Like the Boers, the Ulstermen were in the mood to fight for their rights. They had formed, with the approval of Conservative leaders at Westminster, the nucleus of a private army. Its commander was a retired regular soldier of field rank, General Richardson; and its moral supporters included such men as Field-Marshal Earl Roberts, the most eminent military hero of the day. Asquith's government stood firm, however. Bonar Law, the leader of the Opposition, actually considered moving an amendment to the annual Army Act "in such a way," to quote his biographer, "that the Government would be unable to use the army in Ulster until after a General Election,"[9] but decided against it on reflecting that Ulstermen might not accept the electorate's verdict if it went against them.

It was now that Seely blundered on stage, saving Bonar Law's face and forcing the crisis to a head.

On instructions from the War Office, the General Officer in Command in Ireland, Sir Arthur Paget, assembled all his officers at the Curragh on 23rd March, announced that military operations in Ulster were imminent, suggested that those whose homes lay north of the border might "disappear" now and be reinstated later, with no questions asked, and warned any who might have conscientious objections to the operation that they would be dismissed the service. At once Brigadier Hubert Gough and fifty-seven out of seventy officers in the 3rd Cavalry Brigade chose to tender their resignations, an act of defiance which struck consternation into the Cabinet and confusion into the army. Asquith's subsequent statement that there had been "an honest misunderstanding" of the Governments' intentions only partly allayed public shock and concern.

Gough was reinstated with a written guarantee from Seely that the "forces of the Crown in Ireland or elsewhere" would not be used "to crush political opposition to the policy or principles of the Home Rule Bill," and with a further specific assurance that his own 3rd Cavalry Brigade would not so be used.

Such a clash between the military and the civil power was bound to shake any soldier of Trenchard's simple outlook and classically rigid code of values, eighteen of whose twenty-one years' service had been spent abroad. While he held that it was totally wrong to put officers in a false position by admitting their right to choose between conflicting loyalties, as Asquith's Government had done, he was equally convinced that officers who allowed themselves the luxury of a conscience in complex political questions had no place in the army.

It relieved him greatly that the Flying Corps was too small and compact a branch to be seriously affected, though for that reason, perhaps, the case of Gordon Shephard, a brilliant airman and a friend of Erskine Childers, who combined "gun-running" operations on behalf of the Southern Irish with some discreet espionage on behalf of the Admiralty, assumed a disproportionate significance in Trenchard's mind. The mistrust engendered in the army by accentuating the divided loyalties of individuals was bad enough: far worse was the pall of suspicion which inevitably descended between Ministers and their military advisers, and which tended to deepen with the coming of hostilities. A deplorable series of alleged plots, counter-plots and factious disputes bedevilled relations between politicians and generals from the beginning to the end of the First World War; and though Trenchard was a soldier of minor consequence in 1914, his rapid rise to leadership and his heavy fall from political grace as the victim of one such "plot" a mere four years later, makes it imperative to show where he stood when the seeds of unrest were sown.

The agitation caused by the Irish controversy dragged on into the last summer of peace. Asquith took over the War Office when Seely resigned; but the Prime Minister's tenure was that of a temporary caretaker only and the supplies of the R.F.C. lagged farther behind its needs.

On 28th June, the heir to the Austrian throne, the Archduke Francis Ferdinand, was assassinated by Serbian nationalists in the Bosnian town of Sarajevo, but attention in Britain was not distracted from the animosities of the Irish deadlock. " Such was the frenzy provoked by Home Rule politics," admits Bonar Law's biographer, " that this grave event seems to have been scarcely noticed in Unionist circles." The Cabinet had fewer illusions. Asquith alerted the War Office and undertook one final attempt to solve the Home Rule issue by negotiation.

From late June onwards, when the four under-equipped

squadrons of the Flying Corps' Military wing were concentrated at Netheravon in instant readiness for emergency transfer overseas, Trenchard guessed that war would come. He carried on at Upavon, plagued with a restless desire to know what would become of him on the outbreak of hostilities.

It is recorded that as late as Friday, 24th July, when the all-party conference summoned by King George V to find a compromise solution for the Irish dispute had failed, three of the participants sat on in an ante-room at Buckingham Palace. Bonar Law, and Lord Lansdowne, the chief Opposition spokesman, were waiting with Lowther, the Speaker of the Commons, to take leave of their royal host.

The King's reminder to delegates at the outset of their "great responsibilities" in halting the drift to anarchy and civil war had apparently been in vain. Nobody knew what would happen now.

Lowther's face was buried behind the newspaper which he had brought with him, unread, that morning. Suddenly his voice broke in on the thoughts of his companions. Did either of them know, he asked, that Austria had sent an ultimatum to Serbia? They sat up with a start. Neither of them knew; and in that instant, according to Lowther's own account, the cold light of reality began to seep in from the remote outside world.

" We agreed that it portended something very grave indeed— how grave we did not then realise."

Within a week the major powers of Europe aligned themselves, Russia in support of Serbia, Germany behind Austria, and France against Germany. Would Britain, torn by her internal feuds, stand aside, bound as she was to France and Russia by treaty? Opinion in the Cabinet and country was divided almost to the end.

The issue was settled in Berlin. Heartened no doubt by the symptoms of political uncertainty in London, by the manifest unpreparedness of the British Army, and by the distinct possibility of civil strife in Ireland, the Kaiser ordered his General Staff to take the short-cut through Belgium into France in accordance with a pre-determined plan. The British ultimatum to Berlin, condemning the violation of neutral territory and calling for the instant evacuation of Belgium, expired late on 4th August. All passion over Ireland was stored away for the duration. The British expeditionary force planned by Haldane, and the four barely serviceable squadrons of the Royal Flying Corps, moved to their embarkation points. Britain was at war again; and, apart from the fleet, she seemed as unready for it as ever.

6. The Improviser

"It was only on 3rd August that I was told I would not be going to France with the Expeditionary Force, but to replace Sykes as commandant of the Military Wing," Trenchard wrote in his autobiographical notes: "I handed over my duties at the Central Flying School on the 7th. . . .

"At Farnborough the squadrons were being made up to strength in aeroplanes from all sources, many being taken from the C.F.S., others being bought from private owners and makers. Transport was hurriedly collected from wherever it could be found. I soon realised that the only thing for me to do was to help the Force sailing overseas.

"In the commandant's office Lieutenant-Colonel Frederick Sykes handed me two keys and a confidential box with an air of solemn mystery. The box, he said, contained detailed plans for dealing with any German attack on this country by airships, and the smaller key fitted it. I put that key carefully in my pocket and slept with it under my pillow that night. Next morning, on arriving at the office, I saw that the box had gone. I hunted round until, in one of the billets, I came upon Major Brooke-Popham kneeling on the floor with the box open in front of him.

"Brooke-Popham seemed astonished at my attitude of concern. I, in turn, was astonished to find the confidential box stuffed with shoes. Then he explained that he'd always used it for that purpose, and I understood. Remembering Sykes's instructions, I went to the safe and opened it with the other key. There were no papers whatever inside; but I was already prepared for that."

These words of Trenchard's, set down about ten years after the event, do less than justice to his own deep disappointment or to the cheerful confusion that reigned at Farnborough until the last flight of the Military Wing moved out.

The Army Council had decreed quite logically that the R.F.C. should be led by Sir David Henderson, who had nursed and reared the fledgling force from birth; Henderson just as logically decided not to deprive himself of the services of Sykes as his chief staff officer. The latter might have his faults, lack of originality and human warmth being perhaps the most conspicuous; but his administrative competence was unquestioned. Trenchard's protest at being sent to Farnborough instead of the front did not move Henderson, who reminded him that there was equally important work to be done building up new squadrons at home.

That oldest of excuses seemed less thin when Trenchard took stock of the Military Wing's depleted resources. The strain on the skeleton staff was not eased by the arrival of scores of civilian volunteers, some of whom cycled in to enlist "from miles around." The quartermaster's cupboard was bare. It had been ransacked of boots, blankets, uniforms and other necessities to provide the 105 officers and 755 men of the Military Wing with a generous emergency reserve.

Trenchard organised his recruits into fatigue parties, promising in the Government's name to reimburse them for any wear and tear to their civilian clothes, and paid hard cash for their bicycles, probably the only means of transport on which he could depend for some time to come.

Sykes paid a final visit to Farnborough on 15th August and spent an uncomfortable hour briefing his successor on his duties. Trenchard, who was not particularly pleased to see him, found nothing to quarrel with in the programme of training. This was standard. Only when Sykes ventured to add that its object in future would be to provide replacements for the R.F.C. in the field, and that no new squadrons would be wanted, did Trenchard contradict him. This was a fundamental issue which he had discussed fully with Henderson, though he was careful not to mention the fact to Sykes.

" Don't talk damned rubbish," he said. " My job here, as you should know, is to produce squadrons. You'll get reinforcements but not at their expense."

An altercation followed. The temperature rose in the commandant's office. The two men argued as bitterly over a point of policy as if honour and the fate of the Flying Corps depended on it. Nowhere in his autobiography has Sykes referred to an incident which, however petty in itself, served only to deepen his dislike of Trenchard.

That Sykes did err on a principle of policy is undeniable. The squadron was the basic fighting unit of the Flying Corps, and the building of new squadrons had been laid down by Henderson as

Trenchard's prime task. It is not unfair to suggest that Sykes possibly succumbed to the temptation of scoring cheaply off a rival whose strength of character seemed an inadequate substitute for other imagined deficiencies, and whose loud voice seemed to betray a permanently vacant mind. Trenchard, for his part, gladly seized the chance to deflate this "most conceited and indecisive staff officer." The rift and its pathetic occasion reflected little credit on either man, perhaps, but the simple facts must be noted. For their indirect bearing on the careers of both proved disproportionately great.

Sir David Henderson, en route to France, had more immediate preoccupations than the trivial antipathies of two of his best officers. His small force could afford to dispense with the services of neither Sykes nor Trenchard when so many others were applying to rejoin their parent regiments in order not to be left behind in the headlong race to Berlin.

Remembering how events had falsified the plans of the military optimists in South Africa, Trenchard reserved his judgment about the duration of the new emergency. It was a relief to think that Henderson took a more adult view of the uncertainties than his chief staff officer; and he wondered how far it coincided with the appraisal of Kitchener, the new Secretary of State for War, whose prestige had not been matched by any soldier since Wellington's day. To Trenchard's gratification, Kitchener confounded nearly everyone by predicting before the end of August that the conflict would probably last three years and that seventy divisions, not seven, would have to be raised to ensure victory.

The plans envisaged by the Secretary of State allowed little room for deviation to a stunned and still sceptical War Office staff. Expansions, limited now only by the organisation available to turn untrained volunteers into fully equipped soldiers and airmen, became the order of the day.

Major Sefton Brancker, an even-tempered, good-humoured administrator, who affected foppish manners and a monocle but shared Trenchard's taste for swift improvisation, was left behind in sole charge of supply and equipment at the Military Aeronautics Directorate. Trenchard both liked and trusted Brancker; and during the first ten days of muddle they were in frequent consultation by telephone. Accommodation had to be found for the steady stream of recruits, new instructors to drill and train them. The only aeroplanes free for use in England were those discarded by the Military Wing as unserviceable; and at the beginning there were less than half a dozen mechanics, none of them experienced, on the strength.

Far from being downcast by the fantastic problem of creating a semblance of order out of this chaos, Trenchard and Brancker were inspired to employ drastic measures of opportunism.

Deciding that the Central Flying School must be enlarged, they commandeered Netheravon as an annexe; and with the assistance of Captain Charles Lee, a retired officer whom he had lately known as a capable master of hounds, and who needed little persuasion now to join him at Farnborough, Trenchard settled down to display a fine flair for administrative ju-jutsu. The instructor shortage was surmounted by the unusual expedient of buying up Brooklands, complete with hangars, machines, equipment, trained civilian pilots and a neighbouring public house, the landlord of which insisted on disposing of all the contents with the goodwill. The deal went through during the last week-end of August, a month before a meticulous accounts' officer began to bombard Brancker with humourless minutes questioning Trenchard's judgment in overrating the military value of a second-hand piano, a quantity of bed linen and cutlery, and several casks of beer.

On the whole, however, surprisingly few obstructions were met with. Under the influence of Kitchener, with his predilection for implicating himself in any question that took his fancy, the staidest officials vied with one another in interpreting or anticipating as commands his known wishes. The stinginess and neglect which had been the lot of the R.F.C. since birth were replaced by what can truly be described as unlicensed generosity.

To attract technicians, Trenchard and Brancker opened their own recruiting centre in the West End of London and fixed rates of pay as high as those offered to the best army tradesmen. By mid-September 1100 trained men had been enrolled as riggers, fitters and mechanics. Meanwhile, at Farnborough, Trenchard set himself a target of twelve squadrons, a target which, Brancker assured him, would never satisfy the grandiose ideas of the Secretary of State:

"Brancker thought I should try to raise thirty squadrons. At a later date Lord Kitchener doubled this to sixty."

The details of the provisional expansion scheme were worked out with methodical care on the basis of "one artillery reconnaissance squadron for each new division, and two or three fighting and reconnaissance squadrons for each Army Corps." Months passed before Brancker's paper filtered through the various interested departments, finally reaching Kitchener in the spring of 1915 with the innumerable comments of War Office critics scribbled in the margins. It is a matter of history that the Secretary of State silenced all further sniping with the imperious comment: .

" Double this. K."

The next step was to speed up the training schedule. Trenchard did so by reserving for his best instructors and pupil-pilots the few airworthy machines at his disposal, staggering the tuition of the rest as the supply of aircraft increased. When his first squadron had completed its training, he broke it up into three constituent flights, the hard cores round which another three squadrons could be the more quickly formed. Extending the system he had mastered at Upavon, moving about unceasingly to "keep an eye on things," Trenchard spared neither instructors nor pupils, cajoling and driving them on to better his own exacting programme. The incentive he offered them was ample.

" The harder you work," he told them, " the sooner you'll be in action."

2

The official news from the Western Front was extremely disquieting. Caught up in the precipitate withdrawal from Belgium of the British Expeditionary Force, the R.F.C. sustained remarkably few losses in men or machines. Activity in the air was fortunately extremely light, yet Henderson's demands imposed an immediate drain on Trenchard's almost non-existent reserves.

On 18th August, for instance, he was asked to dispatch two pilots. On 22nd August, five more were ordered to fly out with their own machines. At that rate, Trenchard complained, it would soon be impossible to build for the future as Kitchener commanded. The policy of piecemeal supply must be slowed down, he argued; Brancker agreed and promised to raise the matter at the highest level.

" Lord Kitchener wishes to give you all the replacements possible," Brancker wired Henderson a few days later. " At the same time he wishes to continue organising squadrons at home for use with the divisions of the New Army. Please say if you want flights of R.E. 5's and Maurice Farmans, but if they go other pilots must be sent home to keep things going here."[1]

Two of the R.E. 5's were brand new, and Trenchard detailed Lieutenant (now Air-Marshal Sir John) Baldwin and Lieutenant Gordon Bell to test them. Bell, a shy-looking man with a stutter that did nothing to impede his mordant sense of wit, had been one of the most accomplished civilian aviators in Britain before the war, despite the thick-lensed spectacles he wore. Neither Baldwin nor Bell cared for the R.E. 5 and said so in their reports to Trenchard.

That afternoon, while sunning themselves on the airfield, they heard an uncertain droning overhead and scarcely bothered to glance up as Lieutenant Fox, who tested machines for the Royal Aircraft Factory over the way, flew past in another R.E. 5. Then the sound of car brakes applied at speed a few yards behind them on the road brought them scrambling to their feet, and Trenchard strode towards them with a face as ominous as a thundercloud.

" Why aren't you up there? " he said, pointing to the sky.

" We were this morning, sir," said Baldwin. " Didn't you get our reports? "

" Yes, and I don't believe a damned word you wrote. I'll see you both about that later. Now where's Fox."

Gordon Bell showed sudden animation, and Trenchard curbed his tongue as the slow syllables formed. " F-F-Fox, s-s-sir, is at th-th-this instant j-j-jaunting with J-J-Jesus in m-m-my craft."

Trenchard looked hard at Bell's studiously composed face and grinned faintly, recalling how this same young imbecile had once scared off a crowd of curious children after an emergency landing with a stuttered warning to " G-go away, b-b-because I-I-I've b-b-been kn-known to eat m-my y-y-young."

Trenchard finally said:

" You've a point there, Bell. But I've a better one. I can't ask you to fly to France in a machine you don't trust, and that's that."

Bell protested so much that Trenchard eventually let him go; but Baldwin, who had lately formed the habit of breaking bounds in a hideously noisy sports car, was packed off instead to the Central Flying School for a spell "to learn manners."

The piecemeal calls for reinforcements continued until mid-September when the German "avalanche of fire and steel" was halted on the Marne, then pushed back by the classic action of Gallieni, the Paris garrison commander. The invader fell back to the Aisne and there began the relay race to the sea, with each side striving to outflank the other. The news came through in censored snatches well after the event, but gloomy enough to quicken the pulse of the most apathetic learner-pilot. Apathy was, however, a stranger at Farnborough, as at Brooklands, Netheravon and Upavon. Men watched the clock only in the sense of counting the days stretching between them and a posting abroad.

Early in October Trenchard was urgently summoned by Kitchener who stared hard at him as soon as he entered the room. It was one of the Minister's private boasts that he rarely forgot a face; on this occasion he impressed his visitor by recalling the precise circumstances of their meeting in Pretoria over thirteen years earlier. Then Kitchener got down to business. The War Office and the Admiralty, he said, intended to land a combined force at Antwerp. If the fort could be held, it would block the way to the Channel ports and become a sallying point against the flank and rear of the enemy armies. Trenchard's job would be to provide one battleworthy air squadron in two days.

The training flights were scoured for pilots and machines, and the first of Farnborough's new war squadrons flew to Belgium on 7th October under the command of Major J. H. Beck within thirty-six hours, to be denied the chance of proving itself above a battlefield that was lost before the Allies could effectively intervene. In due course, on the Western Front, No. 6 Squadron amply justified Trenchard's expectations of it.

By the end of October five reserve squadrons were forming; by mid-November the number had doubled to ten, each embryonic unit being conscious only of its own invincible superiority. The training establishment was gradually decentralised as new centres at Catterick, Norwich, Castle Bromwich, Bealieu and Northolt began to absorb the floods of local volunteers. Both Trenchard and Brancker had cause to be satisfied with the success of their free-booting methods. The organisation which they had improvised between them was equal to every ordinary strain, though now and then Kitchener was capable of asking the impossible.

"When I come down to inspect you," the Minister told Trenchard at the War Office one day: "I want to see a full squadron of machines flying past in formation."

Trenchard did his best to explain that this was beyond the art of his finest pilots. Few machines were of the same type or performance; and the rest could not be regimented into line like men on the ground or ships at sea.

It was a good example of that overbearing approach which frequently unnerved weaker subordinates into accepting Kitchener's lightest expressions of opinion as infallible judgments. At the political level, too, he enjoyed with Asquith and Churchill unquestioned responsibility for the conduct of the war. Cabinet decisions were accepted as being in the national interest mainly because Kitchener's endorsement was regarded as a prerequisite

of acceptance. Condemned to-day as a grossly overrated administrator who was allowed to shoulder too much, he is less frequently
criticised for arbitrarily shedding burdens which he could not
immediately carry, though here he was sometimes more gravely at
fault.

Thus, at a Cabinet meeting on 3rd September, 1914, the
Secretary for War invited the First Lord of the Admiralty to undertake the air defence of Britain. As Churchill wrote:

" I thereupon undertook to do what was possible with the wholly
inadequate resources which were available. There were neither
anti-aircraft guns nor searchlights, and though a few improvisations had been made, nearly a year must elapse before the
efficient supplies necessary could be forthcoming. Meanwhile, at
any moment, half a dozen zeppelins might arrive to bomb
London, or what was more serious, Chatham, Woolwich or
Portsmouth. . . ."[2]

Wars, in Kitchener's view, were won by armies and navies;
flying machines were useful accessories which at best smoothed the
path to victory. The First Lord's livelier strategic insight none the less
did him a serious political disservice. For the Royal Naval Air
Service was too weak to discharge its new duties unaided. What was
far more crucial, this almost unnoticed Cabinet decision solemnly
ratified the existence of two independent air services in a country
which could barely hope for many months to supply the needs of one.

Though the bombing of zeppelin sheds at Cologne, Dusseldorf,
Cuxhaven and Friederichshafen, and the patrolling of the sea
approaches to South-East England, illustrated Churchill's pristine
enthusiasm, the naval air defence effort gradually petered out. Leaders
like Murray Sueter lacked not a policy but the authority to enforce
it. And the Sea Lords disliked Churchill's air-mindedness, conceiving
it as no business of theirs to foster a campaign that seemed quite
unrelated to the classic traditions of naval warfare.

These political complications totally escaped Trenchard. Missions
by naval crews, disjointed and infrequent as they were, tended to
rouse his admiration and made him unreasonably critical of the
humdrum patrol duties allotted to the Flying Corps in France. He
listened to the complaints of returning squadron commanders and
pondered the looser denunciations of army officers, drawing the
unfair conclusion that Henderson, acting no doubt on the cautious
advice of Sykes, " had taken to wrapping his machines and pilots in
cotton-wool."

The commander of the R.F.C. visited Farnborough towards the end of October, on the very day that Trenchard's mother died, and tried to remove his misgivings. The R.F.C.'s record was nothing to be ashamed of, said Henderson. During the retreat and later, its response to the many calls on it secured invaluable information of enemy dispositions, a fact to which the Commander-in-Chief had alluded in his dispatches. Trenchard retorted that air ascendancy had still to be fought for; whether or not the morale of R.F.C. pilots and observers stood up to the test, it could only be weakened meanwhile by allowing enemy aviators unhampered initiative. He did not propose to stay on and watch that happen. And he concluded his outburst by demanding to "be sent back to my regiment."

Fortunately for him, Henderson was a man of almost excessive calmness and forbearance.

The implied criticism of himself he chose to ignore. The Flying Corps's difficulties could be overcome, and he explained his proposals for doing so, proposals of which Kitchener and the High Command in France already approved.

The essence of the plan was to decentralise the squadrons so that the rapidly growing ground forces would be better served than in the recent past. For this purpose three operational wings were to be formed, one for each Army Corps. The command of the First Wing was reserved for Trenchard. Would he accept it?

Trenchard longed to say "yes," but one uncertainty deterred him. Where, he inquired, would Sykes fit in? Suppose Henderson were transferred. Would the Flying Corps's fate be committed to the control of this secretive, overcautious man whose views would sooner or later clash with those of the wing commanders? Henderson assured him that Sykes would have no operational jurisdiction; there was nothing ambiguous about his place in the new scheme of things. It would remain unchanged.

" Henderson added finally that he would make me next senior to him," Trenchard recorded.

The challenge to come and do better was clinched by this parting pledge of confidence. Unable any longer to resist the one or spurn the other, Trenchard accepted with an easier mind. On 18th November he embarked at Dover for France.

3

On the quayside at Bologne the unloading of stores and vehicles
from the ship went on in the dying light of the raw November day.
Captain Maurice Baring, the A.D.C. to Henderson, stood well back
from the gangplank, scanning the face of each descending officer.
He was looking for a distinctively large man; but the few to whom
the rough description so far applied were of the wrong rank. Then
he noticed someone "standing quite by himself on the deck of the
boat, with a small head and a Scots Fusilier's cap on. This, I said
to myself, must be Colonel Trenchard. It was."

Darkness fell before they left the dimly lit, cobbled streets of the
town for the R.F.C. Headquarters at St. Omer. The petrol tank of
the second-hand Rolls-Royce brought by Trenchard from England
was empty, and they took an hour to persuade anyone to fill it.
Baring concealed his mounting anxiety as they sped along in the
track of their headlight beams. He fervently prayed that the driver's
bump of locality might be better than his own. Trenchard appeared
wholly unconcerned and kept plying Baring with "a great many
pertinent questions, few of which I could answer."

Then the car came grinding to a halt inches from a barrier drawn
across the road, and Baring got out stiffly to ask the one pertinent
question which had been troubling him for half an hour. A French
officer assured him genially that they were travelling in precisely the
opposite direction to St. Omer; the front-line lay a quarter of a mile
beyond this check point; if they went on they might end up dining
with the Germans.

Trenchard, on hearing this, grunted an uncomplimentary
remark and sat back impassively. Baring was plainly an impractical
muddler. Months passed before this unfavourable impression was
altered.

They reached St. Omer two hours late, but the small headquarters building was so overcrowded with visitors that nobody
seemed to notice their arrival. The place bristled with rumours;
and before turning in on the hard floor of the guest-room, Trenchard
casually overheard a conversation which kept him pondering half
the night. Was it credible that Henderson, after all he had said, could
have relinquished his command and nominated Sykes as his
successor? If so, the conclusion was inescapable; he himself had
been lured to France under false pretences.

Next morning Trenchard's apprehensions were confirmed.

Apparently every gossip in the mess knew the reasons for impending changes which were solemnly spoken of as accomplished facts. During the closing phase of the fighting around Ypres, the commander of the 1st Division had been severely wounded when his conference room at Hooge Château was raked by German shell-fire. Sir Douglas Haig, the Commander of the First Army Corps, was not entirely satisfied with Landon, the brigadier who replaced the injured Major-General Lomax; so French, the Commander-in-Chief, suggested Henderson; and, as a corollary, Sykes was on the point of taking over the Flying Corps.

Trenchard reacted at once with characteristic impulsiveness. The thought of serving under Sykes, his junior in years and rank and someone he distrusted as a colleague and despised as a man, was intolerable. He would prefer to sever his connection with the Flying Corps and rejoin the Royal Scots Fusiliers as a mere company commander.

At French's headquarters a senior officer listened to Trenchard's account of a predicament which could not have been invented or foreseen, and decided after some hesitation to telegraph his request for a transfer, with the reasons, to the War Office in London. Before dusk an angry, disillusioned Trenchard left St. Omer for First Wing Headquarters at Merville to await the answer. He had no intention now of impugning Henderson's good faith or of stimulating Sykes's vanity by seeing either man. Nor did he reflect that his attempt to cut his losses with the little dignity left by circumstances might be similarly misconstrued. He acted with the same headstrong consistency as once in India, when a Viceroy's edict prevented him from hurrying off to the Boer War, and again in Nigeria, when an obstructive colonel had tried to thwart him.

This time, however, his action had the disturbing effect of a pebble hurled from a distance into an empty pond. The wire was certainly shown to Kitchener, for it was Kitchener who personally countermanded Henderson's transfer, informing the Commander-in-Chief that he "would not sanction Sykes's being in command" on grounds of inexperience. Sir John French, quick to resent any unwarranted interference on the part of Kitchener, retorted that he was unwilling to demote Henderson who had earned his preferment and was actually installed at his new divisional headquarters.

Not unnaturally, Sykes suspected Trenchard of pulling strings behind his back, and made no secret of his suspicions. Only Henderson, "bitterly disappointed" as Baring knew him to be, voiced no protest and bore Trenchard no lasting grudge.

Weeks passed before Sir John French would act on Kitchener's veto. Trenchard grew weary of waiting and feared the worst. In seeking permission to rejoin his regiment, his main wish was to present Sykes with the accomplished fact of his departure and thus avoid recrimination. In his self-willed way he had committed his future into the hands of his superiors and was content like Henderson to abide by their verdict. But, until specifically ordered to do so, he refused to count among those superiors a rival in whom he had no confidence whatever.

At last, on 20th December, confirmation came through that Henderson and Sykes had resumed their former posts. And less than a month later, on 18th January, as a token of Kitchener's regard for his success in reconstructing the R.F.C. at home, the promotion of Trenchard to brevet lieutenant-colonel was announced in the *London Gazette*.

At First Wing Headquarters Trenchard's known distaste for scandalmongering discouraged open conversation about an episode which younger and more flippant officers took as just another sign of the congenital inability of the generals to agree among themselves. The cynically minded suspected a plot at lower level but were prepared to exonerate Trenchard, whom they judged to be incapable of stooping to intrigue. Perhaps half a dozen of the more senior officers, who knew his aversion for Sykes, unravelled the truth by intelligent guesswork. Like Samson enchained, Trenchard had acted in accordance with the correct but violent impulse of his own nature, pulling down the roof on Sykes in the process. The passage of years often softens the edges of such mysteries; and Trenchard's subsequent rise seemed, in retrospect, to most of his contemporaries something almost inevitable and predestined.

None knew him closely enough to do more than admire at a distance what they took to be his instinct for self-preservation; a few could not help suspecting in January, 1915, whether beneath their new leader's poker-faced impassivity there might not be lurking the arrogant pique of a *prima donna*. Such critics were wide of the mark, but Trenchard's reticence and indifference to other men's opinions did little to enlighten them. He would sooner have cut off his right hand than take advantage of other men's weaknesses, and the idea of using Sykes or anyone else as a stepping-stone for his own ambitions repelled him: Trenchard knew his own too well.

He had more to do than gloat or brood over such matters, even had it been in his nature to do so. John Salmond and Webb-Bowen, the commanders of Nos. 2 and 3 Squadrons at Merville, were as

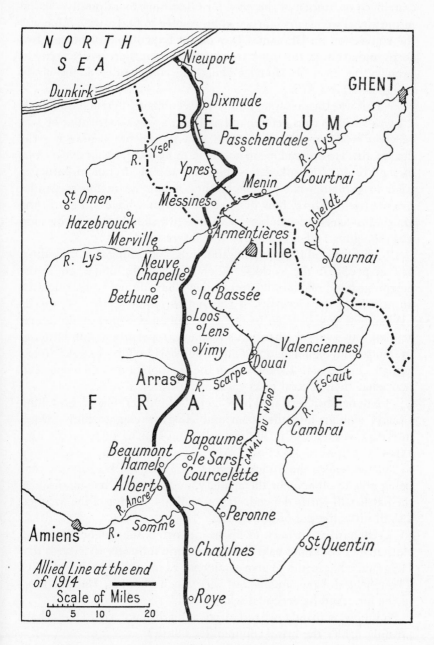

The Front Line at the end of 1914

convinced as himself of the need for organising more positive action in the air. Two events sharpened his resolve to find a way. One was the conversion on Christmas Day of the Expeditionary Force's two corps into armies; the other was a summons at short notice, early in January, to meet Sir Douglas Haig, the commander of the newly designated First Army.

" This was the first time I had ever seen Haig," Trenchard noted. " I was very nervous beforehand as I had always heard that he was very reserved, austere, severe and that he did not believe a great deal in air. He ordered me to go round to his H.Q. about five o'clock in the evening and asked me about the use of aircraft in battle. I tried to explain what I thought they would do in future besides reconnaissance work, how our machines would have to fight in the air against German machines and how we should have to develop machine-guns and bombs. He was interested.

" Then he said he was going to tell me something that only three or four people in the world yet knew; in March, somewhere in the neighbourhood of Merville and Neuve Chapelle, we were to launch an attack on the Germans. I was not to tell anybody. He asked: ' What will you be able to do? ' I explained rather badly about artillery observation (then in its infancy), reporting to gun batteries by morse and signal lamps, and of our early efforts to get wireless going. On the map I showed him the position of my squadrons and said what their several tasks could be.

" I remember very well his Chief Staff Officer, General Sir John Gough, coming into the room and Haig's saying to him, ' Don't interrupt me now. I'm finding out what can be done in the air.' When I'd finished he said: ' Well, Trenchard, I shall expect you to tell me before the attack whether you can fly, because on your being able to observe for the artillery, and carry out reconnaissance, the battle will partly depend. If you can't fly because of the weather, I shall probably put off the attack.' "

Trenchard went back to his headquarters that night filled with elation. " I could not help feeling then and for years afterwards that Haig said what he did to give confidence to me and the whole R.F.C. Though he did not understand very much about it, Haig believed in the air. And he accepted what I said."

But how, with only two squadrons at his disposal, could Trenchard possibly justify the army commander's faith?

Haig had sworn him to secrecy. Even Henderson could not be consulted directly until mid-February, when confidential information about the preparations for an attack at Neuve Chapelle reached

Above: tobogganing at St. Moritz. *Left:* after winning the Freshman's and Beginner's Cups for the Cresta Run, 1901

Above: the staff of the Central Flying School in January 1913. Paine is standing on Trenchard's left and Longmore is seated in front of him

Below: during the autumn manœuvres of 1912. The officer with the deer-stalker, sitting next to Trenchard, is his pilot Longmore

R.F.C. Headquarters. By then the two squadrons of First Wing were half-way through a concentrated training schedule in techniques which were still untried and experimental.

Since November a lull had set in over the entire front. The German and Allied Armies, separated by muddy irregular widths of no-man's-land, were dug in for the winter. The entrenched positions faced each other in an almost unbroken line nearly six hundred miles long from the English Channel to the Alps. The lull was a godsend to Trenchard. He had much to learn; and both in the mess and on the squadron airfields, his teachers were the men who had been his nominal pupils. Their opinions weighed more with him than the technical generalisations from Henderson's headquarters; for with an air policy still unformulated and with equipment lagging far behind actual demands, progress by the trial and error achievements of the men who flew seemed the only sane system.

" Most of what you tell me as individuals is unmitigated rot," he said to his men so often that they cherished it as a catch phrase. " But what you tell me collectively is often sound common sense."

His knack of "picking winners" was put down to his unwearying curiosity and vitality. The light in Trenchard's office always burned late; still there when the bar closed and everyone else was either in bed or thinking of going, he was invariably first down to breakfast in the morning, as in Upavon days. On his bedside table he kept a scribbling pad and pencil, but only Charles Lee, his adjutant, could decipher the spidery hieroglyphics concealing ideas that had come in the wakeful small hours, ideas which took priority when the routine of the new day began.

The technical difficulties loomed larger as the offensive drew nearer. Signalling by wireless, for instance, was an exacting and apparently unprofitable novelty. The first airborne sets were cumbersome, weighing nearly five and a half stones each. When carried aloft in the slow, light aeroplanes then in use, the observer had to stay below in the interests of safety, leaving his pilot to handle both the machine and the clumsy set. Aerial combat was happily still an undiscovered art, but anti-aircraft guns were multiplying on both sides of the winter-bound line; and the approach of even one undermanned wireless machine was a standing invitation to a little target practice which German and Allied gun crews seldom denied themselves.

In the beginning, when rifle bullets were the chief hazards, Union Jacks had to be painted on the underside of the lower wings

T.   E

of machines so that trigger-happy infantrymen could distinguish friend from foe. These marks of identification served no useful purpose now that shells were driving reconnaissance pilots higher and higher. The Union Jack, clearly recognisable only in good weather and at low altitudes, had made way during the Ypres engagement in October, 1914, for the triple roundel of red, white and blue which remains the distinctive symbol of the Royal Air Force. Introduced then in self-defence, it was to be treasured later as a precious battle honour.

The higher Trenchard's overworked wireless pilots flew, the poorer became their chances of identifying and signalling back the bearings of military objectives. This drawback applied equally to the flights which preferred to send observers armed with pad, pencil and good eyesight rather than overburden machines and pilots with transmitting sets. For enemy guns outreached and outnumbered the British; and once they found the range, sketching from the air the approximate site of German dumps and guns and strong points became futile. The airborne camera was the answer to an increasingly hazardous problem, and it was Sykes, to his credit, who drew Henderson's notice to the success of the French in developing a fixed lens capable of taking clear pictures from heights of 3000 feet and more. Early in 1915 a photographic section was formed at R.F.C. Headquarters under Lieutenant J. Moore-Brabazon (now Lord Brabazon of Tara). And when Henderson learnt officially of Haig's plans of attack at Neuve Chapelle, he attached this tiny unit of one officer and two N.C.O.s to Trenchard's First Wing at Merville where it would be needed most.

Moore-Brabazon was an outstanding example of the fertile individualism which abounded in the Flying Corps and was quickly turned to account. Yet he felt "about as welcome as the measles," on arriving at Merville and falling foul of his new commanding officer almost at once. It happened at lunch in the crowded mess when someone asked the time and someone else, casually consulting his watch, said it was ten past one. Moore-Brabazon, a man of many talents who, before launching into photography, had been a member of Captain Hugh Dowding's experimental wireless squadron and regulated his own watch by the time-signal from the Eiffel Tower, broke in at once: " Oh, no," he contradicted. " It's just one o'clock. You must be fast here."

Conscious that the penetrating eye of Trenchard was on him, he explained defensively why he could not be wrong. Then he lapsed into nerve-stricken silence.

" You're Moore-Brabazon, aren't you? " said Trenchard, still staring fixedly at him.

" I am, sir."

" And you only got here to-day? "

" I did, sir."

" Well, remember this, Moore-Brabazon. The correct time here is what I make it."

It was, Moore-Brabazon confessed, a "shattering and oracular utterance." Somewhat stunned, he sat quite still, determined not to say another word. At that moment the main dish was served. The cutlet looked none too savoury, and his fork confirmed that its texture was rubbery. It also exuded an abominable smell which he could not immediately place. One bite was enough to tell him the worst. Evidently the cook, perhaps inadvertently or perhaps for flavour, had mixed a little paraffin with the gravy. Stealthily pushing his plate aside while Trenchard's eye roamed elsewhere, Moore-Brabazon wondered with a touch of malice what this ogre of a man would do when he sampled the cutlet. Would he even notice? It would be interesting to see. Trenchard presently turned to his plate. One mouthful of cutlet sufficed. His face turned deep crimson as he swallowed the morsel. Then with a shout and a clatter of cutlery he called the cook and cursed him for his poisonous handiwork. Suddenly the fascinated Moore-Brabazon found himself under fire again.

" You were the first person to sample—this muck," Trenchard said, withering him with another look. " Why in God's name didn't you say it had been stewed in paraffin? "

It was no rhetorical question. Trenchard wanted an answer. Plucking up courage, Moore-Brabazon countered with another question.

" Don't you think, sir, I'd already spoken enough for one meal? "

The sally took Trenchard unawares. Snorting indignantly, he seemed to grin slightly before rounding on the mess president. He made a mental note of Moore-Brabazon's name as that of a young man of quick wits well worth encouraging on a more suitable occasion.

Moore-Brabazon was pleased to discover, as others were fast discovering, that Trenchard's flexible mind belied his overbearing and stern exterior. He wanted results, not pretensions; he badgered people for suggestions, and was willing to try anything once, however crankish it might appear on the surface. He haunted the hangars at all hours questioning squadron and flight commanders, pilots and

observers. He preached the doctrine of picking the brains of the
French to anticipate the Germans, whose air service was still an
uncertain quantity. Yet it was not part of his practice to let self-
styled experts run riot, preferring to whip up emulation by setting
the camera enthusiasts at odds with each other, and allowing the
wireless or lamp-signalling amateurs to learn from their own mistakes
in a keen, friendly rivalry. Exceptional men like Don Lewis, one of
the most gifted radio specialists in the Flying Corps, were only too
ready to oblige; others needed the occasional prod if only to remind
them that diffidence was a vice in Trenchard's eyes.

One day Lieutenant C. C. Darley, an observer of No. 3 Squadron,
showed his squadron commander a set of passable prints which he
had recently developed for his own use. John Salmond studied the
long, blurred lines of trenches, as recognisable in miniature as old
faces in a family album. The landscape for miles around had grown
familiar in the weeks of unending scrutiny from the air; its features
stood out plainly on these extraordinarily clear photographs, which
Darley claimed to have taken with his own private camera. Salmond
almost snatched them from him; and Trenchard immediately
decided to entrust Darley with one of the photographic section's new
hand cameras.

The observer was briefed next day to concentrate on a particular
sector of the front south of the canal at La Bassée where, of late,
there had been more enemy ground activity than usual. It was a
factory district easily identifiable by the tall chimney stacks and a red
rash of abandoned brickyards. Haig's intelligence staff were not sure
in what strength the Germans were entrenched; all they could say
was that casualties inflicted on British patrols there had been rising.

Darley's aerial pictures more than justified the risk. The evidence
they disclosed of enemy fortifications induced Trenchard to seek
Haig's approval for an emergency conference of local corps and
divisional commanders. The meeting was held early in February:
Darley interpreted his photographs, with Salmond, the squadron
commander, prompting him and Trenchard looking on. The
generals were impressed by the labyrinth of hidden trenches and
strong points inside the disused brickworks; but the eye of the
camera also disclosed a few vulnerable positions which might be
turned by a carefully timed flank attack.

On 6th February, after Allied plans had been revised in the light
of this unfamiliar evidence, an assault by daylight caught the
Germans unprepared. The brickworks were captured; and the
completeness of this minor local action put fresh heart into every

observer, technician and planner at First Wing. Trenchard's influence
on the tactical preparations for Haig's spring offensive thus amply
repaid the army commander's gesture, of allowing a lowly lieutenant-
colonel so free a hand in advance. In the words of the official
historian:

" The pioneer work of Nos. 2 and 3 Squadrons had given Sir
Douglas Haig a picture of much of the Neuve Chapelle area. This
picture was completed before the end of February to cover the whole
German trench system in front of the First Army to a depth of from
700 to 1500 yards. The entrenchments which the photographs
recorded were then carefully traced on skeleton maps of a scale of
one in eight thousand, and on these maps the plan of attack was
based."[3]

The abnormal passivity of the enemy puzzled Trenchard.
Not once did a German machine climb to challenge the slow but
new B.E.2c biplanes which were gradually replacing his antique
collection of Maurice Farmans. Using cameras fixed by bolts to the
fuselage, the squadron observers loitered until shellfire interrupted
them, but hostile aeroplanes still kept their distance. Occasionally
pilots or observers on both sides had been known to fire a few
tentative rounds at a passing machine; now, it seemed, the Germans
were shrinking from offering unnecessary provocation. It was a
truce as grotesque to Trenchard's mind as one between two undeveloped scorpions, neither of which would attack the other owing
to doubts about the lethal power of their stings. One day soon, he
vowed, the Germans would be made to fight in the air.

4

Henderson inspected First Wing towards the end of February. The
harbouring of grudges was foreign to his nature. Since his return to
the R.F.C. he had never referred to the incident which prevented
his departure from the R.F.C. and the promotion of Sykes. His
pensive pleasure in the amenities and the general air of contentment
at Merville was carefully noted that night by Maurice Baring in his
diary:

" The house was steam-heated and like an oven. The billiard
table was boarded over, and had maps on it. Every kind of newspaper seemed to be taken in. When we came away the general said
to me: ' It's extraordinary how happy they are in that mess.' "

From his meagre reserves at St. Omer Henderson grafted two

flights together and sent them as a fresh squadron, No. 16, to
reinforce First Wing; and in keeping with the battle plan the
squadrons of Second and Third Wings were instructed to carry out
tactical bombing raids in support.

On 7th March, Trenchard was informed that the offensive would
begin two days later, weather permitting. Haig set aside for him
as an advanced headquarters a small house in Merville village, next
door to First Army's intelligence centre. The squadrons were keyed
up; their operational schedules were so arranged as to provide
maximum support to artillery and infantry. Nobody doubted that
the enemy would be overwhelmed.

Haig and French, differing as they did on much else, were at
one in maintaining that only by concentrating all available forces
at the decisive point on the one vital battlefield, namely, the
Western Front, would victory be won. Costly diversions from
France to Gallipoli and the rocky shores of the Eastern Mediterranean might yield political benefits; but they would not deceive or
distract a foe possessing undoubted superiority in numbers, fire-power
and the mobility conferred by shorter internal lines of supply and
communication.

The fact that there were no flanks left to turn did not dishearten
them. The notion that even small sectors protected by barbed-wire
thickets and fixed machine-guns could not be overrun without a
minor holocaust seemed too pessimistic for acceptance in that hopeful
spring of 1915.

At midnight on 8th March Haig sent for Trenchard as he had
promised. It was an unusual hour for briefing, but Trenchard was
too grateful for his trust to question his simplest decision. The
general was already waiting, wearing a great-coat over pyjamas,
when Trenchard arrived. Bare-headed and with coat collar turned
up, Haig strolled with him across the wet village square, past the
sentries, over the canal bridge and back, discussing the one imponderable factor which could not be controlled. He had been
pinning his hope on finer weather, he said. He doubted whether the
R.F.C. would be able to direct the fire of the artillery and follow
the progress of the infantry in poor visibility.

" I want one of your pilots to go up early in the morning. If his
report is favourable, the fight will be on."

Just after six o'clock in the morning Trenchard stood with Haig's
Chief of Staff, Sir Richard Butler, watching a biplane slowly gaining
height overhead. Later they questioned the pilot and observer and
were reassured. As Haig recorded in his diary:

" About 6 a.m. . . . . an aeroplane had made a short reconnaissance and reported clouds low but day fairly satisfactory. So I ordered the plan to be carried out as arranged, viz bombardment to begin at 7.30 a.m. and attack by infantry at 8.5 a.m."

The stillness after the thunder of the barrage was shattered every few minutes by the metallic buzz of the telephone in the small operations' room where Trenchard had installed himself. As the operational reports from squadrons began to stream in, excitement grew apace. The clipped, colourless accounts sorted out by the clerks appeared at first to emphasise the probability of a break-through: the infantry were advancing according to plan. Exhilaration lingered and slowly died. The intervals between messages lengthened, the information in them grew scrappier and more confused until, by noon, it was sufficiently clear that the Germans had recovered from the first shock of the onslaught. Trenchard ordered his car and spent the rest of the day touring the squadrons.

At each airfield he asked similar questions, letting the pilots and observers unwind their emotions in answers which sometimes rambled infuriatingly off the point. For once he was in no mood to bark; he drew them out patiently, and from this jumbled array of first-hand impressions he composed his own picture of a battle that had gone wrong before the eyes of these disappointed men.

The highest common factor in their accounts was the least agreeable. Many British batteries either disregarded or misread the target bearings signalled by R.F.C. observers, engaging the enemy gun positions unsighted. Weeks of laborious teamwork had gone by the board in half a day. Banking and turning again and again above the smoke of battle, ignoring the shell bursts blossoming like puffs of thistledown about them and causing their frail machines to shudder in the blast, the pilots had held to their courses, while the observers repeatedly signalled by lamp or wireless the sites of more than a dozen German guns. Yet none of their signals evoked a response from the British batteries.

The clock-code technique of pinpointing target positions from the air owed nothing to Trenchard but willing acceptance when proposed. As in the case of photography, he had offered every encouragement to the two enthusiasts who hit on the scheme, and to Salmond who sponsored it. Once he gained the ear of local artillery commanders, rehearsals were arranged and co-operation improved. The system evidently had its drawbacks in battle, but not through any fault that he could find in his air observers.

Lee, the staff officer, took notes throughout these informal cross-examinations which proved so simple and painless a short-cut to the hidden roots of failure that Trenchard decided there and then to adopt it permanently.   Long a standard procedure in the air forces of the world, the origins of "debriefing" can be traced back to the spontaneous post-mortem carried out by the leader of First Wing, with the help of his flight and squadron commanders, when the Neuve Chapelle offensive began to peter out.[4]

The foul weather persisted. There were prolonged spells in which no flying was possible. During these lulls Trenchard called in turn on the senior artillery officers of First Army; their attitude of unconcern convinced him that his aircrews were not exaggerating the degree of non-cooperation on the part of most British gunners.

" I could not get these gentlemen to take any interest. In fact, one of them said to me: ' Don't you see, Colonel Trenchard, that I'm far too busy fighting to have time for playing with your toys in the air? ' "

He knew then that the weather, on which Haig had banked too much, was not the only or the worst culprit. The bombing raids, on which Trenchard had built unreasonably high hopes, were mostly ineffective. John Salmond had flown in the observer's seat of the leading machine of three early on the first day of battle; in this attack an enemy brigade headquarters was knocked flat from little more than roof-top height. A few direct hits were scored by squadrons of the two supporting Wings on stationary enemy troop trains. But piecemeal blows falling almost at random could not influence the main land battle, since even their nuisance value was small. And the first bombing sortie carried out in darkness proved wholly abortive: all four machines briefed to attack the rail junction at Lille crashed without reaching the target.

After the offensive was called off, Haig visited Trenchard and listened impassively to his account of the cavalier attitude of the artillery in general, then reacted with a vigour which stilled Trenchard's uneasiness. Assembling all his senior artillery commanders, Haig rounded on their "early Victorian ideas." He intended, he said, to use the air service. They must either follow suit or go.

" By the way, I've received a strong complaint about you," Haig said to Trenchard afterwards with one of his rare, flickering smiles. " Colonel Sykes has protested to Sir John French that you incurred too many unnecessary casualties at Neuve Chapelle. I promised French I'd let you know, though this isn't a reprimand."[5]

The information momentarily stunned Trenchard. Henderson

had fallen ill during the battle, and his doctors had since sent him to the South of France for a complete rest. Preoccupied with operational matters, Trenchard had completely overlooked the fact that Sykes was left in temporary charge of Flying Corps Head-quarters. It was scarcely surprising that Haig refused to take his strictures seriously, for R.F.C. losses were light. Only six aeroplanes had been shot down or badly damaged in action, and a dozen pilots and observers killed or injured, compared with the thirteen thousand British soldiers who suffered wounds or death on the ground.

Haig was far more exercised over the second half of his limited spring offensive. Once again he disclosed the general plan to allow First Wing as much time as possible for preparation. The next push would be across the same scarred sector towards the wooded slopes of Aubers Ridge.

Early in April, Trenchard paid a quick business visit to London only to find that the growing pains of the Flying Corps were not confined to France. At the War Office Brancker laboured on, over-burdened with demands for aircraft and equipment which he lacked the authority, the staff and the resources to meet. The Government-owned Royal Aircraft Factory at Farnborough still monopolised the design and supply of army machines, though private manufacturers under contract to the Admiralty were turning out better engines and airframes for the Naval Air Service. Brancker could not compete with the purchasing power of the Senior Service, which had virtually cornered the market in raw materials; and these were growing scarcer with each passing month.

Kitchener could do little to help, having enough administrative troubles of his own. More addicted to giving advice than seeking it, inclined to settle major policy decisions without reference to his political colleagues, his obsession with building the new army blinded him to related questions of man-power and production shortages.

The name of Kitchener still inspired the public with an illusion of superhuman energy and efficiency; but better informed critics had begun to weary of the popular image and to deplore the complacency it engendered.

The first of the new formations reached France for their baptism by fire and poison gas at Ypres in April, 1915; others were held back in readiness for Haig's drive towards Aubers Ridge in May. Before-hand, Trenchard's camera crews flew far behind the lines, providing the army with comprehensive details of the German defence system.

The battle itself was inconclusive, despite closer liaison between gunners and air observers.

" During this period," wrote French in his dispatch, " there have been more than sixty combats in the air, in which not one British aircraft has been lost. In spite of the opposition of hostile aircraft and the great number of anti-aircraft guns employed by the enemy, air reconnaissance has been carried out with regularity and accuracy. . . ."

The weather helped and hindered both air forces with splendid impartiality. Mist grounded the R.F.C. when the Germans finally withdrew, unobserved, to fresh positions. But earlier, on the second day, when hope ran high and conditions were almost perfect, the human element again led to repeated errors of judgment.

Against this, of course, could be recorded individual instances of gallantry which moved Trenchard to pride while filling him with grief at the wanton waste of war. The episode which moved him most occurred at the end of April, when he had to interrupt his battle preliminaries and sent reinforcements north to Ypres, where the Germans had launched a local attack. On the 26th, four pilots took off to bomb railway stations behind the lines. The only machine to reach Courtrai was piloted by Second-Lieutenant W. B. Rhodes-Moorhouse, who dropped to 300 feet amidst a hail of bullets before releasing his 100-pound bomb plumb on the target.

Blood was flowing from a deep abdominal wound as he turned away; more bullets struck him in the thigh and hand as he flew clear. Fighting off the pain and giddiness all the way back to Merville, he insisted on gasping out in Trenchard's hearing a full account of the raid. Rhodes-Moorhouse died in hospital next day; and Trenchard's instant recommendation for a posthumous Victoria Cross was upheld.

The first air V.C. set an example of heroism which would one day become a tradition, so that a quarter of a century later another Rhodes-Moorhouse, the son of the same man, displaying the same contempt for danger, died fighting against similar odds in the Battle of Britain.

Trenchard had no reason to doubt the generous valour of his pilots. In the glum aftermath of the R.F.C.'s tactical failure, he merely doubted whether they yet had the weapons they needed or the leadership they deserved.

5

On 17th May, the day on which the grounding of the squadrons enabled the enemy to disengage in the mist, Henderson called on Trenchard at Merville. He was taken aback to find the downstairs office empty and its tenant lying fully clothed on his bed upstairs with a violent headache.

Intermittently for fourteen years, ever since returning from death's door in South Africa, Trenchard had suffered from agonising bouts of migraine. Brought on as a rule by overwork or worry, they partly accounted for the fitful savageness of mood which subordinates, ignorant of his past, ascribed to natural testiness.

Trenchard well remembered this particular onset. It seemed to lift of its own accord as Henderson sat on the end of the bed, first sympathising with him then speaking with unwonted freedom of the R.F.C. and of certain changes which he intended to introduce. This was a different Henderson; someone had clearly flicked him on the raw, rousing him from that gentlemanly detachment which was his most distinctive grace. Trenchard realised that something serious must have occurred to upset him so badly. Henderson was not in the habit of fumbling for words. At length his visitor said deliberately:

" I'm looking for a new staff officer. Have you any ideas? I'm getting rid of Sykes."

He explained that Sykes had been actively scheming to replace him in his absence. Damaging insinuations had come back to him from the highest quarters. It was said, for instance, that the Flying Corps would be better off under a commander with youth as well as robust health on his side. He had traced the whisper to its source, though Sykes, when confronted, was smoothly evasive, and even commiserated with him. This had only deepened Henderson's embarrassment and hardened his heart.

" I'm afraid I've come round to your way of thinking about Sykes," he told Trenchard. " When he leaves I'd like you to come as my staff officer."

" I'm sorry, sir, but I don't want the job," said Trenchard. " I've criticised policy and organisation before and will no doubt criticise them again, but that's not because I want to be your staff officer. You need a man who is able as well as loyal. Why not try Brooke-Popham? "

Henderson seemed disconcerted by so definite a refusal, but

agreed to consider Brooke-Popham for the vacancy. They then surveyed more general problems, dissecting the lessons of the recent battles and passing on to more general matters. There appeared to be little that the Flying Corps chief did not know of the tensions and conflicts going on behind the scenes.

Henderson, who was on friendly terms with Sir John French, mentioned, for instance, the worsening relations between the latter and Kitchener. The Commander-in-Chief, critical of all War Office rulings which remotely impinged on his authority, saw his political master as an ineffectual Pooh Bah combining off-hand membership of the Cabinet with domination of the General Staff. Most senior army officers were opposed to the Dardanelles project to which Kitchener, after some vacillating, had lent his approval. Even Haig, who saw eye to eye with French on few fundamental issues, was apprehensive that the diversion would reduce still further the unsatisfactory flow of equipment to the Western Front.

Such apprehensions were well founded. The preparations for the Dardanelles expedition, throwing as they did an extra burden on the War Office, depleted the supplies, especially of heavy ammunition, that were necessary for the British spring offensive. And the failure of that offensive moved French to retaliate by touching off a political time-bomb under Kitchener. The repercussions of the "shell scandal" were still reverberating loudly at the time of this conversation between Trenchard and Henderson. The appearance of an article in *The Times*, divulging confidential information which could only have been "leaked" from G.H.Q., caused a major sensation in France as well as London. Neither Henderson nor Trenchard cared for gossip. Temperamentally dissimilar in many ways, they equally loathed political intrigue.

Nevertheless, they could not ignore the fact that for more than a month R.F.C. messes had been buzzing with speculation. Allegations of neglect against Kitchener roused stronger passions than the livelier quarrel between Winston Churchill and his First Sea Lord, Admiral Jackie Fisher, who sought too late to dissociate himself from the muddles and missed opportunities in the Dardanelles. Though it would be futile to pretend that Trenchard knew more than was good for him about the intricate moves and counter-moves which led to the hasty broadening of Asquith's Government into a coalition of convenience, it would be still more futile to pretend that he failed to draw his own baleful conclusions from the little he learnt.

One result of the political changes at home was, indirectly, beneficial to the R.F.C. The appointment of Lloyd George as

Minister of Munitions obliged Henderson to consider how best to
strengthen the bargaining position of the undermanned Military
Aeronautics Directorate in London. The decision he finally reached
was at variance with his own aspirations. Only a senior officer of
high esteem, proven battle experience and sound technical knowledge
could hold his own at the War Office. Reluctantly but with
characteristic unselfishness, Major-General Sir David Henderson
ordered himself back to London.

He had now to decide who should succeed him in France.
Scrupulously impartial in his judgments, he could see no rival to
Trenchard, whose dynamic leadership had found an influential
backer in Haig. Henderson's recommendation went forward. It
was immediately endorsed by Kitchener. And on 19th August,
1915, Trenchard's appointment as General Officer Commanding
the Royal Flying Corps was published in the *London Gazette*.

Of Henderson's choice and the reasons for it, the official historian
of the Flying Corps wrote with dispassionate insight:

" He found that to meet the world-wide flood of demands which
came to him (the R.F.C. had squadrons in West Africa, Egypt
and other parts of the Middle East), he needed the full use of the
qualities with which he was endowed. He had often to fight for
his Corps in an atmosphere where there was no air tradition and
where the role of the new arm was imperfectly understood. To the
end he remained unruffled and kindly in judgment of those who
did not understand, but he alone knew what his serenity cost him.

" In one great respect that serenity was never disturbed. He knew
that in its new chief in France, the Flying Corps had an officer
whose personality must impress itself in the difficult days ahead on
a service responsive to a degree to the inspiration of its leaders."[6]

7. The Aggressor

Nobody regretted Henderson's departure more keenly than Captain Maurice Baring, his A.D.C. and a close friend for nearly twenty years, who returned from an Italian mission in August, 1915, to find Trenchard already installed at St. Omer. The disconcertingly gruff man whom he had originally met at Boulogne, and all but misdirected to a German prison camp, sent for him at once. " I'm prepared to let you stay for a month," he said. " If you're no good, you'll have to go."

Baring, a modest and unpretentious being, could not disguise his embarrassment. As he expressed it to himself, in his diary: " I felt adrift, like a stranded bondsman brought face to face with a new Pharaoh, and a bondsman who felt he had no qualifications."

Perhaps, he suggested diffidently, Colonel Trenchard would not mind his discussing the position with General Henderson in London.

Trenchard acceded readily; he had heard enough of Baring's reputation as a writer, of his virtuosity as a linguist, of his social gifts, his family connections and his dapper if somewhat extravagant mannerisms to write him off there and then as utterly useless. Nor was this due entirely to the prejudices of an impenitent philistine: what Trenchard feared most was that a man of such pronounced artistic temperament as Baring would have too little common sense. St. Omer needed a "second memory " more than a court jester.

" I intended sacking him," Trenchard admitted, " yet in conversation that day I was startled by his unselfishness and the loyalty he showed to Sir David Henderson and others."

The man's eccentric humility made Trenchard almost sorry for having spoken too harshly and hastily. " I'd also like you to give *me* a trial," he said. " I think you'll find I'm not so hard to work for, whatever you've heard to the contrary."

Henderson persuaded the reluctant Baring to work out his month's probation; and so began, in faltering style, an apparently incongruous partnership between two oddly dissimilar men, each of whom gradually proved to be the perfect complement of the other.

On paper, Baring's duties were as uncompromisingly dull as those of any clerk. " Wherever I go, I want you to come with me and take notes," Trenchard told him.[1]

Baring did so unobtrusively and conscientiously during the regular inspections of squadron and wing headquarters which became an integral part of working routine. Trenchard noticed that his new assistant was much sought after as an intermediary; and soon he felt himself falling under the quiet spell of this rather tall, sallow, bald man with the acquiline nose, the shambling walk, the deceptively ineffectual look, and the effortless wit, whose eye seldom missed any detail that truly mattered.

On the morning after Trenchard admitted to a wistful liking for Oxford marmalade, for instance, he found a jar beside his plate when he came down to breakfast. Staring at it with unaffected pleasure, he said sharply: " I see you've got a memory, Baring. Don't worry, I shall use it."

On a foundation of significant trifles of this kind tolerance ripened into affectionate understanding. Trenchard's singularity as a leader of men lay in the direct impact of his tyrannical but unconventional personality on colonels or privates at the airfields, aircraft parks, depots and repair shops they visited. Because he believed that men could not be inspired or commanded at a distance, he broke with Henderson's practice of letting subordinates run their own shows with a minimum of supervision. Even though he himself had thriven on it, the drawbacks had betrayed themselves in the ill-co-ordinated work of the R.F.C. during the spring offensives. The Flying Corps was about to expand, and he was determined that efficiency should not be diluted in the process. His first aim was to impose a more strictly co-ordinated tactical training programme, his second to make good as far as possible all material shortages. He chose to combine the functions of inspecting, directing and administering because, to him, the three were inseparable.

The notes which kept Baring busy on their long outings together are as uninspiring to-day as the inventory of a canning factory. They embrace all manner of supply needs, from fish-tail clips, hot-air pipes for carburettors, and cross-tubes under the fuselage or aircraft, to cam-release gear for bombs, and gun mountings. Baring had less knowledge of machinery than Trenchard; both were devoid of any natural taste for engineering in the narrower sense; for that very reason, perhaps, no complaint or suggestion ever passed unnoticed or unchecked.

Eventually, with scant regard for the misgivings of the experts, an extra machine per squadron was ordered from London so that every innovation, however whimsical, could be incorporated and tested by pilots before being rejected. Orthodox specialists muttered darkly that Trenchard was only indulging the cranks and creating unnecessary work for everyone. They underrated his uncanny skill for fastening on the single sound brainwave which justified a hundred unsound " Heath Robinson " contrivances. The squadrons repaid his regard for their opinions by vying with each other in elaborating ingenious and often worthwhile improvements.

" In the evening," Baring wrote, " the notes used to be put on his table typed, and then he would send for the various staff officers who dealt with the matters referred to in the notes and discuss them.

" The first thing he would ascertain was if the matter mentioned in the note had a real foundation; for instance, whether a squadron which complained that they were short of propellers had not in fact received a double dose the day before.

" If the need or the complaint or the request was found to be justified and reasonable, he would proceed to hasten its execution and see that the necessary steps were taken. If the requests were found to be idle or baseless, the squadron or the petitioner in question would be informed at once.

" But where (he) differed from many capable men was in this: he was never satisfied with investigating a request or a grievance or a need or a suggestion. After having dealt with it he never let the matter rest, but in a day or two's time he would insist on hearing the sequel. He would find out whether Squadron B had received its split pin or what Mr. A had answered from England when asked for it. This did not conduce to our repose, but it did further the efficiency of the R.F.C."

Baring knew at the end of September, 1915, that he had risen from disfavour into critical approval. Trenchard's prejudice against him had vanished. He was disarmed by the fastidious insight of this self-effacing individualist who presumed on nothing and gave the whole of his mind to an exacting job. Baring could be trusted; and the realisation of his utter constancy slowly induced Trenchard to treat him as a friend.

In a more impersonal way the headquarters' staff was equally dependable. It had to be. Officers like Festing, the temporary quartermaster, or Brooke-Popham, whom Henderson had appointed in Sykes's place without further prompting, adapted themselves without demur to Trenchard's autocratic yet flexible methods. He set the pace; they followed, slightly put out at first by his perverse disregard for "office hours." He had a roving eye for matters which commanders of comparable rank usually left to others.

Not that Trenchard was unwilling to delegate responsibility. His staff, though small, was efficient; his operational commanders, though good, were not yet as responsive as they would become with a little pushing. He could carry in his head for days at a time assortments of facts and figures, gleaned almost casually on his rounds. The inquisitiveness of an essentially orderly mind allowed himself and the staff no rest until the marrow had been sucked out of these scraps of information.

" What's wrong with now? " he would say, demanding instant answers to questions before another day brought its fresh accumulation of data to be rendered down.

The stuffy pretentiousness of parades and set inspections he abhorred and cut to the minimum. His car would usually arrive unannounced, the two men inside would get out, neither particularly formal in manner or attire. Baring invariably cut a slightly comical figure beside Trenchard, " tall and straight as a ramrod, covering ground quickly with huge strides, and forcing his shorter aide to move in a quaint kind of turkey-trot at his side, trying to keep up with him."[2] The pair hugely enjoyed worming out the sort of information which, in accordance with unwritten convention, had been withheld from visiting commanders since armies were invented. Trenchard insisted on being shown everything; and he would tread hard on subordinates who attempted to head him off.

Supplies of aircraft and spares were Trenchard's gravest problems. While Henderson was struggling to reorganise the uncertain sources at home, the Flying Corps had to lean heavily on the good will of the French, buying what could be bought and sometimes descending to rough forms of barter. Baring, with his idiomatic French and consummate tact, seldom emerged empty-handed from deals of this kind.

In July, 1915, when Henderson was on the point of returning home, the R.F.C.'s Paris office acquired a stock of new French propellers. Some were sent to No. 16 Squadron, then equipped with Maurice Farman reconnaissance machines; but the commander, Major Hugh Dowding, immediately complained that the propellers were of the wrong size. They were not designed for the squadron's 80 horse-power engines but for the smaller 70 horse-power version.

The complaint caught Trenchard at a bad moment: local air
activity was then vigorous, his reserves of spare machines were low,
and Dowding's air of superior wisdom displeased him. While he
admired the other's technical efficiency and might have deferred to
it in ordinary circumstances, he was aware that the plaintiff's own
flight commanders resented his "pernickety primness" and that
several of his pilots and observers "were almost in open revolt."[3] The
knowledge did not predispose him to treat a reasonable grievance
fairly.

" You'll fit those propellers," Dowding remembers him as saying.
" I want no argument. That's an order."

Dowding compromised, and spent hours fitting one propeller
with extreme difficulty. His doubts as to the final airworthiness of
the machine were so serious that he decided to risk his own neck
rather than anyone else's on a short test flight next day.

" I'm sorry you were put to unnecessary trouble," Trenchard
allegedly said when Dowding reported back. " You were quite right.
The Paris office let us down by sending the wrong replacements."

The incident was seized upon by Dowding as an indication of
the technical stupidity of Trenchard, who, by contrast, dismissed it
as a manifestation of Dowding's self-righteous stubbornness. It was,
unquestionably, a case of unnecessary misunderstanding which would
never have arisen had Baring been at Trenchard's side in July, 1915.
Acutely observant, totally lacking in conceit, amused yet endlessly
fascinated by the comedy of life, the savour of which was not tainted
by his sophisticated worldly wisdom, Baring's restraining influence
on the Flying Corps commander was considerable.

The fortunes of war had landed him a part so richly improbable
that Max Beerbohm, his friend, might well have hesitated to weave
it into one of his fantasies. Baring's veneration for "the General" as
a phenomenal personality went hand-in-hand with an extraordinary
flair for interpreting him at his most inarticulate. The results are
evident in the scores of official papers which stand out like milestones
in the development of the R.F.C. The strain of prophecy in these
is Trenchard's, the clear measured prose Baring's. In the routine
letters dictated daily by Trenchard to Corporal Bates, his clerk, the
grammar and phraseology often pall, if the thoughts still glow with
originality in places. It was Baring's unique achievement to succeed
in capturing Trenchard's best ideas without blunting their pristine
force, a feat comparable to bottling a mountain torrent while yet
preserving the tingling fury of its natural state.

" He was a man I could always trust," Trenchard wrote of him thirty years later. " He was almost my second sight in all the difficult tasks that came. . . . He knew more about what really mattered in war—how to deal with human nature, how to stir up those who wanted stirring, how to damp down those who were too excitable, how to encourage those who were in need of it—than any man I ever knew."

2

The pattern of their future partnership was fixed during the five weeks of intense activity which preceded the Battle of Loos in late September, 1915. Trenchard's first step was to reorganise his operational command. Brancker, relieved by Henderson, came thankfully from London to lead the Third Wing; the coolly efficient John Salmond was promoted to control the Second: and "Trenchard's own," the First Wing at Merville, was confided to Lieutenant-Colonel "Splash" Ashmore, an artillery expert who seemed specially fitted to continue the close collaboration already established with Haig's First Army. Baring attended a lengthy conference with the three new wing commanders in early September when air plans for the battle were worked out. Bombing had a high place on the agenda for the first time.

As was his custom, Trenchard devoted much time to tours of squadrons engaged in mapping the sector where the next British blow was to fall. One morning, after a stimulating discussion with Don Lewis, the commander of No. 3 Squadron near the village of Auchel, on the latest methods of linking up by wireless with the artillery, he was accosted by a kilted soldier who saluted him smartly, begged permission to speak, blurted out a condensed version of his service career to date, and said he wished to become a pilot. Baring, aware that Trenchard's crowded schedule allowed for no hold-ups of this sort, looked understandably anxious, as though disowning responsibility for the safety of the intruder. Trenchard, however, waited impassively until the monologue ceased.

" What's your unit? " he asked briskly.

" The London Scottish, sir."

" Take a note of that, Baring. Now, do you hold a Royal Aero Club certificate? "

" Yes, sir. Here it is." The man fumbled in a pocket and produced it.

" You say you applied to join the R.F.C.? "

" Repeatedly, sir. But my C.O. won't forward the application."

" Have you an application form on you? "

" Yes, sir."

Trenchard was handed a grimy, folded piece of paper. He passed it on to Baring.

" You'll hear more about this," he said enigmatically. Then he hailed a thunderstruck N.C.O., standing by at a respectful distance.

" If there's transport going this soldier's way, see that he gets a lift."

A few minutes later, seated next to the driver of a tender heading for the line, the soldier was left in no doubt as to his own temerity.

" Lumme," said the driver. " You've got a bloody nerve. What d'you think the general is, a recruiting sergeant? "

Air-Commodore D. W. Clappen, C.B., as he afterwards became, returned to the line, hardly expecting that the answer would come from Trenchard himself. Yet, in his own words:

" Three weeks later, at roll call, I was instructed to report to the orderly room. I had just come out of the trenches with the remnants of my battalion after the chaos of Loos. Within three hours I was on the train for Boulogne to report to the War Office and start training as a pilot."

It was one isolated but characteristic example of Trenchard's method of acting on a snap judgment, however great the pressure of work, and of following the action through.

The pressure on himself before the battle was certainly heavy, for the Flying Corps's strength had risen now to twelve squadrons, few of them ready or fully equipped for their task. Haig once wrote that "the problem of warfare consists of three M's, men, munitions and movement." It was an axiom to which Alexander the Great or Napoleon would have fully assented; yet, considering the balance of the opposing forces at Loos as well as the hardening conditions of siege that restricted movement to retreat or head-on collision, Napoleon and Alexander would undoubtedly have questioned Haig's set-piece preparations. He aimed once more at breaching the enemy line along a limited front of about six miles, then throwing in his reserves of infantry to exploit the break-through. Because his stocks of heavy ammunition were limited, he placed inordinate reliance on the still imperfect spotting techniques of the Flying Corps to ensure that precious shells would not be squandered. This touching faith was shared by few of Haig's subordinates; yet before the artillery bombardment opened, on 25th September, 1915, every important target had been fixed. The gunners knew more clearly than the infantry what lay "on the other side of the hill." The aerial pictures continued to pour in when the earth emplacements around vital enemy objectives had begun to spout and shake in the storm of shellfire that reached its controlled crescendo as zero hour approached.

Trenchard spent many hours during the first two or three days of the assault with his four target-marking squadrons. From dawn to dusk pilots and observers flew unimpeded high above the battle-line. New wireless receiving stations lay behind the front to forestall the failures in communications which had hampered the spring offensives, and messages were fed to the batteries with a smoothness that raised Trenchard's initial hopes. Barbed wire thickets and machine-gun nests, gun emplacements and trenches were pounded unmercifully.

The first tactical bombing raids in land warfare were executed according to plan. For three successive days Brancker and Salmond dispatched machines to drop 100-pound loads on trains, stations and railway lines between Douai, Valenciennes and Lille, the enemy's main supply route. The slow, unarmed raiders encountered fierce but erratic fire from the German guns, surprisingly little from interceptor aircraft. With excellent visibility random hits were registered on trains, sheds and signal boxes. Then the weather broke. The infantry swarmed over the top on 25th September under rain clouds that hung sombrely over the rich, already sodden earth; the makeshift bombers were still flying, despite the conditions, swooping down again and again to release their loads on troops, rolling stock and marshalling yards nearly forty miles behind the front. The attempt to dislocate the forward movement of German reserves was Trenchard's most ambitious undertaking yet.

But at the end of a week, the ground fighting was bogged down. Free activity was confined to the uncertain skies, where Ashmore's artillery machines hovered and signalled tirelessly but with diminishing effectiveness. More responsive than in past offensives, the British guns had to ration their cannonades, leaving the toiling infantry to their own devices. Confusion took charge in the fiery cauldron below as the momentum of the advance slackened, and with it the initiative. In desperate efforts to avert stalemates, Trenchard ordered out flights of low-flying machines to sectors where the fighting seemed thickest, the air observers straining their eyes for white cloth arrows laid out to mark the exact position reached by the attackers.

It was an agreed contrivance to help the artillery correct their

aim on the confused battlefield, where the destruction of forward
telephone wires often split men from each other and from their
formations, robbing headquarters of information on which control
of tactical developments depended. At Loos, Trenchard's pilots and
observers strained their eyes in vain. There were no white markings
on the churned-up soil. The men charged with laying them out had
probably been killed outright, and the survivors no doubt thought
better than to reveal their location to passing aircraft on the off-
chance that these were British.

Trenchard's determination to "help the staff by keeping them
informed" produced similar primitive experiments. The official air
historian describes, for instance, how an R.F.C. major and a flight-
sergeant were struck down while advancing with the infantry to
signal their position to a patrolling machine.

" There is a record of three messages, one on the 25th, another
on the 27th, and the last on the 28th, which had reference to the
attack by the Guards on Pit 14 bis. Flight-Sergeant Burns, soon
after this last message was sent, was hit in the head by shrapnel and
died of his wounds. Major Furse, however, carried on; but on the
30th he, too, was wounded in the head whilst making signalling
arrangements from a forward position."

Loos, however, proved less important to Trenchard than its
political aftermath.

Sir John French published a special order of the day during
the closing phase of the struggle praising Trenchard and his small
force for "valuable work . . . (in) . . . extremely adverse weather
conditions which entailed flying under heavy fire at low altitudes."
The Commander-in-Chief singled out for honourable mention the
pilots and observers whose "plucky work in co-operation with the
artillery, in photography and the bomb attacks on the enemy's
railways . . . were of great value in interrupting his communications."

Trenchard was not deceived by a eulogy which bristled with
exaggerations and was acceptable only as a fillip to morale.
Recognition of valour, of endeavour, even of status, could not alter
his disappointment that the Flying Corps had fallen short of his
own expectations yet again. The only consolation, a somewhat
grim one, was the honest doubt whether air tactics alone could have
influenced the outcome of a battle which, as he knew, had been
prematurely staged for mainly political considerations. In the month
of August, Kitchener, to the vexation of Sir John French, had paid
one of his infrequent visits to the front. By then, G.H.Q. had agreed
in principle to support a proposed French thrust in the Champagne

district towards Noyon with a limited assault on a narrow front opposite Loos. Sir John requested Haig, who was to deliver the assault, not to confide in Kitchener: otherwise, as French put it "he would tell the others in the Cabinet and then all London would know." Kitchener, however, was not to be fobbed off so easily. Indeed, he took the chair at an important conference in St. Omer shortly before his departure, a conference which Trenchard was asked by Haig to attend.

Still only a colonel, he felt exceedingly out of place. There was no chair for him at the long table among the generals, corps commanders, senior staff officers and lesser fry, so Trenchard sat on the window-seat, apparently unnoticed, listening in some amazement to the exchanges.

" They were talking about the future course of the war," he recorded. " The Government were apparently very anxious to secure a victory now for political reasons. After the failure of Neuve Chapelle and Aubers Ridge they wanted this action to bring a break-through." Kitchener, beyond stressing the political desirability of a victory, said little. And Haig, when turned to, said guardedly that he would do his best with the limited means at his disposal.[4]

Now Loos was over. Decimated divisions were marching out of the line. The R.F.C. had won a citation, Trenchard promotion to brigadier-general. Behind the scenes a tortuous, oddly one-sided argument was going on between French and Haig; it concerned the question of responsibility for withholding reserves from the front at a turning point in the battle; and since the battle had been undertaken for political reasons, the Cabinet was presently drawn in. Reputations were already at stake when the Commander-in-Chief published his dispatch. That part of it which panegyrised the R.F.C. caused less excitement than the section implying that Haig, far from being denied the reserves he needed, had actually mis-handled them.

3

It was an insinuation which Haig could not allow to pass uncon-tradicted. The dispatch of the reserves divisions, he claimed, had been absurdly mistimed by French himself. His version of what had gone wrong was forwarded to Kitchener; and a government reeling under a series of Allied reverses had no alternative but to intervene. Militarily and diplomatically, a victory in the West was badly wanted to offset the dispiriting news from Russia, the costly deadlock at Gallipoli, the recent subjugation of Serbia, and the accession of Bulgaria to the camp of the Central Powers. The British public were entitled to some explanation of the latest failure in France; and critics of the government were demanding satisfaction no less resolutely than Haig and French.

Haig had no occasion to discuss the dispute with Trenchard; yet the latter was neither sorry nor surprised when French finally tendered his resignation. His own contacts with the latter had been slight and impersonal, but the evidence of intrigue as well as indecision at G.H.Q. was too circumstantial for comfort. Moreover, Trenchard, who looked askance at anyone who was not complete master in his own house, knew that some corps commanders thought little of French's leadership. The attitude of Haig, his superior during these weeks of uncertainty, remained outwardly correct; he reserved for his diary stray flashes of mordant humour such as characterised the following entry on 6th November, 1915:

"Sir J. French has returned from England and is in bed with a heart attack. We wonder whether this is a result of my letter to G.H.Q. asking that paras. 11 and 13 (9) of his last dispatch may be corrected."

Haig exerted all his personal influence to clear himself of the charge of mismanagement. As his diary shows, Esher, Haldane, Kitchener, Robertson and the King himself were apprised in turn of his unflattering opinion of a superior whose position had gradually become untenable. On 10th December, Asquith notified Haig that, "subject to the King's approval," he had nominated him as the new Commander-in-Chief, "satisfied that this is the best advice that could be made in the interests of the army and the country."

Trenchard's incomprehension of Haig's lobbying methods was not entirely due to political naïveté. That the differences between his seniors transcended personal rivalries became unmistakably plain as the Loos inquest prolonged itself after the military lessons had been exhaustively analysed. The Flying Corps's work had to go on; and the temporary lull on land, aggravated as this was by the quarrel and its widespread repercussions, merely intensified his own difficulties in face of a major German threat to the continuance of that work. A new enemy fighter machine, lethal in its striking power, had begun to appear in growing numbers over the British end of the Western Front. Its name was the Fokker.

" It may be asked," noted Baring in his diary, " why we had not got the equivalent of the Fokkers in great quantities at this time, and the answer is that everything in aviation during the war was a compromise between progress and supply. As it took more than nine months for anything new in the shape of a machine or an engine to be available in any quantity, it generally happened that by the time a machine or an engine or the spare parts of both were available in sufficient quantities, the engine or machine or spare parts in question by that time were out of date. . . .

" It is said that we might have had the Vickers fighter in 1914 instead of in the summer of 1915, in which case our pilots could have shot the Germans down like sparrows. I remember hearing a friend of mine, who was himself an excellent pilot, exposing this fact. It was true we might have had the Vickers machine in 1914, so I ascertained; but what the pilot omitted to say, because he did not know it, was this: that the Gnome monosoupape engine, which was the engine of the Vickers fighter, was not in 1914 a reliable engine. It was only in the spring of 1915 that it could be used safely."

Baring fully appreciated Trenchard's dilemma because it was his unpleasant duty to explain it quietly and informally for the benefit of the critical and often resentful pilots. The dilemma was one that had long been foreseen. Henderson had warned Trenchard in July that the Germans were using the Fokker against the French in the centre with conspicuous success; and before Loos individual R.F.C. pilots had reported that a few monoplanes of distinctive appearance and tremendous fire-power were active on the enemy side of the line. The Fokker picked off its first victims among the improvised bombers of Brancker and Salmond during the battle itself; but not until October, when the Germans counter-attacked to recover lost ground, did R.F.C. casualties begin to soar. What oppressed Trenchard most, apart from the Fokker's ability to fire an uninterrupted stream of machine-gun bullets through its propeller, was the ironic recollection that a similar revolutionary device had been produced and offered to the War Office in pre-war days only to be rejected on grounds of expense and complexity. To one inventor who called at the Military Aeronautics office with a working model of a synchronising gear for spitting bullets safely through a spinning propeller, Captain Bertie Fisher regretfully explained one day early in 1914 that the R.F.C., though interested, had no money to spend on its development: every penny of the miserly funds available had already been allocated to other purposes.

Trenchard was thus placed at an immediate tactical disadvantage.

Though, on paper, the Flying Corps was numerically as strong as the enemy's, the bulk of its machines were of the same slow unarmed types as had crossed the Channel with Henderson in August, 1914. One incomplete squadron of the latest Vickers fighter was his only answer to the Fokker; and the Vickers which carried machine-guns, manipulated in the old way by pilots unskilled in the art of close combat, were not grouped together but spread in "penny packets" among the front line squadrons. The decision to dilute assets in this ineffectual fashion had been taken by Henderson in the early summer of 1915, against his better judgment, because of the prevailing opinion among his subordinate commanders, of whom Trenchard was the most insistent, that only thus could the offensive spirit be inculcated in all squadrons, irrespective of function.

In the words of the R.F.C.'s official historian:

" Pilots in the squadrons often alternated reconnaissance or artillery work on the rifle-armed two-seaters with fighting patrols on the machine-gun-armed single-seater tractor or two-seater pusher (machines). . . . Sir David Henderson held the view that the fighting type aeroplanes should be concentrated in one or more squadrons but the opinion was strong in the Wings that they should be distributed so that each squadron should have a leavening of offensive aircraft. Henderson gave way and the fighters were split up, although the policy of grouping (them) was adopted later on. . . ."

The advent of the Fokker forced Trenchard on to the defensive. The Flying Corps could not match its rapid rate of climb or manœuvrability in the hands of "aces" like Max Immelmann, whose famous rolling turn made sitting targets of the eminently stable but excessively slow and under-armed B.E. machines. Many were shot out of the skies unawares; others were outpaced, outfought and destroyed piecemeal on occasional bombing missions beyond the line.

The French Air Service, in support of Joffre's latest abortive attack over the Champagne country, had already suffered severely from the so-called Fokker "scourge"; and its leader, Commandant du Peuty, readily put all his knowledge and advice at the disposal of Trenchard.

" They talked and argued over the experiences of the two air services," records the air historian. " They came at last to the conclusion that the corps aeroplanes could best be protected by what one might call the strategic offensive, that is, by fighting and subduing the enemy airmen far away from the aeroplanes flying in direct co-operation with the army."

Du Peuty, however, was against any immediate attempt to restore the tactical balance by aggressive action, preferring to play a waiting game until the Allies were ready to answer the Fokker in kind. There was, perhaps, a flavour of "sour grapes" about this cautious attitude. For du Peuty suspected that the Fokker's interrupter gear partly owed its development to the mischance which permitted a rudimentary French contrivance to fall intact into German hands in February, 1915, when engine trouble forced down Roland Garros, the pilot of a Morane monoplane, on the enemy side of the line. Alert pickets seized him before he could set fire to his machine, which was immediately identified from its markings as the one which had lately shot down at least a dozen Germans with almost insolent ease. The Morane, on closer examination, was found to have protective triangular steel wedges on the inner edges of its propeller blades. An automatic rifle was still mounted, undamaged, on the front of the cockpit. Here, in this crude hit-or-miss device for deflecting bullets forward, lay the explanation of Garros's run of victories. Its capture seems to have indirectly inspired Anthony Fokker, the Dutch born engineer and aircraft designer, to adapt and harness an improved, automatic and much safer device to the engine of his own fighter, the Fokker E.1.

Only gradually, as R.F.C. losses outstripped replacements, did Trenchard cut down his routine commitments on behalf of the army, and only then for the sake of operational efficiency and not from squeamishness or any slackening of purpose. His main worry as 1915 drew to its close sprang from the depressing effect on squadron morale of the misleading and often alarmist accounts of the "Fokker scourge" that were beginning to appear in the British Press. In fact, the struggle to maintain local air superiority, despite the tactical and technical odds, was far from being the one-sided affair which de Peuty had originally feared and which some of the more sensational newspapers mistakenly supposed.

Brancker, in command of Third Wing, replied to the enemy challenge in typically bold style, using flights of speedy Vickers biplanes with their fixed Lewis guns to escort his patrols.

"My command," he wrote, "consisted of three squadrons of B.E.2c's and one of Vickers fighters. The B.E.2c was not a good bombing machine, as in order to carry a good load of bombs it was necessary to fly it single-seater. This made it a somewhat easy prey for the Fokker. . . . We used to send two or three machines together and try to keep the air clear of the enemy by patrolling with Vickers fighters. I believe that these operations mark almost the first time in the British Army that any effort was made to fly in formation and to employ fighting patrols."

A sharp decline in air co-operation with the ground forces inevitably resulted from the systematic grouping together of Martinsyde, Bristol and Vickers scouts as well as of the few Moranes obtained from du Peuty. The effective strength of the Flying Corps all along the front was thus depleted; but Haig, engrossed in his unsettled quarrel with French, proved understanding and forgiving. There was, fortunately, little serious activity on the ground as the winter deepened.

Only in the clouds overhead was there constant fighting from which Trenchard did not flinch. His contention from the beginning had been that air supremacy would sooner or later have to be fought for; the fact that the enemy possessed a "flying gun" vastly superior to anything the Allies were likely to produce in the near future did not deter him. There could be no "standing on the defensive" in the skies. Survival in three-dimensional warfare depended on maintaining the offensive, whatever the odds or the cost. It was a choice between destroying and being destroyed on the ground. Such technical modifications as could be introduced to lessen the odds were swiftly carried out: the Lewis gun, for instance, replaced the observer's rifle in the B.E. biplanes, though the ammunition drums were small and the weapon itself was prone to jam. Pilots in single-seater fighters, accustomed to manœuvring for position until they could open fire on an attacker without risk of fouling the propeller and shooting themselves down, now fought on slightly less disadvantageous terms with a machine-gun fixed to the upper wing and controlled by a cable.

The most delicate factor in the long run, as Trenchard realised, would be the morale and stamina of his crews; so long as he could watch over these, all would yet be well. He had no need of the solaces of popularity or liking; he simply knew that he was right. His contempt for what he called "interfering busybodies," uniformed or civilian, coupled with a reluctance to defend himself against mis-informed criticism, was one of the glaring defects of his monolithic integrity. An old regimental friend, who met Trenchard again during that grim period, said of him with some perception: " He looked to me more than ever like a man who had mislaid affection somewhere along the line." There were occasions, however, when Trenchard could be stung into hitting back.

While on official business in London towards the end of 1915, he was sitting one day in the Green Park, enjoying the feeling of anonymity in mufti, and delighting in the peace that stole over him on his bench under the trees. Even the newspapers seemed in that mood and setting to reflect the doings of a world far removed from the violent realities of his. There were two domestic topics in particular which, he noticed, appeared at the time to be generating a lot of heat. One was an alleged glut of unwanted war babies, the other a campaign conducted by ardent females to shame able-bodied men of military age into enlisting by presenting them publicly with large white feathers.

It amused him to think that anyone in authority should treat this excessive manifestation of jingoism with any seriousness; yet he had noticed the silver discs shining like badges of merit in innumerable buttonholes, and had learnt that these were issued to men engaged on essential work as an insurance against public insults and embarrassment. It was a strange war, a very strange war, he reflected. He was on his way back towards his Berkeley Street flat, still musing, when a waspish woman of uncertain age accosted him.

" May I ask you, sir, where's your war badge? " she inquired.

Trenchard hesitated only for a moment.

" And may I ask you, madam, where's your war baby? " he barked, and stumped off into Piccadilly.

4

It had never been Henderson's intention to remain indefinitely at the War Office. All that autumn he had been hastening the training and equipping of new squadrons, seeking both to satisfy Trenchard's urgent calls for replacements and to broaden the basic structure of a Flying Corps which he hoped soon to command again in battle. The Army Council had already accepted the principle of his scheme to merge wings, two at a time, into new brigades. This fitted in exactly with Kitchener's wishes; and the moral support of the Secretary of State overrode the orthodox opinions of staff officers who thought it outrageous that comparative juniors should be jumped up to the temporary rank of brigadier in a specialist arm, the operational value of which they strongly questioned.

Letters passing between Henderson and Trenchard towards the end of 1915 confirmed that they had agreed to change places at the beginning of the new year, Trenchard with some reluctance,

Henderson with considerably more eagerness. The latter had quickly tired of the incessant vexations inseparable from his task. He wanted Trenchard to relieve him, with the appropriate rank and powers of a major-general. Unfortunately for Henderson's hopes, the Admiralty, the Kaiser and Kitchener—roughly in that order—intervened one by one to thwart him. To understand how and why this should have occurred, we must go back in time.

The Gallipoli set-back in the previous spring had broken up the triumvirate of Asquith, Kitchener and Churchill. The resignation, in melodramatic circumstances, of Admiral Fisher, Churchill's own choice as First Sea Lord, precipitated the departure of Churchill from the Admiralty and his replacement by Balfour, when Asquith formed the Coalition Government in May, 1915. Churchill, the *bête noire* of the Conservatives, was made to atone, among other sins, for his "sinister" part, on the wrong side, in the pre-war Ulster crisis; he could only watch the dignified but halting efforts of his successor to trim some of the innovations which he and Fisher had contrived together in the heyday of their partnership.

The surrender to the War Office of the Royal Navy's armoured trains, armoured car squadrons (containing the germ of the idea which produced the tank) and anti-aircraft units was a justifiable reform. The reorganisation of the Naval Air Service, which took longer and was undertaken in the name of naval discipline, produced a specialist arm so rigidly controlled from above that it promised to wither away. Unlike the Army Council, the Board of Admiralty was careful to appoint to the highest posts officers more distinguished for age, rank and length of service at sea than for practical experience of air matters.

Murray Sueter was replaced as Director by Rear-Admiral C. L. Vaughan-Lee. Exceptionally, an airman was given command of the operational squadrons at Dunkirk; but Wing Commander C. L. Lambe came under the orders of Vice-Admiral R. H. Balcon, whose interest in flying was somewhat limited. The fate of Sueter was symbolic. In trying to serve Churchill, he had antagonised his own superiors, incurring open hostility from "several of the Sea Lords", who tried, he declared, "senseless blocking tactics to hinder air development."

These changes in the policy and structure of the Naval Air Service could hardly have happened at a worse moment for the Royal Flying Corps. While air efficiency was being sacrificed as a kind of burnt offering on the high altar of Admiralty tradition, the Fokker was beginning to take toll of the old-fashioned, easily outmanœuvred reconnaissance machines of the R.F.C. Henderson's efforts to produce better trained pilots and improved types of aircraft were indirectly hindered by the conflicting wants of the eight Admiralty departments with an interest (among many others) in the raw materials necessary to maintain two separate air services in being.

"Of these eight," comments Sir Walter Raleigh, the official historian of the Air War, "only two were officers of the original Royal Naval Air Service. Most of the newly appointed administrative officers had no previous knowledge of aircraft or aircraft operations."

As if to put paid to the initiative of Churchill, Balfour allowed himself to be persuaded of the merits of a revised air policy that would need all the luck in the skies, millions of public money, and ample time to succeed. It was decided in late 1915 that airships would serve the fleet better than aircraft; and one effect of the upheaval required to implement that decision was an increase in Henderson's supply difficulties.

"Had I had my way," wrote Churchill, "no airships would have been built by Great Britain during the war (except the little 'Blimps' for teasing submarines). After I left the Admiralty this policy was reversed, and forty millions of money were squandered by successive boards in building British zeppelins, not one of which on any occasion ever rendered any effective fighting service. Meanwhile, the alternative policy of equipping the fleet with aerial observation by flying aeroplanes lagged pitifully with the result that at the Battle of Jutland we had no British airships and only one aeroplane in the air."[5]

The Admiralty was, however, a realm within a realm. Lord Kitchener, as keen as ever on the principle of an expanding R.F.C., had less time and opportunity to ensure that Henderson's practical demands were met. The crucial political problem of the hour was how to extricate a Government and an army from the fiasco of the Dardanelles with a minimum loss of face. The beginnings of the "Fokker scourge," like the ordinary growing pains of the R.F.C., had not yet assumed in the eyes of the politicians the significance attached to them by Flying Corps' commanders at home and in France.

It was typical of the prevailing spirit of indecisiveness in Whitehall that, though the War Office agreed to take over the air defence of Britain in the summer of 1915, not until the following January was this former naval commitment surrendered to the R.F.C.

"Nobody at the War Office can in any way comprehend our

difficulties and the huge amount of work there is to be done,"
Henderson wrote to Trenchard on 17th January, 1916. " Very few
will take the trouble to learn."

Henderson felt hopelessly isolated. The War Office, prodded
from behind by Lloyd George, now Minister of Munitions, had fallen
too far behind Kitchener's over-ambitious supply programme for the
army to concern itself with the parallel needs of the Flying Corps.
Nor was Kitchener's token sympathy for Henderson an adequate
substitute for the magic wand he had waved at will over less elaborate
shortages in the days when Trenchard was at Farnborough. Then
the R.F.C. had drawn freely on the nation's unorganised plenty,
now its greater necessities clashed at a dozen points with those of
army and navy and were, at best, only imperfectly understood.

Henderson had three equally pressing difficulties to surmount:
first, the provision of fresh squadrons to match the expansion of the
armies in France; second, the creation of a skeleton Home Defence
system of ground stations and aircraft against zeppelins; and third,
the improved training of pilots and the production of new machines
and weapons of higher performance to meet the dual challenge of
night raiders over England and Fokkers over the Western Front.
In spite of everything, perhaps because of everything, he still clung
to his dream of changing places with Trenchard.

" I shall want a lot of suckling flight commanders soon, as I have
to produce at least four squadrons a month," he wrote towards the
end of December. " I might start the New Year with you, if that
would suit. I hope we shall soon have plenty of machines for you,
but the lack of a big engine is turning my hair grey."

Practically every moonless period in 1915 had brought enemy
raiders to London and the east coast. Militarily ineffective the
zeppelins might be, but their nuisance value could not be ignored.
About two hundred people were killed; over one million pounds
of damage was caused. It needed only a lengthy bomb-free lull of
three months followed by one long night of scattered bombing over
the Midlands to alarm the public seriously. This happened,
to Henderson's chagrin, on 31st January, 1916.

" We had some zeppelins last night, and did a good deal of
flying," Henderson wrote to Trenchard. " Our young men are a
little too intrepid. Their interpretation of suitable weather was a
little vague. . . . I have read your memorandum on the fighting in
the air at the front and have told the C.I.G.S. (Robertson) that I
agree with it entirely. I have also appended a note showing what
steps we are taking to cope with the new activity and I understand

Maurice Baring

Haig, Joffre and Lloyd George together in France, 1916

Trenchard as Chief of Air Staff

it will be discussed at a War Council to-morrow, which I am to attend."

Henderson had every reason for dismay at the repercussions caused in Whitehall by a few off-chance zeppelins. Overnight, popular clamour obliged the Government to seek the basic cause of inadequate air defences: they found it, quickly enough, in the breakdown of co-operation between the War Office and the Admiralty. Thus, indirectly the Kaiser and his zeppelins did the Flying Corps a good turn; for the Cabinet was in full and rare agreement with Kitchener as to the next steps. It was decided to keep Henderson at home and give him a permanent seat on the Army Council as a pledge of the Government's newly awakened anxiety to settle the conflicting air interests of army and navy. A select Committee charged with investigating their rival responsibilities and claims was also set up at once.

" I'm so tied to the War Office at present that I can't even get away to see new machines," Henderson wrote on 25th February. " The establishment of the Government's new Joint War Air Committee is going to give me a lot of work, and I think very useful work, as we are bound to get the navy more or less into line. Lord Derby is an ideal chairman and I'm sure will do a lot of good."

In reply, Trenchard expressed deep personal relief. " At last I hear I am to stop out here, for which I need hardly say I am extremely thankful. . . . I am very glad you are going on the Army Council. It is funny, but that is what I suggested three months ago. . . . I am very much of the opinion that Brancker ought to be made a Director, not necessarily a Director General, to enable him to do the large amount of work you haven't time to do."

There is no evidence that Haig, who succeeded French in December, intervened at any stage on Trenchard's behalf, though the field-marshal's reluctance to part with him was privately well known to Sir William Robertson, the newly appointed Chief of the Imperial General Staff, whom the Government had invested with exceptional authority in order to curb the powers of Kitchener. The old order was passing. The political influence of the Secretary of State for War was on the wane, even if his popular prestige was not.

" I see lately they have been talking in the House as if I was afraid of being shot at—and stating that I never go over the line," Trenchard wrote to Henderson on 28th February. " I hope, when you get the chance, that you'll ask these political people whether they're prepared to come as my passenger."

T.   F

What both amazed and heartened him during the last weeks of
that winter of endurance was his certainty that the Germans had
failed to exploit the Fokker's enormous technical superiority. Had he
been in command of the enemy's fighters he would have striven to
drive the R.F.C. out of the sky by an unremitting onslaught until
every squadron was destroyed on the ground or over its own airfield.
The Germans had mishandled their chances; Fokkers seldom
pounced together, except in random or misdirected swoops; and not
all of their pilots were of the calibre of Immelmann or Boelcke.
Between January and March, 1916, Trenchard restored a difficult
situation which, under an enemy leader of his own single-minded
ruthlessness, could well have ended in disaster.

The aggressive temper he instilled into his commanders and
aircrews was his finest consolation. Despite an open grumpiness,
which he was at pains to stimulate, about the imperfections of the
machines and equipment on which their very lives depended, he
never forfeited their respect and confidence. Every death above the
lines cut him to the heart, as Baring and Bates could testify when his
vigilance relaxed and his carefully guarded feelings betrayed
themselves.

It was not a callous insensitivity to casualties but a degree of
prescience unmatched among air leaders of the day which convinced
Trenchard of the necessity of trying to hold his own. He knew that
if he changed his tactics too suddenly, the enemy might follow suit
by concentrating Fokkers and Albatrosses in overpowering strike
groups and sweeping the air clear of the Flying Corps, as he would
certainly have done in their place months before. So Trenchard
drove his squadrons on, convinced that he had no other course.

Nearly fifty pilots and observers perished in combat between
early November and early January, the two worst flying months of
all. Most of the victims were ambushed on the "milk runs," those
long-distance bombing and reconnaissance flights which the armies
still expected as a matter of routine, though Trenchard had to ration
such missions more and more rigorously.

"Until the Royal Flying Corps is in possession of a machine
as good as or better than the German Fokker," he declared in an
instruction to all squadrons on 14th January, 1916, "it seems that
a change in the tactics employed becomes necessary. . . . It must be
laid down as a hard and fast rule that a machine proceeding on
reconnaissance must be escorted by at least three other fighting
machines. These machines must fly in close formation and a
reconnaissance should not be continued if any of the machines

becomes detached. This should apply to both short and long reconnaissances. Aeroplanes proceeding on photographic duty east of the line should be similarly escorted. From recent experience it seems that the Germans are now employing their aeroplanes in groups of three or four, and these numbers are frequently encountered by our aeroplanes. Flying in formation must be practised by all pilots."

The change paid gradual dividends. Instead of opening an immediate counter-offensive and pinning the R.F.C. to the ground, the Germans spent themselves trying to break up rigidly held R.F.C. formations with small flights of Fokkers. By the last week in February, two new squadrons of the latest F.E.2 and de Havilland fighters arrived from England, a welcome if overdue reinforcement for the battered but unbroken R.F.C. Equipped with fixed machine-guns but not yet with the interrupter gear, they nevertheless quickly proved a match for the Fokker.

Meanwhile, at home, critical voices were raised in Parliament and unfavourable comparisons drawn between the immunity enjoyed by raiding zeppelins and the heavy casualties suffered by the R.F.C. in France. Trenchard's tactics came under fire; but Trenchard himself was unmoved by allegations founded on what he regarded as emotionalism and ignorance. Towards the end of January, when the Prime Minister himself wrote expressing certain misgivings about the handling of the R.F.C., Haig replied to Asquith:

" As to aircraft, I enclose a note from General Trenchard with which I agree. We must continue to reconnoitre. The remedy is not to stop sending machines out for this purpose but to send them out in groups rather than singly.

" Our present experience with aeroplanes is somewhat similar to Napoleon's in the matter of cavalry patrols before Jena in 1806. I think then the German cavalry was very efficient and regularly mopped up the French reconnaissances until the latter went out in double strength to the enemy's patrols. Distant reconnaissances are not sent out without some object sufficiently important to justify the risk involved. . . ."[6]

Trenchard was less concerned with drawing neat parallels from military history when the turn of events had begun to prove him right. The sky was a battlefield where orderly retreat was impossible, standing on the defensive unthinkable, and any strategy but an offensive one completely insupportable. Unlike the land or the sea, this new three-dimensional arena was one and indivisible, with no fixed lines to hold or flanks to turn.

It was rare for a shaft to pierce his composure; even then it was usually an imputation on his courage to which he could not personally reply. His only course was to work off his feelings in letters to Henderson or Brancker in the way that more articulate men let off steam in their private war diaries.

8. The Prophet

The broad lines of Allied strategy for 1916 had already been formulated at a meeting between Joffre and Sir John French in November, when they agreed to abandon the limited offensive methods of recent months for something altogether more ambitious. Instead of trying to punch small holes in the enemy defences by heavy preliminary bombardments, then pouring infantry through on a narrow front to exploit the breaches, it was decided to concentrate everything on one gigantic blow to drain enemy reserves, the ultimate obstacle to success. By synchronising their attacks, the French, British, Russian and Italian Armies would stand a better chance of ending the strategic deadlock on land and so create the open conditions necessary for victory.

Haig, on replacing French, accepted the project with one main reservation: he disliked the subsidiary role assigned to himself. A series of short, sharp pushes by the British in support of Joffre did not quite commend itself to Haig, who favoured conserving his resources for a single stroke timed for delivery immediately before the French assault. The dispute proved as unrealistic as the master plan on which the leaders' vain hopes of an early knock-out were pinned. For the Germans, turning Allied complacency and their own internal supply lines to swift advantage, got in first at Verdun on 21st February, 1916.

Trenchard heard of the opening of the battle on the night of 22nd February, after driving from Paris in a snowstorm. The news came as no shock to him.[1] Evidence of an impending German move had lately been increasing; and he assumed that the French High Command were as prepared as du Peuty appeared to be. The French air commander, with his customary economy of words and gestures, had confided his dispositions to Trenchard only a week previously. The two men, thanks to Baring's subtlety as an interpreter, were by now good friends as well as close collaborators, esteeming one another's courage and integrity without allowing that to prevent spirited arguments about tactics. The R.F.C.'s refusal to let the Fokker dictate exchanges had not yet converted du Peuty to Trenchard's belief in "forward action" as the only proper way to "use and win the air."

The logical Frenchman, drawing on his experience as a regimental soldier, contended that defensive tactics might sometimes be inevitable even for airmen. While respecting Trenchard's calculated recklessness in pitting his strength against technically superior but indifferently organised enemy fighters, recovering local air ascendancy in the process, he had no immediate intention of emulating him. Du Peuty viewed the heavy enemy concentrations along the nine-mile stretch of the lower Meuse, opposite Verdun, as too complex and sinister a threat for incaution in the air. Opinion had been sharply divided at French General Headquarters in Chantilly as to the imminence of a serious German attack; and Joffre himself seems to have been more unready than anyone. His stolid serenity on the eve of the storm was not, however, entirely due to complacency. Some of his staff were guilty of telling him only what they thought it good for him to hear. If the unfavourable signs were also pointed out to him, he gave no hint of having understood them when he discussed with Haig as late as Tuesday, 14th February, their joint plan for an offensive in the spring. Before the week-end General de Castelnau, Joffre's virtual second-in-command, was begging Haig to extend his line and release the French Tenth Army for transfer to Verdun.

De Castelnau proved himself the man of the hour, and the saviour of the situation. On returning from Salonika in January, he had prudently taken heed of the gloomier critics, inspected the Verdun salient himself and authorised drastic steps to fortify it; but his personal warnings were powerless to dispel the atmosphere of enchanted optimism reigning at Chantilly. It was as if Joffre's henchmen were unwilling to rouse the irrascible but somnolent old warrior until the alarm went off.

The storm descended with a violence which Chantilly could not misinterpret any longer. Haig fell in at once with de Castelnau's representations and took over more of the line; the French Tenth Army was moved east; du Peuty combed his squadrons on the Western Front to strengthen those behind Verdun, and sent to St. Omer a young pilot called la Ferrière to act as his liaison officer, Trenchard reciprocating by sending Captain Cooper to the battle-front so that du Peuty's needs could be passed back to him direct.

Until the last week of March, the onslaught ran true to the

expectations of von Falkenhayn, the enemy commander at Verdun. The French author, Jean de Pierrefeu, who spent the First World War writing the official *communiqués* at Chantilly and saw more than was salutary for any staff officer of happenings behind the scenes, has left a graphic account of the belated change of outlook at G.H.Q. Joffre was sufficiently shaken to sanction the dispatch of the Second Army, under Pétain, in addition to the Tenth, and to confer on de Castelnau the plenary powers he sought to prevent a collapse and a disorderly withdrawal behind the Meuse. Having secured the river-line, de Castelnau handed over to Pétain, who proceeded to reoccupy and rearm the Verdun forts.

Von Falkenhayn's uncanny sense of anticipation could scarcely have been improved upon had he known the Allied plans for 1916. The aim of these, as stated, was to draw Germany's man-power reserves into battle and destroy them. Quite independently, the German High Command, by forcing the French to defend a half-moon of ground before a ring of forts previously rendered harmless by the removal of guns and magazines, tempted France to bleed herself white instead.

The prize, in retrospect, seems hardly to have been worth the tremendous pains and losses of the attackers and defenders. Its capture would not have opened any vital new communications; its surrender after an orderly, prepared withdrawal behind the Meuse, which cut through the salient, would have exposed no indefensible French flank.

Verdun formed an unnatural bulge which simply asked to be squeezed flat. Yet von Falkenhayn, in mounting a limited assault in enormous strength, gambled on catching the French off guard and luring them into a desperate holding action. As the initial gamble paid, he redoubled the first hammer blow again and again with the set aim of sucking more and more French reserves into the arena. Between February and June, 1916, some sixty-six French divisions (or nearly half the effective strength of Joffre) saw action at Verdun.

This was attrition with a vengeance and on an unprecedented scale. It was made possible by von Falkenhayn's fearsome array of siege guns and heavy artillery, under whose cover three corps of picked troops were matched with twice or thrice as many defenders. In point of time the Germans set an example in the gruesome art of modern siege warfare which Joffre and Haig, often vilified as its inventors and arch-exponents, would copy in turn. Barbed wire, the shell and the machine-gun, concentrated at selected points, were, with the almost impassable ground conditions in winter, the factors which fixed the pattern of this negative, destructive strategy for the next two years.

The air services could not affect the outcome yet, and du Peuty's squadrons were caught up at once in the maelstrom. The watchword, " They shall not pass," on which Pétain's title to greatness rested for a generation, was ill-suited to the tussle for air ascendancy above the torn battlefield. Trenchard, with shrewd appreciation of du Peuty's material shortages, ransacked R.F.C. depots for every Lewis gun, tracer bullet and bombsight that could be spared, dispatched them to Verdun without being asked, and pestered Henderson in London to replenish his stocks. With one hundred extra square miles of the Western Front to patrol now that the British had taken over more of the line, and with few machines and men in reserve, he deliberately increased local pressure on reduced enemy squadrons, knowing that du Peuty's air battle was his, too.

" I'd like you to thank General Trenchard again for his machine-guns," du Peuty wrote to la Ferrière early in April. " We've had trouble with some which jammed during combats. This seems due less to the tracer bullets he gave us than to the precarious and poor conditions of maintenance at Verdun. I've had one of his Lewis guns fitted to my own aircraft. It proved most useful in an attack with two other Nieuport fighters on two Fokkers and five L.V.G.s about four miles behind their lines. We had them cold; they were picking their noses in a disgusting fashion. Navarre (an 'ace' fighter pilot) has shot down four Boche machines in a single day. . . ."

Only a major in rank, du Peuty remained in command at Verdun until the summer. There was, it seems, no air leader of comparable experience or resource to replace him. His letters, like the fuller reports Trenchard received from Cooper, his R.F.C. observer, were evocative of a fierce and fluctuating contest with enemy squadrons roughly equal to the French in numbers. By trial and error, du Peuty slowly learnt for himself the truth of Trenchard's earlier assertions that offensive action was the key to air superiority.

" The most characteristic facts about the fight so far are, first, the new importance of night reconnaissance, and second, the improvements resulting from organising our fighters into separate groups outside the ordinary army co-operation squadrons," he wrote to him through la Ferrière in April. " By flying together in threes, our army machines have shown that they can protect them-selves, so freeing the real combat aircraft for independent offensive action against enemy fighters which are already organised in such groups.

" I'd like you to draw General Trenchard's attention also to the following point: in the near future the advantage will go to the group which can carry its striking power the farthest. . . ."

This tallied exactly with Trenchard's belief and experience. He had never questioned the bravery or competence of the average French pilot, whose equipment and training were on the whole better than the British, but distrusted the rigid control exercised by French army commanders with no understanding of air tactics. Du Peuty was evidently striving to terminate this bad tradition by progressively creating his own, as Trenchard had done, in conditions of extreme adversity.

" We are beginning to improve on our new methods, though over and over again we have to start from scratch, teaching new squadrons that keep coming and going with the constant relieving of units at the front. I may say that my *official* reports, which are meant to plant a few ideas in the heads of some noble but very old-fashioned gentlemen, call for a real reorientation of thinking at G.H.Q. I'm drawing up a detailed account of my conclusions which I'll let you have."

This considered document reached St. Omer in mid-April, after du Peuty's "new methods" had been subject to the severest testing. It was regarded by Trenchard as the most significant paper on air fighting so far produced. Even to-day, as a historical curiosity, it is worth quoting at length:

" Aircraft can be divided into two," wrote du Peuty, " army machines and combat machines. And these aircraft can be employed in two separate ways: either by using the combat machines to protect the army machines, or by letting the latter fend for themselves so that the combat machines can do their real job of fighting.

" We've employed both methods, and here are the results. Like the Germans, we began by adopting the second method, and thanks to our offensive efforts we attained a material and moral superiority so marked that the enemy were forced to protect their army machines.

" We were proud of this. It made us a little complacent; we yielded to the demands of our own army corps which wanted close protection for their hard-pressed co-operation machines. We in turn were driven to adopt the first method, and were barely able to hold our own with the enemy. The strongest formations of aircraft proved themselves masters of the situation.

" We then resumed the second method—and immediately recaptured local air superiority by going after it. There were two

main drawbacks. The first was this: the corps commanders, misunderstanding what was at stake, protested shrilly at being left in
the lurch, despite the fact that their corps machines, by flying in
formations of three, as ordered, managed to do their work, protect
themselves and suffer relatively few casualties in the process. The
second drawback has been the acute nervous strain imposed on our
combat pilots, who are carrying the fight non-stop to the enemy's
back areas, fighting and dropping their bombs far from their own
bases and within constant range of the German anti-aircraft defences.

" Our losses in the air may be heavy, but they are much less than
those we are inflicting on the enemy. And our air mastery is proving
of enormous advantage to the troops on the ground."

At the start Fokkers were attached like sheep dogs to German
reconnaissance flights. The skies above the German Fifth Army
were neatly divided into four sectors, each with its own dawn-to-
dusk patrols. These "barrage flights" were, as du Peuty and
Trenchard eventually realised, a gross misuse of air strength. For
the Germans never deviated from their fixed courses. The policy
was self-defeating, and its first effect, in the measured words of the
R.F.C. historian, "was to divert these aeroplanes from their proper
duties and to deny the attacking German infantry much of the air
support which they ought to have received. . . ."

What gradually tilted the balance against du Peuty was the
ignorance of his army superiors, who echoed the panic-stricken cry
of the beleaguered ground troops that the only aircraft they ever saw
were German. While the enemy, quick to learn from failure, regrouped their squadrons, the French were forbidden to continue
their successful air offensive against the German rear. Du Peuty
was ordered instead to protect his own infantry and artillery. Then
Fokkers began to arrive in growing numbers from other sectors.
They were reorganised into strike-units under the command of
a young veteran named Oswald Boelcke, who had served his
apprenticeship under Immelmann. The sequel was much as
Trenchard expected. During March the Germans set about
harassing the French ground defences, bombing rear supply lines,
shooting up installations, and repeatedly inflicting casualties, in
passing, on the army co-operation machines. In answer to further
calls from his superiors du Peuty reluctantly provided further cover,
until his own artillery and reconnaissance machines, pinned behind
the French lines, were unable to do their work; and his combat
aircraft, held back for tight escort duties, became easy targets for
Fokkers.

Realising the futility of argument, du Peuty, with a splendid disregard for the prejudices of the military mind, decided in desperation to reverse his tactics, and led several long-range intruder raids in person. Trenchard warmly approved.

He recalled how, at the height of the " Fokker scourge," lightly escorted R.F.C. bombing raids had banished the old illusion that raiders flying in close formation were more vulnerable than individual machines to anti-aircraft guns and fighters. With nicely judged daring, Trenchard had on more than one occasion concentrated what, for late 1915, was a large force of twenty aircraft and sent them with impunity to attack a single important target at a time. He was relieved that du Peuty had learnt to hit back with similar ruthlessness until, by the end of April, he regained the initiative, never to relinquish it. As the air historian noted:

" The experience of the French Air Service at Verdun confirmed the value of the strategic offensive."

The rigidity of French resistance on the ground resulted, by contrast, in appalling losses. A total of 442,000 men were killed, wounded or captured, against German losses of 278,000, before the Verdun battle ended. The premature death of Gallieni, the Minister for War, forestalled the possibility of an inquiry that might well have led to the arraignment of Joffre, who instead retained supreme command and shared the palm of a dubious victory with the gloomy Pétain; ironically, de Castelnau's contribution was overlooked.

How far du Peuty's success in the air assisted the French stand it is impossible to say: what must be said is that he attributed much of it to Trenchard. Routine exchanges of information between the two air services had become so well established that, in la Ferrière's phrase, " the word of Trenchard carried weight in time even at Chantilly." When du Peuty relinquished his command and was killed in action with his regiment the following year, cooperation was too firmly rooted to wither away. According to la Ferrière, who in 1918 served as a liaison officer between Foch, the Supreme Allied Commander, and Trenchard's bomber force in the Nancy region: " the question put to me by Weygand or Foch in all cases of doubt was usually this: ' What is General Trenchard's opinion? ' Even when they disagreed with it they knew his efficiency too well to ignore it. It has always seemed odd to me that this fact never seems to have been appreciated in Britain. Effective collaboration between the Allied air forces must be traced back to Verdun, and to the interplay of ideas between two leaders, who, thanks largely to Maurice Baring, implicitly trusted one another."

2

There were several reasons why Trenchard had meanwhile
become an object of contentious misunderstanding at home, reasons
which, as we shall see, he did not always sufficiently allow for in
exchanges with Henderson, his chief.

Trenchard's liberality in throwing open his stores to du Peuty's
pilots in their hour of need was repaid many times over by the
French later that spring by Colonel Regnier, the French air equipment controller in Paris. More powerful engines like the 110 h.p.
Le Rhone, and improved fighters like the Morane and Nieuport,
were turned over to the R.F.C.; but more than once Trenchard was
embarrassed by having no spare pilots to accept delivery.

On average, trained replacements were reaching St. Omer at the
rate of about ten a week, barely sufficient to cover casualties.
Volunteers for flying duties were all too numerous; good instructors
too few; while a prolonged spell of bad weather at home so hampered
training that new arrivals with the statutory fifteen hours of solo
flying to their credit were seldom fit for action. Trenchard repeatedly
complained to Henderson that "insufficiently trained" men were
more of a liability than an asset to their squadron commanders.
The worst he sent back for further tuition; the more adaptable were
initiated gradually to their lonely and dangerous calling through
improvised courses of day and night flying behind the lines.

" Would it be any use my writing officially to know whether you
can send four pilots to Paris to fly up Morane biplanes and then go
home again? " he wrote to Henderson in March. " I have thirteen
biplanes waiting but no pilots to go down and bring them up—and
I badly want them. I don't dare have them packed in cases as we
don't know enough about erecting them yet, though we are learning
how."

It frequently happened that new machines were wrecked before
ever crossing the line.

" A reserve pilot has just smashed his fourth machine, so I'm
sending him back for further training," he remarked in another
letter.

Yet storm, entreat or cajole as he did in correspondence with
Henderson, whose readiness to respond imperceptibly cooled with
time, Trenchard never lost heart or perspective. He wrote always
as his feelings dictated, simply, often constructively, and invariably
at the pitch of his voice. He knew no other method of communica-

tion. It was his suggestion that at least some pilots should be trained in Egypt, the South of France, or Canada in order to avoid the rigours and delays of the British winter. The idea was eventually adopted. Both Henderson and Brancker, who was recalled home early in March as acting director of " Air Organisation," were refreshed by Trenchard's cheerful vitality on his occasional visits. Politics he abhorred; but he could not pretend to be wholly uninterested, since the problems of meeting R.F.C. demands from home sources had been taken quietly out of Henderson's hands. The zeppelin raids of the winter forced Asquith, as was shown above, to appoint a special committee with the aim of ending the unedifying scramble for scarce components by the rival military and naval wings. Within six weeks of accepting the chairmanship, Lord Derby gave up in disgust.

" It appears to me quite impossible," Derby told the Prime Minister in his letter of resignation, " to bring the two wings closer together . . . unless and until the whole system of the Air Service is changed and they are amalgamated into one service, as personally I consider they must be. To make this great change would be a difficult and lengthy operation in peacetime. . . . I am inclined to think it would be practically impossible in wartime."

" So the Derby Committee has ceased to be," Trenchard commented to Henderson early in March, 1916. " I wonder what will be the next move."

It was not long delayed. Derby had lacked executive authority; his patience was worn down by the unavoidably obstructive attitude of the naval representative, Vaughan-Lee, who could commit the Admiralty to no changes, great or small. Asquith responded by inviting Lord Curzon to conduct an inquiry into the shortcomings of air administration as a whole; but before the Lord President of the Council could summon his first witness, a more sensational public tribunal was hurriedly convened, at the express request of Henderson, to examine grave allegations that R.F.C. pilots were being "murdered" daily through the blundering incompetence of their leaders in Britain and France.

Trenchard was mildly astonished that Henderson should stoop to defend himself against an irresponsible charge, or that Brancker should be just as keen on a futile investigation. Nobody, he believed, could prevent Members of Parliament with axes to grind from uttering privileged slanders against Flying Corps leaders if they felt so inclined; but nobody, least of all the slandered, should pay any attention to such utterances. Trenchard's perennial insensitivity to criticism allowed too little in this instance for political complications; not merely did he under-rate the disinterested shrewdness of Henderson, but he wholly discounted the public impact of assertions which struck him personally as more frivolous than damaging.

Mr. Pemberton-Billing, who first levelled them in the Commons early in March, was an independent backbencher well known for the flamboyant eccentricity of his opinions. On air questions, however, he posed as something of an authority. Early in the war Pemberton-Billing had indeed distinguished himself as a brilliant pilot and planner of the Naval wing; and so pronounced was the current ignorance of air matters at Westminster that when this self-styled " First Air Member " condemned R.F.C. commanders for inexperience amounting to criminal negligence in fattening young pilots as " Fokker fodder," his words produced a considerable stir.

" Billing's last speech brought things to a head," Henderson informed Trenchard on 1st April, 1916, exactly two years before the birth of the Royal Air Force. " I was fortunately in the House and urged Tennant (the Under-Secretary for War) to promise a judicial inquiry, which he did. If the Government grant one, I shall ask to be relieved. I don't think the sailors want (it) at all; but even if they stand out I must insist on one for our side. . . . I am thankful to get a chance of clearing things up."

The Government agreed to hold the inquiry, but would not consider "relieving" Henderson. Dubious as he was about the propaganda value of the affair, Trenchard understood why the Admiralty disapproved. The status quo suited the Sea Lords. For it ensured them the lion's share of available aero engines, components, machines and equipment to which their liberal funds and steady patronage of private manufacturers gave them readier access than the War Office. This, rather than Pemberton-Billing's malicious charges, struck him as the most crucial aspect of the affair since the Admiralty's plenty conditioned his own difficulties on the Western Front.

Around Arras, where du Peuty's machines had once supported the French Tenth Army, Trenchard's depleted squadrons filled the gap as best they could. Not all the Fokkers had gone to Boelcke's assistance at Verdun; and though R.F.C. losses stayed below the peak they had reached in December, Trenchard was less able to afford any while regular replacements were denied him.

Trenchard's correspondence with Henderson in March and April emphasised the acuteness of the dilemma.

" We cannot send out the squadrons promised this month and

at the same time keep you up to strength in pilots," Henderson wrote early in March. " I am sorry for this but the combination of bad weather and casualties has brought us down for the moment to bed-rock in pilots.

" The casualties must give you a lot of worry. I am trying to ginger up the political crowd here to see that casualties are inevitable and that the only surprising thing is that we escaped them for so long."

Trenchard replied by return:

" I am, as you say, frightfully worried over the loss of pilots out here. You can imagine it is not quite an easy game at present. . . ."

Towards the end of the month Henderson wrote again:

" At your suggestion I asked the Director of Air Services at the Admiralty whether any pilots of the Naval Air Service could be spared to assist you at the front. I was first informed that some fifteen pilots could be made available, but this morning Admiral Vaughan-Lee told me that the pilots who had been warned for this duty were unwilling to fly our aeroplanes, as they considered them unsuitable for flying in the presence of the enemy."

One of Lord Derby's few successful deeds as chairman of the now defunct Air Commitee had been to persuade the Admiralty to lend four volunteer naval pilots, complete with their own Nieuport machines, to the Flying Corps. Recalling an agreement which had never been acted upon, Henderson now said:

" I demurred to this, knowing that you wanted pilots, not aeroplanes . . . but the attachment was still considered desirable. . . . Three beastly Nieuports with their attendants are going to you at once. Gawd help you."

" It will be a great nuisance," replied Trenchard, " but as you ask it I will do it. Please send out at once the four de Havilland scouts of 29 Squadron I asked for and I will put the four Nieuports with them in Second Army, where they will get a lot of fighting. . . . I sometimes think it would be better if Pemberton-Billing was put in command out here and C. G. Grey (the pugnacious editor of *The Aeroplane*) at home. What are your views on this? "

He was more troubled than he cared to admit about the harmful effects that the public inquiry might have on the morale of his men, fearing that insinuations of bad leadership would be magnified out of all proportion. If mud was thrown openly and indiscriminately, some would be sure to stick. Sometimes he wondered whether Henderson's self-righteousness was not running away with his sense of perspective.

" Regarding your second paragraph about (sending) two or three people from here to answer specific charges," he replied to a casual request from Henderson for witnesses. " I hope this will not come about at a time when the question of beating the Hun is in progress. I will send you the actual facts regarding the amount of work done and state the number of German aeroplanes reported by the anti-aircraft guns and the number of hours flown, but I am not going to give information for political agitators to pull to pieces unless I am ordered to do so. I hope to goodness the two services will be put on a better footing and work more together. I suppose that mountain of conceit G. N. C. (Lord Curzon) will be put in as head of it. He is an able man, but he does not like me and I do not like him."

Trenchard, however, was not foolish enough to underestimate Curzon. During May, with Verdun still invested, Haig recasting his plans for an earlier summer offensive to assist Joffre, and the overpublicised Air Tribunal under Mr. Justice Bailhache raising the roof of Westminster Hall, the Lord President of the Council was busily completing his own fact-finding inquiry into the adminstrative shortcomings of the two air arms. The Cabinet, well pleased with his report, acted on its recommendations with commendable speed. A new body called the Air Board was appointed and Curzon chosen as its first head. Its brief seemed to Trenchard as absurdly ambitious as its powers were studiously vague. It was intended to carry on the unfinished labours of Derby and prevent "overlapping between two great Departments of State," as Curzon told the House of Lords on 19th May. Man-power, long-range offensive operations, Home Defence, air training, inventions, and the future of the Royal Aircraft Factory were among the numerous questions within its scope. The Board would examine them one by one.

" In the further distance," said Curzon, " there will always loom the possibility and desirability of creating a single department under a single Minister."

This, as Trenchard knew, was a favourite dream of the Lord President. One snowy morning in February, on the crossing from France to Folkestone, he had listened to an interminable monologue from Curzon on the need for an Air Minister—"a man on whose broad back the slings and arrows of outrageous criticism would fall harmlessly." The person he had in mind for the job was so obviously himself that Baring could not resist remarking later on Trenchard's self-restraint, having seen the wire thrust into his chief's hands at Boulogne before they embarked, stating laconically that the latest in a long line of French Air Ministers had resigned that very

morning. The Air Board seemed to Trenchard a typical product
of Curzon's pedantically tidy mind: it was "all gloss and no go";
and he was prepared to wager that its creator would become the
first victim of his own cleverness. For though the Board had the
theoretical right to formulate policy, as well as reorganise supplies,
it could only advise, not command. Its sole course in the event of
disagreement with the War Office or the Admiralty would be an
appeal to the War Committee, so squaring the former vicious circle
of indecision and compromise.

It was, of course, quite characteristic of Trenchard to prejudge
the Air Board's prospects by the shortcomings of its director; it must
be added in fairness to Curzon that Asquith was unwilling to move
faster than public opinion forced him. Bonar Law perhaps expressed
the Government's attitude most clearly when he informed the
Commons shortly before the Board's opening meeting on 22nd May:
" The right way to get an Air Ministry—and I think an Air
Ministry may come out of it—is to make some arrangement of this
kind, to let it grow, and gradually absorb more and more the work
of the air services."

Neither the War Office nor the Admiralty paid much attention
to the Air Board. Kitchener contented himself with observing that
it would commit him to nothing he disapproved; Balfour, with a
keener appreciation of the risks of inertia, remarked that "if the
Government refuse to do anything of their own free will, some
dramatic change may be forced on them by the House of Commons."
But the Western Front was a hundred miles away; and distance lent
detachment to Trenchard, whose letters increasingly reflected his
disenchantment. If Henderson simultaneously frittered too much
energy on inquiry hearings, only the Germans would benefit. As for
testifying himself to clear the R.F.C.'s good name, Trenchard shied
away from the suggestion.

" It will not be easy for me to give any evidence or statements
with regard to present inquiries about the Flying Corps out here
without the sanction of the Commander-in-Chief," he told Henderson
flatly before visiting London in early May. " I very much want to
go to Farnborough and other places in the flying world. I don't
want to see any politicians, judges, or lawyers. . . . I don't know who
makes the silliest remarks in the papers. Pemberton-Billing thinks
everyone is sent up to be killed, and the members of the Air Enquiry
think the war can be conducted without casualties."

For the life of him Trenchard could not yet grasp the sense of
it all.

3

He was invariably happy to leave Whitehall and its pettifogging
side issues behind him. The biting cynicism of Flying Corps crews,
being mainly on the surface, never failed to refresh him, especially
after interviews with politicians. In France, at any rate, he felt truly
at home among his own. Issues of life and death were relatively
simple and undisputed so that issues of strategy could be squarely
faced. Trenchard believed that victory on land might still be
attained in 1916, despite Verdun, if the Flying Corps gained the
upper hand while Haig's armies were preparing for their biggest
push since the outbreak of war. From April onwards Trenchard
called on the Commander-in-Chief at least once a week to discuss
his problems and plans. When the British lengthened their line in
March, R.F.C. Headquarters were transferred to St. André, a
château of pink brick, high narrow rooms, and immensely thick walls,
standing in its own wooded grounds near the village of Hesdin. Haig
lived and worked in a beautifully appointed, much larger establishment outside Montreuil; and Baring during the twelve-mile drive
often noticed Trenchard's sombre nervousness beforehand and
his cheerful effusiveness afterwards. Having once recognised the
symptoms, Baring would put off untimely visitors with the advice:
" I'd wait a day or two, if I were you. Your problem isn't urgent,
and the general's rehearsing his lines for the Chief."
    Haig was invariably " the Chief " to Trenchard who tended to
idolise him for his personal qualities: such detachment, rock-like
steadiness, agility of mind and devotion to duty were qualities
seldom found together in soldiers of the highest rank. Trenchard's
admiration bordered on hero-worship: week after week he would
deferentially submit his plans to Haig, knowing them to be sound
in his bones but lacking the fluency of expression to elaborate them
fully.
    Haig never rushed him, never interrupted. He was a patient
listener. According to members of the staff at G.H.Q. the Commander-in-Chief liked the plans for their simplicity and respected
their author for his integrity. From occasional remarks Haig
dropped, Trenchard gathered that his relations with Joffre were
somewhat frayed; more than once he expressed open contempt for
soldiers who let political calculations influence their strategic
thinking. His diaries bear witness to a remarkable fixation on this
point; and his critics could well say that in dealings with his own

Government he was anything but a model of consistency. Perhaps to atone for this deficiency, the field-marshal favoured the dissipation of misunderstandings at lower levels, and was genuinely pleased with the valuable tactical lessons which emerged from the air fighting above Verdun. Trenchard's assurance that far more decisive results could be obtained, provided the R.F.C. were sufficiently reinforced in time for the summer offensive, Haig accepted without reservations.

The field-marshal's only criticism of the Flying Corps concerned the uneven distribution of duties at headquarters. On several occasions he cautioned Trenchard against overtaxing himself, offering a choice of excellent staff officers to take routine burdens off his shoulders. Then, one April morning, a young man whom Trenchard's long memory immediately identified as an acquaintance of his polo-playing days at the end of the Boer War arrived unannounced at St. André. It was Lieutenant-Colonel Philip Game, whose repressed fury at being "removed from the army" to an organisation in which he had little faith did not prevent him settling down to win Trenchard's confidence as "my shrewdest and most competent administrator."

Within five minutes of his arrival, Trenchard had his new staff co-ordinator on the airfield. "I was not in a very receptive frame of mind," Game recorded. "After letting me inspect half a dozen different stationary machines on the ground, he suddenly pointed to one several thousand feet up in the air on the horizon.

" 'What's that?' he asked.

" Completely at a loss, I replied a trifle testily, 'I think it must be liver.'

" He snorted and looked hard at me, then his face creased into a smile. 'You'll learn, Game,' he said, and left it at that."[2]

Game had to learn quickly. He fitted in well as G.S.O. 1, relieving Trenchard of the incessant paper work and drafting clear, neat statements of R.F.C. requirements which were incorporated in the daily letters to Henderson and Brancker. Trenchard, determined to keep abreast of the latest technical improvements, but refusing to be blinded by science or to mistake "the latest" for "the best," tried to strike a reasonable balance between the claims of the experts and the sometimes fickle enthusiasms of his pilots. There were occasions when he erred in conceding too much to the collective judgment of aircrews and had bitter cause to reproach himself for going against his own.

In April, for instance, the French offered him sufficient Morane

" Bullets " to form an entire squadron. Trenchard compromised at first by taking only six on approval, though shortages had recently obliged him to curtail operational activity and the scale of Haig's preparations for the forthcoming Somme offensive meant that the Flying Corps would need every machine it could get, from whatever source, to perform its proper function. Nevertheless, his gratitude to the French was tempered by doubt, which the ecstatic reports of pilots who tested the Morane " Bullet " did little to allay.

Well aware that the " Bullet " handled easily, that the Fokker was almost an exact copy of it, and that its new synchronising gear was probably as good as the German, Trenchard instinctively disliked the machine because, in his own words, "it suffered from the defect of all monoplanes built at that time—namely, the very real difficulty of seeing out of it except by banking."

In yielding to the unanimous pleas of the pilots, Trenchard openly voiced his misgivings.

" He proved right and they proved wrong," was Baring's verdict. " The Morane proved to be the most expensive in pilots and cost us more in casualties than any other during the whole war. The squadron which had these machines was the only squadron which had to be taken out of the line for a prolonged period."

This squadron, No. 60, was one of the four led by Dowding, who returned from England before the Somme battle to command the Headquarters Wing at Fienvillers, Trenchard's advance headquarters. Since Loos, new squadrons from home had been reaching France at the rate of about one every three weeks; and by June, 1916, the R.F.C. had nominally doubled its size inside nine months to twenty-six and a half front-line squadrons. On paper, such expansion looked impressive. In fact the force was a shadow of its token self. Most of the squadrons consisted of reconnaissance machines, few were at full strength. For the drain on men and equipment had gone on through the winter, easing only slightly in the spring; and the Flying Corps's area of responsibility above the extended British lines had increased.

It was Trenchard's boast that no call ever found the squadrons wanting; but efforts to support ground forces in local actions, on top of duties carried out daily as a matter of course in all but the worst weather, ate into reserves. The official records compiled at R.F.C. headquarters show that, on average, one pilot or observer and one aircraft were lost every day during the first six months of 1916, the costliest periods being March and June when casualties rose to forty per month. A less confident leader might have hesitated about committing his straitened squadrons to full-scale battle without further respite or delay; but Trenchard believed that a force as deeply imbued as his with the offensive spirit would let neither him nor Haig down.

Besides, he knew that the Commander-in-Chief had no intention of going over to the offensive unless French resistance suddenly crumbled at Verdun. " I have not got an army in France really," Haig wrote in his diary on 29th March, " but a collection of divisions untrained for the field."

Two months later, still far from satisfied about the battle-worthiness of his men, the Commander-in-Chief yielded to Joffre's urgent request that the British should bring forward the day of attack. French casualties at Verdun were then approaching 200,000; and the French generalissimo insisted that at that rate his army would soon be "ruined." 1st July was therefore fixed as the latest date for the main British assault in conjunction with a minor French thrust, under Foch, on the right, against the heavily fortified enemy positions between the Somme and Ancre rivers.

The Fourth British Army, commanded by Sir Henry Rawlinson, was to deliver the main blow; and during May Trenchard reorganised his squadrons to provide the maximum support. Each of the four British armies under Haig was now supported by a Flying Corps Brigade; each Brigade comprised two wings, one of fighters, the other of army co-operation squadrons, but varied in size. The best-equipped squadrons and most experienced squadrons were naturally grouped in the two wings attached to Fourth Army.

Lieutenant-Colonel Edgar Ludlow-Hewitt, the wing commander responsible for guiding Rawlinson's gunners and troops, began work at the end of May with four undersized squadrons. One of the most practised " gun-spotters" among the R.F.C.'s pioneers, he was also one of the few men of his rank who flew over the line daily to encourage his overworked pilots and to short-circuit their practical difficulties. Within a month Ludlow-Hewitt's squadrons were at full strength on the new eighteen-machine basis which Trenchard had advocated for months past; but with reinforcements from home still lagging behind requirements, this was achieved only by "borrowing" from reconnaissance wings in quieter sectors. Counting two fighter squadrons held in reserve for special tasks, the R.F.C. on the eve of battle mustered a first-line force of 105 assorted aircraft in the rear of Rawlinson's army.

Trenchard's operational plan was devised to bring every squadron systematically into play. Because bombing bulked large in his list of preliminary targets, he could, without fear of protest, allocate objectives to other wings. Unfortunately, the only machines at his disposal were unsuited to his purpose. The "utility" B.E.2c, even when driven by the most powerful engine available, could carry no more than four hours' petrol and a maximum bomb load of under 500 pounds; and this entailed sending the pilot off alone and virtually defenceless. The task of escorting these makeshift bombers was allotted to Dowding's fighter squadrons of headquarters wing; it was an invidious task, but Trenchard judged the opportunities to warrant the risks. His doubts about the Moranes with which they were equipped had not abated, though the pilots of No. 60 Squadron, on whom most of the escort duties would fall, did not share them.

Beneath their wings Ludlow-Hewitt's reconnaissance pilots could see, during the last sunlit days of June, the green and brown patchwork of landscape that lay, lozenge-shaped, between the winding ribbons of the Somme and Ancre rivers. Behind the Allied trenches all was bustle and movement; the comparative stillness on the German-held ridges opposite seemed oddly unreal. Only the flash of an occasional gun spoke of enemy watchfulness, but the emplacements were not easy to locate in the vivid white chalk of slopes into which the Germans had tunnelled deep to fortify their positions. When the savage, preliminary shelling began, and enemy batteries intermittently replied, there was still no interference from enemy fighters. Observation was left to men in kite balloons which Trenchard set down as targets for immediate destruction in rivalry with the French squadrons on his right.

" We had our great strafe to-day," he wrote to Brancker on 25th June. " Three Nieuports met their balloons with rockets and brought them down, a fourth missed. . . . One phosphorous bomb hit a balloon as it was being hauled down very quickly. . . . There was one hell of an explosion which blew everything into the air. . . . Just heard that another has been seen burning."

The poised and waiting armies had a grandstand view of the fireworks that day and the next. It was a spectacular overture, no more; but Trenchard had a double reason for jubilation, having laid a bet with Pugo, the staff officer to General Barès, now the administrative chief of the French Air Service, that his pilots would score more " kills " than theirs. When he collected his one-franc wager, the air was temporarily empty of enemy kite balloons; the singling out of German batteries and the photographing of wired aprons about visible enemy strong points had begun. It seemed at times that nothing could survive the deluge of British shells, yet the reconnaissance pilots did, and still the Fokkers held off.

" The weather report is favourable for to-morrow," Haig recorded in his diary on the last night of June. " With God's help, I feel hopeful."

The British Fourth Army went over the top at dawn on 1st July. R.F.C. machines swooped low over the slowly advancing troops, signalling progress to corps and army headquarters at regular intervals and braving the shellfire and bullets of both sides. Surprisingly few aircraft were lost on these "contact patrols." But among the bombers and fighters operating far behind enemy lines casualties were heavy. The reserve squadrons of Trenchard's headquarters wing suffered most.

" I spent all that first afternoon at Vert Galant," noted Maurice Baring. " I saw the pilots of No. 60 Squadron start, and then one waited and waited . . . Who would come back? Who would not come back? At four-thirty Ferdy Waldron came back with his machine riddled with bullets. I went home at four-thirty and reported to the general, and then went back again at six and stayed till six-thirty. This time I saw a lot of pilots hot from the fighting and in a high state of exhilaration, as they had had a grand day."

Many Moranes came back holed. Then the squadron was sent to act as an offensive decoy for several pairs of heavily-laden, low-flying B.E.2cs bound for St. Quentin. This time the Fokkers rose to accept the challenge: over Cambrai, Waldron was sent crashing to his death in flames, his companions returning to base badly shot up; the bombers, separated from their escorts, were pounced upon at leisure and shot down by the enemy almost at will.

A less resolute commander might have cancelled his bombing programme. Trenchard decided instead to revert immediately to escorted attacks in big formations, realising as he did that there would be fewer machines for reconnaissance and that more fighters would be needed.

" I have lost, as you know, eight machines at low bombing," he wrote to Brancker at the end of the first week of July. " I am afraid some of the pilots are getting a bit rattled, and it's not popular. I have put in for two V.C.s. The fighting is going on well, and the pilots are doing splendidly. We have crashed a good number of Fokkers and brought down a good many more than they admit. We have done 1200 hours' flying a day which makes you think a bit, as a lot of the pilots have to do five or six hours day after day. . . . It's a bit of a strain with so many hostile machines and anti-aircraft guns about. . . . The depots are getting overworked mending machines that are shot to pieces and crash, issuing stores and repairing transport."

Criticised even then, Trenchard has been condemned since for refusing to relax the pressure on his pilots, especially those engaged, day in day out, irrespective of weather or alternative tactical needs, in offensive sweeps so meticulously timed that Fokker intruders were said to "set their watches by them." Like " Bomber " Harris at the height of the Second World War, he has been pilloried as an unfeeling apostle of the bludgeon, splendidly unswerving in aim but devoid of humanity and tactical flexibility. Few of his subordinates were more upset by the early losses on the Somme than Dowding. By early August half of No. 60 Squadron's original rota of pilots had been killed or wounded, and Dowding requested that the unit should be temporarily withdrawn from the line and rested.

Trenchard agreed, but the interview left him uneasy—not so much about the squadron's morale as about Dowding's own. If the self-confidence of the pilots had been shaken, it was unlikely to be restored by a wing-commander who gave him the impression of being obsessed by the fear of further casualties. Dowding he informed Brancker in his next letter home, was a "dismal Jimmy" whom he proposed to replace as soon as that could be conveniently arranged.

The following comment by Ludlow-Hewitt made at the time of the publication of Dowding's biography goes to the root of a misunderstanding that was to come between Trenchard and Dowding for many years:

" Trenchard at this time was bearing a stupendous burden, persevering in his offensive policy despite terrible losses. In this he proved the greatness of his faith in his men and his own strategical vision. By this he created an 'offensive' tradition which the R.F.C. and the R.A.F. would never lose. That tradition stood all the air commanders in good stead during the Second World War. Trenchard later recognised that he had quite misjudged Dowding. Though normally a good judge of men, Trenchard was liable at times to be misled by his own prejudices: and then, as in this case, he could be unjust. He hated complaints which he thought could be bad for morale and even when they were fully justified he was inclined to react against the complainant. Trenchard seldom admitted a mistake but when he recognised it would quietly do his best to make amends. He was a most consistent and reliable friend."

Trenchard's offensive policy was openly questioned in certain circles at home, as Haig's drive lost its initial momentum. Henderson and Brancker discovered, without surprise, that Sykes was damning it in private at a time when the unfinished Air Enquiry provided an easy platform for the disgruntled and misinformed. Trenchard was more incensed, however, by the increasing obstructiveness of the War Office to any further expansion of the Flying Corps.

With the Somme battle consuming his slender reserves at an alarming rate, Trenchard forwarded through Haig an estimate of his front-line requirements for 1917. These included, significantly enough, ten squadrons specially equipped for long-range bombing in addition to fifty-six fighters and army co-operation squadrons as well as sixty observation balloon units. By mid-August, when his pilots had vindicated his judgment by sweeping the Somme skies clear of Fokker intruders and enemy camera and artillery machines, for the loss of fewer R.F.C. bombers and fighters, Trenchard's estimate of future needs gathered thumb-marks and unsympathetic comments in a succession of War Office pending trays.

The Adjutant-General is at his wits' end to find *men*, let alone skilled mechanics," Brancker warned him. " The Expeditionary Force have put in further enormous demands for heavy artillery, and neither the Master-General of Ordnance nor the Quartermaster-General know where to look for the necessary skilled artificers. . . . Heavy guns and aeroplanes need the same class of men to maintain them in the field and to manufacture them.

" The R.F.C. at home is a tiresome institution which, by means of a good deal of push at the beginning of the war, has encroached on everyone else's vested interests. Its value is not realised on the Army Council, nor can it be realised by anyone who is not getting direct assistance from it. We assist no one at home; we compete with everyone. At present you have a weak D.G.M.A. (Henderson) and a bored D.A.O. (Brancker himself)."

Trenchard's pride in attaining undisputed air mastery over the Somme hardened him in his resolve to move heaven and earth on behalf of his pilots. They had not striven and conquered, sacrificing life and limb at his behest, only to be pushed aside unceremoniously by a "pack of military bureaucrats." The Flying Corps had already earned more than could ever be repaid in terms of better machines and weapons. It was fortunate indeed that the Commander-in-Chief, disappointed as he was at the slowing down of his own attack on land, endorsed Trenchard's valuation of the R.F.C.'s triumph.

Haig had achieved only part of his objective on the Somme, that of lifting the seige of Verdun. Owing to the natural strength of the defences and the stubbornness of German resistance, he was slowly robbed during August of that greater tactical prize, catching the enemy off balance before reinforcements could be rushed up from Eastern France.

"I knew by early September that the Germans would not collapse because our army was unable to take advantage of the situation," Trenchard stated. "I also foresaw that the Germans would recover in the air . . . and might even wrest supremacy from us unless our reserves increased and our weapons improved. Generals like Rawlinson thought I must have got jumpy, worrying in case the enemy would do to us what we had just done to them, but how true my forebodings turned out to be."

So strong were his forebodings that Trenchard, with Haig's consent, committed them to paper. The result so impressed the field-marshal that his commanders were urged to study the sombre but unshakable conclusions derived from Allied experience of air fighting since the heyday of the Fokker. In due course the War Office received copies; and senior staff officers there might have been pardoned for thinking it Haig's own copyright, so earnestly did he commend it to their attention. The memorandum in fact owed nothing to the Commander-in-Chief. It was rendered into lucid English by Baring, who here surpassed himself in reproducing the thoughts of Trenchard without sacrificing a jot of their prophetic content. Because this first summary of the basic principles of air strategy has remained valid for nearly half a century, and is unlikely to be superseded until manned aircraft are finally discarded in favour of guided missiles, it must be quoted at length:

"Owing to the unlimited space in the air, the difficulty one machine has in seeing another, the accidents of wind and cloud, it is impossible for aeroplanes, however skilful and vigilant their pilots, however powerful their engines, however mobile their machines and however numerous their formations, to prevent hostile aircraft from crossing the line if they have the initiative and determination to do so.

"The aeroplane is not a defence against the aeroplane. But the opinion of those most competent to judge is that the aeroplane, as a weapon of attack, cannot be too highly estimated. A signal instance of this fact is offered to us by the operations which took place in the air at Verdun. . . .

"On the British front, during the operations which began with the battle of the Somme, we know that although the enemy has concentrated the greater part of his available forces in the air on this front, the work actually accomplished by their aeroplanes stands, compared with the work done by us, in the proportion of about four to one hundred. From the accounts of prisoners, we gather that the enemy's aeroplanes have received orders not to cross the lines over the French or British front unless the day is cloudy and a surprise attack can be made, presumably in order to avoid unnecessary casualties.

" On the other hand, British aviation has been guided by a policy of relentless and incessant offensive. Our machines have continually attacked the enemy on his side of the line, bombed his aerodromes, besides carrying out attacks on places of importance far behind the lines. It would seem probable that this has had the effect of compelling him to keep back or to detail portions of his forces in the air for defensive purposes. . . .

" The question which arises is this: Supposing the enemy, under the influence of some drastic reformer or some energetic leader, were now to change his policy and follow the example of the English and French. . . . Should we abandon our offensive, bring back our squadrons behind the lines to defend places like Boulogne, St. Omer, Amiens and Abbeville, and protect our artillery and photographic machines with defensive escorts, or should we continue our offensive more vigorously than before? . . .

" It has been our experience in the past that at a time when the Germans were doing only half the work done by our machines their mere presence over our lines produced an insistent and continuous demand for protective and defensive measures. If the Germans were once more to increase the degree of their activity even up to what constitutes half the degree of our activity, it is certain that such demands would be made again. On the other hand, it is equally certain that were such measures adopted they would prove ineffectual. . . . If the enemy were aware of the presence of a defensive force in one particular spot, he would leave that spot alone and attack another, and we should not have enough machines to protect all the places which could possibly be attacked behind our lines, and at the same time continue the indispensable work on the front. . . .

" But supposing we had enough machines both for offensive and defensive purposes. Supposing we had an unlimited number of machines for defensive purposes, it would still be impossible to prevent hostile machines from crossing the line if they were determined to do so, simply because the sky is too large to defend. We know from experience how difficult it is to prevent a hostile vessel, and still more a hostile submarine, from breaking a blockade when the blockade extends over a large area. But in the air the difficulty of defence is still greater, because the area of possible escape is practically unlimited and because the aeroplane is fighting in three dimensions.

" The sound policy would seem to be, if the enemy changes his tactics and pursues a more vigorous offensive, to increase our offensive, to go farther afield, and to force the enemy to do what he would gladly have us do now."

The date of this paper, which Baring began drafting during August and finished in early September, is of some interest. For on 29th July, Haig reacted forcefully to a letter from Robertson alluding to the increasing restiveness of "the powers that be" who were questioning "whether a loss of say 300,000 men (on the Somme) will lead to really great results," now that the primary object of relieving enemy pressure on Verdun had been attained. The Commander-in-Chief, in admitting that British casualties for July alone amounted to 120,000 men, contended that these could not be counted "sufficient to justify any anxiety as to our ability to continue the offensive" which he intended to maintain "well into the autumn." On 9th August, Haig learnt that he could expect "full support" from the Cabinet War Committee in carrying out this intention. It seems more than probable that Trenchard, with Haig's blessing, seized the opportunity to justify his own offensive policy for the benefit of sceptics and scoffers at home. In doing so, he incidentally produced a historic document.

No clearer or sounder exposition of air policy could have been formulated. That its conclusions were founded on hard facts, Haig, Rawlinson and other responsible leaders knew beyond doubt: for the most convincing tributes to its effectiveness came unsolicited from the Germans themselves. Enemy papers recently captured on the Somme confirmed the unanimous testimony of enemy prisoners that the impact on morale of low-flying Flying Corps machines was out of all proportion to their numbers, engendering a sense of defencelessness which defied official attempts to check or suppress it.

Du Peuty, who had meanwhile resumed command of the French squadrons operating to the right of the British, shared Trenchard's fear that Allied air ascendancy was almost too complete to last, and that the Germans would learn from their own mistakes.[3] So it proved, and quickly.

On 29th August, Hindenburg was appointed Chief of the German General Staff. One of Hindenburg's first acts was to suspend offensive operations at Verdun and switch his ground and air reserves to the Somme, while Haig pressed on with his marathon assault. It was in mid-September that the R.F.C. pilots identified several pursuit squadrons of new Halberstadt and Albatross machines, the pilots of which had evidently been ordered to attack at sight.

" German machines are multiplying in these parts," Trenchard wrote to Brancker, adding darkly that he wanted to "beat the Boche in this war, not the next." Anticipating as much opposition from Curzon and the Air Board as from the enemy, he next put in an official request (through Haig) for the loan of a full squadron of naval Sopwith fighters idling upcountry at Dunkirk. This provoked mild consternation among the Sea Lords, who deprecated so presumptuous a demand for help. Unable to await their pleasure, he appealed in writing to Balfour himself, explaining his predicament to the First Lord without troubling to notify Henderson. The latter rebuked him sharply for an unconstitutional act.

" I cannot understand why the demand (for more pilots) calls forth letters of protest," Trenchard commented impenitently to Brancker. " We are fighting a very big battle and the struggle in the air is becoming intense. The fighting will increase, I regret to say, not decrease, and it is only a question of our keeping it going longer than the Huns.

" If we cannot do that, we are beaten; if we do it, we win. . . . It is only by keeping up the pressure that we can hope to keep the Huns under to the extent we have him under now."

To Trenchard's mind, the stiff prerogatives claimed by Air Board members were, like the rules which bound them, as meaningless as the arithmetic of those other critics who measured success in air warfare by the smallness of the casualty lists. Every man's death hurt and saddened him, but it was a point of honour with him never to betray what he felt: there were better ways of helping, and few pilots who lived through the violence of the next few months could think of him entirely as a butcher without a heart. Yet, according to Viscount (then Mr. J. C. C.) Davidson and the late Viscount Weir, this was the bleak image which the very name of Trenchard conjured up in political minds between September and mid-November, 1916.

It must be confessed that most of Trenchard's men knew him better. He was too human to deceive them with soft words or buoy them up with false promises. " I want you to be real heroes, not *Daily Mail* heroes," he would tell them bluntly. They trusted him because he understood and could read their doubts in advance; they respected and listened to him because he had been so often right before. The sudden sight of him standing, legs thrust apart and hands in pockets, as a flight was taking off or returning, never lost its oddly heartening effect; and when he praised or commiserated with the pilots, the words he used seldom failed to carry a ring of assurance that heightened their pride in themselves and their regard for him. Even when he looked into a casualty clearing centre and would say, as he often did, to lightly wounded men: " Now get well soon. I hate sick people," the harsh ring of a quaint remark that gradually assumed the familiarity of another catch phrase mattered less than a certain tone of solicitude which he could not so easily hide under mere gruffness.

At St. Omer Trenchard kept a large pool of pilots. It was his unbreakable rule that casualties should be replaced on the very day machines limped back with a dead or injured pilot or observer on board, or failed to return at all. His commanders interpreted it rigidly, aware from past experience why his insistence on "a full breakfast table, with no empty chairs" was utterly sound. In Trenchard's own words:

" I always looked on the R.F.C. as a family. I tried to put myself in the others' places and to consider the feelings of those who flew as if they had been my own. If as an ordinary pilot you see no vacant places around you, the tendency is to brood less on the fate of friends who have gone for ever. Instead your mind is taken up with buying drinks for the newcomers and making them feel at home. It was a matter of pride and human understanding."

Nor were pilots allowed to overlook the less spectacular but vital work of the mechanics and technicians on the airfields, in the depots, and at repair centres behind the fighting line. These men, he repeatedly reminded the squadrons, "are the backbone of all our efforts." Without their ingenuity and toil at all hours and in all weathers, he would have been shorter still of weapons and of men to use them. To their craftsmanship, the pilots owed at least half their victories. And as "father of the family," Trenchard respected the obligation of recalling to its members how much they depended on one another.

At the same time, and on a higher level, he fought hard to protect his family from the wrong-headed interference of officialdom. The impotence of the Air Board, the jealousy of the War Office, and the war-weary complacency of a Government which seemed increasingly loth to take unpleasant decisions, had to be taken into account as never before during October and November, 1916.

9. The Rock

All through the autumn the battle raged on, swaying this way and that over the same sixteen miles of front between the Somme and Ancre rivers. Whole divisions were decimated in repeated assaults on fortified villages and redoubts. Ground changed hands continuously; losses soared on both sides; twice, in mid-September and again in mid-November, before the war's third winter clamped down on the prodigious blood-letting, Haig threw in powerful reserves and temporarily recovered the initiative by switching the course of his advance, but hopes of a break-through soon wilted. The German defences were as impregnable as the British Commander-in-Chief's faith in the ultimate triumph of such methods of attrition.

Wellington's saying that it is easier to describe a ball than a battle applied with terrible truth to this costly collision of closely matched forces, in which, for five months, some two million men were engaged. As far as the Flying Corps was concerned, enemy aggressiveness increased as the autumn days shortened. The air battle developed into a losing race for supplies, with the R.F.C. once more at the mercy of an Air Board apparently too engrossed in its own struggles and intrigues to heed Trenchard's demands.

Being simultaneously engrossed in his own problems, he tended as usual to think the worst of the politicians when he thought of them at all. He had never liked Curzon, for instance, "that mountain of conceit," as he called him; and their characters were so dissimilar that Trenchard was probably quite incapable of understanding him at all. Yet he admitted to astonishment at the transformation in Curzon's attitude to the R.F.C. before the end of 1916. This man whom he discounted as a power-seeking pedant seemed willing to befriend the Flying Corps in its need to the point of bringing down the Government itself.

" I believe the Air Board are going to get all their demands," Brancker informed Trenchard on 2nd December. " There has been much effort to compromise and dodge, but George Nathaniel has his back to the wall prepared to die fighting—and the Government are afraid to let him die."

Within a week of Brancker's note, to the intense consternation of contemporaries and the bafflement of political students since, Curzon deserted Asquith and joined Lloyd George. The extent to which his sufferings at the Air Board moved him to change sides lies outside the scope of this book. Yet the Trenchard-Brancker correspondence and the relevant Air Board documents suggest that his mounting frustrations as arbiter between two rival air services were a contributory cause. It was doubly unfortunate for Curzon that he had to work in accordance with a set of unworkable rules devised by himself. His more than ordinary vanity and a sublime sense of his own dignity could not endure such restrictions indefinitely. Curzon put Trenchard in mind of a pedigree dog chasing the tin can tied to its tail like any back-street cur; but he scarcely expected the animal to turn on its master in a fit of savage oversensitivity. It seemed that Curzon was avenging himself on a Prime Minister who would neither release him from the Air Board nor heed his repeated threats of resignation. Once drawn into the fine web of cross-purposes and mixed motives spun by those who were already plotting Asquith's downfall, the Air Board President displayed a final consistency of temperament for which historians give him too little credit.

There is no ambiguity whatever in the record of his deepening dissatisfaction during the last quarter of 1916 with Asquith's lack of drive. This disposed him to act with premeditated disloyalty. Alone among the analysts, Robert Blake has portrayed Curzon in this light, quoting, in his biography of Bonar Law, part of the telling letter which the President of the Air Board wrote to Lord Lansdowne: " We know that with him (Asquith) as chairman either of the Cabinet or War Committee it is absolutely impossible to win the war."

The name of Curzon is often linked with those of Austen Chamberlain and Robert Cecil as one of the " Three Cs," immovable pillars of Conservatism whose allegiance to Asquith was an insubstantial thing born of mistrust for Lloyd George. This convention should not obscure the fact that Curzon's humiliations at the Air Board prepared him for the part he played, ostensibly without rehearsal, as a turncoat.

Weary of his lack of authority in trying to reconcile the expanding needs of the R.F.C. with the claims of its unco-operative and rather stingy naval counterpart, despairing of the Prime Minister's unconcern, and highly conscious of his own neglected merits, Curzon responded in the end to Lloyd George's tempting offer of a seat on a smaller and more flexible War Committee with an alacrity otherwise impossible to explain except in derogatory terms. The element of opportunism in his behaviour was blended with scorn for Asquith's leadership and eagerness to see himself employed to better advantage. The information that Balfour, having yielded to similar overtures from Bonar Law, had been promised the Foreign Office, helped to clinch the deal.

Curzon began to fall foul of his own rules at the Air Board in August, 1916. The Somme assault was then at full blast; and his anger on learning that the Admiralty had been authorised by the Treasury, behind his back, to spend nearly three million pounds on an independent programme of air expansion was self-righteous indeed. Summoning an emergency meeting of the Air Board, he rebuked the naval members for usurping his authority. They heard him out in silence because, in the words of the official air historian, they "were not empowered to offer either explanation or protest," being subject to the decisions of the Sea Lords. A more formal protest was clearly in order. Curzon sent one forthwith to Balfour, whose dusty reply indicated that the Admiralty had no intention of adapting its policy to suit the convenience of the Air Board.

Curzon took his grievances to the solitude of his study. He laboured for some weeks on a lengthy indictment of naval intransigence and its interference with Trenchard's offensive in France. This was submitted to the full War Committee on 23rd October; but as a bombshell designed to shake Asquith out of his detachment it utterly misfired. Its effect was merely to widen the breach between the Admiralty and the Air Board and the supporters of both in the Cabinet.

Balfour, suspecting that Curzon's plan for closing the breach was aimed instead at increasing his personal powers, rejected the recommendation that the Air Board, in the name of efficiency, should control supplies of engines and equipment. He further questioned Curzon's right even to suggest that the Admiralty would help the nation by appointing a single naval officer to act as Henderson's equal and opposite number. This seemed to Balfour an unpardonable intrusion into the affairs of the senior service.

" I do not propose," he dryly replied, " to discuss the constitution of the Admiralty. It was created some generations before the Air Board, and its framers had not the wit to foresee it would some day be required to carry out its duties in subordination to another department. . . .

T.   G

" In the Air Board's report, a proposal is made, which, if carried out, would hand over to that body the whole design and provision of aeronautic material. The easy task of criticism would then be exchanged for the difficult labour of administration. . . . I do not dogmatically deny, however, that the time may come—perhaps indeed has already come—when a single Air Supply Department may be desirable. But, when such a department is established, I hope it will not be on the model of an Air Board with extended powers. . .

" The Admiralty would view with the greatest misgiving a system under which they would have to use aeroplanes and seaplanes whose numbers and design were determined for them by an independent and (I suppose I must now add) a hostile department— a department which would have the right to criticise, the power to embarrass, but no direct responsibility for military or naval action."

Balfour's austere sincerity persuaded Asquith to temporise; but Curzon was not to be fobbed off so lightly. Determined not to let Asquith fall asleep over a question of military urgency, Curzon was helped by the publication, in November, 1916, of the Air Tribunal's report on the alleged criminal incompetence of R.F.C. leaders. While exonerating the leaders, it underlined the same fundamental flaw as Curzon, quite independently, had pointed out:

" Our first recommendation, and that to which we attach greatest importance, is that the equipment of the Royal Flying Corps should be entirely separated from the executive command."

The position of Henderson, the report declared, was "impossible." No man, however gifted, could hope to discharge the incompatible functions of "Commander of the R.F.C., responsible for it as a fighting arm" and " Director-General of Military Aeronautics, responsible for its equipment." It went on significantly:

" Whether there should some day be a united air service combining the Royal Flying Corps and the Royal Naval Air Service we are not in a position to say. However that may be, we see no reason against having one Equipment Department, charged with the equipment of both the army and navy flying services. There would no doubt be inter-service jealousy to contend with, but that should not be allowed to stop a much-needed reform. It would make for increased efficiency."[1]

Curzon had found unexpected judicial support for his point, but Balfour would still not concede it. If the Government insisted, but not otherwise, the First Lord retorted, supply should be handed over not to the Air Board but to the Ministry of Munitions. The deadlock was now complete; yet Asquith refused to impose a decision which could no longer be delayed without a rift in the Government. The situation remained confused until the end of November.

" It is just a toss up which way the thing will go," runs a typical extract from one of Brancker's numerous letters to Trenchard. " They may find some form of compromise, but Curzon is quite strong on being determined to control supply and will resign unless the Government agree. If he resigns, it is quite possible that the Government will go altogether."

The political implications seemed remote and theatrical to Trenchard, who despised politics as a dishonest game and politicians as players whose motives were seldom anything but shady, and had no interest in their tricks for steering in and out of trouble. He therefore wholly overlooked the fact that his latest appraisal of future battle needs, the corollary of his brilliantly accurate forecast of what would happen once the Germans took to offensive methods in the air, had meanwhile become one of the best cards in Curzon's hand.

At the outset of the Somme attack Trenchard had a total of 410 aircraft distributed among twenty-six and a half front-line squadrons. More than half were slow, army co-operation aircraft, which he also used for bombing; the rest were fighters. By mid-September, when Haig had pushed back the enemy line two or three miles and was about to launch a new drive forward, the German Air Service showed signs of having recovered from the hammering it had sustained since July. Roland and Fokker fighters swarmed up to intercept Trenchard's improvised bombers; daily reconnaissance patrols were no longer unmolested; and R.F.C. casualties rose higher. The evidence suggested that the "drastic reformer" predicted by Trenchard was already at work. Haig promised to support whatever expedients Trenchard proposed; and early in October Brancker was notified of an immediate and very obvious step that had long been overdue.

" I have written to Henderson on the subject of the Air Board once more suggesting that the Admiralty send us a squadron of eighteen fighter machines from Dunkirk," Trenchard wrote.

One squadron represented a mere drop in the bucket; but Trenchard had been casting envious eyes for weeks on the eighty machines, half of them fighters, held by the Naval Air Service at Dunkirk. Were they earmarked for some private war of the Admiralty's which nobody had bothered to tell him about? Sometimes he wondered.[2]

A day or two later Brancker came back delightedly.

" Most things are accomplished in this world by unexpected means. Your letter to Henderson had no effect at all. . . . But Douglas Haig's letter to 'Wully' (Robertson, the C.I.G.S.) has borne fruit in that the latter has put up an extract of it to the War Council saying that, in view of the shortage of aeroplanes for the Expeditionary Force, it is quite time we took stock of the resources of the Naval Air Service and put them to some useful purpose. The War Council has circulated this to the War Office, Admiralty and Air Board, and matters look like moving."

Curzon, who was at that moment preparing his own broadside against an unhelpful Admiralty, seemed relieved to find a temporary ally in the C.I.G.S. Armed with a copy of Haig's letter, he lectured the War Committee on 17th October about Trenchard's shortage of fighters, which could and should be supplied out of naval abundance. His plea was not ineffectual. Within ten days, to Trenchard's amazement, a naval squadron was sent to him from Dunkirk.

Haig's private letter to Robertson is a document of unusual interest. For though it bore the signature of the Commander-in-Chief, it appears to have been drafted entirely by Trenchard. It is worth quoting as an example of the circuitous ways which had to be followed, in the very teeth of a hurricane, to obtain decisions from London.

" My dear Robertson," it began (and these words, like the signature, were in Haig's own handwriting):

" With regard to Sopwith aeroplanes, I know the navy have them and just at present they would have been invaluable here in order to help the one Sopwith squadron we have got, which has too much work to do and has had very large casualties on account of it. I hear now that we are likely to have a squadron of army Sopwiths sent out in October.

" With regard to engines, I am glad to hear that a large order is being placed in America, but I do not know what Henderson means by saying he is sending out new engines as fast as he can, unless he calls the R.A.F. (Royal Aircraft Factory) 3, which is not very high powered and none too satisfactory, a new engine. The only really new engine we have got out here is the Rolls-Royce with which only one squadron is equipped, and that squadron is only just being kept up to strength.

" It is not, however, a question of getting engines immediately but of supply next spring. The Germans have already developed a new type of machine which is superior to anything we have got except in three squadrons, and one of them is composed of French machines. In spite of this, however, I do not anticipate that we shall fail to keep the predominancy in the air this year. It is the situation next spring which makes me nervous, unless we have sufficient fighting squadrons.

" According to captured German orders and prisoners' statements, the Germans apparently fully realise the importance of increasing their number of fast fighting machines. They have already done so to some extent, and beyond doubt will do so to a far greater extent during the winter.

" I enclose a slip showing the casualties we have had during September in the squadrons that have to go and fight behind the enemy's lines in the battle area. I enclose another slip which shows the number of officers killed, wounded or missing during the three months the battle has lasted. I would like to point out that during the last month the majority of casualties have been *in the last fortnight, the period when the new German fighters have appeared.** The result of these casualties is that we are not doing as much fighting far behind the enemy's lines as we were, with the result that an increasing number of German machines now come up to our lines and a few cross them, whereas practically no German machines crossed the lines in the first two months of the battle. It is fighting far behind the lines which tells most."

Was Trenchard guilty of improvidence in dissipating his resources during July, August and September, 1916? The charge has often been levelled against him; yet the contemporary testimony of critics as well placed to judge as General Fritz von Below, commander of the First German Army on the Somme, whose memorandum on the air fighting fell into British hands before the battle ended, proves that the enemy saw no reason to support it.

" The enemy's aeroplanes enjoyed complete freedom in carrying out distant reconnaissance," von Below declared. " With the aid of aeroplane observation, the hostile artillery neutralised our guns and was able to range with most extreme accuracy on trenches. . . . By means of bombing and machine-gun attacks from a low height against infantry, battery positions and marching columns, the enemy's aircraft inspired our troops with a feeling of defencelessness."

---

* The slip showed that nearly 75 per cent of R.F.C. casualties in September, which totalled 170, occurred in the second half of the month. Comparative figures for the last half of 1916 compiled from contemporary records are as follows: July, 140; Aug., 90; Sept., 170; Oct., 125; Nov., 95; Dec., 60.

Nearly two-thirds of the 600 Flying Corps casualties occurred between September and November, when the new enemy fighters outclassed and gradually outnumbered Trenchard's best machines. By early November, according to the records in the official German archives at Potsdam, the enemy had regrouped their single-seat fighters into twenty-five squadrons of fourteen aircraft each. By December the number had risen to thirty-three squadrons. Against these Trenchard could pit at first only two squadrons of comparable performance. Under operational leaders of the calibre of von Boelcke and an organiser as ruthlessly competent as Colonel Thomsen, the German Air Service paid Trenchard the compliment of imitating his tactical aggressiveness. This was achieved all the more rapidly with a supply organisation far more efficient than that behind the R.F.C.

" I am perfectly certain," Trenchard wrote to Brancker on the second last day of October, " that the only thing to do now is to fight to a finish and have an Air Minister to control all our supplies."

2

Haig had not yet abandoned his dream of a break-through in strength. One hammer blow after another fell upon ruined but heavily fortified villages like Courcelette, le Sars and Beaumont Hamel, synonyms of dread and grief rather than of pride or glory in homes throughout Britain and Germany. Under the relentless will of the British Commander-in-Chief, these localised attempts to feel out weak points in the defences degenerated into the longest battle of attrition ever fought on earth. British losses, running to 10,000 men on a very good day, could not deter a man so convinced that the Germans were losing more heavily still.

Yet the Flying Corps's ability to give Haig that superiority in accurate artillery support which Ludendorff has noted in his memoirs, and thus cut casualties on the ground, was progressively impaired as new enemy pursuit squadrons came into service. Trenchard had to reorganise his own now that a dozen fighters had become necessary where one or two had sufficed before—and this at a time when reserves were very limited. He knew the temper of his pilots by maintaining constant touch with them. When the going was roughest, the distant thunder of his voice rumbling in a mess, a hangar or a workshop, conveyed its own peculiar reassurance to aircrews and maintenance men alike.

He could never abide barriers, however courteously interposed, between himself and his men. " Get this into your thick head," he barked early one morning at an overzealous officer whom he caught punishing some mechanics for infringing some minor regulation by sending them on a wet cross-country run before breakfast. " This is a technical corps. Our job is to shorten the war. You're not in the army now, you know."

He detested people who stood on ceremony or tried to impress with pompous formality. In addressing more than a dozen men at once, his words came "off the cuff." Indiscreet, often angry, seldom dull, he rivetted their attention because he was recognised as a man who spoke only when he had something definite to say.

" I'm not asking you to do anything I wouldn't do myself," was a common opening gambit. " Just because I'm condemned to ride about in a big Rolls-Royce and sit out the fighting in a chair, you mustn't think I don't understand."

Words like these could easily have rung false in any other man's mouth. In his they sounded natural because he never meant less than he said. To see him at dawn on some outlying airfield, standing apart from his retinue, staring upwards and obviously counting his machines returning from a line patrol or a bombing raid, was to appreciate why this phenomenally perceptive leader, whom some disparaged for having a heart of stone, had lost none of his power to infuse all with his dauntless vitality. Abrupt, rude, jovial, unflattering or "plain contrary" he might appear at times; but he never erred by playing down the role of the Flying Corps in a struggle which frequently seemed more pointless than dangerous.

The day before Haig's second big push on 15th September, when tanks were first used, Trenchard assembled the officers and men of his Headquarters Wing and explained in detail why German machines approaching the line must be attacked on sight and driven off: the lives of untold soldiers, even victory itself, might depend upon it.

In the words of one officer who heard him:

" He said more in five minutes than the rumour mongers had said in five weeks."[3]

Dawn was breaking next day when a car drew up unexpectedly outside the mess of No. 60 Squadron: Trenchard and Baring got out quickly. The waiting pilots learned that in the small hours three enemy observation balloons had been hoisted into positions overlooking the British tank-parks. Nobody was sure how much the

Germans had already discovered;* but No. 60 was the only squadron in reach possessing the necessary machines and rockets to destroy the balloons before zero hour. A deathly pause followed his final words: " Now I want three volunteers."

" Good luck, Gilchrist," he said to one of them. " But remember this: it's far more important to get that balloon than to fail and come back." It was a death knell of a farewell. He repeated it to the others; yet none took the words amiss, perceiving how much it cost him to utter and mean every brutal syllable. He was watching when the trio took off with Le Prieur rockets fastened beneath the wings of their Nieuport fighters, hoping that their speed might carry them through unscathed, but aware that rockets could not be aimed with any degree of accuracy except in a steep power-dive through the field of fire about the targets. Trenchard was still waiting when, after a short eternity, the telephone rang. Army Headquarters were on the line, reporting that three balloons had just fallen to earth in flames. Presently the miracle happened. All three aircraft returned, badly damaged but intact.

" Twenty years later," Gilchrist recalled, " I was dining with Boom. Rather lightheartedly and by way of a respectful leg-pull I reminded him of his farewell that morning. He had not forgotten. Indeed, the look of pain that crossed his face, betraying for once that almost feminine sensitiveness which he took such trouble to hide, made me wish I had kept my mouth shut."

This episode was far from unique. It typifies many others that could be cited. Like Aristides the Just, Trenchard, for all his inner core of compassion, could offer few concessions to human frailty. The heart which he could have cut out in sending the bravest and best to daily rendezvous with death was hardened against the contagion of doubt spread by the despondent or the waverers. As far as the rule could be enforced, he packed off to their regiments men who lost their nerve; men recovering from honourable wounds were alone sure of "soft jobs" on the ground. Though the first successful experiments with parachutes were carried out in late 1916, Trenchard's considered attitude to this innovation was characteristically spartan. His balloon observers, being defenceless, were issued with them as a matter of course, but never his airmen. He was more interested in armouring vulnerable parts of their machines against bullets so that they could fight with easier minds. Even allowing for the fact that the compact parachute harness had not

* A German balloon observer had in fact reported tanks moving up the day before.

yet been developed, it must be said that perhaps one in every three or four R.F.C. pilots and observers killed in action might have survived had they been able to bale out. On several occasions the political authorities expressed concern at the death roll. When the Air Board suggested, for instance, that specific losses should not be listed, Trenchard's sense of honesty was affronted. Henderson and Brancker broadly agreed with his sentiment which amounted to saying: " Publish the figures and be damned to Curzon's hair-splitting." However, Curzon got his way: R.F.C. casualties were not published separately.

Where the letter of King's Regulations was concerned, Trenchard steered an arbitrary middle way between the extremes of rigour and laxness. First things, as he saw them, always came first; and his healthy sense of proportion helped to preserve sanity and reduce unnecessary paper work.

On receiving from Brancker a set of instructions prescribing what officers should and should not wear in public, he commented:

" It makes me laugh, but I will see this matter is insisted on. I think, however, you ought to give me two months' warning out here from now, so that officers can get properly dressed to go home on leave."

Again, when Brancker inquired, at an awkward moment, if one of the recently issued arm-bands worn for identification purposes by R.F.C. officers at the front could be posted home for his inspection, Trenchard replied:

" Is the war over, or have you made a deal with some tailor? . . . Why not get all your lady friends to make them for you? I'm having a stock of them made ready, so that you can put them on both arms and both legs when you arrive. How many hundreds do you want? Can you send out some more sailmakers to cope with the extra work? "

Trenchard contributed much to the common contentment by exerting his uncanny insight into character with deliberate tolerance and restraint. Perfectionism in battle he regarded as an ideal vigorously to be shunned. He had a saying which Baring, for one, knew to be an essential prop of his simple but dynamic philosophy of life: " The best is the enemy of the good."

The rule implied a preference for risking the life of a good pilot or a good machine to-day rather than risking the loss of the war to-morrow by holding back until all factors were in conjunction to produce the perfect pilot, the foolproof machine, and the unrepeatable tactical moment.

Sometimes the dividing line between the dreaming perfectionist and the practical genius was hard to draw justly; but Trenchard never budged from his belief that geniuses in the air war were, in the main, impossible customers best left to discover themselves. Yet, in a sense, Trenchard did discover the great Smith-Barry, who contributed more to the art of airmanship as a result than any other pilot on earth.

Trenchard had known him since Upavon days as an opinionated individualist far more interested in the technique of flying than in the tactical developments of air fighting. He had given him command of No. 60 Squadron after its early losses over the Somme to test the quality of his courage. He had listened, apparently unmoved, to Smith-Barry disparaging the antiquated, sketchy training methods still in vogue. And when casualties began to rise steeply during the last phase of the staggered offensive, Trenchard unexpectedly sent for him and said:

"It's about time you went home to try out these ideas you've been pestering me with. I've told the training people. So don't let me or yourself down."

There was enough of the rebel in Trenchard to welcome challenges from younger men eager to expose the faults of their superiors. Smith-Barry returned to England. From December, 1916, onwards, he was accorded a completely free hand by John Salmond, his former instructor at Upavon and now the Director of Air Training. The innovations introduced by Smith-Barry at Gosport were startling. They revolutionised the existing hit-or-miss system of tuition; and out of them sprang a school of instructors then unrivalled anywhere. Pilots selected for his courses learnt to analyse and master, one by one, the mysterious hazards of flying, which, under pressure of man-power demands, none before him had found time or intellectual curiosity to explore. Smith-Barry developed a basically simple routine. With the object of applying first principles in the air and inculcating them by trial and error until they became second nature, he threw existing rules out of the window and taught his pupils "every possible manœuvre, including flying in a wind, landing and getting off across wind, spinning, etc.," by dual control.

Original, unconventional but practicable, the Smith-Barry technique grew into a uniform system which spread from Britain to other countries. If its founder has been largely forgotten, its sponsor, Trenchard, has never even been recognised. Some may argue that a genius of such calibre should have been cultivated long before 1916; but the fact of Smith-Barry's "discovery" at all during a desperate battle disposes of the charge that Trenchard was blind or indifferent to training deficiencies. Nobody felt more keenly the dreadful waste of life inseparable from sending untried, half-instructed men over the line to learn. And nobody was happier than Trenchard when Smith-Barry made good his eccentric claims.

Trenchard's critics, especially in recent years, have also asserted that had he done more to resist the interminable calls for reconnaissance from the various Army Headquarters, R.F.C. casualties could have been substantially reduced. They contrast his methods with the alleged economy and effectiveness of enemy counter-tactics which were, simply, to retaliate when conditions favoured them.

It must be said first that Flying Corps casualties over the Somme are usually misinterpreted. Admittedly some 800 machines were officially struck off squadron strength during the five months of the battle; but more than a third of these were not battle casualties at all, but out-of-date machines systematically withdrawn from service as newer types arrived. A careful analysis of the figures shows that only 190 Flying Corps machines were shot down by the Germans, and that a further 173 limped home, or crashed, so badly damaged that they had to be completely rebuilt. 499 pilots and observers were killed, wounded or missing in these 363 aircraft. Though enemy losses in men have not been given, they were probably as high as the British. For the German archives show that 359 enemy machines, including two-seaters, were destroyed or forced down on the Somme.

So long as his machines were roughly equal in performance to their opponents', Trenchard's tactical grip on the air fighting remained vice-like. It slackened, as has been stated, in October, when squadrons of new fighters capable of outmanœuvering his were once more concentrated behind the German line. And during the final two months of fighting British casualties reached their peak, exceeding the losses of the previous three. Trenchard held that no parallel could be drawn between conditions of survival in the sky and on the relatively static battlefield beneath. His was a war of no fixed lines or salients; to sit on the defensive would be inviting the enemy to batten on the Flying Corps's technical inferiority. Unless he kept "bustling" the Germans, they would increasingly "bustle" him, until his bases became untenable and Haig's forces were harassed at will. Meanwhile, nobody could accuse him of failing in foresight. He had often reminded Brancker that "the air war will be won or lost at your end, not mine." Nor did the warnings from France exactly fall on deaf ears, even if Curzon was struggling not so much for aircraft as for the authority necessary to let his emasculated Air Board provide them.

The evidence that the technical balance had swung in the enemy's favour almost as decisively as in the case of the " Fokker menace" twelve months before strengthened Curzon's hand, just as Asquith's reluctance to accept the Air Board President's exclusive advice gradually weakened his standing as Prime Minister.

3

The Admiralty revealed its capacity for tactlessness and bad timing by inviting to London in October, 1916, the head of the French Air Service, Colonel Barès, to discuss long-term plans for bombing German munition centres. Trenchard, who knew Barès fairly well, saw him at St. André beforehand and emphasised the futility of a separate bombing offensive while the enemy was regaining the upper hand at the front. Barès stuck to his brief, however, and won over the Sea Lords at Whitehall.

His suggestion that British orders for engines should be restricted in future to powerful versions of the Hispano-Suiza and Clerget impressed the Admirals; the French were already committed to this policy; the Russians, he intimated, would probably follow suit. His ideas were set down precisely in a paper which the Admiralty representatives submitted to the Air Board, adding a rider that "it should be definitely laid down that the navy should keep an effective force of at least 200 bombers in France, to include Dunkirk."

Curzon at once opposed the scheme. Henderson poured cold water over it on the reasonable pretext that, however desirable in principle, long-range bombers, and the re-allocation of overtaxed materials for building them, were a luxury while the Flying Corps lacked the necessary fighters to hold its own in France. Balfour, for the Admiralty, refused to withdraw until Trenchard appealed to Haig, whose remonstrations to the War Committe again proved decisive.

" Sir Douglas's letter is a real snorter," Trenchard reported to Brancker. " I hope it will make the Admiralty sit up and cough."

The crisp style of this letter is unmistakably Haig's, though the facts and arguments are just as clearly Trenchard's.

" I disagree entirely with Colonel Barès's view of the proper proportion of fighters, reconnaissance machines and bombers," wrote the Commander-in-Chief. " The fighters are of the first

importance, for it is evident that we shall have to face a new struggle
for the command of the air in the spring of 1917; and if we lose that,
then neither reconnaissance machines nor bombers will help us. . . .

" Therefore I cannot accept the Admiralty proposal that 200
naval aeroplanes should be devoted to bombing in France. . . . All
air duties, except airships, should be carried out by the Royal Flying
Corps, and it is for the military authorities to decide the relative
numbers of the different types of aeroplane to be used for these
purposes."

Trenchard's disapproval of naval zeal for long-range bombing
was hardly surprising in the circumstances. He had objected to it
since the spring of 1916 when naval squadrons began to assemble
for the purpose at Luxeuil, near Nancy, in eastern France. So costly
and cumbrous a diversion of military and industrial effort could not
be justified, he maintained, until battle needs were met.

Why mount a few, desultory raids on distant munitions centres
just to prove that no British machines had the range or bomb-
carrying capacity to sustain a proper offensive? Why claim that the
Allies would shorten the war by such a programme as Barès's, when
they stood in growing peril of losing air supremacy in France? The
sky, as Trenchard saw it, was one and indivisible. Britain's paltry
air resources were still tragically divided; and while the Admiralty
paid lip-service to "co-ordination of effort" through the Air Board,
the Flying Corps was left to fight alone.

Trenchard abominated politics for distracting men's minds from
real issues to the bickerings of factions, yet the life-and-death interests
of the R.F.C. gradually drew him towards the political arena in spite
of himself. And the grudging respect he felt for Curzon's persistence
outstripped doubts about Curzon's motives. The climax of the
struggle inside the Air Board came in November when, once more
through Haig, Trenchard pressed the Government to allot the
R.F.C. twenty extra squadrons of fighters. Curzon took up the new
demand as though his reputation depended on it. It soon became
plain that the Air Board President would, in Brancker's phrase, be
"prepared to die fighting" unless the Government granted it.

It did not necessarily follow, as Brancker further hinted, that the
Government were by now "afraid to let him die," for Asquith
apparently mistook the seriousness of Curzon's threat by indicating
that he had no intention of meeting R.F.C. needs at the expense of
the Naval Air Service. This proved the last straw for Curzon who,
was easily persuaded to throw in his lot with the major conspirators
then engineering the overthrow of Asquith. No doubt Curzon had

other motives, not least ambition, for deserting the Prime Minister and so precipitating the downfall of his Government early in December, 1916; but one need look no further than the Air Board for a cogent explanation of his conduct.

Trenchard paid one of his infrequent visits to London on 12th December, to appeal in person for an immediate increase in fighter strength. At the Air Board the President's chair was vacant, and the sensational but mysterious turn of events which had swept Asquith from office the previous week seemed to be the only subject which anyone wanted to discuss. Curzon was evidently concluding some political business elsewhere, having already driven his bargain with Lloyd George, the new Prime Minister. Reflecting that he might just as well have stayed in France, Trenchard addressed a rather listless audience about his unchanged difficulties. These were summarised in a letter circulated next day to the War Office, the Admiralty and the War Cabinet.

" The British forces from the Somme to the sea," he noted, " comprise 36 squadrons, including the naval squadron recently lent by the Admiralty, or about 700 machines in all. Of these 36 squadrons, eighteen are fighting squadrons and eighteen are artillery squadrons. Opposed to us the enemy have from 500 to 600 machines of all sorts, but their proportion of artillery machines to fighting machines is considerably higher than ours." In other words, the Germans, with a smaller force, were doing more work for their armies than the R.F.C. And, owing to the tactical inferiority of his more numerous fighter machines, Trenchard was unable to prevent this.

" Three months ago," he explained, " it was discovered that the Germans were in possession of two or three very fast types of aeroplane. One of these has now come into our possession and has been proved, by trials, to be faster than the majority of the fighting machines at our disposal. The number of these fast enemy machines has increased with great rapidity, and it is estimated that 150 of them are now employed against us.

" The R.F.C. has at this moment one fighting squadron, besides the naval squadron lent to it, of a performance equal to that of the German machines. It is hoped that nine further squadrons of equal performance will be available before the end of March, making a total of eleven squadrons. This is the most that can be expected from army sources and falls far short, as will be seen, of the Commander-in-Chief's request for twenty additional squadrons."

The letter also asked, "on behalf of the Commander-in-Chief," for four naval squadrons, 100 Rolls-Royce engines and 50 Hispano-

Suiza engines from Admiralty stocks "which would give us sufficient machines to enable us to hold our own."

At the Admiralty the request fell upon stony ground; the Sea Lords did not like it, and said so. Fortunately for Trenchard, his words carried weight with the new and smaller War Cabinet, thanks again to the initiative of Curzon, now Lord President of the Council, who on 19th December drew Lloyd George's attention to the plight of the R.F.C. and urged that the ministerial powers formerly denied him by Asquith should be conferred immediately on his successor at the Air Board. On the understanding that these powers would be no longer withheld, Curzon then withdrew his long-standing objection to the transfer of air supplies from the Admiralty and War Office to the Ministry of Munitions.

Under the terms of an obscure, hurriedly revised Bill which became law on 22nd December, the New Ministries and Secretaries Act, it was categorically stated that the President of the new Air Board "shall be deemed to be a Minister appointed under this Act and the Air Board a Ministry established under this Act." This was the most significant change of all.

Curzon obtained the additional satisfaction of ensuring that the Admiralty would henceforth be represented on the Board by a fifth Sea Lord with the necessary powers of decision. On any reckoning he had won more than his pound of flesh.

Whether Trenchard would get his fighters seemed more doubtful. Henderson and Brancker were happier than himself about the prospects. The Lloyd George Government, with so many other problems in store, would need more time to settle than the R.F.C. could afford. Neither Acts of Parliament nor the simplifying of Air Board procedure would enhance its front-line strength, and the enemy would not await the House of Commons' pleasure.

Days passed before Curzon's successor was named, then on 2nd January, 1917, Brancker wrote to Trenchard:

" Lord Cowdray has been appointed President of the Air Board, and we had our first meeting this afternoon. I think he will be all right; he is certainly quick on the uptake. We talked hard for about two hours and meet again to-morrow. I will try to get him out to see you as soon as possible."

" I have heard nothing from Cowdray," Trenchard replied about a week later, " and I am uneasy that we shall not get the squadrons I am certain could be got if everybody looked for that, instead of for high policy, now that we have got the real change that matters carried through."

As an organiser, Cowdray demonstrated a swift, firm grasp of essentials. By the end of January his Board had moved into new headquarters, the Hotel Cecil in the Strand, where offices were providently found for Weir and Martin, the two men from the Munitions Ministry co-opted to control air equipment and supply. William Weir, a taciturn engineering expert, had been producing engines for the R.F.C. at his Glasgow works since 1914, when Trenchard at Farnborough, desperately casting about with Brancker for reliable manufacturers willing to accept orders, had first brought this tricky business his way.

Weir's diffident manner and almost painfully laconic turn of speech concealed a knowledge of air problems which ranged far beyond the technical niceties. His ambition was to build bombers by the hundred to carry the war into Germany, for Weir regarded long-range aircraft as weapons potentially more devastating in their direct impact on the enemy's economy than the U-boat would prove on that of the British.[4] Weir had long ago come to the approving notice of Lloyd George at the Ministry of Munitions; and both Cowdray and Trenchard were about to learn, months before the same chance came Churchill's way, that whenever Weir advocated something, in nine cases out of ten his matter-of-fact logic was borne out by events.

" I think the W.O. are delighted to get away from the responsibility of aviation," Brancker wrote in January. "The Army Council really took extraordinarily little interest in this, and since Sir David Henderson has been away they have only asked me to attend one meeting—and that was to try and prove that guns were more important than aeroplanes. Don't repeat this or I shall be crucified! "

Trenchard, obsessed with the present, implored Brancker to "push out those extra squadrons . . . which are more important even than putting your shop on a sound footing." The difficulties, however, were hardly of the politicians' making. Delays in producing, testing and refitting new aircraft retarded the already funereal progress of withdrawing time-expired machines. And bad weather had so slowed up deliveries that in December only five artillery aircraft reached France out of seventy-two promised.

" In one month you have found your estimate as much as four squadrons out in one type of machine alone," complained Trenchard. " We cannot carry on a war like this! "

The Admiralty for its part was in no hurry to disgorge the promised engines and the four fighter squadrons at Dunkirk. Though

Trenchard's old friend and colleague, Godfrey Paine, had mean-while been promoted to Fifth Sea Lord, with a seat on the Air Board, the latter had to reconcile the strategic requirements of the Admiral at Dover with the wants of the R.F.C. in France. Not until the end of March, 1917, in fact, on the very eve of the Allied spring offensive, was the Admiralty's pledge redeemed in full.

When Brancker ruefully confessed in mid-January that no Bristol fighters could be dispatched owing to an industrial dispute at the factory, Trenchard flew into a rage.

" You are asking me to fight the battle this year with the same machines as I fought it last year," he wrote. "We shall be hopelessly outclassed, and something must be done. I am not panicking, but the Hun is getting more aggressive. I warned you fairly as far back as last September, and the Chief also warned you in November. And I warned the Air Board personally on 12th December. All I can say is that there will be an outcry from all the pilots out here if we do not have at least these few squadrons of fast machines, and what I have asked for is absolutely necessary."

Trenchard was surer than ever that the Germans were lengthen-ing their lead in the air. In December, 1916, a relatively quiet month, 17 of the 27 Flying Corps machines shot down came to grief behind the *British* lines. He was all the more thankful that January brought thick weather which grounded and spared the squadrons on both sides, offering him more leisure to reflect on happenings in the overlapping spheres of politics and strategy. Within days of the unseating of Asquith's Government the French Cabinet also under-went a reshuffle. General Lyautey came in as War Minister, Joffre was removed from Supreme Command, and the operational plans for 1917, which the ageing Marshal had agreed with Haig in November, came in for drastic revision. For a new military broom had come to sweep away the sedative influence of Joffre. His name was Nivelle, one of the younger French generals, who owed his preferment over experienced leaders like de Castelnau to his success in recapturing Fort Douamont from a depleted German force, thus ending the ten-months' siege of Verdun on a heroic note.

Nivelle, flushed with victory, unceremoniously discarded his predecessor's battering-ram policy. By meticulously detailed plan-ning the Allies, he held, could storm and engulf the German lines. By methodical timing, a huge *masse de manœuvre* could then be deployed to exploit the gains and finish the war in a single action. What he had achieved on a narrow sector at Verdun, Nivelle proposed to repeat along 100 miles of the Western Front. Haig confessed himself none too sanguine about a project whose chief merit in Trenchard's eyes was to afford the R.F.C. a respite while the two Commanders-in-Chief argued. Then he took a step which seemed wholly uncalled for. On the rashly mistaken assumption that Henderson was less concerned with Flying Corps's needs than he should be, Trenchard sent a personal letter to Cowdray, the Air Board President, and Henderson retaliated by rapping him sharply over the knuckles. Trenchard was piqued at what he deemed pettiness in a superior whom he admired for breadth of mind.

"Things are too hopeless," he fumed to Brancker. "To think that we are in the middle of the war, and the only letter I get for six months from the man responsible does not mention machines at all but only remarks about my conduct and military usage and 'the usual channels of communications.' It is really as good as a comic opera and, as you say, we deserve to lose the war."

He was rather more circumspect in justifying his conduct to Henderson. Recalling the Flying Corps's critical lack of up-to-date machines, he invited him to reconsider whose judgment was at fault. Henderson ignored the letter, so Trenchard returned to the charge a few days later:

"I would emphasise once more," he wrote with impenitent, ungrammatical defiance, " that if everybody thinks I am attacking them when I say the supply is hopeless, and they begin to defend themselves instead of trying to improve the supply, I am afraid we shall never get the supply to what we ought—and the result is we shall continually fall behind the Hun."

This regrettable incident had a distinctly cooling effect on the hitherto warm, if intermittent, exchanges between Henderson and Trenchard. The latter began to confide increasingly in the resilient Brancker, whom he had once advised "not to put me in leading strings." From the spring of 1917 onward, Brancker replaced Henderson as the safety valve for Trenchard's pent-up feelings and nearly all official criticisms and demands.

"Keep going on and don't be depressed," he urged him in February when Brancker admitted that the gap between Air Board promises and military needs was almost unbridgeable.

"You are, I was going to say, my only hope, and don't forget that your work influences work out here as a whole more than anything else I can think of."

Trenchard's main supporter on the spot was still the Commander-in-Chief. Haig had again warned the War Cabinet in January, when Nivelle's short-cut plan to victory was first seriously considered, that the R.F.C. would be unable to support a spring offensive. In February he renewed the warning: owing to inexplicable delays in deliveries, he said, the Flying Corps was at least seven squadrons short of establishment.

" Our fighting machines," wrote Haig, " will almost certainly be inferior in number and quite certainly in performance to those of the enemy. . . . It appears that we cannot expect to gain supremacy in the air in April, and it is even possible that it may pass to the enemy."

The War Cabinet was not perturbed. Lloyd George's long-held doubts about the Haig-Joffre strategy of attrition disappeared with capricious suddenness now that a French general of engaging ways had emerged with a simpler and cheaper expedient. Nivelle's method of attack sounded doubly attractive: if it failed to rout the enemy within forty-eight hours, the offensive would forthwith be called off.

Characteristically, the Prime Minister welcomed it for a reason less directly connected with strategy; so deeply did he distrust Haig's generalship that he was prepared to accept Nivelle on trust as Supreme Commander in France.

Lloyd George's abortive manœuvering to attain this end at the Calais Conference of January, 1917, need not detain us. Few apologists have yet succeeded in giving it a virtuous look, though some have defended it on the disingenuous pretext that Lloyd George lacked sufficient ministerial support to demote his own Commander-in-Chief by open methods. What most impressed Trenchard, who learnt of the attempt to undermine Haig's authority from the Commander-in-Chief himself, was the composure of the victim and the studied hypocrisy of his assailants. The episode stamped itself on his politically unformed mind as a remarkable instance of shabby dishonesty.

The incident also strained relations between the British and French High Commands without, however, affecting Trenchard's smoothly working partnership with du Peuty. The two air leaders were summoned separately to Beauvais on the same day in late February to hear from the lips of Nivelle their complementary roles in the coming offensive. Trenchard's interview with the French Commander-in-Chief was, incidentally, his only consultation with a leader whose control of the allied armies had meanwhile been limited by hasty compromise to the duration of a single battle, a battle which Lloyd George still hoped would turn the tide in the West.

Trenchard detected something too plausible in the overpowering charm and glibness of the Frenchman who tried to put him at ease by allowing him in advance "a completely free hand" in the air (and by claiming, over lunch, that his English mother was a Trenchard).[5] Listening to his recital of the recent French triumph at Verdun, Trenchard found himself wondering at Nivelle's presumption in expecting to repeat it at short notice on a massive scale. To rupture the enemy front at a stroke would call for absolute surprise, perfect planning, superhuman force, and unprecedented good fortune. Of one fact he left Nivelle in no doubt: the R.F.C. could no longer keep prying German aircraft at a respectful distance, so that the scope and direction of Nivelle's drive might be partly robbed of the element of surprise.

Trenchard's scepticism was tinged by his own anxieties. He could not afford to risk his new machines; on the other hand, he could not skimp his commitments to Haig's artillery and infantry. The brunt of the air fighting therefore fell, in March, with the return of spring-like weather, on weakened squadrons, and offensive activity was cut to the minimum. Even when flying in close defensive formations his machines could do little to protect themselves against enemy fighters emboldened by the R.F.C.'s odd unwillingness to hit back. Diehard critics of Trenchard may care to note that nearly one in every four of the 120 R.F.C. machines lost that month were destroyed while supporting the British infantry in its cautious advance to the Hindenburg line, or while registering for the artillery in routine battle preparations. This was the price which had to be paid for having to stand on the defensive.[6]

4

As if fate had not bludgeoned him enough, Trenchard went down with German measles at the end of March. Baring noted how Philip Sassoon, Haig's private secretary, complimented Trenchard one morning on his unusually rosy complexion.

" I've never seen you looking so well," he said.

Trenchard, who had long schooled himself to ignore the strain of overwork and incommunicable worry, grunted uneasily. Perhaps the symptoms were beginning to show. That night Haig's doctor ordered him to stay in bed; but he could not refrain from stealing down to his desk on the floor below while the staff were at meals or asleep. On 5th April, the day he had chosen to pay off some recent

scores by committing his new fighter squadrons to battle, Baring
discovered that Trenchard had "got up and had a good rummage
in the operations office" during lunch. His "graveyard cough"
echoed dismally through the thick-walled château. Nobody seemed
surprised to learn that he had developed severe bronchitis; but
nobody, least of all the harassed doctor, was allowed to discover
that Trenchard had only one congested lung with which to draw
breath.

Two mornings before the British push in support of Nivelle on
7th April, Trenchard rose from his bed and advise his medical
adviser to go to the devil. He announced that he was leaving by air
to visit squadrons that had become embroiled in some of the fiercest
fighting of the war. Baring, aware that Trenchard " still had a touch
of bronchitis," mildly rebuked him. The doctor, eager to avoid prolonging the scene, merely said, " Flying may do him good or it may
kill him," and departed gratefully to visit less tiresome patients.

That day Trenchard visited eleven squadrons to grapple with
problems which had lain unattended for days while he was tossing
about in bed. Du Peuty had again put at the R.F.C.'s disposal an
entire squadron, with spares, of Nieuport fighters, though these
machines were more vulnerable now than formerly against élite
enemy formations led by technicians as versatile as Voss and von
Richthofen. Within a single week of clashes with German aircraft
among the lowering snowclouds south and east of Arras, 75 R.F.C.
machines of all types were shot down and a further 56 wrecked.

Artillery squadrons equipped with the new R.E.8 suffered worst.
This two-seater machine had been dogged by ill-fame ever since it
left the Royal Aircraft Factory in 1916 for proving. Designed to
replace the long outmoded B.E. biplanes, it was faster, heavier and
armed with two machine-guns, the first synchronised and the second
on a movable mounting for the observer. Despite these improvements the R.E.8s run of almost uninterrupted misfortune had killed
off test pilots, ferry pilots, and trainee pilots, causing numerous
delays for modifications. Above Vimy Ridge and the Arras sector
that spring, it added dozens more victims to its credit through a
tendency to spin down out of control.

Trenchard upheld, within reason, the right of temperamental
airmen to damn their equipment. Individual complaints, he found,
had a habit of cancelling each other out; collective grievances were
always the better for being aired, sifted and sometimes exploded.
Earlier that winter, when the first of the Admiralty squadrons on
loan from Dunkirk reached Vert Galland, he had listened with

poker-faced attentiveness to naval pilots condemning the lubricating oil for their machine-guns.

" It's Admiralty issue," they said caustically, " and it's useless. It makes the guns jam. Why can't we have oil that doesn't freeze up, like the R.F.C. across the way? "

" Take a tin of the stuff, Baring," said Trenchard. " We'll have it analysed," he promised.

He managed to conceal his amusement on questioning a neighbouring R.F.C. squadron, whose guns were alleged never to freeze. They were having similar trouble, and they knew why.

" These naval fliers, sir, are luckier with their oil. Their guns never jam. The Admiralty may not know much about flying, but they organise these things better than we do."

" Take a sample tin, Baring," said Trenchard.

That night both containers were sent for checking, one marked in blue the other in red. Within the hour the analyst confirmed that the contents were identical. Trenchard received no further complaints about lubricating oil.

The prejudice against the R.E.8 was much graver. For the newspapers had seized on it; there were public demands for an inquiry; and, worse still, many pilots had lost confidence in something they regarded as a death trap, regardless of the fact that it could not be replaced for months. One morning, while visiting a bombing squadron commanded by Major (now Air-Marshal Sir John) Baldwin to congratulate him and his men on several effective raids in their new De Havilland 4s, a grim message reached Trenchard. Another squadron of R.E.8s had been caught in the toils that morning; eight had gone out on a routine line mission only to be intercepted by enemy fighters. None had returned. Trenchard decided at once to call on the survivors, whose spirits were reported to be mutinously low. He arrived ostentatiously enough as a passenger in one of the doomed and detested machines.

They were expecting him. Even the squadron commander looked guilty as Trenchard's R.E.8 taxied towards the pilots standing stiffly beside their machines. He startled them all by asking: " Who arranged this parade? I want lunch, and so do you." He seemed in good humour now, after sounding so stern on the telephone. Apprehensiveness gave way to puzzlement as the meal progressed. Trenchard sat at the top table next to Baring, talking with animation. Conversation elsewhere lagged. The old devil was playing with them, saving up the fireworks until the end. Some noticed how he stared about him, sizing up individuals as they ate.

At last he rose to his feet. The room was immediately hushed. Still without a word, he pushed back his chair and walked towards the door. Baring closed it behind him and immediately repressed speculation relieved itself in a crescendo of noise which, in the words of one witness, "seemed to raise the roof." "The old so-and-so must have suffered a blackout in transit." "Serve him right for risking his bloody neck in an R.E.8."

They saw rather than heard the door swing open, framing the reproachful figure of Trenchard.

"There's nothing wrong here," he thundered. "I've been watching you. Now go to work properly and give the Hun hell in your R.E.8s."

He was *willing* them to do better, and they rose to his challenge. Within a week that squadron had regained its fighting spirit and recovered confidence in its equipment.

The gallantry and resilience of his pilots were his sole consolation in April, the bleakest month of all for casualties. An enemy who enjoyed all-round superiority was never permitted to flaunt it. Trenchard had often heard the saying at the time of the Somme:

"A V.C.? Who wants a V.C.? We want to get Boelcke."

Now it had changed to "We want to get von Richthofen."

There was no malice in their ruthlessness. To see those one loved disappear or return dying and mutilated did not excite generosity; but hatred of the Germans was rare, and of this Trenchard approved. Values were changing with the increasing mechanisation of warfare; but while Trenchard remained in command wreaths and messages of condolence, which must read strangely to our later, more callous generation, continued to be dropped on either side of the line as spontaneous tributes to adversaries who had died bravely.

The offensive on the Aisne River was launched on 16th April, 1917, by three French Army groups. "*L'heure est venue,*" Nivelle declared in a preliminary order of the day. "*Confiance. Courage. Vive la France!*" The forty-six French divisions massed along the hilly, wooded front between Soissons and Rheims had drained his reserves; but the attack from the outset fell short of expectations, a fact obliquely reflected in *communiqués* that were evasively non-committal.

"I could get no details from the French Mission as to the results of to-day's fighting," Haig recorded on the evening of the second newsless day. "This is always a bad sign and I fear things are going badly with the offensive."

Over a week before, Haig's forces had moved into action. Progress about Arras had slowed down after the early storming of Vimy Ridge. One British gun to every twenty-one yards of churned-up earth had provided better cover for the advancing infantry, and casualties on the ground were light.

The advance was not maintained. In heavy sleet and snow, the few British tanks failed to penetrate the enemy wire; and the Germans held off successive attempts by infantry to reduce the first line of the Hindenburg defences. Overhead, fierce air fighting broke out whenever the weather brightened; but Trenchard's ability to influence the battle below was hampered by scanty reserves. Nevertheless, he devised a novel if slightly desperate means of forcing the pace in the fighting zone: flights of improvised bombers and fighters were sent in very low to attack German trenches, gun sites and assembly points, but bullets and bombs alone, far ahead of the straggling British infantry, were as ineffective as a spearhead split from its shaft.

The nuisance value of such tactics was demonstrated when the enemy paid Trenchard another compliment by adopting them. Then complaints from British divisional commanders crowded thick upon him. Why must he seek trouble farther afield, leaving his own lines unguarded and the Germans free to wreak vengeance on *them*? There had been no comparable outcry since the early winter, when the Albatross and Halberstadt first appeared in strength. He had then had to placate the gunner generals and resist a determined attempt on their part to dismember the Flying Corps by taking over the artillery machines. That dispute had been settled in his favour by Haig; but now the Commander-in-Chief had worries enough without springing to Trenchard's aid again.

Soldiers, he concluded, were nearly all alike. Their horizons were earthbound. Whether Germans, French or British, most of them seemed quite incapable of appreciating the flexibility of aircraft as weapons until, as helpless spectators, they experienced the demoralising effect of a few low-flying hostile machines. How could he begin to explain? To the few who understood and believed, no explanation was necessary; to the vast, prejudiced majority, no simple explanation appeared possible.

Du Peuty had written to him in the first flush of victory at Vimy Ridge:

" These results of yours have not only contributed to the great success of your armies, but in close co-operation with our own efforts they have relieved us of a large part of the German aviation. I hope to be able to teach what is left of the German aviation that the French intend to apply the same methods in the same manner."

Du Peuty's intentions were, alas, doomed by a resolute enemy with precise knowledge of Nivelle's. By the last week of April du Peuty could do nothing in the sky to revive broken hopes of a French break-through on the ground. The annihilating victory on which Nivelle counted had eluded him.

Few in high authority yet knew that well before the battle, by treachery or carelessness, the Germans had come into possession of the campaign directive.* The French were repulsed by an enemy who anticipated every move. The career and reputation of Nivelle hung in the balance while nearly half a million of his men spent themselves on behalf of an offensive plan that would not work. Disillusion spread among the shredded French divisions, with demoralisation at its heels.

"The irony of the situation was sublime," commented Haig's biographer, Duff Cooper. "Two months earlier the French Government had been seeking to compel the British Commander-in-Chief to become a mere automaton under the inspired guidance of his more gifted French colleague. Now the French Minister of War was almost on his knees to that same British Commander-in-Chief to furnish him with material that might help him to get rid of that same French colleague."

By the first week in May it was clear even to Lloyd George that Nivelle had failed. Nearly 100,000 of his men had fallen to disprove the worth of a grandiose strategic theory, while farther north, on the Arras front, nearly 160,000 British soldiers had suffered wounds, death or internment in subsidiary attacks wished on Haig from above. The casualties were only part of the price of failure. When Pétain took over from Nivelle on 15th May and informed Haig for the first time of the growing indiscipline in the French Army, the consequences of bad faith and faulty propaganda became more evident.

The extent to which Haig's plans for the rest of 1917 were determined by Pétain's secret disclosures has been disputed ever since. The official British and French war histories should by now have demolished the pretensions of those who assert that nothing could have deflected Haig from undertaking his Flanders offensive; that only afterwards did he try to justify it by exaggerating or inventing the excuse of a pledge of secrecy to Pétain; and that the

* On 17th April, Haig, whose sources of intelligence were better than his detractors have often implied, referred in his diary to the "carelessness" of this breach of security.

demoralisation of the French Army was far less critical than Pétain, a pessimist by temperament, seems to have alleged.

Haig had sound reasons for preparing to mount the Ypres campaign of the autumn without delay. The first and most important was the alarming toll taken by unrestricted U-boat warfare at sea. In the first six months of 1917, over two million tons of Allied shipping went to the bottom, a fact which drove Jellicoe at the Admiralty to warn the War Cabinet in June, in Haig's hearing that "if the army cannot get the Belgian ports, the navy cannot hold the Channel and the war is lost." This, as the Commander-in-Chief wrote in his diary, was a "bombshell for the Cabinet and all present." The second reason was the darkening military outlook in Russia, where the April revolution had begun to sap the ordinary soldier's will to fight. The Americans, it is true, had redressed the military balance on paper by declaring war on the Central Powers; but months would pass, as Haig well knew, before the vast, untried forces of the United States were ready for action in France.

These factors weighed heavily with Haig. They did little to reconcile Lloyd George to another large-scale British offensive, though after some hesitation and heart-searching the War Cabinet at length assured the Commander-in-Chief of their "wholehearted support" on 25th July.[7] If, as seems probable, definite evidence about the French mutinies had at last reached London to tip the scales in Haig's favour, the information certainly did not come from the Commander-in-Chief, who honoured Pétain's confidence to the end.

Whether any military leader has the right to withhold from his own Government vital information of the kind is debatable. When, as in Haig's case, the withholding of such information leads to misconstruction of his motives and aspersions on his professional ability and personal integrity, the expediency of saying nothing would appear as doubtful then as it is unthinkable to-day.

It was largely by accident that Trenchard discovered more than any other senior British officer, apart from the Commander-in-Chief, about the broken spirit of the French Army in the summer of 1917; and until his death he remained immovably certain that Haig saved France from defeat and Britain from probable capitulation by refusing to dishonour a military secret and following his own conscience.

How did Trenchard form this judgment? To answer that question the time-sequence of events must, for once, be ignored. For Trenchard's understanding of Haig's dilemma affected him so profoundly that it led to his own eventual collision with the Lloyd

George Government in circumstances which have never been fully
explained. Because he, too, was instinctively mistrustful of politicians,
secretive by nature, more addicted to doing than to explaining, and
almost unnaturally indifferent to the good opinion of others, the
prelude to that collision must be adequately described. And because
Trenchard's reputation has suffered by default in the process, the
underlying causes must now be traced to source.

5

Trenchard had never taken seriously the talk in London of an early
long-range bombing campaign against Germany. The proposal was
put forward by Weir, still only a technical adviser to the Air Board,
endorsed by Cowdray, the President, and placed high on the
planning agenda in the spring of 1917. It seemed to Trenchard a
delusion even to contemplate such operations while the R.F.C. in
France could not rely on reinforcements for its bread-and-butter
business with the Army. Yet it is worth recording that as long ago
as June, 1916, Trenchard had ordered ten squadrons of long-range
bombers in a composite force of 86 squadrons for all purposes, none
of which had yet reached him. His scepticism can thus be appreciated.

" You prove that your factories can deliver the machines," he
told Weir, in effect, at St. André in May. " Then leave the bombing
to me."

The fact that Weir, whose honesty and competence he admired,
was the prime mover in the bombing enterprise did not displease him.
Deliveries of fighting machines and engines had lately improved,
and for that Trenchard rightly gave most of the credit to Weir.
But he begged him not to let the Air Board forget that the struggle
for air superiority above the battlefield must take precedence
over everything else.

Weir's exceptional talent as an organiser had unblocked within
four months the industrial bottlenecks representing the negative half
of Curzon's legacy to Cowdray. The latter had meanwhile vindicated
the early hopes of Brancker and Henderson by leading his team of
experts and advisers on a loose rein with the confidence of a man who
knew exactly where he was going. A good if critical listener, the
President of the Air Board was a ready convert to Weir's faith in the
bomber as Britain's answer to the U-boat. The Royal Navy had its
work and resources cut out hunting the submarine at sea: and both
men agreed that the Flying Corps alone possessed the flexibility,

experience and leadership to shoulder the added responsibility of striking hard at the enemy's industrial vitals before the end of 1917.

Trenchard was someone whom the President of the Air Board had learnt to accept on trust. Until mid-1917 the two did not meet, yet each understood and liked the other at a distance. For Weir was their intermediary; and Weir not only spoke Trenchard's language but respected him as a "natural organiser, a very strong personality and an unrivalled leader of men." It was an unmixed pleasure for Trenchard, on his side, to welcome a "real expert" who never had to be reminded that a squadron meant 33 machines, allowing for training, wastage and reserves, not the literal eighteen listed for convenience on the order of battle. What a blessing to deal with a specialist who "kept his promises and could count"; what balm to credit Weir with enabling the Flying Corps to dominate the Western Front before and during the short, breath-takingly successful British action at Messines in June, 1917, the prelude to Haig's forthcoming offensive at Ypres.

Maurice Baring recorded at the time:

"The air reports read like a fairy-tale. It all went like clockwork. It is the finest day in the air we have ever had."

Messines would have been a different tale altogether had Weir failed to deliver the long promised, new squadrons of S.E.5 and Bristol fighters which, with the De Havilland 4 medium-range bomber, transformed the tactical situation and took the heartache out of operational planning. Though R.F.C. reserves were still low in view of the build-up for the Flanders push, Trenchard was satisfied that his ordeal had all but ended. From now on he could depend on Weir to forestall the kind of "staggered" production crisis which had almost crippled the R.F.C. between March and May, 1917, when proportionately more machines and men perished in pursuit of Nivelle's strategic will-o'-the-wisp than in any earlier British action.*

Could the Air Board improve on its recent record by doubling the number of squadrons in France, as Trenchard was demanding with 1918 in mind, and yet have slack enough for a separate force of bombers, as Weir insisted would be practicable? The Flying Corps' commander still doubted it, in spite of Messines, owing to a new complication: the antagonism of the War Office to R.F.C. encroachments. Reading between the lines of Brancker's recent letters he

---

* 1,270 Flying Corps aircraft were shot down or failed to return during those three months.

knew that Robertson was up in arms. The Air Board was competing too successfully with the War Office for man-power and raw materials which could no longer be readily bought on the American market now that the United States was mobilising for war.

According to Brancker, the C.I.G.S. had grown as obdurate and unreasonable as the Admiralty in Curzon's day. It was, he wrote, as though Robertson and his advisers had come to the conclusion that "the spirit of independence which they had encouraged had gone far enough—perhaps too far—and that it was necessary to shackle this precocious infant, the R.F.C., to its old mother, the army." The Whitehall atmosphere was sultry, the outlook heavy with foreboding. It seemed that little short of a national catastrophe could force the Air Board and the War Office to compose their differences.

With an obliging touch of brutality which shook Whitehall to its foundations, the Germans accidentally provided the semblance of one out of a hazy sky on 13th June, 1917. Nobody was prepared for the descent on London in broad daylight of a squadron of twin-engined Gothas. The raid caused minor damage to property, major havoc to morale; nearly 600 people were killed or maimed; none of the fourteen raiders was brought down; and the manifest ineffectiveness of the anti-aircraft defences, to say nothing of the ensuing public outcry, led the Government to react vigorously. Not since early 1916 had this unpleasant aspect of the developing air war been rammed so crudely home. Trenchard was recalled from France for immediate consultations. He travelled over with Haig, who had a long-standing appointment to discuss with a nervous War Cabinet the imminent British offensive in Flanders.

It was Trenchard, rather than the Commander-in-Chief, whom Lloyd George and his colleagues were really anxious to see. The Flying Corps' chief came armed with a five-point appreciation of the general air situation; and at a special Cabinet meeting on 20th June, he expounded the facts as he saw them. His brief was as constructive and concise as Baring could make it, shirking none of the questions then agitating the Government and public; yet it embodied principles of airpower which have lost little of their grim validity even to-day. The arguments deserve to be quoted at length:

" The capture by us of the Belgian coast," he declared, " would be the most effective step of all, as, in addition to increasing the distance to be traversed, it would force the German machines either to cross territory occupied by us, when going and returning (a considerable advantage to us), or to cross neutral territory, where our

Secret Service could doubtless establish means of giving us warning quickly.

" The next most effective step is to inflict the utmost damage on the enemy's sheds and machines behind the Western Front. The amount which can be done is limited by the number and capacity of machines and pilots available in France. Increased activity on the Western Front serves the double purpose of assisting the armies in overcoming the enemy and at the same time reducing his power to send expeditions to England. To the Germans this reply would be most disappointing.

" Any system of patrols [over the English Channel] would entail the use of a great number of machines and pilots. To justify any hope of such a system being effective (except by sheer luck) the number of pilots and machines required would be entirely beyond our present power of supply. . . . As a temporary measure, a modified system of patrols might be tried, working on both sides of the Channel. To give this its best chance of success, an extensive system of communications, by wireless and other means, would be required; and it is essential that there should be unity of command over the whole system of patrols and communications. . . .

" Reprisals on open towns are repugnant to British ideas but we may be forced to adopt them. It would be worse than useless to do so, however, unless we are determined that once adopted they will be carried through to the end. The enemy would almost certainly reply in kind—and unless we are determined and prepared to go one better than the Germans, whatever they may do and whether their reply is in the air or against our prisoners or otherwise, it will be infinitely better not to attempt reprisals at all. At present we are not prepared to carry out reprisals effectively, being unprovided with suitable machines."

Lloyd George wanted Mannheim bombed at once. Under questioning, Trenchard stated that any attempt to bomb Mannheim would result in failure. Privately, he was against theatrical counter-measures merely to slake the popular thirst for revenge. Though he had no scruples about attacking German industrial targets, none were within range of his bases in northern France. Indeed, Mann-heim was barely within range of the French airfields behind the front in East Central France. However, as a pledge of his readiness to organise a sustained offensive as soon as suitable machines could be provided, Trenchard offered to approach Pétain at once for the lease of bases there.

The War Cabinet insisted, however, that two "crack" fighter

squadrons should be detached from the R.F.C. for daylight defensive patrols above the English Channel, disregarding his contention that the Germans would retaliate against the weakened R.F.C. in France. Events speedily proved him right. For the next ten days, Gothas bombed with relative impunity several towns behind the British lines, including St. Omer, where Trenchard had reopened his old head-quarters in preparation for the Flanders battle, as well as trenches, dumps and depots. And von Richthofen's fighters showed rare determination in holding off Flying Corps intruders while the raids were in progress.

There was little comfort in being shown how well the enemy had profited from their harsh experience over the Somme; for, having calmed the politicians, Trenchard now had to face charges of negligence from corps commanders, few of whom relished his uncompromising refusal to interfere with normal preparations for Haig's offensive. Air protection now, he stressed, would be false economy. If the R.F.C. failed to register enemy guns, blast wire entanglements, or bomb the German rear, many British soldiers would die unnecessarily when battle commenced.

He felt sufficiently stung by hostile criticism to circularise, with Haig's consent, a simple explanation of what the German Air Service was up to.

" By bombing raids against London and in England," he declared, " they have tried, trusting to their effect on public opinion and to the political agitation which was bound to follow, to make us dislocate our flying forces in the field. . . ."

But the enemy had not quite finished with London. Trenchard was rather surprised when the two fighter squadrons, which had been patrolling above the Channel for nearly a fortnight, were suddenly restored to him. This was done at the express request of the Commander-in-Chief; but owing to a clerical blunder at the War Office the Cabinet was not informed. The Germans responded with a promptness which demonstrated their ruthless simplicity of aim. No sooner had the R.F.C. fighters ceased patrolling than the Gothas were dispatched from Flanders to bomb London again.

The capital's renewed ordeal came unhindered out of a clear sky on 7th July. Air Board members, on hearing the alert, abandoned their desks for the balconies of the Hotel Cecil and watched the machines wheeling three miles above the skyline of spires and buildings, nonchalantly shaking off the few fighters which managed to climb close enough. Henderson and Brancker were aware, as they looked on in silence, that attempted interception by obsolete machines was as futile as the desultory firing of the ground batteries.

The psychological shock of this second daylight attack within a month was prodigious. Alarm and anger re-echoed in the Press, affecting public and politicians alike. The War Cabinet met a few hours after the all-clear in an atmosphere of such glum recrimination that Robertson commented later to Haig:

" One would have thought the whole world was coming to an end."

The weakness of the defences had shaken Lloyd George and his colleagues. Clearly, a wholesale overhaul was imperative; but first, as a face-saving gesture, the squadrons borrowed from Trenchard and prematurely sent back to France must return home for an indefinite period. Another top-priority wire went to Haig which also recommended the bombing of Mannheim by way of reprisal, if this could be arranged without disrupting battle preparations. The fighters flew north at once to stand guard again, but the citizens of Mannheim were left undisturbed. As Trenchard informed Henderson:

" We must stop the bombing of London, but the only way to do it is to knock out completely the German aviation here. . . . At the same time there is no doubt we ought to do bombing, and directly you can get me out a squadron of De Havilland 4s with B.H.P. engines, I will strongly recommend that we start bombing the factories of Mannheim."

The B.H.P. (Beardmore) six-cylinder engine had the range and power he needed. Weir had often spoken cheerfully of its development, and other engines of comparable thrust were at last in production. But none was immediately available; indeed, nearly six months would pass before the B.H.P.'s "teething troubles" were cured. Trenchard was too conditioned by past disappointments of the kind to make an exhibition of his frustration. This latest air crisis was merely a domestic variation on the theme of "too little and too late" which had haunted him and the R.F.C. since 1915.

The French, though better equipped, were more optimistic to Trenchard's mind than circumstances warranted about the results to be derived from bombing Germany. Du Peuty had a nucleus of fairly reliable, long-range machines, and his pilots had been visiting the industrial belt of the Saar at infrequent intervals since 1916, when machines of the Naval Air Service joined them in the brief honeymoon at Luxeuil. The chronic shortage of unevenly divided equipment had killed an experiment which Trenchard had then dubbed a "luxury of war." Now it had overnight become a political necessity.

Du Peuty was definite enough about the advantages of an air offensive of the kind, but was too seasoned a commander to underrate the hazards of sustaining it. Distances were at least twice as great as those which the Gothas had to cover. To the dangers of interception on the way had to be added the risks of drift, head winds and blind navigation, which imposed unpredictable strains on men and machines alike. Once again, however, this remarkable Frenchman placed himself entirely at Trenchard's disposal, offering the benefits of his experience and the leasing or sharing of French airfields closer to the German frontier.

Meanwhile, the repercussions in London passed over Trenchard's head. The anguish of the politicians smote him less than the sudden change in the outlook of Robertson, no well-wisher of the R.F.C., as he knew. At another War Cabinet meeting on 21st June, Trenchard had scarcely been able to believe his ears when the C.I.G.S. calmly advocated a massive and immediate expansion of the Flying Corps.[8] On the strength of Robertson's *volte-face* the Air Board had hastily doubled its current programme to include no less than forty long-range bombing squadrons. Haig, of course, took the liberty of protesting. Was the C.I.G.S. losing his grip? Trenchard wondered. Or was he playing an artful diplomatic hand of his own, as Brancker suggested?

In his heart, Robertson detested the upstart Air Board. A stickler for correct procedure, he had never gone in for fussing over the Flying Corps foundling which everyone else seemed to spoil. Yet Robertson struck Trenchard as above subterfuge. And Haig's mystification turned to grief when the C.I.G.S. further asserted that the time was ripe for a full-bottomed Department of State for Air.

" I doubt if any real progress will be made," Robertson wrote to the Commander-in-Chief on 9th July, "until a different organisation is established. The army and navy now say what they want, the Air Board considers their wants, and then Addison (the Munitions Minister) makes the machines. I am inclined to think that we need a separate air service, but that would be a big business. . . ."

The evidence of chaotic compromise drove the essentially tidy-minded Robertson to a disagreeable but inescapable conclusion which Haig dismissed as absurdly far-fetched. Even Cowdray, the President of the Board, was taken aback. In fact, only the unobtrusive, sensitive Henderson, who for two years had seen the undernourished R.F.C. stagger from crisis to crisis while a succession

T.   H of guardians haggled over its rations, was certain that nothing less than an Air Minister would do. Whether Haig, Robertson, Trenchhard or the Government liked the idea or not, Henderson could see no other way out of a bewildering maze which had already cost the country dear in treasure, and the Flying Corps in blood.

When Haig wrote querulously at the end of July, demanding an answer to the rhetorical question: "Are these mythical bombers to get priority over the fighters and other machines I've been awaiting for months?" it was Henderson who replied for the last time as Director of Military Aviation. Unofficially and discreetly, this far-sighted staff officer, who had founded the original R.F.C. and led it to France in 1914, was already advising General Smuts, whom Lloyd George delegated to frame the future birthright of a separate Royal Air Force. Henderson assured Haig that the Air Board intended to meet all outstanding orders for aircraft in full. He was, however, unable to comment on the latest plan to provide forty bomber squadrons for two reasons:

" Firstly, because such plans will be dependent to some extent on the military situation when the squadrons become available, and, secondly, because the War Cabinet are now considering the establishment of a separate department of State to control and administer the air service. . . ."[9]

This was not, for Henderson, a matter of the wish being father to the thought. The concept of a separate Air Ministry was far from new. Ministers, politicians and journalists had been toying with it off and on since the outbreak of war. A belated object lesson in the effective use of air-power, provided by a single squadron of Gothas based in Flanders, had now impelled the Government to study the implications for the first time and act on them. They could have deputed no wiser man than Jan Christian Smuts for the task: his status as a *de facto* member of the War Cabinet was less important than his acknowledged impartiality. Lloyd George found him reluctant at first to become embroiled in an issue bristling with controversy, but the Prime Minister hit on a formula which placed Smuts "above the battle" and still guaranteed a systematic inquiry.

6

The two Smuts Reports, the first on the deplorable state of London's defences, the second on the best method of reorganising the British air effort to suit all parties, are complementary documents of historical interest. Yet the South African statesman spent little more than a month compiling both. While he was in London collecting, sifting and compressing the oral and written evidence of many witnesses, Trenchard in France was stealing time from his duties at the front to survey likely bombing bases, in keeping with his promise to Lloyd George in June. He had not been bluffing or merely "showing willing." Trenchard believed in bombing sufficiently to know that airfields were as vital to him as suitable machines. The latter might or might not be manufactured in time, the former had to be inspected, selected, then begged or borrowed and prepared. And du Peuty had already assured him that available sites were few and far between.

Brancker, who had now taken over Henderson's duties in all but name, appreciated Trenchard's anxiety to push on. The dispute between Haig and Robertson over the size of the future bomber force was academic and did not stir him.

" Do your best to get this out," Trenchard wrote to Brancker, asking for detailed estimates of Robertson's forty-squadron plan for the Commander-in-Chief, "because I must get to work expanding the depots . . . I should like to be able to include in my scheme one or two groups of bombing squadrons, if they're coming to us before the spring. This matter is very urgent as I want to do it in the next fortnight."

The time factor influenced him above all else. While Haig was wrangling with Robertson, and Henderson was "guiding" Smuts, Trenchard was travelling hundreds of miles through eastern France on odd days in July and early August, whenever the opening phase of the Flanders offensive was interrupted by the torrential rain and he could leave with an easier conscience.

The slow progress of the latest British push was the least of Trenchard's worries. He was far more appalled by the sombre proof he encountered on his journeys farther afield that French morale had not yet recovered from the Nivelle fiasco of four months ago. One unforgettable late July day, Trenchard and Baring were delayed for hours outside the village of Provins, some thirty miles east of Melun, by a disorderly mob of French soldiers marching officerless from the front. The men had thrown down their arms. Some were hostile; most were apathetic. At one stage he and Baring had got out of the car in an imprudent attempt to clear a path through the ragged lines of men choking the road like a disorderly football crowd. This provoked a minor demonstration. Trenchard decided that it would be better to wait.

That had been the worst episode, and it branded itself on his mind. He had sworn Baring to say nothing about it to anyone. *En route* to more distant French airfields they witnessed similar scenes, the total effect of which confirmed past rumours of mutinies. The French authorities had evidently striven to conceal the facts from their Allies in the interests of military survival. Trenchard reached that conclusion before reporting his experiences to Haig. The Commander-in-Chief's dry, unsurprised comment told him everything: he had no further need of explanations. This new battle in the north, he realised, was more than another round in the interminable war of attrition. Haig dared not slacken his drive, lose the initiative, and allow the enemy to fall prematurely on the French. If he failed to keep the Germans at full stretch, they would cut through France like a knife through butter before the year was out.

It is doubtful whether more than a dozen senior officers, including Robertson, were fully aware of the British Commander-in-Chief's motive for concealing from Lloyd George and the War Cabinet the real reason for maintaining the offensive to the bitter end that autumn. It is certain that few realised more vividly than Trenchard why Pétain had insisted on absolute security. Only the British Army could buy time to stop the rot in the French forces.

The official British historian, Sir James Edmonds, drawing on unrivalled sources of information, wrote thus of Trenchard's experiences in his detailed account of the aftermath of the Nivelle offensive:

" He was quartered behind the French Aisne front at various times in the summer of 1917 for reconnaissances in connection with the establishment of a base for an independent air force in an eastern area, and saw soldiers and civilians alike continually streaming back southwards along all the roads in fear of a German attack. His car was held up for six hours in a village, the road being completely blocked by a rabble of soldiers and refugees with their belongings."[10]

What Trenchard had seen served only to deepen his understanding of Haig's lonely difficulties and to sharpen his contempt for the latter's political enemies. It did little to blunt his practical faith in the merits of a well-planned bombing offensive: he merely questioned whether an offensive on the scale he knew to be necessary was yet within the realm of possibility.

10. The Hostage

It took the Smuts Committee barely two months to interview witnesses, sift contradictory evidence, then marshal and draft conclusions with a sense of urgency rarely surpassed in Whitehall. The report of 6000 words was a masterpiece of compression which could not wholly conceal the marks of hasty composition. What finally saved it from the wastepaper basket was not the logic of its demand for an independent air force, but the fears of the Cabinet about the general military outlook. It seemed, towards the end of August, 1917, that the conflict would drag on indefinitely unless the strategic monopoly of Haig and Robertson could somehow be curbed.

A later generation like ours, which has seen vindicated in the Second World War the apocalyptic vision of air-power usually ascribed to Smuts, may wonder why the report begot strenuous opposition at the time. Few would quarrel now with its central assumption that "the day may not be far off when aerial operations, with their devastation of enemy lands and destruction of industrial and populace centres on a vast scale, may become the principal operations of war, to which the older forms of military and naval operations may become secondary and subordinate . . ." Yet many quarrelled with it then, and rightly so, as something totally irrelevant to the strategic opportunities and supply problems of a land-locked war approaching its climatic point. Trenchard, with his unmatched experience of the effects and limitation of air operations, including bombing, quickly proved the sceptic *par excellence*, much to Henderson's annoyance and Smuts's distress. He received an advance copy of the report from Lord Hugh Cecil, a staff officer at R.F.C. Headquarters' staff until his recall to assist the Smuts Committee, and was not in the least put out by the prophetic passages. He was at one with the joint authors, for instance, in accepting without reservation the "almost boundless" potentialities of aircraft as future weapons. Where he disagreed with them was on the expediency of forcing development prematurely, above all through a separate Ministry, at such an hour of acute danger.

On the night of Tuesday, 28th August, Haig noted in his diary after a conversation with Trenchard:

" The War Cabinet have evidently decided on creating a new department to deal with air operations, on the lines of the War Office and the Admiralty. Trenchard is much perturbed as to the result of this new departure just at a time when the Flying Corps was beginning to feel that it had become an important part of the army. The best solution would be to have one Minister of Defence with the three offices under him, viz: Admiralty, War Office, Air."

Trenchard was not alone in fearing the dislocation that would be caused by placing the naval and Flying Corps squadrons under an independent Air Ministry. Several members of the Government, including Milner and Cowdray, took the same view, as did all senior R.F.C. officers, with the distinguished exception of Henderson. Knowing this, any smaller or more prudent man than Smuts might have tempered his verdict to the prevailing current of opinion; but the South African had sufficient insight to understand why Henderson despaired of the system of dual control under which the R.F.C. and the Naval Air Service continued, as separate and competitive forces, to impair each other's efficiency. A merger would end that wasteful process; more important still, a combined air staff would be better able to reallocate resources so that the bombing of Germany might become feasible in 1918. From this last proposition Trenchard most strongly dissented. For he knew, if Smuts did not, that it rested on false promises; and impulsively he blamed Henderson for not warning Smuts against accepting the lavish production estimates of the optimists at their face value. In Trenchard's opinion, only a genius with absolute powers could carry out the changes proposed without serious danger to the fighting efficiency of the Flying Corps. Revolutions on paper were, he felt, poor prescriptions for winning battles.

At the end of August Lloyd George left London for Criccieth, suffering from overwork and depression. Bonar Law, who presided over the Cabinet in his absence, had little taste for strategic controversy, and no mind ever to commit himself when in doubt. So far Haig's offensive before Ypres had achieved so little that the Prime Minister was again said to be toying with the idea of replacing him. Meanwhile the attitude of his colleagues to Smuts's controversial proposals had lost none of its tepidity. Only Curzon and Churchill, whom Lloyd George had installed at some political risk as Minister of Munitions in July, seemed anxious to act on them; but the careful Bonar Law had no immediate intention of fomenting unnecessary trouble.

Derby, the Secretary of State for War, blew hot and cold in turn. Balfour, true to his beliefs as a former First Lord, opposed any changes that diminished the Royal Navy's right to regulate its own affairs.[1] The judicial view of Balfour influenced that of Sir Eric Geddes, who had lately superseded Carson at the Admiralty and did not relish further aggravating Sea Lords resentful of certain reforms he had just introduced in the cause of greater efficiency. Much depended therefore on the view of Cowdray; but the President of the Air Board, flattered as he was by the prospect of unprecedented powers, doubted whether these should be used to build a separate bomber force for the immediate waging of war on German cities.

" I am driven to request," he wrote, " that the Air Board should now be turned into a permanent Ministry, presumably by Act of Parliament, so as to place it in a position to secure a war staff of recognised experts."

These staff experts would certainly not be employed planning air operations which might well cut across the tactical requirement of army and navy. Cowdray was determined for practical reasons to let sleeping dogs lie.

" It appears to me beyond question," he concluded, " that during the war the administration of the Naval and Military Air Services as they at present exist, or will exist when their imperative needs are satisfied, should not be changed. . . ."

Despite these divided counsels, the Cabinet accepted the Smuts plan in principle when the professional heads of the War Office and Admiralty belied the doubts of Derby and Geddes by giving it their guarded blessing. Brancker, whose letters to Trenchard in July and August were peppered with scathing references to what he termed "the Royal Imperial Air Service," was frankly incredulous. The disarming reasonableness of Robertson was beyond comprehension. Admirals, he implied, were benighted enough for anything; but the C.I.G.S., he suggested, was not running with the hare and hounds merely for the exercise.

Early in September, Trenchard thanked Hugh Cecil for sending him the Air Report and asked pointedly whether he had written it.

" Smuts's report to the Cabinet was drafted for him (I think) by Major Storr of the Cabinet Secretariat, certainly not by me, though I was consulted about it," Cecil replied. " It states the policy pretty cleverly. I thought the bombing plans rather visionary, but I was so anxious for a change that I did not pour cold water."

In Trenchard's opinion, the plans were simply out of tune with the facts of production and the strategic realities. Only a giant combining administrative genius with absolute authority could make them work; and there were no giants in Whitehall so far as he knew, only myopic men who evidently still believed that wars could be won by shuffling papers. Trenchard's mistake was an understandable one. He underestimated the mental stature of Smuts, whom he yet hardly knew. And he had the grace to say so in his autobiographical notes.

" I thought," he wrote, " that if anything were done at that time to weaken the Western Front, the war would be lost and there would be no air service, united or divided. I wanted to unify it, but later on at a more suitable opportunity. Smuts thought it should be done at once, and he proved right. It was a fearful risk at the time, but we managed to work it and yet not get defeated in the field on the Western Front.

" This made it possible to form the air service on a sound basis when the Great War was finished, and I doubt now that we could have unified it then, with the opposition from the army and the navy we would have had, bearing in mind the terrific efforts made by the two older services to break us up *after* we had been amalgamated."

Trenchard's attitude was less detached in 1917. Then, it seemed, he was being invited to barter everything he had learnt and gained in action against the enemy for a planner's pipe dream. The R.F.C.'s *raison d'être* was to support the army. What military advantages could there be in forcing its squadrons, at shotgun point, into an illtimed political liaison with those of the Royal Navy? Little by little, under pressure of events, Trenchard had succeeded in squeezing piecemeal reinforcements out of the Admiralty. He nursed the delusion that by the same process the Naval Air Service, in which the Sea Lords appeared to have small faith, would be absorbed into the Royal Flying Corps. A less single-minded leader would have realised that such miracles of expediency seldom happen, least of all in a crisis of military confidence, without political direction from above.

The only senior officer who welcomed the prospect of a united air force under its own Minister was Henderson, whose present appreciation of supply problems in Britain confirmed his earlier experience of the military difficulties in France. The extent to which his opinions weighed against those of Haig and Trenchard has never been fully acknowledged. Yet Smuts trusted him implicitly and leaned on him increasingly as the debate waxed fiercer from September, 1917, onwards.

" Henderson had twice the insight and understanding that I had," Trenchard admitted in retrospect. " He was prepared to run risks rather than lose a chance which he saw might never come again. He did so with no thought of self-interest, and it is doubtful whether the R.A.F. or Britain realises its debt to him, which is at least as great as its debt to Smuts."

Haig wasted little time in dismissing the scheme for a separate air force as militarily unsound. In mid-September, when invited to comment, he emphasised "the grave danger of an Air Ministry, charged with such powers as the Committee recommends, assuming control with a belief in theories which are not in accordance with practical experience."

What he chiefly disliked, and here Trenchard sympathised, was the implication running through the Smuts Report that total victory would come by means of an air campaign. At a time when the French were unready for offensive action, the Italians tottering, the Russians in disarray, and the British alone struggling forward yard by yard to clear the ridges overlooking Ypres in one of the muddiest, bloodiest, most gallant, most necessary yet apparently most pointless of preventive actions in military history, such wishful thinking hardly bore examining. Haig contented himself with the acid reminder:

" After more than three years of war our armies are still very far short of their (air) requirements, and my experience of repeated failure to fulfil promises makes me somewhat sceptical as to the large surplus of machines and personnel on which the Committee counts in its report."

Some of the most inspired discoveries owe their origin to misconceptions. If Aristotle had not wrongly assumed, for instance, that the sun moved round the earth, mankind, for good or ill, might have been deprived of his theory of causation. If Smuts had not been misled into supposing that Britain's aircraft industry in late 1917 was capable of producing a surplus big enough to sustain a separate force for independent bombing operations, it is questionable whether he would have listened to Henderson or signed the Air Report that bears his name.

It is therefore worth analysing the reasoning which led him to conclude that air-power could become a war-winning instrument. Trenchard accepted the conclusion, rejecting only the time-premise on which it rested. Haig rejected both the premise and conclusion.

" In our opinion," Smuts declared, " there is no reason why the Air Board should any longer continue in its present form as practically no more than a conference room between the older services, and there is every reason why it should be raised to the status of an independent ministry. . . .

" The urgency for the change will appear from the following facts. Hitherto aircraft production has been insufficient to supply the demands of both army and navy, and the chief concern of the Air Board has been to satisfy the necessary requirements of those services. But that phase is rapidly passing. The programme of aircraft production for the following twelve months is far in excess of army and navy requirements.

" Next spring and summer the position will be that the army and navy will have all the air service required in connection with their operations. . . . This means that the Air Board has already reached the stage where the settlement of future war policy in the air war has become necessary. Otherwise engines and machines useless for independent strategical operations may be built. The necessity for an Air Ministry and Air General Staff has therefore become urgent. . . ."

Smuts's optimism about supplies gave generous rein to his imagination. He felt safe in predicting that the air war would transform itself within twelve months.

". . . While our Western Front may be moving forward at a snail's pace in Belgium and France," he said, " the air battle front in 1918 will be far behind on the Rhine. . . . Its continuous and intense pressure against the chief industrial centres of the enemy as well as on his lines of communication may form the determining factor in bringing about the peace. . . ."[2]

Trenchard realised that Smuts was arguing from an unwarranted assumption. Who on earth, he wondered, was going to build this new bomber fleet? The Americans?

Not until the end of September, when he in turn was pressed to comment, did Trenchard openly pose that question. He could not have chosen a more dramatic or a less happy moment. For the Germans again intervened in the discussion by resuming their air-raids on Britain. A few naval zeppelins joined forces with the Gothas in bombing London and towns on the East Coast by moonlight. Damage and casualties were slight, but industrial output in scores of war factories suffered heavily. Public alarm was not lightened by allegations, which inspection substantially confirmed, that as much damage had been caused by the shells of the defenders as by the bombs of the intruders. On 1st October, after the capital had endured four noisy and sleepless nights in succession, a weary War Cabinet deliberated its next step. That evening Robertson wired Haig:

" Cabinet desires immediate action against those German objectives which can be reached from neighbourhood of Nancy. Send Trenchard over at once to me to discuss scale on which you can undertake these operations and necessary arrangements for them. Cabinet wish for at least one squadron to be employed and with least possible delay."

Trenchard's flight from France the following morning, 2nd October, had the makings of a slightly farcical melodrama. After being delayed by mist, the three R.E.8s containing him and his staff took off in visibility that worsened as they approached the English coast. The pilot of the second machine, carrying Baring, lost touch with the pilot of the first, carrying Trenchard, though both were flying at only 800 feet; and the tentative gropings of the third R.E.8, which tried vainly to trace them in the murk, overtaxed the nerves of the commander responsible for various anti-aircraft units scattered across Kent and Sussex. A general alert was sounded; spasmodic firing broke out; Trenchard eventually motored into London from Lympne, where his aircraft had made an emergency landing, amazed at the half-empty pavements and thoroughfares. As a portent of nervous confusion in high places, the spectacle was not reassuring. He was still less amused to learn that the business of the capital had been slowed down for several hours because of his arrival by air.

That afternoon Trenchard explained to the War Cabinet that his first bomber airfield at Ochey, near Nancy, was ready. Lloyd George, looking ill and drawn despite his recent holiday, was relieved to hear it. How soon, he asked, would R.F.C. bombers be able to operate from Ochey?

Trenchard replied: " Six days after arriving there."

The Prime Minister stressed the urgency of replying in kind to the enemy's assaults on England. Trenchard, he hoped, would speed these operations for which two flights of de Havillands and another of naval Handley Pages were promised in addition to the squadron that was about to be detached from the Flying Corps' Headquarters Wing. The bombing from Ochey would not fail, Trenchard assured the Prime Minister; success, however, must be related to the size of the force, to its lack of experience, and to the obstacles of distance and weather. If Lloyd George was seeking cheap propaganda triumphs, he might be disappointed.

Before returning to France, Trenchard had his first lengthy conversation with Smuts, whom he had met briefly twice before. He was impressed by his obvious sagacity, sincerity and candour. Smuts announced at once how shocked he had been to find that Trenchard's scepticism about production prospects was better founded than anyone else had led him to suppose. The scheme for establishing an Air Ministry, he admitted, hinged on estimates which had turned out to be wildly high. He had been budgeting on a surplus of 3000 machines; he had since been informed that these would not be available when needed. Discrepancies between Air Board figures and actual deliveries could be put right; Weir no doubt would do his best; but it was for the Cabinet to rouse itself first from its torpor of indecision, and he would do his utmost to that end.

" I am," he wrote in a restrained memorandum to the War Cabinet shortly after Trenchard left London, "somewhat alarmed by the backwardness of our preparations. . . . General Trenchard is quite clear that the enemy has never been stronger in the air than he is to-day, and that relatively we are not so strong as we were some months ago. . . . General Trenchard, therefore, presses for an acceleration of our aircraft programme so that this position may be improved instead of worsened before the winter. . . . As regards the bombing campaign of next spring and summer, the fear amongst officers is chiefly that the enemy is making very great preparations to recover ascendancy in the air, and that success for him in that respect may have far-reaching consequences on the course of the war.

" Even from a purely defensive view, therefore, we are called upon to make a very great effort in the air. But our preparations should be on such a scale as not only to make our defensive position secure, but to enable us to gain a decisive superiority on the battle fronts so that the road may be clear for our offensive bombing policy against the industrial and munition centres of Germany."

The additional reminder that Trenchard still awaited bomber and fighter squadrons officially approved as long ago as 1916 did not, however, stir Lloyd George as Smuts had hoped. The Prime Minister appeared listless and despondent; events seemed momentarily to have got on top of him. Smuts's original idea had appealed to him as the germ of an alternative strategy, immediately exploitable and more economic in outlay of lives and weapons than methods of attrition on the ground. Now, it seemed, the practical effectiveness of the plan had been exposed by no less a person than Trenchard, whose feeling that the R.F.C. had been badly let down and possessed only a bare sufficiency of weapons for its immediate tasks, was upheld by Smuts.

Lloyd George's memoirs are significantly reticent about the hesitancy which beset him and most of his colleagues at this time. An atmosphere of gloom enveloped Cabinet discussions. Parliament was still in recess, and the censorship obscured official uncertainty from the public. This fortunate circumstance was due to the prescience of Smuts, who had suggested at the outset that too much publicity, good or bad, would hamper progress and possibly spur the Germans similarly to reorganise their own air resources. The restriction of exchanges to Ministers and experts was unappetising to Lloyd George, who liked an audience, and was not wholly at ease playing the impresario in an empty theatre. That he finally resisted the temptation to drop the scheme can be largely attributed to the persistence of Smuts.[3]

Unlike Trenchard, Smuts had begun to question the competence of Haig, whose refusal to call off the Ypres offensive despite appalling conditions, staggering losses and negligible tactical gains, struck him as the abnegation of good generalship. A break-through along the wooded ridge which ran from Staden to Passchendaele village appeared beyond hope. Unofficial accounts spoke of armed deadlock in a vast man-made marsh heaped with the killed and drowned. Yet the exaltation of the official *communiqués* spoke only of steady progress. The long, doleful lists of casualties and the evidence of interminable stalemate conveyed a different message as the weeks wore on: the original purpose of the offensive, that of pushing back the Germans and opening the way to the Channel ports, had not merely been overtaken by events but sacrificed by Haig to the ends of attrition. Gunfire and practically incessant autumn rain had reduced the salient to a quagmire in which the wounded often sank without trace as the battle to consolidate a few square miles of bog squelched mercilessly on. Lloyd George's distaste for the primitive pattern of Haig's strategy was more fiercely emotional than Smuts's; but the Prime Minister lacked the moral courage to will as he wished. Instead of an ultimatum, the Commander-in-Chief received a congratulatory message "upon the achievements of the British Armies in Flanders," on 16th October, the day after Parliament reassembled.

The Government's misgivings about Haig were still masked. Behind the scenes, Smuts accepted the commission to head another Cabinet Committee—that palliative for all but the most hopeless emergencies—charged with the still harder task of scrutinising war production and reordering industrial priorities so that aircraft output should be doubled. As committees went, this one was representative and well balanced. In addition to Geddes from the Admiralty and Derby from the War Office, Smuts enlisted Churchill and Cowdray to advise him. The inquisition was bound to take weeks, if not months, and would not necessarily commit the Government in the end, but Lloyd George needed the interval badly: for though Smuts had reawakened his desire for an air force liberated from the dead hand of Haig and capable of carrying the war into Germany, the rest of the Cabinet had still to be persuaded. Unlike Churchill in 1940, Lloyd George had no assured backing in Parliament or Cabinet, no comparable personal standing in the country, which enabled him to snap his fingers at waverers. His enemies were powerful, his friends few and fickle, his leadership, therefore, still a thing of sufferance. To force through the sweeping changes advocated by Smuts might precipitate a political crisis.

Yet time itself was against Lloyd George, badly as he needed it. Hints of the Cabinet's infirmity of purpose had begun to creep into the Press even before the reassembly of Parliament in mid-October. People were growing restive. When did the Government intend to hit back at the enemy? It was no idle question. The continued ordeal of London and other towns within range of Gothas and zeppelins could no longer be brushed aside with smooth parliamentary answers. Committees, even committees headed by the redoubtable Smuts, were no substitute for British bombs on German towns. The Cabinet were partly in Trenchard's hands. What was *he* up to? Had he not promised to start his air offensive from Ochey "almost at once?"

On 5th October Smuts asked the Cabinet whether any decision had been reached about the air force. The Prime Minister hedged. The time was "not ripe" he said, for any "premature disclosure" of plans. On 10th October, Cowdray disclosed in strict confidence to Admiral Mark Kerr, a fairly new and spirited member of his board, that the War Cabinet had virtually decided against a separate Air Ministry. Kerr was horrified. Since being seconded from the Admiralty in August, he had specialised in the study of enemy war production. His researches convinced him that in Germany the highest priority was being given to aircraft. So Kerr impetuously put pen to paper, imploring the Cabinet in vigorous terms to think again. There was little in his unexpected broadside that had not been said or written before; but its sharp timeliness carried inordinate weight and evidently induced ministerial waverers to reconsider well.

On 15th October, the day before Bonar Law rose to inform the Commons that an Air Ministry would *definitely* be created, the Leader of the House treated the subject with guarded vagueness. The Government, he said when questioned, intended to introduce a Bill to "co-ordinate" the air services of army and navy. Then, sensing perhaps the impatience and dissatisfaction of many M.P.s, Bonar Law went beyond his brief. Few parliamentarians had a finer perception of the undercurrents of opinion at such moments; fewer still would have responded on impulse and boldly committed the Cabinet to a plan which hitherto it would have gladly shelved. Within a month the necessary Bill was drafted and presented to a Parliament more willing for a change than Lloyd George had imagined.

2

On 17th October, Trenchard kept a promise. Exactly six days after reaching Ochey from the north, two flights of de Havilland bombers took off for the Flying Corps's first long-range attack on a German target, the Burbach iron foundry, near Saarbrücken. Direct hits were scored on buildings and railway lines in broad daylight without serious opposition. A week later, naval pilots of the Handley Page squadron joined R.F.C. crews in the first night raid of the war on this distant objective. And before October ended the citizens of the Saar were imbued with the same feelings of angry defencelessness which had filled Londoners since the summer. Defying variable winds, intense cold, bad visibility and the hazards of primitive navigation aids, the new 41st Wing at Ochey achieved more in a fortnight than Trenchard had expected in a month. Whenever it was humanly possible to order them off the rain-soaked ground, the overburdened machines would roar east to drop an average bomb-load of ten tons on each trip.

Lieutenant-Colonel Cyril Newall, the commanding officer, knew his business. And Trenchard had been more than generous with weapons and advice. His broad directive—"learn as you go, but don't give the enemy time to draw back "—stirred many memories. Ever since the summer of 1916, when Newall replaced Dowding as leader of the Headquarters Wing on the Somme, bombing by night as well as by day had gradually become the special task of this élite force under Trenchard's personal control. Then they had hammered away at the airfields of Richthofen's fighter formations behind the battle front.

Now, without landmarks or escort, the F.E.2s of 100 Squadron flew thrice as far afield after dusk in search of factories unmarked on the maps. The longest missions in the past had carried pilots 160 miles into Belgium and back. Many of the same crews were now being schooled to disregard the discomfort, boredom, monotony and dragging uncertainty on round flights of 300 miles and more.

For the D.H.4s of 55 Squadron, daylight missions were at least as perilous. Nobody could ever say with any assurance: " This is my point of no return," and calculate accordingly. Even with extra fuel tanks these machines left little margin for navigational errors, let alone for clashes with fighters. The bigger Handley-Pages were better off in that respect. Yet luck, skill, phlegmatic determination and enemy unpreparedness balanced the odds at first. When wintry weather shut out the November sky and grounded the squadrons, only five bombers had gone missing. A windfall of 50 new D.H.4s, originally earmarked for a Russian front that had rapidly disintegrated after the Bolshevik Revolution, provided Trenchard with an immediate reserve.

The Government seemed inordinately pleased with him. The propaganda value of the raids at that moment was the dominant factor, and Trenchard's personal stock as a commander and organiser had never stood higher in Whitehall.[4] Yet he himself took a less rosy view than the politicians of the Ochey experiment. Newall's Wing was a small but integral offshoot of his command; the targets, like the machines and pilots, were of his own choosing, but he disliked having to split and spread his relatively meagre force for two distinct and unrelated bombing campaigns; nevertheless, he deliberately set out to convince the War Cabinet by deeds that the R.F.C.'s greatest need was a steady flow of supplies to increase the Ochey Wing's effectiveness, not an Act of Parliament to declare its independence.

His attitude was tempered by common sense and a political simplicity bordering on naïveté. While suspecting that the plan for uniting the air services was founded on political expediency, he accepted it as his duty not to obstruct development unless he could usefully advise or criticise. Smuts's error in overestimating aircraft output was more excusable than the hallucinations of those who supposed that after three years of war an air force could be made to perform the impossible by legislation.

Trenchard wished at times that his views were better understood by senior army officers, many of whom deplored the sight of R.F.C. machines swarming on distant missions, while the bitterly contested

Left: Sir David Henderson, photographed before the outbreak of war. *Below:* Winston Churchill after a flight in 1915

Above: the Fokker E1, which had more effect on aerial warfare in World War I than any other 'plane. This was the first fixed-gun fighter, with a device enabling the bullets to pass between its propeller blades. *Below:* the Gotha G 5, the German bombers used in the raids over London in 1917

A Nieuport Scout, over No Man's Land between the lines

The British night bomber FE 2B in flight

advances from Polygon Wood and the Menin road to the ruins of
Passchendaele were slowed down further by unopposed attacks of
low-flying German fighters on the hapless British infantry.

" Other arms will in time be no more surprised at seeing a low-
flying aeroplane than they would be by the explosion of a shell,"
he stated in a reply circulated with Haig's permission. " And just
as no defensive measures against shells will enable us to master and
silence the enemy's artillery, so no defensive measures either on the
ground or in the air will enable us to defeat the enemy's low-flying
aircraft. . . .

" As aviation develops further new factors are certain to arise.
Aeroplanes will not only fight in formation, but formations will be
led and commanded by one machine by wireless telephone or
wireless signals. But whatever new developments arise, one thing is
sure and certain. The aeroplane is a weapon which has no other
exact counterpart any more than a submarine, a cruiser, a destroyer,
a gun, a tank or a horse. It has its own definite limitations and powers,
but the principles which guide it in warfare . . . are those which guide
all other arms in all other elements of warfare, and the most important
of these is the will and power to attack the enemy, to force him to
fight and to defeat him."

To Trenchard's mind, the politicians were as reprehensible as the
soldiers for refusing to acknowledge the limitations of aircraft.
Recent events at Westminster, where the Air Force Bill was going
through unquestioned, had re-emphasised that fact. Trenchard
wondered how far distrust of Haig and Robertson entered into it. The
C.I.G.S. had so far not raised a finger against the scheme for an
independent air force, possibly hoping that it would collapse of its
own accord. This, no doubt, explained why Robertson had quietly
avenged himself on Henderson and (more unjustly) on Brancker for
having assisted Smuts during "school hours." Trenchard was not
surprised to hear of the ensuing purge; but his sorrow at Henderson's
removal from the Army Council hardly matched his apprehension at
Brancker's demotion as Acting Director General of Military
Aeronautics. Trenchard endorsed the latter's protest to Derby at
being abruptly replaced by an elderly army general who lacked all
practical knowledge of aviation.

" My interview with Derby was amusing," Brancker wrote.
" He told me that he'd wanted to get you here and me to France,
but that Douglas Haig wouldn't part with you."

It was quite true, as Trenchard knew. The craze for reshuffling
key men like aces in a pack of cards was an affront to any sane man's

intelligence. Trenchard had been dumbfounded when Derby, on a
recent visit to France, confided that the Cabinet were anxious to
recall him at once.[5] No prospect could have attracted him less; and
he proceeded to tell Derby so in such immoderate language that
Baring, who was present, indignantly rebuked him afterwards. The
little contretemps blew over quickly. For Haig officially notified
Derby a day or two later: " I cannot spare Trenchard."

Robertson, for different reasons, seemed equally anxious to be
rid of Brancker. And Derby did not lift a finger to save him, despite
Trenchard's intercession.

In mid-October a splenetic farewell note reached R.F.C.
Headquarters from the man who had co-operated so selflessly and
effectively with its commander for two chaotically trying years:

" They have got me all right at last! " Brancker wrote. " I am
to go to Egypt—Jack Salmond is to take Henderson's place on the
Army Council, Henderson is to go to the Air Ministry permanently.
It's very clever, and I don't know how far you have helped them
indirectly. ' Wully ' (backed up by you) is up against the Air
Ministry. He *thinks* I am an ardent supporter of it (I am not very
much really). . . . He has never seen Salmond and knows nothing
about him; but he gets rid of Henderson and side-tracks me with one
blow and I have no case against the move this time. . . . It makes
me smile. Of course, your everlasting criticism of everything at home
has given them a good lever—and as I always told you, everybody's
sins have eventually fallen on my head."

Trenchard did not reply. He saw no point in raking up dead
embers. The C.I.G.S. was not the easiest of overlords; and
Brancker's outspokenness, a quality which endeared him to Trenchard, had been his undoing at Robertson's hands. How would
Salmond, so inexperienced by comparison, fare in an atmosphere so
poisoned by misunderstanding? The least Trenchard felt that he
should do was to offer him some timely advice.

" Remember in your dealings with the War Office that we are
part of the army and that we are not trying to run a separate show
at their expense," he wrote. " Although at times the Flying Corps
conflicts with other arms, at the same time remember that there are
two sides to every question and be certain that what you ask for is
really necessary. . . . Don't forget that you must decide in favour of
a machine or engine, etc., which some technical experts are against.
No two technical experts agree. I listen to one and am guided only
by one and never more than one, and sometimes go against his
opinions. . . .

" You can do nothing with a rush. Take your time over everything and make up your own mind and keep to it, unless there is a
sound argument against your decision which you had not thought
of before. With regard to discipline, the Flying Corps has not got a
very good name in England, I'm afraid, owing to so many scandals.
Deal with these cases fairly drastically, even if the man is not to
blame. It's a good thing to put him somewhere else as he can't do
his best work if people think there's something against him. As to
my duds which I have been sending home from time to time, it's
useful to return them to their units. . . .

" Burn this letter, and the best of luck to you in your new job."

John Salmond, however, was nobody's fool. His personality
might lack fire and colour, but his brain was quick and cool. Within
three weeks of taking up his unfamiliar post, he put a sharp finger
on the cause of half the R.F.C.'s production troubles. The supplies
and contracts branch of the Air Board, he complained, consisted
of people who lived permanently in clouds of bright, theoretical
figures.

" Practically not a single one of their estimates has been met,"
he told Trenchard in astonishment. " Consequently, programmes
which had worked in the past on (their) expectations have not had
the slightest chance of being fulfilled."

Salmond, for one, was aware that these were the men who had
inadvertently misled Smuts. And though Trenchard advised him
to hold his tongue, Salmond stored up a peck of trouble for himself,
first by counselling the supply experts to review their calculations
which "were so seriously interfering with programmes and, consequently, with operations in the field," then, when this was ignored,
by prodding Cowdray and Robertson until the issue was brought
into daylight.

In spite of himself, Trenchard was delighted; he joined in the
Air Board exchanges with relish. The pot was being stirred so
vigorously by so many self-styled cooks that nobody in his opinion
could tell what was brewing. Trenchard expected no thanks for again
questioning air production estimates from the operational point of
view. His intervention, indeed, roused more hostility than Salmond's.
He was accused by the more fanatical experts of splitting technical
hairs, of delaying the bombing programme and, by implication, of
sabotaging Cabinet policy.

Characteristically he ignored the insults and bombarded the Air
Board with incontestable facts. His confidential letters to Salmond
echo the longer official arguments he used in his efforts to dissuade

the unteachable from pursuing the unreachable. The forty bomber squadrons planned for 1918 would, he feared, never materialise.

" I do not think it can be done in the time," he explained. " I think if you got only twenty up to the end of next year we should have some chance of carrying through the programme properly."

Quite apart from numbers, the quality of the new and heavier de Havilland bomber which had been ordered in unseemly haste seemed to Trenchard an added reason for caution: " I saw de Havilland to-night (25th November) and he said he was very uneasy on the subject of what we were going to use the D.H.9 for in these large numbers. He also told me he was afraid the D.H.10 was not much better in performance. . . .

" I want to bomb Germany, but please remember that if we lose half our machines doing so, the good morale effect which is three-quarters of the work will be on the German side and not ours.

" I am in no way trying to upset the policy of the War Cabinet for bombing Germany with a large number of machines. What I am trying to do is to do it efficiently, and the crux of the whole matter seems to be whether we are going to have efficient machines to do it with."

This was hardly the language of a man whom certain critics still thought of with disapproval as a butcher who had brought to air fighting the gory finality of the knacker's yard. Yet those who believed that his view merely reflected a wayward desire to obstruct were almost as numerous as those who felt that the old blood-letter was on the rampage again, vainly trying to convert experts to his ludicrous theory that twenty squadrons could do the work of forty.

On 29th November, Trenchard returned briefly to a London gloomily regretting its premature jubilation over Haig's recent tank victory at Cambrai. He appeared once more before the Air Board to press his argument. Go ahead if you must with the new de Havilland, he advised; but in the name of reason treat it only as a stop-gap. It would be useful enough in the New Year, while the enemy's guard was down; but commit me to it in excessive numbers, and "we shall lose so many pilots as to make the continuation and extension of long distance bombing almost impossible."

David Henderson openly disagreed. If the new bombers were unfit for their task, he retorted, " it may be inadvisable to attempt any bombing until a better machine is produced, by which time again the German machines may also have improved. If the D.H.9 is fit for day bombing, then the more of them we use the better." Rather unfairly, Henderson went on to upbraid Trenchard for opposing a policy which the Government had underwritten. The familiar accusation, coming from such a source, grieved Trenchard. Could not two men honestly differ, he asked, without impugning one another's good faith?

While this technical wrangle was in progress, an event of more momentous significance was being staged without fanfare in another part of Westminster. On the afternoon of 29th November, the Air Force Bill received the Royal Assent. The measure which owed so much to the initiative of Smuts had become law after a passage through Parliament of remarkable speed and smoothness, in view of its many unsettled and conflicting implications. The Minister charged with welding the unmalleable elements of two services into a single whole was too busy that day with formalities to hear Trenchard's views. The chair which Cowdray had occupied with distinction for nearly eleven months was symbolically empty; but unlike Curzon nearly a year before, Cowdray had been unseated. And Lord Rothermere, the man who had succeeded him a few days earlier in grotesque and shameful circumstances, was busy elsewhere.

3

Everyone was agreed that Cowdray had been a successful President of the Air Board. Equable and decisive, he held the respect and trust of the Flying Corps. No officer who crossed his path could have disliked him; and only once had Trenchard irritated him. That had been in September, when Cowdray, paying a long-deferred visit to R.F.C. Headquarters, regaled him with a list of improvements he intended to introduce shortly as Air Minister.

" What makes you so sure *you're* going to be Minister? " Trenchard had inquired. Thrown out of his stride, Cowdray had stared balefully at him, momentarily speechless.

" Why did you say that? " he demanded.

" Because you talk as though the job was in your pocket. I haven't the least idea who's going to be Minister, but my information is that it's not going to be you."

In the ordinary way, gossip was the bane of Trenchard's life. He rarely indulged in it. On this occasion he did so provocatively to shake the complacency of a man whom he deeply admired and longed to go on serving. Cowdray fell broodily silent; the subject was not raised again; and Trenchard never troubled to ask afterwards whether a hint, dropped originally by the indiscreet Derby, returned to Cowdray in all its funereal significance when the latter opened *The Times* on 16th November, 1917, and in effect read his own obituary notice.

It was contained in an open letter addressed to Lloyd George by Northcliffe, the proprietor of *The Times*, who mockingly thanked the Prime Minister for his "repeated invitations that I should take charge of the new Air Ministry," explaining that he must decline the honour of serving Lloyd George and his wobbling Government which were quite unworthy of the people of Britain, its valiant soldiers, and their great Commander-in-Chief. Whatever whim induced the writer to publish such a letter in his own columns, the evidence of political treachery was clear: the Prime Minister had gone behind Cowdray's back, with a knife in one hand and an olive branch intended for Northcliffe in the other, only to be spurned and publicly branded for villainy by the giant of Fleet Street.

" I would as soon go for a sunny evening stroll round Walton Heath with a grasshopper as try and work with Northcliffe," the Prime Minister said on another occasion. But, on 15th November, 1917, Lloyd George not only strove to coax Northcliffe to work with him, but actually persuaded himself that Northcliffe was willing. Over lunch at No. 10 Downing Street, the bait of the new Air Ministry was dangled invitingly under the nose of the powerful Press lord whom the Prime Minister secretly scorned as " Haig's kettle-drum." Cowdray was a minor obstacle. Though he also owned newspapers, his immediate and potential influence for good or evil was smaller. Any upset caused by Cowdray's departure from the Government would be outweighed by Northcliffe's accession.

Late that night, after presenting Bonar Law with the cheerless news that Northcliffe had been squared with the new Air Ministry, Lloyd George discovered that he had mistaken both his man and his price. Beaverbrook telephoned him to say that the proprietor of *The Times* and *Daily Mail* had changed his mind, and in public. The final sentence of Northcliffe's "open letter" left the world in no possible doubt the following morning exactly where he stood politically.

" In present circumstances," it declared, " I can do better work if I maintain my independence and am not gagged by a loyalty I do not feel towards the whole of your administration."

When Weir walked into Cowdray's office at the Air Board, it was to find him already "fuming over an unprintable letter of resignation." It says much for Cowdray's forbearance that, at Weir's suggestion, he tore up his first draft and sent round to No. 10

Downing Street instead a curt but dignified note in reply to the Prime Minister's glib "explanation" that Northcliffe was better qualified for the job.[6] Northcliffe's report to the Government after an extensive tour of the slowly developing American aircraft industry had demonstrated, to Lloyd George's satisfaction, an instinctive flair for the problems that would eventually confront the Air Force.

Trenchard had been no more impressed by that report than Cowdray. Its sole points of interest were, first, a somewhat superfluous reminder of America's potential as a producer of aero-engines; and, second, a warning that the American Air Service would be unready for the spring campaign on the Western Front. (" It is unlikely that more than 5000 fighting planes fitted with Liberty engines will be in France before July, 1918," Northcliffe had written, provoking Trenchard to question whether there would even be 500, which was incidentally more than the grand total of American-powered machines in front-line service by the Armistice.)

Northcliffe's motives for spurning the Prime Minister's bait need not detain us. Those of Lloyd George are relevant to this story, since he and most of his biographers have thought fit to neglect them. Cowdray's expendability was certainly not due either to lack of drive or to any superiority in Northcliffe, except perhaps as a political mischief-maker. Nor was the Air Board President marked down for extinction merely because he honestly and persistently doubted the administrative wisdom of merging the air services during the war. It would seem that Cowdray accidentally earned the Prime Minister's spite when his two newspapers, the *Westminster Gazette* and *The Star*, published a brief, inaccurate item on 25th September, implying that Lloyd George had left London for the country the previous evening in time to avoid an air-raid. The Prime Minister sued for defamation of character; but the damages and unreserved apologies he extracted from the defendants, including the news agency which had circulated the original message, did not placate the plaintiff. Lloyd George had not quite settled with Cowdray; left to himself, he would probably have done so in his own time. He had good cause to regret Northcliffe's macabre taste for sensation in holding up the avenger's knife for everyone to see.

To Trenchard and others, this squalid episode confirmed that there could be no honour among political desperadoes. The sequel, however, was stranger and less comprehensible. For, after being publicly insulted, the Prime Minister went through the motion of meekly turning the other cheek by inviting Rothermere, Northcliffe's younger brother, to become Air Minister instead. According to Beaverbrook, Rothermere had little in common at this time with the brother whom he had helped to found a newspaper dynasty unrivalled in influence before or since. His friends, tastes and sympathies were different; and, unlike Northcliffe, he wanted to serve the Government, not dictate to it. Whether Beaverbrook is right or wrong in his recollection, the military situation presently drew the Harmsworth brothers closer together than at any period since their early business days.

The piercing of the German front by the massed tank attack at Cambrai early in November came to nothing; Haig was short of reserves to consolidate a local success; the cruel losses sustained farther north about Passchendaele, and the emergency withdrawal from France of five divisions to rally the shattered Italian Army at Caporetto, foiled him yet again.

" I gather that the Prime Minister is dissatisfied," the Commander-in-Chief wrote to Robertson at the War Office on 9th December, when fighting had all but ceased for the winter. " If that means that I have lost his confidence, then in the interests of the cause let him replace me at once."

If Northcliffe instead of Rothermere had joined his Government, Lloyd George might well have risked removing Haig there and then. At G.H.Q., senior staff officers were half expecting it. One of them, Brigadier John Charteris, the Chief of Intelligence, noted in his diary on 12th December:

" The attack on D.H. is in full swing. All our information is that L.G., Curzon and Churchill are out to down him, and will try to do so by attacking him through his staff. . . . If D.H. were to go, I, personally, think there is only one man with the strength to replace him, and he is Trenchard."

This improbable solution, coming from a man so dissimilar in temperament that Trenchard usually contrived to avoid discussing anything serious with Charteris, may be taken as an oblique reflection of the Flying Corps chief's sterling reputation in France. Aware as he now was of the political campaign to undermine Haig, Trenchard never considered himself as a candidate for the succession, and would have ground the whisper underfoot had he heard it. For him, Haig towered above everyone, dwarfing in stature the groups of politicians and "gossips" who seemed to drift endlessly in and out of G.H.Q., presumably spying out the land.

During the autumn of 1917, Major (now Sir) Desmond Morton, who later became one of Churchill's intimates and was his personal assistant at No. 10 Downing Street throughout the Second World

War, served as A.D.C. to Haig. On several occasions he observed Trenchard and Haig in consultation, sometimes standing over battle maps, sometimes poring over official reports and papers spread out before them on a green baize table. Morton, a dispassionate but sensitive witness, discerned the curious bond of sympathy between the pair: " They seemed to read one another's thoughts by some form of instinctive telepathy, expressing themselves aloud with gestures and agricultural grunts rather than with words."

With his personal knowledge of the rot in the French Army—and of Pétain's past insistence that the British must maintain maximum pressure on the enemy—Trenchard was scandalised by this latest attempt to oust Haig. Italy was reeling, Russia out of the ring, the United States not yet in it. France was largely a bystander. Only the battered but undaunted British, led by a resolute Commander-in-Chief, stood between the Germans and complete mastery of the field. Yet so mistrustful was the mood of the War Cabinet that reinforcements were being deliberately withheld from a front which, said Lloyd George, was already "over-insured." The war could be lost on land; it could not conceivably be won at sea or by a sudden knock-out from the air. It was in a morose frame of mind that Trenchard opened a letter from Salmond on 9th December:

" I saw Rothermere. David (Henderson) is in as Chief of (Air) Staff for six months. It is then open for you. This has been arranged by Smuts. Ellington (who at Trenchard's suggestion had gone home to assist Salmond) is to be Liaison between the Air Council and War Office. Brancker has been wired for, in my absence. Rothermere says the Chief of Staff had been arranged by Smuts before his arrival. All I can say is CURSE, and happier days will dawn in six months' time."

" I am very uneasy about David being Chief of Staff," Trenchard replied, " and I am afraid we shall go rapidly backwards, beside making it very hard for you and everyone."

So little was Trenchard addicted to speculating about himself as a movable pawn on the Whitehall chessboard that a wire from Rothermere less than a week later, recalling him at once, caught him wholly unawares. The peremptory nature of the summons seemed a black omen. What had gone wrong? Had Salmond, who confessed to a keen dislike of the new Minister's manners and methods, come to grief so soon? Trenchard was pensive and untalkative as he crossed the Channel with Baring aboard a destroyer on the morning of 16th December.

That afternoon, he entered Rothermere's private suite at the

Ritz Hotel, London, with an odd sense of foreboding. He had not met the Minister before, and was immediately put off by his hearty affability. Rothermere clasped him warmly by the hand, sprayed him with flattery, then introduced two other people whom Trenchard recognised. One was Northcliffe, who emulated his brother in greeting Trenchard like a returning prodigal; the other was Major John Baird, Rothermere's Parliamentary Private Secretary designate, who knew Trenchard better than to fawn on him. Baird wore the slightly strained air of a man with the premonition that a storm was about to break.

Rothermere came to the point briskly. Exuding a charm which was wholly lost on his visitor, he announced that the War Cabinet had upheld his suggestion that Trenchard should be appointed Chief of the new Air Staff. He had not formed too favourable an impression of Salmond, who was unequal to his responsibilities; as for Henderson, there were other plans for his employment. Before the startled Trenchard could speak, Rothermere calmly explained why he wanted him at his elbow rather than anyone else.

" My brother and I are about to launch a Press campaign against Sir Douglas Haig and Sir William Robertson," he said, " quite apart from the fact that you're the best man for the job, your presence at home will greatly assist us."

The words sank deep into Trenchard's memory. He never forgot them nor the feeling of sickening unreality they momentarily caused him. He reacted in a way which neither Northcliffe nor Rothermere had bargained for. He turned the job down flat.

What should have been in normal circumstances a polite, formal interview lasting a few minutes degenerated into an acrimonious argument which continued for twelve and a half hours. Meals were served in the suite as the night wore on. The two brothers, realising that they had misjudged where Trenchard's true sympathies lay, threatened, bullied, cajoled and implored him to change his mind. Boiling with the bewildered wrath of a political innocent, Trenchard realised too late that he had been lured into a web of intrigue by a pair of scoundrels invincibly confident that everyone had his political price.

" I met them at 3 p.m. in the afternoon and the arguments carried on until about three-thirty the following morning," Trenchard wrote. " Rothermere and Northcliffe told me that they were going to start their Press attacks on Haig and Robertson, that they were going to say that neither Haig nor Robertson knew how to use the air, and that if I did not come home they would use that to attack

Haig still more. Major Baird simply listened. I did not know what to do. It was an impossible situation. I warned them that I would not fight the army and navy during the war, but the argument got hotter and more unpleasant, and I was exhausted."

Under Cowdray, it would have been hard enough to unite the air services without friction; under Rothermere it would be quite impossible. The new Minister had only one end in view: to use him (Trenchard) to promote a policy opposed to the interests and needs of the army on the eve of its most arduous trial. The separate air force principle was apparently to be used to break a field-marshal whom the politicians were afraid to break by more straightforward means. Lloyd George had decreed it; Rothermere would contrive it; the megalomaniac Northcliffe, wearying of his old part as "Haig's kettledrum ",[7] yet loth to play second fiddle to a leader of Lloyd George's despicable quality, was deriving vicarious pleasure from composing an improved score for his less creative brother to follow.

Beaverbrook told this author that Lloyd George did not deliberately set a Harmsworth to catch a Harmsworth; Beaverbrook may be right or wrong. Trenchard, judging only by appearances, wondered whether the brothers had not perhaps agreed to share the Air Ministry, Northcliffe settling for what, to him, was the more enticing role of Rothermere's Grey Eminence.

To his own satisfaction at least, Trenchard succeeded in showing them both that neither his soul nor his convictions were for sale. He was less successful in his attempts to defend Haig from their calumnies. He took them back in time on a noisily conducted tour of every battlefield since Neuve Chapelle, finally explaining as best he could Haig's paradoxical reasons for pressing forward, to the last ruined barn of Passchendaele, the offensive which had begun so hopefully at Messines the previous June. He cited his own terrible casualties (nearly 33 per cent in every squadron) as a pledge of his own certainty that the strategy of striking, even at a disadvantage, was preferable to standing on the defensive. His assertion that France had probably been saved to fight again, that six months of precious time had been bought from the enemy at the price of over quarter of a million British dead and wounded, left the Harmsworths unmoved.

He could not reason with them, nor shout them down. So they abandoned the battlefields at last and returned to the original subject. Eventually the brothers wore down Trenchard's resistance: he agreed to accept the post of Chief of the new Air Staff on condition that he must first consult the Commander-in-Chief, who had so far refused even to consider parting with him.

They did not demur. Quite mistakenly, they seemed to imagine that Trenchard had succumbed to threats where persuasion was of no avail. If he rejected the job, they would denounce Haig a little sooner; for the obnoxious pair made that disagreeably clear. They had him either way. The choice lay between two evils, and Trenchard chose the lesser.

" I thought that I might be of more use to the nation, the R.F.C. and the R.N.A.S. if I accepted the post. At the same time I knew that I should have to fight Rothermere and Northcliffe from the day I took the job. I remember so well saying in the end: 'All right, I'll agree to come home, but don't forget I'm not the man you think I am. Don't forget also that I'm neither a good writer nor a good talker.' "8

Then they talked more calmly. Baird, the silent onlooker, at last joined in. Trenchard unfolded his ideas. The air force, he said, must be reconstructed on rational lines. The process must cause the least possible interference with the operational commitments of the other two services. He stated his views on the limitations of bombing as an independent instrument of strategy; surprisingly, they did not dispute these, even when he reminded Northcliffe that it was easier to bomb Berlin in headlines than from the cockpit of any machine likely to be constructed for years.

It must be admitted that Beaverbrook, in *Men and Power*, puts a different construction on these events and their sequel. Had he been better informed, Beaverbrook might have thought twice before pillorying Trenchard as another "army man" who "did not want the divorce of the Royal Flying Corps from the army organisation." The fair-minded reader must judge for himself. It is the first of two flimsy strands of evidence which Beaverbrook, lacking anything better, has twisted into an insubstantial hangman's noose for the neck of Trenchard, that miscreant and miscalled " Father of the Royal Air Force " who by wilfully obstructing the merger of the flying services "tried to strangle the infant at birth." The second strand is an extract from Haig's diary, dated 16th December, 1917:

" General Trenchard also came to see me on his way to his H.Q. from London. Lord Rothermere (head of the Air Board) insists on him (T.) going as Chief of Staff. T. stated that the Air Board are quite off their heads as to the future possibilities of aeronautics for ending the war. I told T. that it was evidently necessary that he should become C. of S. of the Air, much as I regretted parting with him."

Trenchard's version of his interview with Haig that morning runs as follows:

" He asked me what happened. I could not tell him that he was going to be attacked and that he had bitter enemies in Rother-mere and Northcliffe, so I just said: ' I think I had better go home.' He said: ' Do what you think is right.' He then suggested that I should be made G.O.C. in France as well as C.A.S. at home, but I said that would be impossible. He then said: ' If you think you can help the war by going home, I trust you.' Those were the most heartening words I ever heard at a time when I felt pretty sad and miserable." [9]

It should be added in common justice to everyone that Trenchard, as usual, carried his practice of conscious reticence too far. His resemblance to Haig in this respect was remarkable. Beneath the silence lay a dogged presumption which in a more self-centred or ambitious man might have blossomed into an overmastering conceit. Baring, no mean or unkindly critic of his fellows, felt that Trenchard was guilty of extreme political naïveté in choosing to head off so slippery a customer as Rothermere single-handed, without breathing a syllable of his intentions to another soul.

Salmond was the first to object to Trenchard's self-imposed secrecy.

" For better or worse," he wrote on the day Trenchard left London, " I am Director General of Military Aeronautics at the moment. If I am kept in the dark, I feel as if I am standing on water."

Two days later, having still heard nothing from Trenchard, Salmond rang him up to say that he was on the point of tendering his resignation. Trenchard begged him to be patient, for everyone's sake; and in a letter to him that evening he stated contrarily:

" You cannot resign in war. I know it is impossible sometimes when nobody will give you a definite answer, but then you must let it slide until somebody does—you can do those things which can be done. Please believe me, and do all you can to avoid trouble for the time being or else things will be infinitely worse."

Only Rothermere expected a definite answer; and within forty-eight hours of their meeting at the Ritz Trenchard wrote to him as follows:

" I got back and saw Sir Douglas Haig at once. He was going away from G.H.Q. for a couple of days, so I just caught him. I told

him what you wanted me to do and he will agree to it. He thought
it would be the best thing which could be done, but he thought that
I must still remain Chief of the Flying Corps in France as well. In
other words, I think he agreed to the suggestion that it was one front
from Switzerland to London, and that I should come here constantly
to look after things, so I hope this is all right.

" I have been thinking over our long discussion a lot, and I am
still a little uneasy that as you do not know me very well you will
find that I am not altogether up to what you expect. I have very
decided views on how to run the air service, and to what extent it
can and must expand, but at the same time I am equally decided
that the expansion of the air service which is necessary in a very
large way—and should be started very early—must not be allowed
to jeopardise the whole of the Western Front.

" I quite think that I ought to go home under these circumstances
—not that I want the job in any way—but I do feel that I have more
experience than anybody else at this present moment, and that
I have the confidence of the whole Flying Corps at present.
Vast improvements are necessary in the service, and they can be
carried out and must be looked at in a large way and taken up
early.

" I must have people as my subordinates, regardless of seniority,
whom I think best for the appointments, and then I am certain I can
carry through the task you ask me to undertake.

" I accept the proposals you mentioned of the naval and military
members of the Air Council who will be under me, and I also agree,
feeling as you do though I think you are wrong, that Salmond must
come abroad.

" I would ask that you tell Baird to send me out the organisation
of the Air Council as far as it has gone in order that I can study it
now . . . and also the conditions you propose (unless you are going
to leave them to me) as to running that part of the Flying Corps
which has to do with the army primarily, and that part which has
to do with the navy primarily, and how it is to be worked with the
War Office and Admiralty.

" The last point and the most important is I am quite clear as
to how you want eventually to run the big aerial offensive of bombing,
and that is under the Air Council after we have got it going. Will
you also let me know what is in your mind for aerodromes, the
medical service and the wireless service."

So much for the fantasy, propagated with puckish malice by
Beaverbrook, that Trenchard opposed the creation of a separate

air force in principle and strove to destroy it in practice. The conflict concerned military means, not ends; though a Minister committed out of his own mouth to an unworthy political conspiracy against Haig could hardly be expected to notice the distinction.

4

Trenchard's letter of acceptance crossed one from Rothermere which hardly promoted understanding. The War Cabinet were worried, he said, "about the adequacy of the preparations for the long-range bombing offensive." Lord Milner had called at the Ritz to tell him this shortly after Trenchard's departure on 16th December.

" I said that I had discussed the matter with you and that you had convinced me that you were doing all that was possible with the means at your disposal, and that more labour and material were essential. I subsequently saw General Smuts and we came to the conclusion that I must have a report on the whole situation. . . . I am accordingly asking the Commander-in-Chief to agree to Commodore Paine going out with a representative of Sir John Hunter, who is taking over responsibility for the construction of aerodrome and buildings here. . . ."

This was a new side of Rothermere's nature—the tendency to conceal ignorance under a brisk show of energy. Trenchard could not refrain from replying bluntly:

" I am uneasy about other people being uneasy about the adequacy of preparations for long-range bombing. I am responsible for it, and of course you will be, but if they cannot trust me then I cannot see any object in your asking me to come as C.A.S. . . . I delayed writing this letter for a day until I had seen the Committee. I am delighted that you sent out a Committee to look into it, although what has been done down there up to now is—and will be—well ahead of the machines we shall get by the time my preparations are ready."

The Committee's subsequent report endorsed Trenchard's words. The bases were almost ready, with room for ten times as many bombers as were then available. Yet the undersized force of three squadrons at Ochey had already drawn enemy fighters from other sectors to protect a widening arc of targets between Saarbrücken and Mannheim. Enemy bombers, too, had been pulled out of the line: four times in November and December, the Germans had betrayed anxiety by vainly trying to destroy Ochey's hangars from the air.

Trenchard could not be blamed for neglecting his part of the programme. He had begun the draining of marshes and the flattening of meadows in the Nancy region to accommodate thirty bomber squadrons, not three, as an independent group under Newall; and half a dozen times that winter he had flown down to check progress. Once Baring had stood with him, watching squads of Indians from a Labour Battalion sweating in the rain to convert " what looked like a Scotch moor " into an airfield near Ramber-villers. " The ridges and furrows were so enormous, the ground so marshy, that it did not seem possible that this stretch of bleak, sopping country could ever become an aerodrome," noted Baring. " It did, nevertheless."

Nor was Trenchard content with leasing land, preparing it, and using simultaneously the few bombers he had. He took it upon himself to open preliminary discussions with the French and the Americans on the necessity of joint bombing operations.

" I want to meet the Americans," he informed Rothermere on 20th December, " and fix up a definite programme of what they will do and how much they would like us to run for them. It is of vital importance that I do fix up this matter with the French and Americans for bombing Germany efficiently, and I am perfectly convinced that we can make a very good start by getting control of the whole of the long-distance bombing in a big way."

His reputation for straight dealing was so secure that the im-mediate French response was favourable, though du Peuty was no longer in command. In the tightening up of discipline that followed the army mutinies of the previous summer, several conservative-minded officers with no experience of air matters were wished on him, despite his protests. Rather than stand passively by and watch his squadrons misused, the French air leader applied for transfer to his regiment—a request that was promptly granted. Bereft now of an operational commander of du Peuty's outstanding abilities, Duval, the administrative head of the reorganised French Air Service, welcomed Trenchard's offer to organise and direct a combined air offensive.

The Americans, having no front-line machines and few trained pilots, were grateful to be asked for their co-operation.

" With regard to squadrons," Trenchard was able to tell Rothermere, " I proposed that they (the Americans) should put theirs as they come out under my bombing wings with all their own officers, etc. If a time came for me to choose officers for any appoint-ments, I should choose the best, either American or English, to command the different wings or brigades. The whole of the command in the Nancy area will, however, be under me as long as the British are the predominant partners, that is to say as long as we have more squadrons than the Americans. When they have a greater number of squadrons, the command will automatically pass to them. I feel certain that this will be the best way to run it, and it will save long discussions as to who is going to command. I am certain by the way the Americans talked to me that they will do it. This means no delay in our arrangements. . . . The only question is whether the machines will be efficient. I can assure you the organisation will be."

All this tentative planning presupposed War Cabinet approval for Haig's request that Trenchard should be allowed to combine the two apparently incompatible functions of Chief of Air Staff in London and overall Commander in France. Trenchard himself was not counting too much on it, little though he relished the thought of being severed from the men whom he had schooled and led and integrated, through good times and bad, into a fighting arm bigger than the entire British Expeditionary Force in 1914. So far, Rothermere had carefully avoided defining the actual terms of his home appointment; and since Trenchard did not trust him an inch, he raised the matter without more ado.

" The only conditions I feel that I am entitled to ask for," he wrote, " are that I am the only adviser to the War Cabinet and yourself on the carrying out of aerial operations, that all orders with regard to aerial operations will be issued through me, and that (in order to give you a free hand) I shall not be expected to remain in this appointment when the war is over."

Rothermere was not to be drawn so easily; but rather than lose his man he fell in with Haig's unrealistic proposal that Trenchard should divide his time between the Air Council and Air Headquarters in France. On the last day of 1917 the Minister wrote to Derby:

" It appears to me to be most desirable that the direction of the Royal Flying Corps should be transferred to the Air Council as early as possible, and that General Trenchard should retain his position as G.O.C., R.F.C., on the Western Front in addition to that of Chief of Air Staff. This point appears to me to be vital, and I trust you will agree with me. . . ."

On receipt of a separate request to this effect from Haig, Derby assented willingly enough; but the War Cabinet would not confirm the double appointment, which, apart from its irregularity, seemed

T.   I

likely to strengthen, not weaken, the bargaining power of the
Commander-in-Chief. The fact that Haig expressly wished it
virtually doomed it.

" As I told the War Cabinet and yourself," the Commander-in-
Chief wrote to Derby as soon as he heard of the War Cabinet's
decision, " I consider that the coming four months will probably
be the most critical of the whole war in France; I therefore again
ask you to reconsider this decision before ordering Trenchard to
hand over to another."

But Derby, so eager to please and so easy to overrule, could offer
Haig only fulsome expressions of regret, provoking the latter to
comment irritably in a letter to his wife on 14th January:

" I am still corresponding with Derby over Trenchard. D. is a
very weak-minded fellow, I am afraid, and, like the feather pillow,
bears the marks of the last person who has sat on him. I hear he is
called in London 'genial Judas.' "

It has been suggested without malice that Judas, at any rate, did
lead the soldiers of the High Priest to the right place, whereas
Derby would probably have "got the assignment wrong." That may
be so; but it may also be questioned whether Derby or anyone else
would have prevailed on the War Cabinet to reverse normal practice
and allow a senior officer to hold two appointments at one and the
same time. All precedent was against it; and the fact that Haig
was pressing for it made Lloyd George and his colleagues less likely
than ever to comply.

Trenchard spent Christmas, 1917, at his old headquarters,
surrounded by his staff and by scores of commanders and pilots from
squadrons; it had long been his habit to invite the latter regularly
to his table as a means of "sounding the hearts of my men." Rumours
of impending changes were rife; if it was hard not to overhear them,
it was harder for him not to be touched by the genuine expressions
of hope on every hand that the Flying Corps would be spared its
chief.

Only Baring and Sir John Simon, a former Attorney-General,
and the latest "gift" wished on R.F.C. Headquarters by Haig, would
accompany him to London: the rest would have to stay and help
Salmond, his heir-presumptive in France.

Simon, a future Lord Chancellor already recognised as possessing
one of the finest legal brains in Britain, had adjusted himself well to
his new role as a junior staff officer, after a start as unpromising as
Baring's. Indeed, he had likewise felt the rough edge of Trenchard's
tongue on his first morning at St. Omer in October, 1917. One of

the bells which jingled incessantly whenever Trenchard was at his desk, filling the narrow central corridor of the château with an answering scurry of feet, had summoned Simon to his presence.

Handing him a telegram, Trenchard said:

" Let's see how you'd deal with this, Simon. It's a case for instant action."

Simon scanned it judicially while Baring nervously looked on.

" I shouldn't say for *instant* action, sir," the newcomer commented primly. " Perhaps, after studying the relevant facts, some form of future action may be advisable."

" Get out," thundered Trenchard, startling the clerks in his outer office. " We've no time here for your pretty distinctions, Simon. If you don't know the meaning of instant action, Sergeant Bates will explain."

Another bell echoed down the corridor. Before entering Trenchard's room, Bates noticed Simon pacing furiously up and down, his usually calm countenance working with emotion. Presently Trenchard rang for him again.

" I've spoken to Bates here," he said more quietly. " If you want to know anything, ask him. Don't take offence, there's nothing humiliating in that. I do so myself."

Simon dutifully swallowed his pride and, in Baring's words, was soon "assimilating aviation problems with incredible speed." His respect for Trenchard's "astounding energy and mental alertness" grew apace; Simon's loyalty and intimate experience of the political world, qualities which Trenchard would need increasingly in the uncertain days ahead, were at his command.

The "tepid turkey, cold bread sauce, flat champagne and port made of furniture polish," Baring's description of the Christmas dinner, did not mar the gaiety of the celebrations at St. Omer. R.F.C. mechanics, electricians and performers trudged through deep snow to the château afterwards to stage a farewell concert in honour of the man universally known as " Boom," whose posting home had only to be confirmed.

The star of the evening was a superbly muscled airman who demonstrated his controlled skill and stamina with massive dumb-bells. All went smoothly until his under-rehearsed assistants nearly killed him by jumping up and down on the wrong parts of his prostrate body while he was straining to raise a 2000-pound weight above his quivering head. Through the deafening laughter Trenchard experienced a fellow-feeling with this victim of circumstance whose plight seemed unpleasantly symbolic of his own.

On the night following his departure for London, a mysterious fire broke out and burnt the château of St. André to the ground. As if of their own accord, all the bells in the blazing building suddenly rang out together for the last time above the roar and crackle of the flames. Relays of men rushed through the smoke to salvage papers and furniture; others manned pumps and fought a hopeless battle to extinguish the blaze which reddened the snowbound landscape for miles around. A wag was heard to shout above the frenzied jingling: " Boom's ghost's come back."

Next morning, as senior officers surveyed the blackened shell of the building, it seemed as though fate itself had taken a hand, sealing the irreversible decision of the political war lords.

5

Trenchard was human enough to be warmed by the congratulations which showered down on him with the announcement in the 1918 New Year Honours List that he had been awarded a knighthood for his services in the field. He was also hard-headed enough to shrug off the glamour like a hair-shirt that did not fit. With deprecating honesty, he informed the R.F.C. that the honour was theirs, being "entirely due to the exertions of the officers under me." No man, perhaps, had been better served; but few leaders anywhere could have bent to his will so many individualists without surrendering in the process a jot of his personal popularity or, more important still, without cramping their generous spirit of adventure.

Whether he yet recognised the fact or not, the Flying Corps was a force indelibly stamped with his own image.

He felt like a man in fetters during the first month at home. January, 1918, confirmed his fear that any differences that arose with Rothermere would not be easily bridged. His own position remained one of ill-defined scope: for the Minister had never answered Trenchard's original request that his duties should be clearly specified. Other members of the Air Council were in similar straits, Sir David Henderson, the Vice-President, exerting all his patience and diplomacy to settle policy disputes which affected Godfrey Paine, the Master-General of Personnel, nearly as much as Trenchard. Brancker, again responsible for equipment, and Weir, still in charge of aircraft production, were less directly implicated, but their sympathies were decidedly not with Rothermere, whose attitude to normal rules of service procedure was one of active contempt, possibly as a result of his youthful experience as a Government clerk before going into partnership with Northcliffe. According to his private secretary at the Ministry, Sir Evelyn Wrench:

" Rothermere, like his brother, was always on the lookout for subordinates of promise. At Carmelite House the junior of twenty-five, if possessed of exceptional gifts, who had hitherto been earning £300 to £400 a year, might suddenly find himself in a position of responsibility with a salary running into four figures. . . . Was it surprising that Rothermere found the rigid military caste system in force at the Hotel Cecil uncongenial? "

Trenchard, hugging his secret knowledge of Rothermere's ulterior political aims, was quick to protest at a cavalier disregard for the canons of orderly administration which he found not only uncongenial but wasteful and confusing. When he had been master in his own house, Trenchard was never a slave to form-filling or minute-writing and often cut the procedural corners in the interests of efficiency; likewise he had his own favourites, though these had to earn their keep by merit. Now, however, as a restive tenant in someone else's house, nothing the master did was above suspicion.

" Rothermere and Northcliffe introduced a lot of people to the Air Ministry without consulting anybody," Trenchard wrote. " Rothermere preferred any advice to that of his professional advisers. It is a well-known characteristic of a certain type of Secretary of State, just as there is a type of general, air marshal and admiral who hates listening to anybody but professional servicemen. Both are equally dangerous."

He had been in his new office only a week when Rothermere sent for him, and said:

" You will go to the meetings of the Chiefs of Staff and claim every man that is available for the R.A.F."

" That isn't my job," Trenchard retorted. " I must listen to the arguments and see where man-power could be most usefully employed for winning the war. If the navy and army arguments are sound in my opinion, it would be unsound to demand more men than are necessary for the air force."

" No," said Rothermere. " Your job is to get them all."

This was the second of two constant sources of friction. The third and most significant was their conflict of opinion as to the proper use of air-power for ending the strategic stalemate on land.

" I tried to point out to him that whatever the future of the air was—and I believed in that—practically the whole British Army was engaged in a desperate struggle along the Western Front, and it was no good his saying that he took no interest in it. . . .

"I remember pointing out to him that never again would it be necessary to have these enormous armies locked in a death grip along a line of trenches if the air was used properly—though we had not arrived at the proper use of air-power then, or anywhere near it, and the air was only trying to find its feet [sic] and what it could do.

"We had many such discussions and disagreements."[10]

Despite these basic differences, the detailed committee work involved in harmonising the rival traditions and distinctive customs of two air services was relatively free of rancour. Here, Rothermere did not intrude: and Trenchard's gift for quick improvisation prevented many awkward little deadlocks. For instance, when senior naval officers threatened to boycott any reforms imposed by a Chief of Staff with an army background, Trenchard promptly inaugurated what Brancker impartially described as "a very sound system of co-ordination. . . . Captain Scarlett from the Admiralty, General Ellington from the War Office and Commander Groves from the Air Staff . . . met continually and discussed the endless questions outstanding between the three departments. They were nearly always able to arrive at an amicable agreement. . . . It ran perfectly until Trenchard's retirement under the new régime, when it quickly ceased to operate."

Owing to the atmosphere of intrigue engendered by the wider dispute, however, cliques inevitably sprang up and multiplied at the Hotel Cecil, an ill-designed warren of a place with over a thousand rooms, and an ideal breeding ground for factions. It was natural, perhaps, for some disgruntled soldiers and sailors to look askance at the new régime and at each other; but it was rash and unworthy of the Minister to intensify discord by playing off their advice against that of his own Chief of Staff. Sir Evelyn Wrench has put as virtuous a face as possible on this persistent failing of Rothermere's.

"He made a point of talking to flying officers home on leave. He wanted to find out at first hand what the average pilot was thinking of the organisation of the force and the Air Board hierarchy; he took into his confidence two or three young colonels. Now in the fighting services there is rigid etiquette and seniority counts for much. Rumours began to circulate that the President of the Air Board [sic] was listening to—nay, even seeking—the views of junior officers. Such action on the part of the official head of the Air Force horrified some of the more punctilious generals and admirals connected with the force: it was subversive of discipline."

At heart, however, Rothermere was unsure of himself. Given to flaunting his authority, yet easily rattled by firm opposition, he increasingly tended to accept only what he wanted to hear.

The late Mr. Colin Brook, Rothermere's literary executor and a very close confidant during his declining years, admitted to the author that Harold Sidney Harmsworth was by nature "a pessimist" who could "manage statistics better than men." When his aims were frustrated, he would cover "his fear of failure, or criticism, or of ridicule by compromising with the strong or bullying the weak." Even Beaverbrook, who was on intimate terms with Rothermere in early 1918, acknowledged that the Minister lacked staying power. Unlike Northcliffe, he shrank from notoriety. His head for figures had blended perfectly in the past with the other's journalistic flair and lust for power; he was happy enough now as a Minister to let Northcliffe's wayward genius for mischief shine: there was more comfort for Rothermere plotting in the shadows.

Trenchard confided some of his problems to Haig during a short visit to France. On 26th January, the Commander-in-Chief noted in his diary:

" Lord Rothermere (brother of Lord Northcliffe) who is Air Minister is quite ignorant of the needs or working of the air service, and is in great terror of newspaper criticism. Money is being squandered and officers and men wasted by being employed in creating units for performing work hitherto done by the army (or navy) for the air service. For example, Hospitals, Detention Barracks, etc.

" All this is very sad at a time when officers and men are so badly needed. Trenchard thinks that the air service cannot last as an independent Ministry, and that Air Units must again return to army and navy."

In private letters to Salmond, his successor in France, Trenchard deplored the misdirection of effort which flourished under a Minister apparently incapable of seeing or thinking straight.

" The great curse of this place," he wrote on 11th February, " is that there are too many officers doing different jobs. It's too ridiculous, and everybody always thinks it's necessary to increase the staff everywhere to increase efficiency. . . .

" I am very uneasy about the friction which will be caused between the navy and the army as we get down to the air service. I hope it will all be over in six months, but I am doubtful. I fear the navy will think they have joined the R.F.C.; and every department put together under two heads, either a naval man under an army man or vice versa, will cause trouble at first. . . ."

"My worries at home are increasing," he wrote again on 15th February. "I am trying hard to cut down the enormous establishments. I come up against snags every day in making this air service. . . . It is almost an impossibility to run, and I am spending most of my time trying to bustle up the cause of delays, machines, and the development of new types. . . . I miss very much the small, self-contained staff in France. . . .

"Another point which is troubling me a lot is that I am only a Member of the Air Council and I have not even got the power the D.G.M.A. (Ellington) has. I have nine colleagues and one Secretary of State, and at the Council the Secretary of State can veto anything. . . .

"I am still on the brink of stopping, but if I stop I do not know whether I shall be doing right to the Flying Corps. I am certain I could get this show running perfectly if I only became more of a dictator at home and everywhere, but of course this is impossible."

An additional member of the Air Council, Sir Henry Norman, was appointed early in February. His duties were unspecified, but service cynics decided that Norman had been sent either to spy on Rothermere or to assist him in dislodging certain senior officers on trumped-up charges of incompetence and in replacing them with "sound" nominees of his own. Dowding and Ludlow-Hewitt, future Chiefs of Fighter and Bomber Command respectively, were two among many victims; but it was the case of Longcroft, who had been running the R.F.C.'s huge Training Division at home since November, 1917, which stung Trenchard into action.

On his return from France towards the end of 1917, Longcroft had set about "smoking out the multitudes of able-bodied young officers" already installed at his headquarters in Masons' Yard, behind Piccadilly, heedless of complaints from the dispossessed and of pleas from applicants who wished to fill the abolished vacancies, some of whom were sponsored by M.P.s and even by Ministers of the Crown. Longcroft tore up all the applications.

The Training Directorate staff was down to manageable size by the time Trenchard arrived as Chief of Air Staff; but presently Longcroft began to receive "a daily barrage of petulant minutes" from no less a person than Rothermere. Surmising that some of the disappointed and more influential applicants must have taken their cases higher, Longcroft, normally the mildest of men, finally lost patience and minuted an indirect reply. " The less I get of these senseless queries, the better off we'll all be," is a fair statement of its gist. That afternoon Rothermere sent for him.

As Longcroft walked along the corridor towards the Minister's office, Godfrey Paine stopped him.

" What have you been up to? " he asked Longcroft. " He's absolutely livid."

Longcroft explained his recent troubles.

" Is that all? " said Paine. " I might have known. Just keep your head. I have a committee on now, but if I can break away I'll look in."

Rothermere was not alone. Sir Henry Norman sat beside him, pencil poised and note-book open like a magistrate's clerk. The Minister began by accusing Longcroft of antagonising "influential people" at a moment when the air service needed every ounce of public confidence, and threatened to send him back to France at once.

" I'd like nothing better," said Longcroft.

They both stared in astonishment.

" You understand that it would mean demotion? " said Rothermere. " We've no room for two major-generals in France."

" Send me back as a squadron commander, as long as you let me go."

Longcroft's desire to escape at all costs appeared to disconcert his inquisitors. Norman was cross-examining him about his purge of the Training Directorate when Rothermere suddenly interrupted with an ancient conundrum. Why, asked the Minister, were the monthly casualty returns from the Gosport Instructors' school so much lighter than in other training centres? Before Longcroft could reply, a deep voice rang out from the back of the room.

" Really, Lord Rothermere. If that's the best you can do, I suggest you waste no more of the general's time."

It was Godfrey Paine. He had entered unnoticed. And this was a question he had heard once too often.

" Sir Godfrey," snapped Rothermere, " I'd trouble you to mind your own business. Try to remember that you're not pacing your own quarter-deck."

The exchanges grew fiercer. Longcroft sat back enjoying himself until Norman crossed to his side and muttered in some embarrassment:

" I think that will be all, general. We shan't need you any more to-day."[11]

Trenchard was unable to prevent Longcroft's posting, much to the latter's relief. A few days later, however, he was rung up by a bewildered Ludlow-Hewitt, who had just come back from a tour to find someone else installed in his place as Inspector of Training. Trenchard instantly summoned the usurper, Smith-Barry, and ordered him back forthwith to his command at the Gosport Instructors' school. Then he stormed past a bodyguard of secretaries and assistants and bearded the Minister in person. Such underhand behaviour, Trenchard warned, could not go on: it was disrupting work, instigating unrest, and sapping the confidence of the whole department.

To hear the Minister admit that Smith-Barry had proposed several radical suggestions for reorganising the Training Division in a series of private letters staggered Trenchard less than Rothermere's bland acknowledgment that he had encouraged the correspondence. The Chief of Air Staff retorted that there were better ways of running a ministry than stimulating the restless brain of a young man who "though a genius among pilots was an eccentric among administrators." Trenchard left in a towering rage but was partly mollified by the wire, marked "personal", which reached him that evening:

" Brigadier Smith-Barry left London 4.30 p.m.," it ran. " Major Smith-Barry arrived Gosport 6 p.m."

It was consoling to find at least one willing collaborator-turned-victim who knew how to climb down without forfeiting dignity or humour.

From mid-February onwards, Rothermere became notably less accessible to Trenchard. The phrase " I'm not in to that man' became a jocular password among members of his staff. As a result avoidable misunderstandings, big and small, increased: minutes flew back and forth like venomous paper darts and tempers grew more and more frayed. On balance, the more accomplished logic choppers at Trenchard's elbow, led by Simon and Hugh Cecil usually got the better of these petty exchanges; but this in itself fortified the Minister in his dark belief that Trenchard was an intolerably arrogant and obstinate man.[12]

One example must suffice out of dozens. When a member of the public wrote to say that he had heard a Gotha over his house during a recent raid on London, the Minister passed on the letter for the Chief of Staff's comments. The reply from Trenchard was that usually " it was no more easy to hear than to smell a particular type of aeroplane."

The Minister, gravely displeased, decided that the point was worth pursuing further, for after several days he wrote again:

" The matter was referred to the Home Defence Authorities, who stated that it was quite easy to detect by hearing certain types of aeroplanes. A certain number of young practical airmen were asked, who returned exactly the same reply. . . . What I wish to make clear is that in view of a grave conflict of opinion on such a matter as this, it is impossible in the early days of a new service for a Secretary of State to accept the advice of any professional adviser entirely without demur."

Aversion to the heavy-handedness of Trenchard only partly accounted for Rothermere's determination not to be winkled out of the shell into which he had retired. Inconsolable personal sorrow was now preying on his mind as well. On 12th February his eldest son died in hospital from the after effects of war wounds; another had already been killed in action. Beaverbrook and Wrench independently remarked on the change in him: ill with distress, Rothermere lost all appetite for work. Trenchard felt for him as a man, but sympathy could not over-ride the distrust he felt for the politician now that the campaign against Haig was approaching its climax.

A new C.I.G.S. was settling in at the War Office, Robertson having chosen to resign rather than surrender any of his powers to the Supreme Allied War Council. Despite Haig's persuasions, he spurned the alternative offer of becoming Britain's permanent military representative at Versailles. Lloyd George accepted Robertson's resignation without regret, appointing the garrulous, scheming Sir Henry Wilson in his stead. It seemed only a matter of time before the Prime Minister would force a reckoning with the isolated Haig.

The prospect appalled Trenchard, who knew that a German offensive was imminent against an attenuated British line, recently lengthened again to sooth the French, yet still denied the minimum reinforcements in men that were consistent with safety. Could the Government be willing to risk losing the war just to spite the Commander-in-Chief? The least Trenchard felt that he could do was to maintain his grip on air planning and on the husbanding of aircraft reserves.

The final break with Rothermere followed the discovery that in this vital but undemarcated sphere of responsibility also the Minister had been trespassing behind his back. Towards the middle of March, Geddes, the First Lord, asked Trenchard why he would not release

the 4000 aircraft which the Minister had offered the navy a week
before for anti-submarine patrolling. Trenchard assured his visitor
that, though this was the first he had heard of it, the deal was off.
Whatever the Air Minister might have said, there were not even
400 spare aircraft in the length and breadth of Britain.

The Minister had arrived at his mythical grand total of 4000
battle-worthy machines by adding together all the reserve engines
and airframes in stock, irrespective of the fact that "over 3000 of the
engines had no aeroplanes suitable for them in reserve, and that over
3500 of the aeroplanes, some completely out of date, had no suitable
engines to fit them."

Geddes at once complained to Rothermere that "it is a little
disturbing to hear that General Trenchard is not quite so clear
on the point as you were," so the Minister belatedly passed the
question officially to the Chief of Air Staff with the face-saving
comment:

" I cannot understand his reference to the 4000 aeroplanes. The
figure may have been mentioned in conversation but I have no
recollection of having myself mentioned such a figure."

Whether Rothermere's memory was as bad as his conscience
Trenchard would not have cared to say. The man was undoubtedly
a centipede for "putting his foot in it"; and fresh signs of blundering,
duplicity, or both, were soon forthcoming. On 18th March Trenchard
made a short list of three or four recent examples and drew the
moral in a sharp personal letter:

" The failures and shortcomings and delays of the past were
supposed to be due to these very methods," he told him in an
indignant letter. " I am your adviser on these matters and I am able
and willing to obtain for you all the information you desire. I am
far from denying that you have a perfect right to see whom you like,
but at the same time if you have not sufficient confidence in me even
to tell me what is happening in the branches of my own department,
I consider—and I feel sure you will agree with me—that the
situation created is an impossible one."

Rothermere was stung into replying with equal firmness and
more than a hint of sarcasm:

" There has never been any question here as to what your
position is. You are Chief of Air Staff and are my principal, not
necessarily my sole adviser in all matters pertaining to the employment of personnel and material in all the various theatres of war,
and at home in association with the naval forces and the forces of
the Home defences.

" I have shown great confidence in you. . . .

" My conception of the work of your department is that I should be the recipient—at not infrequent intervals—of all kinds of plans for the employment of aeroplanes, strategically and otherwise. These I am hoping to receive.

" In regard to the various matters mentioned in your letter, I must tell you that it is always open to the political heads of any departments to confer at any time they like with whomsoever they please without consultation with their Chiefs of Staff or anyone else."

This letter clinched Trenchard's half-formed decision to resign. After dark on 18th March he left his Berkeley Street flat, walked the length of St. James's Street and crossed the cobbled courtyard of the Palace at its foot to York House. With no better outside judge to turn to, he knocked on the door of Robertson, the ex-C.I.G.S. The taciturn field-marshal admitted him, listened in silence, and then said:

" Come back in the morning. I'll sleep on it."

Early next day, Robertson answered his knock, still in dressing-gown and slippers; he looked impassively at Trenchard and barked out the words:

" Consult your own conscience." Then he slammed the door behind him.[13] The advice was not very much to go on, but it was enough: Trenchard had spent many lonely hours doing just that.

Before noon on 19th March, Trenchard's letter of resignation reached Rothermere's desk. The Minister sent for him at once and begged him to reconsider his decision.

" As I'm soon going myself," Trenchard heard him say, " I'd like you to withdraw your resignation now."

" Certainly not," said Trenchard.

" Surely what I've told you in confidence must make some difference? "

" Why should it? If you must know, I don't trust you to resign."

The last frayed strands of understanding were thus irreparably severed. Each had driven the other into a position from which there could be no retreat. Trenchard left the room insisting that his resignation must stand, and stressing that if Rothermere were serious about resigning then it would be for his successor to decide whether to retain the present Chief of Air Staff or appoint another.

In the considered opinion of Baring and Hugh Cecil, this was a fatal tactical error. For though it was with some reluctance that

Trenchard agreed to the Minister's request and deferred the effective date of his resignation, Rothermere probably never forgave him for the last insulting stab to his pride.

The War Cabinet were presently discussing the conveniently mortgaged head of Trenchard, wondering when or whether they would foreclose and claim it on a platter.

11. Bomber Baron

A single date, perversely chosen in Trenchard's view, obsessed Rothermere throughout the interview: 1st April, 1918. On that day, regardless of impediments, the unhappy affair between the Flying Corps and the Royal Naval Air Service was not only to be solemnised but blessed with the child of Smuts. It seemed to Trenchard a suitable charade for All Fools' Day. He hardly cared whether he stayed on for the ceremonial birth of the Royal Air Force as the Minister earnestly pressed him to do for appearances' sake.

In a letter dated 13th April, formally accepting Trenchard's suspended resignation, Rothermere adopted an altogether more sanctimonious tone.

" Every man is the best judge of what he does, but I believe that your act in resigning your post of Chief of Air Staff twelve days before myself and the large staff here were going into action to accomplish the gigantic task of the fusion of the Royal Naval Air Service and the Royal Flying Corps is an unparalleled incident in the life of the country. . . . I was filled with profound anxiety lest your resignation might become public and rumour with its thousand tongues might allege you had resigned in protest against some policy of mine which would be disastrous to the interests of the 25,000 officers and 140,000 men who were just going to become the Royal Air Force. . . ."

Rothermere's indignation was unquestionably influenced by the military catastrophe which had since overtaken the Allied cause. The interview with Trenchard took place on Tuesday, 19th March, 1918. Two days later, on 21st March, the German offensive, which the Cabinet partly discounted as a figment of Haig's unhealthy imagination and which Rothermere had all along regarded as the poorest excuse for Trenchard's "stalling," smashed the Allied line at its most vulnerable point.

Surging forward in dense mist, nearly a million Germans infiltrated and overran the Fifth and part of the Third British Army on the extreme right. Here stood the hinge that could be broken by a single gigantic push: for the point of junction on the Somme between the French and British forces was the very point where Haig had foreseen and warned that the blow might fall. Yet repeated pleas for fresh drafts to reinforce his tired and weakened divisions had gone unheeded because Lloyd George wanted no more blood-baths. Physically incapable of retrieving the situation, the Commander-in-Chief had to pull back and reform his battered force behind the river. Only the French had reserves enough to exert counter-pressure and prevent the hinge from snapping.

Pétain hesitated to throw them in. His orders, he told Haig, were "to cover Paris at all costs." He believed that the Germans had still to reveal their true strategic aim; a sudden change in the direction of the assault would catch the French on the wrong foot; the road to Paris might be opened if Pétain committed himself too soon. In desperation, Haig appealed to London. The emergency arrangements that followed are a matter of history.

Milner, the Secretary of State for War, accompanied by Wilson, the C.I.G.S., crossed at once to France. On 26th March, at Doullens, they conferred with Poincaré and Clemenceau, the French President and Premier, and with the two Commanders-in-Chief. Unity of strategy was ensured after more than three years of shifts and plots and uneasy compromises when Haig himself proposed that Foch, whom he had so often criticised, should take over as Supreme Commander.

The early reports from the battlefield confirmed Trenchard's presentiment that immediate Allied survival depended on three factors, all of them British: an outnumbered army still capable of resistance, an intact Flying Corps inferior only in size to the enemy's, and the imperturbable faith in both of Haig, the Commander-in-Chief.

The shock of crisis also heightened his resentment against Rothermere for attempting to immolate the R.F.C. on the altar of a bogus, politically inspired strategy. The attempt had mercifully failed; and the Minister's belated anxiety to mend his ways grew suddenly marked. Colleagues at the Ministry noticed and welcomed the perceptible improvement in his personal relations with the Chief of Air Staff.

Rothermere certainly consulted Trenchard several times during the black week-end of 22nd-24th March, when the censorship was lifted gingerly to inform the public that though much ground had been yielded Allied resistance was stiffening.

"I remember my Secretary of State saying: 'No more reinforcements for Haig. Get back as much of the Air as you can from France for the defence of England, whatever the army do.' As far as I could gather, he intended leaving the army to its fate, but he was so excited it was hard to listen to him. I remember recommending him to go away to the country for ten days and I would carry on and things would go all right."[1]

After that, Rothermere ceased trying to influence military decisions. For the first time since November the Air Ministry pulled together as one man; the bickerings and strivings of the factions ceased. At Trenchard's direction, all available reserves of pilots, observers, engines and aircraft were rushed to France.

"You are splendid," Trenchard wrote to Salmond, the Flying Corps Commander, on 25th March. "When I recommended your name to the C.-in-C. to succeed me, and when I previously recommended you as my predecessor here, I told them that I would stake my reputation on your being the right man. . . . The struggle is not over yet by any means, and therefore I would earnestly ask you to watch as much as ever you possibly can the question of keeping your squadrons up to strength. If for any reason we cannot keep them up it is essential, in order to keep up the morale, that you boldly pull a squadron bang out of it altogether so as to save being under-strength in several. I hope this will not become necessary and I hope we shall be able to keep you going, but the full breakfast table is one of the roots of confidence of the Flying Corps, although of course it is not the only one. . . ."

Sir John Simon was dispatched to the front with two other staff officers to strengthen the links between the flying brigades and headquarters. Their liaison work was invaluable. Salmond notified Trenchard on the night of 26th March that at two danger points that day massed machines of the Flying Corps had joined in the ground battle and halted enemy advances.

"2nd and 1st Brigades together with 3rd Brigade were concentrated on low-flying west of Bapaume. 9th and 5th were concentrated on the Chaulnes-Roye area. When I was at G.H.Q. to-night I heard a telephone message from Percy to Dill saying that without doubt the concentration of aircraft in the south had frozen up the attack there temporarily. Similarly Cox (Intelligence) told Davidson he considered that the concentration of aircraft west of Bapaume had had the same effect. They were so thick over the ground that I fear some collisions occurred, but, of course, this must be put up with."

The bombing squadrons at Ochey were meanwhile attacking objectives far behind the front. Cologne was raided; so was Mannheim, at last. So also were Luxembourg, Thionville and Metz, all on the same night.

"For the moment," Newall wrote from Ochey, " I am trying to interrupt the main railway lines feeding the present battle front. . . . To-day I am having a try at the railway congestion about Liége. . . . There is no doubt the Huns have had to draw back a lot of machines for the defence of the Fatherland, and I trust that their aviation is as annoyed at having to do so as we were when two [fighter] squadrons had to be sent home to protect London [in July, 1917] . . ."

Trenchard paid a lightning visit to France himself on 5th April, inspecting a score of squadrons and marvelling at the exalted spirit of the pilots.

" ' We are giving them hell in the air,' they kept saying, and so they were. They asked for no more aeroplanes than they were getting. They said they were quite certain they would fight it out and win. I remember then going on to the French, and they were very different. They said, ' You will come and help us, won't you? You will send more squadrons to help us. We can't stand the pressure.' I pointed out that that was not what their British comrades felt."[2]

Lloyd George invited him to No. 10 Downing Street on his return to ask about the fighting. Other Ministers joined them in the Cabinet room; Milner looked ashen and rather drawn; Bonar Law, gazing into space with his head slightly tilted to one side, reminded Trenchard incongruously of "a psalm-singing saint." Only the Prime Minister, unpredictable as ever, looked and talked " like a man who had not lost heart."

" He met me in the passage, though I knew he disliked me, and said, ' Well, general, though we shan't win this year, we shall win next year instead.' He showed courage at that moment far outweighing that of all the rest of them."

In his political immaturity, Trenchard had scarcely paused to reflect on the ambiguity of his own position. Rothermere's injured vanity, his own stiff-necked defiance, even the resignation which he had placed in the Cabinet's hands, seemed meaningless incidentals now beside the overriding problem of staving off defeat. Trenchard had so far said nothing to any member of his staff about the irrevocable step he had taken. Had it been his nature to unbend, to confide in the shrewd Cecil or the sympathetic Baring, he might have been less unconcerned. For Lloyd George was embarrassed and scandalised by the uncompromising letter of resignation which did not reach him until the struggle for survival on the Somme was several days old.

The Prime Minister, weighed down with far more critical burdens, deputed Smuts to examine the rights and wrongs of the Rothermere-Trenchard dispute. By the end of the first week in April the South African advised that the simplest solution in the changed circumstances would be to let Trenchard go. It was advice which, according to Beaverbrook, the Prime Minister gladly accepted.

"Lloyd George," Beaverbrook wrote later,[3] "had been hearing rumours of conspiracies directed by Asquith, Leader of the Liberal Opposition, and supported by Trenchard, Robertson, Jellicoe and possibly Haig. It was said that these soldiers were meeting with Asquith and considering plans for driving Lloyd George out of office. Lloyd George believed these stories. Certainly his position was being challenged by the military faction with growing force and strength. He had no doubt on that score. The removal, therefore, of Trenchard must have been regarded favourably for no other reason than for the benefits and advantages he would gain in his struggle to hold his own place against the assaults of the political and military alliance against him. Here was a bird Lloyd George could kill with a stone, the stone being Lord Rothermere. He threw it gladly."

It may well be that the Prime Minister's weakness for ascribing his own tortuous motives to others led him to believe in the existence of a fantastic plot to unseat him, in which case the timing of Trenchard's action and his extraordinary silence afterwards could arguably be construed as evidence of complicity. What Lloyd George "believed" would be sounder evidence if Beaverbrook, as defending counsel, had provided chapter and verse for his cloak-and-dagger insinuations. Unsupported speculation, however fascinating, is hardly the stuff of history.

A more credible witness, who kept a diary record of the sequel to the Rothermere-Trenchard fracas, was Sir Maurice (now Lord) Hankey, the Secretary of the War Cabinet. His interpretation is somewhat less melodramatic than Beaverbrook's; but as he assisted Smuts throughout the inquiry, Hankey's account throws new and impartial light on these events.

"I was practically living with Lloyd George at this time,"

Hankey informed this writer, " and my diary becomes a journal.
The Prime Minister was too engrossed in the life and death problems
of the moment to give much time or thought to the tiresome
Trenchard business, which is mentioned only three times in my
diary."

In his elected isolation, Trenchard learnt of the inquiry only
when Smuts's verdict was brought in against him. The South
African chose to base his judgment entirely on Rothermere's version
of the dispute without approaching Trenchard. Then Rothermere,
possibly after consulting the C.I.G.S., Sir Henry Wilson, suggested
the name of Sir Frederick Sykes, Henderson's former staff officer,
as the candidate best qualified for the vacant post of Chief of Air
Staff. Sykes, who had until recently served on the military side of
the Supreme War Council at Versailles, was by now on friendly
terms with Wilson. These tentative arrangements must have
been settled before 10th April, for on that day Rothermere sent
for Trenchard and told him that the War Cabinet had been
pleased to accept his resignation. The Minister was rash enough
to add that the Government wanted him to resume command in
France.

Trenchard was thunderstruck.

" You must be off your head if you think I'd agree to replace
Salmond in the middle of a battle," he said. " I've never heard
anything so damnable."

He reproached Rothermere bitterly for having temporised so that
the world would receive the false impression that he (Trenchard)
had "resigned during the battle." Finally, he demanded and
obtained a few days' extra grace for Salmond so that the Cabinet
could think again.

The sequel is outlined in Hankey's diary. On 11th April, Lord
Hugh Cecil was invited to lunch by Smuts and Hankey "to discuss
Rothermere's decision to replace Trenchard by Sykes. . . . Hugh
Cecil violently opposed the removal of Trenchard. If he had to go,
Brancker, in his opinion was the only possible man. He was
altogether opposed to Sykes. Smuts is much perplexed.

" 12th April: I have a note that at the end of a very long
meeting devoted to urgent war questions, the War Cabinet approved
that Sykes should replace Trenchard.

" Late that evening, as I was leaving for home, Smuts turned
up at Whitehall Gardens to see Milner and myself about the *affaire
Trenchard*. He had seen Rothermere, who had suddenly got cold feet

about the proposed change.* After a long palaver, we all went off
to the P.M. at the House of Commons, where we gradually collected
Henry Wilson and Rothermere.

" I was asked my opinion and did not conceal that I thought it
was a mistake to make a change. Trenchard, whatever his faults,
had created the greatest air force in the world; it is absurd to
remove him during a great battle when he has all the strings of a
difficult situation in his hands, and is conducting his affairs with
conspicuous success. Sykes, whatever his merits (and they are many),
is unpopular with a part of the air force, and rightly or wrongly was
superseded in France early in the war and later in the command in
Gallipoli.

" Eventually they decided that, before confirming the appointment of Sykes, they must clear up the mystery of why he had been
got rid of in 1915, and I was sent off to see General (Sir William)
Roberston who had been C.I.G.S. in France at that time and might
be expected to know the facts. Robertson, however, could throw
no light on the matter.

" 13th April: When I arrived at the office, General Smuts rang
me up to say that Rothermere had seen the Adjutant-General,
Macready, who had been French's A.-G. at the time of the Sykes-
Henderson affair; that he considered Sykes to be the best man
available; and that accordingly Rothermere was to make the
appointment."

The first intimation Trenchard had of his successor's identity
came with a quiet tapping on his office door later that same day.
He was dumbfounded when Sykes, the last man in Britain he wanted
or expected to see occupying his chair, walked into the room.

" Lord Rothermere has sent me," said Sykes, adding hastily to
cover up his own embarrassment: " I didn't ask to come."

" I'm not interested in your explanations," said Trenchard. " Is
there anything you want to know about the work? "

" No, thank you, nothing."[4]

Trenchard cleared his desk and left the room. Rothermere's
hand-written minute, confirming the name of his successor, was
delivered to him that night.

At Buckingham Palace next day, the King gathered from the
Sunday Press that major changes had already taken place on the

* That morning, Henderson had been at last asked for his opinion of Sykes
as a likely Chief of Air Staff. It was his first hint that Trenchard had resigned.
Henderson's unfavourable verdict on Sykes evidently left Smuts and Rothermere
wondering about the soundness of their choice. Hence Rothermere's attack of
"cold feet."

staff of the new Air Ministry without his knowledge or consent. By a curious oversight, the official War Cabinet memorandum, tentatively drawn up two days previously, did not reach him until the Sunday evening. Trenchard was summoned to the Palace on the Monday, and the King listened with sympathy to his account of the circumstances leading up to and following his letter of resignation. Lord Stamfordham, the King's secretary, saw Trenchard out, and offered a word of advice.

" Say nothing to anyone," he said.

It was a stiff counsel of perfection. Henderson, for one, was exceedingly vexed to discover that Sykes had been promoted Chief of Air Staff over the week-end and rebuked Trenchard for having kept his friends unnecessarily long in the dark.

" Why couldn't you have told me? It might have been possible to avert this calamity. I doubt whether I can go on now under Sykes."

Before the end of another week of heart-searching, Henderson tendered his resignation, too.

Lord Hugh Cecil, another friend who had learnt too late what was impending, also reproached Trenchard for his absurd secretiveness: it had allowed, he said, too much play to Rothermere's vindictiveness. Cecil vowed that, whatever happened, he would demand a full inquiry in his capacity as a Member of Parliament. Trenchard implored him not to engage in public controversy; but Cecil was adamant. A wave of despondency was sweeping through the new service at the news of their leader's downfall. It convinced Cecil that the nation and the air force had been put to a greater loss than even Trenchard himself.

2

For the guidance of the War Cabinet, and to clear his name with posterity, Trenchard prepared a baldly factual statement of his unheard case, and sent it to the Prime Minister with a copy of the correspondence which had passed between himself and Rothermere.

" As will be seen," he wrote, " I ventured to point out that the Chief of Staff was not allowed to carry out his work unfettered and without outside interference, and that the Secretary of State has encouraged the intervention of various people without responsibility in decisions concerning operations and the means of carrying them out.

" I would also like to record that I resigned on 19th March, two days before we knew the battle in France had started. On handing my resignation to Lord Rothermere he told me that he himself was going to resign before 20th April, and he wanted to know if that would make any difference. I said of course it would make a difference, in as much as it would be for his successor to decide whether to accept my resignation or not. He then asked me if I would defer my resignation so as not to embarrass him or the Government and I stated that I had no wish to embarrass him or the Government. He also asked me if I would give him further time before my resignation became effective. This of course I agreed to do, and eventually 20th April was settled as the date.

" The battle began on 21st March, and so just before I went to France on 5th April I informed him that I had not pressed the appointment of a deputy as in the event of my resignation my successor might want to appoint another man.

" On 10th April in the afternoon the Secretary of State sent for me and told me the War Cabinet had accepted my resignation and had offered me the command of the air force in France. This was repeated two or three times. It seemed to me that it was out of the question to think I could turn out General Salmond to make room for me, for I felt very strongly it would have undoubtedly lost me the respect and confidence of the whole air service. Still less could I do this in the middle of the battle.

" I had no wish to take any action during the battle and I deeply regret that the Secretary of State has considered it necessary to do so."

The Prime Minister was disconcerted to learn that Rothermere had entered into a kind of suicide pact with Trenchard, a pact due to expire in less than a week. The Air Minister had not been quite candid about this mutual resignation offer in conversation with Smuts; the problem of removing and replacing a recalcitrant Chief of Staff apparently became an end in itself, as the following note suggests. Dated 17th April, it was addressed by Rothermere to his private secretary, Wrench, then at home recuperating from an attack of mumps.

" You have been out of all the fun. Sir Henry Norman and I have had really the time of our lives. We simply rounded them up and then clubbed them remorselessly. I am so sorry you were out of the fray."

The idea of resigning himself no longer seemed so imperative. The taste of undisputed power was sweet. With Trenchard safely out of the way and the more malleable Sykes in office, why should Rothermere not remain as Minister? Alas, Lloyd George, the stern political realist, was not so accommodating. If Trenchard's claim were true, and news of it leaked out the Government would have even more explaining to do when the Parliamentary storm broke out. It would be wiser, in the circumstances, if Rothermere did some explaining first.

Acknowledging the receipt of Trenchard's statement, Hankey wrote:

" The Prime Minister asks me to say that he thinks Lord Rothermere ought to have an opportunity of preparing his remarks for circulation at the same time. I am accordingly sending your memorandum to Lord Rothermere."

The Air Minister responded with a fervour which antagonised at least one leading member of the Government. Mr. J. C. C. (now Viscount) Davidson, Bonar Law's private secretary, distinctly remembers drawing the deputy Prime Minister's attention to Rothermere's reply which had struck him personally as "an evasive, vindictive and thoroughly indefensible attack on Trenchard's integrity." Bonar Law read it, then turned to his secretary.

" Get me Harold Rothermere on the telephone at once," he said. " This really is too much."

According to Davidson, the call was more in the nature of a lecture than a conversation. For Bonar Law, "made no secret of his anger and disgust." After telling Rothermere exactly what he thought of his "apologia," the deputy Prime Minister added these chilly words:

" Harold, I'm afraid that you must go."

Davidson still holds that Rothermere "did not resign but was really sacked" as a result of Bonar Law's prim view of a matter less of principle than of propriety. Beaverbrook, who was not present, dismisses Davidson's opinion as "most unlikely." On the balance of evidence, it would seem that neither Beaverbrook nor Davidson is wholly right. There is reason to think that Bonar Law's staid reaction depressed the fickle Rothermere far more than it impressed a Prime Minister who did not readily take scandal from defamatory statements of the kind. Besides, Lloyd George now had a second and bigger bone to pick with Rothermere.

The Parliamentary Under-Secretary for Air, Major J. L. Baird, had meanwhile presented the Prime Minister with what amounted to an ultimatum. Baird had just seen a copy of a Cabinet paper on future R.A.F. policy, dated 9th April, which Rothermere had composed and circulated without reference to any responsible adviser. The reorganisation plans were a compound of wildly optimistic hopes and grossly inaccurate facts, as Baird confirmed on checking them with Weir and other experts.[5]

Baird's indictment against a Minister for whom he had "covered up" once too often was far more damaging than Trenchard's. In a brief covering letter to Lloyd George, the Parliamentary Under-Secretary dissociated himself from "some of the views expressed by Lord Rothermere," declared that he "could not support them in the House of Commons," and asked to be given the opportunity of "laying my own views before the War Cabinet." When this last request was granted, Rothermere wisely took his cue and resigned in the nick of time.

The public manner of his going was dignified and decorous, thanks largely to Beaverbrook's skill in expurgating all contentious matter from the final letters which passed between Lloyd George and his erstwhile Secretary of State. Some good reasons were listed in these published letters to account for the Minister's urgent desire to go rather than face the music. Undeniably, Rothermere was in no fit mental or physical state to stand trial; sorrow for the loss of his eldest son and the struggle to hide his own self-pity and uncertainty in office had overtaxed his nervous strength. Nevertheless, the anxiety of Lloyd George to spare him further strain was swayed by political rather than personal considerations. Knowing that Rothermere had hardly a leg to stand on, the Prime Minister was concerned to deny Baird the opportunity of exposing that fact to the world.

When Rothermere's resignation was announced on the afternoon of Thursday, 25th April, passers-by in the Strand looked up in curiosity at the windows of the Hotel Cecil where scores of R.A.F. officers were leaning out, cheering and waving newspapers.

" What is it, a victory in France? " someone shouted.

" No," answered a reveller on the first floor. " A victory at home. Lord Rothermere has gone."*[6]

Next morning, Trenchard, who had asked Milner, the successor to Derby at the War Office, to let him return to the army and the command of an infantry brigade offered by Haig, received this note from Godfrey Paine:

" Sit tight, my friend. Nothing can be done or settled until the new Secretary of State is appointed which I understand will probably be to-day or to-morrow morning. I am feeling years younger and see daylight again."

* A similar account is recorded by Colonel Repington in his diary.

3

For hours on end during the next three weeks, Trenchard "sat tight" on a bench in London's Green Park, communing with himself. In times of desolation the advice and the company of others had always been his hardest cross: now, by spending most of the day under the freshly budding trees, in anonymous civilian clothes, he could avoid the attentions of intriguers and scandalmongers, whose invitations gathered dust on the mantelpiece of his living-room, as well as persecution by journalists. At midday and dusk he would walk to his ground-floor bachelor flat in Berkeley Street to answer any important letters or telegrams which had turned up in his absence.

The conspirator of Beaverbrook's fancy went in fact to the other extreme, lying low like a fugitive from the hurricane of controversy that had begun to blow about his head. He had no wish to add to the Government's cares while the second phase of the German offensive was in train, though he hated sitting out the battle in idleness merely because Lloyd George could not immediately decide what to do with him.

Trenchard was thankful that the air debate in Parliament on 29th April fizzled out in anti-climax. He was sick to death of a dispute that profited nobody. After breakfast each morning, he would walk into the park with the daily newspapers under his arm; for time hung heavily and there was little else to do but read and brood. He rejoiced for everyone's sake at Rothermere's unexpected departure, though it amused him that Lloyd George should have felt obliged, even as a perfunctory duty, to extol the ex-Minister's imaginary achievements.* It vexed him also that Simon should have joined Cecil, in a useless crusade on his behalf at Westminster.

Trenchard read Lloyd George's speech again and again, not to relish the superlatives heaped on himself from that unlikely quarter, but to search for hidden clues as to how exactly the Government proposed to re-employ him.

"I am most anxious," the Prime Minister had told the House,

*Lloyd George had written to Rothermere, acknowledging the receipt of his resignation: "It is the more to be lamented that, having set the Ministry on its legs, you cannot remain to enjoy the fruition of your own brilliant work. But I feel on reading your letter that I cannot press you to stay, much as the Government must suffer from your retirement." Lord Hugh Cecil dismissed the letter in the House of Commons as "the effort of a strong Celtic imagination. It was not a statement of fact but an essay in hagiology. . . ." (*Hansard*, 29th April 1918)

" that nothing should be said which would appear to be derogatory to the distinguished services of General Trenchard or his great ability. If the Committee listened, as I know they did, very carefully to the description given by the noble Lord [Cecil] of General Trenchard, it was the description of a great leader. He said something about Nelson and Wellington. I am not sure that either of them could be the Chief of the Air Staff.

" This is not a criticism of Nelson. I agree with the noble Lord that the qualities of General Trenchard are of the Nelson type—his highest qualities are Nelsonian qualities of mind and inspiration. . . . I can assure the noble Lord that there is an essential difference between the kind of qualities which you require for a man who sits in an office to think out slowly, perhaps laboriously, plans not merely for to-morrow, not for the day after to-morrow, but for next year— because that is the business of the Chief of Air Staff—to think out the work for the months to come, for this year and for next year— there is a vast difference between the qualities you require for that and the qualities you require for great leadership and inspiration of the air force. . . ."

And so it rambled on, a cleverly misleading speech, liberally sprinkled with praise of the victim, in which the Prime Minister had drawn off his own assailants one by one. The reasons for the Air Ministry crisis, of course, went unexplained in the smoke-screen of verbiage. Trenchard could not withhold his grudging admiration. Lloyd George even succeeded in turning the tables on Cecil and Simon by accusing them of abusing their privileges as M.P.s. What right, the Prime Minister asked, had these two Members of Parliament to use information obtained as temporary service officers for waylaying the Government? The question helped to side-track the course of the debate. Only one remaining paragraph in the speech held Trenchard's interest, momentarily rocking his diminished faith in human nature.

" When you come to consider," said Lloyd George, " whether it is desirable to turn out the present Chief of Staff of the air service [Sykes] and put General Trenchard [back] in that post, instead of using his services where they can be of more advantage to the air force, then the opinion of Sir William Weir must necessarily count with the Government. . . . He has absolutely no doubt on the subject, none, that that is not the best way of using the great services of General Trenchard, and there is no man with greater admiration for General Trenchard than Sir William Weir."

So Weir, it seemed, after only forty-eight hours in Rothermere's shoes, had fallen for the line of least resistance and confirmed Sykes in office as his Chief of Staff. The disclosure grieved Trenchard; yet typically, he never raised the grievance with Weir then or later, though they remained intimate friends for the next thirty-eight years.

"I was not invited by Lloyd George to choose my own Chief of Staff and had no idea Trenchard thought so," Weir explained to the present writer. "Sykes was part of the legacy I inherited from Rothermere. I was simply told by Lloyd George to find another air force appointment for Trenchard. What the Prime Minister told the Commons was untrue, of course, but then I didn't write his speech."

Weir's own appointment had surprised nobody but himself. He was inspecting new aircraft at Hendon one misty, late April morning when a huge car drew up and an official approached with the message:

"You are wanted immediately, Sir William, at No. 10 Downing Street." Weir was whisked away, wondering what new wind of change was blowing. Max Aitken, better known as Lord Beaverbrook, joined him as he waited in an ante-room. "Bonar would like to see you first," he said. "They want you to take the Air Ministry."

Weir, who had known Bonar Law slightly since their early business days in Glasgow, respected the other's political judgment as a rule, but listened unmoved on this occasion to his laborious efforts to make an unenviable post sound slightly more congenial. Weir had kept aloof from Rothermere, whose passion for intrigue had distressed him. He did not want his job now, but did not feel it right to add to the Government's embarrassment or the nation's troubles by refusing it. Incongruously, at that moment, he recalled a cryptic remark of Rothermere's on the latter's first day at the Air Ministry.

"You know, Weir," he said, "if only you'd been three inches taller, they'd have picked you, not me." Had he meanwhile put on the necessary inches? Or was it only Rothermere's stature which had shrunk to vanishing point? Weir wondered as he accepted the post.

His first act was to arrange a meeting with the elusive Trenchard. This took place on the second-last evening of April in Weir's Embankment flat at Westminster; and it proved, in the new Minister's words, "a difficult and inconclusive encounter." Nothing, apparently, would induce the ex-Chief of Air Staff to terminate his self-imposed sentence of solitary confinement in the park merely to salve what passed for Lloyd George's conscience. He reminded Weir of the Prime Minister's promise to the Commons that it was not proposed "to create a post" for himself, and of the further assurance that the appointment the Cabinet had in mind would be "one associated directly with his (Trenchard's) own aerial policy."

Weir replied that he had advised Lloyd George to say just that. He was not ashamed of it. At least three new openings were crying out for men of Trenchard's experience and authority. He could choose whichever he liked, though the one to which Weir personally attached most weight was the Bombing Command at Ochey. Trenchard seemed as hesitant about all three jobs as he was doubtful about the terms, but did agree to consider them.

In a letter to Weir on 1st May, he explained why he felt unable to accept any of them. Referring first to the Ochey proposal, he wrote:

" You say the man in charge should devote his entire energies to the development of bombing. There is one of the best generals in the air service, Newall, already in charge of this bombing and the whole point is whether he should work under Salmond (the G.O.C. in France) or under the Air Ministry. Let me ask what this really means.

" Do you mean all the administration should be done from England as well as the operations? If it is to be administered from England, do you realise what this involves? In my opinion it will mean a great waste of man-power, overlapping of work in workshops, etc. If you mean operations, what sort of orders could the Air Ministry send? I take it they are to bomb German towns.

" I cannot conceive why any officer in London should think he is in a better position or more capable to say which particular towns should be bombed at which particular moment. It would be fatal in my opinion to direct the actual carrying out of orders from London. . . .

" Another point that should be borne in mind is the question of the French. The French bombing is under their army commander, and they deal with our commander. Their aviation is part and parcel of their army, and if they have to refer some questions regarding aviation, aerodromes, supplies, operations, etc., to the Commander-in-Chief and some to the Air Ministry it will lead to all sorts of trouble as the war goes on and aircraft increase."

Trenchard's argumentativeness did not displease Weir, who challenged the soundness of his reasons for rejecting the two other posts, that of Grand Co-ordinator of British and American air policy, and that of Inspector General of the R.A.F. overseas. So Trenchard referred him to an exhaustive paper on American air problems drafted in Rothermere's time and reiterated some of his original objections. These are very revealing.

" I am certain it would be fatal to lay down for the Americans their policy of organisation and the methods of their supply," he wrote. " We can but advise them, which we have done in the past; but a big nation will not surrender its right of evolving its organisation according to its views after it has gained a certain amount of experience and taken a certain amount of advice, which America has already done from us.

" I am certain they will never agree to handing their organisation, which is the chief difficulty, over to a British officer, lock, stock and barrel, but they will undoubtedly in my mind, when they are ready, hand over to a British officer in the early stages of their work a force available for bombing." As for the proferred post of Overseas Inspector General, Trenchard said firmly:

" Before I left the Air Council I drew up the whole of the organisation for this—and that as far as I am concerned is finished with. It is on simple, straightforward and sound principles. All that is necessary now is to send the scheme out with an officer . . . and bring it into force, which I had intended to do about 1st May."

The exchange of letters, punctuated by further inconclusive meetings, continued like an exercise in administrative logic until even the long-suffering Weir grew a trifle testy. Every fresh suggestion the Minister put up, Trenchard seemed to enjoy knocking sideways. It seemed impossible to break through the thought-barrier and persuade him that these were not artificially created jobs designed to keep an awkward customer quiet, so Weir finally ruled that the correspondence must cease:

" I have again reviewed the situation and make you the following alternatives," he wrote tersely on 6th May:

(a) Position of Inspector General already referred to. . . . I am really at a loss to understand your view that such work is of 'no real value.' . . .

(b) The command of all air force units in the Middle East.

(c) The independent command of long-range bombing forces in France, the strength and final development of which will represent a big command, particularly if associated with America. It is also possible that at a later date this might be combined with the command of the bombing force operating from another base (in Norfolk, England) which we have discussed.

(*d*) Inspector General of R.A.F. areas and commands at home, including training.

" If you accept (*c*), which I would very much like you to do, I would ask you before taking over command to carry out the American mission on the lines indicated to you on Saturday.

" Now I trust I have made it clear to you that I will not create a position specially for you. The above are positions requiring men, and I want you to accept one of them so that your experience may contribute to the success of the Royal Air Force and not on any ground of quelling what you call 'the agitation.' Any of these positions in my opinion answers your test of 'being of value,' and, moreover, fully covers the promise I made through the Prime Minister. If there are any points not clear in the above, I shall be available for half an hour between nine-thirty and ten to-night."

Trenchard did not call on Weir that evening. He was still in a quandary. The post of bomber commander at Nancy, the only big operational vacancy available, tempted him for paradoxical reasons to which Weir still shut both eyes. If the so-called independent air force were both to retain its independence and expand, its commander would have to temper diplomacy with thrift. Neither Foch nor Haig, he knew, would tolerate a separate force which consumed Allied men and supplies without contributing directly to the waging and winning of local battles. The challenge to go out and square this particular circle had its own appeal. For Trenchard was aware that both Foch and Haig trusted him.

What helped to clinch his decision was a stinging remark he overheard in Green Park early on 8th May. He was settling down on his usual bench with the daily newspapers and a book to while away another empty day when two senior naval officers approached on their way to Whitehall. There had been recent moments of frustrated envy when he would gladly have changed places with the obscurest staff officer. His status as a displaced general of notoriety had become a source of depression rather than of satisfaction. Yet Trenchard's longing for the easy way out rarely survived reflection. The opinionated, self-willed and dominant half of his nature renounced the idea that peace of mind could be secured by surrendering on a point of principle. Weariness with a false part could never obscure the fact that peace purchased at such a price would bring greater humiliation and remorse.

Trenchard pricked up his ears as the pair passed by. They were discussing his case so intently that neither of them so much as glanced at the man in civilian clothes on the park bench, his face screened behind a newspaper, who hung on their every word. The shorter and older naval officer was the more loquacious. He had no sympathy for anyone, however badly victimised, who abandoned his post in a crisis.

" It's an outrage," Trenchard heard him say. " I don't know why the Government should pander to a man who threw in his hand at the height of a battle. If I'd my way with Trenchard I'd have him shot."

The less voluble of the two murmured assent, and presently both were out of earshot. It startled Trenchard to think that many others probably shared this view of his conduct. He found it suddenly unbearable to sit dumbly on, doing nothing. Believing that he had held out long enough, Trenchard walked home and wrote to Weir accepting the command of the Independent Air Force.

" Out of the four alternative appointments you offer me, one of these I have already refused as it has no power or responsibility. Another is of a similar nature, and the other two are based on a polciy against which I have stated my objections several times, and which I think will lead to efficiency being lowered.

" At the same time, as you have apparently decided to bring in this policy, and are apparently anxious to retain me for it, then I can only say I will accept the command of the long-distance bombing in France and do my best to make it a success as far as possible."

Weir was enormously relieved. Trenchard would, in his view, be far happier dropping bombs on Germany rather than outsize bricks in London; for if any man could put teeth into the inter-Allied bombing plan, that man was the ex-Chief of Air Staff.

" I'll back up anything you decide," Weir told him eagerly. " If you're ever in need or doubt, get on to me direct."

Trenchard could have asked for nothing better. Though he had so far refrained from mentioning it, half his uneasiness about the appointment sprang from distrust of his successor. He had seen Sykes only once since resigning; and once was quite enough.

4

The following entry in Trenchard's operational diary scarcely conveys the distress he felt on breaking his journey at British G.H.Q. to discuss his new role with Haig and Salmond, neither of whom was exactly overjoyed at the prospect of being deprived of heavy bombers.

" 17th May, 1918. Discussed the separation (of the Independent

Force). It was arranged that I should go down to Nancy and whilst there should remain under General Salmond until he and the French Government receive their orders from the Air Ministry. Stayed the night with the C.-in-C."[7]

Yet he quickly recovered his spirits on reaching his destination. The wastes of moorland were now flat, grassy airfields. The half-finished depots and roads, the virtually completed loop railway, and the scores of tented camps, reminded him that this island of teeming activity was the fruit of his forethought. He soon learnt that its insular character was more than physical, and that his new bases were set in an ocean of French suspicion which he would have to plumb at once.

Trenchard's first confidential report, which reached Weir towards the end of May, made fairly stimulating reading.

" I have started visiting the French and Americans fairly freely," it began, " and as you know, we are pushing the bombing. Provided that the C.A.S. (Sykes) lets me know what is going on, I am perfectly certain that in time I shall get the thing going as an independent show. If I am not told I shall have an impossible job. . . . I have not yet got a headquarters or any staff and am doing all the work myself."

Weir had long recognised Trenchard as peerless in energy and ingenuity when confronted with the problem of creating something out of nothing. It had been so at Farnborough, in Flanders, and more recently at Ochey when the 8th Brigade's bombers had begun to repay the enemy in kind for the Gotha raids on Britain. Since early 1917, the two men had frequently compared views on the feasibility of long-range air operations; and though Trenchard disagreed with the Scot for exaggerating the probable impact of a bombing campaign on German industry, his respect for Weir's sure grasp of an intricate subject had grown with time.

Nearly a year before Smuts undertook his air inquiry, Weir had stressed in an official report that "bombing aeroplanes will drop more high explosives behind the German lines, for the same cost and at a longer range, than howitzers, since a bomb needs less steel than a shell, and petrol is cheaper than cordite." Now his chance had come as the responsible Minister to test the theory in partnership with Trenchard.

Spring was ending with no tangible promise of early victory. Only Haig clung to the seemingly unfounded belief that the Germans had shot their bolt on land, for his estimates of enemy man-power wastage were by now as discredited in the Government's

T.   K eyes as his strategy of attrition. In the air, as on the ground, the hopes of political leaders turned on the fresh reserves of men and material still only trickling from the United States. The plan devised by Trenchard in January for incorporating American bomber crews with his own was the very plan which Weir now wished him to carry out as commander-designate of an embryonic inter-Allied bombing force.

That it could not make its influence felt before the summer of 1919 both men were agreed. And it was with this provisional date in mind that Trenchard approached the American and French High Commands, glumly aware that British output of big horse-power aero engines had not yet reached the conservative level which he had forecast as necessary the previous autumn when Smuts was basing his case for a separate air force on an expected glut of them.

" I have told Sykes that you are to have a very free hand and all help and information so that you can push ahead," Weir assured him in his first letter from London. " Do not worry about the French and the Air Ministry until the matter is raised by them, when we will be prepared to meet strongly any objections which may come up. . . . The French must give you ground. If you have any trouble, I will get the Prime Minister to convince Clemenceau."

Weir, in fact, had moved briskly to anticipate "trouble." In mid-May, as soon as Trenchard accepted the Nancy command, the Minister submitted for instant War Cabinet approval a paper advocating the formation of an inter-Allied bombing force on grounds of military necessity. Its most intriguing feature was a postscript, tacked on in deference to Trenchard's emphatic warnings that Foch would insist, as Allied Generalissimo, on the bombers being placed directly under him.

" I would represent most strongly," ran Weir's postscript, "the possible dangers of such an arrangement, and would point out the necessity of supporting the independence of this command to a similar degree as a naval command."

Clemenceau's first reaction was one of easy compliance. Towards the end of May he replied that Duval, the deputy Chief of the French General Staff with administrative control of the air service, had been instructed to introduce the required changes. Weir was delighted, until Trenchard's next letter arrived. This suggested either that Duval was playing a double game or that an inexplicable failure in communication had occurred between Paris and Nancy.

" It's very hard to explain on paper the various difficulties that arise if it's not clearly laid down what I am," Trenchard complained.

" For instance, if I ask the French railway authorities for facilities
to bring trains into the neighbourhood with my stores, the answer
I may get is ' What are you? We know nothing about you.' This
will take place over all matters, roads, supplies, maps and other items
too numerous to mention. . . ."

It seemed a simple enough request; but neither Weir nor Lloyd
George was in any position to grant it, and even Clemenceau, "the
Tiger," appeared strangely reluctant to intervene. The explanation
was simple. The question of Trenchard's status had meanwhile been
referred to Foch by Duval on receipt of Clemenceau's instructions.
And the Allied Generalissimo simply refused to recognise the
existence on French soil of "an irregular air force" claiming to take
its orders from London. Only the Supreme War Council at Versailles,
the cumbersome instrument intended by Lloyd George for the
frustration of his own Commander-in-Chief, had the right to judge
Foch's decision, but an emergency meeting could scarcely be called
at a moment's notice. It so happened that a sub-committee of the
Council, consisting of five men from each of the interested Allied
powers, was then considering the implications of long-distance
bombing. The position of Trenchard's force was passed over to it
for examination; and an extraordinary session was hurriedly
arranged for the last day of the month. Invitations went out to
Duval, Sykes and Trenchard.

" It was an extremely delicate position," commented Baring,
who had rejoined his old chief after a prolonged leave, "as we had
not been recognised by the French Government and we were neither
under the orders of the Generalissimo nor of Sir Douglas Haig.
Therefore our unique and undefined position depended, as far as
practical results were concerned, on the goodwill of the French. . . .
The French had only to put the slightest spoke in our wheels, and
our work became impossible since every square inch of aerodrome,
every arrangement for the transport of each gallon of petrol,
depended on their goodwill. . . . Luckily this goodwill was given to
us in an overflowing measure by General de Castelnau, the
commander of the group of armies of the east. He and the
General understood each other at once after their first conversation."

This meeting with de Castelnau reprieved the Independent Air
Force. For de Castelnau was no conventional leader, either. A man
of culture, a Catholic and an aristocrat like Baring, he also had
something of Trenchard's monumental integrity and lack of rigidity.

" He seemed," wrote Baring with deep feeling, " to belong to a
nobler epoch than ours, to be a native of the age of chivalry, of that

time when Louis IX, who is known as St. Louis, dispensed justice under a spreading oak tree. He had the easy familiarity, the slight play of kindly irony, the little ripple of humour, the foresight and forethought, that *politesse de coeur*, that complete remoteness from what is common, mean, base, self-seeking, which are the foundation and substance of God's gentlemen. . . ."

For de Castelnau's capacity as a commander, Trenchard had the highest regard. He thought of him, and not of Pétain, as the saviour of Verdun, just as he would always remember du Peuty's role there in proving the doctrine of the air offensive. Now du Peuty was dead. No public clamour had prevented *his* premature return to the front after protesting in vain against changes in the structure of the *French* Air Service. They had found and identified his body somewhere in no-man's-land after the recent Chemin-des-Dames battle, still clutching the walking-stick he had held while leading his Zouaves through the enemy wire.

It was during the air talks at Paris at the end of May that Trenchard first heard that the Germans had recaptured the Chemin-des-Dames, turning the French line on the Aisne, and advancing unchecked to a point some ten miles north of Château Thierry. Haig, whom he unexpectedly met in the French capital, commiserated with him in his difficulties, and expressed doubt whether political talks alone would settle them in his favour. Foch had preoccupations enough, he suggested, without assuming responsibility for a bombing force over which he would exercise no direct control. It was for Trenchard to demonstrate in practice that his command was a help, not a hindrance, to the Allied cause. Then Foch might be reasoned with. It was good advice, though Trenchard hardly needed it.

An atmosphere of unreal calm pervaded the meetings of the air conference, except when " Big Bertha " spoke in the distance or when raiding aircraft gleamed like silver in the unclouded sky overhead. The Germans had not been so close to the French capital since the late summer of 1914.

" Many people," wrote Baring, " thought we should never see Paris again, and we looked at the beautiful buildings, and the Champs-Élysées, and the glittering dome of the Invalides, and the delicate trees which had just put on their fresh summer apparel, and we wondered whether in a fortnight's time all this would be one with Ninevah and Tyre, and Ypres. . . . As someone aptly quoted from the classics, we were chattering and the enemy was at the gates of Rome."

Duval proved less despondent than other French staff officers about the latest German break-through on the Marne. The military situation, he assured Trenchard, would be established before the week was out. What irked him more than this minor tactical set-back was the inconsistency and inconsiderations of the British in trying to foist the independent bombing force on Foch.

At the conference table Duval poked fun at the misuse of the word "independent," asking ironically: " Independent of what? Of God? ", and rebutting the argument of Sykes, the new Chief of Air Staff, that Trenchard's primary duty was to bomb Germany and to assist the Allied armies only if the need arose. That, said Duval, was putting the cart before the war horse.

" The committee is being asked to say that the primary object is to bomb Germany and the secondary one merely to defeat the enemy in the field. We need unification of effort, not dissipation."

Yes, protested Sykes, but in an emergency Foch need only *ask* for support and all Trenchard's bombers would be unreservedly at his disposal.

" From the military standpoint," remarked Duval dryly, " orders are usually better than requests."

He was quite unimpressed to hear that the British Government had weighed all the factors well, and that the highest priority had been given to bomber output, since the estimated future needs of the army and navy were already catered for.

" I shall be grateful," retorted the Frenchman, " to any authority capable of determining the limit of what is necessary to the winning of a battle. Great commanders have always solved this problem by making use of every resource within reach."

The breakdown of the talks came as a grievous disappointment to Weir, who had not expected the Allied representatives to yield so passively to Duval. Yet, the French Air Chief responded amiably enough in private to Trenchard's suggestion that he should be allowed to shift for himself at Nancy. " If General de Castelnau will let you go on bombing, I shan't interfere," he said. " But don't expect official recognition."

Clearly, Foch would not relent until the Germans were thrown back on the defensive. Trenchard's only course in the circumstances was to convert local French commanders one by one.

" I am certain Pétain, from what he said to me, is very keen on the bombing of Germany," he informed Weir, "and so is de Castelnau here and the majority of the French, but the French aviation people with Foch, I fancy, are very much against it, because they see a number of squadrons slipping from their grasp."

In fact, Foch's attitude in the summer of 1918 almost exactly resembled Haig's the previous autumn, when the Smuts Report was published. The attitude of Trenchard had not altered; though he believed in air-power heart and soul, his original doubts as to whether sufficient aircraft of the right types could be produced soon enough to build a separate air force, and so justify the colossal administrative and operational upheaval entailed in letting it fight its own battles, remained hard and clear cut. His scepticism had been borne out by events. Under Rothermere, Trenchard had become a convenient scapegoat for the other's administrative incompetence, while the promised aircraft surplus had failed to materialise. Weir alone had refused to be distracted or deterred. As Director of Aircraft Production, he had scaled down his earlier estimates, kept the army and navy supplied, and yet contrived by rigorous economies to lay down more bombers than Salmond would ever need on the Western Front.

Now, as Air Minister, Weir was determined to harvest the rewards of his thrift. Knowing that Trenchard was well thought of by the French, he supported him resolutely in his private overtures. His greatest fear was that Lloyd George, as he put it, would "wobble again" and reverse the bombing plan by seeking a compromise with Foch.

" I need hardly say," Weir wrote to Trenchard, " that I would not sit in my chair for five minutes longer if the Government agreed to come to terms on bombing. More than that, I feel sure the country would turn them out."

Trenchard reciprocated the Minister's trust by keeping nothing back from him. At least twice a week the two men exchanged long, frank letters which mirrored their difficulties and still more their close understanding. It is arguable whether this partnership between a service Minister and an active commander has any modern parallel in war; and while one cannot but pity Sykes, whose authority was thus by-passed, the Chief of Air Staff did not feel disposed to challenge an irregular procedure which Weir persistently encouraged. It did little to allay Sykes's personal dislike of Trenchard; it did much, given the anomalous position of the independent force, to secure prompt decisions.

For his part, Trenchard saw no contradiction in egging on Weir to commit the very sin which he had found unforgivable in Rothermere. The mitigating factor now was Sykes, the epitome of indecisiveness, to by-pass whom could be accounted both virtue and duty.

Salmond broadly shared Trenchard's opinion.

" I made a point of getting through personally to London when I knew Sykes wasn't there," he told this author. " It was the simplest and quickest way of getting results."

Salmond, however, had reason to dislike the privileged status of Trenchard, which made him a potentially serious competitor for aircraft, spares and men. As commander of the biggest air force in the field, Salmond's wants were considerable; and fully aware that Trenchard, in a similar predicament, would have brooked no refusals, he protested more than once at the diverting of bombers from the Western Front to Nancy.

The clearest evidence of Trenchard's consistency of view is contained in a memorandum he sent to Weir on 23rd June, 1918, for the attention of the War Cabinet:

" In my opinion," he wrote, " once our aviation is strong enough to hold and defeat the German aviation, the extra effect on the battle front of still further bombing would not turn a defeat into victory or a victory into defeat. . . .

" It seems to me unanswerable that if it is possible to hit the German Armies in France and at the same time hit the Germans in Germany, this is a better concentration of effort than if we hit only one part of Germany.

" This has always been my view from the beginning of the war against Germany. As long ago as June, 1916, I asked for a certain number of squadrons for fighting the German armies in France and for a certain number of squadrons for fighting the Germans in Germany. I said the first necessity was to provide those machines which were necessary for fighting and bombing the Germans in France, and that the others were a luxury until sufficient machines were provided. I said it was a necessity to have long-distance bombing machines for fighting the Germans in Germany.

" It may still be said that we have not enough machines to beat the German aviation. If this is so, then all our public claims at present are false. We are stronger in the air relatively to the enemy at the present time than we have ever been before, and we are stronger than I expected to be when I put forward the programme of what was necessary two years ago. In my opinion, the British aviation is now strong enough both to beat the German aviation in France and to attack the industrial centres of Germany. . . ."

It would have greatly simplified matters if Weir had not tried to rush Foch at the outset. This was the Minister's one mistake. The reluctance of the Generalissimo to waive any part of his authority was certainly logical; but it equally exposed the slowness of the army mind to grasp the strategic opportunities of air-power. Duval, alas, was no du Peuty; on the few occasions French machines raided the Rhineland cities, it was always emphasised that such attacks were in the nature of reprisals. Trenchard was against retaliation; his sole concern was to cripple Germany by means of a sustained air offensive. Weir had promised to let him have fourteen extra squadrons by August; and though it was not Trenchard's practice to count bombers before delivery, the diplomatic deadlock between Paris and London convinced him that a successful bombing campaign on a small scale would be the best method of weakening Foch's resistance—and ultimately the enemy's.

5

As it turned out, Trenchard did not get those fourteen extra squadrons before the Armistice, though this was not entirely due to production set-backs. Had he insisted on grabbing every delivery earmarked for him, his force would probably have outgrown its five huge airfields about Nancy. None the less, his brief was to form not a British but an Allied force; and because of unrelenting French opposition, half his time and energy was expended on helping the Americans.

" I had a visit last week from Colonel Monell, whom General Patrick (the U.S. Air Commander) has designated as Chief in Command of American night-bombing squadrons," Weir wrote at the end of June. " He's rather a good chap and is anxious to get in touch with you as soon as possible. . . . He fully understands that he will work under you and with you, although it is also understood that nothing in the way of a formal agreement should be discussed at the moment unless absolutely necessary. I mean an agreement embracing the French also.

" General Patrick, through him, will require advice from you as to the composition of squadrons other than Handley Pages, that is the future day-bombing squadrons, and perhaps some of the extreme range squadrons. . . ."

Sykes was paying one of his rare visits to Nancy a few days later when Monell arrived with another senior colleague, Colonel Van Horn. It was "a very satisfactory meeting," Trenchard told Weir.

" They want a large amount of assistance to organise their air service in this country. I gave them three alternatives: I would do nothing except use any squadrons they gave me: I would organise and run joint depots for them: I would organise, plan the layouts, and supervise at the start the American organisation of their depots, etc., and then by about February or March next year hand the lot over to them to run.

" The latter is undoubtedly the correct solution if they are not capable of carrying out the first. . . . It means the building of three or four depots for fifty or sixty squadrons each."

Before July ended, a detailed plan, complete even as to the sharing of financial costs, had been drafted. Trenchard undertook to supply and repair at his Courbon depot all American Handley Page and de Havilland machines operating east of Rheims, laying it down that "for purposes of accounting, 3 D.H.4s or D.H.9s shall be equivalent to one Handley Page." His proposals for training American crews were adopted without argument.

" The British will take two bombardment teams every two weeks for instruction in their service squadrons and will usually form them into a flight," Weir was informed. " These teams can be withdrawn by us to form a nucleus for the pilot and observer personnel of a new squadron."

Thus was conceived and shaped, under the stress of war, the embryo of the future United States Strategic Bombing Command. Fed by British machines, nursed by British technicians, its first members were enrolled and initiated in Trenchard's exacting school. When Weir spent three days with him towards the end of July, Trenchard pressed him to set aside special flights of Handley Pages and F.E.2bs for the advanced tuition of dozens of Americans stationed with the new R.A.F. in Britain, though this meant sacrificing machines for his own command. He was thinking in terms of the future, of the destruction which would rain down on the industrial vitals of Germany the following spring; and he felt sufficiently strongly about the unsoundness of investing only in the present to raise the subject again with Weir in writing.

" I know the training of the Americans in England has nothing to do with me, but in my opinion it is of the most vital importance to them and me to get some of their squadrons going on some of the long-distance bombing."

There had been a more urgent reason for the Minister's sudden journey to Nancy than co-operation with the Americans. Trenchard had lately received a copy of Sykes's revised programme for dividing future aircraft supplies between army, navy and independent squadrons; and his reaction at being allotted on paper twice as many machines as his command could accommodate was scornfully critical. He objected in particular to overstocking his depots with twenty fighter squadrons which were evidently to be filched for that purpose from the army and navy wings. For he had not yet decided which type of machine would be most suitable for long-range escort duties. At his insistence, therefore, the 104 "paper" squadrons which Sykes and the planners would have wished on him were whittled down to a more realistic fifty-four. It is of interest to record that only five of these fifty-four reached him before the Armistice.

The Americans were, in contrast to the French, extremely eager to co-operate and delightfully frank about their inexperience. Trenchard's only criticism, an unusual one, was that leaders like Foulois and Patrick were too easy to persuade, tending to lean too heavily on him and betraying at times their "army-mindedness," as he called it. Indeed, Pershing, the U.S. Commander-in-Chief, admitted to Trenchard that he had selected them for that very reason in preference to "natural airmen" whose visionary faith in three-dimensional warfare owed more to intuition than to the canons of West Point. By far the most engaging of these young enthusiasts, and certainly the one for whom Trenchard developed the greatest respect and affection was Billy Mitchell, who had first driven up to R.F.C. Headquarters in May, 1917, at an inconvenient moment, demanding to see him. When Baring politely suggested another day, Mitchell coolly remarked that as an official observer attached to the American General Staff, he had no mind to waste his own or anyone else's time. Trenchard, who was just leaving to inspect outlying squadrons, had entered the room at that moment.

" What can I do for you? Have you an appointment? "

" No, General, but I still want to see as much of your organisation as you can show me. I'd like to see your equipment, your stores, and the way you arrange your system of supply. Also, I need to know all you can tell me about operations, because we will be joining you in these before long."

Trenchard stared quizzically at the business-like, absurdly boyish-looking intruder.

" That's quite a large order. How many weeks have you got to spare? "

" We could take in the equipment and supply part of it to-day," said Mitchell. " Then to-morrow we could start——"

" One minute, Major," interrupted Trenchard. " Do you suppose I've got nothing better to do than chaperon you and answer questions? "

Mitchell shrugged and grinned in the friendliest way.

" I don't suppose anything, General. I just know you've got a good organisation here. It won't miss you if you take a day or two off, no matter how bad you say things are."

The explosion expected by Baring did not follow. Trenchard was intrigued by Mitchell's good-natured impudence.

" All right," he said. " Come along with me, young man. I can see you're the sort who usually gets what he wants in the end."

For the best part of three days, Mitchell seldom left Trenchard's side. A good listener and a shrewd interrogator, he made no apology for "picking other men's brains." He visited artillery and fighter squadrons, watched the F.E. bombers of the Headquarters Wing take off after dark to attack targets behind the German lines, and went away convinced that everything he had heard from the French in praise of Trenchard's leadership was an understatement.

The biographer of Mitchell, Roger Burlingame, quotes one saying of Trenchard's which deeply impressed the American:

" The Germans still think of the airplane as a defensive weapon. That is why the work they have actually accomplished on the British front is about four per cent of what we have done. The one exception is their night bombing. They have inflicted thousands of casualties on our troops in bivouac by a new twin-engined aircraft called a Gotha. We must learn this."

Mitchell's occasionally extravagant methods of dramatising his needs in the twelve months since had not gone down well with Pershing, who appointed Patrick, an engineer, as head of the American Air Service with Foulois as his Chief of Staff. Mitchell, now a colonel, controlled the squadrons attached to the 1st U.S. Army Corps, but in a system of command which seemed to Trenchard more rigidly centralised than the British the scope for air leaders as gifted as Mitchell was scant.

" He's a man after my own heart," Trenchard remarked to Baring one day. " If only he can break his habit of trying to convert opponents by killing them, he'll go far."

They met officially and unofficially several times that summer. Twice during August, 1918, Mitchell called, uninvited, to let

Trenchard run a paternal eye over the preliminary details of his first big "air show" in support of the American First Army. His tactical plan for sweeping German opposition out of the sky above the St. Mihiel salient, a few miles north of Nancy, was ingenious and boldly conceived. Mitchell had only a bare dozen squadrons of Nieuport and Spad fighters of his own, but these were to be reinforced liberally by the French before the attack. At the express request of Foch, Trenchard gladly directed nearly half his bomber force to play an indirect role by pounding selected railway junctions, airfields and supply centres behind the enemy lines.

The timing of the St. Mihiel offensive was kept a close secret, Trenchard being informed less than half a day before zero hour, at dawn on 13th September. The 400 tanks and half a million men flanking both arms of the enemy salient, a V-shaped dent in the Allied line, were under the orders of Foch. Despite poor visibility Mitchell was able to use most of his machines. These were assembled in two groups behind each arm of the wedge; and while the first tremendous mêlée was taking place, the second formation of aircraft swept down on the unprotected far flank, splitting the outnumbered German airmen and giving them no respite. Resistance both on and above the ground quickly weakened. By 18th September, Foch had gained all his objectives.

" I have been doing my best to assist the Americans very largely in this battle," Trenchard reported to Weir. " This was just as well, since the weather was such owing to strong winds and clouds that it was impossible to do long-distance work."

Thirty-two tons of bombs were dropped on the station and marshalling yards of Metz alone.

" Enemy scouts for the most part were comparatively inactive," Trenchard noted, " except on 15th September, when our machines were heavily engaged over Metz."

Yet British bomber losses during the battle were negligible.

The success of these loosely co-ordinated efforts by Allied squadrons on and behind the battlefield pleased Foch almost as much as they appeared to displease Sykes. The Chief of Air Staff complained to Weir that Trenchard was neglecting his first responsibility for strategic bombing in thus concentrating on purely tactical targets, but the Minister chose to trust Trenchard's judgment rather than Sykes's. In fact, Trenchard was content to comply with Foch's request for aid on military as well as diplomatic grounds because he had not ceased to believe in the value of tactical bombing. Air supremacy had to be established, and seen to be established, over the battlefields before Foch would authorise an Allied air campaign against Germany, a point which the Generalissimo had recently made in a personal interview.

" He told me we were doing very good work and that he recognised my special position," runs a current entry in Trenchard's operational diary.

The overcaution of American staff officers occasionally taxed his patience more than the inflexible logic of Foch. He admitted his concern to Mitchell in the final stage of the St. Mihiel advance.

" Discussed various points with him," runs the relevant diary entry. " Also informed him that I was going to stop co-operating for the time being."

If the American leaders insisted on misusing their small bomber force, then they would have to learn from their own mistakes. Mitchell fully sympathised, as became a man who had once written rebelliously in his own diary:

" The (American) General Staff is now trying to run the air service with just as much knowledge of it as a hog knows about skating. It is terrible to have to fight with an organisation of this kind. . . ."

When Pershing's air advisers repented, it was too late. The appointment of Mitchell as operational chief of the American Army Air Corps on 1st October could no longer influence the outcome of a war already racing to a victorious climax on land. From Ghent in the north to the Argonne in the south, the Allied armies, with overwhelming tactical air support, were converting the German retreat into a rout. By Armistice Day no American bombers had taken part in a single long-range mission alongside Trenchard's Independent Force, a matter of deep and lasting regret to Mitchell and himself.

6

It must not be supposed that, because of Foch's veto on the plan for an independent Allied air offensive, little was done by the small core of available British squadrons. On the contrary, Trenchard drove these as hard as he dared in the hope that a ton of bombs on a German target would move Foch more quickly than all the arguments of politicians and self-styled experts. Within the restricted margin for action allowed by optimists in London and sceptics in Paris, he set about fashioning a physically minute force of less than seventy long-range bombers into a psychological weapon of unprecedented deadliness. So long as the Independent Air Force remained officially the creature of the War Cabinet in London alone, unrecognised except tacitly by local Allied commanders like de Castelnau, Trenchard had to fend for himself. This entailed great waste. For the Nancy base required 10,000 officers and men who were all combed from other establishments, an example of the price that had to be paid for dismembering an organisation as highly technical as the new R.A.F. Most of the specialists, the rail and road engineers, the ordnance men, the anti-aircraft and searchlight teams, the meteorologists, the craftsmen and the tradesmen, were "borrowed" on indefinite terms from the reluctant Haig and Salmond. Runways, hangars and depots were expanded to accommodate a force of sixty squadrons, since Weir's still plan envisaged not a British but an inter-Allied air fleet which, once Foch agreed, Trenchard would unleash on the Ruhr, the Rhineland, and eventually Berlin itself.

Because he hated the encumbrance of a long administrative tail, Trenchard shortened it wherever practicable. The subordinates he selected were men of proven competence; and while charging them with the details of development, he kept them on a tight rein and never gave notice of his sudden inspections.

The straight dusty roads of the Nancy region, blazing white in the sun of that idyllic summer, were lined with newly laid telegraph poles linking the airfields with his headquarters at Autigny-la-Tour. In this once peaceful hamlet, perched on a spur of the Vosges, an empty seventeenth-century château was requisitioned for his small personal staff.

" It's interesting starting a new force," he admitted to Weir. " The petty worries are always the worst."

Some of his worries were anything but petty. The engines which powered the three daylight squadrons of de Havillands were defective; spares of all kinds were virtually unobtainable at first; new pilots and observers took a week to come from England, letters longer still. One day, during the move to Autigny, a sackful of mail was discovered in an attic where it had been stored with a pile of trunks. Trenchard caustically asked Brigadier Gordon, his chief Staff Officer, to have the garden pond dragged "in case some harebrained person has stowed another there for safety."

Once his operational scheme was in order, administrative muddles had to take care of themselves. As early as 27th May, Trenchard's diary recorded the unchanged importance he attached to inculcating the offensive spirit.

" Explained to brigade, wing and squadron commanders what the Independent Force is and what I expect of it, that cloud flying must be practised, that we must be able to *bomb* in clouds very, very shortly, that we can't always do fine weather bombing, that we must fly long distances on dark nights without a moon as long as it's clear, and also impressed on them the importance of keeping in friendly touch with the French and Americans."

The administrative machine he had inherited from Newall was still only a small test model; but no sooner was he in control than he gave it full throttle. The crews expected this: so long as he stayed, willing them on and firing them with his faith in the impossible, all would be well. He prescribed the end and somehow provided the means. The rest was up to them, in theory at least.

" We could never be quite sure with Trenchard where the dividing line came between the flexibility he preached and the dogmatism he often imposed," fairly summarises what three of his squadron commanders separately told this writer. " He certainly inspired us; he could be generous and warm-hearted; but he could also be terribly touchy when contradicted, even if he happened to be wrong. Perhaps this was because he was a decisive man in a hurry."

A single incident will convey something of the mingled apprehension, respect and puzzled affection which Trenchard habitually stirred among his men. The waiter who served breakfast one morning in the mess of a bomber station where he had spent the night, produced coffee in a brown earthenware pot with a detachable and rather loosely fitting lid. Immersed in his papers, Trenchard did not even look up when Baring sat down beside him. But half a minute later there was a clatter of breaking crockery and a throaty bellow of rage. The lid of the coffee-pot, tilted at too sharp an angle, had crashed into Trenchard's cup, spilling the contents into his lap. The waiter returned in time to see Trenchard striding towards the nearest window, flinging it open with his free hand and hurling the coffee-pot into space with the other. Not a word was spoken; Baring did not even turn his head, but went on munching his toast, smiling disarmingly at the petrified waiter as if to say:

" Rather the pot than you. Now fetch something unbreakable." The waiter seemed to receive the message; for he withdrew, and reappeared with a fresh supply of coffee. Trenchard examined the pot.

" That's better," he said to the waiter. " Bury the other one— and any others you have like it."

Impulsiveness of the kind had its oddly human as well as comic appeal. A waiter had been treated to a spectacular display of temper instead of a cold stiff reprimand. An obsequious brigadier or an officious squadron commander might be less lucky. It was almost as if Trenchard regarded every cog in the machine as his personal property, to be used for a purpose which he alone fully understood and therefore had the sole right to judge.

Lacking the resources to concentrate attacks on one target at a time, Trenchard so spread his raids that no city within range could feel entirely safe. The bombers might cause little destruction; what counted was their impact on the spirit of the German people. The cumulative effect on morale would far exceed the actual toll of damage inflicted, provided the bombing went on, day and night, with few interruptions. On the other hand, Trenchard had to protect his own bases; and since expediency ruled out any approach to the French, half his bombers were employed in attacking enemy airfields between Nancy and the frontier.

Despite the constant plaintiveness of Sykes in London, Trenchard could not forget how, in a single night the previous autumn, the naval air depot at St. Pol and its reserve of heavy bombers had been virtually wiped out by a single squadron of Gothas. There would be no surprises of that disastrous kind so long as his daylight raiders struck hard and often, keeping the defenders spreadeagled and guessing. By thus confining the Germans to their own air space, Trenchard eased the way for his night raiders whose targets, though numerous, were seldom easy to find and hit.

" When it was impossible for squadrons to reach their objectives well in the interior of Germany," he wrote, " I decided that railways were first in order of importance as alternative targets, and next blast furnaces. . . . The Germans were extremely short of rolling stock, and some of the main railways feeding the Germany Army in the west passed close to our frontier. They were also fairly easy to find at night. I chose blast furnaces as they were also easy to find, although it was difficult to do any really serious damage to them owing to the smallness of the vital parts of the works."

The selection of targets was a matter of expediency. He needed quick results; for Foch had to be convinced that the bombing project was sound. Trenchard therefore doubled and trebled everyone's work during the crucial period from June to September. In his own words, "my job was to prod, cajole, help, comfort and will the pilots on, sometimes to their death. It wasn't pleasant. They were a new breed of fighting men grappling with unknown forces in the loneliest element of all. They had no precedents, no book of rules, nothing else to lean on but their pride of squadron, their corporate spirit of endeavour and unlimited personal courage, which made me feel humble and thankful. I think it was the sense of being tossed head first into the most impersonal type of battle any group of men had ever faced in history which helped them to rise above the risks and write their own traditions in the skies."

Trenchard, who often appeared at briefings before raids, knew each man by sight and wrestled harder than in the past to memorise all their names. The self-conscious mannerisms which newcomers and veterans alike adopted as a cover for uneasiness were easily recognisable. He felt for them, but rarely betrayed how deeply. Some thought him a stranger to fear, others as merely unimaginative, others again as an insensate, calculating ogre. At least he was immune to their opinion, good or bad; his supreme power to judge and to decide would never be swayed by that consideration. The duty of reminding them that what they were about to do was more important than life itself was one which he hated but could not shirk.

" If I knew for a fact that this raid would shorten the war by a day," they often heard him say, " you'd go and be glad you were going."

In cold print, those words assume the cold, brutal overtones of a death sentence. Yet that was not how the bomber crews of 1918 heard or understood them. They were mostly men who had matured young, some through the unexampled self-sacrifice of a dead comrade, others in a burst of avenging anger, others again through the gambler's adventurous love of risk for its own sake. Courage was the knot binding them together; all of them felt that they were serving life in the very act of facing death; and most of them sensed that Trenchard envied them the privilege. His booming overtones were not made for expressing noble subtleties. And even the few who feared or detested him for his overmastering ways refused to judge him by his words alone.

The tyrant who had sent them off would usually be waiting, grey and heavy-eyed with fatigue, to welcome the survivors at some out-lying airfield. The first faint throb of returning engines would signal the beginning of the end of suspense; his happiness was greatest on the rare mornings and evenings when he could count home every machine. Baring was certainly not speaking for himself alone when he wrote:

" Of all the experiences we had in connection with aviation, there was none more trying, more harassing and more hard to bear for those who were responsible, than waiting for these long-distance raids to return. . . . It was not a question of losing one or two machines. One knew only too well that a change of weather might occur when the machines were at a great distance, and one might quite easily lose the whole formation."

The night vigils were in a class apart; but Trenchard endured agonies as sharp in intensity every time he watched a squadron take off.

" Doesn't it make your heart beat when a machine goes up? " he commented one day to the commander of a French bombing wing as flight after flight roared overhead towards a horizon glittering in the early sunlight like a newly honed knife.

" Yes," said the Frenchman. " Some people call aviation sport. I call it war."

They were standing together on a hill, and Trenchard stared hard at the last machine in the formation.

" He's going to crash," he said.

Seconds later the left wing dipped, struck the far side of the hill, and was torn off. The aircraft turned turtle and broke up with a rending, shuddering crash. A thread of black smoke rose up, then tongues of flame enveloped the wreckage. Trenchard was first down the slope. Somehow both the pilot and observer had struggled free or been thrown clear. The former lay motionless in a crumpled heap, the latter was dancing like a madman, his fur-lined clothing blazing like a torch in the wind. Trenchard seized the man bodily, flung him down and rolled him about until the flames were smothered. Then he cut away the smouldering clothing with the small gold pocket knife he always carried and knelt beside the man, cushioning his raw, burnt head until the ambulance came. The bombs in the debris exploded while they were walking towards the car.

" Aviation is war, Chalcroft, not a sport," Trenchard said to his driver who was hastily putting his field glasses back into their case.

" Seems like it, sir," said Chalcroft. Baring remembered the words to his dying day.

7

More British bombs fell on enemy targets during the single month of May than in the previous six, though Trenchard was still only feeling his way. In June he speeded up the tempo; over seventy tons of bombs hit German cities and tactical objectives on the French side of the Rhine. The bomb load dropped increased to nearly eighty-five tons during July.

Bomber losses at first were relatively light. Only nine machines failed to return in June, sixteen in July. Most of these were shot down by fighters over enemy airfields within striking distance of Nancy; interference with night squadrons bound for the frontier and beyond was negligible. Weir, who studied the campaign with a careful eye, seemed pleased that thirty-eight German fighters had been accounted for as well as a dozen "probables" (all bombers) destroyed on the ground. However, many of the bombing claims made at this time, both by squadrons and by the H.Q. at Nancy, were certainly exaggerated.

"You may be interested," wrote Trenchard, "to know how much my last two days (30th and 31st July) have confirmed my view regarding the amount of petrol machines should carry. On these two days it appeared to the ordinary observer as if there was not a breath of wind, though Met. said there was 19 to 20 m.p.h. at 14,000 feet. We therefore made two attempts to get Cologne; on the first day one squadron got as far as Coblenz, although it took very nearly five hours there and back. . . . They ran out of petrol when crossing our lines but managed to glide into various aerodromes. This, as you can imagine, frightens the pilots. . . . And this is only Cologne, and only done these last two days by continual pressure to run their distance to the limit.

" The raids on Stuttgart the last two nights were satisfactory, but the Handley Pages only got there by dint of pressure, pressure and pressure. . . .

" It was bad luck No. 99 losing so many machines yesterday. . . ."

In an attempt to bomb Mainz in daylight, No. 99 was intercepted over the Saar by a mixed formation of Fokker triplanes, Albatrosses and Phalz scouts more than thirty strong. After a running battle lasting an hour, the squadron commander ordered an attack on Saarbrücken instead. Seven times on the way home the back of the ragged formation was broken, and the dwindling survivors saw yet another victim hurtling down out of control in a plume of smoke. Only two machines returned to base.

" They had a great fight," Trenchard told Weir. " I went round at once and told them that as long as they kept up their spirits it was a victory for us. This, I said, is what defeats the Hun so much: when we suffered casualties we went out and bombed again. I promised the squadron that you and I would do everything we could (to replace the losses at once) and I hope they'll be up to strength to-morrow."

It was not, however, a light matter to recoup while Salmond was losing de Havillands not by the dozen but by the hundred, many in accidents behind his own lines.

" The crashes on Salmond's D.H.9 squadrons have been exceptionally heavy," Weir had warned Trenchard at the end of June. " Consequently there will be some delay in getting out your next few squadrons."

Shorter of bombers than he liked, Salmond told Colonel Repington, the garrulous but observant military correspondent of the *Morning Post*, that the "serious" drain on his air resources was attributable to the Independent Force, which profited from the "strong individuality and enthusiasm" of Trenchard who "floods the Air Board with his views, and Sykes does not know enough of our position in France to guide the Board. . . ."

Happily Weir stood in no need of guidance from Sykes or anyone else. He ran "the Board" with a business-man's skill, deputing Sykes, who enjoyed the sense of authority this gave him, to present or interpret policy in council or committee. The Minister gleefully confided that he had found the perfect formula for keeping Sykes out of mischief. Trenchard congratulated him sardonically.

" Weir was the finest Chief of Air Staff, and Sykes the most willing stand-in Minister, the R.A.F. ever had," was his terse summing up.

Salmond had another grievance. He told Repington in the same interview that had he had the bombers of the Independent Force at his disposal, he "could have made 8th-10th August [when Haig smashed the German lines before Amiens and the final Allied advance in the west began] a Boche rout this year." The Independent Force commander was of a different mind, as Repington discovered soon afterwards at Nancy.

" Trenchard the same as ever, brilliant, full of ideas, alert, combative and a mine of information. He has 120 aeroplanes, mainly Handley Pages, for long-range bombing, and the squadrons are scattered round partly concealed in the woods. The Huns have 600 aeroplanes for the defence of the Rhine towns, of which 400 were there before he came. . . . He thinks he has done much moral and material damage and showed us photographs of the bombs falling on various towns. His planes now have to fight all the way out and back again. . . . He declares that he has not changed his views that

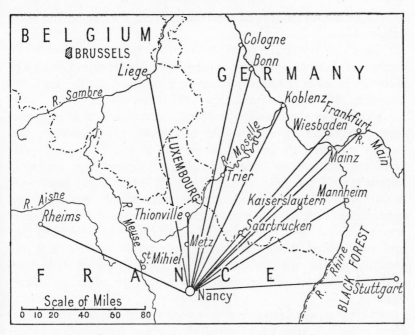

The targets for Trenchard's Independent Bombing Force in 1918

bombing is necessary and the force is about the same (size) as he intended. . . ."

Two extra squadrons reached him at last in August; and though over 1000 tons of tombs hit German targets that month, there were fewer sorties than before. Trenchard gave Weir this explanation:

" First of all it still takes five or six days for pilots to get from England when telegraphed for. After they arrive, if they are new pilots, we cannot use them over the lines for two weeks and they spend this time in practising flying in formation. This saves a large number of casualties. We cannot send less than twelve machines over the line in formation, and they must be able to fly together before they go.

" Then, in a squadron, there are usually a couple of pilots on leave as they have two weeks' leave every three months. This is very necessary to keep them fit. In addition there are generally one or two pilots sick in hospital and an occasional case of a pilot having gone to England owing to a (nervous) breakdown and yet not replaced. This as you can easily see, reduces the establishment of twenty-one pilots to under twelve. . . ."

The fault, he owned, was his alone.

" I blame myself for the shortage of pilots, for not having asked England in sufficient time to get them, and for not seeing sufficiently far ahead. I am afraid we must count on losing one machine on every raid, as when you come to think of twelve machines going well into the interior of Germany and fighting hard all the time, it's expecting too much to think they will all come back."

Some junior commanders believed, nevertheless, that casualties were unnecessarily high, owing to Trenchard's insistence that beginners should fly on the shorter but invariably more bitterly contested missions to enemy airfields. Handley Page sorties of approximately 300 miles to the cities of Germany and back were mainly reserved for seasoned veterans and normally took place on calm, moonlit nights, when newcomers might arguably have gained time to quicken their reflexes and lengthen the odds against sudden and unprovided death. Nobody, these critics alleged, had the temerity or the moral courage to challenge Trenchard's rule-of-thumb decree; yet he had his reasons for adhering strictly to it.

In his eyes, the Handley Page crews were the least expendable. Hard to replace, they were the main carriers of destruction who had to defy incalculable hazards in delivering their cargoes of incendiaries and high explosive. Trenchard's habitual refusal to discuss his decisions no doubt misled a minority into supposing that he lacked imagination and human warmth. The error was natural. How could he, with so many issues of high policy to nag him, be expected to appreciate the comparative risks, they wondered? Had his mind been less burdened with the difficulties created by the intransigence of Foch, difficulties which unfortunately persuaded Newall, a somewhat cautious deputy, not to worry him with inessentials, Trenchard would probably have answered for himself. The long haul of the bombers through the night was the hardest way to the stars. He did not underrate the risks of his daylight raiders; but what could they know of the monotony, of the cramping cold, of the steady endurance and skill required to keep a set course, hour after hour, with primitive navigational instruments, often in the teeth of adverse winds and through dense curtains of cloud that blotted out the stars above and the earth four miles beneath the cockpit? Then, at the climatic moment, with guns blazing up from far below or night-fighters groping after them, the stop-watch, the crudest of bomb sights and the coolness of their collective nerves were the factors on which the timely release of the bomb-load and the success or failure of a whole operation hinged.

" All of you have perilous parts to play, but long-range bombing isn't meant for newcomers," epitomised his policy and thought.

As it was, sceptics had to rely on impulsive gestures of insight, like the visit Trenchard paid to the base hospital at Chaulmes to sit by the bed of a young de Havilland pilot hovering between life and death. Dennis was his name. A bullet had plunged into his chest during a dog-fight fifty miles from base. Anger rather than pain or fear had apparently possessed him at the sight of his observer sprawling over the machine-gun, and that upsurge of fury made Dennis clench his teeth and fly on, regardless of his agonising weakness and giddiness. When the machine touched down, it was several minutes before the squadron commander discovered both pilot and observer unconscious and apparently bleeding to death.

At the hospital, the doctor was not very sure whether even Trenchard should be admitted.

" It's touch and go with him," he said.

Trenchard went in. Dennis opened his eyes. He could not talk; but he looked faintly astonished and pleased when the D.F.C., an instantaneous award, was pinned to his pyjama jacket where he lay. Everyone who heard of it praised the touching spontaneity of the act, especially as the pilot pulled through. The tyrant whom some suspected of having a calculating machine instead of a heart had demonstrated his unpredictable human touch once more.[8]

Of the seventy-four bombers lost between August, 1918, and Armistice Day, nearly half were claimed by the vagaries of wind, fog and storm. Some, circling low with empty fuel tanks and exhausted or badly wounded pilots at the controls, were wrecked within earshot of home airfields shrouded in the mists that so often rose without warning in the hills and bogs of that half-tamed wilderness. The records also show that not once did German machines damage a single British bomber on the ground. Enemy bases were immobilised, enemy fighters challenged in their own air space; the burnt-out remains of 122 of them strewn, over the French countryside, marked the passage of formations pressing on overhead towards the German frontier.

A captured letter, one of many in the records of the Independent Force, evoked the terror sown in the Rhineland and Saarland cities, a terror which indirectly affected husbands, sons and brothers in uniform as well:

" My eyes won't keep open while I'm writing. In the night, twice in the cellar, and again this morning. One feels as if one were no longer a human being. One air-raid after another. In my opinion, this is no longer war, but murder. Finally, in time, one becomes horribly cold and one is daily, hourly, prepared for the worst."

It was still only the experimental overture to a dreadful revolution in warfare. No squeamishness for the fate of civilians distracted Trenchard's mind. His sole purpose was to weaken the enemy's will to resist. It was for moralists and lawyers to argue whether a munitions' plant and the workers' houses about it should be struck off the list of legitimate war targets; it was for statesmen to act on their verdict. Only then might there be a truce—until the statesmen recanted or fell out among themselves again. Trenchard consoled himself that his bombs were not aimed indiscriminately at civilians but at factories which supplied the armies and so prolonged the slaughter of the battlefield. He prided himself on strictly professional thinking unclouded by vindictiveness or mawkish sentimentality.

Weir was less pernickety than Trenchard.

" I would very much like if you could start up a really big fire in one of the German towns," he wrote in September, suggesting that incendiary bombs could be used to spectacular advantage in older built-up districts where there were few "good, permanent, modern buildings."

And again:

" If I were you, I would not be too exacting as regards accuracy in bombing railway stations in the middle of towns. The German is susceptible to bloodiness, and I would not mind a few accidents due to inaccuracy."

On the score of precision at any rate, Trenchard entertained no false pretensions.

" I do not think you need be anxious about our degree of accuracy when bombing stations in the middle of towns. The accuracy is not great at present, and all the pilots drop their eggs well into the middle of the town generally."

8

The wrangling between Foch and the British War Cabinet continued until the autumn, with Trenchard in the oddly privileged position of unofficial counsel for both defence and prosecution. His sympathies were with Foch, his loyalties with London.

" I must say, to put it plainly to you, that this has hung on so long and nothing has been decided that I feel it can't drag on much longer," he told Weir on 21st September. " I fancy you'll find the

Independent Force will be abolished as such for purely bombing Germany. It will be put with a lot of polite words under General Foch to use where he thinks fit, and it will, of course, bomb Germany at times. Please keep this quite private."

Impressed as he had good reason to be by Trenchard's ability to hammer nails in the German coffin, Foch was summoning all his strength to close the lid with a final bang. His armies were everywhere advancing. In its last phase, the war on land had rapidly developed into a war of movement against a reeling foe; Nancy in consequence again became an isolated base, far in the rear of the onrushing Allied ground forces. Trenchard's supply chain, once broken, took time to repair; worse still, his personal liaison work with army leaders, the secret of his earlier success, was interrupted.

Then Foch proposed a tactical task which suited Trenchard admirably: the disrupting of German communications between Rheims and Verdun. The worsening weather and the uncertain state of supplies was grounding the squadrons and preventing all but a few long-distance raids.

Only the heady scent of victory persuaded Weir and Lloyd George to yield at last with a good grace and accept the terms which Foch had been demanding for six months. Not until 26th October, 1918, was Trenchard's appointment announced as Commander-in-Chief of an inter-Allied Air Force, comprising French, Italian and American as well as British bombing squadrons. A group of French and Italian machines came under Trenchard's orders immediately, but none took off from Nancy before the Armistice. By then the original nucleus of five British bomber squadrons had risen to nine, virtually the figure which Trenchard had predicted a year previously in the light of the British aircraft industry's known difficulties and the growing man-power shortage. And none of the new " super Handley Pages," four-engined machines capable of carrying a crew of six and a bomb-load of nearly three tons to central Europe and back, was ready before 11th November. So Trenchard's plans for 1919, which included "shuttle-raids" from Allied bases in Norfolk, Nancy and Prague against every part of Germany, including Berlin, came to nothing.

Would Foch have misused the bombers if the British Government had given way six months earlier? Trenchard did not think so; and this is borne out by the contemporary writings and sayings of Foch, whose strategic ideas were in some ways far in advance of those of most Allied military leaders, for whom air units remained as indivisibly part of the army as artillery. Had better harmony prevailed between the French and British Governments, and had the Versailles Council functioned less as a conference for the discouragement or suppression of refractory generals and more as a genuine inter-Allied executive, Foch's logic would probably have been displayed to greater advantage.

His intention was to form into a single reserve the separate air forces of the Allied armies. The Royal Air Force might thus have been reunited in the field, and a similar unity imposed on other national air arms, under Trenchard's operational control. The experiment had to be shelved until 1944, when the political leaders of a more tightly knit Alliance were mercifully less hesitant in allowing Eisenhower, admittedly a more pliable Supreme Commander than Foch, to select as his deputy in charge of the Allied air forces for the liberation of Europe an Englishman called Tedder, who was one of the youngest squadron commanders on the Western Front in 1918.

Trenchard was seated at his desk late on 10th November when the telephone rang. Baring answered the call in voluble Italian. It was the commanding officer of the Caproni squadrons a few miles away, passing on the rumour that a cease-fire had been arranged. Trenchard did not go to bed that night. Sleep was out of the question while his own aircraft, laden with over five tons of bombs, were wheeling in the eerie light of their own flares, possibly for the last time. above the guns of Metz, Mohrange and Frescaty in the valley of the Moselle. A grey dawn brought every man and machine home safe. It also brought belated confirmation of the overnight report. The war was over.

Trenchard immediately telegraphed Foch asking permission, now that his task was done, to hand back the squadrons of the Independent Force to Haig. This was granted on 14th November, to the baffled indignation of Salmond who misconstrued Trenchard's gesture as prompted by a selfish desire "to pass on an unwanted baby and clear out with all speed." [9]

Weir understood its symbolic meaning because he was better informed. The Minister's last piece of advice to Trenchard was to "keep your final operational dispatch educational" for the benefit of arm-chair critics; partly to assist him with background material, Weir passed on his own first-hand observations regarding the disruptive effects of tactical bombing behind the German front.

" Cambrai and Douai, for example, show first the very considerable damage done to the railway stations and railways in the town,"

Weir wrote. " The bombing has been quite accurate and has definitely handicapped the movement of stores, apart altogether from the deaths caused to enemy troops. Next it shows that in a town occupied by the enemy bombing has the immediate effect of causing the German to dig like the devil. . . . This means a vast expenditure of man-power. . . . I estimate that in Bruges alone he has expended the work of 10,000 men for two years on account of bombing. . . . When I apply this to the numerous towns of the Rhine, then I know we have done right. . . . In no direction of war effort are we able to obtain such a good dividend. It is not the destructive effect but the effect of what we cause the Germans to do."

Bomb-inspection teams, which went to Germany after the Armistice, amply confirmed Weir's conclusions. Here, however, far behind the fighting line, it was the relative intensity of the bombing campaign which had counted most: the lost man-hours in Rhineland war factories, the fraying of public nerves, and the clamour for more guns and deeper shelters, far outweighed the physical damage caused, as had happened during the lighter air-raids on England. Trenchard's counter-blows were not, however, spread thin over three years and hundreds of thousands of square miles. They had been more highly concentrated, in time and space.

The aircrews, apprentices to a new and ultimately catastrophic form of warfare, had made it possible with the unwearying support of the maintenance men on the ground. Trenchard left Weir in no doubt on that score.

In reply to the Minister's victory message Trenchard wired back his thanks, adding with heartfelt sincerity:

" No one knows as well as I do how thoroughly they deserve your congratulations."

His farewells over, Trenchard drove through the great iron gates of the château one mid-November morning, bound for home. The frank astonishment on his face yielded to a rarer and softer look as the car moved down the main street. The narrow pavements were lined with cheering men. All had come of their own accord from miles around to demonstrate their affection for a man who had unwittingly earned it. He had never expected to carry away from Autigny-la-Tour more than the memory of their magnificent loyalty and achievement, and he could only wave back in acute embarrassment, muttering at intervals to Baring: " I don't believe it. There must be some mistake."

It was as though the sleep he longed for had taken him too soon, and that this parting was all a dream: for Trenchard felt suddenly old and sad and unbelievably tired. He had written privately to Weir on Armistice Day to tell him so and to ask a favour.

" Put me on half-pay for a year," he pleaded. " This will give you a chance of pushing on some of the younger men as you must not forget that although I am not old, I am forty-six, and most of the other officers are six or seven years younger. I am perfectly certain I am right in having a good long rest as my head gets very bad at times now."

Weir had no intention of remaining in politics himself; but he had no intention either of letting Trenchard slip away and vanish in the blue. So he tore up the letter and persuaded Trenchard by return to take a holiday before deciding anything.

12. *The Comeback*

So far the turning points in Trenchard's career formed a curious catalogue of unexpected things. The telephone call which roused him, irritable, from a late sleep about ten o'clock one mid-January morning in 1919 proved no exception. The caller, an officer on the staff of Robertson, the Commander-in-Chief, Home Forces, expressed regret for disturbing him, yet sounded unmistakably relieved to find him in. Sir William would have rung himself, he explained, had the Cabinet not summoned him to another meeting on the army mutinies. Further disorders had broken out, this time at Southampton, and Robertson thought these the worst of all.

" His staff officer told me," Trenchard noted, " that the docks were in the hands of soldiers, that everything was in a bad way down there, and that 20,000 men were refusing to obey orders. He added that the field-marshal wanted me to go down and take charge.

" ' What as? ' I said. ' Sir William must know I've no official position. Do I go as an army or an air general? Who am I to take my orders from? ' Eventually he said he didn't care tuppence what I did, as long as I went, so I said, ' All right, I'll go as an army general.' I got hold of Maurice Baring, put on a general's uniform, and took the afternoon train to Southampton."

Rooms were procured with some difficulty at the South-Western Hotel. Later, as he changed for dinner, Trenchard pondered on his unsought predicament and his characteristically slender resources for extricating himself from it. He had a staff of two, Bates, his former clerk, having joined him at Waterloo, no headquarters, no car, the vaguest possible commission, and no knowledge of the lie of the land.

Walking downstairs to the lounge, Trenchard was warmly greeted by a Royal Air Force officer, who had apparently driven straight from his neighbouring Group Headquarters in response to Baring's discreet S.O.S. It was Smyth Pigott, the pupil-pilot who had almost killed himself on his first solo flight at Upavon in 1914, and whose path had crossed Trenchard's again more recently, in similar if less catastrophic circumstances. An expert night-bombing instructor, Smyth Piggott had wrecked the Handley Page he was ferrying from England the previous summer in a forced-landing near Paris, and had been mercilessly flayed for negligence on reaching Nancy.

Smyth Pigott, still thinking of Trenchard as an absolute ruler, was taken aback by the magnitude of his present needs. His former chief's spontaneous gratitude for the offer of a typewriter and an old staff car touched him strangely.

" I associated him with fleets of cars, typing pools and everything he wanted," Smyth Pigott wrote of the episode. " Once he was all-powerful, now he had nothing. The hotel was packed with hordes of junior officers and as, in the post-Armistice period, discipline had disappeared, the noise was dreadful. There in the lounge sat this old eagle amidst a squealing flock of parakeets.

" I had very comfortable digs in town, so I rang up my landlady to see whether she had any free rooms. She had, so I moved into them and gave mine to Trenchard. . . . It was just the shock of seeing him deprived of everything. As far as I could make out he was finished." [1]

Trenchard would have been amused by Smyth Pigott's readiness to write him off by overestimating his material needs, or judging these without reference to his rock-like self-sufficiency.

Before breakfast next morning, he walked alone through the dock area. Groups of soldiers were standing about in the rain, picketing the gangways of deserted troop-ships. From a customs shed on the quay came sounds of indescribable pandemonium.

Trenchard, who was in uniform, drew near enough to catch a glimpse of the kit-bags and blankets strewn in heaps over the vast floor space where half a dozen braziers glowed amidst a profusion of unswept litter. The place stank. Whoever the ringleaders were, they had little sense of orderliness. Hundreds of men seemed to be milling aimlessly about; hundreds more slouched or squatted in the shadows; some jeered and shouted abuse at a few haggard officers standing together passively, looking on. One of them, a captain, saw Trenchard and approached him, bitter in his complaints, only to be curtly dismissed. Trenchard was less interested in the symptoms than in the causes of mutiny. He had read the newspaper accounts of similar outbreaks of indiscipline at Folkestone and Calais, Luton, Glasgow and Belfast. The disorders had a sensational but somewhat improbable flavour in print, rather like bad fiction; but here on the wet quayside, confronted by the latest and possibly the gravest, he could understand why the Cabinet and the War Office were torn between panic and guilt.

Servicemen, in Trenchard's experience, rarely kicked over the traces without reason. The demobilisation scheme, which Lloyd George had sprung on the country after the Armistice, seemed to provide its own special incitement to discontent. The principle of "key men first," irrespective of the human and domestic claims of those who had served longest and often suffered most in the firing line, had inflamed the feelings of servicemen. The authorities, in his view, were as culpable as the so-called mutineers: the Government for an unjust system of release, the War Office for its inability to maintain discipline. It required little imagination to see how a widespread sense of grievance among the troops, feeding on the administrative chaos and lack of supervision in the depots and transit camps, had rapidly turned to disaffection.

In Trenchard's code of military values, the unforgivable sin against the light was neglect of the average man's welfare and morale. The sombre signs of it stared him in the face at the rest camp, on the outskirts of Southampton, which he inspected after breakfast. The commandant, a lieutenant-colonel in his late seventies, he recognised as a man long set in his ways, who had lorded it over his battalion with no great efficiency when he himself had been a young subaltern. The camp adjutant and quartermaster appeared to be as far out of their depth as their aged superior. Between the three of them, Trenchard calculated, they probably mustered a century and a half of service experience and less than a grain and a half of wisdom. Because their applications for extra staff had been so frequently ignored they had finally ceased to care. The commandant complained that not once in four years of war had he set eyes on an inspecting officer, and that his entire clerical staff consisted of two men.

Trenchard moved Bates into an adjoining office with the borrowed R.A.F. typewriter. The muddle of the rest camp, he said, would have to wait until the "rabble at the docks" came to heel. If the commandant's figures were correct, nearly 5000 men were in the customs shed.

Late that afternoon Trenchard drove beyond the town along a flat, open road where, one by one, the gas lights were coming on, deepening the moist desolation of the dying January day. Entering the dock gates he ordered his car to be parked in full view of the soldiers, got out and marched straight into the customs shed, followed by Baring. There was nothing to use as an improvised platform, but at his loud summons the men slowly formed a wide, uneven circle round him. At first they were comparatively attentive; curiosity at the arrival of a general silenced them. Then, as the uncompromising burden of his message assailed their ears, the murmuring gradually swelled into a roar of heckling. Trenchard tried to shout his interrupters down. He had been put in charge, he said, and would hear every grievance even if the process lasted a month; but, first, they must return to their duty or take the consequences. The booing and cat-calling drowned his words, and as he stopped speaking a section of men surged forward, almost knocking him over.

"It was most unpleasant," Trenchard wrote of the incident later. "It was the only time in my life I'd been really hustled. They said they did not want to listen to me. They told me to get out and stay out. They wanted either the Prime Minister or the Commander-in-Chief. They would listen to no one else."

Words had failed; only the threat of force would move them now. According to the camp commandant a hard core of mutineers had reason to fear embarking for France where courts-martial already awaited them. Clearly, these were the ringleaders: they would somehow have to be segregated from the rest. Trenchard spent part of the evening alone, weighing the merits and risks of the only quick solution that presented itself. Finally he emerged with his mind made up, telephoned Portsmouth, and after some delay spoke to the army garrison commander:

"I want two hundred and fifty men immediately," he said. "Issue them with rifles and ball ammunition."

The garrison commander hesitated before committing himself.

"If you insist, I'll send them. But I doubt whether there are two hundred reliable men in the whole place," he said.

"I'll have to chance that," said Trenchard. "Send an escort of military police with them. Put them all on the first available train. I'll be expecting them."

Baring and Smyth Pigott tried not to look too disconcerted as he picked up the receiver again, talked briefly to Robertson in London, then asked for Southern Command Headquarters. The ensuing conversation was sharp and one-sided. The only words which Trenchard used twice were the ominous ones "to shoot, of course." He explained as he hung up that the duty officer at the other end had been slow-witted enough to inquire what two hundred and fifty armed men could be wanted for. Trenchard's answer had apparently

Prince Albert and Trenchard at a dinner after the war. Baring is
sitting in front of them

Lord Rothermere

dumbfounded him as much as Baring and Smyth Pigott. The
telephone rang again several times.

"Let it ring," Trenchard said. "Southern Command will get
tired before I do."

It woke him up in the small hours of the following morning,
however, and he finally got out of bed and answered it. The
G.O.C. was on the line, short-tempered and querulous. Trenchard
offered him no quarter. Having assumed responsibility for the
armed men, who were already on their way, he would know what
to do if the need arose. The G.O.C. retorted that the position was
too grave for misunderstanding. On no account must Trenchard
open fire. He, the G.O.C., refused to answer for bloodshed at
Southampton or anywhere else in his command unless he personally
were present to authorise the use of force.

"I'm not seeking your support," said Trenchard. "I'm informing you of my intentions, so there's nothing more to be said." He
was resolved not to be side-tracked by another's timidity.

Soon after dawn next morning Trenchard commandeered a
small draughty office on the quayside and dispatched one of the
officers "displaced" by the mutineers to meet the troop train from
Portsmouth. The day was again damp with drizzle. One hundred
yards away, through the grimy office window, the customs shed
stood outlined against a murky sky. A medley of protest rang out
suddenly when, by previous arrangement between Trenchard and the
dockyard authorities, a master switch was thrown in a neighbouring
power-house and every light within half a mile was extinguished.
Half an hour passed, then Baring pricked up his ears at the clatter
of heavy boots on cobble-stones. Someone was running hard from
the customs shed towards the office. Trenchard pulled open the door
and a breathless lance-corporal saluted awkwardly and said that he
had come to give himself up. Trenchard cross-examined him with
deliberate restraint, aware that he was dealing with a thoroughly
cowed youngster whom frustration and fear had led astray. Six
months ago, he had deserted, only to be arrested after the Armistice;
but he so disliked the idea of going back to France under escort that
he was glad of any excuse for putting this off, and that was why he
had joined the mutineers. Now he did not care what happened.
The uncertainty was too much. Most of the other men in the shed,
he said, felt themselves to be victims of War Office muddling. They
had been easily persuaded to disobey their officers and picket the
troop-ships.

Trenchard listened reflectively. If this boy were telling only half

T.   L the truth, the mere sight of the armed men would probably do the trick.

The train from Portsmouth had evidently been delayed. Noon came grey as dawn; Trenchard and Baring were finishing a scratch lunch when the column of armed men marched in from the station, escorted by a dozen military policemen. He inspected their rifles, stood them at ease, issued ten rounds of ammunition to each soldier and handcuffs to the red-caps, then briefed them.

" I don't have to tell you why you've been brought here. This nonsense must stop, and we'll stop it together now. If there's firing to be done, I'll say when."

The plan of approach, as he elaborated it, was simple. They would advance in single file from both sides of the great open front of the customs shed to form an unbroken line, thus sealing off the mutineers' only escape route. They would load almost underneath the noses of the men inside, and as noisily as possible. Trenchard would carry on from there. On no account must they do anything further unless he gave the order.

" Any questions? "

There were no questions.

He led them across the cobbles, standing back to watch as they split into two columns on either side of the open shed. A volley of abuse from the unlit, cavernous interior greeted them as they moved across with stiff precision to meet in the centre, cutting the floor space in half and penning the mutineers between the shouldered rifles and the rear wall.

On Trenchard's word of command, there was an impressive clash of steel as two hundred and fifty bolts slid into place. Almost at that moment, an officer stationed in the distant power-house looked at his watch and turned on the current again. Light blazed down on the scene, dazzling the eye and gleaming coldly on the brass buttons and pointed rifles of the riot squad.

Trenchard expected no riot. And there was none. His carefully contrived stage effects seemed first to stupefy, then to paralyse the ringleaders. The hush that fell as the lamps shone down again on every corner of the shed did not last; now, however, he noticed that the yells had an unconvincing overtone, like the whistling of boys in a graveyard after dark. Trenchard stepped forward to address the crowd, the red-caps clearing a path on either hand.

" The last time I came," he said, " you howled me down. I'm

prepared this time. The men who started this trouble will be on the troop-ships to-day, even if they have to be carried. My advice to you all is—surrender quietly now."

A big sergeant waved a truculent fist, obscenely inviting Trenchard to drop dead.

" Grab that man," he said. " Put him aboard below decks."

The military policemen pushed through resentful but passive rows of mutineers and seized him. Nobody lifted a hand to defend him. Handcuffs were slipped on, and the man was dragged away, struggling and cursing.

" All right," said Trenchard. " The rest of you had better decide quickly. Will you do as I order or not? "

He stared round the circle of uneasy faces. There was silence, then a shuffle of feet and a slow movement forward as one man, then another, then a trickle of them, moved towards him.

" Stop," he shouted. The movement stopped.

" You're sure you've had enough? "

There was a muttering of assent.

" In that case, form into ranks. I want to hear your stories in turn."

For the rest of that day, Trenchard sat at a table placed just inside the customs shed. Baring took down statements until his hands were cramped with fatigue. There were few men without excuses.

" The majority," Trenchard noted, " were quite ready to return to France but naturally objected to being sent back as prisoners for having overstayed their leave by perhaps a couple of days."

These he discharged conditionally. Only the ringleaders interested him.

Baring and Bates later compiled a factual report to the War Office which served as a commentary on the injustices to which many other servicemen were subjected by a bad demobilisation scheme and inefficient administrators. His sympathies were mainly with the victims, most of whom had been told that they were going to Southampton for discharge. This palpable falsehood had rebounded like a boomerang when their escorting officer arrived and calmly admitted that he had been misinformed and that a troop-ship was standing by to transport them to France.

Trenchard exonerated them without further questioning, castigating instead the individual who had deceived them. These men, in his judgment, were not recruits lacking in discipline and unfamiliar with the ways of the service, but veterans who deserved better than they had received for their part in Haig's last victorious campaign in France.

One hundred and seven soldiers under open arrest had instigated a rebellion among 5000 good men with reasonable grievances, according to the figures in Trenchard's official report; and of those one hundred and seven, only fifty-three were confined aboard the troop-ship. The docks were peaceful again, but scores of soldiers were still defying authority behind the barricaded doors of billets in the inaptly named rest camp. After stacking the unused rifles and ammunition and requisitioning a dozen firehoses, Trenchard paraded his riot squad again.

" We'll soak them out," he said.

It was all over in half an hour. When the resisters ignored a last call to yield unconditionally, he ordered the windows of the huts to be smashed; the jets were trained through, the hydrants turned on at full pressure. Drenched to the skin by ice-cold water which numbed them to the bone and knocked the breath out of their bodies, all but a few of the mutineers had to be helped out. Eventually about a hundred bedraggled men in blankets formed outside the office where Trenchard sat waiting for each of them to shiver out his excuses.

A demand for more officers and N.C.O.s to fill the camp's long-depleted establishment was met with alacrity by the G.O.C. Southern Command, who had complained prematurely of Trenchard's high-handedness only to be snubbed by Robertson for his pains. A régime of parades, inspections, fatigues and games was gradually introduced by Trenchard, who decided to remain for a week "just to see it work." At night he would relax now with Baring and Smyth Pigott, discussing old times and only rarely betraying any anxiety about the future of the Royal Air Force. When he touched on this at all it was with the plain indiscretion of someone no longer involved, though the Government's decision to saddle Winston Churchill with the double burden of War Office and Air Ministry affairs perturbed him. He could not say that he envied Sykes his job of presiding over the probable dissolution of the third service.

His own future, he thought, would probably remove him beyond recall to East Africa. If the Colonial Office gave him the appointment he had applied for, he would spend five years at least in Abyssinia, advising on the economic development of that wild, backward land. Otherwise, something else would turn up: several offers to join the boards of city companies had already come his way.

Smyth Pigott particularly noticed Trenchard's annoyance and

perplexity on opening the official telegram delivered while they were at breakfast one morning early in February. The wire was from the Secretary of State for War and Air. It requested Trenchard to return forthwith to London on "urgent air force business." Not even Baring, normally so quick on the uptake, knew quite what to make of this sudden echo from a past which, for Trenchard, had already been abandoned without apparent regret.

2

It was chance, not choice, which led Churchill to the War Office when the Cabinet was re-shuffled after the "coupon election" of December, 1918. Had circumstances permitted, he would rather have returned to the Admiralty, as this passage from *The Aftermath*, the final volume of *The World Crisis*, clearly shows.

"The Prime Minister," he wrote, "reconstructed his Government with masterful dispatch. At the end of a conversation on various topics he said to me in so many words, ' make up your mind whether you would like to go to the War Office or the Admiralty, and let me know by to-morrow. You can take the Air with you in either case. I am not going to keep it as a separate department.'

"I spent the night at Blenheim, and from there accepted the Admiralty together with the Air Ministry; but when I reached London the next afternoon I found the position had changed. The temper of the army and the problem of demobilisation caused increasing anxiety. I could not refuse the Prime Minister's request that I should go to the War Office. The new Ministry was announced on 10th January, and I quitted the Ministry of Munitions and became responsible for the War Office on the 15th. I was immediately confronted with conditions of critical emergency."

The "critical emergency" was handled by Churchill with moderation and good sense. By abjuring force, discouraging the death penalty for proven acts of mutiny, and amending the late Government's ill-advised demobilisation programme, he succeeded first in checking the spread of distemper among the troops, then in restoring calm. By early February, 1919, Churchill was free to consider the fate of the R.A.F., the second and less urgent portion of his new responsibilities.

Because of the disturbances, few people outside the Government and none inside it questioned the anomalous appointment of

Churchill as Secretary of State for War and Air combined. What
Lloyd George intended by it has never been explained, defended or
even mentioned in the many biographies and books of contemporary
history that have been published since. His apologists and detractors
alike seem to have overlooked the point entirely; yet because of its
importance, not only to Trenchard's career but to the history of the
Royal Air Force, the mystery must be examined in the light of the
evidence available.

To say the least of it, the Prime Minister's decision to wind up
the Air Ministry as a separate department in January, 1919, seems
in retrospect an extraordinarily clumsy and arbitrary step. What was
his aim? Did he intend to end the separate existence of the new third
service as well? If so, what were his motives? If not, why did he
invite Churchill to administer the air force as an offshoot of the
War Office?

According to Hankey, Lloyd George was "so immersed in the
details of the coming Peace Conference that he had little thought for
anything else." This suggests that in seeking to cure the ills of the
wartime Air Ministry by removing its head, the Prime Minister was
actuated only by indifference to it; yet decapitation is so unusual a
method of surgical treatment that Hankey's explanation alone hardly
stands up. Churchill, who has recorded what Lloyd George said
when offering him the job, preferred to leave it at that: his writings
are bare of further references to the subject. Bonar Law, Lord
Privy Seal and Leader of the Commons, did attempt to clarify the
matter nearly twelve months after the event by explaining what the
Prime Minister had in mind. On 15th December, 1919, in answer
to a spirited attack by Major-General Seely, who had recently
resigned as Churchill's Under-Secretary of State, Bonar Law said:

" I do not suggest that this is a permanent arrangement, nor do
I suggest that my Right Hon. Friend (Churchill) was made
Secretary of State for Air merely because he was Secretary of State
for War. That is not so. It was discussed between the Prime
Minister and myself at the time the appointment was made, but the
ground on which it was recommended was not that he was filling
the position of Secretary of State for War, but that he was competent
to fill the position of Secretary of State for Air and to do the War
Office work as well. This is not any question of principle at all.
There is no idea in anyone's mind that the air force is not to be an
independent force. The sole question is whether or not my Right
Hon. Friend (Churchill) is capable of fulfilling the duties of both
offices. . . ."

This belated defence of Government intentions cannot be accepted at face value. It bristles with after-wisdom. By December, 1919, the Lloyd George Government had in fact yielded to second thoughts. The decision to keep the R.A.F. as a separate service, and the belated hint that in time it might eventually be controlled once more by its own Minister, had little in common with the Cabinet's original purpose in February, 1919. It was fortunate indeed for Britain that Churchill, on taking office, kept an open mind on strategic issues and was prepared to be guided by the advice of Weir, his predecessor at the Air Ministry, who was both "horrified and scandalised," to quote his own words, by the Prime Minister's indifference to the survival or disappearance of the R.A.F.

Weir was familiar with the official excuses for what he could only regard as an outrage. Lloyd George was determined to economise on the fighting services; and air force needs in the closing months of war had cost the taxpayer close on one million pounds per day. The Prime Minister was also short of experienced ministerial candidates after the Coupon Election, and here Weir felt a twinge of guilt for declining the Prime Minister's invitation to stay on a moment longer than was necessary to see his successor securely in harness. Possibly Weir, who had no political ambitions, underestimated the extent to which Lloyd George relied on him, as he certainly underestimated the dearth of available talent to fill the service and other departments.[2]

Lord Riddell, one of Lloyd George's intimates, noted in his diary on Christmas Day, 1919, after a lengthy conversation with the Prime Minister:

" He said that next week he proposes to take a short holiday to consider the reconstruction of the Government. The difficulty is that there are so few men available."

In the event, Weir was shocked by the Prime Minister's irresponsible method of repairing this deficiency at the expense of the R.A.F. As the "caretaker" of a department about to be abolished, he held his tongue and was thankful for two small mercies; the unrest in the army, which prevented any precipitate move to wind up the air force, and the amenable attitude of Churchill himself. The new Minister for War and Air took Weir into his confidence and welcomed his advice.

" I was glad of the army troubles as a breathing space," Weir told this author, "just as I was pleased to be dealing with Winston rather than with anyone else. Had he been at the Admiralty instead, the R.A.F.'s chances would, I'm afraid, have been quite negligible."

It is doubtful whether many yet appreciate the extent to which Weir's advocacy influenced Churchill while the latter was contemplating what to do with the Air Department. Uncertain how deeply the Minister believed in a separate air force as a military necessity, unwilling therefore to risk any argument in which Churchill would have had the last word, Weir took care not to provoke one. He harped instead on the dangers of the new release plan: the army, he knew, was being reduced from $3\frac{1}{2}$ million to 900,000 men as fast as the ships and trains could carry them. Under the revised demobilisation terms, a wartime air force of some 300,000 officers and men was likewise being dismantled without thought of tomorrow.

A new Chief of Air Staff with a mind and will of his own was the first essential, in Weir's view, if the R.A.F. were not to disappear before its future could be decided; and he did not hesitate to press this opinion on Churchill. Sykes, he suggested, lacked the resilience and force of character to salvage what was necessary from the wartime wreckage.

" Trenchard's your best man for that," he insisted. " He can make do with little and won't have to be carried."

The proposal intrigued Churchill, for Trenchard happened to be in his thoughts for a different reason. When Southern Command protested that the former Chief of the Air Service had demanded, and obtained, arms for possible use against the mutineers at Southampton, the Minister's immediate response had been one of alarm. Since then Trenchard's report, justifying an irregular technique which had restored a difficult situation without bloodshed, had reached him. It predisposed him to consider favourably Weir's bold plea that Trenchard be reappointed to the very post he had relinquished less than a year before. At any other moment, Churchill might well have scotched the idea as outrageous; instead he promised to think it over, decided to invite the ex-Chief of Air Staff for an informal discussion, and promptly wired him to that effect.

They met at the War Office towards the end of the first week in February. The Minister was most affable, complimenting Trenchard on his handling of the Southampton disorders and steering the conversation round to the air force. Because he had nothing to gain or lose, Trenchard was more outspoken than he otherwise might have been, when Churchill said that his mind was open on the question of maintaining the R.A.F. as a separate service. Then the Minister mentioned Sykes, who, as Trenchard knew, had left for the peace talks in Paris with the Prime Minister's large retinue of advisers.

Churchill, who evidently did not relish having to grapple single-handed with a multitude of vexing details, suddenly staggered his visitor by lightly inquiring:

" How would you like to come back as my Chief of Air Staff? "

" That's impossible," said Trenchard. " You have one already whether you like him or not."

" You leave Sykes to me," Churchill retorted. " Civil flying is going to be under the Air Ministry. We'll call Sykes 'Controller of Civil Aviation' and console him with a G.B.E."

Trenchard felt distinctly uncomfortable. Honours, in his eyes, were part and parcel of the royal prerogative, not spoils or political consolation prizes. Fortunately he refrained from saying so, merely pointing out that since nobody could accuse Sykes of being a failure, to remove him without explanation in favour of the very person he had supplanted eleven months or less ago was an unheard-of proposition.

" I want time to think it over," said Trenchard.

Churchill, however, refused to leave the matter suspended indefinitely in mid-air. After assuring Trenchard that there would be no opposition within the Cabinet, he persuaded him to commit to paper an outline of his ideas on reorganising an Air Ministry that was top-heavy.

" You do that, and I'll do the same," he said. " Then we can exchange notes."[3]

The Minister's criticism of the detailed plans already submitted by Sykes was extremely withering. The country, he said, could not afford the organisation necessary for a post-war R.A.F. on the Sykes scale of 154 squadrons, 62 of them for front-line service, at home and overseas. The project lacked realism. It would probably cost far more than the seventy-five million pounds a year mentioned by the author, a sum in excess of anything the Treasury or the public would stand.

It dawned on Trenchard that Churchill had decided in advance to part company with Sykes; and he vaguely recalled a letter from Weir in December, suggesting that Lloyd George no longer questioned his (Trenchard's) ability as an administrator. He had ignored it at the time.

" As you know," Weir had written, " I found it impossible that you and I should work together in London. Circumstances were too strong, although I fully realise it would have been a complete success. I also wish to say that, before my departure, I took the opportunity of seeing the Prime Minister and—as the Americans say: Put him wise as to my opinion of what you had done for the air service. I feel that he now realises it."

Weir's persuasiveness since had helped to sway Churchill, if not Lloyd George. That at least was certain. So Trenchard promised to let the Minister have his ideas in writing, set them down that same evening on a side and a half of foolscap, and posted them to Churchill with a wry covering note, expressing every confidence that the Minister would find much to disagree with in them. Nearly a week went by. Then came a message from the War Office asking him to call on Churchill next day.

He found him at his desk in an amiable mood.

" I got your notes," said the Minister.

" I notice I didn't get yours," said Trenchard.

" I haven't had time to write mine. I've been in Paris. You'll be pleased to hear, however, that there's little in yours I can quarrel with. Broadly speaking, I like them."

They disagreed that morning only on such minor details as the new styles and titles of the various ranks of the air force. At the end of their talk Churchill said:

" Well, that's settled then. You must come back and I won't hear of any refusal."[4]

Trenchard still hedged. How could he be sure that Churchill was not going behind the Prime Minister's back? How would Lloyd George respond when presented with the accomplished fact of a Chief of Staff he did not want, carrying out a revised air policy he apparently did not like?

Churchill seemed to sense the reasons for Trenchard's misgivings. There would be no Cabinet objections, he promised, to the reinstatement of the first Chief of Air Staff over Sykes's head. The R.A.F. was the one accomplished fact in the case, harder constitutionally to do away with than to remodel. As the Minister responsible, his main interest now was to ensure that the remodelling was as efficient as possible with the limited money available; and since Trenchard's ideas were sounder than Sykes's, he (Churchill) would accept no further refusal.

Another factor which considerably reduced Trenchard's resistance was the reaction of Salmond and other ex-colleagues whom he had meanwhile sounded in the strictest confidence. They were unanimous that personal considerations mattered less than the integrity of the R.A.F., which would be safer in his hands.

One morning, during the second week of February, Churchill, on an impulse, humoured the curiosity of his private secretary. When

Mr. (now Sir) Christopher Bullock asked diffidently how far the
delicate business of settling the future of the air force had progressed,
the Minister's reply was to cross the room, open a dispatch-box and
beckon him over to inspect the contents. There were two papers
inside, one of which Bullock recognised as Sykes's detailed plan of
reorganisation. The other, generously spaced out on two foolscap
sheets, was Trenchard's laconic statement of essentials. Churchill
seemed highly amused at Bullock's mystified reaction. It was quite
simple: he had set Trenchard some homework, and the results had
bettered all expectations. Sykes would be staying on, of course, but
not as Chief of Air Staff. There would be scope for his talents in
another position.

Bullock felt sorry for Sykes, when he ushered him into the
Minister's room later that week, by appointment. The visitor was
clearly unprepared for the bombshell awaiting him within.

3

It was not so much the style as the pith of Trenchard's proposals
that captivated Churchill. The paper was less than 800 words long,
but it covered the essentials without wasting words. Of seven
numbered paragraphs the third provided the key to the rest.

" It seems to me," it stated, " that the Air Ministry should be
as small as possible. The force will be small and it will not be
beyond the capabilities of a few carefully chosen officials to run.
I am therefore of the opinion that the Air Ministry should consist of
the following:
Air Council
Secretary of State.
Under-Secretary of State, Financial Under-Secretary.
First Lord (Military), Second Air Lord (Civil), Third Air Lord
　　(Production).
Office of the First Air Lord (Military).
Deputy First Air Lord (Naval); he'd also be responsible for
　　operations.
Assistant First Air Lord (Military).
Director of Personnel to be Naval.
Director of Material to be Military.
(I am not definite in my opinion as to whether these should not
　　be changed round.)

Office of the Second Air Lord (Civil).

Deputy Second Air Lord; Civil Laws and Regulations.

Assistant Second Lord; Inspection of Civil Material and Supervision.

Deputy Assistant Second Lord; carrying out of above arrangements for Civil Aerodromes and Sheds.

Office of the Third Air Lord (Production).

The service would thus require only three branches and less than a dozen senior officers to carry on. It seemed an absurdly small administrative price to pay for efficiency; yet Weir had assured Churchill that the division of duties was realistic. For the rest, Trenchard confined himself to a few issues about which he felt most keenly. One was a plea for preserving the identity and, with it, the *esprit de corps*, of certain R.A.F. units.

" By changing the titles and making completely new squadrons, (squadron) traditions, built up through four years of war, will be lost. This would be very unpopular inside and outside the air service and would cause inevitable wasting of time. And it is for wasting time that the Air Ministry has been constantly attacked. . . ."

As for future recruiting and training:

" The Royal Air Force would be composed of officers with permanent commissions and officers from the navy and army seconded for four years. The men would be permanently in the air service. All new officers would have to learn to fly, and no officer joining after this date would be considered for an appointment in the air force who had not learnt to fly.

" Training would have to be specialised and I would recommend that one should, as far as one can see at present, train pilots as fighting pilots (land and sea), reconnaissance pilots (land and sea), bombing pilots (these would probably be common to both), and torpedo pilots. . . .

" It is important to keep the training units distinct from the service units. Some would be at full strength and some only cadres —and these should be periodically changed, i.e. full strength squadrons reduced to cadres, and cadre squadrons increased to full strength and sent to certain camps for war training."

" There should be an Inspector-General of the air force, but he should not have a seat on the Air Council."

On 17th February, two days after his return to the Air Ministry, Trenchard informed Salmond:

" I am working on a strength, as you know, of 75,000 for the armies of occupation and about 50,000 for the post-war army. This is all the money we shall get.

" I propose (in Britain) to do away with the four areas in time. There will be three brigadier-generals and one major-general. Eventually I propose to reduce them to two areas, North and South.

" I propose that the air force should be capable of extending to double the size.

" I am taking it that the nation will allow for only small wars at present.

" I am very strong on the point that for the next six months we must try to make the Air Ministry as powerful as we can with the best people."

He easily persuaded Churchill that Egypt was the ideal base for an immediate nucleus of front-line squadrons; the strategic value of aircraft for patrolling the deserts that flanked Britain's ocean life-line to the Far East greatly appealed to the Minister.

Salmond, Ellington and other officers were next asked to let Trenchard have their views by return. He wanted as many constructive criticisms as possible. The sooner a permanent scheme could be produced, the less readily would an absentee Cabinet, wintering in Paris and becoming engrossed in the early procedural squabbles of the Peace Conference, tend to quarrel with Churchill's somewhat free interpretation of Lloyd George's brief to close the Air Ministry. To save as much as possible from the doomed remnants of the wartime air force, he kept a careful eye on the half-dozen "reconstruction committees" headed by picked staff officers. Just when these were beginning to show results, misfortune intervened. Trenchard fell ill with Spanish influenza.

At first he tried to walk it off, all his animosity towards "sick people" turning against himself. The thought of seeking medical advice was as repugnant as that of taking to his bed and "sweating it out." The fact that an epidemic was raging far and wide, killing thousands each week in Europe alone, was something he preferred to ignore until sheer exhaustion forced him at length to rest. Then Baring defied Trenchard's phobia for doctors by calling one in. The patient was found to be suffering from acute pneumonia. Disregarding all advice, medical or otherwise, to relax, Trenchard used the sickroom as an office and continued to dictate letters and transact official business as though he had never left his desk. His condition worsened. When it began to appear distinctly improbable that he would recover,

Trenchard's method of acknowledging this was not uncharacteristic of a man suddenly brought face to face with utter loneliness.

Through his batman, he sent a series of urgent messages to Katharine Boyle, the one woman for whom he secretly cared. The wife of the colleague who had befriended him at Londonderry on his return from Nigeria had been a widow since the death in action of her husband during the retreat from Mons; Katharine, left with three young children to support, had met Trenchard once or twice since 1914; occasionally they had corresponded, but never until now had he admitted even to himself the depths of his feeling for her. Unfortunately, she was out of London. Only on reaching her mother's home in Lowndes Square late one night towards the end of February, tired out after a long journey through northern France and Belgium to visit the family war graves, did she discover the messages begging her to call. Fearing that her late husband's friend must be dying, if not already dead, she set off at once for the flat.

The door was opened by a bald, politely solemn man in a white overall whom she mistook for a rather eccentric doctor. He was unwilling at first to admit her, saying that the patient was too ill for visitors. Then his face brightened.

" Are you by any chance the new nurse? " he asked. " The patient has already got rid of three."

She explained that she had come at the patient's request. She was a friend.

Several R.A.F. officers sat reading or talking on a row of chairs in the hallway which reminded her of a dentist's waiting-room. They rose to let her pass. The small flat seemed to bulge with people, all in uniform, all preoccupied with matters that had nothing to do with sickness or death. Outside Trenchard's bedroom her quaint guide whispered that though the patient was still conscious he could hardly speak. He was in a bad way with his chest, found difficulty in breathing, and helped nobody, least of all himself, by his reluctance to stop talking and working.

Trenchard screwed up his eyes, unable to believe them. Katharine Boyle had not given herself time to change and wore the Red Cross uniform in which she had travelled from France. Was this woman, standing now at the foot of his bed, a mirage, he wondered, or just another uninvited nurse? He recognised her only when she removed her hat, and he pulled the sheet over his unshaven face in a clumsy gesture of embarrassment. Remarking that it would be better if he lay quite still, Katharine took his temperature. It was over 104. He did not protest at her injunction to lie still and seemed too tongue-tied to comment when she added that the officers outside ought to leave. As she gathered up the litter of papers strewn over the counterpane and bedside-table, piling them neatly out of reach, Trenchard remained strangely docile. Katharine Boyle gave a few nursing instructions to the stranger who had shown her in, assuming that he must be the sickroom orderly. Next day she accidentally overheard that his name was Maurice Baring.[5]

For most of March, Trenchard lay prostrate. The overstrain of the war years seemed to have sapped his stamina, and the crisis prolonged itself. Katharine Boyle called regularly, seeing to his daily wants with something more than the impersonal care of a trained nurse. In her experience of wartime Red Cross work, she had never encountered a more unwilling patient. She was present on several occasions when he fell into a restless sleep and his pent-up worries came tumbling deliriously off his lips. Always it was a variation on the same theme: grief at the new and hateful duty of abandoning so many of the survivors he had once led, grief at remembering the violent ends of the many more who had not survived. His anguish was all the more harrowing because of his helplessness. It told her more vividly than any words what the war had cost this man, and what pain its aftermath would cause him if he survived to rebuild the R.A.F.

The crisis passed. Then one day Trenchard sat up, called for pen and paper and laboriously wrote to his Secretary of State. So far he had been only a liability: illness had prevented his doing any of the urgent work that had to be done. In the circumstances, it might be advisable to appoint another Chief of Air Staff, particularly as he would probably be inactive for weeks to come. The straightforward honesty of the letter touched Churchill.

" I could not think of losing your greatly valued services until I was satisfied you were physically unfit," he replied. " I am looking forward so much to working with you."

But pleasure at Churchill's patience soon gave way to a depression so profound that Trenchard's colleagues were mystified. How could they know that his first act on rising to convalesce had been to offer his hand in marriage to Katharine Boyle, who had laughingly turned the proposal down? The thought of marrying again had not occurred to her; and Trenchard, of all possible suitors, seemed utterly incongruous. He had never declared his true feelings; and the current vogue of leading war widows to the altar, out of pity or chivalrous sentimentality, was wholly repugnant to her. How could she know that Trenchard had set her on a high pedestal in his heart and had secretly worshipped her for years? For this reticent bachelor had no words to explain how distant admiration had ripened slowly into affection since early 1915. Katharine, in fact, fitted his preconception of the ideal wife.

It was hardly surprising that nobody, not even Baring, who had in any case recently left the service, could plumb the depths of Trenchard's glum listlessness. He did not reappear at the Air Ministry until May, 1919; but as he insisted on handling all important policy questions personally, he had kept abreast of developments. The few letters he scrawled in pen or pencil from the Northamptonshire country house of Robinson, the solitary friend of his schooldays who had since achieved riches and distinction in the business world, are small classics of good judgment and bad grammar. The handwriting might be shaky; but the decisions were invariably firm and commanded assent.

It shocked him on his return to discover that scores of brilliant officers, young and old, had been allowed to leave the R.A.F. as wartime establishments were cut down. Freely cursing for negligence those who, from considerations of kindness, had kept the facts from him, Trenchard imported a belated element of arbitrary selectiveness into the release scheme by deciding himself who should be offered permanent or temporary commissions. It was the way he had always ruled, autocratically but very personally. To him the air force was not a faceless entity but the sum of its living parts, each individual being more or less necessary, more or less likeable. Too late now to prevent Festing, for example, one of his best staff officers, from disappearing into civilian life, he returned just in time to dissuade Salmond, the commander of the R.A.F. in France, from following suit by telling him rudely what he thought of him.

" Your taking this job rather disgusts me as you were one of those who pressed me very hard to come back. I was offered a job—not in commercial aviation—worth four times what I am getting now, and besides this I have been offered two other fine jobs. I declined all of them directly I accepted this. Unless I am kicked out, I intend to see it through at whatever pecuniary loss to myself and in spite of a very hard, difficult and not too pleasant task. . . ."

Salmond replied with icy restraint. It was his intention to resign, he said, when the Germans accepted the Allied peace terms, not before. " Perhaps," he suggested, "some day I may be more use to the Air from outside than I ever could be from within." It was a sentiment which Trenchard had heard too often to be impressed. Neither of them raised the matter again in the many letters that

passed between them during the next few weeks. Then, quite unexpectedly, Salmond wrote to say that he had changed his mind.
Trenchard was overjoyed and told him so plainly.

In a service as highly mechanised as the R.A.F. more confusion
and waste accompanied the process of demobilisation than was the
case in the army; and liberties had occasionally to be taken to
maintain in fighting trim a small core of front-line squadrons. The
massive striking force of ninety-six squadrons in France on Armistice
Day had shrunk to twenty-three in six months, yet less than ten of
these were serviceable, because most of the maintenance crews had
been discharged.

To watch the extinction of an unmatched weapon was a disagreeable business; but Trenchard could not abide the humbug or
self-deceit of commanders who complained that more could have
been salvaged. It was enough that Churchill, acting on an inspired
impulse, should have ignored Lloyd George's intentions and offered
the R.A.F. a chance to work out its own salvation.

This was the "soft option" which Trenchard had mistakenly
upheld in 1917 as the only sane policy. He now realised that when
the German daylight raids on London induced the War Cabinet to
push hard for the creation of a separate air force, Smuts and
Henderson had been right for the wrong reasons. From the military
viewpoint, the innovation had been an untimely and costly gamble;
but from the political viewpoint, it was then or never. An air force
was at any rate in being. Its separate existence was a fact; and
though Lloyd George seemed uninterested in keeping it alive, no
Cabinet would find it easy to kill.

" I am working night and day on permanent conditions of pay
and service," Trenchard told Salmond in June, " and Mr. Churchill
is doing all he can to help. It is taking time, and it is so important
that I cannot do half of my other work. Directly the War Cabinet
have sanctioned the proposals I will come and see you. I feel certain
you will agree that I must not give way but really make good
conditions. Never again shall we have the opportunity of doing it."

4

The summer brought repeated alarms and false hopes. The Cabinet
was too involved with peace-making to bother about the R.A.F.,
and Churchill's mind was too full of unfinished army business. In
Ireland, terror had broken loose again. In Egypt and India,

nationalism was on the march. As if he had not worries enough, the Minister allowed himself to become unnecessarily embroiled in the Russian civil war, the absence of any firm Allied policy providing him with an excuse for indulging in some highly ineffective anti-Bolshevik crusading.

Trenchard felt that Churchill's prodigious energy was offset by a tendency to shoot off at such tangents without sufficient reason or warning. The man had a mind like lightning and was no easier to control. There were compensating moments in between when the outlook appeared fine, despite the growing opposition of the older services to the revival of the air force.

After some fractious meetings with members of the Army Council, the future ranks and titles of R.A.F. officers were provisionally settled in July, Wilson, the C.I.G.S., incidentally betraying the measure of his enmity by pouring scorn on them. Was it Trenchard's idea, he asked, to bring the rank of Field-Marshal into disrepute by inventing the ridiculous title of Marshal of the Air? Knowing Wilson's obsession with trivialities, Trenchard had come forearmed: one of his young staff officers had spent a fruitful morning combing reference books at the London Library on his behalf.

" You or your predecessors should have thought of that before," he retorted and quoted some of the many existing uses of the word "Marshal," infuriating the C.I.G.S. by tacking provost-marshal, court-martial and Marshall and Snelgrove, the London store, to the end of the list. Churchill, who seemed to find Wilson something of a trial, laughed aloud at his discomfiture.

Later, at Buckingham Palace, King George V questioned the propriety of "Marshal of the Air" on theological grounds.

" Don't you think it tends to poach a bit on the preserve of the Almighty? " he asked. " Why not simply Marshal of the Royal Air Force? "

It was a happy suggestion, promptly adopted by Trenchard, who was equally flattered by the King's unreserved praise for the R.A.F. ensign. Trenchard had selected it in preference to half a dozen more colourful and original designs. The red, white and blue roundels on the wings of the wartime R.F.C. and R.A.F. were, in his eyes, a badge of courage beyond compare.[6]

These interludes were unreal beside the nagging difficulties on essential matters. Were the critics right? Had the old R.A.F. been run down too fast?

" I was left with nothing but two heaps of rubble—one of bricks and mortar, the other of men," Trenchard wrote, in an attempt to describe the problem of reconstructing a new model amidst the ruins of the old. " There were gems in each heap, but I had to pick them out blindfold."

Of the £66,500,000 voted by Parliament in the Air Estimates of March, 1919, no fixed sum was set aside for reconstruction; most of it went on demolition. Churchill was gratified to hear that, according to Trenchard's tentative calculations, the R.A.F. would need less than £25,000,000 to put it on its feet, about a twelfth of the sum spent on it in 1918; but the Commons were sceptical when the Minister offered this solace for the future during August. It was Churchill's present behaviour that disturbed many M.P.s.

With Army Estimates approximately eight times higher than the R.A.F.'s, Churchill's critics wondered how much money he was squandering on preparations for military intervention in Russia. Lloyd George had begun to wonder, too, having noticed the supplementary vote of one hundred and seven million pounds which was added in July to expenditure on the War and Air Department. It seemed to him excessive. Churchill, as he put it, was clearly suffering from " Bolshevism on the brain."

" You will, I am sure, forgive me for saying that I think Russia has cost us more than the hundred millions odd we have spent on her," Lloyd George wrote to Churchill at the end of August. " For an impression is left on my mind that the best thoughts of the War Office have been given to these military ventures in Russia and that the important administrative questions upon which so many scores if not millions depend have not received the same intense study."

The presence on Russian soil of some 40,000 Allied troops, at least half of them British, displeased Lloyd George. Admittedly, the Supreme Allied Council had publicly blessed the cause of the White Russian, Admiral Kolchak, in June, 1919, promising material aid in return for assurances of his democratic intentions. But the Prime Minister was determined privately to let Kolchak fight his own battles, since neither the French nor the Americans showed the slightest inclination to honour the pledge as liberally as Churchill.

Trenchard, too, disliked having to maintain squadrons at Murmansk and Archangel, quite apart from flights of aircraft aboard naval carriers in the Black Sea and at bases on the Caspian in the south. He needed the money and could have spent it more profitably.

Returning from Paris in September, Lloyd George once more admonished his Secretary of State for War and Air "to let Russia be, at least for a few days, and concentrate your mind on the quite unjustifiable expenditure in France, at home, and in the East, incurred by both War Office and Air Department." The expeditionary force at Archangel was at that moment preparing to disengage by striking its one defensive blow against the encircling Red Army before winter closed the port. In other sectors where British units were standing by, similar orders to pull out began to arrive. In the face of popular criticism, Allied apathy, and the Prime Minister's insistence that Britain could not undertake to save Russia from Bolshevism, Churchill reluctantly gave way. He had little opportunity to mourn over the abandonment of Kolchak to his fate. With the signing of the Peace terms, Lloyd George was impatient to reduce all service expenditure to the lowest level consistent with security.

The Prime Minister's faith in the will of the victors to make the world a safer place to live in was proof against disillusion. As the sole active survivor of the original "Big Four," his prestige abroad had never stood higher. The Germans had accepted the conditions imposed on them. There were still disputed frontiers to redraw, reparations to extract, conflicting claims of minority groups to disentangle without violence. Wherever men sought to arbitrate with the sword, as in Russia, the victims always had the League of Nations as a final court of appeal.

In this elevated and unrealistic frame of mind, Lloyd George cast about that autumn for a formula that would bring the spending habits of the service ministries at home into line with his hopes of the New World Order. His "Ten Year Rule" was the result. Embodying the simple proposition that Britain would not have to fight any major war for a decade, it was endorsed by the full Cabinet, which, by October, 1919, had begun to meet regularly again. The "Ten Year Rule's" purpose was to tighten the Treasury's grip on the Admiralty, War Office and Air Ministry. It created despondency among the Chiefs of Staff, Trenchard in particular fearing that it would increase inter-service rivalry and restrict both the development of the air force and its chances of survival. Its introduction had a temporarily blighting effect on the mercurial Churchill, who began to behave as though he regretted his gamble to preserve the R.A.F. as a separate service.

Austen Chamberlain, the Chancellor, provided an indirect foretaste of the rigours to come on 2nd September, when he wrote to Churchill:

" We seem to be moving in a vicious circle. Trenchard wants to know what money he may spend: we want to know what forces he has thought necessary to maintain, and what is involved in individual items of proposed expenditure, and so we each put questions to the other to which neither can give an answer."

The Cabinet, in effect, wanted a detailed inventory of Trenchard's plans before committing themselves to the principle of a separate peacetime air force. A third service now had to be justified in terms of financial outlay. With Churchill behind him, Trenchard had held at bay the combined heads of the War Office and Admiralty.

" The generals and admirals said the air force should use the existing services and their colleges," he wrote. " I had to live and work in a barrage of criticism. I was continually being pressed by the high-ups that the army and navy should train my people to be 'officers and gentlemen.' I could then take them over for flying training in the squadrons and form the R.A.F. that way. I could also use their medical, dental, engineering, clerical, scientific and spiritual facilities. It would save untold money.

" After a little cogitation I came to the conclusion that if I formed squadrons, and built my own bases, schools, and technical institutions as well, there would be a howl for more economies. Equally I knew that if I decided to have a few fighting squadrons and to use all the maintenance and other branches of the older services, I should be guilty of misusing a force that would grow more and more necessary for national defence on its own account.

" I therefore decided—and gradually convinced my Secretary of State—that we ought to defy the other services and risk unpopularity by building foundations with nothing much else to show —but foundations that it would be hard to destroy. I wanted very few squadrons—just enough to gain experience and carry out domestic roles in our overseas territories when local emergencies arose."

But Churchill had suddenly become less reasonable. His "tendency to wobble when attacked" began to worry Trenchard. Had the Minister still been in the Cabinet's good books, he might well have turned a studiously deaf ear to the lobbying of the soldiers and sailors. As it was, he listened to their special pleading on the pretext of "keeping an open mind." The more he listened, the more critical grew his attitude to Trenchard's reconstruction scheme. When the Chief of Air Staff bluntly taxed him for his fickleness, Churchill angrily denied the charge and withdrew into his shell to avoid further reproaches. Trenchard realised that the whole future of the R.A.F. now depended on his adroit handling of the Secretary of State. If he meekly knuckled under to Churchill, as that Minister had apparently knuckled under to Lloyd George and a pennywise Cabinet, the breaking up of the air force would merely be a matter of time. The only honest alternative was to tender his resignation as Chief of Air Staff for the second time in eighteen months, a drastic way indeed to test the Minister's good faith.

One evening towards the middle of September, Trenchard, who had been working late, rang for his private secretary, Captain T. B. Marson, and dictated a short letter of resignation.

" I want this delivered to Mr. Churchill in person," he said. " It should go to-night."

Marson, whom Trenchard encouraged to speak his mind, suggested that he ought to sleep on it, particularly as the letter would probably not reach the elusive Churchill until next day in any case.

Trenchard said nothing, but picked up the sealed envelope laid it in a desk drawer, and turned the key.

The following morning he summoned Marson from the outer office, unlocked his desk, held up the letter, and tore it up before his secretary's eyes without a word. Marson noticed that "he was smiling in a tired sort of way." The ritual over, he pledged Marson to unbroken secrecy, said that he was going to see the Minister without an appointment, and took a taxi to the War Office.

He walked into the Minister's office a quarter of an hour later, unannounced, having brushed aside the cohorts of messengers and secretaries who attempted to bar the way. He had come, he said, to clear up several misunderstandings which could not be allowed to stand between them any longer. Churchill scowled at him: he was not accustomed, he said, to being invaded and shouted at in his own sanctum. Both men promptly lost their tempers, exchanged abuse, and banged the desk at each other for emphasis. Nobody interrupted them, and this was just as well; for light as well as heat was accidentally generated by this uninhibited clash of tongues. Trenchard used a phrase which seemed to stick like a burr in Churchill's mind; later, when apologies were exchanged and the pair began to converse more civilly, the Minister carefully retrieved it.

" You said something just now about the absurdity of trained airmen becoming mere chauffeurs for the army and navy. I like that. It's the best argument I've heard yet."[7]

He asked Trenchard to develop it, cross-examined him like a prosecuting council, and urged him to produce at once a written statement on the same lines. Trenchard drafted it later that day. Some 3000 words in length, dated 11th September, 1919, and couched in Trenchard's characteristically rugged style, it served Churchill well in subsequent Cabinet discussions.

" There is still a great deal of discussion going on now as to whether it is justifiable to retain a separate air force," the statement ran. " This discussion rather takes the form of whether it is necessary to keep an Air Ministry. I hope to show that if a separate air force is necessary it cannot be run without an Air Ministry. This discussion is a great deal in the interests of economy, and it is no doubt essential that the utmost economy be enforced, but I would seriously ask— is it economy to spend, say, ten million pounds or a less sum on a camouflaged Independent Air Force which really means that the country is paying for a force that is of no practical value as such?

" It will be remembered that, owing to the great popular outcry, it was considered necessary to start an air force and form a large Department of State, and a new service, in the course of war, owing to the feeling that the air was not properly understood by the navy and army, and also that there was friction and, therefore over- lapping of work, between the two old and parent services. The air force thus formed was, as is well known or should be, only a temporary one, and practically all the men were temporary, and all the officers were temporary, with the exception of three.

" I think the consensus of expert opinion would be that the power of the air will be an increasing power in years to come—which is right. It seems to me that there are two alternatives.

(1) To use the air simply as a means of conveyance, captained by chauffeurs, weighted by the navy and army personnel, to carry out reconnaissance for the navy or army, drop bombs at places specified by them immediately affecting local operations or observe for their artillery.

(2) To really make an air service which will encourage and develop airmanship, or better still, the air spirit, like the naval spirit, and to make it a force that will profoundly alter the strategy of the future. . . ."

The strategic argument impressed the Prime Minister and Chancellor of the Exchequer far less than the economic premises on which it rested; and here Trenchard's unprecedented proposal that permanent commissions should be offered to only a third of his future officers, the remainder being recruited on a short-term basis, told in his favour. This innovation, condemned by professional critics of the two established services as quite ludicrous, Trenchard never

doubted his own ability to enforce. He did fear, however, that the
Cabinet would be unduly influenced by the scorn of the generals
and admirals. There he misjudged the temper of Austen Chamberlain, whose readiness to let him experiment enabled Trenchard not
only to lay new foundations but to prove himself an excellent
recruiting sergeant years ahead of his contemporaries in originality
of method. The human considerations which led him in that
uncertain autumn of 1919 to recommend the revolutionary concept
of short-service commissions were graphically underlined in a speech
to R.A.F. officers at Uxbridge nearly six years later, in 1926, when
the system was running smoothly.

" First of all I recognised that we should want a larger number
of officers than either of the two other services had—a larger proportion, that is—and then I looked back at my own experience. I
remember presiding at my own regimental dinner and meeting
twenty officers, all senior to me, who had done nothing since they
were fifty except draw their pay. . . . How could we make an outlet
for all the officers of junior ranks who would be needed?

" I took a pencil and paper. I assumed that the air force would
want 4000 officers, then I worked out what promotion they would get.
I found they would have become squadron-leaders about the age
of fifty. I myself was twenty-one years a captain in the army, and
I thought, ' Well, they are going to be thirty years in the rank of
captain, and that's impossible.' It would have been fatal. We
wanted not an older but a younger service than the navy or army.
I then worked out the requirements until I reached a reasonable
curve of promotion. I came to the conclusion roughly that it was
necessary to divide the 4000 by half in order to give a good curve of
promotion to those officers who were permanent."

Churchill, whose outlook was no more bound by established
conventions than Trenchard's, had accepted the short-term commission plan without batting an eyelid when it was first suggested
in the summer of 1919. Then, imperceptibly, as the ridicule and
resentment of army and navy leaders grew, the Minister had second
thoughts for a while. It took a head-on collision with Trenchard to
restore his faith in it. And now even a tight-fisted Cabinet seemed
satisfied.

5

Because of Austen Chamberlain's natural reluctance as Chancellor to bind himself to any fixed sum, Trenchard and his advisers were asked to produce three versions of the master plan. Scheme A provided for 40 service squadrons, with a further 42 for training, at an estimated cost of nearly £23 million; Scheme B for 34 service and 21 training squadrons at a cost of just over £17 million; and Scheme C for 27 service and 18 training squadrons costing about £15 million. Churchill presented them to the Cabinet at the end of October. In a covering paper, he brilliantly exploited Trenchard's basic distinction between true airmen and sky-borne chauffeurs.

"No compromise is workable," he wrote. "If we are not to relegate aviation to a minor position and lose that predominance which we have won at such cost during the last five years, we must create a real air service, not necessarily large but highly efficient. The problem is not, in the first instance, one of how many service squadrons we require to meet strategical needs, as in the case of the army, but one of making a sound framework on which to build. . . ."

When Pepys reformed and saved the navy, he was merely operating with the devoted skill of a surgeon on an institution which had long been part of the national heritage. Corrupt and inefficient administrators might have momentarily weakened it, but an island people could never question the necessity of a strong navy so long as their own security and prosperity were founded on sea-power. The army's title deeds were older still, less romantic perhaps, but equally incontestable. Neither service depended entirely, as the R.A.F. did in 1919, on a recent Act of Parliament passed in haste to meet an emergency of war.

Trenchard had been set the invidious task of drafting a coherent blueprint to justify its arrival and survival. The strategic arguments were new and unfamiliar; few people in or out of the Government wanted to subsidise a third service for its own sake. It is doubtful whether Trenchard could have succeeded in drafting an acceptable charter without Churchill, the opportunist, at his back. Yet, as Trenchard admitted to his biographer on several occasions:

"The same Winston Churchill caused me more sleepless nights while he was in charge of the Air Ministry than any of his successors. His imagination was too strong for comfort and he tended to be too easily swayed by the last devil's advocate he happened to meet. The trouble was that the devil then had too many advocates."

Churchill's resourceful mind, once bent in the right direction, convinced the Cabinet that the Chief of Air Staff had every reason to insist on the "elementary training of all ranks . . . in the bedrock of their professional duties": for if the officers of a highly technical service were deprived of their own centres for acquiring knowledge, and the men of tools, workshops and instructors for mastering their trades, the R.A.F. would be a thing built on sand. The principle that " schools for higher training are a necessity if the flying officer is to become something more than a chauffeur" thus prevailed. The final decision on means still rested with a Chancellor beset by other problems; so Churchill appended this note to the schemes prepared by Trenchard:

" Air-Marshal Trenchard attaches the greatest importance to Scheme B, and he seeks from the Cabinet an opportunity of submitting his reasons for it. I hope this may be accorded to him."

The Cabinet sent for him early in October. They listened politely to his explanations of the relative advantages and disadvantages of the three schemes. Then he sat down and his heart leaped when Lloyd George said:

" Scheme A is obviously the best. . . ."

Just as Trenchard was about to express his appreciation of a wise choice, the Prime Minister leaned forward, and added:

" But it would be better still to run Scheme A at a cut-price— on the money you want for Scheme B."[8]

Though it meant some five million pounds less to spend, Trenchard accepted the hard bargain driven by Lloyd George with relief. It was enough to know that the Cabinet conceded him the principle; the working details could always be adjusted. What Trenchard did not yet know was that Churchill had a more ambitious card up his sleeve which would greatly enlarge the area of his own jurisdiction if only he could play it. Its essence was that service spending could best be regulated by appointing him Minister of Defence and placing all three services under his control.

It was thus hardly surprising that Churchill, while promoting the cause of a separate air force, should still refuse to allow that a separate Air Ministry was necessary to run it. Trenchard was mystified by the inconsistency until Seely, the Under-Secretary of State, discovered the true reason early in November and disclosed it to the Chief of Air Staff.

" Winston's impossible," he said. " He's busy grooming himself for the post of Defence Minister. I'm going to force his hand and the Government's. Either they agree to a separate Air Ministry, or I go."[9]

Trenchard tried to dissuade Seely, from precipitate action, but the latter's combative instincts had been roused. The diaries of Lord Riddell and of the C.I.G.S., Sir Henry Wilson, are more informative about Seely's subsequent resignation than the Government spokesmen who had to account for it to Parliament. These privileged witnesses confirm that conversations between Lloyd George, Churchill and other Ministers did indeed take place on the question of forming a Defence Ministry. Riddell's diary entry for 9th November, 1919, says that after meeting Seely on Cobham golf-course he told the Prime Minister at dinner that Seely intended to resign next day "if he did not get his way." Lloyd George retorted that he would be sorry, but there was no alternative.

" He [Lloyd George] was strongly in favour of a Ministry of Defence to be responsible for the army, navy and air force," Riddell continued. " If this plan were adopted, the efforts of the three services would be co-ordinated and they would not be competing against each other. He thought there would not be another big war, at any rate, for ten years, and that meanwhile we could consolidate our position."

Seely, to Trenchard's mind, martyred himself to no purpose. No matter how keen Churchill and Lloyd George might be on creating a Defence Ministry, it was an impracticable proposition in peacetime; and the Prime Minister was too wily a political bird to spring such a change on the country when no single candidate possessed the heart and stomach for the job, and at the same time commanded the full confidence of the Cabinet. Churchill undoubtedly had the right kind of organs; but his reputation as a "wild man", among Government supporters and critics alike, automatically disqualified him. He had been hard pressed enough to keep the balance between a shrinking army and a small resurgent air force. With Beatty, the newly appointed First Sea Lord, already joining Wilson, the C.I.G.S., to challenge every measure that seemed to trespass on their traditional preserves, even a Churchill at his resilient best, with unanimous Cabinet support, would not have lasted long as Minister of Defence in 1919.

Trenchard was right. In six months of intermittent argument with the Admiralty and War Office, he had usually dealt with the professional heads of those services. Their hostility convinced him of the need for regular meetings so that all prejudices and grievances could be ventilated openly. Hankey, the Secretary of the Cabinet,

whose respect for Trenchard's negotiating talents and political
detachment had lately grown, called on him shortly after Seely's
resignation and mentioned in passing the informal arrangements
which Churchill at the Admiralty and Seely at the War Office had
evolved in pre-war days. The Ministers and their advisers, he said,
used then to meet regularly. There was no reason why the practice
should not be modified and revived. Trenchard was greatly
interested.

"What I need more than anything," he replied in so many
words, "is an official ring where I can face Wilson and Beatty as an
equal. If they intend to destroy me, they'd have to do so under
Queensberry rules."

Hankey doubted whether the "high-level bridge" technique of
Churchill and Seely would work. In that case, said Trenchard,
would the Cabinet ever agree to recognise the three Chiefs of Staff
as a permanent sub-committee of equals, "individually and collectively responsible" for national defence? Lloyd George, replied
Hankey, was too set on a full-fledged Defence Ministry to be easily
moved, but Churchill might be more amenable. Meanwhile,
Hankey promised to bear the matter in mind.[10]

No note of this casual conversation was taken, though both
participants remembered its gist clearly. It need only be added that
the Chiefs of Staff committee, a permanent part of Britain's modern
defence system and an institution which proved a flexible instrument of victory in the Second World War, was established in 1923,
less than four years after this talk at Adastral House. For Hankey
did not lose sight of a constructive idea which Trenchard had formulated largely in the interests of self-preservation.

He feared Wilson much less than he feared Beatty who
succeeded the safe and elderly Wemyss as First Sea Lord in the
last quarter of 1919. The supremacy of the Royal Navy had been
slighted, as far as Beatty was concerned, by the decision to let
Trenchard retain control of all aircraft, including those working with
the fleet. In the Cabinet exchanges, Walter Long, the First Lord,
had been no match for Churchill, who neither forgot nor forgave the
admirals for failing to exploit the wartime possibilities of aircraft at
sea.

Trenchard, nevertheless, saw in Beatty an opponent whose immense prestige made him potentially more dangerous than any
Minister. To public and politicians alike, he was the perfect em-
bodiment of the fighting captain. It was true that, in 1917, Beatty
had swung the Admiralty behind the Smuts plan for merging the

Flying Corps and the Naval Air Service, believing that it was then in the national interest. Beatty was already regretting his decision, causing Trenchard to complain that strategic arguments valid three years ago did not suddenly become invalid because they no longer happened to be convenient.

Once more on his sole initiative, he resolved to head off Beatty in private. Early in December, a few days before the new Air Force Charter was laid on the table of the House of Commons, Trenchard kept an appointment at the Admiralty with the First Sea Lord and the C.I.G.S. When he arrived, Wilson was behind Beatty's chair, lounging nonchalantly against the mantelpiece, his monocle appearing to screw his face into a welcoming leer more cynical than usual. The atmosphere at the start was not propitious. Wilson, knowing what was in the wind, evidently relished the prospect of watching Trenchard grovelling.

The First Sea Lord sat square and stolid at his desk while Trenchard paced the floor from door to window, as he frequently did in his own office when coaxing out a difficult line of thought. He doubted, he said, whether either of them shared his certainty that the " air is one and indivisible." This was the heart of his case for R.A.F. control of squadrons over land and sea. It was a hard doctrine, perhaps; but it did not mean what most critics imagined. For, apart from its own strategic role, the air force existed to co-operate with both army and navy. The tactical details were for the Chiefs of Staff to elaborate in harmony. He looked forward to that, but wanted to be sure of their intentions.

It was one of those sharp, bright December days which belied the time of year. Whenever Trenchard turned at the window and walked back towards the desk, he noticed Beatty shielding his eyes against the slanting sunlight. Presently the admiral rose impatiently, and began to stride purposefully to and fro in the opposite direction. Wilson, who remained propping up the mantelpiece, said little except to endorse Beatty's denial of Trenchard's central assumption with a dry "hear, hear." Since neither of them would budge an inch, Trenchard played his last card.

If the War Office and Admiralty were determined to frustrate the Cabinet's intentions, he said, he could not stop them. It would be easy enough for them to maim the R.A.F. fatally before it had grown big enough to justify even his own faith in its future. All he asked now was a sporting chance.

" Give me just twelve months' grace to get started," he said.

If at the end of 1920 they were still of the same mind, he would not feel hard done by: he would simply admit that he had failed, and he would deserve to have failed.

Wilson would promise nothing; but it was Beatty to whom Trenchard was primarily appealing, and Beatty seemed taken aback by the unexpected appeal to his sense of fair play. After some thought he said:

" All right. I'll leave you alone for a year—on condition that you meet our requirements meanwhile."[11]

It sounded suspiciously like an offer of "heads I win, tails you lose," but an armed truce suited Trenchard better than a one-sided battle. There would be difficulties enough in 1920 without hostility from Beatty and the Sea Lords. Cranwell, the proposed R.A.F. cadet college which had once been a naval training centre, was about to be opened; his plans for recruiting and training boy mechanics, as vital to the reborn service as Cranwell itself, were nearly ready. These undertakings alone would leave Trenchard and his staff little leisure for inter-service feuding. Ever grateful for small favours, Trenchard could only hope that Beatty's promise would be honoured at least in the letter.

Unlike the intolerant Wilson, the First Sea Lord did not underrate the resourcefulness of the Chief of Air Staff. He erred merely in over-estimating his power to break the R.A.F. regardless of the time factor; for in offering Trenchard a year's start he offered more than he could afford.

The labours that had been going on incessantly in Adastral House, just off the Strand, had borne fruit that would not lightly perish. The jumble of ideas thrown up during the past ten months had been rendered down and sifted; nothing of value had been discarded. By December, 1919, Trenchard's blueprint was being prepared as a White Paper; and though ends and means were clearly defined in Trenchard's mind, he felt his habitual inadequacy as others toiled over the proofs. He particularly missed the intuitive genius of Baring, whom he had tried in vain to wheedle back as his permanent mentor. Some of his new "English merchants," notably Charles Evans and Christopher Bullock, who though still Churchill's private secretary willingly lent a hand when necessary, proved exceedingly capable; except for Game, however, they were comparative strangers to the mysterious thought-processes of Trenchard.

The result of their endless redrafting and polishing under his restless, critical eye was no literary masterpiece. Apart from the odd rhetorical flourish, the style resembled that of an average company prospectus, its unevenness betraying the collaboration of several hands. Yet it stands like a towering landmark among military policy statements of this or any century. When it appeared in December, 1919, the reception accorded to it was lukewarm. Few politicians or journalists recognised in it the stamp of a practical visionary who would live to see every one of his proposals carried out. Fewer still believed that the new Royal Air Force could last, or that inside a generation it would save Britain from utter catastrophe in battle. This relatively unknown document has therefore an intrinsic importance equal to the more celebrated Smuts report.

The core of its message is contained in the preface. Referring to the political circumstances which had all but wiped out the air force of 1917-18, it stated:

" The force may in fact be compared to the prophet Jonah's gourd. The necessities of war created it in a night, but the economics of peace have to a large extent caused it to wither in a day, and we are now faced with the necessity of replacing it with a plant of deeper root. As in nature, however, decay fosters growth, and the new plant has a fruitful soil in which to spring.

" The principle to be kept in mind in forming the framework of the Royal Air Force is that in future the main portion of it will consist of an Independent Force, together with service personnel required in carrying out aeronautical research. In addition there will be a small part of it specially trained for work with the navy, and a small part specially trained for work with the army, these two small portions probably becoming, in future, an arm of the older service. It may be that the main portion, the Independent Air Force, will grow larger and larger and become more and more the pre-dominating factor in all types of warfare. . . ."

Neither the War Office nor the Admiralty were likely to overlook the admission that eventually they might recover their own "air arms." This passage was inserted, according to Trenchard, as a sop to their jealousy; he regarded it afterwards as a fatal lapse of judgment, and one which would be deservedly cited against him. The remainder of the paper, defining the place and purpose of the Cranwell cadets, the boy apprentices, the short-term commissioned pilots, and the future "week-end fliers" of an Auxiliary Air Force to be recruited like the Territorial Army from the counties and cities of Britain, could not be faulted if one accepted the basic premises.

The atmosphere at Westminster when Churchill introduced the "Trenchard Memorandum" on 11th December was torpid, the apathy of most M.P.s reflecting the public mood. Belated Government support for the principle of a separate air force raised the spirits of a minority only. For Members like Lord Hugh Cecil, Sir John Simon, Captain Wedgwood Benn and Colonel Moore-Brabazon, who had served Trenchard and trusted him, were easily outnumbered by the partisans of naval and army interests.

Because Trenchard could count on so little parliamentary backing, he was all the more grateful for the occasionally fickle encouragement of Churchill and for the pledge extracted from Beatty. The Press in the main, sounded a carping note about his master plan. And though Northcliffe and Rothermere had still to coin, between them, the mocking term "Royal Ground Force," that thought was already implicit in the attitude of their newspapers. The most balanced comments came from Colonel Repington, one of the foremost military correspondents of the day. Writing in the *Morning Post*, Repington declared that Trenchard's scheme contained "claims of a most contentious kind," even though "nearly all his subordinates, including Generals Salmond and Sykes (who had since accepted the control of Civil Aviation proffered by Churchill), are entirely convinced that the air force must remain for the present under the Air Ministry."

Repington, however, was indignant at Trenchard's presumption in declaring the natural independence of the R.A.F.; and the assertion that the service "will grow larger and larger and become more and more the predominating factor in all types of warfare " seemed to him worse than ludicrous.

" If there is nothing like leather," retorted Repington, "it must be remarked that we seem to be back in the last months of the war, when the air force demands raised its personnel to some 300,000 men at a time when our infantry were so short of men that they suffered a grievous defeat, and when the air force, brilliant as its services were, did not prevent that defeat. It is absurd to talk of any fraction of our armed forces as independent, since unity of conception and control is the leading principle of war. . . . No evidence has been given that the Independent Air Force shortened the war by an hour, and the fact that this force was brilliantly commanded and served with the utmost heroism does not alter that. . . .

" Infantry with its machine-guns is still the Queen of Battles, gains and consolidates victories, suffers the heaviest losses, and is the kernel of the offensive or defensive battle. To label an auxiliary arm predominant entails that in days of straitened means we foster it at the expense of the working infantry. . . . It is a heresy for Sir Hugh

Sir John Salmond

Arriving at 10
Downing Street at
the time of the
Chanak crisis, 1922

Trenchard to suggest that the air force can be a substitute for part of our garrisons overseas, and these exaggerations do harm to the air force itself by turning its friends into enemies."

The "Trenchard Memorandum" had become an open book for the orthodox to read and condemn. Churchill, a characteristic exception to the rule, was sufficiently edified to draw on it extensively for his own Cabinet paper. It was now up to the Chief of Air Staff to convince a massively indifferent public that his new model would work.

13. Poor Relation

Trenchard was probably correct in assuming that, had he failed to restrain Beatty, his master plan would have disintegrated in 1920. That single "year of grace" enabled him to lay the foundations at home in comparative tranquillity while his squadrons abroad, notably in India and the Middle East, demonstrated that air-power could become a cheap and effective means of preserving peace. Of the 25½ squadrons he was allowed to retain, Trenchard decided to base no fewer than 19 overseas: 8 in India, 3 in Mesopotamia, 7 in Egypt, and 1 for division among the various naval bases. Only 2 fighting squadrons were left to protect Britain, after 2½ had been allocated for work with the home fleet and 2 for army co-operation.

Anticipating the objections of those who could not see why the R.A.F. should flaunt its strength overseas, Churchill told the Commons on 15th December, 1919:

" I must remind Hon. Members that we have still an Empire to defend. Odd as it may seem on the morrow of unheard-of victories, we have all those dependencies and possessions in our hands which existed before the war, and in addition we have large promises of new responsibilities to be placed upon us. The first duty of the Royal Air Force is to garrison the British Empire."

Only a Minister equally responsible for the War Office could have thus served notice that the traditional preserves of the army were no longer safe. Neither the Commons nor the General Staff rejoiced at the prospect. Some ridiculed Trenchard's sense of proportion in earmarking £13 million out of a budget of only £15 million on bricks and mortar at home. A mere £2 million for maintenance, research, and civil aviation seemed a pitifully inadequate outlay. The priorities, according to these critics, should have been reversed.

The mood of the hour was against changes in a time-honoured pattern of defence. The task of building a peacetime air force, complete with its own colleges, training and experimental centres,

354

seemed to call for every particle of Trenchard's concentration, without his becoming embroiled in warlike operations on the side. That was poaching. The army resented it; the navy questioned its propriety. Had not Churchill himself admitted that "the R.A.F. is in want of practically every permanent institution of a disciplined service" ?

Mr. Walter Long, the First Lord, was voicing the feelings of his board when he dropped a hint in the Commons that should Trenchard's tentative arrangements for air-sea co-operation prove unsatisfactory he would have no compunction in resigning. And Seely, who had already done so, scoffed at the policy of letting the War Office define what the Admiralty needed.

" This is not government," he declared. " It is *opéra bouffe*."

Churchill's left hand seldom knew what his right intended; and whether his "murderous propensities" were to be employed against the War Office or Air Ministry, Seely could not rightly say, though one or the other would undoubtedly fall victim to those "propensities" before long. It is salutary to-day to recall such early intimations of scepticism about the future of the reborn R.A.F.

Lacking ready cash, Trenchard had to hasten slowly. Unwanted wartime stations could be closed only as fast as the leases and scrap could be disposed of. The delays hardly encouraged cheerfulness or hope among the officers and men obliged to remain as uniformed caretakers. A sense of gloomy desolation swept the service in 1920, affecting high and low alike, at home and overseas. When Sir Oliver Swann, for instance, an ex-naval aviator of distinction, wrote in January from Malta, stating that he had not sufficient men either to justify his rank or to maintain the few weak squadrons in his command, Trenchard replied:

" I admit it all. I quite understand that you are very short. . . . At the same time we now have in England one hundred stations over and above what we should have—and no men allowed for these extra stations. . . . Active service is also going on in India and this has the first call."

Similar complaints were pouring in from scores of others. He could only advise them not to despair.

It would have been disastrous if Beatty had incidentally exposed this state of affairs by pressing Trenchard to fulfil the legitimate demands of the navy, which the R.A.F. was then quite incapable of doing. For the Chief of Air Staff had no friends in Fleet Street; and he had at least one, probably two, implacable foes among the Press lords. Maurice Baring had recently warned him:

" Rothermere and Beaverbrook have it in for you. The former has never forgiven you, the latter doesn't think you're fit for your job."[1]

Squadrons in India were undoubtedly the worst off, materially and financially. Afghanistan had declared a "holy war" in 1919; and the frontier tribes, particularly in Waziristan, had been causing the Indian Government intermittent anxiety since. In response to requests for air reinforcements, bombers from depots in Britain and France were reconditioned and flown overland to the Middle East and Far East. The excuse for salvaging something more from the scrap heap was an added incentive to instant co-operation, for the bombers would be a charge on India. Unfortunately, several Handley Pages crashed *en route*; the news seeped out; questions were asked in Parliament; and the synthetic fury of the popular Press, especially Rothermere's part of it, knew no bounds. Who was responsible for this "trail of blood?" the newspapers thundered.

The cause of truth would have been better served, in Trenchard's view, had the Press lords taken the trouble to examine the appalling conditions under which the R.A.F. had to exist, let alone fight, in India. It was wholly at the mercy of the Delhi Government, whose military and financial advisers were eager to use all available aircraft but less than willing to pay for or maintain them. Negotiations to determine where the Air Ministry's financial liability began and ended dragged on for months in an atmosphere of Oriental bargaining that severely taxed Trenchard's patience, inducing him on occasion to turn a blind eye to the conduct of quite junior officers in India, several of whom, goaded beyond endurance, took the law into their own hands.

One example will suffice. A bristling young Rhodesian called Arthur Harris, destined to become an outstanding wartime chief of Bomber Command, was then in charge of a Bristol fighter squadron on the North-West Frontier. But for Trenchard's "blind eye" policy, the career of this officer would probably have been cut short in 1920 before a court-martial. Growing weary of "having to fly myself and to send my crews in aircraft which were utterly unairworthy," Harris first submitted his resignation, and, when this was not forwarded, announced that he would continue operations against dissident tribesmen at his own discretion. The fact that his machines were so worn that they took off "on wheels with naked rims because there were no tyres, and with axles lashed on with doubtful country-made rope because there was no shock-absorber rope" did not excite official concern in India, though spares of all kinds were commonly known to be rotting in the dumps of Britain or being sold off at bargain prices.

Trenchard meanwhile dispatched as much equipment as he dared to India. Nearly a year passed before he was relieved of this unnecessary burden. Then as a result of a letter to *The Times* by an eminent visitor, who accused them of gross negligence, the Indian authorities bestirred themselves. The most glaring deficiencies were hastily repaired before Sir John Salmond disembarked at Bombay on a tour of inspection ordered by Lloyd George in response to belated criticisms at home. Only Trenchard knew how harshly the morale of his squadrons on active service had been tried during the intervening months. Once, when a visiting general informed Harris that he need undertake no more reconnaissance flights or raids until further notice, he retorted that none were possible in any event, since he was down to his last four serviceable machines. This induced the general to round on Harris and denounce all airmen for shirking their duties unless "coddled to the point of living in the lap of luxury." When he had cooled down, the visitor said more understandingly:

" I suppose you must get back to Peshawar and your spare parts before you can do more."

" Yes, sir," said Harris. " It's high time we got back to our ball of string."

The general promptly exploded again and promised the impenitent Harris that his insolence would not go unrewarded. Possibly to the latter's surprise, Air Headquarters were instructed by London not to take proceedings. Trenchard did not, as a rule, condone impertinence; but, being less in sympathy with the plaintiff than with the defendant, he quietly had Harris transferred to Iraq. No more was heard of the incident.

The R.A.F. was not so well staffed with promising young officers that even one should be sacrificed to the vanity of a general. Too many were inventing reasons for leaving a service which apparently had little to offer them. The hazards of civilian life seemed less uninviting than being endlessly shuttled from one redundant home station to another, while dealers squabbled over the prices of derelict stock like buzzards over a deserted battlefield. It was natural in the circumstances that candidates for short-term commissions should hold back, so that Trenchard's master plan stood for a while in jeopardy. The air force, during that final spell of demolition, not only lost its sense of direction among the ruins; it lost its confidence and self-respect as well.[2]

Whenever he could break away from the office, Trenchard would descend, unannounced, on stations and depots within a few hours' reach of London. He expected his staff likewise to tour commands so that the human aspect of current problems should not become submerged in columns of statistics.

" Be lenient and learn how far a point can be stretched," was his constant exhortation.

" Try to be proud of yourselves," he would tell officers and men on the stations he inspected. " If you don't, nobody else will."

His own early struggles, of which none of his colleagues had an inkling, fitted him admirably for the hard, uphill business of firing young men in doubt with a corporate faith in themselves.

With an insight cultivated during the war years, Trenchard softened formal orders by enclosing personal notes to his commanders that showed plainly how his mind was working. The most candid and illuminating of these exchanges were with the Salmond brothers, John and Geoffrey, with Ellington and with Charles Longcroft, war-time associates whom he accepted now as partners, not as rivals. All of these except Longcroft—and that through no fault on either side —would one day succeed him as Chiefs of the Air Staff.

Relations with the nucleus of ex-naval officers at Air Ministry were somewhat more formal. In passing over the stronger qualifica-tions of several ex-R.F.C. senior officers to secure a leavening of sailors among his key advisers, Trenchard looked farther ahead than many of his subordinates realised at the time. Not even warm admirers would have said, for instance, that Sir John Steel, Trenchard's choice as his deputy, or Sir Cecil Lambert, the Director of Personnel, or Sir Charles Lambe, the Director of Equipment, were so endowed that their superior claims could not be ignored. It was their experience of the senior service and their understanding of the naval mentality, quite apart from their devotion and loyalty to himself, which persuaded Trenchard to appoint them over the heads of others. Beatty had allowed the R.A.F. only a year. He was content, therefore, to be guided up to a point by Steel and Lambe, and to let Lambert, a wrinkled former vice-admiral with a tongue like a lash, inject some of his stern, disciplinarian spirit into the new service, reminding him on occasion:

" Of course, I can balance things up by injecting some humanity."[3]

Trenchard was most troubled by the patronising view of the R.A.F. held by people in the upper spheres of society. It was a common whisper that "nobody who was anyone" would disgrace himself or his family by joining, or encouraging a near relative to join, this "upstart cinderella of the services." Disparagement of the kind could, he knew, be more damaging than the enmity of admirals and generals and their camp followers at Westminster or in Fleet Street. As his own character and outlook, let alone the various stages of a tempestuous career, had been largely fashioned by a lifelong determination to prove that riches and status, titles and blood were not the only passports to fame or success, he set out deliberately to crush the snobbish insinuation wherever he encountered it.

His principal weapon was good-natured derision; and one of his most obliging allies was Lord Londonderry, Churchill's Under-Secretary of State. Among the so-called leaders of fashion and society, the politicians, Press lords, and people of influence who were often entertained in the magnificent town home of the London-derrys, Trenchard sought to undo at every opportunity, in his own direct manner, the harm done by wagging tongues. Courtesy, common sense, and an unlooked-for readiness to mix in any company gradually stamped him in the minds of many to whom he was still only a name as an oddly engaging individualist who was at heart the reverse of a snob. His upbringing and experience had long ago confirmed the truth of a favourite saying of his that "nice things make nice people, nasty things make nasty people." The knowledge spurred his will to raise above criticism the new air force with which he completely identified himself. It must learn to weather its nondescript social reputation by adopting the rules, customs, ceremonies and practices which were deemed not merely "nice" but necessary by the fashionable world.

Rugby, he advised Longcroft, the commandant-designate of Cranwell, as though announcing a scientific discovery, was "the best game on earth" for developing team spirit and manliness. It had the additional advantage of being played in most of the leading public schools. In details of the sort, he was not uniformly guided by convention. Remembering the thrills and rewards of his own brief apprenticeship on the Cresta Run, he wrote to all R.A.F. commanders suggesting that officers should be encouraged to acquire a taste for winter sports and offering to assist any who responded. Silver trophies were more than prizes for skill and ability in his eyes. They were symbols of permanence, possessions to be coveted and treasured, whether the men of a squadron who carried them off came from castles or slums. When he decided that the R.A.F. should have its own band, it was on condition that it recruited only the best musicians possible. The same quest for distinction led him to set particular store by the public displays of the R.A.F. gymnastic teams.

But undoubtedly his most spectacularly successful promotion was the annual air pageant at Hendon, an occasion, as he visualised it, for letting the public see in a huge shop window of his own choosing that they were not paying taxes in vain, whatever the critics of the R.A.F. might say to the contrary. Trenchard was no Barnum; but he did not shrink from the art of showmanship when this served his own purposes.

His punctiliousness about dress or ceremonial was notable; yet he hated to be "fussed," and was quite capable of self-mockery when admiration or flattery were thrust on him for the wrong reasons.

" These? " he was overhead saying at a ball when his rows of medals were being studied by a slightly condescending titled lady through a lorgnette.

" Perhaps two were earned. The rest just grew on me like barnacles."

Attending social or civic functions where his absence would be remarked upon became a duty he shouldered as willingly as the late hours he habitually kept at the office, or the extra work he took home to his flat in order to redeem the hours spent on journeys to airfields where morale needed artificial respiration. Too wise to conceal from himself the truth that the R.A.F. lacked what was sometimes referred to as "dining out power," Trenchard invariably insisted that the Air Ministry should be represented by Steel or Game or someone of comparable standing whenever he himself was prevented from accepting an important invitation.

From one member of the Royal family at least, the young Prince Albert (later George VI), Trenchard consistently received sympathy, encouragement and unobtrusive support. The Prince, who had joined the Naval Air Service at Cranwell in 1917, and served briefly on the staff at Nancy during the final weeks of the war, needed no convincing of the value of a separate air force. His appreciation of the R.A.F.'s teething troubles was genuine; for the Prince had none of his father's obdurate suspicions of a service which, because of its newness and lack of tradition, preached strategic doctrines which were anathema to the orthodox.

King George V required time to adjust himself to the existence of the R.A.F., professing sharp distaste for the style of its early hybrid uniform and retaining to the end his original inhibitions about aircraft as noisy, smelly contrivances. It is possible that the monarch's prejudices dated from an untoward mishap which overtook him in November, 1915, on a brief visit to Trenchard's First Wing in France, when his horse, startled by a lusty burst of cheering from the ranks

of airmen, reared and stumbled on the slippery ground, pinning him
underneath. Even after the air force survived the political perils
of the twenties, and the King learnt to look on it with unmixed pride
at last, he could never bring himself to travel anywhere by air.

" At the notion of entering an aeroplane himself," recorded Sir
Owen Morshead, " he would shake his head."

Prince Albert, on the other hand, belonged to that segment of a
rising generation which could appreciate aircraft as weapons of war.
He was the first royal visitor to the new R.A.F. college at Cranwell,
still the spartan place of huts he had known as a naval cadet, with its
hangars the only permanent structures. Far removed from the
metropolis, and wholly bereft of historic associations or outward
graces, Trenchard nevertheless preferred it to more gracious and
accessible centres for the formation of his future leaders. Cadets, he
felt, would be better off in the Lincolnshire countryside than anywhere nearer London. If he was breaking with tradition, he was
also being realistic. The very future of Cranwell was insecure. The
majority among its first intakes of cadets tended to come from middle-
class homes; barriers of ignorance and snobbery still excluded the
sons of the rich and well born, though riches and nobility to his mind
were no substitute for, or guarantee of, the gentlemanly qualities
demanded of all entrants, whatever their background. However,
(and here Trenchard was reasoning from personal experience) lack
of money and status might prove a handicap to cadets in any college
situated too close to the attractions of London.

" I thought they'd dislike Cranwell to start with, but hoped that
eventually they'd appreciate my intentions," he told his biographer.
" Marooned in the wilderness, cut off from pastimes they couldn't
organise for themselves, they would find life cheaper, healthier and
more wholesome. And they'd have less cause to envy their contemporaries at Sandhurst or Dartmouth and acquire any kind of
inferiority complex."

To Prince Albert, as to Hugh Cecil, de la Bere and others who
offered advice, it seemed at the outset as if Trenchard was resolved
to dispense with entrance to Cranwell by competitive examination.
He was finally overborne; but he retained the right to reconsider
personally the cases of young men who failed to satisfy the examiners,
scrutinising references and character reports from headmasters and
others, and weighing these against his own impressions of the
unsuccessful candidates at special interviews. In the hands of really
painstaking examining boards, he felt, this alternative method might
have become the starting point of a fairer and less fallible selection

system. But Trenchard did not press too hard against the firm opinion of experienced men like Cecil that it would be disastrous to foster the illusion of Cranwell as a haven for the work-shy or the congenital blockhead.

Living quarters at the cadet college were cramped; the playing fields, class-rooms, workshops and community rooms were more spacious. The staff had been meticulously chosen as much for their sense of vocation as for their ability to inculcate specialised knowledge and discipline into their young charges. Trenchard's views were known. To outsiders they may have seemed romantic and far-fetched, but never to the instructors at Cranwell or the earliest cadets. One day these youths would become the very backbone of the new service; one day, in a dire extremity, they might have to prove their fibre by rising to save the nation. This was the most enduring of Trenchard's cherished premonitions; he lived long enough to see it fulfilled. His critics might harp on the indispensability of tradition, on the air force's lack of anything remotely resembling one: they reckoned without the sense of history and achievement in the bones of a leader whom they deemed an "uneducated man." Trenchard found tradition enough in the annals of his wartime squadrons, the brief glory of which was carefully fostered at Cranwell. Art, science and the applied subjects of the new and complex profession of military aviation were taught as a systematic part of Trenchard's dogmatic faith in air-power as he had learnt it in action. His young disciples meanwhile enjoyed all the advantages that he had gone without at their age, coupled with more scope for cultivating individual tastes and hobbies than their army and navy contemporaries were allowed under their stiffer systems. There is no written record of his first use of the expression, but Longcroft and many cadets heard Trenchard say repeatedly on visits to the college during the early years of its existence:

" The Royal Air Force depends on you far more than on me. The service will be really safe only when one of you takes over my chair as Chief of the Air Staff."

Trenchard was spared long enough to witness the accomplishment of this second and happier prediction, too. The case of Dermot Boyle, the son of a widowed Irish woman wiser than her generation in withstanding convention and resisting the pressure of relatives who felt that the natural ambition of a farmer's boy should be to follow his father behind the plough, illustrates it perfectly. Boyle had not been born and bred in the lap of luxury; he came of no particularly privileged or wealthy family; when his father died he was still in his teens. He wanted to become an airman, not a farmer, and his mother supported him against the collective opposition of his uncles who were adamant that the life of an airman was short and unsweet, since airmen had the reputation of either "breaking their necks young or of drinking themselves to death."

At Cranwell, Boyle heard Trenchard say that the R.A.F. would reach maturity only when a cadet became Chief of the Air Staff, never dreaming that one day he would make the saying come true. Nearly twenty-five years later, on 1st January, 1956, when Boyle's appointment to that post was announced, he called privately on Trenchard to remind him of another prediction which time had vindicated. The founder and first marshal of the R.A.F. had then six weeks to live.

Perhaps the finest example of Trenchard's flexibility of approach was his decision to leave six Cranwell places vacant for apprentices from the boys' training wing, then stationed next door to the college. This notable break with custom reflected the rare blend of autocracy and egalitarianism which went unrecognised in him until the end of his days. If, as he believed, it took all sorts to make a world, a mechanised service could simply not afford to neglect its best mechanics. Room must be provided at the top for them, too, places allotted, hidden talents brought forth and developed. Certain Air Ministry colleagues, more conservative in outlook, argued that the innovation would "lower the tone" of the service. Trenchard ignored them, as he had done in establishing the short term commissioned officer.

When, in 1923, an apprentice was denied a cadetship because his prowess in the gym and on the parade ground fell short of his exceptional abilities in the class-room, Trenchard overruled the selection committee which had turned young Frank Whittle down. He chose to listen instead to the special pleading of the flight commander, Robert Barton, his former subaltern at Londonderry, who privately requested that Whittle's case should be reconsidered as the boy had the makings of a mathematical genius.

" Because the Personnel Branch wouldn't listen, I bearded Trenchard in his office," Barton recalled. " He gave me a sympathetic hearing and ended by saying, ' You don't often make mistakes, Barton, but if this is one I won't forgive you.' But for Trenchard's common sense, Whittle might never have got his head; and Britain might have had to wait for the inventor of the jet engine."

Longcroft, as commandant, could be relied on to keep cool fingers on the pulse of the new college, and a watchful eye on the general conduct and qualities of his pupils.

" This (latest) entry is the best we have had up to date," he was able to inform Trenchard in 1921, " but there is still a sprinkling at Cranwell of the hairy-heeled type."

The information pleased Trenchard, implying that Longcroft had acquired at last, as he had known he would, the delicate art of handling young men of all types, the hairy-heeled included.

Yet it is intriguing to note that of the relatively meagre funds voted by Parliament for building purposes, the major portion was lavished by Trenchard not on Cranwell, but on the vast stores, machine shops, and barracks that were slowly rising at Halton Park, Buckinghamshire. This training centre, the largest of its kind in the land, was not completed until 1926. Halton, a temporary depot of the war years, seemed to him the ideal site for the mass of boy apprentices on whom the air force would one day depend at least as much as on the more refined products of Cranwell. So Trenchard promptly purchased the house and estate from the Rothschild family for a reasonable sum. He was determined not to rush the construction of a place meant to last, though many of the 3000 youths between the ages of fifteen and eighteen whom the centre would ultimately accommodate were recruited at once. Halton's proximity to London was a point in its favour. Boy trainees, Trenchard decreed, should be near enough to visit or be visited by their parents and friends; and the relaxations of the cinema and dance halls in their free time would do them no harm.

While his great technical centre was going up, the apprentices were temporarily quartered either at Cranwell or Flowerdown, the R.A.F.'s electrical and wireless school. It was not a convenient arrangement; but it was the most practicable in the unsettled circumstances of the day. The spirit of his boy recruits had to be lifted. This he did by introducing separate "wings," after the fashion of the house system in public schools. The scheme found an enthusiastic sponsor in Churchill, who agreed that no more natural or inexpensive form of incentive existed. Provided the instructors were sufficiently dedicated and understanding, it should, he said, produce excellent results. On the whole, it did. For it became a point of honour with Trenchard to be satisfied with nothing less.

2

The outside world, mercifully, seemed conscious of the R.A.F.'s existence only at intervals. Trenchard, a stern realist, did nothing to disillusion those who had already written him off as a dead duck. It was no part of his nature or duty, as he saw it, to do otherwise. He preferred, as always, to snatch his chances unhelped or unhindered by the fickle breezes of opinion. Whitehall looked on, outwardly impassive, though several officials of prominence, including Sir Warren Fisher at the Treasury, alternately regretted and marvelled at Trenchard's lofty disdain for opponents who could not comprehend why any government should keep a separate air force.

That the memories of newspaper readers tended to be short, and rather shallow, had lately been proved to Trenchard's satisfaction. For, by the summer of 1920 the public no longer recalled the fate of the "Mad Mullah," a terrorist whose long career of spoliation and violence in British Somaliland had been cut short by a single R.A.F. squadron only a matter of months before.

This militant fanatic, who had been a thorn in the side of the War Office since the first decade of the country, was routed and driven into exile in February, 1920; yet it is doubtful whether anyone except Trenchard, and possibly Churchill, saw in his downfall the strongest political argument yet for maintaining the integrity of the new air force.[4] A flat official *communiqué* or two at the time, suitably rehashed in the newspapers with abridged accounts of the Mullah's past exploits, helped to play down the dramatic complete-ness of an air operation planned and executed within six weeks. Such dispatch doubtless engendered its own sense of anti-climax. There was an element of faint incredulity in the public reaction to this experiment in pacification. Millions of pounds and many lives had been spent in the past on what the late Mr. Leopold Amery, the then Colonial Under-Secretary, classified justly as "inconclusive, and more than once, disastrous fighting" against the Mad Mullah.

During the First World War, when British forces were busier elsewhere, the terrorist's grip on this barren corner of Africa had tightened to such a degree that now Milner, Amery's chief, quailed at the thought of bringing him to book.

Stout fortresses of stone constructed by the Mullah's men dominated the few passable roads into the hills. Armed bands controlled half the country, frequently descending on villages in the other half to loot, kill, torture, and kidnap recruits. The police and security forces were too few and ill-equipped to venture far outside the limited areas known to be safe. Early in 1919, Milner studied the situation reports with mounting anxiety. The alternative to another expedition on the pre-war model was to abandon Somaliland to the mercy of this bandit who believed himself divinely inspired. To Milner, with his consuming interest in the civilised development of Africa, such a course seemed unthinkable. But so, for that matter, was armed intervention. Neither the Cabinet nor the public, in the prevailing passion for military economy, would welcome or perhaps even consider it.

By May, 1919, Milner was warning Lloyd George that there was no middle way that he could see; but military action, so imperative in theory, appeared financially prohibitive in practice. The C.I.G.S. admitted that at least two divisions would be necessary. The operation might take anything up to a year. In addition, Wilson stipulated that a railway should be laid behind the advancing troops, to prevent any future recurrence of trouble. Milner was dispirited, realising that the Cabinet, presented with a War Office estimate running into several million pounds, might choose to scuttle rather than to fight.

At this point Milner showed political courage and imagination. One day towards the end of May he sent a note by hand to the Air Ministry asking Trenchard to call on him privately. The invitation came as a surprise. By no stretch of fancy could the Colonial Secretary have been described as a trusty friend of the air force; Trenchard's dealings with him as Secretary of State for War, in the spring of 1918, had been frigidly formal; and their relations since had been somewhat distant. Yet the Milner who received him now held nothing back in his patently sincere desire to solve an awkward dilemma. Intervention in Somaliland could not, he said, be deferred indefinitely. Could Trenchard suggest any way of reducing the cost without imperilling the outcome?

Trenchard countered the question with another.

" Why not leave the whole thing to us? This is exactly the type of operation which the R.A.F. can tackle on its own."

Milner stared back as though he had misheard. Surely some ground troops would be essential, the Minister said at length. Wilson had mentioned two divisions. How many battalions would be desirable for mopping up if the R.A.F. broke the Mullah's resistance?

Trenchard assured him that he saw no necessity for moving in extra troops. There were sufficient for the purpose in Somaliland, unless the Colonial Secretary wanted a reserve at hand against some unforeseen emergency. Two battalions of infantry and the local camel-mounted levies would be ample: the R.A.F. would not waste time or ammunition. Whatever the C.I.G.S. might assert to the contrary, quite possibly the Mullah would surrender without a fight. For ambushes and stone forts would not obstruct bombers. And the rebels, without their forts and ambushes, would be incapable of lengthy resistance, especially when deprived of the lure of easy loot.

" Why not get Churchill's advice? " said Trenchard. " I think you'll find he agrees with me."

Milner promised to do so; and a few days later Trenchard attended a War Office conference with Churchill in the chair, Amery deputising for Milner, and the C.I.G.S. seated beside the Chief of the Air Staff. Wilson was clearly agitated and annoyed. He protested, as soon as the Somaliland project was raised, that he appeared to be the only sane person present. Then he challenged Amery or anyone else to say by what right the Colonial Office, or the Foreign Office for that matter, could presume to plan a military expedition independently of the War Office. Trenchard silenced Wilson with a rejoinder that brought an appreciative smile to the chairman's face.

" I don't know about the Colonial Office," he said, " but I once led an expedition in Nigeria authorised by the Foreign Office."

Wilson quickly changed tack.

Whether there was a precedent or not, he said, the proposal to substitute the air force for the army in Somaliland was "utterly fantastic." He could predict what would happen.

" I shall be asked, when it's too late, to rescue your aeroplanes and clear up the mess. That will mean not the two or three divisions I want now, but perhaps double the number—and a lot of unnecessary alarm and expense."

Trenchard retorted that he had no intention of shouting for help. If the Cabinet asked for an air campaign, it would be conducted competently. Amery then declared that the Colonial Office was willing to let Trenchard try. Churchill approved, and Wilson had to swallow an unpalatable verdict.

The entry in Wilson's diary for 2nd June, 1919, substantially confirms Trenchard's version of what was said.[5]

" This evening," it runs, " Winston, Trenchard, Amery and I had a meeting about the coming campaign in Somaliland, to be conducted by the Colonial Office and the Air Ministry. I had put in a strong objection; but this afternoon both Amery and Trenchard said that under no conceivable circumstances would they ask me for troops, so I withdrew my objection and gave my blessing."

Amery, in the second volume of his political memoirs, has awarded himself full marks as the originator and sponsor of an air campaign in Somaliland. Nowhere is Milner mentioned in connection with it, and Trenchard's part in the preliminary discussions is likewise ignored. The charitable explanation must be that Amery's memory deceived him.

Six more months passed before the R.A.F. was permitted to deal with the Mad Mullah. The second half of 1919, as we have seen, was no easy period for it; its post-war charter was in gestation; its new terms of service were being harmonised with the harsh conditions imposed by the "Ten Year Rule"; while the fickleness of Churchill drove Trenchard frequently to the edge of doubt and once to the point of resignation. Nevertheless, Somaliland beckoned like a beacon when there was the least hope. Success there would outweigh all the disputes in committee, all the cliché-ridden statements in Parliament, about the possibilities of the R.A.F. as a mobile police force abroad. In talks with Churchill, in papers read and rejected by his fellow Chiefs of Staff, Trenchard covered and recovered the ground until his brain reeled and he longed for the final test of action.

" It is said that the air may completely destroy a place but cannot hold a place, and that it will want troops to hold it," ran a typical extract from one of many papers. " I cannot agree. Even in countries which have no roads, it is possible to capture and hold places for a time. This may seem to many a dream, but I would like to point out that if the actual fighting in the war had lasted another month, the Independent Air Force intended to do it.

" It was proposed to send six machines to the big aerodrome at Mannheim—these machines being armed with many machine-guns —and for a party to have landed, burned and destroyed the place and flown away again, and this at night, too."

To wearisome charges that dreams signified nothing, Trenchard had an answer. " An air force can't be built on dreams, but it can't live without them either, and mine will be realised sooner than you think."

The skeleton force of early 1920, which needed work to fulfil itself and Trenchard's dreams, owed much to its first benefactor, the Mad Mullah, for providing some. In January, a single bomber squadron commanded by Group-Captain R. Gordon flew from Cairo to

Somaliland. Gordon studied the orders from London with his staff officer, Wing-Commander (the late Sir Frederick) Bowhill; these were to drive the Mullah's forces into the open by attacking their camps and forts, the primary targets, then to pursue and harry at leisure.

Amery's account of the operation in the second volume of his memoirs is succinct and accurate enough, if one allows for the dominant first person singular.

" There were already in Somaliland an admirable little Camel Corps 500 strong, and an Indian battalion of the King's African Rifles from Kenya," he wrote. " I could also count, if things went well, on a tribal levy some 1500 strong. Cairo lent me a dozen planes. As soon as these arrived they started on 21st January, 1921 (*sic*), bombing the Mullah's main camp at Medishe and his fort at Jidali. By the 28th Jidali was occupied by the Camel Corps with the Mullah in full retreat. Well bombed on the way and harassed by the tribal levy, the Mullah took refuge in his main fort at Tale. This was captured by our tribesmen on 9th February. The Mullah himself escaped with a handful of men, presently reduced to four, and finally, as a solitary refugee, reached Abyssinia where he was killed not long after.

" The borrowed planes flew back to Cairo. The King's African Rifles were sent back to Mombasa. The tribal levy returned to their lands laden with loot. All was over in less than three weeks. The total cost, including transport of the King's African Rifles, extra pay to the Camel Corps and petrol for the Royal Air Force, worked out at £77,000, the cheapest war in history. For the next twenty years, till the Italians invaded it in the last war, Somaliland enjoyed the blessings of an undisturbed peace."

No wonder Trenchard was jubilant. Within two months of being formally re-established, the R.A.F. had justified his claims on its behalf. Here was an object lesson for the future; Milner and Churchill saluted it as such. British garrisons were still occupying large tracts of the Middle East which, for centuries, had been ruled by the Turks. With Lloyd George and the Cabinet pressing the service departments to curb military expenditure, Trenchard's "dream" might have wider application yet. One cheap victory was not enough. The service had to find regular work to earn its keep. Otherwise the "nurseries" of the future at Cranwell, Flowerdown, Halton and elsewhere would be denounced as an excessive charge on the taxpayer.

The R.A.F., in Trenchard's view, was incomparably more mobile and efficient as a "fire brigade" than the army, but there was another aspect to consider: the development of future air routes. An infinite highway arched high above the ancient caravan tracks of Africa and the Middle East. The sky awaited his pilots. It required no capital, no painstaking toil by armies of labourers to open up like the roads of old, only the courage and persistence and navigational skill of his airmen. South Africa, West Africa, India, the Far East, Australia could be brought weeks closer to Britain. The public interest had been already aroused by the achievements of Alcock and Brown, who had flown non-stop across the Atlantic from West to East in a converted wartime bomber during the summer of 1919, and of the Ross brothers, who had more recently flown from England to Australia in a series of long, hazardous hops. What these intrepid individuals had done in the spirit of adventure, the R.A.F., in which these first record breakers had learnt their skill, would shortly perform daily as a matter of routine, if Trenchard got his way with the Government. One day civil airliners would follow the routes mapped out by the R.A.F. But peace was necessary first; and peace in the Middle East was a wasting asset in 1920. Few liked the way the old maps had been redrawn by the victors at Versailles. The spirit of nationalism was rampant; the liberated and the oppressed, taking as their cue the concern of the Allies for "self-determination," were not averse to condemning their protectors as oppressors and rising against them. Iraq, the Mesopotamia of those days, was a case in point. Over eighty battalions of British troops stood guard there and in Palestine alone, an easy target for critics of military extravagance at home and a ready source of grievance to local nationalists burning with political ambition.

The methods currently employed by terrorists in Ireland might have served as a warning that regular garrisons were no match for revolutionary gangsters. The lesson was only slowly learnt; and for that Trenchard partly blamed the War Office. Wilson, the C.I.G.S., believed in static garrisons and old-fashioned punitive patrols, supposing that these would reimpose order in the restless Middle East.

The Cabinet was less certain. The fact that its views were sometimes naïve and ill-digested emerges, for instance, from one fantastic official query to Trenchard. When asked whether he could recommend aircraft for police action in Ireland, or in the event of grave industrial disturbances at home, where the unemployment figures had begun to soar as the post-war boom receded, Trenchard was appalled. A military machine, he stated, was the worst possible weapon for such a purpose, and should never be used except for reconnaissance. Its weapons lacked sufficient accuracy to clear crowds in built-up areas without inflicting indiscriminate casualties. And he expressly urged that if ever aircraft were called out, the civil authorities should first issue specific orders *in writing* before his men were called on to bomb or fire at targets on the ground. Trenchard included Palestine in the same category as Ireland; it was not opportunism alone which caused him to exclude Iraq.

When, in May, 1920, a local rising broke out in the Euphrates valley and quickly spread, he instructed Geoffrey Salmond, the Air Officer Commanding, Middle East, to dispatch an extra squadron from Egypt. Before long, he suggested, this would prove a godsend to the army. Before long, he confided to Air Ministry colleagues, the Government would be begging him to dispatch every squadron that could be spared.

He was right. Soon the British Press was full of alarming accounts of the military situation. A new "Mespot scandal" seemed to be brewing. Despite the strong security forces stationed in Iraq, more battalions had to be sent for. In Churchill's words, a local revolt had spread by a process of spontaneous combustion into "a serious rebellion which was suppressed with much difficulty and with the aid of reinforcements sent from India."[6] The Secretary of State for War and Air had reason for concern. Wilson's methods were more expensive than they were worth. A second opinion was sought by the Cabinet. Churchill, remembering Somaliland, consulted Trenchard and found him prepared with a rough alternative plan for policing Iraq from the air.

On 15th July, as the guest of officers who had served in his Bomber Command at Nancy, Trenchard privately explained why he was not so pessimistic as some felt he ought to be about the R.A.F.'s immediate chances of survival. He recalled the precarious position only twelve months ago, defining the twelve months since as "a year of careful destruction." A separate air force, minute in size but rich beyond dreams in promise, had since seized its opportunities. In Afghanistan, in North and South Russia, on India's North-West Frontier, then in Somaliland, a few squadrons of wartime machines had illustrated that air-power could become a recognised instrument of peace; ministers were certainly less chary than before of using it. In Iraq a greater opportunity might be coming.

It was enough. He sat down amidst rapturous applause. His audience had a double reason for congratulating him; his "off-the-record" talk would, he knew, be passed on like all good secrets, until its contents were known throughout the service. What he had divulged was gratifying enough but far less astonishing than a personal announcement which had appeared in the columns of *The Times* two days before, the announcement of his engagement to be married. Trenchard had not lost his knack of springing the unexpected on those who felt themselves closest to him. Most of his colleagues thought of him as an incurable and often crusty bachelor, so involved in his work that he needed and sought little relaxation beyond Whitehall and Adastral House. They still repeated with relish his cutting remark on hearing that Sykes, the Controller of Civil Aviation, intended to wed Isabel, the eldest daughter of Bonar Law.

" I suppose this means that Megan Lloyd George wouldn't have him," he had growled, to the malicious delight of his staff who wrote him off as insensitive to the pangs of love and to the delicious anguish of courtship. Here, however, his staff had been less than just.

There had been odd rumours, of course, and fragments of circumstantial evidence which lent substance to them. One day two officers leaving the Berkeley Grill heard an unmistakable voice hailing a taxi, and saw Trenchard climb inside bearing a huge bunch of pink carnations. They followed him in another taxi to 56 Lowndes Square, made a few tactful inquiries and discovered that "an elderly widow" lived at that address. Another day, he was seen driving down Piccadilly in the back of an open car with an unknown but not unattractive lady and three children holding large coloured balloons on strings. Was Trenchard leading a double life? Some of his colleagues remembered that Maurice Baring, who was noted for the elaborately contrived quality of his more serious practical jokes, had arranged a series of special lunch and dinner parties during 1919, always placing Trenchard next to some eligible woman of rank or wealth; but thanks to his intended victim's disconcerting habit of saying exactly what was in his mind at any given moment, Baring soon abandoned this untimely experiment in match-making. His delight and astonishment were all the greater when Trenchard told him, six months before the official engagement, that Katharine Boyle had changed her mind and agreed to marry him.

Nearly two months after his illness they had met again by chance in Hyde Park. It was a warm Sunday morning in June, 1919. She and her children were out for a walk when one of the boys pointed to the familiar figure sitting hunched up on a bench, his head bowed in thought. Even from a distance Trenchard looked so worried and lost to the world that she decided it would be heartless to pass by. His surprise at her greeting was as unaffected as his pleasure. He was grateful to the kindly fate which had led her that way, and said so. He was, he explained, then in the thick of a struggle to keep Churchill on his side; he admitted that life was not easy. The army and navy had many friends; he had none. Trenchard was so eager to unburden himself that Katharine Boyle had little trouble in persuading him to join the family for lunch.

A man possessed by a single idea, Trenchard struck her also as something of a solitary with few interests outside his public work. In this he believed with a fervour bordering on passion. Nevertheless, she could not help liking him. They met again; and her admiration for his honesty gradually softened into affection for the man himself. Trenchard proved an extremely thoughtful and attentive friend. Soon he was calling on her regularly with bunches of roses, dropping in unexpectedly for tea, and usually ending up playing on all-fours with her children on the carpet. Often he would call for them to escort them on shopping expeditions to the toy departments of West End stores. And when at length he screwed up courage, opened his heart and proposed again, she could no longer find it in herself to refuse.

They kept their happiness strictly to themselves for months. Trenchard, who had a violent distaste for the publicity which attended fashionable weddings, would have liked to dispense with the formality of announcing their engagement at all. Besides, he had many preoccupations and a back-log of work to clear. His arrangements for the first air pageant at Hendon were not yet complete; and this event, which was due to take place a fortnight before his wedding day on 17th July, consumed much of his spare time and thought. It would be his way of reintroducing the R.A.F. year by year to those who paid for its upkeep; and in the context of 1920 the variety and complexity of its new role abroad was going to be underlined.

For weeks in advance Trenchard kept a careful eye on the preparations of Sir John Salmond, the commander of the small force of home squadrons, visiting stations where pilots were already practising aerobatic stunts, formation flying and dummy raids. The Hendon show embodied Trenchard's conception of practical propaganda at its best. An ounce of performance was always worth a ton of adverse criticism, in his view. And if the split second timing of the performers could be blended with perfect stage management and

a fine day, the R.A.F. would have little difficulty in reminding the
man in the street that "seeing is believing."

Like the producers of most open-air spectacles held in Britain,
Trenchard was more concerned than he appeared to be about the
weather. Meteorology had stood still since the end of the war; and
the Meteorological Office, which came under Air Ministry control
at the end of 1919, did not exactly command his confidence. On the
eve of the 1920 air pageant, Trenchard pressed one of the row of
bells on his desk. The "Met" man on duty hurried in with a sheet
of paper and the strained look of an actor unsure of his lines. His
recital of the weather forecast was halting and lugubrious.

Trenchard let him finish a monologue rich in its promise of
hopeless conditions for a day when sunshine would really matter: the
low clouds, poor visibility and probability of thunder showers might
ruin everything. Fixing the narrator with a steely look, Trenchard
said: " This won't do, you know. It isn't good enough. Go and
brighten it up, then let me see it."

Hovering for a moment before retiring in utter confusion,
convinced now that Trenchard must be crazier than was sometimes
alleged, the expert none the less did as he was told, and half an hour
later returned with a much-improved version. Trenchard read it
carefully.

" That's miles better," he said. " It's probably nearer the mark,
too."[7]

The remorseful young man could hardly sleep that night for
turning over the possibly dire consequences of a forecast forged under
duress. The crowd at the air show would get wet, and serve them
right. But what of the farmers, the fishermen, the sailors, and others
whose livelihoods (if not their very lives) depended to some extent on
the scrupulous accuracy of the "Met" men? Dawn brought relief
and some bewilderment; it held the promise of a flawless summer's
day.

The spectators at Hendon had no thought or fears of rain. The
weather was as superb as the flying. Even Beatty leaned out of the
special box reserved for Important Visitors and congratulated
Trenchard on a display which, he declared, exceeded his expectations. That was an admission worth waiting for, one that conveyed
far more than the compliments of Cabinet Ministers. It did not
surprise Trenchard in the least that nature had smiled at the liberty
he had taken with the weather bulletin.

Mrs. Boyle was with him as he walked among the distinguished
guests with the pride of a man whose party was going better than

planned. Salmond's pilots thrilled the huge throng and made the
critics ponder. The Press that week-end devoted a good deal of space
to Hendon; and the tone of all correspondents, not excluding those
of the Northcliffe and Beaverbrook newspapers, was enthusiastic.
Perhaps, Trenchard hoped, the public would draw its own
conclusions.

He had leisure at last to think of his wedding. He wanted a quiet
ceremony and a small reception; so he chose a Saturday in the
season, when London would be comparatively empty, and dispatched
the invitations late. However, there was standing room only in St.
Margaret's, Westminster, on 17th July; and after the service and
procession down the aisle, Trenchard and his bride had to face a
battery of Press photographers on the inner ring of a multitude of
bystanders. One, more thrustful than the rest, held up progress by
half-squatting in front of the groom until each could see the whites of
the other's eyes. The photographer was possibly too intent on what
he was doing to notice the red gleam in Trenchard's. At any rate,
he was not expecting the sharp nudge which sent him stumbling
and his camera flying.

Trenchard felt better for it, and laughed all the way to the
reception. Both he and his wife were taken aback at the turn out of
guests. More people were there than could ever have been asked to
come, though Baring, the best man, with a wine glass nonchalantly
balanced on his bald, domed head, a posture long familiar to R.A.F.
officers who had ever celebrated any special occasion with him,
assured Trenchard gravely that this was simply not so. The bridegroom had miscalculated his notoriety with some, his popularity with
others, that was all. Churchill, more relaxed and genial than Trenchard could remember, insisted on making a speech, then on button-
holing the bridegroom to talk shop in a corner until Baring, accompanied by Marson, his successor, intervened to escort the couple to
the station. His last duty done, Baring was waiting for the train to
start when Trenchard leaned out and remarked with emphasis:

" All right, Baring. You may go. This is a journey I shan't want
you on."

After dinner that evening, Trenchard absentmindedly handed his
wife a cigar before lighting his own, and talked at length about his
life and early struggles, leaving nothing out. It was the first time he
had unburdened his soul to anyone, though Katharine Trenchard, as
she had now become, was someone rather special. Apart from the
love he bore her, he welcomed her admirable self-possession as a
foil for his own tempestuous nature. She, who would share his

thoughts from now on, had a sense of humour not altogether unlike his own; a woman of striking beauty and vivacity, who had known tragedy and misfortune, her resilience and sympathy were gifts which he would have abundant cause to bless. Katharine, for her part, was content to link her destiny with his. A man whose sense of honour was so finely adjusted that he should recently have used most of his savings clearing the debts run up by his father half a lifetime before might not die rich, perhaps; but the world would be the poorer without his sort, just as her own life would have been drabber and emptier without him.

3

It was not the first time a superfluous shot of melodrama had been injected into Trenchard's life at an absurd moment. Who but Winston Churchill, he thought, pulling off his dressing-gown and getting back into bed, would have sent a dispatch rider hurtling to Cambridge at dead of night with a personal note clamouring for an instant answer. He wondered if his host, the young Duke of York, had slept through the deafening arrival of the motor cycle, or had been rudely disturbed like the household servants and himself.[8]

Churchill, of course, had his reasons. He wished to refresh his memory on the arguments advanced by Trenchard in a recent memorandum for controlling countries like Iraq with fewer ground forces and more R.A.F. squadrons, thereby saving money. The note delivered by hand in the small hours of the last Monday in November, 1920, informed the Chief of Air Staff that the Cabinet would meet on the Tuesday or Wednesday, that a definite decision seemed probable, and therefore that the writer, Churchill, as the newly appointed Colonial Secretary, must have the subject at his fingertips. A scribbled acknowledgment, a mental note to ring Marson, his secretary, after breakfast, and Trenchard dismissed the dispatch rider, wishing that a question which had remained dormant for several months could have been allowed to rest for another few hours. As he had come to realise, Churchill was no respector of civilised conventions once his hunting blood was up.

Unrest had been smouldering in Iraq for so long that the Government could not withstand the censure of its critics. Assailed on all sides, Lloyd George was willing to reconsider his policy of letting different Government departments, guided by conflicting interests, administer the new British mandates of Iraq and Palestine.

That system of bickering rivalries had gone bankrupt. The late Colonial Secretary, Milner, who professed to be above the battle, was never happy about the Prime Minister's evident desire to appease the Arabs in the Middle East at the risk of estranging the French. From the seeds of broken wartime pledges a crop of resentment had sprung, the only common ground between Arabs and French being the knowledge that the British had behaved with customary perfidy. Otherwise they were at daggers drawn.

Under a secret compact with France in 1916, the Sykes-Picot Agreement, Britain had arranged to partition the Turkish provinces of Asia Minor after the war. Either by inadvertence or miscalculation, this was done without reference to the Sheriff of Mecca, who, when presented somewhat brutally with the accomplished fact, counter-claimed that he had been separately promised the keys of an independent Arab kingdom as a reward for his part, with Colonel T. E. Lawrence, in organising the desert revolt against the Turks. At the Peace Conference, in March and April, 1919, France went as far as her leaders felt they could reasonably go towards compromise by accepting the Emir Feisal, one of the Sheriff's sons, as provisional King of Syria.

The French believed as firmly as the British that they had a duty before history to fulfil in an area where their interests and influences could be traced to the era of Louis XIV. Their rights in Syria, they contended, were as good as Britain's in Iraq; and they held Lloyd George to the Sykes-Picot terms, regardless of anything else there might or might not have been promised to the Arabs. Thus was the way paved for violence. In May, 1920, the anti-British insurrection began in Iraq; two months later, King Feisal, the French puppet ruler of Syria, organised a *coup d'état* in Damascus which was crushed at once and with a ruthless efficiency which the British in Baghdad could not emulate.

It is easy to understand why Milner, who was very much an idealist among politicians, should have found so distasteful the complications in which Britain and France had improvidently involved themselves. Lloyd George, a considerably less squeamish person, merely concluded that his Colonial Secretary was still suffering from that "nervous lassitude" which he had noted at the Peace talks of 1919. Churchill, whose vigour and realism compensated for his occasional waywardness, and whose success as Minister for War and Air entitled him to preferment, was appointed to the Colonial Office on Milner's retirement. Having lately fallen beneath the personal spell of Lawrence of Arabia, whom he persuaded to join the new

Middle East section of his department, Churchill lost no time in championing the seemingly defeated Arab cause. Expediency, if not honour, called for a fresh approach to the restoration of order in Iraq; and Churchill was not disposed to imitate the caution of Milner or heed the disapproval of Curzon, the Foreign Secretary, at the Cabinet table.

" A large and costly garrison still remained in the country," he wrote afterwards in *The Aftermath*.

" In the autumn of that year (1920), Sir Percy Cox had been sent out to Baghdad as the first British provisional High Commissioner under the presidency of the Nagib of Baghdad, a venerable figure, who commanded great respect not only in Iraq itself but in the Mohammedan world outside its borders.

" Prior to 1921 different departments of His Majesty's Government had dealt with the different Middle Eastern areas conquered during the war. The affairs of Palestine and Transjordan were in the charge of the Foreign Office; those of Iraq in that of the India Office. Early in 1921 the Government decided to place these matters under a single department, viz., the Colonial Office, to which I had recently been appointed Secretary of State. A new Middle East department was accordingly established at the Colonial Office and came formally into existence on 1st March, 1921. My first step was to summon a conference at Cairo. . . ."

Before taking that step, Churchill forearmed himself against failure by obtaining conditional Cabinet backing for Trenchard's scheme to police Iraq from the air so that army costs could be systematically reduced. The saving of money was not its least attractive factor: aircraft, argued Trenchard, would be as effective in Iraq as in Somaliland. Hence the flash of inspiration late on a November night which induced Churchill to disturb one of Trenchard's rare week-ends off. He knew the general thesis already, but wanted it in his hand, and its author at his side, to rally the more faint-hearted of his ministerial colleagues.

At the vital Cabinet meeting Trenchard was invited by Lloyd George to explain why he seemed so sure of success when Sir Percy Cox, the Government's man on the spot, was adamant that aircraft would be the worst possible instruments of pacification. Cox, he replied, would change his opinion with experience; the High Commissioner in Iraq was merely echoing the views of his present military advisers. At this Wilson, the C.I.G.S., launched into a tirade against an experiment which would retrieve nothing and lead only to humiliation and reverses. It cut no ice with the Cabinet.

Churchill was triumphant. He left the meeting with a free hand. He confided to Trenchard that his intention was to placate the Arabs by wiping out the real or imagined injustice they had endured at British hands. This could be most simply achieved by making Iraq a kingdom and putting the banished Feisal on the throne. Up to a point Trenchard shared in the Minister's sense of elation. If Churchill preened himself as a king-maker, the Chief of Air Staff had been designated palace guard and preserver of the peace. But such romantic notions passed Trenchard by. Iraq, to him, was an arena where the R.A.F. could consolidate its claim to equal treatment with army and navy.

This remained Trenchard's first and deepest concern. Churchill towered above his colleagues when it came to military issues, and his departure from the War Office had created something of a vacuum. Sir Laming Worthington-Evans, the new Minister, had little practical knowledge of service problems. Would the authority of such a man extend to the Air Ministry also, as in Churchill's day? Trenchard felt that he had every right to an unambiguous answer. In a spontaneous letter to Bonar law, the Lord Privy Seal, he put the question in a way that reflected his anxiety.

" It was possible," he wrote, " to run a joint Secretary of State for War and Air in the case of Mr. Churchill with his enormous capacity for work and quick comprehension, at one reading, of the complicated questions that continually arise. But I am perfectly certain that no other man I have met could have done this work without seriously handicapping the development of the air service and militating against economy. . . ."

Bonar Law answered that the Government still had an open mind on the question; Churchill would continue to look after R.A.F. interests at a distance. It was not a reassuring prospect. Nobody knew better than Trenchard of the Colonial Secretary's obsessive preoccupation with the new business of king-making in the Middle East; and nobody distrusted more profoundly the active and passive resistance of the C.I.G.S. and the War Office to that very business. Bonar Law's evasiveness settled nothing.

It seemed to Trenchard a singularly unpropitious moment to pack and leave for a conference in Cairo with military and Colonial office representatives, as Churchill assumed that he would now be glad to do. Writing to Geoffrey Salmond, the Air Officer Commanding, Middle East, in mid-February, Trenchard told him what was in the wind.

" The S. of S. for the Colonies, Mr. C., is probably going out early in March to Egypt to confer with the Palestine and Mesp. authorities. The chief point will be the running of Palestine and M. He (Churchill) is very much in favour of the air taking control, I believe. (Keep to yourself.)

" Broadly speaking, I am in favour of risking a good deal in Egypt and Palestine in order to equip Mesp. early. I am very keen on taking over Mesp. next cold weather, if not before, and I am very keen to insist on the withdrawal of a lot of the little detachments, to accept a certain amount of chaos in parts, but to hold the central line, and by gradual peaceful penetration spread over three or four years to regain what we give up. . . . There is a slight chance of my having to come myself with Mr. Churchill."

There had been less chance of it until earlier that week. Trenchard stung Churchill to a fury by saying that he did not want to go, without giving one convincing reason. Mixing blandishments with threats, persuasiveness with hot impatience, the Minister finally succeeded in changing Trenchard's mind virtually by accident. A day or two before the above-mentioned letter to Salmond, Churchill dined with the Chief of the Air Staff at " The Other Club," that exclusive meeting place which the Minister had founded before the First World War as a gesture of defiance towards political critics who conspired to blackball him socially.

The two men had the table to themselves and immediately turned to the topic uppermost in both their minds: the implications of their plans for the Middle East. Trenchard talked with animation and was busily describing in detail how he proposed to redistribute his squadrons so that army battalions could be withdrawn in quick and orderly fashion from Iraq when Churchill broke in capriciously. They were talking too much shop, he said. There would be ample opportunity for that on the voyage from Marseilles to Alexandria. Why try to rush it over a single lunch and risk indigestion?

Trenchard was taken aback. Did the Minister really expect him to go to Cairo? he asked. Until that moment he had not thought of attending the conference in person. He doubted whether he could afford a month's absence. Would that be wise while Wilson and Worthington-Evans were left free to undermine R.A.F. and Government interests? Churchill pounced at once with eyes flashing and lips pouting. So the Chief of Air Staff could not stir from his office? What was Trenchard so bothered about? Still more to the point, what was he trying to do—wreck in advance an experiment that offered the R.A.F. its first worthwhile job since the war? Who's side was he on?

Trenchard retorted that Churchill was twisting his words, adding that he would prefer the conversation to continue as it had begun, calmly and without these personal innuendos. A touch of indigestion was, after all, less harmful to the system than apoplexy. Churchill rose scowling to his feet, indicated that he had no more to say, and stamped out, fuming with rage.

A sullen silence of several days followed. Trenchard moodily resigned himself to a prolonged absence and made the necessary arrangements. Then, one morning towards the end of February, his telephone rang. It was the other Churchill, full of charm and magnanimity, his voice vibrant with solicitude. *How* was Lady Trenchard? he asked. He had just been chatting to a member of the Air Staff; and, quite by accident, he had discovered the true reason for Trenchard's otherwise incomprehensible reluctance to see Cairo in the spring.

" Why couldn't you have told me, Boom, that your wife was expecting a baby? Have no fear, Boom. It won't be a long conference—I shall be in the chair. You'll be back soon on the very ship that takes us out."

4

As conferences of the period went, it was an incredibly short and fruitful one. Churchill's eloquence, vehemence and firmness, backed by the thorough preparatory work put in before and during the voyage out by his Middle East department, guaranteed that. Unlike many larger gatherings of Allied statesmen in more imposing settings, the Cairo Conference of March, 1921, accomplished its set purpose in a week of daily sittings. And though to-day it is probably no better remembered than the Mad Mullah, it was a historic landmark of sorts. For not only did it save the Arab world from sinking into the anarchy of the pre-war Balkans; it also saved the R.A.F. from probable extinction the following year.

The delegates were not rival politicians seeking rough compromises between national aspirations and international ideals; they were the governors and pro-consuls of British-held territories throughout the Middle East, accompanied by their advisers, who had been summoned in a consultative capacity to discuss a policy settled in advance by Churchill. Nearly all of them thoroughly disliked it and said so. But, having no voting rights, only reservations, they could not prevent it being imposed upon them.

As far as Trenchard could see, most of the reservations concerned the security aspect of the settlement. The conference minutes suggest that although doubts were also expressed about the wisdom of relying too much on the two future Arab kingdoms of Iraq and Jordan as bulwarks of British influence against instability, it was the insanity of handing over their defence to the untried R.A.F. which exercised the pro-consuls. Sir Percy Cox, the High Commissioner in Iraq, Sir Herbert Samuel, the Governor-General of Palestine, and Lord Reading, the Viceroy-designate of India, being directly affected, implored Churchill to think again.

They implored in vain. Churchill, who jocularly referred to them all in private as "The Forty Thieves," stressed that the substitution of R.A.F. squadrons for army battalions was a principle on which there could be no argument. Trenchard had proposed it; he, the responsible Minister, had seconded it because he believed in it; the Cabinet, without dissent, had already accepted it. With practical goodwill on their part, the air plan would provide better insurance against unrest at a fraction of the financial outlay of unwieldy permanent garrisons. There was the nub of the matter— the cost. He deluged them with facts and figures, rubbing in the disagreeable truth that this was the element which weighed most with the Cabinet.

The most outspoken critic was Sir Percy Cox, who had recently performed valuable service in reconciling some of Iraq's most powerful tribal leaders and inducing them to recognise King Feisal's claims to the new throne. Iraq, he warned, was by no means peaceful yet.

In the north especially, where the peaks and wild gorges of Kurdistan merged with those of Turkey along an undemarcated boundary, there was perennial unrest. What would happen when the British Army, the only force capable of holding or penetrating the fastnesses of that inhospitable area, left for good? A few R.A.F. squadrons would, he feared, be insufficient in the event of a Turkish-inspired rising or an actual violation of the disputed frontier above Mosul.

The views of Cox echoed the reasoning of Wilson and the General Staff at home, and more particularly that of General Haldane, the G.O.C. Iraq and the High Commissioner's military adviser. Haldane had recently submitted to the Cabinet an appreciation of the R.A.F.'s local operational value, in which he damned it with faint praise for its co-operative spirit during the prolonged revolt, concluding that its only conceivable role was an ancillary one since, without troops in support, squadrons could not consolidate tactical gains. Trenchard had contested the logic of that deduction at the time, noting in passing that the army seemed to have grown somewhat less sure of its ground. The R.A.F. had come a long way since Sir Henry Wilson contemptuously described it in a speech at the Staff College, Camberley, as a force "coming from God knows where, dropping its bombs on God knows what, and going off God knows where."

Cox's spirited rear-guard action in Cairo also failed. In the end, he fell in with his more docile colleagues and reconciled himself to the principle of a gradual transfer of military control in Iraq from the War Office to the Air Ministry, which should be completed by the autumn of 1922.

A more inhibited character than Trenchard might have been distressed by the tendency of the army leaders to cut him socially out of conference hours. Contrarily, he found the experience amusing and not at all unprofitable. For on the few occasions when he was at liberty to choose his company, he was joined at meals by two of the oddest and most attractive personalities in his experience. Gertrude Bell, a former amateur archæologist turned administrator, was already middle-aged and rather dowdy in appearance and dress; T. E. Lawrence, whose wartime exploits had won him immense renown since the Armistice, seemed a curiously frail and unlikely candidate for the unique role as an Arab leader in which he had excelled. It was Miss Bell, whose life and career had been spent in the service of the Arabs and their culture, who first broke the ice by asking Trenchard one day as they left the conference room:

"How many pencils do you get through in a conference, Air-Marshal? I watched you this morning and counted a dozen broken points."[9]

Trenchard stared hard at her then laughed. This observant woman, who had been seated next to him, evidently admired the way he emphasised his words with a stab of the pencil each time he rose to answer a hostile critic. She was far-sighted, too, and had no sentimental delusions, inclining to his view that, psychologically, the sight of one squadron of aircraft would be a greater deterrent to trouble-makers than a brigade of infantry. Provided the air weapon was used with civilised restraint, she believed it would work: a bomb was certainly no worse than a siege-gun as a means of bringing trouble-makers to their senses. Lawrence, who had seen something of the R.A.F.'s power and mobility in action, went further. Early in the conference, he contradicted Cox by declaring that air control would help Britain as much as the Arabs. A small force, kept out of sight until a cause for its intervention arose, able to supply and reinforce itself from home in days rather than weeks, would safeguard the peace and enable Iraq and Jordan to grow up and prosper.

"Sir Hugh is right, the rest of you wrong," he told Cox and the other delegates with quiet emphasis.

Lawrence was fascinated by Trenchard's intention to blaze a trail high above the desert for the airlines of the future, literally ploughing a straight furrow in the barren earth below for 800 miles, from Baghdad in the south to the region where the scrub and sand of the limitless desert gave way to the volcanic escarpment leading towards Amman and Jordan. Every few miles, the pilot's eye would be guided by the furrow to one of a dozen or more emergency staging posts, each numbered and marked in white, where he could land and refuel. The project was discussed informally over dinner in Churchill's suite at the Semiramis Hotel, and again at the Aboukir R.A.F. base, before the conference opened. The Minister, Salmond, Trenchard and Lawrence were seen poring together over large-scale maps and talking as eagerly as explorers on the edge of a new continent. Lawrence impressed Trenchard by his complete assurance: the man was a visionary, labouring under a mysterious diffidence until properly launched on a subject that interested him. Then he would forget himself for a space. One night, after a lengthy conversation, he told Trenchard with a ruminative smile:

"I'd like to join this air force of yours some day."

"And I'd be glad to have you."

"Even as an ordinary ranker?"

"No, certainly not," said Trenchard testily. "As an officer or nothing."[10]

Lawrence's smile broadened, but he did not pursue the matter. He proposed to raise it again in his own good time.

14. *The Heretic*

" I had a very interesting trip to Egypt," Trenchard wrote shortly
after the conference to General Rawlinson, a wartime associate who
had lately been appointed Commander-in-Chief, India, and who
differed from most of his army contemporaries in accepting the
principle of a separate air force.

" We got through a tremendous lot of work. I was there only
nine days myself. Winston has given up the S. of S. for Air. We
now have our own. I am perfectly certain at the present moment
that an independent air force is the only solution of our troubles.

" I still think that as we get larger and take on more responsibility
—which we must do in time, and it is only a question of time—such
as coastal defence, home defence, protection of shipping in the
Narrow Waters, etc., etc., and even of countries like Mesp. and
Palestine, then it may be that those parts of the air working with the
army and navy will become rather units permanently with the
army and navy—almost in the nature of arms of the older services,
not absolutely but to a great extent.

" I feel that our successors forty or fifty years hence will laugh at
the idea of the whole air being under the army or the navy. But
it is impossible to prophesy and I am not very good at dreaming. . ."

The designation at last of a separate Air Minister, Major
Frederick Guest, a cousin of Churchill's, coming as this did almost
on top of the Cairo settlement, was a less happy augury than
Trenchard supposed. Lloyd George was merely responding to
administrative necessities at an awkward moment. The post-war
boom at home had receded; over a million men were idle; industrial
peace was threatened by the unrequited grievances of miners and
transport workers; and the Prime Minister's stock had slumped to
a degree which disturbed the dwindling number of his well-wishers.
While the drift towards anarchy and civil strife continued unchecked
in Ireland, Churchill's endeavours as an Arab king-maker in Iraq
counted for little, politically.

The alternative policy of disowning all wartime pledges, of cutting losses with responsibilities, and of concentrating exclusively on the solution of domestic issues which alone could reburnish the somewhat tarnished public image of Lloyd George, had its loudest advocates among the popular Press lords. Why should Britain take on further commitments in such circumstances? Where was the statesmanship in creating new kingdoms at the risk of backing the wrong feudal factions in Iraq and Transjordan, and of courting either the ultimate disgrace of forcible eviction or the folly of full-scale military involvement? Could there be any greater nonsense than expecting the untried and puny R.A.F. to keep the peace? What was the point, anyway, in maintaining this third service when a child knew that two services were cheaper to run than three?

The clamour of the popular Press found an official echo in Whitehall. Trenchard's resilience in adapting himself to the stringencies of the "Ten Year Rule" moved the War Office and Admiralty to recurring bouts of jealousy; self-preservation imposed on Beatty and Wilson the obligation to defend themselves against his encroachments. The First Sea Lord had honoured his pledge not to attack the R.A.F. in public; now the "year of grace" was up. The C.I.G.S., it will be remembered, had promised nothing; yet his efforts since to calumniate and impede the development of the air force had been of no avail.

The reason had its core of poetic irony. For Wilson was the "political general" *par excellence* with a capacity for mischief and intrigue which was well nigh inexhaustible. Yet the Irish problem which had set him at odds with many brother officers as a younger man, notably during the Curragh Mutiny, crabbed his judgment again.

The Government disliked his rabid Ulsterman's extremism; and that dislike steadily detracted from his influence. It was a disappointed and aggrieved Wilson who retired in late 1921 to seek a more suitable outlet for his feelings as M.P. for North Down. His career in Parliament was cut short in the summer of 1922 when he died in the entrance of his own London home, shot down by two Irish gunmen of the opposite allegiance.

Wilson's last fling as C.I.G.S. to outmanœuvre Trenchard occurred in the summer of 1921. Parliament had by then given grudging approval to Churchill's Middle East settlement, reserving judgment on the role of the R.A.F. as custodian of the peace. A powerful minority of backbenchers ridiculed the Government's estimate that, within twelve months, there would be a saving of at least ten million pounds in Iraq by reducing the British garrison and leaving eight R.A.F. squadrons to stiffen such levies as the local Government could raise and train. The simplicity of the scheme rendered it suspect. Trenchard could still count on two hands those M.P.s with a firm enough grasp of the potentialities of air-power to realise that the R.A.F. could actually control a vast desert kingdom without occupying it.

The C.I.G.S. began by damning the plan as a conspiracy between the Colonial Secretary and the Chief of Air Staff to dispense with rational advice from the only proper quarter, himself. When argument failed, he grew obstructive. There were ample opportunities for filibustering. A thousand and one practical details of the hand-over had to be arranged between the two services concerned. How far was the understaffed R.A.F.'s writ to run? Should it include "works, ordnance duties and supplies"? Were "repair shops, depots, wireless communications, both internal and with Egypt" to be controlled by the Air Ministry or the War Office? And what of light tanks and armoured cars? Was the air force, in casting out the military, intent on forming a separate army?

Trenchard frequently had to carry Guest, his own Secretary of State, with him in acrimonious disputes over such points of substance. The limitations of the Minister were only too apparent. He had none of the knowledge, the taste for in-fighting or the flair for seizing a quick advantage which characterised Churchill. Guest seemed happy enough to put up endlessly with the delaying tactics of the War Office. At length, when Trenchard suggested that the time had come to call in Churchill, whose policy was being systematically undermined, Guest was equally happy to comply.

" I am afraid the War Office are taking it badly," Trenchard's secretary informed Philip Game in August, 1921. " They are very bitter about it and will do everything in their power to render impossible any sort of co-operation with them. It seems a great pity, but I suppose we are up against vested interests and shall have to fight accordingly. . . . The present situation is that the War Office, the Colonial Office and the Air Ministry finance people are to have a conference. . . ."

The severest blow to army pride was Trenchard's decision to form special armoured car units for security duties in Iraq. Money was not the trouble; he was ready to pay for necessities; but Worthington-Evans, the Secretary of State for War, was just as adamant as Wilson in denying him the right to order army weapons without consulting the War Office as to their tactical worth. The discussion impaled itself less on a point of principle than on a matter of professional prejudice. And Trenchard, rather than appeal over their heads direct to Churchill, circumvented them in his own way. Evans and Bullock, the two Air Ministry officials chiefly implicated in the barren bargaining, left the final meeting wondering whether Trenchard had not bitten off more than he could chew. For the financial secretary to the War Office had just stated categorically that the air force would have to manage without armoured cars since he was not empowered to help them.

" Evans," Trenchard said as he reached his office, " get on to Harris, the financial secretary, as soon as you like. Tell him to pass it on to his masters that we shan't need their precious armoured cars. We'll build our own."

It was a gesture of impulsive boldness. Eventually it broke the deadlock. At R.A.F. workshops in England and Egypt the conversion of suitable vehicles began at once. The first batch was dispatched to Baghdad before Christmas, 1921. By the autumn of 1922, when Sir John Salmond assumed command, there were sufficient reserves to equip every mobile detachment of Iraq levies, led by British officers, on whom the R.A.F. depended for routine ground patrolling. Trenchard did not even then crow over the War Office. Wilson was in his grave; and Cavan, his successor, was proving much less implacable a C.I.G.S. Yet when Cavan offered to revoke an embargo which had never worked, Trenchard demurred.

" No, thanks," he said politely. " We're quite self-sufficient now."

Self-sufficiency based on thrift was the key to all his forward planning. In this, Trenchard displayed great political realism without compromising a jot of an overmastering faith in air-power that still had mountains of prejudice to move.

" We must run Iraq as 'handymen,' " he advised Air-Commodore A. E. Borton, his interim commander in Baghdad, "improvising as we go."

When Geoffrey Salmond wrote anxiously from Cairo, reporting the circumstances of a raid in which two R.A.F. officers had recently had their throats slit by tribesmen after crash-landing in the northern Iraq desert, Trenchard rejected the plea that pilots should henceforth carry cards guaranteeing handsome rewards for safe conducts back to base.

" To my mind, this is contrary to all British ideas of warfare. At one moment a man is dropping bombs and trying to kill the enemy, the next he has to come down and land—and then he asks his enemy not to shoot him. It reminds me of the Boer in South Africa who shot at my servant. My man was going at him with a bayonet, and the Boer opened fire at over 500 yards and missed him every time until the bayonet came within five yards of his throat. Then he dropped his rifle and put up his hands. But he did not insult us by offering us five pounds to get him off. . . ."

Not all the letters Trenchard wrote were to officers of "air rank." Most of the new squadron commanders had learnt how approachable he was, despite his fearsome aura of inaccessibility, during the war. When one of them moaned in a letter about the hazards of operational flying against turbulent tribesmen in the Himalayan foothills, his reply was firm yet understanding.

" You state that it is impossible to see snipers. Nobody ever expected to see them and I should have thought this idea of looking for them ought to have been long since dead in India. . . . I admit all the hardships the pilots undergo. Do not think I have lost sympathy with them, I have not, but I do feel so much, as I felt the whole time I was in France, that the load must be borne without speaking about it. . . . Indiscriminate bombing should never be allowed. Surely this was dead five years ago. . . ."

Accusations of indiscriminate bombing were often raised but rarely substantiated. When, in 1921, Borton's first operational report from Baghdad reached the Colonial Office, describing how flights from three squadrons had successfully quenched the flames of revolt in three Iraqui districts, Churchill pounced indignantly on the following extract:

" The eight machines (at Naseriyah) broke formation and attacked at different points of the encampment simultaneously, causing a stampede among the animals. The tribesmen and their families were put to confusion, many of whom ran into the lake, making good targets for the machine-guns."

Borton's marginal comment that this gave "a vivid if rather ferocious glimpse of the type of warfare we have to wage" caused Churchill to minute Trenchard sharply:

" I am extremely shocked at the reference to bombing which I have marked in red. If it were to be published it would be regarded as most dishonouring to the air force and prejudicial to our work and use of them. To fire wilfully on women and children is a disgraceful act, and I am surprised you do not order the officers responsible for it to be tried by court-martial. . . . By doing such things we put ourselves on the lowest level. Combatants are fair game and sometimes non-combatants get injured through their proximity to fighting troops, but this seems to be quite a different matter."

It was indeed; but Trenchard took Borton only lightly to task, suspecting that there was probably a simpler explanation than lust for blood on the part of a few pilots. The inquiry he immediately ordered confirmed his surmise.

" The *political* handling of the operation," Borton subsequently established, " left much to be desired." District administrators, in nearly all cases civilians unaccustomed to the lethal power of aircraft as punitive instruments, had erred by insisting that a special example should be made of an exceptionally unruly tribe. The air-crews in question, not yet used to their semi-political role, had been merely carrying out to the letter a brief laid down by civilians.

Had such an incident occurred a few months earlier, when Sir Percy Cox was settling down as High Commissioner, the ensuing scandal might have prejudiced everything. But Cox, in spite of his premonitions at the Cairo Conference, had since become as "completely converted as Haldane, the army commander, to the scheme of air control." A humane man of pronounced liberal instincts, zealous in his hatred of undue coercion, Cox at once exonerated the R.A.F. and lectured his political officers on the necessity of restraint.

" The military and political opinions of the results obtained are most gratifying and have a marked effect on our most stubborn opponents here," Trenchard reassured Borton. And to Geoffrey Salmond, his Middle East Commander in Cairo, he laid down three simple principles to be applied in the light of common sense.

" The air force is a preventative against risings more than a means of putting them down," Trenchard wrote. " Concentration is the first essential. Continuous demonstration is the second essential. And when punishment is intended, the punishment must be severe, continuous and even prolonged. . . ."

Such severity was not to be misconstrued as "frightfulness." Warnings were dropped by leaflet before air attacks began; Trenchard's orders to this effect were strict; and villages were never bombed until their inhabitants had received at least twenty-four hours' notice of an impending punitive raid. Often the nerve-racking sight and sound of the demonstration flights alone, when machines would swoop low in warning, sufficed not only to quell unrest but to persuade neighbouring chieftains whose loyalties were suspect to opt for peace.

After the Cairo Conference, Colonel T. E. Lawrence reluctantly accepted Churchill's invitation to serve as adviser to Abdullah, the King-designate of Transjordan, and supervise stage by stage, the artificial construction of the smaller and more destitute of the two new desert kingdoms, and convince his disgruntled and exceedingly tetchy old friend, Hussein, who still nursed delusions of ruling all Arabia from Lebanon to the Persian Gulf, that the new dispensation was a thing of permanence. In Transjordan, as in Iraq, aircraft were the ultimate guarantee of security; and the psychological fear of retribution from the skies infested potential rebels and actual law-breakers alike. One demonstration flight over a remote Transjordan district, where a series of political assassinations had momentarily reawakened the martial instincts of Abdullah's rivals among the sheikhs, restored instant calm.

" Our machines," reported Geoffrey Salmond on that occasion, " were over the scene of the murders on the same day that they took place. This had an immediate effect on the tribe concerned, for one half of them came in at once. I think they realised that Abdullah had a means of asserting his authority which they had never dreamed of."

Playing on the fears even of violent and barbarous men was scarcely the ideal method of inculcating respect for authority, salutary though it might be in a crisis. Sir Percy Cox had returned to that point again and again at Cairo, falsely assuming that any outbreak of Arab violence would automatically bring down a rain of avenging bombs on the miscreants' heads.

It was Gertrude Bell, sitting quietly next to Trenchard, who set a vexed problem in perspective by asking:

" I suppose, Sir Hugh, that your aircraft will drop bombs until the victims surrender? "

" No, of course not," he said. " Bombs won't be necessary. In time we should start dropping bottles of Eno's Salts—to put their livers right."

It was an oblique way of saying that the mere presence of an apparently all-seeing, all-powerful mobile force, however small, would encourage the lawless to settle down and learn civilised ways. Cox considered that Trenchard's imagery was more flippant than the gravity of the question warranted, but not so Lawrence.

" I thoroughly agree with Sir Hugh," he said. " I know that he is right."[1]

Now, within two months of his being overruled by Churchill, Cox had the generosity and honesty to admit that he was wrong. The air weapon, as his official dispatch from Baghdad underlined, was proving to be as flexible as Trenchard and Lawrence had promised. General Haldane, the Iraq G.O.C. was no less impressed than Cox by its sedative effect on the most bellicose of tribal leaders. Even the Eno's Salts were unnecessary, so startling was the change. Air-Commodore Brooke-Popham, the Director of Research at the Air Ministry, referred to the General's changed attitude during a flying visit to the survey teams that were already marking out landing grounds below the first air route across the desert, from Baghdad to the Transjordan border.

"He [Haldane] is very pleased with the air force [and] is certainly doing his best to carry out the [provisions of] the Cairo Conference. . . . He thinks that with three battalions of infantry and a tank or two in the background, the air force can control the country. . . . You remember Henry Wilson's remarks at the Staff College: ' Here's the R.A.F. coming from God knows where,' etc. Well, that exactly expressed the reason for the immense morale effect that aeroplanes are having in Mespot. The Arabs feel utterly impotent against them. In fact, H. W. all unwittingly paid the R.A.F. the best compliment he could. . . ."

Violence was seldom needed; the mere threat was usually enough. As a result Cox had more leisure for constructive work, like Lawrence in Amman. The track over the face of the desert which R.A.F. surveyors were ploughing, mile by mile, meant infinitely more to Trenchard than easy triumphs over tribal chieftains rash enough to defy the law. Remembering how, less than twenty years before, he had toiled through the jungles of southern Nigeria, opening up the forest and letting in the sun, he believed that the air force was adding a new dimension to the civilising arts of his countrymen. The star-shells and fireworks he had once used in tight corners had become airborne and immeasurably more destructive; but now, as then, pacification was only the negative side of an immensely beneficial undertaking. With the aid of a crude wheel and a compass he had once explored the unmapped hinterland; his early dirt roads through the bush had followed, accelerating the course of pacification. The R.A.F. surveyors and working parties in Iraq stood to accomplish more in a matter of months than he in Nigeria had accomplished in years. That was why he thought of these pioneers in the wilderness as the engineers of a new order.

"A track is all we want," he reminded Geoffrey Salmond. "The air will be the road."

The track would be a boon to the drivers of supply trucks and patrolling armoured cars. To airmen in the wide, shimmering oven of the sky above it, it would be a link with life. It was easy for the pilot's eye to be misled by mirages; easier still to run out of fuel, crash, and die of thirst or despair in that ancient waste; rarer

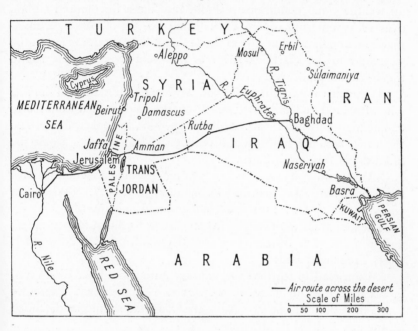

The Middle East, 1921-22

but still possible to fall victim to nomadic Bedouins. Where the desert was soft and flat, the furrow of a plough drew a scar across its dusty face. Where it rose and hardened into lava, long straight ribbons of white paint pointed towards the next staging point, with its emergency stocks of spares and petrol. The track was Borton's special responsibility; he took it as seriously as Trenchard intended.

"I tried white strips every ten miles. I tried petrol tins opened out and painted white at one-mile intervals. I now realise that in the featureless desert the trail must be more continuous and more conspicuous than occasional wheel-tracks," he wrote towards the close of 1921.

The work continued in sandstorms, baking heat, and the short rains. The Bedouins avoided the unguarded dumps, some pausing at first to examine the heavy tins half-buried in the sand, and, finding no use for them, pass on. Within twelve months of the Cairo Conference that illimitable vista of burning emptiness had been crossed; the working parties from Amman and Baghdad met, with the way behind them visibly charted for others to follow. The furrowed shadow, checked again and again by hovering aircraft in all weathers and conditions of light, ran like a discoloured ribbon over rocky outcrops, down the twisting lengths of gorges, a man-made lifeline that led at last to the tawny hills of Transjordan in the west and to the sparkling silver of the great river bending round the Baghdad plain in the east.

Trenchard would talk to his colleagues with animation of the day when it would be feasible to hop across the Middle East from Cairo to Baghdad between meals. More practically, he looked forward to the time, actually fixing tentative dates, when supplies would be lifted down this aerial highway.

" When do you contemplate sending training machines across the desert? " he asked Geoffrey Salmond in July, 1921. " When can you start taking Government dispatches, and how often? "

The first mails were carried from Cairo to Baghdad that summer; and in a cheerfully sarcastic note to Churchill on 17th November, 1921, Trenchard said:

" I am glad to see that the military authorities have discovered at last that [our] air mail . . . is reliable. I suppose that in another year's time they will be suggesting that England should be defended by the air, and not by the army."

Though physically remote, he was invariably thought and spoken of by his men in the Middle East, with a reverence never far from laughter, as a kind of guardian spirit. Trenchard's eyes and ears were always on the men, high and low, who worked the "Desert Run." His pride in their achievement was bottomless. He was never too busy to extol the lesson of Iraq where, in a few months, *his* explorers vaulted barriers which had hampered conquerors and colonisers alike since Biblical days. The turning point in R.A.F. relations with the Bedouins came when, quite spontaneously, a squadron commander picked up and flew to the nearest service hospital, a matter of 250 miles away, a badly scared sheikh suffering from peritonitis. He recovered. His gratitude was both lasting and infectious. But the saving gesture of an officer was no less than Trenchard expected of all his "handymen," who had caught the infection of his own pioneering spirit and were thinking for themselves "instead of being like children at the end of a piece of string which may often break. . . .".

Iraq, under the dynamic influence of air-power, was becoming manageable. In June, 1921, when the Emir Feisal set off for Baghdad, Churchill told the Commons that his nominee for a new throne enjoyed far wider support than that of his British protectors. Though not of Iraqui origin, Feisal belonged to the Sherifian family which, as guardians of the holy places of Mecca, was venerated in most parts of the Islamic world. He was crowned king on 23rd August, 1921; by then the Cabinet in London were readier to accept Churchill's undertaking that Trenchard's security plan would ensure the protection of King Feisal against internal and external foes. It provided for eight R.A.F. squadrons, a supply of armoured cars, auxiliary services, several armoured trains, an air ambulance unit and a few gunboats. The squadrons would be concentrated at two main stations near Baghdad, with an advanced airfield in the north at Mosul and emergency landing grounds elsewhere. The main policing duties would devolve on Arab levies trained and led by British officers; but the rider was added that not until the air scheme had been tested more fully should the remaining army battalions be sent home.

2

The Admiralty was less affected by the plan than the War Office, though naval *amour-propre* was affronted by the recommendation that river gunboats should also be controlled by the R.A.F. Whoever heard of anyone but Trenchard trying to fly a gunboat? The man was a pestilence and a pernicious influence on the Government, especially in conjunction with Churchill. There seemed no limit to his acquisitive instinct. Not content with supplanting the army in the Middle East, he had now begun to question the traditional defence roles of the two older services in the next major war.

Beatty was sufficiently incensed by the minutes and papers with which Trenchard kept bombarding the Committee of Imperial Defence at regular intervals to fire a warning shot or two in reply. When, for instance, Trenchard hinted that the Royal Navy could no longer be regarded as an impregnable shield in the age of air-power, the First Sea Lord countered by disputing the R.A.F.'s claim to be the first line of defence against future air attacks on Britain, since the need for a separate air force had still to be proved. Trenchard, in the Admiralty's view, was an alarmist intent only on making people's flesh creep. Who else would have been so indiscreet as to predict, as he had lately done at the second Independent Air Force dinner in London, that:

" We may yet see governments living in dug-outs and holding Cabinet meetings in the bowels of the earth."

Independence seemed to have gone like wine to his head, a conclusion which Beatty crisply expressed outside Londonderry House after a reception one evening when he and his tormentor picked up one another's hats by mistake and solemnly exchanged them on the steps as they were leaving. The incident had its own piquant symbolism. Yet for all his lack of self-consciousness, Trenchard felt sorry that the First Sea Lord should take so personally a campaign to make the Committee of Imperial Defence a little more "air-minded." Beatty's tendency to treat him with the disdain of an aristocrat seemed an illogical way of answering an adult argument.[2]

As long ago as mid-1920, Trenchard had asked Churchill in writing whether "the growing discontent between the Admiralty and the air" might not be partly due to "personal dislike of myself." His friend Londonderry, who had more recently learnt from Beatty that the Admiralty was setting up its own private air section, dismissed that suggestion out of hand at the time. It was not due to anything personal, he replied, but to "the dread that an air officer may one day be C.-in-C. So far the seaman and landsman have had a clearly marked province. The conquest of the air changes all this. The navy are one hundred years behind the times and the war has not modernised them. . . . The enemy for us to fight is the unwillingness of the present antiquated and semi-antiquated heads to allow the youth of both services to be inoculated with the air idea."

Trenchard confessed that Londonderry's answer "made me purr with pleasure"; it also stimulated him to act in a way that made Beatty growl with rage. Since the Admiralty clearly intended to fight for a separate Fleet Air Arm, he prepared to strike first. Aided by Evans, Game and Bullock, he produced at speed an official paper, the final draft of which was ready by March, 1921. On his return from the Middle East, Churchill read it and was so impressed by the cogency of its thesis that he offered to write a laudatory foreword. The offer was gladly accepted. Then Churchill persuaded Austen Chamberlain, who had lately replaced the sick Bonar Law as Lord Privy Seal and was the Committee of Imperial Defence's nominal chairman, to circulate the contentious document as a Cabinet paper.[3]

Its main premise was the importance to Britain of economising on defence without thereby sacrificing national security. It went on to state that "money spent on the R.A.F. should not merely be an *addition* to army and navy expenditure but to some extent a *substitute*." It elaborated on some of the ways in which this could be done; it tilted at the orthodox preconceptions of all staff officers outside the Air Ministry; and it kindled fires of controversy that smoulder on to this day.

The fixed naval belief in the future of the battleship and the aircraft carrier was dismissed as a costly hallucination.

" Carrier ships are expensive and vulnerable, and with suitable aerodromes the main routes of the Empire can be largely covered." Trenchard's reasons for discrediting battleships were equally provocative: weight for weight, he said, the explosive power of a bomb happened to be greater than that of a shell, and a bomb could be carried two hundred miles before being released whereas a shell had to be fired from a gun only twenty miles away. He admitted that there was disagreement about the efficacy of air attacks on battleships; but nobody who knew how to add and subtract could deny that many squadrons of torpedo and bombing aircraft might be had for the price of a single battleship.

His point in raising such disputable matters was that strategic thinking required a drastic overhaul. In any future war the gravest threat to Britain would come "not from a landing on these islands but from repeated incursions on a large scale by hostile aircraft." Nor could that threat be measured by the insignificant weight of German air attacks in the recent conflict.

" Unless we can put up an adequate defence," he concluded, "we must be prepared for a dislocation of national life to a degree unthought of in the past. . . . The navy and army cannot materially assist us to face this attack and no improvements in guns or other defences will ensure our security. . . . Responsibility should be assumed by the Air Ministry. It should include a skeleton organisation of anti-aircraft gunnery, searchlights, net defences, sound locators and directional W/T stations. . . ."

Both Beatty and Wilson rose to the challenge with vigour. The First Sea Lord counter-claimed that the Royal Navy would be unable to fulfil its traditional role as guardian of the high seas so long as the R.A.F. retained those air squadrons working with the fleet. An air arm wholly administered and manned by the Admiralty was essential for naval efficiency. The War Office advanced a similar claim; and both were debated in secret before the Committee of Imperial Defence during the early summer of 1921. Deadlock was quickly reached, so an attempt was made to break it by calling in an independent arbitrator. The Cabinet invited Balfour, the Coalition's elder statesman, to consider the evidence and present his verdict.

For nearly two months Balfour heard the conflicting testimony of the three Chiefs of Staff and their experts. Trenchard insisted on appearing in person to represent the views of the "Air Staff," as he chose to describe the small inner circle of perhaps a dozen collaborators, both civilian and service, whom he used either as "English merchants" or as chopping-blocks for his own ideas. Then came the sultry August day when Trenchard pressed all the bells on his desk simultaneously and told his assembled staff with elation: " I think we've won. Balfour has conceded our case."

Guest, he said, had just been on the telephone. Trenchard wanted them to have the good news at once. Next day the Minister sent round a marked copy of the Balfour decision.

" I think it's a great victory due to your persistent and clear arguments," he said in a covering note. " The air force will owe you another debt. *C'est le premier pas qui compte.*"

" It is not really *me* who does these things," Trenchard replied. " It's only my voice that communicates to people what our staff has proved. I must say, I am pleased, and a great deal more than pleased, that this our claim has been recognised by a statesman (Balfour) who fought very vigorously during the war against a separate air service. Personally, I think the report is what any fair-minded man must have [concluded]. . . . How can we let the service know that we have been given this sort of responsibility as I presume the Cabinet must support Mr. Balfour? "

Balfour's conclusion was that the difference between the Chiefs of Staff were not irreconcilable. " All would agree, I think, that where the part played by the flying fleet is an auxiliary part, it must be under the general or admiral by whom the army or fleet is commanded," he declared.

" But supposing the roles are reversed—supposing the main operations are carried out by the air force, while the navy and army play a relatively unimportant part in the operations—what then? That such a condition of things is possible seems indeed to be hardly contemplated in the papers submitted to us by the naval and military staffs.

" The military staff, for example, regards the air force as holding a position analogous to artillery: like artillery, it is highly technical and therefore requires a special training; like artillery, it is important because it can co-operate with infantry, cavalry and tanks. To the critics holding this view it is absurd to allow aeroplanes to play an independent part as it would be to confer a similar privilege on guns and howitzers.

" The General Staff indeed dwell with some insistence on the fact that in earlier times a different view was taken, and the artillery was not placed under army control until the necessity for maintaining unity of command forced it into its proper position of subordination, and they appear to think that the same principle will, in the case of the air force, lead to the same result.

" Parenthetically, I may observe that the permanent tendencies have not always been towards unification. Up to the seventeenth century, for example, fleets were navigated by sailors while naval strategy and naval tactics were determined by soldiers. The complete differentiation between the organisations which carried on war by land and war by sea is a relatively late growth.

" Leaving history on one side may we not put our present question as follows: Are there, or are there not, military operations of first-class importance in which the main burden of responsibility is thrown upon the air force, while the other services play either an insignificant part or no part at all? The air force claim that there are; and it seems to me that their claim must be allowed. . . ."

Balfour next summarised Trenchard's basic contention that in the event of air attacks on vital centres like London, aircraft must be met by aircraft.

" Here we have a military operation which not only can be carried out independently by the air force but which cannot be carried out by anything else.

" There is a tendency in some of the papers laid before the Standing Committee to minimise the military effect on this country of air-raids successfully carried out on a very great scale. In the memorandum prepared by the General Staff there is a picture drawn of Great Britain with its capital in ruins and the Admiralty and War Office carrying on their duties undismayed in the safe but obscure retreat supplied by some disused coal-mine. Even such a catastrophe as this, they say, would not force a decision; and perhaps they are right.

" I would, however, observe that as a matter of history, peace has usually been arranged between belligerents long before the worsted party was reduced to so pitiable a condition; and while the position of the General Staffs of the army and navy heroically

carrying on their functions at the bottom of a coal pit might in some
respects be less disastrous than it seems, seeing that in the contingency
supposed they would have very little to do, the enemy aeroplanes
wandering at will over the country could carry out their work
of destruction, however numerous and however heroic might
be the armies and the navies of the country they were reducing to
ruin. . . .

" The conclusion that I draw from these considerations is that
the air force must be autonomous in matters of administration and
education; that in the case of defence against air-raids the army
and navy must play a secondary role; that in the case of military
operations by land, or naval operations by sea, the situation must be
reversed and the air force be in strict subordination to the general
and admiral in supreme command. . . ."

There were, Balfour admitted, border-line cases where co-
operation "like that which prevails between the army and navy "
would be necessary. Here, with the exercise of tact and good judgment, friction need never arise. But, he declared, with a broad hint
that any future efforts by the War Office or Admiralty to side-track
the findings of this exercise in dry strategy were to be deplored:

" I am convinced that any attempt to reduce the new force to
an inferior position will seriously hamper its vigorous development
and may put us at a serious disadvantage. . . ."

By a remarkable oversight this State paper, which bears comparison for insight with the Smuts report of 1917, seems to have
wholly escaped the notice of Balfour's biographer. Lloyd George
and his colleagues, who had held themselves free from the outset to
accept or reject the arbitrator's verdict, endorsed it at once and
without reservation. The Balfour inquiry into the strategic claims
of the R.A.F. must therefore rank as Trenchard's first moral victory
over the Admiralty and War Office. It is very questionable if the
R.A.F. would have long survived if Balfour had brought in a
different verdict.

Characteristically, Trenchard had acted on the belief that the
only sound way of protecting what he held was to attack the old-
fashioned strategic outlook of his opponents. This reflex action owed
as much to the natural doctrinaire in him as to his highly developed
sense of timing and to his instinct for self-preservation; but it also
helped to intensify an atmosphere of hostility in which the right of
the air force to survive would be questioned again and again during
the next six years. Trenchard had won only the first round in a
marathon serial. For Beatty, in particular, was determined to

avenge himself on a Chief of Staff who had turned the "year of grace," 1920, to such outrageous advantage.

Trenchard left for a month's leave in mid-August, 1921, easier in mind than at any time since the Armistice. The heretic of Whitehall had scored a signal triumph, though the secrecy which necessarily hedged it from the public lent it a disquietingly ephemeral look. Only on his return in September from a grouse moor in Scotland did he begin to realise how impermanent such tactical triumphs can be. His jubilation, and that of Guest, had been a trifle premature.

3

The Government, in his absence, had yielded to sustained Opposition and Press criticisms of excessive spending by ordering an altogether more searching kind of inquiry. A Committee had been empowered to poke into the dusty corners of Whitehall, pull out the dead wood, and make a huge public bonfire of it for the edification of all who disliked Whitehall extravagance.

Sir Eric Geddes, the chairman of the new Committee, seemed confident at the start of extracting plenty; and the popular organs of opinion were helpfully plying him with suggestions. Nobody knew where the Geddes Axe, as it was nicknamed, would fall or how ruthless the woodman would be. Unofficial estimates of possible and desirable cuts fluctuated between £150 million and half that figure. Every Government department had reason for alarm; but the pundits of Fleet Street and Westminster were broadly agreed that the first and obvious victims should be the three defence services.

The Lloyd George Coalition, after nearly three years in office, had outrun its electoral credit. Its enemies were not alone in thinking that the record of its domestic failures was lamentable. The continuing trade recession, the plight of the unemployed, now nearly two million strong, the inflationary rise in prices, the violent troubles in Ireland, and the deterioration of relations with France were put down to the Government's incompetence. The charges were no juster than such charges normally are when the times are out of joint; but they were more difficult to rebut because the Coalition itself had started to give at the seams.

With the temporary disappearance of Bonar Law, who had been ordered a prolonged rest by his doctors soon after Milner's retirement in early 1921, the last restraining influence was removed from Lloyd

George. On the rare occasions the Prime Minister turned to others for advice, he turned now to Austen Chamberlain or to those political inseparables, Churchill and Birkenhead (the former F. E. Smith), whose standing with the Conservatives in the Coalition was very low. Junior Ministers like Baldwin and Amery were growing discontented with their lot, a state of mind which the querulousness of their own backbenchers did little to relieve. The widening chasm between ministerial policy-makers and the rest could no longer be bridged by trust or patriotism. For the feeling was abroad and spreading that Lloyd George's mistakes would have to be paid for eventually in lost Tory votes.

The Geddes Inquiry was thus a typically deft move on the Prime Minister's part to placate critics at home while borrowing extra time to win peace abroad. From any administrative standpoint, such an inquiry was unquestionably overdue. The war years had stimulated a riotous undergrowth of bureaucracy. A Parkinson might have analysed and defined the organic process of increase; but only a Geddes could say which were true branches, which suckers, and which of both were wholly unproductive. The commonly held opinion that the service departments should be the first for pruning suited Lloyd George admirably. Had he not anticipated it by introducing his "Ten Year Rule"?

Trenchard had cause to fear. With a few strokes of the new axe, everything he had striven to build since 1919 might well come crashing down in ruins. Even Churchill could not protect the R.A.F. this time. Trenchard would have to justify its expenditure and existence to the last farthing. The ground gained by the Middle East settlement, the technical victory awarded him more recently by Balfour, his very status as the nominal equal of Beatty and Wilson, were no longer safe. For the First Sea Lord and the C.I.G.S. would, he knew, be bound to defend themselves by pleading that any inefficiency or waste uncovered in their departments was infinitesimal beside the annual outlay of about £15 million required to maintain a separate air force. And Geddes, alas, was no strategist.

Trenchard told the Air Staff that if such a propaganda campaign were unleased by the army and navy, the most telling answer would be the truth. Geddes must be shown everything; not an airscrew or a nut must be left unaccounted for. Every penny spent since the Armistice must tally with the books; every argument for and against the creation of a united air force from 1912 onwards must be resurrected. The R.A.F. had nothing to hide, and everything to lose, by suppressing evidence.

The files containing the Air Ministry's written evidence run into scores of thousands of words. Night after night, during the autumn and winter of 1921, Trenchard would leave the office with a bulging brief-case, catch his train from King's Cross to Potters Bar, and work at home until the small hours, annotating the drafts of papers prepared by his branch chiefs.

The Trenchards had moved after the birth of Hugh, their first son, in June, 1921, from a flat in Kensington to Dancer's Hill, an Elizabethan house near Potters Bar which was offered on favourable terms and a long lease. While the infant and the three older step-children were fast asleep upstairs, he would often dictate by the hour to his wife, who seemed as capable as himself in a crisis of going without rest and living on reserves of nervous energy. If the physical and mental strain was considerable, both were equal to it. Trenchard himself possessed an enviable gift of being able to "switch off" and forget his work as soon as he put it aside; as for Lady Trenchard, her adaptability was as remarkable as her stamina and dogged will-power. That she should be allowed to share in his battles was all she asked.

The C.I.G.S., Wilson, now on the brink of retirement, could not contain his delight at the turn of events. The War Office circulated a loaded minute, assuring the Grand Inquisitor that he need look no further than the Air Ministry for immediate economies. It was the first shot, but Trenchard was ready.

" In preference to these unprofitable paper polemics," he fired back, " I shall wholeheartedly welcome any proposal for an independent searching examination of defence expenditure, provided such examination includes the army. . . .

" I am confident that the results will support my contention that the air arm is our cheapest form of defence, and that, if only we are prepared to move with the times and leave the ruts of an obsolete dogmatism, the gradual transfer to the Air Ministry of certain functions hitherto vested in the War Office—and to a lesser extent in the Admiralty—will make for substantial economies."

Fortunately, Geddes was not moved by partisan slogans, though he could not ignore the odium in which the R.A.F. was manifestly held by its elders. Determined as he was to scrutinise the affairs of all three services, he turned first to the alleged deficiencies of the third and most despised. It was providential indeed that Trenchard's keen nose for the scent of danger, his faculty for reading the minds of his opponents, had not failed him. Geddes was agreeably surprised by the co-operative spirit he encountered at Adastral House. His questionnaires were answered fully, and without evasion; everyone seemed glad of the chance to throw open the cupboards just to prove that no skeletons were concealed within.

Gaps in the wartime records were filled in by sheer industry. Written evidence to confirm the spoken word was indispensible. Trenchard, Evans, Ellington and others who had served under Cowdray, Rothermere and Weir, might vividly recollect the gist of old controversies, but the incompleteness of the relevant files was sometimes startling.

The revised and completed records were unimpeachably accurate and spoke for themselves; but neither Geddes nor his Committee had any inkling of the language of air-power. The underlying principles that had guided its development from the beginning were mysteries to them, so that Trenchard's burden was heaviest during the many oral cross-examinations. He had, as he put it, to "educate Geddes without upsetting him." The arming with an axe of a shrewd, intelligent but untutored man "who could not see the wood for the trees" seemed at times an irresponsible departure.

For instance, one of Geddes's earliest proposals, based on the cost of equipping and running a service squadron, was that the $8\frac{1}{2}$ now employed at home for defence and co-operation with army and navy should be abolished forthwith. This, he hinted, would not only serve to patch up Air Ministry relations with the War Office and Admiralty; it would also save the taxpayer an immediate sum of £$2\frac{1}{2}$ million. Trenchard rebuked Geddes for his mathematics, pointing out the odd coincidence that these were Wilson's mathematics. The saving would not be a tenth of £$2\frac{1}{2}$ million; the cost in security might be ultimately catastrophic for Britain.

By what method, he asked, had Sir Eric reached his attractive estimate of £$2\frac{1}{2}$ million saved? Geddes replied that he had taken the total air vote, divided it by the number of squadrons in service, and thus arrived at the basic cost of one. Trenchard smiled, then began to explain, item by item, how far wide of the mark the tentative axe blow had struck.

The $8\frac{1}{2}$ home squadrons represented Britain's first line of defence. It was, moreover, the only reservoir from which trained men could be drawn to reinforce the squadrons in Egypt, Iraq and India. Apart from those considerations, the scrapping of home squadrons would mean "the total and perhaps irretrievable destruction of army and Navy co-operation with the R.A.F." It would strike at the very foundations of the service, making nonsense of Government policy and reviving the possibility of that duplication and overlapping which had led during the war to the establishment of a separate air force.

With infuriating persistence Geddes next suggested that the training centre at Halton should be shut down. Trenchard was appalled. Did Geddes realise, he asked, that despite the current trade slump, the R.A.F. had tried without success to recruit skilled engineers, fitters, riggers and other craftsmen direct from civilian life? Surely that in itself showed the absurdity of amputating this vital limb of the service? Other branches had been starved so that 3000 youths between the ages of fifteen and eighteen could receive the finest technical education it was possible to provide. Eighty per cent of the money earmarked in 1919 for new living quarters and machine shops at Halton had already been spent; and the results of two full years' working needed only slight scrutiny to justify every farthing of it. Where else could the R.A.F. have turned for trained specialists in each of the fifty-four trades then necessary to service and equip a modern air force? A qualified Halton boy was not merely an integral part of the R.A.F.'s specialist backbone: in view of the fact that before the age of thirty he would return to civilian life, every Halton boy should be regarded as a national asset.

Geddes did not disagree. Indeed he gradually shifted his position and leaned hard in the other direction, finally recommending that the R.A.F. should prolong the careers of future boy technicians. Let them sign on, he urged, for two extra years. Though this might well affect his carefully planned recruitment programme, Trenchard eagerly complied. Reduced numbers of trainees would be a temporary handicap that could be borne with a lighter heart than permanent mutilation.

The Committee also learnt that the depots housing unused machines and spares were not the hoard of a miser. The allegation that "reconditioning engines" implied misemploying men for the purpose of "making old machines look pretty" was, said Trenchard, frivolous and quite unfounded. He had not relished approaching one aircraft manufacturer after another with the cheerless news that the R.A.F. would have no money to spend on new models for five years at any rate.

Shortly after returning as Chief of Air Staff, he had personally advised Sopwith, de Havilland, Handley Page, Fairey and the rest not to despair on that account. Their time would come again; but until the R.A.F. was allowed to expand, the British aircraft industry must either find foreign markets or "take to toy-making." It could not hope to prosper on his meagre contracts for replacements.

It was news to Geddes the Air Ministry had saved the taxpayer some £25 million since the Armistice by conserving wartime machines and spares, many of which had been produced in such haste that maintenance officers often had to dismantle and wholly rebuild them.

" At present the life of an aeroplane in store is three years," said Trenchard. " Would it help if I undertook to lengthen it to four? "

Geddes said that he would like time to think it over, bearing in mind not only the wastage of outmoded equipment but the consequences of subjecting the aircraft industry to still harsher privations. In the end, he accepted the proposal.[4]

On balance, the R.A.F. came well out of the inquiry. Despite reductions, many of them voluntary, amounting to some £5 million, which Trenchard decided to implement by a further tightening of belts all round, the Geddes Committee had benefited from his persevering efforts to "educate" the chairman. It was worth re-introducing the wartime scheme of training N.C.O. pilots, postponing plans for rehousing officers and men on home stations, and pruning the small staffs of overseas commands. The Air Ministry, and especially that inner portion of it over which he exerted the closest form of benevolent autocracy, would henceforth be more necessary than ever. Trenchard's strongly paternalist influence, already as sharply felt in India as at Uxbridge, had won the admiration of Geddes. But more significant by far than any minor changes, the strategic value of the R.A.F.'s squadrons (which then numbered $32\frac{1}{2}$ and which would soon be reduced to 31 as an additional gesture of compliance with the spirit of austerity) was grasped by this enemy of waste.

" Economics to an increasing extent ought to result in the older arms from the advent of the air force," Geddes stated in his final Report. " We have in mind not only the substitution of aircraft for certain other arms of the older services, such as light cruisers or cavalry, but a revolution in the method of carrying out certain operations."

And again:

" It can no longer be denied that by the intelligent application of air-power it is possible to utilise machinery in substitution for, and not as a mere addition to, man-power."

4

If a tentative date can be put to the laying of Sir Eric Geddes's doubts about the R.A.F., it would be reasonable to suggest the first half of November, 1921. By then the War Office campaign against the R.A.F. as a military luxury, the most scandalous part of which, according to Wilson, was the duplication of the supply and administrative branches of the older services, had begun to fizzle out. The facts unearthed by the committee belied the charge, heightening Geddes's respect for Trenchard as a man of his word.

The Sea Lords had meanwhile been far from idle. In October, before Beatty left for the Washington Conference on naval disarmament, a new Deputy Chief of Naval Staff arrived at the Admiralty. Roger Keyes was an obvious choice; for not only did he enjoy public acclaim as a hero whose dashing leadership at Zeebrugge on St. George's Day, 1918, rekindled memories of the fighting sea captains of old; he was, as Trenchard knew, practically the only officer of flag rank with any first-hand experience of air command. As admiral at Dover during the final months of war, Keyes had chafed, just as Salmond had done in France, at being deprived of bombers for local operational requirements. The birth of the R.A.F. was, to him, little better than an abortion. The Handley Pages and Sopwiths at Dunkirk, which had once been in effect the private air force of his predecessors, were now controlled by the new Air Ministry. And both the needs and strategic plans of that Ministry, so he claimed, were almost always at variance with his own.

Nothing had happened since to soften his prejudices. Being a man of choleric temperament, he clung with a faith more fanatically blind than Beatty's to the Royal Navy's supremacy of jurisdiction. It followed as a corollary that everything co-operating with a fleet, aircraft included, must be exclusively controlled by the Admiralty. He carried his conviction, in public and private, like a banner in a gale; and Trenchard's troubles with the Sea Lords started in earnest soon after Beatty's departure for the United States. Though Keyes was no orator, no sharp-witted debater, no skilled polemicist capable of making a little logic go a long way, he had tenacity and fervour in abundance. He used both in rash attempts to sway the judgment of Geddes.

Beatty could not have wished for a more pertinacious champion, and there were moments when Trenchard wondered a trifle unkindly whether the stratagem of setting a relative to catch a relative had moved the First Sea Lord in his choice of a deputy. For Keyes, as it happened, was Trenchard's brother-in-law by marriage; and presently his rift with Trenchard, much to the latter's quiet amusement, gave rise to a certain coolness, particularly among the ladies, in both family circles.

The Cabinet had only half an ear for the inter-service dissensions caused by the inquiry. It would be time enough for the reckoning when Geddes presented his findings. One Minister alone was anything but indifferent to the outcome. Immersed as Churchill then was in the delicate, confused and often tense negotiations which eventually led that winter to a settlement of the Irish question, he insisted on weighing in with a statement which helped to demolish the anti-R.A.F. case of Keyes and the admirals.

" We are sure," wrote Churchill, "that if, after a prolonged spell of peace, war on a great scale suddenly broke out again, the Power which had made the most intensive study of aerial warfare would start with an enormous initial advantage, and the Power that neglected this form of active defence might well find itself fatally situated.

" Proceeding on this assumption, we contend that the British policy is to develop the independent conception of the air as an art, an arm and a service; and that this method alone will secure that qualitative ascendancy and superiority which the safety of the country requires. We think that to keep this new arm, with its measureless possibilities, in perpetual thraldom to the army or navy, and confined solely to ancillary and auxiliary duties in relation to these two older services, will be to rob it of its most important developments.

" Moreover, we are inclined to think that the growth of the Independent Air Force will in the future take place largely at the expense of the two older services, and that important economies will be secured thereby."

Churchill added some examples of this trend: air reconnaissance at a considerable distance from land, anti-submarine operations in narrow waters, torpedo attacks on troop transports. These and other duties "would render it possible to substitute air-power for cruisers, destroyers and various types of anti-submarine aircraft, and there should be substantial savings in expense as this development proceeds."

Churchill's intervention seems to have been decisive. Persuaded at last, Geddes turned at last to the War Office and Admiralty establishments with an eye to likely cuts.

He met with considerable resistance. And presently, as if to indicate the strength of public feeling, another campaign to discredit the R.A.F. was whipped up, this time in the Press.

Wilson started it with a widely reported speech at Amiens towards the end of November. It was his last fling at Trenchard. The C.I.G.S., with a bare month to serve before retiring, had nothing to lose in speaking his mind freely. The Government and Geddes might disagree with his assessment of R.A.F. efficiency, just as recent Middle East developments had disproved it; but popular sentiment, always touchy on such matters, would never countenance or condone charges of inhumane methods of warfare. So, in his speech, Wilson concentrated on this aspect, referring ironically to what he called "the development of the aeroplane movement" and defining it as a movement "for killing women and children."

Trenchard flew into a towering rage when he read it.

" I do not wish you to think that I am attacking you behind your back," he informed the C.I.G.S., " so I write this to tell you that I am asking my Secretary of State (Guest) to circulate to the Cabinet a statement on this speech and on your habitual general attitude to the air service. It is impossible for me to sit still under these perpetual attacks—inspired and as it seems to me virtually led by you—to which considerations of dignity and good taste forbid me publicly to reply."

Trenchard's note to the Cabinet accused Wilson of having displayed "implacable animosity against this service from the beginning of 1919." The C.I.G.S.'s policy had been to disparage it at every opportunity, "very often under the cloak of humour which, in my opinion, is usually apt to pass the bounds of good taste." Remarking on the resentment which the public smear of "inhumanity" had provoked throughout the R.A.F., Trenchard commented:

" It is not the right place in this letter to argue as to the humanity of the air as compared with the army, though I am prepared to do this if any responsible Government Committee considered it necessary. No doubt the field-marshal's argument is intended to make a popular appeal which seems better suited to the columns of *The Star* than to the considered opinion of the chief representative of the army."

One point in the speech, however, distressed him still more than gratuitous allegations of brutality.

" According to the *Daily Telegraph*, he suggested that it would be 'better to limit aeroplanes rather than submarines.' That is in effect a public expression of disagreement with the policy of His Majesty's Government as formulated in the instructions given to the British delegates to the Washington Conference (Memorandum by the

Standing sub-Committee of the C.I.D. No. 280b) which, while re-commending the imposition of ' a ban on the unrestricted use of submarines,' reached the conclusion that the effective limitation of aerial argument was impracticable.

" On wider grounds I am afraid that disastrous consequences are bound to ensue if the professional head of one fighting service is to be considered free to state to the world at large his dissent from the recommendations of another, after they have been endorsed by the Committee of Imperial Defence. . . . Rightly or wrongly, the Government have established an air service, and in the air service we have attained some degree of efficiency economically. How much easier our task would have been, and would be in the future, if the older services had always said ' How can we help you? ' instead of saying ' How can we destroy you? ' "

Before the repercussions died away, the "College of Admirals" decided to go one better than Wilson. Their methods were more circumspect, their motives no less mixed; they used as mouthpieces M.P.s and ex-naval officers who could be depended on to relay Admiralty grievances against the R.A.F. at Question Time in Parliament or in the correspondence columns of the Press.

The real reason for the animosity of Keyes and his colleagues lay not in London, but in Washington, where the naval disarmament exchanges were not at all to Beatty's taste. The mood of the conference was against the construction of new capital ships; and with the German Grand Fleet rusting on the sea bed at Scapa Flow and the prospect of a major conflict officially ruled out for ten years by the British Government itself, Beatty's case for modernising the navy gained little support. His right to maintain a limited number of cruisers and other ships for the security of Britain's world-wide trade routes was poor consolation indeed for becoming the reluctant signatory to an international agreement debarring him from building battleships for a decade.

Beatty did not tarry in the United States. For the news from Keyes was still more depressing. Geddes had apparently veered to Trenchard's side, and it was high time for the First Sea Lord to return and break the R.A.F. monopoly of aircraft, one of the few weapons left untouched by the Washington decisions. A little pressure from outside, judiciously applied, might prompt the Cabinet to think twice before ratifying Trenchard's pernicious creed of a single air force, controlling land and sea, which cut across shrinking naval interests. Keyes, who had the same thought, applied the pressure at once.

5

The banner headline in the *Pall Mall Gazette* on 5th January, 1922, shrieked for itself. " CHAOS IN THE AIR FORCE," it asserted in bold black type. The article beneath was padded out with generalisations, the factual inaccuracies possibly being the price that had to be paid for disclosing so startling a discovery. The sales of the *Gazette* temporarily rose. Other journals, not to be outdone, took up the cry. Might this not perhaps be an inspired leak, a hint even of the inscrutable workings of Geddes's mind? Some thought it probable; others, including Trenchard, did not. He saw it as a clumsily camouflaged move on the Admiralty's part to sabotage Geddes's proposals in advance by rousing public feeling against them. Its timing betrayed it. So did its contents.

The anonymous writer claimed that he was inventing nothing. All his information had come from a "distinguished officer," still in uniform, who knew only too well what he was talking about. In other words the R.A.F., notably in its relations with the Fleet, stood condemned out of the mouth of one of its own serving members. It was a cunning line; but at least it narrowed Trenchard's urgent search for the culprit, a wing-commander, who readily admitted under cross-examination that he had been in touch with the Admiralty. A formal naval pilot, the young man was quite impenitent. Squadrons serving the fleet, he said, would be better run by the admirals: indeed, he added, he had called on no less a person than Sir Roger Keyes to say so.

Trenchard confronted Keyes with the wing-commander's evidence and demanded the immediate return of certain confidential papers which the accused had boasted of handing over to him. Keyes did not deny receiving the documents; but he denied all knowledge of what was in them and scoffed at his brother-in-law's oversensitivity to public criticism.[5]

" I had not the slightest idea that the typewritten sheets, which remained locked up in my drawer unread by anyone, formed any part of a confidential memorandum," he wrote immediately after this heated interview with Trenchard. " It did occur to me that in the happy event of our regaining control over the very small air force which we consider essential for the efficiency of the fleet, there might be something of value in them. . . . When I heard that the [wing-commander] was shortly to be tried by court-martial I burnt letters and enclosures unread, as I did not wish to be mixed up in any way with R.A.F. domestic matters.

" I had no idea," concluded Keyes, " that you were under any illusion as to the views held by the Admiralty. . . . I mentioned this to the First Sea Lord and, with his concurrence, send you a copy of the paper which was forwarded to Mr. Churchill's Committee, since the Geddes Report discusses our relations with the air force and attempts to fix the strength of the air units we are to be allowed."

The contents of this Admiralty paper intrigued Trenchard less than the gesture of the Sea Lords in letting him see it. Beatty and Keyes were clearly determined to stop at nothing in their endeavour to undo the work of Geddes. Time was certainly on their side; so, probably, was the ingrained and almost mystical belief of the average Briton that the Royal Navy knew its own needs best. It seemed outrageous to Trenchard that this public test of Admiralty infallibility should thus be dragged into the debate, but he could do nothing to prevent it.

The Press followed up quickly. Not all politicians were deceived, though none could ignore the point that, rightly or wrongly, the admirals were as dissatisfied with the Royal Air Force as the *Pall Mall Gazette* suggested. Critics as well informed as Rear-Admiral Sir Reginald Hall, the wartime Director of Naval Intelligence and now the most cogent exponent of the Admiralty case on the Government back benches, were less easily silenced than serving admirals. The complicity between them was unmistakable, but hard to prove, being rooted in an intense loyalty and pride of service which seemed to affect sailors more than any soldiers in Trenchard's experience.

Hall helped to keep speculation on the boil by alleging in a further *Pall Mall Gazette* article that the Admiralty were "seriously concerned" by R.A.F. inefficiency. The only reliable cure would be to partition the air force and restore to the fleet its own lost squadrons. By a curious coincidence, Beatty and Keyes had taken an identical line in their memorandum to the Cabinet, a copy of which they had obligingly sent to Trenchard.

Their claim that "from the naval point of view the aeroplane and the seaplane are essential auxiliaries in reconnaissance and fire control, whilst the torpedo plane promises to play a most important part in obtaining and disputing sea communications" was *vieux jeu* indeed; it had been repeatedly laboured in the Committee of Imperial Defence during recent months. The one new factor was their conclusion that "the demand for a separate Naval Air Service is logical and reasonable." Trenchard could not see the logic of it, but realised that it had never been stated so unequivocally. The point of uncertainty in his mind was whether the Cabinet would withstand the pressure of outside propaganda.

With the service estimates as well as the Geddes Report almost ready for publication, it was the open season for political controversy. It did not matter that Balfour had arbitrated in favour of the R.A.F. the previous summer, or that Geddes had found no woodworm at the Air Ministry. The politicians had still to decide. Once again, it seemed, all would depend on the steadfastness of Churchill. Only he had resolution and vision enough to rally his colleagues. Trenchard wished he could be absolutely sure how Churchill would turn.

By the end of February, 1922, the inspired whisper was circulating in Whitehall that Lloyd George had veered to the view that the air force must be broken up. Almost simultaneously the long-awaited Geddes Report saw the light of day. Trenchard could do no more than cross his fingers and hope. By Parliamentary questions, letters and comments in the Press, and incessant club gossip, the impression was fostered that a Government decree abolishing the R.A.F. could be expected at any moment. Churchill, to his credit, grew so annoyed at the persistence of these false rumours that he rebuked Lloyd George and Austen Chamberlain for their reticence. On 11th March, just before the service estimates came up for discussion in Parliament, he wrote to Chamberlain saying that he regarded the circulation of these rumours as a studied attempt at blackmail which might well place the Cabinet in an impossible position.

In his letter, of which he sent a copy to Lloyd George and another to Trenchard, Churchill made it clear that he for one was not going to be stampeded by the gossip-mongers. He pointedly reminded Chamberlain and the Prime Minister that the air force and the Air Ministry owed their existence to an Act of Parliament, and that until the provisions of that Act were repealed by fresh legislation, there was no question of the R.A.F.'s present status being altered. It was therefore quite wrong to treat the future of the R.A.F. as if it were still an open question for the Cabinet to decide upon; in fact such an attitude was not only erroneous and irresponsible but one which could prove very harmful to the air force— both in affecting the R.A.F.'s prestige and in prolonging the inter-departmental discord which had plagued it for so long.

Churchill therefore urged that in the interests of the service's well-being Chamberlain should make a clear pronouncement in the forth-coming debate that the Government's present policy was that already embodied in the Air Force Act, which the Government had no intention of repealing. Such a statement would in no way preclude the position from being altered by statute in the future, but unless the Government intended to introduce any changes during the present session, it would be very wrong to allow these injurious rumours to continue.

Churchill was prudent enough not to anticipate the attitude of Lloyd George. For whether the R.A.F. survived or went under no longer bothered a Prime Minister who, from a mixture of motives, had been somewhat more definite about the need for inducing its birth in 1917. The question now was one of administrative detail. It could be left to his colleagues while he reserved his energies for winning the peace. Such insouciance did not altogether please Churchill. However, he proffered no opinion as to the advisability or otherwise of an eventual change in the statutory provisions; he merely pointed out that a move to repeal the Act would probably meet with considerable opposition both in the House of Commons and in the Cabinet, and that its opponents would find weighty support in the Press.

Churchill was possibly drawing the long bow in counting on the good sense of the Commons and the Press lords; he could, however, vouch for some support in the Cabinet.

At a Cabinet meeting on 13th March, the Colonial Secretary, in his capacity as unofficial defence expert, followed up this letter with an emphatic appeal to his colleagues which saved the situation. Chamberlain, so Churchill informed the Chief of Air Staff, was the first to accept the need of an unambiguous statement of Government air policy in Parliament. Lloyd George assented. And Churchill, who volunteered to assist in drafting it, immediately turned to Trenchard for background material. The latter was only too delighted to oblige.

Seated in the Distinguished Strangers' Gallery of the Commons on the evening of 16th March, Trenchard heard Austen Chamberlain's quiet declaration. Its impact on the House resembled that of a high explosive bomb with a delayed action fuse. As the Lord Privy Seal rose in his place, M.P.s who supported the Admiralty case sat expectantly. They had been thoroughly enjoying themselves at the Government's expense, debating a motion in the name of Sir Reginald Hall that "the Naval Air Service should be put under the control of the Board of Admiralty." Chamberlain, in his impeccably polite way, sounded almost sorry for spoiling their fun.

" If the matters raised by my honourable and gallant friends related solely to the navy," he began, " I should not have thought it necessary to intervene. It would be left to the very competent hands of the Admiralty representatives in this House." Unfortunately for the country, however, theirs was a "rather narrow point of view" which he wished to broaden into perspective "on behalf of the Government as a whole."

After retracing the history of military flying in Britain, Chamberlain dwelt on the solid reasons which had led to the birth of the wartime R.A.F. These reasons still held, he said.

" I do not want it to be thought that the Government are blind to the real difficulties which arise out of the present system. I do not pretend for one moment that it works with perfect harmony or smoothness or gives satisfaction to everybody. But our view is that the objections to the reabsorption of the air force by the army and navy are far greater than any objections which can be raised against the existence of a separate Air Ministry and Staff. . . . Sailors and soldiers would continue to think of the force in terms of their own service and would not pursue—and could not be expected to pursue —its development as an independent force. We consider that it would be a retrograde step at this time to abolish the Air Ministry and to reabsorb the air service into the Admiralty and the War Office."

A stunned House heard him through with scarcely an interruption. As Trenchard listened to the closing parts of Chamberlain's statement, the major happenings of the previous twelve months suddenly fell into place like the pieces of an incomplete jigsaw puzzle. Without the Cairo Conference in the spring, nothing of practical value would have now stood to his credit, in which case the R.A.F. could not have weathered the artificial storms brewed up by Wilson and Beatty.

Yet the R.A.F.'s success in the Middle East had turned still more covetous eyes upon it in a period of retrenchment, and his own provocative refusal in committee to play down the revolution in strategy brought by air-power had united the War Office and Admiralty in an unholy alliance against him. Balfour's arbitration had settled an abstract argument only; its terms of reference precluded any guarantee of R.A.F. survival. Nevertheless, there were echoes of Balfour as well as of Geddes in Chamberlain's final words.

" These are the conclusions at which we have arrived. In the first place, that the air force must be autonomous in matters of administration and education. Second, that in the case of defence against air-raids the army and navy must play a secondary role.

Third, that in the case of military operations by land or sea, the air force must be in strict subordination to the general or admiral in supreme command. Fourth, that in other cases, such as the protection of commerce and attacks on enemy harbours and inland towns, the relations between the air force and the other services shall be regarded rather as a matter of co-operation than of the strict subordination which is necessary when aeroplanes are acting merely as auxiliaries of other arms."

There was one other point. In order to appease the Admiralty a special committee would be appointed "to examine carefully into the system of naval and air co-operation." This, implied Chamberlain, ought to improve harmony between the two services. In the circumstances, it was an almost inevitable concession; but the thought of it caused Trenchard's elation to evaporate as he walked away from Westminster in the chilly night air. Beatty and Keyes had suffered another rebuff; neither would rest now until the whole question of dismembering the R.A.F. to provide the Royal Navy with its own air arm had been forcibly reopened.

15. *The Unwanted*

No honest critic could say that the Admiralty's misgivings went by default during the service debates that followed. Even Churchill, who knew how narrowly the air force had escaped extinction, went out of his way to smooth ruffled feelings.

" It will be a great mistake for the Air Ministry not to put the Admiralty at their ease in this matter," he admitted. " The vital part of the great sea battle must be fought by aeroplanes out of the ships. The whole course of that action must be intimately regulated by the aeroplanes which rise from and alight upon ships. Then there is the proportion of the money devoted to naval expenditure which has to be assigned to the air forces operating in the battle, and it seems to me that is a matter which to the Admiralty, which still retains prime responsibility for the safety of this country, must be regarded as vital."

Reasonable as Churchill's attitude was, it only nettled the naval partisans who regarded the Government's decision as weak and inconsistent.

Air-minded M.P.s retaliated in kind, condemning the recent whispering campaign against the R.A.F. as a national disgrace. It might have been understandable and even excusable, suggested Moore-Brabazon, who, as Parliamentary Private Secretary first to Churchill and now to Guest, was unusually well informed about its origin, in the case of "very old generals wearing the medals of Crecy and Agincourt." Otherwise, it was unaccountable for, except as a manifestation of professional pique. The Royal Navy, which had been "the spoilt darling of this nation for a hundred years," was abusing its privileges in attempting to thwart the revolution caused by air-power.

" If the Channel had dried up, would the navy still have taken on the defence of England? " he asked rhetorically. " It would have passed to the army. But a larger miracle than that has happened. The air has been conquered, and consequently, from this moment, the navy cannot be responsible for the defence of these islands."

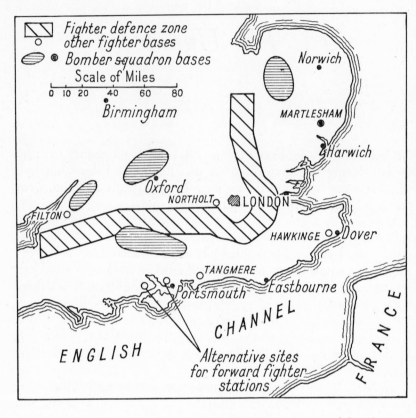

Fighter defence zone
other fighter bases
Bomber squadron bases
Scale of Miles
0 10 20   40   60   80
Birmingham
Norwich
MARTLESHAM
Harwich
Oxford
NORTHOLT LONDON
FILTON
HAWKINGE Dover
TANGMERE
Portsmouth Eastbourne
CHANNEL
ENGLISH
FRANCE
Alternative sites
for forward fighter
stations

The disposition of air-bases in 1923, when France was regarded as the potential enemy

Another R.A.F. supporter whose remarks incensed the Admiralty's champions was Captain Wedgwood Benn; his definition of naval co-operation as the "co-operation of the rabbit with the boa-constrictor" seemed most apt to Trenchard.

By and large, however, the 1922 supply debates were orderly and restrained. For many of the uncommitted M.P.s felt that the Government's decision to preserve the R.A.F. was justified in view of the rapid expansion of the French Air Service. A frontier on the Rhine and the extortion of full reparations from the Germans remained the first objectives of France in Europe; and the recent conference at Cannes had dealt Lloyd George's hopes of a *détente* their severest set-back yet. Then, early in March, 1922, a series of special articles in *The Times* disclosed that the French now possessed the strongest and best-equipped air force on earth. The facts, which had long been known to the Air Ministry, came as a salutary shock to responsible opinion at Westminster, where the discovery that France had the means to impose her will on Germany gave rise to the fear that in her present mood of intransigence she would not hesitate to do so.

The R.A.F. had barely a dozen squadrons for home defence. According to *The Times*, France had at least ten times that number, with adequate reserves to match, and was spending four times as much as Britain each year on air development. There was no official attempt to deny these disagreeable truths when the matter was raised at Westminster during the service debates. And though there was some oblique criticism of Trenchard for lavishing too much money on bricks and mortar, and too little on front-line machines, the common reaction on all sides seemed to be:

" Thank heavens we have an air force at all."

The demands of the Royal Navy fell flat before the unsuspected phenomenon of French air might. One or two M.P.s, notably Lord Hugh Cecil, confessed to some bewilderment at the contemptible logic of their colleagues. Why, in the name of sanity, should the growth of the air force in France commit Britain to a fresh rearmament race?

" We are told by those who advocate a large extension of the air force that you will have quantities of air machines able to carry bombs far heavier than any used in the last war," said Cecil, "bombs containing high explosives which will destroy all the buildings, or poison gas which will kill all the people, men, women and children. Therefore, this great city of London could be totally destroyed, and by way of consolation we are recommended to have corresponding aeroplanes to destroy Paris or Berlin in their turn. Some people say we should then sleep easier in our beds. I do not think I would be any the more comfortable. . . . The only chance would be to be the first to act, and since everyone who knows the British Government may be quite certain that we should not be the first to act, the prospect is not a very prepossessing one. I see no choice except that of retiring to New Zealand or Tristan da Cunha, or to become, as I am, a supporter of the League of Nations. . . ."

The anonymous author of the articles in *The Times* was Brigadier-General P. R. C. Groves, who had been one of Sykes's colleagues on the Air Staff in 1918. No admirer of Trenchard's thrifty policy, Groves could scarcely have foreseen the effect his words would have at Westminster. Indirectly, they deepened the responsible tone of discussion, allowing less scope for frothy partisanship.

"There is no doubt," declared the Labour Party's defence spokesman, Colonel Wedgwood, on 21st March, expressing the misgivings of uncommitted M.P.s on all sides, "that if you went to 99 people out of 100 and asked them what was Britain's first line of defence, they would say the navy. After to-day's debate, there will be more people who realise that the navy is not our first line of defence but that the air service is."

The steps by which the Government, while preserving and even strengthening the air force, now proposed to ensure that Admiralty claims were fairly met, seemed suddenly less urgent than before. Had not Geddes stated in black and white that "economies to an increasing extent ought to result from the advent of the air force . . . not only by the substitution of aircraft for certain other arms of the older services, such as light cruisers and cavalry, but by a revolution in the method of carrying out certain operations" ? And had not Geddes added that a Ministry of Defence was the best means of speeding the revolution—a suggestion that had since found some support ?

Churchill, pursuing his line of studious detachment, refused to commit the Government to such an innovation, though two years previously he had been its warmest advocate and the likeliest candidate for the post.

"A Minister of Defence who had no experts to speak with a measure of authority on the air, land and sea would be in a most difficult position," he told the Commons. "[He] would be such a dazzling super-Minister that he would dwarf all the rest of his colleagues. . . . The practical steps open to us are already being taken. The creation of the brain of a common service is to be the subject of an inquiry by a sub-committee of the Committee of Imperial Defence."

The first necessity, in Churchill's view, was a "college for training that will unite officers of the middle rank." This, he said, "ought not to be delayed by a single year." Meanwhile the special sub-committee would examine the broader question of strategic co-ordination. The Admiralty's demands on the R.A.F. were a separate issue which, he promised, would be considered forthwith by a separate panel of the Committee of Imperial Defence.

On balance, Trenchard was satisfied. The R.A.F. had emerged from its trial at Westminster with more credit than it had entered. Political life was an endless gamble; to-day's principles often became to-morrow's forfeits. That truism had been fortuitously underlined during the air debate. Churchill was defending the

Government's decision not to tamper with the air force, a decision, he said, which "deserved the best of at least a year's experiment," when his former Under-Secretary, Seely, leaped to his feet.

" Why only a year? "

Churchill hesitated before retorting rather lamely:

" Because we shall be able to discuss it this time next year."

" *You* may not be there."

" Well, after all, we only live from year to year."

There, in Trenchard's eyes, lay the half-concealed catch in trying to create so complex an organism as an air force. The R.A.F.'s fortunes were too closely bound up for comfort with the dwindling stock of the Coalition Government. Its survival had been again upheld byParliament; yet Trenchard prudently resigned himself, and it, to another period of living from day to day, from crisis to crisis. The instinct of self-preservation, disposing him to prepare for the worst even at the best of times, proved his ultimate salvation. For though, within eight months, the Lloyd George Government was swept from office and Churchill had temporarily vanished from the Parliamentary scene, the vindictiveness of Trenchard's enemies broke over him in vain.

The causes of the Coalition's downfall were already obscurely at work. Though not directly of Churchill's making, their roots lay in the Middle East. British relations with Turkey, being a Foreign Office responsibility, were outside his province; but his advice, like that of Curzon, the Foreign Secretary, was not sought by Lloyd George, who equally disregarded their strictures on his private and therefore unwarranted policy of backing the Greeks against the Turks in a squalid little war of aggrandisement on the shores of Asia Minor.

" In the quarrel between these two nations," Frank Owen has commented, " Lloyd George was unreservedly on the side of the Greeks. . . . [He] believed that [they] were the rising power in the Eastern Mediterranean . . . and would soon possess all the most important islands in that sea, islands which would be the potential submarine bases of to-morrow and which lay along the flanks of Britain's own line of communication via Suez Canal to the Far East and Australia. Churchill once more (as in the case of Bolshevik Russia) took the opposite view." [1]

The Colonial Secretary's opposition was more realistic this time. He could never forget that the British Empire contained the largest Moslem community on earth. His heart was in his job of developing the new Arab states of Iraq, Transjordan and Palestine which might well collapse if the Prime Minister's improvident dabbling in the Turkish business went too far. Besides, Churchill respected the Turks as soldiers: to humiliate them, even in defeat, as a means of promoting the petty imperialist ambitions of Greece, might eventually plunge the Middle East into chaos. For Churchill had trouble enough already along the ill-marked, wild frontier country beyond Mosul where Iraq and Turkey met, the one district controlled by the R.A.F. where regular punitive action was still a matter of necessity.

Trenchard had warned him several times that here, in northern Iraq, stood the greatest obstacle to the security of the new Arab states. When Churchill asked early in 1922 for a military appreciation of the difficulties of defending Mosul against a possible Turkish invasion, the Chief of Air Staff prefaced his reply with a caution:

" The air is at present under the army generals in Iraq. I have to walk warily, otherwise they will say I am interfering in the running of the country."

Not until October, 1922, would the R.A.F. become formally responsible for Iraq's security, though its eight squadrons of aircraft and new armoured car columns, the latter led by General Tudor and manned, again for want of War Office co-operation, by many ex-members of the Black-and-Tans, had restored calm with a minimum of violence less than a year after the Cairo Conference. Would these units, inquired Churchill, be sufficient to contain a Turkish drive south on Mosul? Trenchard did not minimise the risks.

" There are two or three snags," he replied. " First, Mosul is so close to the French boundary that we might find ourselves bombing French territory, where the Turks are. Second, I do not fear a regular invasion half as much as I fear small parties of men getting into Mosul and various other towns in the neighbourhood and then suddenly rising and cutting the communications everywhere. This, instead of an organised army, is much the greater danger of the two at present—in spite of the War Office."

This danger, he feared, would grow if Lloyd George persisted in his pro-Greek flirtation. For in the highlands of Anatolia a ferment was quickening the martial ardour of those young Turks who in their thousands were rallying behind a new fighting leader. The Prime Minister, jaundiced by prejudice, might discount Kemal Ataturk as something of a military joker; Trenchard and Churchill did not. His very name was unfamiliar as yet to the British public; what it portended was realised in Whitehall by the shrewd and informed alone. The French, ever mindful of their national interests, saw in Kemal a potential ally worthy of secret support as he knit a youthful rabble into a liberating army. For, unlike Lloyd George with his dreams of a Hellenic revival, the French rightly assessed Kemal's ability and determination to drive out the Greek invaders and resurrect his country's fortunes. There could have been no sadder illustration of the rift in Anglo-French understanding, nor of the British Prime Minister's declining powers as a statesman.

2

Throughout the early summer of 1922, the fate of the Government seemed to preoccupy the politically well informed to the exclusion of all else. Even Ministers betrayed their uncertainty. Churchill, Guest, Worthington-Evans, Lord Lee, and Amery, with whom Trenchard had the most frequent dealings, behaved at times like men who had ceased caring about presenting a united front on policies with which, as individuals, they were seldom in tune.

The R.A.F. had its "year's guarantee" from Chamberlain; but, as Beatty hinted darkly to Trenchard more than once, political circumstances might change; and if they did, the guarantee might change with them. Through the special defence sub-committee appointed, as promised, to review Admiralty claims on the R.A.F., Beatty doggedly tried to turn the tables on Trenchard, who countered every move with unblinking mistrust for reasons which he expressed readily enough in this note to Roger Keyes:

" With regard to the 'fact' that the Admiralty have done all they could to make the existing separate air force organisation work, you must allow me to have my own opinion. Papers do not always interpret the spirit."

The spirit of the Sea Lords was against compromise or conciliation. Little headway was made in the sub-committee, yet the Cabinet showed no appreciable concern. Beatty's first set of proposals, at the end of March, indicated that he wanted a separate air force for the fleet in all but name. Trenchard sent them on to Churchill with the following comment:

" This means, boiled down, that the navy will decide on the type of machine; that after we have trained naval personnel as *naval personnel* they will fly and work for the navy afloat as naval personnel, promoted and rewarded and paid by the navy; which amounts to a separate Royal Air Service."

Churchill, the sub-committee chairman, privately agreed with him. Clearly, Beatty was demanding all or nothing. Trenchard whittled down the more excessive claims one by one; and the sterile discussion was adjourned to allow the two sides to deploy fresh arguments. Then an accident put off further exchanges for many weeks. Early in April, Churchill injured himself in a fall from his horse on the polo field at Hurlingham, where, in the months before marriage Trenchard had often played with the Minister in the early morning, reviving the furious enjoyment of their first encounter many years earlier on a dusty field in India. Now, it appeared, Churchill might never play again.

"One does not fall so lightly after forty as before," Trenchard reminded the invalid. "I hope it isn't the old shoulder that's bad again."

He was sorry for Churchill's sake, but glad of a respite from the interminable tetchiness of the Sea Lords. As he informed Churchill in the same note, he had "a hundred and one problems in connection with Iraq and Palestine," to wrestle with. For, owing to the prolonged obstructiveness of the War Office in Wilson's day, a host of administrative loose ends had now to be tied up at speed. It was doubly fortunate that the new C.I.G.S., the Earl of Cavan, was reasonably co-operative.

A short, rotund and cheerful man, Cavan accepted with relatively good grace the appointed role of the R.A.F. in the Middle East. Without overlooking army needs, he was content to ignore the murmurings of staff officers who still pined for an air force completely subordinate to the War Office. But time was pressing; the hand-over in Iraq, Palestine and Transjordan lay less than six months ahead; Trenchard would have all his work cut out.

Colleagues who knew him of old were perpetually amazed at his phenomenal alertness and energy. He seemed to be at the very peak of his powers, leavening his talent as an organiser with a tolerance for the foibles of weaker or less flexible colleagues that was wholly new. To the public, Trenchard was only a name among others far more illustrious in the military sphere; to the Press, it conjured up an enigmatical figure of controversy; in his own circle alone did he stand out like a giant, the incarnation of a new service spirit, and the unquestioned master of a new generation of airmen. Trenchard never lost sight of particular ends, the small as well as the great.

"It used to be said we were quite impossible socially," he remarked to Brooke-Popham, the first commandant of the new R.A.F. Staff College which was opened at Andover that spring. "It is not said nearly so much now."[2]

To the students who assembled to hear him, young men who, he hoped, might live to see an end of the inter-service jealousy which he had so far weathered well, he offered some advice from the heart.

" Don't always be biased in favour of developing the air at the expense of the other services. Think of all the possibilities of substituting one form of force for another. Weigh carefully the balance between cost and efficiency. Take a pride in economy. Learn to keep a sense of proportion over casualties. Acquire the habit of clearly and concisely stating a case—a habit I'm still struggling to acquire myself."

These were not maxims of perfection but the daily and instinctive rule of his own intense life, admired as such by the Treasury as well as the Air Ministry. Indeed, Sir Warren Fisher, the head of the Civil Service, had lately been staggered by an extreme example of Trenchard's willingness to chase an important detail to the ends of the earth and back in the interests of the R.A.F. They were finishing dinner one evening at Fisher's home when Trenchard said:

" I'd like to steal your cook."

He noticed Fisher's face instantly clouding over, and reflected that once or twice earlier his host had not been entirely himself.

" As you've practically stolen my cook from me already," said Fisher, " you're not exactly the right person to compliment me on her skill."

It appeared that Fisher's cook had been associating with a young airman. She was pregnant; her lover had left her in the lurch; and the unhappy girl had just given notice. Trenchard frowned, inquired the airman's name, and begged Fisher not to worry.

Next day the Air Member for Personnel was summoned and peremptorily requested to trace the culprit without delay.

" We're not running this air force for moral delinquents," said Trenchard. " Bring this man to me."

But the airman was very far away indeed, having been posted to Iraq with one of the latest R.A.F. drafts; the flight-lieutenant who informed Trenchard of this drew attention to the inconvenient financial implications. Treasury regulations were quite strict, forbidding the repatriation at public expense of any officer or man, except on compassionate leave, until his tour of service ended.

" Cable for his return at once," came the unexpected rejoinder. " I want a daily report on this. Leave the money side of the business to me."

So every morning for more than a month an officer entered Trenchard's office with a movement bulletin.

" He's due in at Port Said to-day. . . . I'm afraid, sir, that the troop-ship's been delayed at Malta. . . . He should be off Gibraltar now. . . . He'll be in to-morrow, sir; and we've made arrangements to escort him from Southampton. . . . Do you want him brought straight here, sir? "

" Send him to me as soon as he arrives," said Trenchard finally.

When the airman was marched in, pallid and flustered, Trenchard's secretary, Marson, prepared himself for the wrath to come. Yet, as he sat straining his ears in the outer office, only a dull murmur reached him. Not once did Trenchard raise his voice above its booming conversational pitch. The airman left, none the worse for wear, after an obviously one-sided interview which lasted perhaps twenty minutes. It seemed a ridiculously long way to have come, at an exorbitant price, for a piece of fatherly advice.

Beyond hinting that he had administered "the mother and father of all good tellings off," Trenchard did not mention the incident again. But among the junior officers in the personnel branch, there was anxious speculation. Trenchard might have plucked an erring youngster out of Iraq, brushing aside Treasury rules which others were expected to obey with scrupulous fidelity; but the defendant, as far as could be discovered, had been awarded nothing more drastic than a week's leave to make an honest woman of Fisher's cook before being sent to a home station. What had come over the Chief of Air Staff? More to the point, who was going to foot the bill? For Trenchard had scornfully refused to confuse passionate with compassionate reasons to account for the airman's recall.

Gordon Bond, one of the junior officers concerned, watched his salary slip with marked trepidation for three months. As the person who had cabled to Iraq in the first place, he was willing to wager that the fare would be docked from his salary. There were no deductions. And Charles Portal, a more senior colleague, who later rose to match Trenchard for efficiency as Chief of Air Staff, was less mystified by what had happened. With more experience of Trenchard's mentality and methods, he argued that the case was not necessarily evidence of a moral reformer at work.

" Of course he won't ask the Treasury to pay. So you, Bond, needn't worry. Nobody in this branch will have to find a penny."

" But, damn it all, somebody's got to."

" Yes," said Portal. " But I guarantee he's already put his hand in his own pocket without a word to Fisher or anyone."

" But why? Isn't his humanitarian instinct running away with his judgment? "

" Humanitarian instinct my foot! He's just investing in his own air force." [3]

Portal was right. Not for the first or last time, Trenchard quietly took it on himself to insure against the possible cost of someone else's private folly. The good name of the R.A.F. was beyond price to him. Only on rare occasions such as these, when an individual came between Trenchard and his ideals, did stray witnesses discover, with a shock of astonishment that would have brought an understanding smile to the lips of men like Baring who knew him through and through, that the Chief of Air Staff, being one of nature's aristocrats, had his own eccentric but wholly admirable code of honour. The same significant discovery had been made more recently by Lawrence of Arabia.

Towards the end of 1921, Lawerence completed his mission in Transjordan, handed over to Philby, his successor, and returned to the Colonial Office. Churchill was not keen to part with him while danger loomed in the Middle East; but Lawrence, whom Trenchard already regarded as one of the R.A.F.'s least recognised benefactors for his contribution to the success of the 1921 Cairo Conference, insisted that his public life was almost over. Early in January, 1922, he wrote to Trenchard as follows:

" You know I am trying to leave Winston on 1st March. Then I want about two months to myself, and then I'd like to join the R.A.F.—in the ranks of course. I can't do this without your help. I'm thirty-three and not skilled in the sense you want. It's odd being too old for the job I want when hitherto I've always been too young for the job I did. . . .

" You'll wonder what I'm at. The matter is that since I was sixteen I've been writing: never satisfying myself technically but steadily getting better. My last book on Arabia is nearly good. I see the sort of subject I need in the beginning of your force . . . and the best place to see a thing from is the ground. It wouldn't 'write' from the officer level. . . .

" It's an odd request this, hardly proper perhaps, but it may be one of the exceptions you make sometimes. It is asking you to use your influence to get me past the Recruiting Officer! Apologies for making it. If you say 'no' I'll be more amused than hurt."

Trenchard understood, but was not quite satisfied. He had not forgotten Lawrence's remark in Cairo that he would enlist as an ordinary airman, or not at all. The writing business was evidently no more than a plausible excuse; so they met to talk it out. Even then Trenchard refrained from probing too deeply, doubting whether

the highly articulate Lawrence himself could have found words to
describe the compulsions that forced him, like a modern anchorite,
to seek the shade of a decent obscurity. They met again several
times, and with each meeting their mutual respect ripened into
tolerance and lasting affection. Trenchard detected, without pre-
suming to judge, the definite streak of conceit in Lawrence's character
which accounted for his extravagant mock-humility. Yet Lawrence
had humour, untainted by self-pity.

" He was the sort of man," Trenchard told this author, " who,
on entering a roomful of people, would have contrived to be sick on
the spot had everyone stood up to applaud him. Yet if, on entering
the same room, nobody stirred or showed the faintest sign of
recognition, Lawrence might well have reacted by standing on his
head."

The reluctant exhibitionist, with his fatal knack of "backing into
the limelight," was known to Trenchard long before they met in
Cairo. He had heard senior R.A.F. officers indignantly describe how
Lawrence, in 1919, injected an element of burlesque into a Paris
Conference reception by standing guard at the top of a marble
staircase in Arab dress, ostentatiously unrolling yards of toilet paper
until the feet of the statesmen and their minions below were buried
in it. However psychiatrists or conventional people might have
explained this gesture, Trenchard's response on hearing of it was to
roar with laughter. He was disappointed not to have seen the looks
of embarrassed bafflement as Lawrence nonchalantly descended,
after the last roll had uncoiled itself. There was enough of the rebel
left in Trenchard to relish bizarre jokes of the kind.

Lawrence might well become a liability to the R.A.F. if his
exhibitionist impulses were not discouraged; yet Trenchard thought
less of the risk than of the inherent qualities of greatness which, for
complex public and contrary personal reasons, Lawrence now wished
to disown. He had frequently referred in conversation to Britain's
"betrayal of the Arabs"; but the broken wartime pledges had been
partly redeemed, on his own admission, by the creation of Iraq and
Transjordan. Lawrence's conscience was easier, though his contempt
for the machinations of France remained as sharp as a needle. He
confessed to Trenchard that he was partly trying to atone for his
country's misdeeds, partly striving also to escape from his own inner
conflicts, as an anonymous cog in the R.A.F. machine. Trenchard,
who in the words of his closest friend had a gift for "smelling out a
man's soul,"[4] did not disdain as lesser mortals would have done to
comfort this noble but strangely warped spirit.

" With regard to your personal point," he replied by return of post, " I understand it fully—and you too, I think. I am prepared to do all you ask me, if you will tell me for how long you want to join; but I'm afraid I couldn't do it without mentioning it to Winston and my own Secretary of State, and then whether it could be kept secret I do not know. . . . What country do you want to serve in, and how? I would make things as easy as anything."

Lawrence, however, was not yet mentally prepared for a scene with Churchill, who had become too attached to him both as a friend and an adviser to release him without a struggle. Geddes was still stalking through Whitehall brandishing his axe; the Colonial Office was as much under his scrutiny as other ministries; and the strain had begun to tell on Churchill's customary buoyancy. Trenchard let the matter rest until 2nd July, when Lawrence raised it again of his own accord.

" Winston has agreed to let me go after next Tuesday. I have not told him what I want to do next as, since I first wrote to you, Geddes has happened and may make impossible for you what you then thought possible. If there is still a chance of it may I come and see you? "

Lawrence spent the following Wednesday night at Trenchard's home, discussing his future in the ranks of a service which he admired as the most important historical accident to emerge from the First World War. He had used the air force sparingly himself in Transjordan to heal local breaches of the peace which, under the old system of military occupation, might easily have engulfed the new kingdom. He had tested its flexible power and had liked it. He asked now for nothing more than a chance to serve "on the ground floor" under an assumed name.

Midway through August his wish was granted.

" Winston very agreeable," he wrote. " Hope your lord was the same."

Churchill, grieved and mystified as he was, did not oppose the departure of this sympathetic but unfathomable personality who had once declared with a slow smile that when his time came to leave "all you will see of me is a small cloud of dust on the horizon."

Guest, the Secretary of State for Air, followed Churchill's lead, enabling Trenchard to tell his most distinguished and unsuitable recruit that "my lord was very agreeable," too.

In a bare barrack room at the Uxbridge R.A.F. depot, a/c352087 John Hume Ross began life anew towards the end of August, 1922, having promised Trenchard to be of good behaviour, to drop the project of writing a book about the air force, and to further his own avowed aim of "helping to build your new service from below." This had become a standing joke between them; yet Trenchard knew that in a weirdly mystical way Lawrence accepted the R.A.F. as his own child by adoption. There was a looser, more practical sense in which Trenchard, as the omnipotent "Father of the Air Force," could recognise how much Lawrence had already done to save it—and be grateful for this risky way of proving his gratitude.[5]

3

Relaxing on holiday in Scotland at the end of August, 1922, Trenchard sometimes caught himself wondering whether Lawrence yet understood to what he had condemned himself. To a creature of such sensibility and intelligence, barrack-room life and the drudgery of drills and fatigues might bring swift, salutary disillusionment. On the other hand, Lawrence's will to escape the responsibility of living up to his legendary and distorted public image seemed to Trenchard far stronger than his will to go on living at all.

The R.A.F. was no refuge for the socially disabled, unless these had something useful to offer in exchange. It was partly a measure of Trenchard's insight and breadth of mind that he could afford to humour Lawrence and yet go on thinking about him. It was also a measure of the R.A.F.'s improved status. The early summer of 1922 had seen a further swing of sentiment in favour of a bigger air force. The hearings of the special sub-committee appointed in the late spring, after the service debates at Westminster, to review the air defence of Britain, had surpassed Trenchard's hopes. The fact that Britain, compared with France, had sunk inside three years to the level of a third-class power in the skies was considered a reproach to national pride.

" The only question still giving me a lot of trouble," Trenchard wrote in mid-May to Ellington, his new Middle East commander, "is our relations with the navy." This was hardly news, of course; but the tone of the letter suggested that Trenchard was enjoying himself in an atmosphere singularly free from strife.

" The 'Air Menace' sub-committee of the C.I.D. have also recommended an increased establishment at home," the letter added. " That is all to the good."

In June, 1922, when Trenchard delivered his fourth annual

address to his ex-bomber pilots of Nancy days, he was in an unusually jovial mood.

" There was much in the papers a few days ago about the air force and in walking down the Strand I saw many posters," he said. " We were not strong enough, the critics stated, and the R.A.F. was not big enough. And I rather walked on tiptoes with a feeling that whatever might be the controversies of the future, at any rate, the air force had been formed. . . ."

His current letters to overseas commanders, encouraging, criticising, cajoling and wryly reflecting on happenings at home, conveyed a similar sense of cheerfulness. His worries tended to be reasonably little ones.

" The Northcliffe Press have been trying to draw a red herring across the track by saying that the way should be clear to increase civil aviation," he informed Ellington, for instance, at the end of June.

" I think that is finally scotched, but it has been very nice to be abused as 'an old-fashioned military officer.' The army do not think I am old-fashioned, but rather that I am a new air crank. I am having a difficult time because in spite of the increase they'll probably give me, they insist at the same time on cutting down everything that is essential. . . ."

The "Air Menace" sub-committee had set to work with a seriousness all the more diverting to Trenchard who privately dismissed the threat from France as a political chimera of the first magnitude. It was a highly useful one none the less. For the Cabinet's determination to increase the size of the R.A.F. offset the far more realistic "naval threat" to the R.A.F.'s integrity. For weeks on end the sub-committee pored over the difficulties of repelling air attacks by the nearest potential enemy, France. Earlier Air Staff papers were reconsidered more carefully. And what the other service chiefs had formerly repudiated as heresy was adopted now, in the light of French air expansion, as common prudence.

When Trenchard was finally asked, in May, 1922, to submit a fresh home defence programme which would leave Britain less vulnerable he did not fall into the trap of overtaxing the Government's new-found willingness to strengthen his hand.

" There is a big agitation on here, the real object of which is a trifle obscure but the ostensible objective of which is to increase the existing air force by a good number of squadrons," he informed Borton in Baghdad at the beginning of July. "Of course, everybody who has an axe to grind is taking part in it with a view to furthering their own ends—the armament firms, the Admiralty (very active), the Press, and various retired admirals, field-marshals, etc. . . .

" The army say they would sooner have the Air to deal with than the Admiralty which, although it may be a left-handed compliment, is undoubtedly true. . . . There is now no question of breaking up the force. There is bound to be some sort of settlement. . . . Time is on our side."

Deliberately playing down his demands, Trenchard proposed that the present "small nucleus of 14 squadrons, with power to expand to 20 on the outbreak of war" should be raised to a basic 23, with reserves in hand to expand to 50 if necessary. Provided this modest programme was spread over a short period of years, the taxpayer need not be put upon, nor would he be compelled to pare down training or running costs which, he pointed out, were already near rock-bottom. Such a force would *not* render the cities of Britain immune from air attack. On the other hand, if linked with a bomber counter-offensive, it "should prevent damage to the point of paralysis."

Not unnaturally the Cabinet wanted to have it both ways. On 3rd August, 1922, the day before Parliament rose for the summer recess, Lloyd George told the Commons that his Government had approved Air Ministry plans for a "force of 500 machines at an increased cost of £2 million per annum," without prejudice to any further expansion if national security warranted it. He consoled M.P.s who objected to military extravagance that nearly half the money would be found "by economies in the estimates of the Air Ministry."

The Government was giving with one hand only to take away with the other, a likelihood on which Trenchard had wisely budgeted. The essence of thrift, as he practised it, was that quality must never be sacrificed to quantity. That was why he had opposed the sub-committee's recommendation of a large increase in immediate strength, arguing with a conviction born of wartime experience that numerical inferiority to any enemy, real or hypothetical, was preferrable to bigness for its own sake. In the case of France he believed that "the balance would be to a large extent restored by our superior enterprise, *élan* and technical efficiency," though this meant less to Lloyd George than the attractive political bait of two new squadrons for the price of one.

The popular Press did not bite, however, as the Prime Minister would have wished. The Northcliffe newspapers launched a venomous attack on the Air Ministry for squandering public money to little purpose, moving C. G. Grey, the editor of *The Aeroplane*, to comment:

" It is a curious thing that *The Times* and the *Daily Mail* should follow the lead of the *Daily Mirror* in attacking the Air Ministry. It is known that at the present time Lord Northcliffe is not competent to look after his newspapers, and this sudden change in their attitude suggests irresistibly that Lord Rothermere is stepping into his brother's shoes. An attack on Air Ministry policy to-day is in effect an attack on Sir Hugh Trenchard, for the Air Council is very wisely following his policy. And such an attack by Lord Rothermere would be perfectly natural."

It was a pity for the sake of truth that Gray's words were addressed almost entirely to the converted. Beyond the small, charmed circle of *The Aeroplane's* readers, his voice was virtually inaudible.

" Among other mares'-nests, the Northcliffe Press have found that they want to get rid of me," Trenchard wrote in the summer to Rawlinson, the Commander-in-Chief, India. " I don't mind, for I'm having quite good fun and the air force is becoming stronger and stronger and doing more and more work."

The one person he had most reason to fear was Beatty, and Beatty had not been playing a waiting game for fun. Having joined in the clamorous chorus for a bigger R.A.F., the Admiralty changed its tune in August, 1922, as soon as Lloyd George had announced the terms of R.A.F. expansion. Beatty insisted on an immediate improvement in the practical service which his flag officers had been getting from squadrons with the fleet; and his hectoring drew a stinging reply from Trenchard. What cause had Beatty to complain that pilots were being constantly switched to other duties when, despite recent reductions in the number of R.A.F. junior officers, the Admiralty had so far allowed only seven naval officers to volunteer for flying duties, and had "just announced their intention of retiring three of these? " Was this evidence of a desire to co-operate or to kill?

Trenchard went on leave in August, 1922, bored by the repetitiveness of Beatty's tactics but otherwise in excellent spirits. The past six months had so improved his prospects that he could actually afford to forget the tiresome Beatty and muse instead on the self-inflicted trials of T. E. Lawrence at Uxbridge.

The cable urgently recalling him to London in mid-September brought him sharply to his senses. The newspapers and mail from London always reached Argyllshire very late; and though he could

not break his habit of following from afar happenings that interested
him, the sudden turn for the worse of the crisis that had long been
brewing in the Middle East took him unawares. Trenchard realised
its gravity, though he never imagined that it would drag Britain to
the brink of war with Turkey in a matter of days. In that at least
he was not alone.

Political historians agree that the Anglo-Turkish crisis of
September, 1922, culminating in the so-called "Chanak Incident,"
was the direct cause of the Coalition Government's collapse a few
weeks later. Yet none, so far, seems to have noticed that the R.A.F.
barely escaped being tipped out with the debris when Bonar Law
became Prime Minister. Such a turn of the wheel of fate appeared
unthinkable in mid-September; yet it was with an uneasy sense of
foreboding that Trenchard hurried back from Scotland to the Air
Ministry.

The strain on ministerial loyalties of pursuing two incompatible
lines of policy towards the military adventure of the Greeks in
Turkey has already been briefly referred to. In spite of mounting
evidence to the contrary, Lloyd George persisted in his delusion that
the Greeks, being better soldiers than the War Office or Winston
Churchill would admit, were bound to recover from early set-backs
and defeat Kemal in the end, thereby stimulating false hopes in
Athens of British recognition and aid. Such complacency would have
been more understandable, perhaps, in 1920, when Venizelos was
in office. Indeed, it had then suited the convenience of other interested powers besides Britain to connive at the Greek landings
on the mainland of Asia Minor. It was quite inexplicable in 1922,
with Venizelos in exile and the reactionary King Constantine
restored to the Greek throne, an object of baleful suspicion to France
and to liberal opinion in Britain. The incompetence of the Greek
generals in the field had meanwhile served Kemal well. For Lloyd
George's Cabinet colleagues felt less disposed than ever to share his
absurdly high estimate of Greece as potential master of the East
Mediterranean.

The French had devious reasons of their own for secretly backing
and supplying the Turks. On military grounds alone, they questioned
whether the Greeks could win, single-handed, and enforce the
humiliating Peace Treaty of Sèvres. Under its terms, Greece had
been allotted eastern Thrace, including Gallipoli; but the treaty
itself, providing "spheres of interest" for the other Allies, had
become a legal fiction as the Kemalist uprising spread and the ill-led
Greek Army was thrown back on the defensive.

A politician of Lloyd George's experience should have realised
that the British people were no more eager than the French Government to fight for such a cause; but he was too engrossed in his
efforts to harmonise conflicting rivalries nearer home, in Europe,
during the first half of 1922. Even there the tide had turned against
him. His earlier failure at Cannes was repeated at Genoa, and again
in London shortly before the Middle East crisis came to a head.
Moving on from abortive conference to conference, Lloyd George
discovered too late that he was helpless against the intransigence
and mistrust of France.

On 26th August, 1922, Kemal's liberating army forced its
attention on the world by routing the Greeks in Anatolia. The only
pitched battle of the campaign was followed by the pursuit of a
broken and demoralised enemy to the coast. The triumphant Turks
burnt Smyrna to the ground, slaughtering untold thousands of its
Christian inhabitants. By the end of August, Kemal's men were on
the march towards Constantinople. Tension mounted in the
chancelleries of Europe, for the way to Constantinople was
theoretically barred. Strips of land on either side of the Gallipoli
Straits had been declared neutral zones under the Sèvres Treaty;
nominal detachments of British, French and Italian troops stood
guard, a thin and inadequate barrier between the approaching
Turks and their capital. Having publicly repudiated the Sèvres
Treaty as an insult to Turkish honour, Kemal seemed in no mood to
bargain; either the Allies must let him pass or be driven like the
Greeks into the sea.

This was the situation which caused Lloyd George to summon
Trenchard and the other Chiefs of Staff for emergency consultations
with the Cabinet during the week-end of 15th-17th September. The
Turks by then had halted not far from the barbed wire perimeter
enclosing the Allied positions at Chanak, on the southern shore.
Two or three days earlier, the Allied High Commissioners in
Constantinople had warned Kemal not to violate the neutral zone;
now Lloyd George decided to reinforce that warning, leaving to
Churchill the drafting of a note tantamount to an ultimatum. At the
same time, the major powers were informed of Britain's resolve to
stand fast at Chanak; the Dominions were also notified and invited
to assist in the event of war.

The full weight of the crisis descended on an unsuspecting British
public within twenty-four hours, when a more general statement,
also prepared by Churchill with the aid of Lord Birkenhead, was
released to the Press. Unfortunately (and largely through the

slothful habits of the Whitehall week-end) this news reached the Dominions before the official notes reached the heads of governments. The righteous anger of the Canadians and Australians in particular introduced an unnecessary diplomatic complication. Only New Zealand and Newfoundland overlooked the indignity of being drawn into an unwanted war without being formally consulted, both offering unconditional support.

The Dardanelles at the time of the Chanak crisis, 1922

For Trenchard, who had arrived in London by the overnight train from Glasgow about dawn on the Friday morning, that mid-September week-end was the most perplexing he had known since the Armistice. One of his unwritten promises to Churchill in early 1919 had been that in any emergency, the R.A.F. would provide at least one squadron fully mobilised for action at twenty-four hours' notice. Two composite squadrons at home, and a third in Egypt, were alerted; and on the following Monday morning, Trenchard informed the Cabinet that the units were standing by, awaiting movement orders. Churchill at least seemed suitably impressed.

" The Cabinet meet daily and I attend," Trenchard recorded in a private note that week. " Discussions are chiefly on the force necessary to hold our vital points. I don't think we shall get any help from our Allies. . . . Arrangements to send three squadrons, one from Egypt and two from England have been approved. The *Argus* filled up and sailed yesterday."

Trenchard's view, which he justified orally to the Cabinet, was that Chanak could and should be held. Beatty, for once, backed him completely. The First Sea Lord was confident that the *Iron Duke* and other warships could keep the Straits open; and the Chief of Air Staff was emphatic that the two main roads forming Kemal's sole supply route from Anatolia could be rendered impassable from the air. Everything hinged on the resolution and sagacity of General Harington, the British Army Commander on the spot, outnumbered and beleaguered as he was.

The Chiefs of Staff were united on the strategic essentials; but, under cross-examination, they betrayed divergencies of opinion on tactical questions which greatly annoyed Lloyd George. Hankey, with his imperturbable appetite for such details, noticed the Prime Minister's eyes flash with ill-concealed fury when Cavan, Beatty, and Trenchard submitted plans which either contradicted or duplicated one another. According to Hankey, the Prime Minister broke up one discussion which had degenerated into an inter-service argument.

" Gentlemen," he said in effect, " I'm tired of these squabbles. We all know the navy has to protect the Straits, the army to reinforce Chanak, and the air force to cover both. It's your job to tell us how. Come back when you have an agreed plan."

As Secretary of the Cabinet, Hankey had to stay behind, though he longed to join the Chiefs of Staff. Here was the very solution which he had occasionally dreamed about. Lloyd George, of all people, had seized an opportunity born of crisis to make the service heads individually and collectively responsible for military decisions taken in common. Ever since late 1919, when Trenchard had first suggested the need of a "square ring" in which he could meet the First Sea Lord and the C.I.G.S. on equal terms, Hankey had wondered how or when this could best be broached. Now the Prime Minister, in a moment of inspired bad temper, had solved the riddle, setting a valuable precedent.

In what appeared to the Secretary of the Cabinet "a remarkably short time," the trio reappeared with a concerted plan. Each had offered concessions, and the resulting compromise was impressively workmanlike. Trenchard, who described the bargaining process to Hankey afterwards, was as pleased as the Cabinet Secretary with the implications of an unforeseen development rich in promise for the future.

The present still hung heavy with suspense; war with Turkey seemed inevitable; and on 20th September, Trenchard wrote as follows to Harington, the man on whom had fallen the burden of decision for starting or averting it.

" You are having a lot of worry and I don't want to add to it, but I want to tell you that all squadrons are under your command and the War Office. I propose to place the wing that is with you under the Middle East area so that Ellington can come and help you with advice on any situation if you wish it. All supplies and personnel and equipment will be supplied from the Air Ministry direct. . . . Our ambition is to give you a free hand yet free you from worry.

" The feeling at home is that you are the right man in the right spot and that you have done good work. This has seldom been said when once the show had begun and therefore it is a feather in your cap of no mean order."

If Harington felt the weight of his responsibility, his cool manner did not show it.

" This is the rummiest sort of war I have ever seen," he replied. " It is mixed up with diplomats of all nations, soldiers and sailors, Greeks and Turks, infidels of every kind and Bolsheviks, and the town is a seething mass of the dirtiest looking devils you ever saw. . . . I am thoroughly revelling in it so long as I can only get through without any trouble. It is great fun having an Allied force under your command, two parts of which will do anything but ally, but it isn't the fault of the soldiers, poor devils. . . . Thank you so much for all your help. I will do my best to look after the units you are sending me."

The political atmosphere at home, so far as it touched relations with France, was less healthy. It reeked of mutual distrust. Citizens in both lands perceived at last with unmistakable clarity how deep was the underlying crisis of confidence between their respective governments. Lloyd George, the self-appointed apostle of peace, who for the past four years, at conference after conference, had preached moderation to the French in their treatment of the defeated and defaulting Germans, was exposed in his true colours. The Chanak impasse was something of which France desired no part; and few Britons could blame her.

Italy was equally reluctant to fight, a fact noted by the hard-pressed Curzon, who was exerting all his negotiating skill in Paris to patch up an outward semblance of Allied unity; it was to small purpose. For Harington next reported from Constantinople that French and Italian detachments were being moved out of Chanak. As these amounted to no more than a token battalion, the British commander confessed to Trenchard that he was not unduly concerned.

To Major-General Marden, his local commander, Harington sent this directive on 19th September:

" You should hold Chanak as long as possible with the forces I have available. In my opinion, in view of the French withdrawing from Chanak, Kemal will challenge British policy there. In all probability he will stop to reflect, if you hold him there with naval support."

Harington's dispatches to the Cabinet reflected the unruffled mind of a born diplomat as capable of reading his adversary's intentions as he was of concealing the disadvantages of his own precarious military position. Convinced that Kemal would not risk a full-scale conflict and thus forfeit all his gains, Harington avoided provoking the Turkish forces surrounding the Chanak perimeter, while advising their leader against violating the neutral zone.

" Neutral zone? " echoed the Turkish leader in one of his replies. He did not recognise its existence. Nevertheless, Kemal did not advance, reinforcing his front-line troops instead, and paying Harington the compliment of answering his messages civilly.

By the end of September, British troop-ships and their naval escorts were disembarking soldiers and airmen under the very noses of the Turks; yet Kemal still chose to wait. In Paris, Curzon had meanwhile been obliged to accept French and Italian proposals for peaceful arbitration: these included restoring most of eastern Thrace to Turkey and evacuating Constantinople as soon as normal conditions permitted. A joint note to this effect, from which the former claims of Greece were tactfully omitted, was sent to Kemal, together, with an Allied invitation to a conference at Mudania. The Turkish leader slept on it for several nights, an agonising delay which seemed to suggest an arrogant certitude that time was on his side, not on the Allies'.

In London, Churchill, who was now presiding over daily meetings of the Chiefs of Staff, grew short of patience. The arrival at Chanak of British reinforcements had altered the disadvantageous balance of strength. If Kemal attacked, the R.A.F. would command the air without even having to fight for it, while the army's tanks and artillery, supported by naval guns off-shore, would more than cancel out the enemy's numerical superiority. Churchill's aggressive line did not commend itself to the majority of his Cabinet colleagues. Nor did the service chiefs relish his inconvenient habit, already rooted, of rousing them at dead of night to discuss the latest cables from Harington as though the fate of Britain depended on their going without sleep.

The first time this happened, Trenchard was telephoned at home. It was past one o'clock in the morning; and he had not long been in bed. Replacing the receiver, he began rather grumpily to dress. Lady Trenchard, fearing that some very startling development must have occurred, said to her husband:

" How are you going to get to Downing Street? "

Trenchard looked at her in a quandary. Until that moment, he had not given the matter any thought. He seldom used an official car for routine business; his habitual thrift reckoned without major upheavals of this sort in the small hours. Normally he travelled across London by taxi, though Scotland Yard disliked the practice. More than once a detective had returned his brief-case with solicitous expressions of hope that nothing vital had been stolen. But taxis at Potter's Bar were not easily raised after midnight. There seemed nothing for it but to accept his wife's offer of a lift to Downing Street in her rather ancient Ford saloon. For Trenchard, believing that there were too many fools on the road, did not drive himself.

She was soon wishing that she had allowed herself more time to dress. The meeting of the Chiefs of Staff seemed to go on interminably, and she grew steadily more chilled sitting at the wheel of the draughty car waiting for her husband to reappear. His secretary, Marson, came out twice and tried in vain to coax her inside No. 10. She assured him stoically that she was happier where she was. In one sense, this was true. For, in her haste, she had pulled on a long, leather driving-coat over her nightdress and negligee, wound a scarf round her neck and covered her head with a cap belonging to one of her sons. Her hair was in pigtails which hung down over her back. About four o'clock, when Marson reappeared to say that the conference was likely to last another hour at least, she reconsidered her spartan decision. The possibility of being recognised would be less distressing in the long run than the probability of catching pneumonia by staying put.

Lady Trenchard sat huddled by the fire in an ante-room, trying to look inconspicuous. None of the messengers, and only Marson among the secretaries, appeared to know who she was or even to notice her odd attire. After what felt an age, sounds of chairs being pushed back came from the Cabinet room. Through a window near her, the grey light of day filtered coldly in. A door opened, and Churchill approached looking fresh and unspeakably cheerful. He recognised her instantly.

" Lady Trenchard, what are you doing here? " she heard him say.

" I might ask you that," she replied. " Is it war—or only an excuse for keeping hard-worked men who get up early out of their beds—not to mention their wives? "

Churchill smiled ruefully.

" It's not quite as bad as all that."

" Well, what's the explanation—insomnia perhaps? "

Churchill accepted the dig with a courteous bow, turned to Trenchard and said with mock reproach:

" Boom, she's attacking me."[6]

Later that morning, the Chief of Air Staff arranged for a late duty driver to pick him up at home whenever necessary. The night might not be the ideal time for conducting strategic exercises, but neither, he believed, should it be held sacred to the domestic comforts of the service heads.

Churchill's reading of the military omens grew increasingly sanguine as the crisis lengthened. When, for instance, it was deduced from misleading intelligence reports that Kemal would probably attack the Chanak position before the end of September, Churchill advocated taking a perilously strong line and carried all his colleagues, except Curzon, with him. On 29th September, Harington was instructed to issue an ultimatum, warning Kemal that unless the Turks withdrew from their forward positions "all forces at our disposal, naval, military and air, will open fire. . . ."

Harington, pleading for the right to use his own discretion, turned a blind eye to the order, thereby justifying himself as a classic exception to Lloyd George's favourite contention that war was too serious a business to be left to the generals.

" I was convinced," Harington wrote afterwards in his official dispatch, " that I was acting in the interests of peace and in accordance with what I felt would be the wishes of H.M. Government in withholding the warning, as I was alone in a position to judge the situation on the spot."

Owing to the time-lag between messages from London and replies from Chanak, the outlook on this occasion appeared darker than it really was. Again early in October, when all available evidence suggested that Harington's bluff had failed, the Prime

Minister displayed the same courage which had won Trenchard's esteem in the far graver crisis of March, 1918. War with Turkey seemed unavoidable now; and in those last hours of almost unbearable suspense, Lloyd George and Churchill upheld Trenchard's judgment against that of Cavan, who doubted whether the forces at Chanak, supported by three R.A.F. squadrons, would be able to stop Kemal. A troop-ship laden with airmen and supplies was then on its way to Iraq, where Air-Marshal Sir John Salmond would assume command on 22nd October; the C.I.G.S. urged that it should be diverted to reinforce the ground troops at Chanak. Trenchard retorted that Salmond had his own "Turkish problem" above Mosul where unrest was spreading like the plague.

" For a time it was touch and go," Trenchard informed Salmond later, " with the army saying they could not stand a day with the Turks. I argued strongly that we should not run away but fight if they tried to advance, as the air could be relied on to stop them."

The Cabinet leaned towards Trenchard's view but humoured Cavan's fears. In the end the R.A.F. troop-ship Braemar Castle, was ordered to Chanak. The airmen disembarked and remained at Harington's disposal until further notice. The British commander had meanwhile succeeded in arranging truce talks; and early in October, at Mudania, Harington came face to face with the Kemal's envoy, the inscrutably calm General Ismet Pasha, while the bloated corpses of Greek soldiers could be seen and heard, slapping against the supporting piers at the water's edge beneath the open window of the conference room. Harington's fellow commanders, French and Italian, were content merely to look on; and there followed, in his own phrase, "days of incessant work in a network of political intrigue," the scheming of M. Franklin Bouillon in particular, a diplomat of dubious principles who had already secured French recognition of the Kemal régime, almost wrecking his efforts to save the peace.

On 9th October, Harington felt that he could go no further in seeking terms honourable to both sides. Before entering the conference room next morning an urgent signal from Marden was handed to him. It stated that the Turks had begun to envelop the Chanak positions. Was it in order to open fire in self-defence? Harington wired back permission, but deferred zero hour until the afternoon. He then joined Ismet Pasha to offer him a last chance of climbing down. The drama of that encounter between them lives on in Harington's vivid account:

" The scene is before me now—that awful room—only an oil

lamp. I can see Ismet's Chief of Staff—he never took his eyes off
me. I paced one side of the room, saying that I must have that
area (Chanak) and would agree to nothing less. Ismet pacing up
the other side saying that he would not agree. Then, quite suddenly,
he said, '*J'accepte.*' I was never so surprised in my life! "

Harington at once countermanded the order to open fire. His
message reached Chanak an hour and fifteen minutes before the pre-
arranged time limit expired. That afternoon, and far into the night,
he worked with Ismet on the details of the Pact of Mudania. He
had not erred in believing that nobody wanted war; it was not his
concern that people at home were loudly baying for the political
blood of those who had almost caused one. The crisis was over; the
R.A.F. contingent withdrew. Before sailing on to Iraq, however, its
thousand men marched through Constantinople with bayonets fixed
and standard flying, watched by large, undemonstrative crowds.
Their commanding officer led the way, proud of their bearing, until
a stray comment in a loud English feminine voice assailed his ears
from a balcony:

" A smart lot, aren't they? But how in God's name did the
Portuguese in those adorable blue uniforms get mixed up in this
mess? " [7]

It was the old sad story of non-recognition; and it pricked the
commanding officer's elation.

4

Trenchard was not surprised by the subsequent post-mortem on
Chanak. Since it was the prerogative of politicians to score off each
other's mistakes, he did not seriously doubt at first that Lloyd George
would ride out the storm of abuse unscathed. The Government,
he knew, had much to answer for; its opponents, he wrongly
supposed, were rather late with their denunciations. In general
terms of insincerity, he found it hard to choose between them.

Cleaning up after the crisis kept all the service chiefs busy, and
Trenchard knew no more than his colleagues about the inner
workings of the Conservative revolt which presently split the
Coalition and forced a General Election. The details need not detain
us; except in broad outline, they form no part of this narrative.

Public relief at the peaceful settlement of the Chanak crisis was
profound; but its effect on Lloyd George's political enemies was to
trigger off an explosion of discontent, the causes of which had been

accumulating for months. The resolve to have done with the
ministerial clique which had misruled for too long in their name
was not confined to Conservative back benchers. Junior Ministers
like Amery and Baldwin, who resented being treated like errand boys
by the triumvirate of Lloyd George, Birkenhead and Churchill,
sympathised with the rank and file for whom the "Irish Surrender,"
the alleged trafficking in honours, and the dead weight of taxation
in aid of policies which had neither eased economic stagnation at
home nor prevented crises abroad, represented a betrayal of Tory
principles.

A new Party Leader was the first necessity. Chamberlain was too
loyal, Balfour too remote, and both too firmly under the mesmeric
influence of "The Goat," as Lloyd George was irreverently called.
Had not the pair of them agreed to spring a General Election in
November so that the life of the Coalition could be prolonged?

Bonar Law was the only possible saviour of the Party in view.
He had returned to Britain and to spasmodic attendance at Westminster during the previous summer; and at the height of the
Chanak crisis he had attacked the Government in a letter to *The Times*
for acting as though the British were still "the policemen of the
world." Yet Bonar Law now hung back irresolutely, reluctant to
press his claims and seemingly uncertain whether killing the Coalition
was worth the risk of perhaps fatally splitting the Conservative
leadership. Bonar Law's pensive air of indecision dismayed his
backers far more than any doubts they may have entertained about
his health.

The factors which ultimately removed his hesitancy have been
exhaustively discussed in numerous books of memoirs. Ministers,
Party managers, Press lords, friends and family advisers have either
given or taken credit for persuading him, almost against his will, to
appear at the famous Carlton Club meeting on 19th October, 1922,
and wrest the party reins from the hands of its nominal leaders.
When it came to his moment of personal decision, Bonar Law's hard-
headedness and strong sense of atmosphere dissolved his scruples
about throwing Balfour and Chamberlain to the wolves. He was
wildly applauded by a big, enthusiastic majority of Conservative
M.P.s (187 against 87) for saying that he attached "more importance
to keeping our Party united than to winning the next election."
That afternoon Lloyd George accepted the split as irreparable and
tendered his resignation.

Nearly a week passed before a new Government was formed. For
Bonar Law now hesitated to put himself forward as an alternative

Prime Minister until the Party had formally elected him as their leader. This did not mean that he was inactive; only that to satisfy an excessive taste for constitutional proprieties, the centre of political gravity shifted from Downing Street to his home in South Kensington. There he began to pick a Cabinet team. His choice was limited; and his official biographer, Robert Blake, does not quarrel with Churchill's caustic observation that Bonar Law could not but choose "a Government of the second eleven."[8]

The first names were announced on 25th October; next day Parliament was dissolved; the inevitable General Election was fixed for 15th November.

Trenchard watched the successive stages in the downfall of Lloyd George with bewilderment and growing uneasiness, preferring the devils he knew to those whom no one knew. By the time Bonar Law had been sworn in as Prime Minister, the *Braemar Castle* had disembarked its airmen and supplies in Iraq. But by then, as Trenchard had also discovered, the Middle East policy of the Coalition was being reviewed. There were authoritative rumours in Whitehall that the Prime Minister intended, if confirmed in office by the electorate, to jettison British commitments in Iraq, as his friend, Lord Beaverbrook, was advocating in the columns of his newspapers. There were equally persistent whispers that the R.A.F.'s existence was also in jeopardy, though Trenchard could neither scotch these nor trace them to source.

" I still have no Secretary of State," he told Ellington on 30th October. " There was, I believe, an effort made to put us under the War Office. I do not know if it has been defeated—I sincerely hope it has."

The implications of the political changes were ominously uncertain. Trenchard felt like a man groping in the dark. His suspicions were roused but had nothing tangible to fasten on. He knew that he could expect little quarter from Sykes, his former rival, who was said to have gained the ear of his father-in-law, the new Prime Minister, in recommending a general overhaul of the armed forces. If that were so, though he found it hard to credit, then the R.A.F. stood in grave danger. For as Controller of Civil Aviation under Churchill and Guest, Sykes had strongly disapproved of the policy of devoting most of the meagre Air Vote to military developments. Not long after his resignation on that pretext some months previously, there had been talk of his accepting an executive post connected with the London Underground.

" It ought to suit him admirably," Trenchard had commented

with a touch of asperity. " Sykes has been burrowing as long as I've known him."

Not until 1st November did Bonar Law summon the man whom he proposed to appoint as his new Secretary of State for Air. Sir Samuel Hoare, as he then was, has left on record his own account of a rather one-sided interview with the Prime Minister.

> " He told me that he had been passing through several changes of mind as to what office he could offer me . . . and finally had come down on the Secretaryship for Air.
>
> " ' Will you take it? '—these were his words as I noted them down after the interview. ' But before you reply, I must tell you that the post may be abolished in a few weeks. Sykes tells me that the Independent Air Force and the Air Ministry cost much too much, and that there is everything to be said in peacetime for going back to the old plan of navy and army control. I agree with him.
>
> " ' I shall therefore expect you, if you take the post, to remember that it may very soon cease to exist. There will be an immediate inquiry into the whole question by the Cabinet and the Committee of Imperial Defence. Whatever is the result, we shall certainly clear out of Iraq, where the air force has recently taken over the command, and we shall not be able to spare any large sums for a third fighting service. I ought to add that the post will not be a Cabinet post.' "

It was not, as Hoare ruefully admitted, a very enticing offer. He nevertheless "eagerly accepted" it, preferring even a temporary post to no post at all. When he called on Trenchard at Adastral House next day, not a hint of Bonar Law's intention to destroy the R.A.F. crossed his lips, not a word to confirm or deny the whispers circulating in the service clubs that the army and navy would shortly have their own air squadrons restored to them. Hoare was completely non-committal and apparently eager to please. Trenchard's eyes never left him for a moment, and the new Minister had to listen to a recital of the R.A.F.'s trials and triumphs which must have sounded in the circumstances rather like a swan-song.

Writing more than thirty years after the event, Hoare could look back in boundless admiration on the speaker as a prophet.

> " I listened enthralled. . . . I suddenly realised that I might, after all, have come to the Air Ministry not to wind it up, as Bonar Law had suggested, but to help to establish it on an

equality with the Admiralty and the War Office, and to create a peacetime air force as a united and independent service in no way inferior to the navy and army. Each day that followed confirmed this feeling. My mission was to be the prophet's interpreter to a world that did not always understand his dark sayings. . . ."[9]

Hoare was to fulfil that mission with an ardour for which he has not yet received due credit. But his hindsight seems to have been better than his insight, misleading him as to the actual date of his own conversion. Trenchard's impression was different from his own, as the contemporary records show. Hoare, the man, was affable, charming to deal with and therefore "worth educating"; but Hoare, the politician, remained for several months someone "not entirely to be trusted."

Electoral campaigning was now in full swing; the verdict on polling day was conclusive. Bonar Law romped home with a clear majority of 77 seats over all his opponents combined. So Hoare, it appeared, would be staying to wind up the air force. His predecessor, Guest, was not even a Member of Parliament. The same misfortune had overtaken Churchill, once more an invalid, who sat up in bed to scrutinise the returns only to find, in his own pithy phrase that he was "without a job, without a seat and without an appendix." It was the end of a political chapter; and Trenchard felt in his bones that the next would seal the fate of the R.A.F., one way or the other.

16. The Undefeated

Before the end of November, 1922, Trenchard learnt the worst. Hoare called twice to discuss general policy, then looked in again, unannounced, to favour Trenchard with a secret. The R.A.F., he confided, had been under sentence of death for nearly a fortnight; but, he hastened to add, only that morning he had been instrumental in obtaining a stay of execution.

The Minister's account of his role as rescuer sounded quite plausible. Bonar Law had presided at a full meeting of the Committee of Imperial Defence within ten days of taking office, introducing the subject of the Air Ministry's future in the perfunctory manner of a hanging judge with his mind made up. One question alone had to be decided; not if, but how, the R.A.F. could best be liquidated. Hoare, at that point, had plucked up courage and intervened. "Very nervously," he suggested that the Prime Minister should consider holding an impartial inquiry first.[1] Balfour, who had agreed to continue serving on the Committee while declining to join the Government, vigorously seconded him.

Hoare's assertion that, until the moment of intervention, "Balfour had obviously accepted the argument for liquidation," had an improbable ring. Balfour was, of course, "a former First Lord of the Admiralty"; but, as the author of the recent paper upholding the claims of the R.A.F. to autonomy on strategic grounds, Balfour seemed to be suspicious of partisanship.

Trenchard did not attempt to challenge Hoare on such minor details. So appalled was he by the burden of the Minister's story that he listened in utter silence. Now, at any rate, he knew where he stood. Bonar Law, no doubt under the malign influence of Sykes, had begun with the intention of abolishing the service by decree, but had since been persuaded to empower a special sub-committee under Salisbury, the new Lord President of the Council, to settle the issue by more constitutional methods.

Where did Hoare fit in? Trenchard wished he could be sure.

The polished manners of the Minister were not entirely convincing; his mind was smaller and harder to read than Churchill's. Why, for instance, had he dissembled for nearly a fortnight about Bonar Law's original purpose in a way that Churchill would have scorned? Was it due to cunning? Or was his ingratiating smile the mask of a shy man anxious to serve his political masters well, yet equally anxious to spare the feelings of a professional adviser reputed to be exceedingly touchy? Perhaps he merely detested scenes. Guest, who had been Churchill's muted echo, would at least have been franker. Hoare struck Trenchard as a somewhat prim specimen who would never allow enthusiasm to distort his political judgment. A small paragon of correctness, a safe man, he appeared to have more than the average Minister's quota of vanity.

" I can't possibly work here," he said on being shown his office for the first time. " This room's too cramped and inconvenient."

The Minister seemed equally displeased to find a young R.A.F. officer instead of an experienced civil servant already installed as his private secretary. These signs of petulance did little to reassure Trenchard, who made a mental note that a newcomer who fussed over trifles might expect to be humoured over essentials. To do Hoare justice, his attitude reflected a desire to be treated on the same footing as his fellow Ministers, rather than an old-maidish crotchiness. It was all the more ironical that Ludlow-Hewitt, the R.A.F. secretary whom he was impatient to replace on principle, did much to reduce misunderstanding. Trenchard used him to sound out Hoare, who used him in turn to sound out Trenchard; and during his few remaining weeks at the Minister's side, this officer succeeded where nine civil servants out of ten would have failed in interpreting points of policy which, in moments of majestic incoherence, Trenchard did not properly convey to the curious but puzzled Hoare. When Christopher Bullock, probably the most gifted of Trenchard's small band of civil servants, took over as private secretary, this practice of confirming questions at second hand solidified into a tradition.

The Minister raised no objections when Trenchard announced, through Ludlow-Hewitt, that at the forthcoming inquiry he intended to defend the R.A.F.'s case in his own way.

" Our Secretary of State," he informed his commanders in Cairo and Baghdad on 27th November, " is a very able and clever man, but he knows very little about the air—and what little he knows he has obtained from what I may call the Henry Wilson-Sykes-navy side of the subject."

T.   P

He did not conceal from his colleagues abroad the inconvenience of a fresh inquiry in two parts, the first to review relations with the navy as though Balfour and Geddes had never been, the second to consider "the whole reorganisation of the air service." Its work in Iraq, India and at home would also be weighed and judged on its merits.

" I have decided to take the leading part in the discussion," Trenchard wrote, "with a view to trying to get this matter settled by this Government as well as the last. It will mean the air service is safe for all time."

Any doubts he had about Bonar Law's good faith or Hoare's complete trustworthiness, he did not refer to. Candour at that moment would not have helped morale, already shaken by past uncertainties. He had faith enough in himself to bolster up Hoare, if Hoare would let him; but faith alone was no longer enough. He also needed luck; and he hoped that the Prime Minister's unrealistic behaviour might bring a stroke of it. For Bonar Law continued to teeter on the edge of indecision as though unable to choose what to do first in pursuit of his dream of disengagement—pull out of the Middle East, make peace with the Turks, or wind up the Royal Air Force.

Trenchard had discovered which way the wind was blowing even before Hoare disclosed the abortive plan to kill the air force. The Minister, accompanied by his Under-Secretary of State, the Duke of Sutherland, paid a courtesy visit to the Air Ministry shortly after the election, chatted aimlessly about unimportant trifles, then almost as an afterthought, declared that the Government intended to quit Iraq and Palestine as soon as possible. Bonar Law would brook of no undue delay. Trenchard's response was involuntary: to the pained astonishment of his visitors, he hooted with laughter.

" You must remind the Prime Minister of one or two things he's overlooked," he said. " The first is the attitude of Turkey, the second the unrest in Iraq. If we try to leave now, we may have to fight our way out."[2]

Trenchard was not overstating the military dilemma. Every cable and letter from Salmond since late October, when the R.A.F. became responsible for order in Iraq, suggested that Kemal Ataturk, flushed with his triumph at Chanak, had moved into a better theatre for belligerent activity; that long, exposed frontier of chasms and peaks and enclosed valleys above Mosul where northern Iraq melted invisibly into Turkey. Here lay the unconsidered flaw in Bonar Law's policy of immediate withdrawal.

" I emphasised that I thought it would be impossible *without serious military operations*, and without giving up the cross-desert route and Transjordan," Trenchard informed Salmond immediately after the interview with Hoare and Sutherland. " I added that when peace with Turkey is signed, we should be able at once to come down to six battalions (in Iraq), and that when the levies (Arab volunteers under British officers) had their fourth battalion and were a little more efficient we should come down to the Cairo scheme of four (British Army) battalions. After that, I said, I wasn't in a position to say when the country could run itself. This couldn't really be decided for two or three years."

In Trenchard's view, the Prime Minister's indecent haste to scuttle and hang the consequences would adversely affect the bargaining position of his own Foreign Secretary, Curzon, who had gone to Lausanne to negotiate a fresh peace treaty with Ismet Pasha. Trenchard had not only to husband his patience but to counsel Salmond to do likewise. As he explained in a current letter:

> " The change of Government in the midst of negotiations with Turkey rather resembles the operation known as swapping horses in midstream. The new people are, of course, completely out of touch with recent policy—and have to be educated."

Parliament met towards the end of November; but in the short month at its disposal before Christmas there was time only to pass a Bill recognising the Constitution of the Irish Free State. On the surface, the Government seemed to be settling down quietly but industriously. The era of scares and sensations had gone with " the Goat," the era of "tranquillity" promised at the polls had dawned. As far as Bonar Law was concerned, the Anglo-Turkish emergency had ended. Outstanding disagreements with Kemal would be adjusted in a civilised spirit of give and take over the conference table at Lausanne.

The Committee of Imperial Defence had been set the constructive task of putting its own house in order for the benefit of the taxpayer; and the Prime Minister's preconception that the R.A.F. was a superfluous luxury had again become common gossip in Whitehall.

Trenchard had no direct access to the leaders he wished to educate, for the Committee of Imperial Defence, his normal channel of approach, had been temporarily closed for structural repairs, and Hoare was not even in the Cabinet.

Nevertheless, as early as 9th November, Trenchard saw fit to warn Bonar Law, in writing, that a policy announcement on whether or not Britain intended to abandon Mosul was "of the greatest importance." Salmond's forces in Iraq, he pointed out, were endangered "by this uncertainty." It was "for the Cabinet to decide, knowing the risk." Nearly a month later, Trenchard was still waiting for a definite answer, though various excuses were meanwhile offered him for deferring a hard-and-fast decision, the most valid being the delicate stage of the treaty negotiations with Turkey.[3]

On 6th December, Trenchard put the best face on this reasoning in a letter to the harassed Salmond.

" The Lausanne Conference has so far gone more satisfactorily than had been anticipated," he wrote, " and there are not wanting signs that Turkey is beginning to look to this country as the one able to render her the assistance of which she stands so much in need in future, unless she is to become a mere vassal state of Bolshevik Russia.

" As I have previously pointed out to you, you can ignore the newspaper agitation advocating a policy of 'scuttle' (in Iraq). Personally, I think that the present Government, when reviewing the matter, will have regard to our commitments in India and Egypt and will be unlikely to allow themselves to be stampeded into any sudden change of policy."

The future of Iraq in the abstract did not interest Salmond. The Turks, massing above Mosul, were, as he saw it, leading Britain a dance; and however stately the diplomatic pace of Ismet Pasha at Lausanne, the prevailing tempo in the hills was unmistakably that of a war-dance. Besides, as Salmond knew, the Mosul question had not yet been raised at the conference table. When Curzon did bring it up, his façade of magisterial confidence might well crumble. For there was nothing behind it except a Prime Minister without a policy; and Ismet Pasha would quickly grasp that humiliating fact.

While loyally interpreting official policy, Trenchard un-obtrusively insured the R.A.F. against dangers which he foresaw as clearly as the indignant Salmond.

In mid-December, for example, Trenchard wrote to say that he had persuaded the C.I.G.S. to support a "forward strategy" in Iraq and that "an agreed paper between the War Office and ourselves" had gone to the Cabinet. Caught between the complacency of the Government and the exasperation of Salmond, he tried in vain to shake the one and soothe the other. For Bonar Law still refused to accept that his policy of masterly inactivity was egging on the Turks as much as the irresponsible provocation of Lloyd George had ever done. Perhaps events would open the Prime Minister's eyes before it was too late: that remained Trenchard's only solace. Good might come out of evil as so often happened in politics. If Kemal did over-

play his hand again, only the R.A.F. could foil him. For only the
R.A.F., which the Prime Minister wanted to bring home prematurely
and destroy, stood between Turkey and Iraq, between Iraq and
anarchy.

At the time of Chanak, the British Army Commander, General
Fraser, with rather more prudence than foresight, had evacuated
the frontier area about Rowanduz, a town in the hills of Kurdistan,
where a rebel leader of notoriety, Sheikh Mohammed, had formerly
disputed the occupation rights of the British and, more recently, the
jurisdiction of King Feisal. The Rowanduz district was now in the
Sheikh's control, his irregular bands swollen with Turkish regulars
who infiltrated across the unmarked border in hundreds. Salmond's
first act on assuming command in Iraq had been to inspect this savage
no-man's-land personally from a low-flying reconnaissance aircraft.
Fraser had told him that the spirit of the Iraq levies, mostly
Assyrians, who formed the bulk of the ground security force, was
poor. They certainly needed "a fillip," Salmond assured Trenchard.
And so, for that matter, did "waning British prestige."

On returning to Baghdad, Salmond confronted Trenchard with
the accomplished fact that three levy columns were on the way to
Rowanduz; it was not his intention, he declared, to abandon Mosul
to the tender mercies of Sheikh Mohammed and his Turkish backers.

" We can put up a substantial fight in the Mosul area," wrote
Salmond. " There should be no reason to clear out at the first sign
of hostilities. In this I fear I am contrary to my predecessors. From
what I hear, such a plan will upset the War Office if they see it
without you behind it."

Trenchard urged Salmond not to rush anything, meanwhile
steering a careful middle way between the restiveness of his colleague
and the indolence of a Cabinet apparently still half hypnotised by
its electoral slogans.

If this time Kemal meant business, then the R.A.F. must guard
against stretching its lines of communication too far.

" Concentrate at the centre of Government," he advised Salmond.
" Use air action from the centre outwards. That's the soundest and
safest and cheapest method of routing an invader without air cover
of his own. . . . What does Rowanduz matter? Why should it matter
" this small area on the boundary is turbulent and nominally under
the Turks? What I said at Cairo was that I would leave some of these
truculent places until I was in a position to deal with them."

But Salmond stuck to his own tactical appreciation. His Arab-
speaking political officers, all of them reliable men chosen, trained

and posted at strategic points throughout Iraq by the retiring High
Commissioner, Sir Percy Cox, were positive that Kemal had set his
heart on Mosul and would seize it unless forcibly forestalled.
Salmond proposed to forestall him by marching every available
soldier and airman north to defend Mosul and by taking the calculated
risk of leaving his rear communications open and virtually unguarded. The alternative was the path not of safety but of self-
destruction. By standing fast hundreds of miles from the centre of
trouble and depending entirely on his few squadrons to dam back
an invasion, he would surrender the initiative to Kemal and to the
revolutionaries within Iraq known to be in league with him.[4]

Trusting him too much to argue further, Trenchard put the facts
before the Government, in writing, only to find that Bonar Law
chose to discount them. The Prime Minister was still obsessed with
a desire in a vacuum, that of avoiding trouble with Turkey at any
price, which his biographer, Robert Blake, has condoned by
remarking that "a war with Turkey" would have been "a bad start
for a policy of 'tranquillity.'" Bonar Law, according to Blake, "was
anxious to get out of Iraq and very anxious to avoid even the mere
appearance of risking a war because of British oil interests."[5]

In fact Mosul oil had as little to do with the Prime Minister's
negative policy of appeasement as Moscow gold. Not once is it
mentioned, even as an outside factor, in Trenchard's voluminous
correspondence with Salmond or in the record of his dealings with
the Cabinet.

Trenchard had as good cause as Curzon to accept the simpler
and more human explanation that Bonar Law had chronic "cold
feet" about any moves, diplomatic or military, that might aggravate
the Turks.[6]

Well aware of the Prime Minister's disability, Trenchard felt
obliged to warn Salmond in December:

"You'll have to be prepared with an alternative scheme in
which the British battalions will not be moved north to Mosul, in
case the Cabinet say they can't take the risk. . . . You should be ready
to pull them farther back in order to avoid any chance of being cut
off from your main camp in case of defeat. . . . I hope this will never
occur, and I hope I shall not have to send you these instructions, as
I'm quite prepared to leave it to the man on the spot."

Salmond's "forward plan" was discussed by the Committee of
Imperial Defence during December and still no final decision was
reached. Bonar Law would give no definite lead, other Ministers
being content to brood on the problem as if convinced that, if left

long enough, it would hatch itself. Then came a major jolt from quite another direction. It forced the Cabinet to act. The culprit this time was France.

At the end of December Bonar Law joined Curzon in Paris, vainly hoping to persuade the French to settle for less than their full pound of flesh on arrears of German reparations. The talks foundered as usual on the rock of Gallic logic; the Prime Minister gloomily left for home, Curzon for Lausanne. A week went by, then France distrained on her debtors and marched into the Ruhr. This heavy blow to Franco-British relations might almost have been pre-arranged with Kemal, so sharp and quick was the Turkish reaction.

The hitherto amenable attitude of Ismet Pasha at Lausanne seemed to harden overnight. His demand for the immediate cession of Mosul was promptly rejected by Curzon; deadlock ensued; for a few days the conference appeared to be on the verge of collapse; then the Foreign Secretary received an insistent message from Bonar Law. " We cannot go to war for Mosul," said the Prime Minister. " If the French, as we know to be the case, will not join us, we shall not by ourselves fight to save what remains of the Treaty of Sèvres." Salmond alone was in a position to save what remained of that treaty, though his sole intention was the tactical one of safeguarding his own position in Iraq. Acting with the utmost secrecy, in the belief that if he delayed further out of deference to the cautious bleatings of Bonar Law his power of initiative would pass by default to the Turks, Salmond put his "forward plan" into operation.

The arrival of his laconic signal towards the end of January, 1923, stating that his land forces were already on the move towards Mosul, threw the Cabinet into a state of nerves bordering on panic. Bonar Law rounded on Trenchard, who said that he would stand or fall by the actions of his subordinate. Salmond, he recalled, had submitted his operational plan weeks before. Both the Committee of Imperial Defence and the Cabinet had had ample opportunity to pronounce on them, so why blame the man on the spot for their failure to do so in time? Pressure was brought to bear on Trenchard. He was instructed to cable Salmond at once, ordering him to with-draw passively in the event of any Turkish attack. On no account must he seek, or be drawn into, a preventive battle. The Chief of Air Staff complied, knowing that his colleague could turn a blind eye with the best to insipid directives of the sort. A private letter to Trenchard, dated 2nd February, described the local circumstances which had induced Salmond to move instantly:

" Since last writing to you, the situation in this country has altered considerably. The pro-Turkish propaganda has increased definitely with the threat to take Mosul, although at Mosul itself I believe the feeling to be for inclusion in Iraq. . . . Owing to the increases on the Jezireh front and to the fact that a large number of (Turkish) villages had received orders to evacuate, with the exception of the troops, I ordered a concentration north. This should be completed in two or three days' time and will for the present safeguard any possibility of a move against Mosul.

" If hostilities do break out, I hope to deal the Turks a severe blow which will put matters right on all fronts and in the interior (of Iraq). . . . Should it go wrong matters will become extremely difficult. I note the policy indicated to me is that of continuous retirement in the face of a superior enemy. As you know," Salmond concluded dryly, " that is a most difficult manœuvre once we become engaged, and I do not anticipate the possibility of retiring continuously, even in the face of a superior enemy, without firing a shot. . . .

" I note that I need expect no reinforcements."

Trenchard was delighted. Reinforcements or no, it would be an honour to stand or fall with Salmond. The General Staff, like the Cabinet, had expressed its fears of the "forward policy" at the twelfth hour, Cavan's line being that British troops should never have been entrusted to the reckless charge of a senior air force officer. The C.I.G.S. went so far as to damn it in the circumstances as a military gamble and was rebuked by Trenchard for "playing safe" politically. Cavan took umbrage at this, but could not gainsay the fact that in Colonel Vincent, the local ground commander, Salmond had a military adviser of considerable experience whose assessment of the situation coincided completely with his own. The Chief of Air Staff merely concluded that the virus of inertia must be catching.

Neither the War Office nor the Cabinet were yet persuaded that revolution might break out in Iraq, though the dispatches of the new High Commissioner, Sir Henry Dobbs, to the Colonial Office did not disguise that this was a greater risk than invasion by the Turks. Perhaps the soundest counter-measures he adopted after consultation with Salmond was to raise a "Central Force" of tribal recruits. King Feisal's assent had not been easily obtained. The intrigue and corruption in Baghdad made the monarch pitifully uncertain of himself, as this note in Salmond's operational diary for 6th February suggests:

" It is amusing now to see him sitting on his crossed legs in the palace shouting ' I will defend my country to the last drop of my blood—forward, forward the vast legions of King Feisal,' when a month ago I was pricking him into activity and he was haggling over the price. No doubt he has spasms of idealistic enthusiasm but they are of no practical value being sporadic and unsustained. . . ."

To supplement his meagre Colonial Office grant, Trenchard allowed Salmond to draw freely on the R.A.F.'s local imprest account for recruiting, arming and training the emergency force. He did so only because the Cabinet left him with no alternative. Having refused to consider sending reinforcements from home, they would certainly have refused to pay for the mustering of Iraqi mercenaries. The Chief of Air Staff preferred to let the financial arguments wait until he could present successfully accomplished facts with the bills.

Up at Mosul, where the upper Tigris cut Salmond's front in half, the tactical difficulties were undoubtedly real. The defending troops, roughly six battalions strong, were spread so thin that a Turkish assault down both banks might have been disastrous. Salmond chose to mass his main force on the right, leaving only a detachment on the left. It was a deliberate gamble, as Trenchard well knew; for Salmond had prudently dispatched his chief staff officer to Syria where the French High Command at once guaranteed that no infiltrators would be permitted to cross French territory and enter Iraq down the unguarded left bank of the Tigris. General Gourand's solemn assurance that, despite the Rupture Cordiale between Paris and London, Turkish trespassers would be prosecuted with all the means at his disposal, was all that Salmond wanted.

By the end of the first week of February, the last units of Salmond's British and Indian battalions were in position beside the Iraq levies, after a forced march of fifty miles from Shergat to Mosul in a blinding rainstorm.

He was now as confident as Trenchard that he had little to fear from Kemal. But whereas the Chief of Air Staff maintained that the Turkish leader had never intended to fight, Salmond held that it was his forward policy which finally called the Turkish bluff.

2

Meanwhile, far away in Delhi, where he had lately assumed command of the squadrons on Indian soil, Philip Game pondered over a letter from Trenchard, the final paragraph of which contained a clear hint that a younger man would do better as Chief of Air Staff.

Ellington, in Cairo, received a similar depressed note; but it was Game who responded first with the right mixture of fact, flattery and abuse.

" You know perfectly well," he wrote by return, " that the R.A.F. is in a much stronger position than we had any right to expect after such a comparatively short time. This result is one man's work —yours—and to talk of resigning is pure bunkum and shows you are losing your nerve."

It was not loss of nerve that afflicted Trenchard so much as loss of all sense of equilibrium. February, 1923, had opened as tediously as the previous three months of that interminable winter, with the knowledge that the Government was still in hibernation and that another birthday lay just behind him; when or whether Bonar Law would stir from his slumbers, Trenchard no longer cared. At fifty he felt suddenly old, bored and utterly useless.

Three factors had produced this uncharacteristic state of mind: the continuing inertia in Whitehall, the continuing irresolution of the Cabinet, and his own increasing isolation. Hoare had not yet achieved Cabinet rank, so that official information dribbled through to the Air Ministry seldom and slowly.

As far as he could gather, the two ministerial committees studying the issues that affected him most, Iraq and the R.A.F.'s future in any scheme of national defence, had made little progress. So much hung upon the outcome of Salmond's unfinished business at Mosul that no detached witness could have blamed either committee for sloth; but Trenchard, though isolated, could not pretend to be detached. Too many Ministers for his liking were too ready to conclude that the R.A.F. had dug its own grave beside the Tigris.

" We never know whether it's war or peace with the Turks," he complained to one of his commanders. " Salmond is having a very difficult time. . . . We can't give him any guidance because we can't obtain any ourselves."

To crown his frustration, the Cabinet continued to cloak its irresolution in a discreet silence. As far as the public were concerned,

Mosul and the mountain strongholds of Kurdistan might have been situated on the dark side of the moon. Remembering the fatal way in which the Chanak crisis had been overpublicised, Trenchard could understand the expediency of reticence; but dangers could not be abolished simply by averting the popular gaze from them. No doubt, if Salmond kept his end up at Mosul, the Chief Air Staff would be blamed for having embarrassed the Government. If Salmond were defeated, Trenchard would be condemned and probably asked to go for conniving at the impetuosity of his commander. In either case, the R.A.F. would bear the guilt. Official silence in these circumstances seemed to him the enemy of truth. It conveniently coupled itself to the censorship imposed in Baghdad for valid security reasons, and hoodwinked national and world opinion for invalid political reasons.

Salmond had started censoring news from Iraq in mid-December, and Lord Beaverbrook created something of a commotion when a dispatch filed by the *Daily Express* correspondent was stopped. The wires between London and Baghdad buzzed with confused recriminations until the crossed cables were sorted.

To Trenchard's surprise, and possibly Beaverbrook's, Bonar Law defended Salmond's action from a desire to sustain the illusion of tranquillity. Not to be outdone, before the end of December Beaverbrook was proclaiming to the world through the *Daily Express* that Lawrence of Arabia was skulking in the ranks of that service. Against his will, Trenchard yielded to strong Government pressure and discharged the one man whose identity and whereabouts he had striven to conceal.

Lawrence once more gave proof of his loyalty in a manner which deepened Trenchard's affectionate respect.

" I am never burdened with big politics, it is always that the little politics are the burden to me," wrote the Chief of Air Staff on 30th January, 1923, in an attempt to explain what had happened. " The trivial circumstances have been too much for me and for you. It is the smallness of it that has brought about the decision to finish it, and I know you will accept it however much you hate it. To my way of thinking, the only thing that would be of any use would be an armoured car officer—short service. One of the drawbacks to you is that you have been a bit of a friend of mine, and that has made it so hard for me to deal with. . . ."

Spurning the bait of a direct commission, the sole concession which the Government would make to Trenchard's special pleading, Lawrence spent his first weeks of unsought freedom haunting

influential acquaintances in the political and literary spheres
Amery was one of several Ministers whom he approached, primarily
in search of an alternative retreat. When questioned, as he some
times was, about developments in the Middle East, he invariably
spoke his mind. The Iraq Committee, though not yet in sight of a
decision, was predisposed to accept Bonar Law's defeatist proposal to
evacuate forthwith. Lawrence's advice to those committee member
who sought it was simple: the facts deserved a more studious hearing
than they had yet enjoyed. Amery was not alone in judging the incisive
views of this eccentric celebrity on the run to be "essentially sane
and well balanced."

It would be easy to exaggerate the influence of one man, and
an unhappy outsider at that, in improving the climate of opinion
within a cautious and still uncommitted Government Committee
Yet Trenchard confirmed Amery's impression that Lawrence contributed something positive to the Iraq Committee's deliberations,
almost in spite of himself, because his frankness was accepted as being
based partly on experience, partly on disinterested conviction
Trenchard found not a little irony in the fact that Hoare, whose
propriety had been outraged by the unmasking of "Air Mechanic
Ross", and only slightly placated by his dismissal, presently began
to benefit indirectly from Lawrence's free-lance advocacy.

His expulsion "as a person with altogether too large a publicity
factor for the ranks," to use his own phrase, was the only sensational
happening that winter which brought the R.A.F. to the public eye.
Its real problems were almost universally overlooked, just as the
precariously fluid situation in Iraq went unrecognised, because of
Bonar Law's tendency to make a virtue of procrastination and a
policy of drift. To judge by the flattering attentions of the Press,
there was little wrong with a service which could produce such
formidable sportsmen in so short a time. In the week following
Game's letter accusing Trenchard of "loss of nerve," the R.A.F. beat
the Royal Navy for the first time at rugby; and on the following
Monday, 19th February, *The Times* passed over any number of more
important subjects to devote a sententious leading article to this
"remarkable feat." Straining the legendary link between Waterloo
and the playing field of Eton, the leader writer hailed the victory at
Twickenham as a classically bright omen for the future of the
"youngest of the fighting services."

It caused Trenchard to wince, proud as he was even of a sporting
triumph over the navy during that period of gathering gloom. It
left him sardonically wondering what leader writers were coming to.

This particular tract from *The Times* might have been composed on another planet for any bearing it had on the present, let alone the unsettled future, of the R.A.F.

Yet within forty-eight hours, Trenchard had reason to thank his stars that Fleet Street knew so little. On 21st February, an excited Hoare told him that Beatty had visited No. 10 Downing Street the day before to present an ultimatum to the Prime Minister. Unless the Government agreed to hand back to the navy its own air service, the First Sea Lord would resign at once and carry on his fight from the cross-benches of the House of Lords. Trenchard's first, unguarded reaction was to compliment the Minister on maintaining his record as a "bringer of bad tidings"; but bad as the news might be, its effect in restoring the equilibrium of the Chief of Air Staff was instantaneous.

Hoare spent the morning with Trenchard, committing to paper, at his request, the opening moves and counter-moves in what promised to be a less gentlemanly affray than that at Twickenham the previous week-end. Bonar Law, who sent for Hoare as soon as the door of No. 10 closed behind the departing First Sea Lord, seemed beside himself with anxiety.

" The Prime Minister, who said that Lord Beatty was not to be moved in his decision to force the issue to a point, seemed quite hopeless as to arriving at an agreement, and asked *me* to see Lord Beatty," runs Hoare's confidential account written at the time. " This, of course, I undertook to do. In the evening, Colonel Amery (First Lord of the Admiralty) came into my room at the House of Commons and had a long talk with me. . . .

" After pressing the naval case as strongly as he could, he made a proposal, as a compromise, that in order to retain the outward integrity of the air force the naval units—manned by naval personnel and a certain sprinkling of air force officers—should be shown on both the Admiralty and air force lists and that the Admiralty should make a grant-in-aid for the naval personnel.

" I told Amery that I was particularly anxious for peace, and that it was on that account that I had pressed postponement on the Prime Minister. As to the merits of his proposal, I said that I could express no opinion whatever, but that I would consider it and discuss it with the Chief of Air Staff and the Secretary. . . ."[7]

Trenchard told Hoare plainly that there was nothing to discuss. If Beatty imagined that by blackmailing this Government as he had tried to blackmail the last, he could break up the R.A.F. without a finger being raised against him, then the First Sea Lord was due for another disappointment. Admittedly, Beatty could not have chosen a better moment. The service estimates were about to be debated in Parliament; the Air Staff was under a cloud for alleged war-mongering in Iraq; and the rights of the R.A.F. to any part in national defence were being considered afresh by the Committee of Imperial Defence. With the British Press otherwise distracted, Beatty had some reason to expect that the Cabinet would submit tamely so that the breaking-up of the R.A.F. could be settled in principle before being publicly announced. The Admiralty plot to reverse the judgment of Austen Chamberlain, nearly twelve months ago, had been extremely well thought out. The one forgotten factor was Trenchard's will to resist.

Hoare kept his promise to the Prime Minister and saw Beatty alone at the Air Ministry on 22nd February. The meeting lasted an hour and was quite inconclusive. The First Sea Lord, according to the Minister's contemporary account, "pressed the case for the naval units quite pleasantly, but in its extreme form." When Hoare again suggested to Bonar Law and Amery that the matter should be postponed, Beatty became openly disagreeable.

" He said that when he took up his appointment, the Chief of Air Staff had asked him not to press the issue, as in a short time the air force would be strong enough to stand by itself without the naval units. Year after year he had waited, and year after year he had been put off. In view of this he could not wait again and insisted on the issue being joined at once. I told him that, if that was his view, the only course to be taken was to refer the question to an impartial inquiry."

Amery, whom Hoare saw for a second time later that day, agreed that "the controversy had gone too far to be settled from inside." The two Ministers decided there and then to demand the appointment of "a small outside committee to whose names we would also agree."

Bonar Law confessed that he was "much disappointed" at their failure.

" I have been thinking a great deal about the question," he said. " And I have come definitely to the view that it can't be settled without raising the whole issue of national defence. Any *ad hoc* inquiry into the navy's case will be impossible."

To this Amery retorted that a quick decision was imperative. Beatty's patience had all but run out. The Admiralty had gone to the limit of concession. Hoare protested that they had come to discuss the merits of their cases; as the Prime Minister knew, he had argued from the start in favour of postponement, and with reason, too. The R.A.F. expansion scheme passed by the Coalition Government in 1922 had only just been confirmed; at home there were barely twelve squadrons. " In a year's time," he pleaded, " the situation might be entirely different and it might well be that the problem of national defence would be materially changed."

Bonar Law veered one way and then the other. Finally, after Amery declared that he would accept a postponement on condition that the proposed committee of inquiry examined the controversy from the point of view of national defence as a whole, and that the R.A.F. assumed immediate responsibility for training 1100 naval officers and ratings who were on the point of being axed, Hoare yielded.

" It was clear to me," he wrote, " that it was quite impossible to get better terms without a crisis in the Government and probably in the House of Commons and the country. . . . Moreover, the Prime Minister, who was very worried with the whole political outlook, was determined to avoid a crisis if he possibly could. Accordingly I told him that I would accept the proposal."

The crisis which Hoare tried to avert by compromise was not over, however. Beatty was so enraged at being cheated of his prey that he declined to withdraw his threat of resignation. Considerably more tension marked the next meeting between Amery and Hoare, which took place on 23rd February, with Beatty and Trenchard in attendance. The Ministers took back seats as the two main protagonists openly confronted one another for the first time. Trenchard told Beatty exactly what he thought of people who used "empty threats" to bend others to their will. He reminded him that two could play at that game. The meeting broke up in some confusion, with the First Sea Lord implacably angry. That afternoon, Trenchard received an unexpected summons to 10 Downing Street. The Prime Minister wanted to "consult" him privately on a practical issue of some consequence.

" You're something of an expert on resigning," Bonar Law began. " You know that Beatty has threatened to go if we don't give way to his demands. Now I hear that you are threatening to go if we do. Is this true? "

" I made no threat," Trenchard replied. " But I won't stay on for a day longer if the R.A.F. is carved up just to suit Beatty. There's a difference, you see. I believe in resigning only on questions of principle or when my hand is forced."

Bonar Law seemed amused in a faintly startled way.

" You ought to write a treatise on the subject,"[8] he said dryly.

Trenchard returned to his office convinced that he had won the opening round on points; soon he received confirmation. The terms of the forthcoming inquiry were circulated, but the resignation of the First Sea Lord was not announced.

Beatty, like the Turks at Mosul, had evidently had second thoughts about staking everything against an opponent who was prepared to stand his ground.

The postscript of a long letter to Game in Delhi, dated 12th March, referred briefly to these events.

" The controversy with the navy has raged very bitterly lately. In fact it came to Beatty seeing the Prime Minister and my refusing to budge an inch, and between ourselves, stating that I was prepared to resign at once if Beatty got his way. As a result of this another inquiry has been ordered, which will decide once again in favour of the air force. It's a nuisance, but really it was a question of brute force being used by the navy—and I could not resist by any other means than brute force on our side. It has been a bitter fight and it will be still more bitter. You ought to have seen Hoare and myself, with Amery and other navy people sat round the table! "

Whatever had been wrong with Trenchard's liver, Game concluded, he sounded more like his old self now that he was up in arms again.

3

Bonar Law's insistence that the air-naval dispute should be arbitrated as part of a wide reappraisal of national defence needs was inspired by caution not by vision. Indeed, had circumstances permitted, Bonar Law would probably have acted already on the incomprehensible advice of his son-in-law, Sykes, and imposed the measures necessary for dismantling the R.A.F., though equally, being a man of sickly will, he might have shrunk from seeing them through against really determined opposition.

The war-like manœuvres of Kemal at Mosul had thwarted the first destructive impulse; the chauvinism of France in seizing the Ruhr had since exposed it as both inopportune and unwise. Much as it went against the grain of his tidy business-man's mind, Britain's security could not be mortgaged indefinitely to the Prime Minister's longing for tranquillity with economy. Yet without Beatty's personal threat to resign and thereby instigate an internal political crisis, it is hard to believe that Bonar Law, left to himself, would have ordered an inquiry into national defence just then. As Trenchard saw it, the Prime Minister was surrendering to Admiralty blackmail in Whitehall as he had been ready to yield without a murmur to Turkish bluff at Mosul; now the Committee of Imperial Defence was to be empanelled like a jury largely because of the First Sea Lord's antipathy for the R.A.F. Against Trenchard's somewhat baleful view of these half-hearted political developments must be set the crucial decisions on strategy to which they led. By saving the air force alive, those decisions would enable Britain to survive the peril of military extinction less than a generation later.

Trenchard's rough but passionate advocacy was not the least memorable factor in the protracted hearings that followed. He was conscious of standing secret trial not for career, good name or professional reputation, but in defence of an unwanted infant service's right to its own strategic existence.[9] The indifference of most members of the jury to the very principles of air-power spurred him on as nothing else could; but the swaying of the verdict, which ensured the survival of the Royal Air Force to fight and save the nation in 1940, owed still more to the procedural subtlety of an unobtrusive counsel behind the scenes. His name was Weir; his part was crucial. For Trenchard cut a strange figure in the dock, wearing the mantle of an unfashionable prophet almost too willing to revile the entrenched beliefs of the military establishment.

At the outset, Trenchard was uncertain whether strict justice would be done. There were, alas, no Churchills on the jury. Lord Salisbury, the chairman of the parent committee on national defence, he knew slightly as a somewhat aloof patrician, endowed with a good deal of common sense but wanting in practical knowledge of military affairs. Salisbury's aristocratic taste for detachment might prove an asset, but his hereditary instinct of attachment to what was old and tried and true might equally prove a liability. Balfour, whom the Prime Minister had chosen to conduct the subsidiary and parallel investigation into specific Admiralty claims against the R.A.F., was a more experienced specimen of the same breed. Balfour had invented, some twenty years before, the very machinery of the Committee of Imperial Defence; as a young Prime Minister, horrified by the evidence of maladministration that came to light after the South African War, he had designed this typically British device for removing one of the roots of inefficiency: the lack of any effective liaison between political and military leaders which had ossified into a bad tradition since the heyday of Wellington.

An elder statesman now, in poor health and beyond the hurly-burly of factional strife, Balfour had seen the C.I.D. gradually pushed into the background between 1910 and 1918, then restored to partial service when peace returned. It bore some resemblance in 1923 to a vintage tandem, with a third pair of makeshift pedals added for the Chief of Air Staff. As a machine for controlling the services, regulating their relations, and co-ordinating strategic ideas, it lent itself too easily to abuse or neglect, in Balfour's view. Trenchard was thus taken aback when Weir, who, as a permanently co-opted member of the C.I.D., had a shrewd working insight into the idiosyncrasies of his colleagues, advised him "not to depend too much on Balfour." The sub-committee chairman, he said, had returned from the Washington Conference on naval disarmament thoroughly indoctrinated with Beatty's ideas; and there had since been no change in his outlook. Cynics put down the transformation to the fact that Balfour was an indifferent sailor. On the outward voyage to America he had suffered so much from sea-sickness as to be incapable on arrival of resisting naval propaganda.

Weir liked the story, but thought it more probable that at a time when the Admiralty were foredoomed to lose, under the new system of international rationing, their right to construct more than a bare quota of capital ships and aircraft carriers, Balfour had too easily swallowed the case for arresting any further naval decline at R.A.F. expense. Whatever the reason, the elder statesman who had once arbitrated in Trenchard's favour, and had supported Hoare against Bonar Law's impulsive plan to abolish the R.A.F. by decree, would not necessarily do so again. The third member of the sub-committee was Lord Peel, the Secretary of State for India, and a passenger in comparison with Balfour and Weir, though his respect for air-power had lately grown with evidence of its success in imposing peace on the turbulent North-West Frontier.

The majority of Ministers with a direct stake in the inquiry were, as far as Trenchard knew, biased against the air force. Derby, once more the Secretary for War, had little nuisance value by himself. In combination with Amery, the Duke of Devonshire and Curzon, Derby might, however, become a stumbling block to progress. For Devonshire held the Colonial Office and was as sceptical of the air experiment in Iraq as Curzon and the Foreign Office had been from the beginning. (In fact, at that moment, early in March, 1923, Curzon was complaining that Salmond's advance to Mosul threatened to unstitch all his neat diplomatic handiwork at Lausanne.)

Cavan and the General Staff still maintained that Trenchard had overreached himself at Mosul. What Bonar Law thought was a matter of guesswork; in the Chief of Air Staff's irreverent opinion, " Bonar Law was so foxed that he hardly knew what to think or whom to believe." As for Baldwin, the genial but somnolent Chancellor of the Exchequer, his interest seemed to be as limited and impersonal as a cash register's.

During the first half of March, the Air Staff received from Hankey, the C.I.D. Secretary, a list of questions bearing on the main strategic issues to be settled by the main Salisbury Committee. At once Trenchard prepared his defence, briefing his colleagues, farming-out " homework," and dictating the rough drafts of most of the written replies.

" The navy," Trenchard informed Salmond, " do an immense lot of propaganda work and, of course, Amery is an old hand at this. Our own man, Hoare, though doing well, is quite new."

The new Minister was engagingly philosophic about his deficiencies, at any rate to Trenchard's face. What concerned him most, he stressed, were the uncertain political complications. The scales at that stage appeared to be heavily loaded against the R.A.F.

" It soon became evident," Hoare wrote, "that the two sides, if left to themselves, were irreconcilable. The only hope therefore of avoiding a crisis that might well split the Government depended on Ministers who had not yet taken up final positions in the battle. This was the origin of the special (sub) committee of Balfour, Peel and Weir, with Balfour as its chairman. The main committee was in the meanwhile left free to concentrate on wider questions such as . . . the place of air-power in national defence."[10]

Under Hankey's rules, each side was heard separately. But the very breadth of the questions made for controversy. Trenchard's analysis of the weak state of Britain's air defences was contested in the main arena as well as the smaller, though Hankey's expert prompting and Salisbury's firmness as chairman usually kept disputes within manageable bounds. It must be stressed that Hankey, even more than Balfour, was the mainstay of the Committee of Imperial Defence; as its servant for nearly twenty years, his memory for facts and precedents was encyclopædic. His private sympathies, attracted by Trenchard's record of being more often right than wrong, were partly with the R.A.F. His framing of questions, therefore, like his background guidance to the members of both committees, ensured that the air force case should not only be heard but understood. As the naval staff had equal opportunities to reply, none could tax him with partisanship. His purpose throughout was to guarantee that justice would be done through an exhaustive reappraisal of all the relevant facts.

What follows is not even a summary of the arguments produced by nearly two dozen witnesses on both sides. The hearings lasted many weeks; and the time scale, apart altogether from the often involved technical questions in dispute, defies compression into anything shorter than a longer-than-average novel. Stripped of its superfluous fat, the air inquiry of 1923 can best be presented as an uninterrupted duel between the two chief protagonists, Beatty and Trenchard, with their rival staffs as seconds in the background providing the ammunition, and the tribunal in the foreground keeping one eye on the rules and the other on the score. This remarkable contest was as much a clash of wills and of personalities as of strategic doctrines; but who will say to-day that Salisbury erred at the close in giving the verdict to the man who had rebuilt the R.A.F. and was battling against almost overwhelming odds to save it?

Here and there Trenchard's actual words were quoted in the record of proceedings. Because there is a regulation that suppresses the details of such inquiries until the interest of the living has perished from the earth, I, as the biographer of Trenchard, must here and now state that I have not consciously infringed it. My sources are not the verbatim minutes of the Committee of Imperial Defence but the draft notes used in evidence by Trenchard. I have his word for it that the two are substantially the same.

It was accepted, for argument's sake, that France should be treated as the potential enemy in Europe. In their written and oral testimony, Trenchard and the Air Staff insisted that in a war with France the survival of Britain would hinge on retaining command of the air at home.

" In a democratic country like ours," the Chief of Air Staff declared, "power rests ultimately with the people and war cannot be continued unless the bulk of the people support it. If the people are subject to sufficient bombing they will compel the Government to sue for peace."

Eminent soldiers could be cited in support of this unpalatable prediction. Had not Foch publicly stated some months previously

" The potentialities of aircraft attack on a large scale are almost incalculable, but it is clear that such attack, owing to its crushing moral effect on a nation, may impress public opinion to the point of disarming the Government and thus become decisive."

And had not Sir Ian Hamilton recently written:

" Surely we who have witnessed the Germans doing star turns over London and the second exodus of the Jews, surely we will be worse than Thomas Didymus if we do not put the conquest of the air above the conquest of the sea? "

Sir Ian's concern was commendable, admitted Trenchard, but the committee should remember that only 242 tons of bombs were dropped on the whole of Britain between 1914 and 1918, a mere fraction of the load which could be expected in a conflict with France.

" With their proposed expansion by 1925," said Trenchard, "the French could drop 325 tons in *one day*. With our strength in 1925 we will be able to drop *only* 67 tons per day."

Since Britain had an army strong enough to defend her from invasion, and a navy capable of destroying the enemy's seaborne commerce and of providing "limited protection" for her own, " France's primary object would be the destruction of British air-power, and her secondary object to cause as much destruction as possible to British seaborne trade."

Therefore air superiority was the first condition of military survival. And Britain's primary strategic aim must be to destroy the enemy's air-power.

Could a defending air force, inferior in numbers, ever be expected to defeat an attacking air force? Salisbury and his colleagues seemed eager for a straight answer to the question. They got it.

Defending aircraft undoubtedly had "a small tactical advantage," Trenchard conceded. They would be fighting in a prepared zone above their own bases. On the other hand, the attackers would have choice of time, place, direction and height of advance, in the absence of any early warning system, for crippling and probably decisive blows on British bases.

" It is not feasible to keep a large force of defenders in the air continuously," he stressed. " In consequence the defenders must have *sufficient warning* of an impending attack to enable them to reach a sufficient altitude before the attack takes place. In the future, increased means of defence against aircraft may redress the balance, but they are not in sight yet."

R.A.F. fighters, in the conditions of 1923, were disposed over an area "some 35 miles inland for warning purposes" so that the approach of a powerful bombing force could not be impeded, except by anti-aircraft fire, from attacking coastal towns or industrial centres a short distance inland.

It followed that, in aerial warfare more than any other, the second age-old principle of warfare applied:

> " It is on the bomber offensive that we must rely for defence. It is on the destruction of enemy industries and, above all, on the lowering of morale of enemy nationals caused by bombing that ultimate victory rests. . . . In consequences superiority in the air will be necessary in a single-handed war against France. Provided the facilities for expansion are greater in Britain than in France, this superiority need not be provided before the outbreak of war."

Britain's first strategic aim, therefore, depended on building an air force big enough to match that of any potential enemy. There were, he admitted, manifest dangers as well as disadvantages in this. No Government would face for long the cost of maintaining a large air force in peacetime; for without a comparably large outlay on research, on modern machines and weapons, and on the training of more men to operate and maintain both, such an air force would swiftly become an emasculated giant. Nothing must be allowed to dilute the present skill and fighting spirit of the service; what the R.A.F. needed most, said Trenchard, was a man-power reserve of equal quality. He still believed that this could be easily raised through an Auxiliary Air Force of part-time fliers, a course he had vainly urged on the previous Government.

On the equipment side, immediate measures should be taken to revive an aircraft industry that was slowly withering away. R.A.F. squadrons were still flying obsolescent wartime types; and the restricted budget for civil aviation was insufficient to keep the Sopwiths, the de Havillands, the Bristols, the Handley Pages and the rest in business. It was imperative for national survival that the British aircraft industry should "be able to expand rapidly and achieve a large rate of production in some months."

Salisbury seemed startled at first by the stark simplicity of Trenchard's strategic doctrine. Even in an exercise of military logic, it was disconcerting to be told, in effect, that if war with France broke out next morning the Royal Navy, Britain's sure bulwark since time immemorial, would be unable to save her. The R.A.F. in 1923 had only three fighter squadrons for home defence. The machines then attached to the fleet, fifteen flights of them, would be adequate for protecting naval ships from the "attack of hostile fleet aircraft." On that point Trenchard was quite definite. But he added the rider:

> " It is when the fleet ventures within radius of shore-based aircraft that the Air Staff have serious misgivings as to its safety."

The Naval Staff at once repudiated this as a ludicrous assertion. Most major sea battles of the past century and a half, they asserted, had been fought far from land; that being so, the likelihood of shore-based aircraft, British or enemy, coming within range of a naval battle, was remote. Trenchard retaliated by quoting chapter and verse from a naval paper, less than a year old, which stated the contrary and pinned Beatty helplessly down. " All I can say is that the admiral's compasses must measure differently from mine," he commented.

On that earlier occasion, the Admiralty had admitted that "co-operation of air forces would be essential" in a big sea battle. The R.A.F., Trenchard now warned the committee, would not necessarily be tied to its home bases in a future war. " It is unlikely," he added, "that diplomacy will fail us to the extent of depriving us of Allies," or the R.A.F. of overseas bases within striking distance of an enemy fleet.

Trenchard could not afford to draw back, just to humour Beatty.

" I want to avoid, if possible, the introduction of the naval controversy into this bigger question (of defence)," he assured Salisbury, " but there are certain points in the evidence given by Lord Beatty on which I wish to comment."

No fleet, in the world, he said, was now safe from air assault. He did not claim that a heavy battleship could yet be sunk by bombs. Practical evidence from R.A.F. experiments at sea was too inconclusive as yet, though fuller trials carried out in 1921 by the U.S. Joint Army and Navy Board suggested that this feat had come "within the realms of possibility."[11]

It was, in fact, General Billy Mitchell, Trenchard's American associate at Nancy, who had personally instigated and conducted an unorthodox publicity campaign in the United States until the authorities reluctantly consented to test his theory that "sea-power was done for." The former German battleship *Ostfriesland* and the cruiser *Frankfurt* were used as experimental targets. And beforehand the ex-Secretary of the navy, Mr. Daniels, had scornfully volunteered, in the hearing of a Congressional Committee, to stand bare-headed on the bridge of any battleship during any bombardment by any aircraft—"and, by God, expect to remain safe."   It was just as well for Mr. Daniels that he was aboard neither target ship on the day that Mitchell's flights of Martin and de Havilland 4 bombers took off from Langley Field, Virgina, to deliver the test attacks. These were extraordinarily successful. The *Frankfurt* was hit several times and sank in eleven minutes; the *Ostfriesland*, listing badly, remained afloat for a few minutes longer. Trenchard regretted that the facts had since become obscured in controversy.

He reproached himself, in a sense, for not having kept in closer touch with the brash young American who, in his own uphill struggle for the recognition of air-power, had relied too much on publicity, a weapon which the leader of the R.A.F. distrusted for its boomerang effect. Mitchell, the showman, seemed to be at greater odds than ever with Mitchell, the air prophet. And this last fantastic piece of showmanship was ruined in advance, to Trenchard's mind, by the unchanged inclination of the prophet to "convert his enemies by killing them first."

Subsequently demoted and silenced, Mitchell and his experiment had become the subject of interminable dispute among military planners on both sides of the Atlantic. Trenchard raised it before the Salisbury Committee only to remind members that certain vital conclusions had been omitted from the official American report issued for public consumption. He quoted, for instance, the later verdict reached by the U.S. Joint Army and Navy Board, which, being confidential, was probably more honest on that account than its much-advertised predecessor.

"Aircraft carrying high-capacity, high-explosive bombs of sufficient size," it said, "have adequate offensive power to sink or seriously damage any naval vessel at present constructed. Furthermore, it will be difficult if not impossible to build any type of vessel of sufficient strength to withstand the destructive force that can be obtained with the largest bombs that aeroplanes may be able to carry from shore bases."

He quoted also from the equally telling secret report of the British naval attaché in Washington, who acknowledged that the trials, in which smaller warships and submarines had been bombed from the air as well, substantially vindicated Mitchell's contentious thesis:

" The effects of the 2000-pound bombs bursting alongside the *Ostfriesland* and some of the 1000-pound bombs under the *Frankfurt* were so immediate and overwhelming as to render it immaterial whether these ships were possessed of 'watertight integrity' or not."

This was the very point which, for many months past, the Air Staff had been vainly pressing the Admiralty to allow for in assessing the results of mock attacks on warships by R.A.F. bombers during manœuvres with the fleet. To Beatty, Keyes and the Naval Staff, a near miss by an aerial bomb always spelt failure.

" It is true," said Trenchard, " that the percentage of direct hits in high bombing at the last Agamemnon trials was five per cent, but if close misses are counted the percentage was eighteen. It is on the close misses we depend to sink ships (for) it is against the unprotected bottom that the force of the delayed action bomb develops."

Nor could the fleet depend on gunfire for immunity against low-level torpedo aircraft.

" In relying on the high rate of fire of the multiple pom-pom, the Admiralty have practically no experience of hitting an aeroplane in flight with these small calibre weapons," said Trenchard. " The torpedo plane approaches at a rate of 120 miles per hour. Assuming it is sighted four miles away (a liberal assumption) the defenders have but two minutes in which to bring it down at a minimum range, for some few seconds, of some 400 yards. The time taken to launch a torpedo attack of 12 machines is about 2 minutes. Our experience is that the fleet have the greatest difficulty in avoiding complete surprise even when they are actually expecting attack. . . .

" It is not contended that the attackers will escape unscathed, but we hold that the dangers of torpedo plane attack are merely commensurate with those of an ordinary operation of war. . . . Casualties may and will occur, but the majority will certainly achieve their object. . . ."

Why, then, inquired Salisbury, had the Royal Navy not been attacked at sea by German aircraft during the war? Did he explain that immunity in terms of the relative equality of strength between Britain and Germany?

Trenchard replied that naval immunity had been "mainly due to the fact that zeppelins were used for reconnaissance and not offensive purposes. The enemy heavier-than-air force was more usefully employed with the armies and for bombing raids on towns."

It would be a different tale altogether in a future conflict with France, or any other modern nation, "where the army has the preponderating influence in air matters and the navy takes a very subordinate place." The Royal Navy might be lucky again if the enemy were France. For it was questionable whether the French High Command would bother to divert squadrons against naval bases until its primary strategic aim of destroying Britain's air-power had been accomplished.

4

The corroboration of ex-naval officers like Steele, the deputy Chief of Air Staff, Vyvyan, the A.O.C. Coastal Area, and Kilner, the operational commander aboard the flagship of the Atlantic Fleet, was hard to refute. Beatty did his best; but under cross-examination his performance was none too convincing. The committee wanted facts; the First Sea Lord usually obliged with blunt assertions or denials. His high and mighty attitude to anything that touched his personal infallibility or the Royal Navy's invincibility irritated Salisbury, for one.

" It was clear from the start," says Hoare, " that Salisbury's hereditary talent for dialectics reacted against the dogmatism of the admirals. Beatty gave the impression that his case was so simple that it needed no argument to support it, and that all that was required was to repeat the commandments that had been brought down from the naval Sinai.

" The Lord President was getting restive under these pontifical utterances. Trenchard and I redoubled our efforts to convince him that our case was based both on the actual lessons of war and on the certain developments of the future. Step by step, and in many talks, we succeeded in converting him, and in the end he became one of our strongest supporters."[12]

Proceedings were held up towards the end of May by a major political upheaval. There had been rumours for some time that Bonar Law was thinking of retiring. His almost complete in-audibility in the Commons had given further rise to speculation about his health. At first rumours of impending retirement were officially squashed; the Prime Minister, it was stated, had nothing worse than a relaxed throat and would rest abroad for a month, then return refreshed to his duties. When he did return, it was, in fact, to resign. The ailment of which he had been complaining was diagnosed as a symptom of malignant cancer. The patient, according to Lord Horder, who was called to Paris for the critical consultation, would be lucky if he lived for six months.

The first wave of public sympathy was followed by a scurry and flurry of lobbying, letter writing and private bargaining in high places. The most important political post in the land had fallen vacant, yet none of the obvious candidates seemed wholly suitable. The qualifications of Curzon looked incomparably better than anyone else's; and George Nathaniel flattered himself on his chances as few others who "knew the form" did. He badly wanted to become Prime Minister; he was serenely confident of achieving his greatest ambition; but a grievous shock awaited him. Robert Blake's definitive account of how Curzon lost hands down to Baldwin is an instructive commentary on the vanity of human wishes, as well as on the tortuous way in which chance and miscalculation can sway the judgment of a constitutional monarch. In this case a lengthy memorandum, drawn up not by Bonar Law but by an assistant who took it on himself to pronounce on the respective merits of the two candidates, somewhat to Curzon's detriment, was unwittingly misinterpreted by King George V as the humble advice of the retiring Prime Minister himself.

Trenchard's interest in the succession was anything but detached so that his surprise at Baldwin's wholly unlooked-for preferment was tinctured with relief. A Government headed by Curzon, who had little sympathy for the R.A.F. and its strategic pretensions, might have closed the unfinished Air Enquiry without ceremony, leaving Britain permanently and fatally weak in the air. Baldwin might lack energy; but indolence was preferable to supercilious enmity. Moreover, Baldwin for all his alleged allergy to hard work, could scarcely fail to improve on Bonar Law whose indecisiveness, in retrospect, had a tragically human explanation.

The inquiry's hearings were resumed towards the end of May; and progress in the main Salisbury Committee was rapid. By 6th June, Trenchard was writing enthusiastically to Salmond:

"The political people have at last wakened up to the importance of the air force and of Air Defence to the United Kingdom, and as a result I think we shall be asked to prepare a scheme of expansion for the R.A.F. This scheme will, of course, take time to prepare; and, if and when it is accepted, still more time to carry out. I will not go into details, but briefly the idea is to expand the regular air force by a number of squadrons and to supplement these by auxiliary squadrons and a strong reserve."

The turning point in the marathon review of strategy came suddenly. The clearing of the political atmosphere at home had helped; so, to a surprising extent, had Baldwin; but the clinching factor, psychologically speaking, was the profound impression on the Salisbury Committee of Salmond's victorious spring-cleaning operation in Iraq. The R.A.F. commander had done better than contain the Turks above Mosul as promised; he could now report that Sheikh Mohammed's rebels, aided by Turkish infiltrators, had been utterly routed. Ten thousand British, Indian and Iraqi levies, advancing in two columns, had combed out the trouble centre of Kurdistan in a brilliantly conceived and executed spring campaign. Salmond's forward squadrons, which had been patrolling the entire disputed border since the start of the Mosul crisis, opened the way into the mountains, scattering Turks and Iraqi insurgents alike with scant discrimination.

A note in Salmond's private diary, dated 12th March, discloses how he justified the operation to himself in advance, in spite of Curzon's current protests to the Cabinet about the diplomatic niceties:

> " I decided that the situation in Kurdistan had to be tackled at once. If let slide, war or no war with Turkey, it's a grave potential danger. In the event of war with Turkey it's on our rear right flank—and very weakly held. The peace prospects (at Lausanne) seem fairly good so I've taken what I think is a justifiable gamble."

His Vickers Vernon transport machines were put to various uses. Some ferried Indian troops across the northern Iraq desert in the R.A.F.'s first major operational air-lift; others, as flying ambulances, carried back the sick and wounded; the rest carried bombs. The resourceful Arthur Harris, with his two flight commanders, Ralph Cochrane and Robert Saundby, had rough holes sawn in the noses of their Vernons; racks were fitted beneath the bellies; and No. 45 Squadron anticipated the future by establishing itself as a pioneer long-range bomber team.

" By sending us straight on to the Turkish columns as they crossed the border," says Harris, " Sir John Salmond very quickly impressed upon the Turks that they were not getting the place without a fight. . . ."[13]

That had been in the beginning, before the end of February, 1923. The end of Sheikh Mohammed's resistance was considerably quicker and less dramatic than expected, once Kemal and his local military commander bowed to the inevitable. The R.A.F.'s success was barely noticed by the British Press; ironically, Salmond's censorship arrangements blunted its significance as news. But the new Prime Minister recognised the completeness of Salmond's triumph by approving his instant promotion to the rank of air marshal. As Trenchard had foreseen, the Treasury did not query the bill, nor did the Foreign Office spurn the fruits of victory. £100,000 was a small price to pay for an expedition, lasting nearly five months, which simultaneously pacified the frontier of Iraq and dissuaded Turkey against snatching a prize which she would have had to risk her all to hold.

The future of Mosul was no longer in question. Nearly three months later, on 6th August, 1923, Turkey renounced all claim to sovereignty over Mosul in the new Treaty of Peace ratified at Lausanne. Historians may argue whether this would or could have resulted without R.A.F. action, but Trenchard had no doubts in early June, 1923, about the remarkably useful repercussions in London. " I cannot emphasise too much," he wrote to Salmond, " the value your successful command in Iraq has been to us."

5

Only the War Office reacted with a bad grace. The General Staff, which disapproved of Salmond's unorthodox campaigning methods, were inclined to disparage his success as a fluke. Nor did they let it rest there; when Baldwin's Government endorsed the recommendation of the main Salisbury Committee that the R.A.F. should be expanded, Cavan responded by officially resurrecting an old demand. Army co-operation squadrons, he claimed, ought now to be administered and maintained by the army. The R.A.F. would not miss them; alternatively the R.A.F. would not run them properly if allowed to keep them. Trenchard was far from dismayed at this apparent *volte-face* on Cavan's part.

" We were not unprepared for this attitude," he informed Salmond. " Although, in view of the proposed expansion, the Cabinet might have been prepared to give the navy their air service, I am confident that public opinion . . . will never permit any government to break up, much less abolish, the Royal Air Force.

I think therefore that the very fact that the General Staff are, so to speak, joining forces with the Admiralty will strengthen the hand of the Government in maintaining our integrity, and I am certain we shall win."

From Cavan's point of view, it seemed a reasonably propitious moment to revive a claim that had not been heard since early 1922 when Wilson retired as C.I.G.S. Trenchard could hardly complain of mutilation since the R.A.F. was going to be doubled at least. Both services would benefit if the army co-operation squadrons were sliced off the parent body. There would be no loss of efficiency; on the contrary, Cavan argued, the Air Staff would be shedding a burden which it had neither the interest nor the competence to go on bearing alone.

From another point of view, however, both Derby and Cavan misjudged the changed mood of the Government. Trenchard's detailed analysis of the implications of air-power was based on the hard lessons of war. Its impact on the majority of Ministers had been salutary; so that this hasty War Office counter-proposal for vivisecting the R.A.F., while a similar but more serious demand by the admirals was still *sub judice*, invited summary refusal.

A chastened Cavan accepted the ensuing verdict without demur. Yet the intervention of the C.I.G.S. put the Admiralty at an immediate psychological disadvantage. For "jumping the queue" without good cause, the War Office had been rebuffed. And a rebuff at that moment could not fail to cast a slur of something like reproach on the naval case for a separate air arm.

Amery, the First Lord, insisted in his memoirs that War Office intervention "added to my difficulties"; the evidence presented to Balfour's sub-committee shows equally well the unexampled rancour of the proceedings as Balfour's sub-committee moved on towards the close of its separate inquiry.

The rival staffs, in this narrower debate, displayed a withering and unfailing contempt for one another's strategic principles. Seldom can the jargon of the staff paper have been turned in time of peace to such uncompromising purpose. Seldom can three committee members as experienced as Balfour, Weir and Peel have derived so few crumbs of comfort from such a feast of contradictory evidence. The standpoint of the Admiralty was expressed at the outset in oracular terms which set the tone for everything that followed.

" The great principle on which the Admiralty base their case is that the Admiralty should be solely responsible for the efficiency of the fleet. . . . At the present time, the Admiralty have not full control of the unit for duty above the sea, namely, the Fleet Air Arm, with the result that the Admiralty cannot be held responsible for its efficiency, thereby destroying this fundamental principle."

Never a man for swallowing *ex cathedra* pronouncements, Weir complained that this begged the question. It was only the indigestible *hors d'œuvre*, however. As he and his colleagues studied Trenchard's reply, then the naval rejoinder, and then the counter-rejoinder to that, they began to grasp the almost hopeless task of arbitration confronting them. Trenchard treated the "great principle of Admiralty" as an irrelevancy invented by the Sea Lords for want of anything better; what it meant, in basic English, was "that the Admiralty cannot be expected to admit the necessity of co-operation with any other department of Government. . . . They have forgotten, or hope (you) will forget, that we've had experience of two air services before, and that so much confusion resulted that committee after committee had to be appointed, which by gradual steps brought about the present single R.A.F."

Had the R.A.F. in fact abused its stewardship since by neglecting the navy? Trenchard anticipated that objection too.

" The Naval Staff," he said, "refuse to recognise that the extension of warfare to the air has introduced a new and permanent complication in the problem of national defence. If at some future date the British Empire is compelled to fight in the air for its existence, as in the past it has been compelled to fight on land and sea, it is vital that our air forces should be reared on a single policy and trained on a single system, imbued with a single doctrine, not only at home but throughout the Dominions." [14]

Few would now challenge a statement which has admirably withstood the supreme test of war, above all, in the Battle of Britain. Only Weir accepted it without qualification in the cantankerous atmosphere of the 1923 hearings. But the principle was soon lost in a welter of detail; the sub-committee had to work twice as hard as the contending staffs which kept snowing them under with conflicting evidence, with fresh points for consideration, and with revised versions of earlier points that lay buried in the rising drifts of paper.

Upstairs, in the main committee, Salisbury added to their burden by passing on anything that seemed to reflect naval grievances rather than the broad Admiralty view of defence strategy. Inevitably, there-

fore, such differences of opinion as whether or not warships could
fend off air attacks were ventilated in Balfour's sub-committee a
greater length and with considerably more venom than Salisbury
would allow. Witnesses, primed with facts which Salisbury had ruled
out of order, loosed them off later and without restraint at the heads
of Balfour, Weir and Peel. To make matters worse, the chairman
went down with phlebitis after a few meetings, leaving his overworked colleagues to manage as best they could and inform him of
progress.

Weir took over the chair, hoping that Balfour would not be
indisposed for long; confined to his bed at Sheringham, nursing his
thoughts and inflamed limbs in isolation, the elder statesman would
hardly be in a receptive mood to judge the merits of the dispute on
the confusing written evidence alone. Nobody was more skilled than
Balfour at cross-examining witnesses until, by a surprise supplementary, he extracted the grain of meaning from a load of verbiage.
With Balfour well and in command, justice would have taken
precedence over everything, including his own opinions. With
Balfour unwell in Norfolk and out of touch, justice might not so
easily be done.

" The army fight is over at last," Trenchard informed Game in a
hurried note towards the end of June. " They are frightfully sore that
their proposals for doing away with us have been turned down so
quickly. The expansion is sanctioned, and an announcement is to
be made next week. The first step is an increase of thirty-four
squadrons on to the fifteen already sanctioned. . . .

" The Navy fight is not over, and it is very bitter and intense at
the present moment. . . ."

6

By staggering its hearings, the overburdened sub-committee of
two on naval-air relations gradually reached the core of Beatty's case
against the existing system of naval-air co-operation.

The First Sea Lord declared that it was inefficient in principle
and almost unworkable in practice. Any good results, claimed the
First Sea Lord, had been achieved not because of it but in spite of it.
According to Trenchard, the Admiralty could hardly condemn as
unworkable a system which they had consistently boycotted. If it
was inefficient, which he denied, the explanation must partly be that
the Naval Staff had overrated their powers of sabotage. Their

ttitude seemed to be "heads I win, tails you lose"; their remedy
as to dismember the air force rather than co-operate with it; and
ich a remedy would invite national disaster in the event of war.

Weir and Peel preferred to draw their own conclusions about
hat; and by mid-May they had done so. After sifting the evidence
or and against the existing system—in regard to "policy, supply of
naterial, research, supply of personnel, reserves, training and
ducation, operational and administrative control at headquarters,
1 the fleet, and at the fleet's bases, discipline, and the relations
etween the two services on board aircraft carriers"—they brought
n their verdict.

" The evidence shows conclusively that the Air Ministry has
made every possible effort to ensure success for the existing
system. They have provided everything which the Admiralty
have asked for, both in material and personnel. The quality has
not been questioned, nor has there been any unavoidable delay
in supply. There is no weight of evidence that the aerial
functions required by the fleet have not been carried out
efficiently. The Air Ministry are clearly looking ahead in
research and in the provision of new types of aircraft, and the
needs of the navy are being anticipated and progress is being
achieved. In certain types of aircraft and in flying from and to
aircraft carriers, we are unquestionably ahead of other nations."

Why, then, all the fury and the fuss? Had the admirals fabricated
a case out of excessive pride and self-righteousness? Was there
nothing to be said for Beatty's grievances and pretensions?

The sub-committee found that there was something to be said,
out not much.

" The Admiralty clearly indicated that, if they had complete
control, they would expect to achieve greater efficiency through
the unification of control and the complete identification of the
naval arm with the navy. They pointed out that unless there is
a leaven of officers with personal experience of air work among
the higher ranks in the navy, then the staff at the Admiralty will
not make the most intelligent and progressive use of the air arm,
and there will be a danger of defective naval air policy and of
defective tactical use of the air arm. They say that life on board
a ship, and the efficiency of the ship as a unit, depend on all on
board speaking the same language, thinking only in terms of ship
and naval efficiency, and of a single service, and that consequently

T.   Q the importing of officers and men wearing another uniform and not being an integral part of the navy militates against the achievement of maximum naval efficiency."

In the judgment of Weir and Peel, there were certain minor fault in the R.A.F.'s present handling of the squadrons with the fleet These, they suggested, could be eliminated by the exercise of good will on both sides. They were at a loss to understand why, for instance, so few naval officers had yet volunteered for the R.A.F.'s naval wing to acquire that "personal experience of flying" which the Sea Lords rightly regarded as essential. The Naval Staff objected to temporary attachments; whether they had tried to sabotage the system by actively discouraging attachments, as Trenchard alleged was hard to prove; but the sub-committee exonerated the Air Staf from all blame on this count.

Was there any practical solution? Trenchard had complained that the Air Staff could scarcely keep up with the bewildering shift in Admiralty demands.

" One month they want a separate air service. The next month they don't. One day they say they want to break up the independent air service, the next day they say they don't. One day they say they do not fear the air and can protect themselves. The next day they ask for an enormous number of machines for their own protection. Two years ago they asked for torpedo machines for their carriers. Now they say these can be no value whatever in damaging a ship. At one time they say aircraft should have the right of search of merchant shipping. Shortly afterwards they refuse this. It is impossible to compete with this constant change of Admiralty policy."

The sub-committee, labouring under the same uncertainty, decided to take at face-value the Naval Staff's vague declaration that if their proposed remedy called in question the independent status of the R.A.F., then that, too, must be judged. It was a decision which, for totally different reasons, suited Beatty and Trenchard; the former, because a loaf of his own was always preferable to any number of slices from someone else's; the latter, because he wanted the Admiralty's real intentions brought into daylight for the sub-committee to see. The Admiralty could not have it both ways. Let Beatty and his friends accept a "clean cut," pleaded Trenchard, "or try to work a system which has so far worked well enough in spite of them."

The consequences of a "clean cut" either way appalled the sub-committee. If they agreed to the principle of a separate naval air arm, they must accept the consequences of duplication and waste. Beatty asserted that there would actually be a saving; Trenchard estimated that it would almost double existing costs. Weir and Peel, after analysing the two balance sheets, concluded that "the duplication must necessarily be substantial," leading in time of war to "a repetition of that departmental competition in the same markets which brought about the formation of the present Air Ministry."

Should book-keeping objections alone be allowed to outbalance the undoubted dissatisfaction of the navy with the existing system?

There lay the crux of the sub-committee's dilemma. They could only recommend, not command; and Balfour would have to endorse their findings. It would then be for Salisbury and the Cabinet, in turn, to decide, allowing always for the probability that Beatty might resort to intrigue or blackmail, if thwarted, as in the days of Bonar Law.

" We cannot ignore that the existing conflict of opinion is to a great extent the resultant of psychological elements of pride of service, prestige and loyal service conviction," their report stated. " While we fully appreciate the importance of these considerations, intangible as they seem, we do think they may be overstressed and that there has been a tendency on the part of the Admiralty to think more of means than of the end.

" The main reason for the creation of a national air service was to achieve unity of air development, policy and administration. If the predominating value of this is seriously impaired, as it would be by breaking off the naval part, then there would exist a reasonable case on grounds of economy for abolishing the Air Ministry and placing all other air work under the army, in fact, a reversion to the previous situation. Are we justified in breaking up an existing common service merely on psychological claims? . . .

" We feel that consideration of the foregoing wider issues compels us to elect for a continuance of the existing system with essential modifications, rather than a reversion to a system which was departed from during the war on well-considered grounds. Accordingly we recommend:

1. That the Admiralty submission for the creation of a separate naval air service should not be agreed to.
2. That the original Admiralty proposals for the administration of the naval air arm personnel be not agreed to.
3. That the Admiralty should take whatever steps are required

to ensure the seconding of naval officers of all ranks to the naval air arm of the R.A.F. . . ."

Other technical recommendations followed. These were aimed at removing small specific defects in a dual system which, after four and a half years, had still to function. The last of the sub-committee's recommendations made no bones about the reason.

" That as no decision which is not wholeheartedly accepted by both services will bring about the necessary spirit of amicable working it is essential that the final decision be heartily and publicly accepted in the national interest by the political and professional heads of both services."

Salisbury and the Prime Minister were ready to endorse the sub-committee's report as it stood; but Balfour, the absentee chairman, still confined to bed in his Norfolk retreat, announced that he would not sign it. The inquiry, after weeks of unremitting labour, was apparently back where it started. There was only one way that Weir knew of influencing a man of Balfour's rare intellectual calibre: the rest of the sub-committee must visit him without delay, take him through the evidence step by step, and defy him to produce a different answer. The personal approach was always best, in his experience, when dealing with someone so addicted to the astringent delights of metaphysical abstraction. Correspondence would not have narrowed the gap of misunderstanding between the sick chairman and his colleagues. Balfour, as Weir realised from long experience, was a stickler for the precise word in its logical context.

One day early in June, 1923, the sub-committee met again in Balfour's bedroom at Sheringham. The invalid sat up, his shoulders propped against the pillows, with Weir and Peel perched on either side of the bed, and Hankey on a chair in the background, note-book at the ready. The three visitors had driven from London that morning. The documents, representing the output of nearly two and a half months of inter-service wrangling, littered the counterpane. Weir and Balfour did most of the talking. The improbable setting contrasted sharply with the feeling of tension in the air. Neither man was in any mood to be trifled with, Weir because his patience had been sapped by the other's chilly scepticism, Balfour because there seemed no more to be said on either side of a case which, he observed, seemed to have been well and truly loaded against the navy.

" From his reading of the evidence," Hankey told this author, " Balfour felt that Weir had been less than just. The latter naturally resented the implication."

They waded together through the evidence, pausing to discuss or dispute the occasional point without uncovering anything new. On strategic grounds, Balfour finally conceded, the R.A.F. certainly had the better case. Similarly, Admiralty charges of Air Ministry mismanagement could not be upheld. On most of the technical questions, Balfour was prepared to defer to Weir's expert knowledge; if the latter said that there had been material improvements in training, weapons, design, research and the practical performance of squadrons with the fleet, that was good enough for Balfour. But how could Weir square all this with the extraordinary psychological fact of the Admiralty's deep and abiding aversion to R.A.F. control?

That mystery was still unsolved; and there, in Balfour's view, lay the heart of the controversy. Some rational explanation must exist. His colleagues left him unconvinced that their efforts to disinter it had gone far enough. Surely they did not expect him to accept it entirely as a manifestation of naval hubris? And even if this proved, after further inquiry, to be the melancholy truth, he doubted if in that case the Admiralty alone were culpable.

The deadlock was almost complete again. It seemed hopeless to continue; for everything led back to the same parting of the ways. More than ever Weir regretted Balfour's untimely infirmity, for all their sakes. If only he had been well enough to hear the witnesses, study their demeanour, measure the ever-widening gulf between naval allegations and ascertainable facts, instead of judging everything from afar in the cold and imperfect light of written notes, this impasse would have been unthinkable.

It was Hankey, hovering in the background, who hit upon a possible way out. His suggestion was providential though hardly novel. Trenchard had put it to Weir weeks before as a practical method of checking Beatty's assertions. Why not arrange, said Hankey, for the sub-committee to inspect aircraft carriers in home waters? Since it was aboard these carriers that friction between R.A.F. and naval elements was alleged to be sharpest, where better could they choose for seeking symptoms and causes? Nobody at the Air Ministry or the Admiralty need get wind of it; the visits would be unannounced, and the sub-committee would judge for themselves without being influenced by either side.

Their faces fell when Balfour remarked that his doctor would certainly forbid him to go. Then he added an afterthought: since the matter was urgent, perhaps Hankey might care to take his place? Hankey eagerly assented. The sub-committee was in business again, with an immeasurably important observation test before it.

To keep up appearances, the routine of re-examining witnesse: and trimming the loose ends of the inquiry was lengthened. Renewed discord broke out over a revised Admiralty estimate of what it would cost the taxpayer to create, run and maintain a second (naval) air service. Trenchard, as Weir had reason to remember, was an old hand at breaking down round figures into component parts; he enjoyed proving that the Naval Staff's grasp of aeronautical expenditure was anything but sound. Through his last piece of oral evidence ran the unbroken thread of an old theme:

" No staff officer can define the frontier between air and sea . . . a division of responsibility for organising the country's air-power is wrong in principle and has already in the past proved satisfactory in practice. . . .

" If the Admiralty get what they ask for now, they will in future continually encroach on the work of the air based on the shore— and with much more reason. . . . I won't be able to advance arguments against it."

What Trenchard did not yet know was how close to breaking point the sub-committee had come on the merits of that theme.

Before the end of June, Hankey organised the outing to Portsmouth where the carriers *Eagle* and *Argus* awaited an unusual inspection that provoked some curiosity but no marked suspicion. The trio spent many hours touring the carriers separately, so as to form independent opinions. Weir attached himself to the captains, Peel to the R.A.F. commanders, Hankey to the officers in command of marines.

" So far as I had any views of my own," said Hankey, himself a former colonel in the Royal Marines, " they were mildly pro-navy. This was perhaps fitting for Balfour's stand-in, since his sympathies were as firmly with the Admiralty as Weir's were with the Air Ministry. Peel's was still a floating vote. When we compared notes together afterwards, we were unanimous about one thing: working relations between the two services were far better than had been alleged to the contrary in the war *communiqués* from the rival headquarters."

Another visit to Balfour at Sheringham followed early in July. The invalid appeared put out by the unanimity of his colleagues that the naval case for a separate air service was founded largely on propaganda. His error had been grave, he admitted, but not so grave as Beatty's. He quickly endorsed Weir's suggestions that the whole sub-committee should at once confirm the R.A.F. in possession and concentrate on tightening any unwritten or loosely worded rules governing its working partnership with the navy. These, he stressed, were obviously the main source of unrest. Weir then handed to Balfour a report he had drafted since the visit to Portsmouth; here and there the old man queried a word, struck out a phrase, or inserted a balancing clause of his own. The sub-editing did not matter. The absentee chairman had come round to the principle. The sub-committee could at last bring in its formal verdict.[15]

Baldwin seemed pleased that the sub-committee had composed its differences. Had they failed, and had the news prematurely leaked out, there would have been the devil to pay politically. A further inquiry would have been virtually impossible to arrange; and the split among Ministers might easily have widened until the ground caved in beneath the Government's feet. There was only one uncertain hazard more to negotiate. How would Beatty react when the report was published? Having forced Bonar Law to hold this inquiry in the first place, he might conceivably force Baldwin to disown it. The possibility was always there; but Weir consoled himself that a united Cabinet would handle Beatty more firmly than a disunited one.

On 21st July, a Saturday, the recommendations of both committees were circulated to the departments concerned before being published as a White Paper. There was instant pandemonium at the Admiralty. The following Monday, Trenchard wrote apologetically to Salmond in Baghdad:

" The naval controversy has kept me hard at work. . . . I am afraid there will be a great row this week as the verdict has just been given in our favour."

Later that week, Trenchard heard that the entire Board of Admiralty were considering resigning in protest. When Hoare confirmed this, Trenchard said:

" Well, let them. It would be a good riddance, but I'm afraid it's just another piece of Beatty's bluff."

Hoare disagreed. From what Amery had told him, Beatty and the Sea Lords were in deadly earnest this time.

" The Board of Admiralty," Hoare has written, " decided to resign en bloc if the committee's recommendations were accepted. On my side, I said that I would resign if they were not accepted. Baldwin was at his wits' end. It looked for several days as if the Government would break up. Hoping still for a compromise that would prevent catastrophe, the Prime Minister asked Amery and me to make a final effort for peace.

" We accordingly met our advisers in the House of Commons

on the Friday morning after the report was published and spent several hours trying to find a way out of the impasse. All that we could do was to smooth off some of the rougher edges, but upon the main settlement Trenchard and I could not and would not budge."[16]

Baldwin spent the week-end of 27th–29th July at Chequers. The Press had meanwhile caught the whiff of a new political crisis-in-the-making. By Monday, 30th July, most of the national dailies were busy speculating, beneath big headlines, on impending resignations and rumours of resignations: now it was Trenchard, now Beatty, now all the Sea Lords together, now only the Ministers. The Committee of Imperial Defence had given its blessing to the Balfour report; but ministerial approval had not been unanimous. It remained for the Cabinet to speak.

The second trial of strength between the admirals and the Government within four months was imminent, the difference now being that the Press and public, which mainly sympathised with the naval view, had wind of it. Would Baldwin succeed in resisting the pressures of coercion and propaganda and rally his divided colleagues, or would he buy off Beatty by shelving the Balfour sub-committee's verdict? At the end of the week Parliament would be rising for the summer recess. A statement by the Prime Minister one way or the other was unavoidable. Questions had been tabled to ensure that the Commons would be informed of the Cabinet's decision, petitions organised by Admiralty supporters to help Baldwin reach the right decision. Government back benchers were confident that Baldwin would yield to Beatty's ultimatum.

On Thursday, 2nd August, the Prime Minister confounded the prophets behind him by announcing that the crisis had been settled. The Cabinet, he said, had agreed to uphold the verdict in favour of the Air Ministry.

" The reasons in favour of a single air service which have had weight with the Government," said Baldwin, " may be summed up as follows:

" In the first place, the air service, although it must have intimate relations with the other armed forces at sea and on land, and must be familiar with their requirements, differs in its conditions essentially from both. On the other hand, aircraft, whether flying above the sea or elsewhere, are broadly speaking, governed according to the same principles.

" In the second place the whole science of air-power is in a condition of rapid development. The application, therefore, of

experience both as to personnel and as to material, wherever that
experience could be obtained, whether at sea or on shore, is vital
to success in either case. We cannot afford to break up the lessons
of this experience.

"In the third place, it is clear that in certain contingencies the
shore-based aircraft and the air force of the fleet may be called upon
to act together. Such common action may be very difficult without
a unity of method in both services. Efficiency, therefore, prescribes
common knowledge, common training, common material provisions,
and a common service. Economy points in the same direction. From
this last point of view the conclusion against the duplication of
training schools and aerodromes and building plant is evident.

"For these reasons, the conclusion of the sub-committee and of
the main committee that there should be a single air service must,
in the opinion of the Government, be accepted, subject to the
conditions which are necessary to meet the detailed objections of the
Admiralty."

These conditions were simply administrative trimmings: naval
uniform and a distinguishing badge would be worn by naval officers
attached to the parent R.A.F.; a new code of regulations governing
pay, discipline, staff liaison would be drawn up; and fleet reconnaissance would henceforth be entrusted to navy recruits alone.
The concessions cost Trenchard little. Whether Beatty admitted
it or not, they had been honoured in the spirit by the R.A.F. from
the beginning. Baldwin omitted to mention what was, politically,
the most significant reason of all for the Cabinet's endorsement of the
Balfour findings: the final calling of Beatty's bluff. Why did the
First Sea Lord and his fellow admirals suddenly withdraw their
joint threat to resign *en bloc*? Amery, the First Sea Lord at the time,
is the only informed commentator who has so far touched on the
point.

"There was bitter disappointment in the Admiralty when the
Cabinet endorsed this report," he wrote in his memoirs. "And it
was only with great difficulty that I dissuaded Beatty and the Sea
Lords from resigning in a body, and that only by insisting that
Baldwin, in his statement in the House, should make it clear that the
Balfour decision was not final." [17]

Baldwin's statement in the House gives the lie to that explanation;
it was quite unequivocal. And still Beatty did not resign. Amery
seems once more to have exaggerated. In fact, something else came
to the Prime Minister's notice which enabled him to call Beatty
shortly to heel.

Before Baldwin's statement in the House, a number of newspapers carried remarkably detailed and accurate accounts of the Admiralty case against the Air Ministry and, indeed, against the Government. On 30th July, for instance, a signed article by Lord Rothermere appeared in the *Daily Mail*, which was too well informed for Weir's taste. He did not mind that Rothermere should have chosen such a moment to take sides with the navy against the R.A.F.; Rothermere could not help repeating himself. What Weir objected to most strongly was Rothermere's bare-faced use of secret information culled from the actual sub-committee proceedings to stiffen his arguments. Weir took the liberty of drawing Baldwin's attention to certain extracts from the article which tallied word for word with Admiralty evidence. It was extremely unlikely, he pointed out, that the Air Ministry should have seen fit to betray itself to the proprietor of the *Daily Mail*. In his view, the information, which had since been picked up by other journals, including *The Times*, could only have been supplied by the Admiralty.*

According to Weir, Baldwin took a very grave view of the leakage and confronted Beatty with the facts when the latter arrived to discuss his threatened resignation. The Prime Minister said, in effect, that he would not dream of coming between the First Sea Lord and his conscience; but whether Beatty was serious about resigning or not, the Government would not hesitate to investigate the disclosure of secret information and take vigorous action against those responsible. Such a course, he stressed, would not help Beatty in his avowed intention of continuing the struggle from the benches of the House of Lords.

"The First Sea Lord," said Weir, "apparently decided on reflection that he had better stay."

The affront to Baldwin's lofty sense of moral rectitude served its political purpose. Weir never saw the Prime Minister so aggressively determined about anything again. Had Beatty resigned, claimed Weir, Baldwin would certainly have called him to account for turning secret information to his own ends. Rothermere, without knowing it, had also served a purpose rather different from that which he intended or desired. A special Cabinet committee was appointed, under the chairmanship of the Home Secretary, to "ascertain how certain newspapers were able to publish last week

---

* The chief complaint "leaked" by the Admiralty to the Press was that their letters-patent as Lords Commissioners of the Board expressly laid down that they—and they alone—were responsible for the fighting efficiency of the navy. Under the existing dual system of air control, they could no longer, they argued, discharge this heavy constitutional responsibility.

he pith of an official document outlining the Admiralty's case";
ut no subsequent action was taken against any individual.

"You must be pleased that the great naval battle is over and
ery proud of the result," Philip Game wrote to Lady Trenchard on
rd August. "The more I think of what he has done in the last few
ears, the more I am completely overcome with astonishment.

"With anyone else as Chief of the Air Staff, the air force would
ave broken up long ago. He, on the contrary, entirely by his own
fforts, has trebled it, secured its position, and induced the Government to do what no Government has dared to do for a century—
nake a stand against the navy. It is really stupendous and words
ail me. . . ."

The reader will have gathered that it was not quite so simple as
hat. Trenchard had certainly fought with spirit. His staying power
vas as prodigious in its way as his vision; but, refusing to stoop to
he ways of intrigue, the mistakes of his opponents and the unfailing
lertness of allies like Weir were his only political shield. Trenchard,
t must be said, was singularly lucky in his allies.

17. The Master-Builder

The time of year alone encouraged Baldwin to be magnanimous. For if Beatty, by giving him a fright, had finally roused the Prime Minister to an uncharacteristic pitch of resolution, it was also the end of the session at Westminister; and the public had had its fill of inter-service feuds. Parliament rose, Baldwin vanished to Aix-les-Bains, and the Press abandoned itself to topics better attuned to the "silly season" mood. The Admiralty had clearly sustained a narrow defeat on points; and the moral drawn by *The Times*, when the future of the Government had seemed uncertain indeed, remained the shrewdest commentary on a squalid episode. No longer a mouthpiece of Harmsworth opinion (*The Times* regained its traditional freedom of expression shortly after Northcliffe's death in 1922, when Rother-mere's bid for ownership was defeated by Colonel Waldorf Astor), that newspaper had declared on 28th July:

" However strong their [the admirals'] case, it can only have been weakened by the tactics which have been adopted, with or without their knowledge and approval, in the effort to force their convictions on Parliament and the public. Their mistaken partisans, who have been getting up petitions against the report in the House of Commons, or spreading rumours that the Members of the Board had threatened to resign in the event of its adoption, have impaired instead of helped their case."

As the excitement faded into anti-climax, the most momentous Cabinet decision of all, which went furthest towards explaining Baldwin's lenient treatment of Beatty, was generally ignored. This was the endorsement of Salisbury's proposal that the Chiefs of Staff should henceforth sit as a permanent sub-committee of the C.I.D., thus consolidating Lloyd George's experiment during the Chanak emergency. For Trenchard and the air force, the decision meant more than a narrow points victory over the Sea Lords It meant that the status of the Chief of Air Staff had at last been recognised officially as equal to that of the C.I.G.S. and the First Sea Lord, and that, in future, the three would be expected to advise the Cabinet on defence issues as one. Having discovered, after Churchill, that only a superman could adequately serve as a peacetime Defence Minister, Salisbury concluded, quite rightly in Balfour's view, that the Committee of Imperial Defence must be strengthened by gearing it to the collective "brain" of the three service chiefs.

In future the trio would be expected to concert their views and confine their energies to fighting the King's enemies rather than each other, in keeping with the formula drawn up by Salisbury, at Hankey's suggestion:

" In addition to (their) function as advisers on sea, land or air policy respectively, to their own Board or Council, each of the three Chiefs of Staff will have *an individual and collective responsibility* for advising on defence policy as a whole, the three constituting as it were a Super-Chief of a War Staff in Commission."

The operative words, it should be noted, were those originally suggested by Trenchard in 1919 when, in conversation with Hankey at Adastral House, he had voiced his longing for a "square ring and Queensberry rules." Beatty might find it harder than Cavan to start confiding in him; but opportunities of sabotaging air development would be less plentiful, too.

Experience would teach Trenchard the unpalatable truth that the new status of the service chiefs had its drawbacks. It had been relatively easy at the time of Chanak to reach agreement because the difficulties then were clear-cut and the psychological pressure was great. Now, however, their discussions on such imponderables as the best means of protecting the proposed naval base at Singapore, were almost bound to generate less light than heat. For the Chiefs of Staff were still at odds on most strategic matters; their rival doctrines were incapable of immediate proof; and Trenchard was invariably the odd-man-out, since neither Cavan nor Beatty shared his total faith in air-power. Forced to choose between dissenting and conforming, increasingly uneasy under the scrutiny of Ministers who naturally wished the defence trinity to speak with one voice when it spoke at all, Trenchard would soon learn that his position was not a comfortable, nor a particularly simple one.

His one thought that summer, none the less, was to "get away and cut the office altogether," for as long as he decently could. He was physically and mentally tired; and he owed his family a holiday. When he returned to Air Ministry in October, the detailed arrangements for a gradual expansion of the R.A.F. at home had been roughed out. These he had left in the capable hands of Brooke-

Popham and Philip Game, whose term in India had recently expired. Land for new airfields and depots had to be surveyed and leased, often at unfavourable prices, after much prospecting and hard bargaining. As for recruiting, Trenchard decided that this must wait till last. By spreading development evenly over six or seven years, meanwhile securing ground, machines and "capital goods" in easy stages, the Air Staff would not scare this or any future Government into repenting of a measure purely because it oppressed the taxpayer. Thrift was still Trenchard's order of the day.

Salisbury's defence trinity intrigued some of the Dominion Prime Ministers who descended on London in October, 1923, for talks which promoted important changes in the relationship between the mother-country and the self-governing countries of an Empire that was already emerging as a Commonwealth in all but name. Even the Admiralty, clinging to its nineteenth-century principle of a single fleet to which each Dominion would contribute men, money and ships according to means, had to moderate its old demands. Amery persuaded the Sea Lords that the separate right to existence of Canadian, Australian, South African and New Zealand navies must be recognised forthwith.

In a private speech to the visiting Premiers, Trenchard returned to the disquieting thesis which had so impressed Salisbury when the R.A.F. was struggling to maintain its right to exist in the summer. Air-power concentrated in the wrong hands, he warned, could "bring Britain to the verge of destruction in the next war." An over-crowded island off the European mainland could no longer depend for protection on the narrow seas about her; she must be as strong in the air as her nearest potential foe. The pattern of Empire or Commonwealth security, too, had altered. Navies alone were no longer enough. For "air interference with British sea communications" across the globe would be the first objective of any enemy worth his salt. Yet aircraft justified themselves on other counts.

" Aircraft," Trenchard said, " are the only weapon of war on which the money you spend is not wholly unproductive. The judicious use of service machines in peace will refund no small part of your war insurance."

Few of his distinguished listeners were scandalised by his words. Trenchard's reputation for realism was better known overseas than he himself realised. The many Canadians and Australians who had served under his command on the Western Front included several outstanding leaders, young in years but mature in the wisdom of air strategy and all imbued with their chief's fiery enthusiasm. They had benefited since 1919 from his precarious uphill battle for recognition. The prejudices of the older services were evidently less influential in the newer lands. Canada, for instance, after challenging the stiff Amiralty doctrine of "One Empire, One Navy," had gone further in 1920 by establishing a small independent air force modelled on the struggling R.A.F. The others would follow that lead; of that he had no doubt.

Always diffident about addressing audiences, however small and select, Trenchard wondered afterwards whether his "message" had "got through." Hoare reassured him. Balfour, observed the Minister, might have appeared "somnolent," but nobody could judge him by appearances even when the theme of the sermon was as familiar as this undoubtedly was to him. None of the visitors had nodded off in any case; the speaker's dark strategic predictions held their attention to the end.

Any repercussions, favourable or otherwise, were precluded by appalling frankness of another kind ventilated by Baldwin on the same day, 26th October, in another place. The Prime Minister, who had been long brooding on the chronic problem of mass unemployment, startled a Plymouth audience, his own Cabinet colleagues, and members of all parties, by proposing a drastic and politically unacceptable remedy for the disease: protection duties against cheap imports. The proposal was probably most distressing to his conservative followers, who could not forget Bonar Law's promise not to tamper with the fiscal laws during the lifetime of that Parliament. The flouting of that pledge by Bonar Law's successor, an ironmaster's son with a social conscience and a fixed habit of thinking aloud at awkward moments, had disturbing consequences. Baldwin had carelessly slung an outsize political brick through his own window; and his supporters did not relish having to foot the bill.

This second political contretemps of 1923 was more sensational than the first. Baldwin's fall from grace came as suddenly as his rise, but was all the more embarrassing for being so palpably avoidable. It was not every year that a cortège of Commonwealth Premiers could watch their host commit political suicide and attend the obsequies. For the dissolution of Parliament on 26th November was followed by the last election fought on the classic nineteenth-century platform of free trade or protection; and with the Conservatives split, and many voters disconcerted by Baldwin's lack of discretion, the final returns showed a Free Trade majority of over ninety in the new House. Baldwin had in fact been counted out. The one lingering uncertainty was which of his opponents, Asquith, Lloyd

George or Ramsay MacDonald, could secure enough support to form an alternative Government.

On 8th January, 1924, two weeks before Ramsay MacDonald accepted the King's commission to head the first Labour administration, Trenchard wrote to a former R.A.F. colleague in retirement:

" The longer I stay, the more difficult it is to go. Now I try to make the excuse that this change of Government precludes my going. I wonder if it does. After the Labour Government has come in (if it does come in) I think we shall have more friends than ever before. I may be wrong but that is my impression."

It was an impression founded on something more durable than the sneaking fellow-feeling of one underdog for another. Trenchard liked the Labour M.P.s he had met. He also liked the trade union leaders whom he had consulted when preparing his Halton apprenticeship scheme. Their advice had been sound; he had adopted it readily; and union recognition of the Halton system had followed. The official Labour attitude to his own difficulties as Chief of Air Staff was unmarred by hypocrisy or cant. The pacifist wing of the Party opposed him on principle; Trenchard rejected the principle while respecting its honesty. On the other hand, most Labour back benchers were unaffected by the service prejudice which blinded so many others. Why, then, pretend that the revolution was at hand because Baldwin seemed unwilling to reach an understanding with the Liberals to keep Labour out?

Trenchard felt quite sincerely that a period of responsibility would do MacDonald good and the nation no harm. It was true that the Liberals, with 158 seats, and the Conservatives with 258, could "dish" him at any moment by joining forces. That possibility was remote, however, since Baldwin had gone to the country protesting that he would not carry on without tariff protection, the Liberals had sworn to deny him the chance, and the electorate's equivocal verdict had disappointed them both. Whatever happened, the life of this new government would probably be short. Defence controversies might well be put into cold storage for the duration, though this did not necessarily imply, as some professed to think, that MacDonald would be the death of the air force. Trenchard took pains to squash the suggestion wherever he met it. There was no virtue that he could see in borrowing other men's antipathies.

The award of the G.C.B. in the New Year Honours mildly astonished him. As he confessed on 22nd January in reply to a congratulatory note from Ellington:

" I was extraordinarily lucky to get it without being kicked out at the same time, and some people asked me if it had been given to me because I was going.

" The political situation is very uncertain, but I personally do not think this is the end of all things, as apparently some do. I believe the country will go on in exactly the same way as in the past —gradually getting better, just as much better in the next fifty years or so as it is now compared with what it was fifty years ago."

Later that day, Ramsay MacDonald became Prime Minister without entering into any arrangements with other parties. His Cabinet team was strengthened by a number of former Liberals, notably Lord Haldane, whose reforming zeal at the War Office before 1914 had remodelled the old British Army. As Lord Chancellor in early 1924, Haldane appeared to be no more than a figurehead; and yet, as the only available expert on defence matters, he was destined to become the arbiter of all strategic disputes, for the service Ministers were comparative novices. The credentials of Chelmsford, an ex-Viceroy of India unexpectedly transported to the Admiralty, were as nebulous as those of Stephen Walsh, the new Secretary of State for War, or of Brigadier Birdwood Thomson, Hoare's successor at Air Ministry. It was Haldane who, from the start, jockeyed them along, just as it was Haldane who steered the Committee of Imperial Defence out of trouble with the ease of an accomplished veteran who knew the course and the limitations of his vehicle.

MacDonald's greatest dilemma was how to govern without causing the disintegration of his Cabinet and Party alike. He was bereft of allies; most of his colleagues lacked experience of admini-stration; and the first three months were exceptionally trying because of industrial unrest. There were strikes on the railways, in transport, and among London busmen; the miners agitated for a minimum wage guaranteed by law. Hostile critics regarded these symptoms of economic discontent as ironic proof of Labour's unfitness to rule, and recalled the Party's empty boast on the hustings that MacDonald alone had some magical cure for unemployment.

In these circumstances Haldane could handle service Ministers and Chiefs in his own quiet but masterly fashion. Like a seer born out of due time, he firmly appropriated the effective powers of a Minister of Defence in 1924 without once having his unique position of authority called in question. When, for example, Beatty con-ducted his first experiment to test how far the Labour tail in the Commons wagged the Government dog, he discovered something of Haldane's supple skill in rallying the Cabinet. In February, 1924, a Press campaign was launched on behalf of the Admiralty's plan to lay down five new cruisers as fleet replacements. The ultra-Conservative newspapers naturally supported the Sea Lords' case, but a few organs of Liberal opinion sounded a more hostile or carping note.

"They try to represent that I am a dictator and have bullied two Cabinets into swallowing schemes for the aggrandisement of the British Navy," Beatty complained. "But now I am up against the Labour Party I am to face defeat. . . . I am having a rotten time. . . ."[1]

Beatty's difficulty, which becomes plainer in other letters he wrote at the time to his wife, was "the amount of real ignorance" he encountered among Ministers on issues of defence. In fact, the question whether or not the navy needed those cruisers almost split the Cabinet. For nearly a month the stern pacifism of Snowden, the Chancellor of the Exchequer, was proof against Haldane's reasoning; but Snowden finally yielded, the naval estimates for 1924-5 provided for the cruisers, Ramsay MacDonald managed to placate his own back benchers, and even Beatty, whom Haldane had meanwhile reprimanded for his propagandist activities, had to admit that "on the whole, we came out of it very well."

The First Sea Lord, a week before the Commons' debate on 21st February, acknowledged the fairness of the elder statesman behind the scenes.

"Old Haldane," he informed Lady Beatty, "has been a great help to us and supports us on every occasion."

There was less controversy over the air estimates which had been prepared before Hoare's departure. Trenchard had certainly not misjudged the sympathetic temper of the Government: an extra £3 millions for eight new Home Defence squadrons was voted without a murmur. Greatly heartened, the Chief of Air Staff approached Haldane in person with a simple, ingenious and cheap proposal for speeding his expansion programme. Why not raise auxiliary squadrons of week-end pilots and technicians? It worked in the case of the army, so why should it fail in the case of the R.A.F.? Haldane was interested and not a little flattered.

Territorial Army units had flourished ever since he had founded them over fifteen years before, during his term at the War Office; the suggestion of winged "Terriers" appealed to the Lord Chancellor, who confessed his inability to understand why Churchill, of all people, had turned up his nose at them, particularly as provision for such a reserve had been specified in Trenchard's post-war Charter. The

Chief of Air Staff said that he, too, could not account for Churchill's allergy, though it was possibly due to a temperamental reluctance on Winston's part to allow that young men could succeed where he had failed and become fully fledged pilots in their spare time.

The Cabinet approved the Auxiliary Air Force project without delay. Its inexpensiveness was a commendation in itself. The detailed plan submitted by Trenchard so attracted Snowden that the Chancellor had it classified in March as a Cabinet paper. Haldane was authorised to institute the necessary legislation at once.

" I will just try and give you a few points of interest," Trenchard told Ellington on 19th May, in a long discursive letter. " First, the expansion scheme of the Royal Air Force to bring it up to fifty-two squadrons for home defence: it's proceeding apace and nobody is trying to stop it. They are all keen on it. The actual organisation of home defence is also going on at a great pace, and we have a big War Office and Air Ministry Committee reporting (to us) on their various responsibilities. We are operationally responsible for the whole thing. . . ."

The physical energy of Haldane at sixty-eight was as impressive as his easy command of the intricacies of inter-service relations which had altered out of all knowledge in the decade since he was hounded out of office. In a matter of weeks, he assimilated the salient facts of controversies which had bedevilled the C.I.D. since the R.A.F.'s formation.

Professional evasions cut no ice whatever with him. He preferred views served up in straightforward style without sauce or trimmings, which may explain why he treated Trenchard with avuncular affability. Yet to bracket Haldane with Weir as a natural champion of the third service would be absurd. Haldane held aloof, a philosophic figure above the battle, but well able to detect every false move through the smoke and din beneath.

He was probably the most underrated statesman of his time, not only because of the odious Press campaign which had once impugned his patriotism, but because he fought shy himself of all publicity. In this latter respect, at least, he might have been Trenchard's twin.

Haldane was also a political realist. Having pressed for the Admiralty's new cruisers he pressed no less diligently for the R.A.F.'s expansion, recognising both as essential for national security. The inhibitions of colleagues like Snowden could not deflect him; and to grasp this point is to grasp half the reason why an inexperienced Labour Government, living largely on sufferance, lasted for nearly a year without alienating the confidence of Parliament in its defence

policy. The one blot on its record, in the judgment of many, was
the decision to shelve the ill-fated plan to build a new naval base at
Singapore. Perhaps it is time to reconsider that verdict, too.

When Beatty formally invited the Cabinet at the end of March,
1924, to approve the Singapore project, he received an unexpected
rebuff. The First Sea Lord had hoped that Haldane, having handed
him his cruisers, would be willing to throw in this important naval
extra. There he misjudged the pliability of Haldane—and the
temper of Trenchard. Beforehand, Beatty noted complacently that
the Singapore plan had been "accepted reluctantly by three Cabinets
representing Liberals and Conservatives in Coalition, and by two
Conservative Governments, and has been endorsed by two Imperial
Conferences. So to reverse the whole decision will not be easy."

It was reversed none the less; and one reason for this was
Trenchard's decision to oppose the existing Singapore plan with an
abandon that would have been most ill-advised while the R.A.F.'s
continued existence was still in doubt. With the noose of anxiety no
longer round his neck, Trenchard felt free to voice misgivings which
he had carefully repressed since 1920, when the Naval Staff began
to shape the elaborate scheme for transforming Singapore into the
Gibraltar of the Far East. It was not the naval base itself he objected
to, but the alarmingly old-fashioned methods proposed for its
protection.

The need for a Far Eastern base had been reinforced by the results
of the Washington Conference in 1921.[2] Partly to appease Canada
and the United States, the Anglo-Japanese Naval Treaty had to be
scrapped; then the contracting powers agreed to reduce their fleets
in accordance with a sliding scale. Ratios of capital ships and aircraft
carriers were carefully fixed, entitling Japan to a battle force only
three-fifths the size of the British or the American. It looked safe and
neat enough on paper; but the tearing up of the Anglo-Japanese
Treaty tilted the strategic balance in the Pacific where an uncommitted Japan now emerged as potentially the strongest naval power
east of Suez. Henceforth India, Burma, Malaya, not to mention
Australia and New Zealand, would depend more than ever on the
mobility of a Royal Navy so weakened by international agreement as
to be incapable of discharging its traditional role of policing the
world's oceans. A naval base was an obvious necessity for the future
security of the Western Pacific; Singapore was the obvious site; but
there was little public enthusiasm for a long-term plan that would
cost the taxpayer dear.

" This project of putting Singapore in order so that it shall be

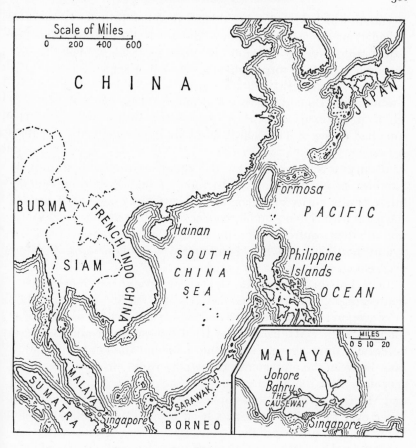

Singapore

of use to the navy has been attacked by many as if it was something new," Beatty said at the Lord Mayor's banquet in November, 1923. " This is far from the case. For many years it was a naval base, a base recognised by many of the most astute [he mentioned among others Sir Stamford Raffles, the colony's first settler] as being the best strategical position in the Far East."

It was not the location that troubled Trenchard. Nor did he quarrel with the estimated outlay of £23 millions on a floating dockyard, modern storage and repair facilities, and an arsenal. What perplexed and vexed him was the contrast between these modern installations and the antediluvian system proposed for their defence. Beatty seemed to be breathing the air of the nineteenth century, betraying a disregard for the strategic realities of the twentieth which Trenchard could not condone. Into the Admiralty's calculations the facts of air-power did not begin to enter. The Sea Lords still chose to discount the increasing range, mobility and hitting power of the torpedo bomber, a weapon which was not theirs to control, as though it did not exist, seeking instead to impress Ramsay MacDonald, as they had impressed his predecessors, with the strategic value of 15-inch fixed guns pointing out to sea. The time had come, in Trenchard's view, to expose the fallacy of their reasoning.

Beatty was infuriated by the counter-proposal that torpedo bombers should replace at least some of the 15-inch guns in the interests of security and economy. The Chief of Air Staff pressed the point with vigour; and it reopened, as he intended that it should, the unsettled controversy on the relative striking power of bomber against battleship which had embittered the Balfour sub-committee proceedings of the previous year.[3]

The Labour Cabinet had better, or at any rate more urgent, matters on its mind than rival methods of defending an unbuilt base at Singapore. Since the Chiefs of Staff could not agree on fundamentals, neither MacDonald nor Haldane saw any reason to impose agreement from above. Too astute to sound the gong for another bout between the protagonists of sea-power and air-power, Haldane suggested that the scheme should be deferred for the time being and MacDonald gratefully complied. A storm of Conservative wrath broke over the Prime Minister's head in the Commons as a result. He weathered it successfully.

During that debate, and a second the following July, the military grounds for a decision which Opposition extremists falsely condemned as an example of Labour's lack of patriotism were submerged in the tide of political abuse. The Conservatives could not or would not see that a plan supported in principle by the Dominions, and one in which both Australia and New Zealand had a direct interest, might have been set aside for arguably sound strategic reasons. No doubt Ramsay MacDonald felt that this aspect of the matter would have come less credibly from his lips than the woolly generalisations with which he favoured the House instead. Even a Churchill at his most eloquent would have been hard put to it in 1924 to convince many M.P.s that the fault lay as much in their own shallow thinking as in the alleged anti-militarist sentiments of certain Labour leaders.

Haldane's role as judge was never appreciated, though Trenchard's as devil's advocate was suspected by a few.

It is a curious fact that the political mist enveloping this early phase of the Singapore tragedy has been allowed to persist until the present. It is no part of the present writer's task to dissipate it entirely. That would require a book as long as this again; yet it must be shown that the seeds of disaster were sown, not primarily by the wavering and appeasing policies of the thirties, but by the wantonly narrow military planning of the twenties. It will also be shown how Trenchard, who never deviated from his grimly prophetic views as to the hollowness of the naval defence project, finally allowed himself to be overborne. There are limits to the physical and moral resistance of any man permanently at odds with his partners in a "defence trinity," particularly when that trinity is regarded as authoritative only if it speaks with a single voice. The struggle which he started in 1924 continued intermittently for the next three years. The causes and circumstances of Trenchard's ultimate surrender in the interests of a bogus harmony will be considered later.

His own standards of self-criticism were so unsparing that he went to the grave thirty-two years later still unable to forgive himself for an error which appeared to him all the more heinous in the light of the inglorious military debacle at Singapore in 1942. But, as the contemporary evidence should make clear, his failure in the twenties was one of persuasion, not of conviction; his guilt, if any, lay in not persevering against the indifference and scepticism of Ministers and against the intolerance and obstructiveness of rival Chiefs of Staff who thought him incorrigible or slightly mad.

2

The shelving of the Singapore project in March, 1924, was thus partly due to Trenchard's exercise of the veto as a member of the Chiefs of Staff sub-committee. Beatty and the Naval Staff retaliated in kind by requesting the Cabinet to consider the intolerably bad relations between the Royal Navy and that part of the Royal Air Force whose duty it was to co-operate with the fleet. Haldane promptly examined the naval charges of inefficiency and bad faith; invited both Beatty and Trenchard to explain why there had been no joint meetings to stimulate the "goodwill on both sides" which Balfour had described as the root cause of misunderstanding; and refused to accept that the recent political changes were a sufficient excuse for bringing the business of the C.I.D. to a virtual standstill. This was largely true, but the reminder did not mollify Haldane.

" I give you three months to settle this dispute between your-selves," he told the two Chiefs of Staff. " I'll arbitrate where necessary, but I'd like you both to remember that you've wasted nine months already."[4]

Haldane was equally adamant that there would be no further inquiry along the old lines advocated by Beatty. The Balfour award, he insisted, had confirmed the R.A.F. in its control of squadrons with the fleet, and that was that. But it had also recommended certain administrative reforms. The two staffs should have made a start on these months ago. They must codify an agreed list without delay. Now a written code was the last thing Trenchard wanted; it would offer the Sea Lords endless occasions of mischief by lending a legal plausibility to frivolous charges of inefficient management. Imaginary grievances could be blown up with a little ill will to look real and serious. But Trenchard's protests in this respect were as ineffective as Beatty's about the validity of the Balfour award. Haldane simply told them both that a written agreement must be ready for his signature by the end of July. If they did not produce it, he would impose his own.[5]

The mere threat of a Judgment of Solomon was sufficient, and Trenchard could not but admire, in his aggravation, the austere impartiality of Haldane who picked his way mentally from one subject to the next with the calm and sure-footed grace of a cat crossing an unpaved street.

" Beatty was just as stunned as I," said Trenchard. " Haldane had knocked both our heads together—hard."

The psychological result was strangely gratifying. Keyes, whom the First Sea Lord deputed to act for him, seemed to undergo a miraculous change of heart.

" I do so intensely want to settle this business satisfactorily for the good of the services," he wrote to Trenchard on 30th March, "and I am trying very hard all the time to see 'the other side.' . . . I promise I will do all I can to bring about peace."

Trenchard's reply next day was also framed in a relatively conciliatory spirit.

" I do really want to settle this controversy, but I will be quite honest and say I want to settle it on the lines of the integrity of the air service and of giving the Admiralty all they want."

The negotiations went on almost uninterrupted through the early summer months of 1924. There were thirteen heads of agreement to draft, regulating every practical point of contact between sailors and airmen on ship and shore. The disciplinary powers of the ship's commander, the duties and working conditions of the lowest ranking fitter, the attachment to Air Ministry of naval officers for closer liaison, the supplying of equipment designed to Admiralty specifications—these were some of the technicalities which had to be regulated one by one. Naval demands were not all unequivocal. Trenchard and Keyes wrangled, for instance, over the Admiralty claim that fleet squadron costs should be included in their estimates; there was another tussle over the percentage of seconded naval officers to be trained by the R.A.F. as pilots, Trenchard refusing to alter the figure of "not less than 30 per cent of air force officers, whether regular or short service" to serve aboard the carriers. He had no intention of allowing naval pilots to outnumber his and develop as units of a floating Trojan Horse from which the Sea Lords would debouch one day, when the mood of conciliation had passed, to present some other Government with the accomplished fact of a Fleet Air Arm already established in all but name.

It was a pleasant change within the wider family circle to have Trenchard and Keyes on reasonably amicable terms again. Being temperamentally very dissimilar, it had been simpler for them in the past to avoid seeking one another's society for the sake of domestic peace.

Much of Trenchard's resilience flowed from his practice of keeping the public and private sectors of life as far apart as was practicable. He loved good company, particularly that of younger people, and his house at Dancer's Hill saw a continuous procession of visitors. Junior air force officers often came to dine; and the distant awe in which many of them held a chief known, usually by hearsay, as an omnipotent slave-driver, melted in the warm and informal atmosphere of his home surroundings. Those who were older and remembered him in France, marvelled now at the mellowing effect on him of a supremely happy marriage. The Trenchards were not rich; and they disdained the false airs often worn by the class-conscious. The Chief of Air Staff's salary barely covered his public and personal expenses; for the lowest paid of the service heads, drawing less than £3000 a year, had no private income. His wife had a small annuity which went further towards providing comfort than would have been possible in the hands of a less capable manager. This was particularly noticeable when those ungovernable cycles of misfortune which are part of the human condition upset the rhythm of their ordered, lively and intensely crowded existence.

They now had two children of their own, in addition to Lady Trenchard's three by her late husband. Hugh, the eldest, was born three months after the Cairo Conference, in June, 1921; Tom in December, 1923. Trenchard's affection for them was tender in the extreme and would probably have astonished those who recollected him as the hard and apparently incurable bachelor of old, wedded only to the business of conducting war in the air. There was none of that chilly and almost abashed remoteness that so often mars the growth of understanding between a father leading an active public life and his children. During the recurring bouts of Government austerity, when he denied himself the use of an official car "just to encourage the others," he took to cycling morning and evening between Dancer's Hill and the station at Potters Bar. He seldom looked entirely safe to his wife as, with bulging brief-case balancing on the handle-bars, he would go wobbling down the drive into the narrow two-mile stretch of lane and road to the train. Sometimes, if he remembered to telephone before leaving the office early, Trenchard could rely on a family reception committee at the ticket barrier and an escort of children in the back seat of the car on the way home. As a rule, however, he returned long after their bedtime.

The references to home life in Trenchard's voluminous correspondence with R.A.F. commanders are almost negligible. Ellington, who was godfather to Hugh, the elder boy, was given occasional glimpses of the gay background from which Trenchard drew refreshment of spirit against times of stress. At week-ends large cars would appear now and then with important callers. Ministers or ex-Ministers, distinguished soldiers or key civil servants whose advice he valued or whose support he needed, often came to dine. Churchill, Hoare, Weir and Hankey were among the regulars. For it was Trenchard's rule never to lose sight of the original few whose friendship and sympathy required no proving. He was fond of saying that "a man may learn or understand after forty but he won't absorb." And since most influential politicians were considered young at forty, though he thought of them as non-absorbent, there were many to be stimulated, reasoned with or inspired.

It probably would not have surprised him had he ever discovered that Haig, who on a visit to Dancer's Hill in the early twenties, declared in a rare outburst of confidence that the Great War produced only two new things of importance, "barbed wire and Trenchard," personally disapproved of the separate air force his host was then striving to consolidate against tremendous odds. Characteristically, Haig did not divulge his opinion to Trenchard, but let it out grudgingly on one occasion to Marson who thought better than to repeat it. Yet it is doubtful whether Trenchard would have been affected by the knowledge since, in his silence and virtually complete seclusion from public affairs, the "Chief," whom he still admired as the greatest living Englishman, had long lost the faculty of absorbing anything new. Haig's work was done.

Sickness in himself and others continued to be something of a phobia to Trenchard. The stoical cheerfulness of a wife who never complained or spared herself was a correspondingly sweet consolation to him throughout his married life. When a colleague wrote in April, 1924, briefly condoling with him for having caught 'flu, he replied with a touch of impatience:

" I really am quite fit. Marson was incorrect in telling you I had it. I think he must have had it himself."

However, he began to see sickness in a more compassionate light when Hugh, his two-year-old son, fell ill with a complaint that grew steadily worse without appearing to fit into any of the normal categories of childish ailments. The boy would lie awake crying in excruciating pain. For nights on end, Trenchard walked the nursery floor with his son in his arms, trying to soothe him. A consultant was called in. He diagnosed the disease as advanced mastoid and recommended an immediate operation rather than risk removing the child to hospital. The surgeon came; and Trenchard's wife had never seen her husband so beside himself with nerves as he stood near the door, listening to the faint chipping sounds of the instruments. His relief at the success of the operation was as radiant as his joy at young Hugh's fight for life and slow recovery.

" Your godson is now absolutely fit and well again," he assured Ellington, then grappling with the political and supply problems entailed in mounting the R.A.F.'s first independent campaign on India's North-West Frontier. " He had a really bad time and everyone was very anxious indeed about him for a fortnight or more. . . . He is a great boy and has quite got back to his old form."

The illness had an accidentally beneficial effect in another direction. It brought out the affectionate side of Roger Keyes's nature at a moment when Trenchard most needed it. Their joint bargaining progressed at a rate which would have been inconceivable a few months earlier; and the various points at issue between the Admiralty and Air Ministry were settled well inside Haldane's time-limit. The agreement was accepted by Trenchard as a necessary evil. Certain clauses, however hedged about with reservations, might serve as loopholes which any group of Sea Lords, then or after a discreet interval, could widen at will.

" All our illnesses at home are now over," Trenchard had

informed Ellington late in May. " My wife got very ill on top of it all but we are again gadding about like anything. With regard to the naval dispute of the past, we are getting on and if the Admiralty play the game, as I think Keyes certainly wants to do, I see no reason why everything should not work out all right; but of course if they turn round and attack us again in two years' time, they have an advance stepping-stone. I really expect goodwill."

The token evidence of goodwill seemed to be enshrined in the joint letter accompanying the agreed report which was submitted by Trenchard and Keyes, through Haldane, to the Cabinet on 4th July, 1924. One question only remained outstanding: whether the navy or the air force should be finally answerable for financing the fleet squadrons, and this was passed on for arbitration to the Treasury.

" We both recognise," stated the covering letter signed by Keyes and Trenchard, " that in trying out the scheme, amendments will no doubt from time to time be required in the light of practical experience, but we hope that the main principles of the scheme will provide a lasting and satisfactory settlement of the questions which have been at issue between the Admiralty and the Air Ministry. A bright augury for the future is the fact that there are at the present moment fifty-three naval officers undergoing flying training at Netheravon."

The Cabinet put on record their "congratulations to the Lord Chancellor on the happy result of this inquiry." Before Parliament rose, Thomson, the Secretary of State for Air, announced the terms of peace. At the back of Trenchard's mind lay the half-formed thought that an augury could be too bright, like one of those summer mornings, glittering with vivid blues and golds, when a wise man will leave the house armed with an umbrella in case of rain. This was a trial-and-error settlement. It would have to be watched.

3

A subject which seldom failed to work some M.P.s into a lather of indignation at Question Time in the Commons was the alleged barbarity of the R.A.F. in crushing local disorders in Iraq and on its borders. Bombing from the air connoted terrorism to a vocal minority of Labour back benchers, who continuously badgered the Government to ban a method of warfare unworthy of any civilised nation. Charges of excessive cruelty and of callousness riled Trenchard, all the more so since he could not answer back.

" I've had a certain amount of bother here at home," he reminded Salmond's successor, Sir John Higgins, in July, 1924. " The Labour people always bring it (bombing) up as brutal and try to stop it, but so far I've held off all attempts to give an order to stop it. The Ministers thoroughly understand."

But if the Ministers understood, their efforts to enlighten others were singularly half-baked and unsuccessful. Like a sore point of religious controversy, the question rankled with believers and unbelievers alike. For some it was an affair of principle, for others a question of emotion; but official explanations that in backward countries the sparing use of air-power was a more humane form of coercion than dispatching a military expedition seemed face-saving humbug to all who had convinced themselves that bombing was intrinsically wrong. As early as November, 1923, Trenchard had written to Salmond :

" Sometimes remarks come to my ears, not from officers but friends I meet who have evidently inside information (the ordinary back-biting that is always going on), that the policy (of air control) is becoming too brutal. The expression is sometimes used ' Why are we bombing these tribes? ' and very often 'and women and children' is added.

" I don't want to worry you with all this. It seems to me you have kept the country quiet and saved a lot of bloodshed by your efficient handling of the show, but I would like you to spread yourself on this a little so that if the question crops up in Parliament or elsewhere I can use your letter to deal with it."

Salmond's detailed reply at the end of November delighted him.

" It is one of the finest letters I've seen and has received praise from everybody here. You interpret Air Ministry policy splendidly."

The letter came in handy the following summer when MacDonald began to show signs of wilting under the barrage of the anti-bombing brigade at Westminster. As an authoritative contemporary account of the procedure of control, Salmond's letter deserves to be quoted :

" No action is ever taken except at the request of the British civilian advisers on the spot, and only after this request has been duly weighed by the Minister of the Interior and the British adviser and by the High Commissioner. Even after a request has passed this three-fold scrutiny, I have on more than one occasion, as the

High Commissioner's chief military adviser, opposed it on military grounds. . . .

" It is a commonplace here that aircraft achieve their results by their effect on morale, and by the material damage they do, and by the interference they cause to the daily routine of life, and not through the infliction of casualties. The casualties inflicted have been most remarkably small. . . ."

Air action, Salmond noted, was aimed less at people than at property.

" It can knock the roofs of huts about and prevent their repair, a considerable inconvenience in winter-time. It can seriously interfere with ploughing or harvesting—a vital matter—or burn up the stores of fuel laboriously piled up and garnered for the winter. By attacks on livestock, which is the main form of capital and source of wealth to the less settled tribes, it can impose in effect a considerable fine or seriously interfere with the actual food source of the tribe—and in the end the tribesman finds it is much the best to obey the Government."

As for dropping propaganda leaflets "with the object of educating the tribesmen or bringing them to a reasonable frame of mind," Salmond could only say that he had tried this repeatedly without avail. The personal visits of officials and inspectors were far more effective, since over 99 per cent of Iraqi tribesmen happened to be illiterate and tribal "scribes" had been known to garble official messages, thus causing worse misunderstanding. Nor were R.A.F. bombs the only means of restoring order.

" Where I consider it tactically suitable, having regard to their numbers and state of efficiency, I make use of the Iraq Army with or without air co-operation. I may on another occasion use levies or mounted police with air assistance, or air action alone or the air mainly, followed up by action by one or other of the above local ground forces. Again, where conditions have been suitable, armoured cars in co-operation with local forces have been used and restored without bloodshed a situation which might otherwise have resulted in serious disturbances and loss of life. . . .

" No two outbreaks as yet have been exactly similar and each one has to be carefully examined from its various aspects before the best means of dealing with it is finally decided. . . ."

Salmond's analysis of air control as an instrument of policy was doubly useful. For shortly before drafting it, his Chief Staff Officer, Air-Commodore L. E. O. Charlton, embarrassed his superiors by first protesting against, then dissociating himself from, the bombing of the Iraki rebels. Conscious of the political difficulties that would arise if Charlton publicly posed as a martyr, Trenchard displayed uncommon perception in handling him. After tendering his resignation and returning to England, Charlton went on leave, somewhat surprised that Trenchard had not sent for him, and finally had to ask for an appointment with the Chief of Air Staff. He began by saying that he could not understand why he, Charlton, should have been obliged to seek an interview.

" Indeed," said Trenchard innocently, " and I can't understand why you want to see me."

" About my reasons for resigning."

" Look here, Charlton. You resigned, and I accepted your resignation. There's nothing more to be said."

" Won't there be an official inquiry, then? "

Trenchard could detect a hint of dismay in Charlton's manner. " An inquiry into what? Your conscience? Certainly not."

" He seemed rather hurt that he was not on a pedestal," Trenchard informed Salmond immediately afterwards. " I hope it will not cause a lot of trouble, but at the same time I wanted to get his views about bombing. I send you a copy of his paper. It is very vague, and the only points that call for comment from me are on the question of dropping pamphlets from the air not only as ultimatums but for educational purposes."

Charlton, whose personal courage was beyond reproach and whose skill as an air leader had won Trenchard's respect during the First World War, was debarred from holding any further posts in the East as long as bombing remained an official instrument of policy. In due course Trenchard offered him the responsible post at Air Ministry of supervising the home defence expansion scheme. Trenchard never referred again to this " little kink of conscience," and took care that nobody victimised Charlton because of it.

The security of Iraq was once more menaced by the Turks in September, 1924, when troops crossed the north-west border and moved towards the town of Amandia. Higgins, under the misapprehension that they were " irregular marauders," ordered his squadrons to attack. Severe casualties, running to several hundreds, were inflicted on the intruders. Consternation rose in Baghdad when it was reported that many of the dead and wounded belonged to the Turkish regular army; but Higgins, having inadvertently frustrated another attempt by Kemal to isolate and possibly seize Mosul, resisted pressure from the Iraq High Commissioner and the local Government to drive home his military advantage. Even when an ultimatum was sent to Turkey over Higgins's head, the R.A.F. commander refused to act on it, insisting that he had done all that was necessary to deter the invaders. The ultimatum expired; the Turks withdrew in their own time; and Trenchard agreed with Higgins that it was not Kemal but a "panicky" High Commissioner who had been spoiling for a fight.

The Committee of Imperial Defence and the Cabinet in turn commended the R.A.F. commander for displaying "coolness and mastery" in a situation as explosive as that which had confronted his predecessor after Chanak. Thomson, the Secretary of State, who happened to be visiting Iraq when the 1924 emergency was at its height, testified to Higgins's moderation in the face of excessive political pressure.

"The great temptation which confronts commanders handling the air arm is its power of immediate action of an overwhelming and decisive character," Trenchard reminded the Cabinet. "The A.O.C. was altogether proof against this temptation; and there is no doubt at all that the credit for keeping off the Turks and yet tiding over a crisis whilst the League of Nations made up their minds as to the *status quo* frontier is primarily due to him."

Despite the vociferous, who abominated air control for its own sake, Trenchard could claim that the R.A.F. was still the main stabilising force for peace in the unstable desert kingdom of Iraq.

4

Budgeting for his first auxiliary squadrons was Trenchard's most rewarding preoccupation during late 1924 and most of 1925. The relief he had known after weathering past storms was as nothing compared with the joy of it. Making Britain air-minded in spite of itself was a new venture in military history; and he was glad that, in the contrary way of politics, it was a Labour Government, guided by the unobtrusive Haldane, that firmly took the initiative. For he had never seen eye to eye with right-wing diehards who regarded Transport House as a political outpost of hell; and the popular hysteria that greeted the publication of the Zinoviev letter, contributing to Labour's defeat at the polls before the end of 1924, did not greatly edify him.

Though the downfall of MacDonald by hook or by crook, had been in the offing for months, the Prime Minister and his colleagues, by acquiring a taste of responsibility, had virtually ensured that they would return to power one day on more advantageous terms. Diehard anti-Socialists might question whether the experience had done the Labour Party or the nation any good; Trenchard, who was no socialist, did not. Within his own restricted sphere of action, he knew that much ground had been cleared by men of common sense whom only fools or fanatics impugned as strangers to patriotism.

" I have served in my time under six different Secretaries of State and fourteen or fifteen Under-Secretaries," he said at a public dinner in his honour when he retired in 1930. " I see that most of them are here to-night." (Pause.) " I hope none will take offence if I say that I never saw much difference between any of you."

There was as much truth as impishness in the remark. The main differences he recognised were not of party but of mental agility and of capacity for intrigue or expediency. Weir stood at the top of his list, perhaps because he had held office for only six months of war. Churchill scored heavily on the first count, only to squander half his marks by inconsistency on the second; while Hoare, good-hearted, well meaning and faithful after his fashion, but with too fine a conceit of himself, was bracketed in Trenchard's mind as Churchill's equal.

On returning to the Air Ministry at the end of 1924, Hoare found astonishingly little to undo. The R.A.F. had certainly not stagnated while he had chafed on the Opposition front bench; and his old anxiety to please had become less suspect now in Trenchard's eyes. For the Minister responded with alacrity to the Chief of Air Staff's resolve to strengthen the service by letting it take deep roots in the minds and hearts of ordinary people; and it should be said without hypocrisy that if Hoare only half succeeded, the fault was less his than Trenchard's. The point is of substance and of uncommon psychological interest. Too few members of the public in 1924 yet understood "what the air was all about"; Trenchard willingly acknowledged the fact, but his aversion to cheap publicity, bound up as this was with his lifelong secretiveness, handicapped half his efforts and those of Hoare to secure public confidence in the R.A.F.

How could he begin to win esteem as well as recognition for his child? The first need, he felt, was for an interpreter to set in historical perspective its arrival in war and its survival since, and then to show by what strange alchemy the very element in which airmen flew seemed to raise the pitch of endeavour and disciplined individualism at every level. The Cinderella of defence had sat too long huddled in a corner of the kitchen. It was time for the transformation scene. Trenchard realised that only a poet or a first-class historian of

T.   R

sensitivity could do justice to the theme. Yet the right man was never found, not for want of searching, but because Trenchard, despite his new-found enthusiasm for a study of the R.A.F., sternly refused to allow free play to his own capital role in its arrival and survival. He wanted to have it both ways, and the loss was not his only.

The question had become one of some urgency. For Sir Walter Raleigh, the gifted Oxford professor, who undertook the task of describing the origins of air development in Britain shortly after the Armistice, had died in 1923 of an illness contracted in Iraq. He had completed by then the first volume of his *War in the Air*, a volume sparkling with all the sad promise of an unfinished epic. Raleigh, alas, died too soon. The short-list of candidates to complete the work soon grew shorter under the terms imposed by the Cabinet Office at Trenchard's instigation until the best were eliminated altogether. Finally, the task went by default to an industrious civil servant, H. A. Jones, who had assisted Raleigh in his researches and who laboured for a decade to produce five more volumes of pains-taking fact dressed in the drabbest of prose. The raw material of perhaps the most romantic chapter in our military history since the first Elizabethan age was dutifully stirred to the consistency of a suet pudding, partly through Trenchard's refusal to permit the necessary licence to writers of Raleigh's brilliance.

Maurice Baring was the first to be approached. He turned down the commission, but suggested the names of two or three more suitable authors, including Hilaire Belloc; nowhere, however, did Baring state the real reason for "my grand refusal." The fact is that he had always intended to publish a memoir of his own on the war, including the birth of the R.A.F. By 1924, he had drafted the early chapters; but these were not to the liking of Trenchard, whose distaste for personal praise influenced him unduly against the proposed volume. When asked to cut the main character from his plot, Baring ruefully complied by discarding the idea of a detailed account. A watered-down version, consisting almost entirely of edited letters and leaves from his wartime diary, appeared in 1931 under the title of *H.Q. R.F.C.* Its most notable feature is the omission of all fulsome references to Trenchard. It is hardly surprising that Baring had little stomach for an official chore, involving as it would arduous research in which he was expected to produce a Hamlet of sorts without the Prince.

Belloc's qualifications did not appeal to Hankey, who had a remarkably small opinion of his objectivity and accuracy. Whether Belloc would have accepted is beside the point: he was not even invited. Still authorless, Trenchard suddenly remembered T. E. Lawrence, who had enlisted in the ranks of the moribund Tank Corps under a fresh pseudonym. His hope of regaining sanctuary in the R.A.F. was still strong. Every February (his "supplication month," he called it) Lawrence wrote to Trenchard asking to be reinstated, though that favour was no longer Trenchard's to grant. MacDonald's Government had proved as reluctant as Baldwin's to humour the sensation-hungry Press lords by revoking Bonar Law's expulsion order. When, therefore, in the spring of 1924, Trenchard told the suppliant that he could re-enter the R.A.F. in the sense of settling down as its chosen historian, the Chief of Air Staff was dispirited by the promptness with which Lawrence looked this gift horse in the mouth.

" I took thought for a night and then declined," Lawrence explained to his friend, D. G. Hogarth. " The job is a hazardous one (T. wants a 'literary' history, the C.I.D. a 'technical'), attractive, very, to me by reason of its subject. The terms (three years) compare unfavourably with the six which the army offers; and the responsibility is one which I'd regret as soon as I shouldered it."

Completing its history was not Lawrence's idea of recovering liberty from responsibility as an anonymous cog in a beautiful and useful machine. It was still his ambition, he reminded Trenchard, to consolidate the new service in the only worthy way—"from the ground floor up."

The names of other authors were suggested, but Trenchard seemed to lose personal interest in the project after Baring and then Lawrence spurned his offer. Lawrence, with his discerning eye for the surface flaws, which mattered less than the solid virtues that lay beneath, would, so Trenchard believed, have composed any enduring masterpiece. The new slang and customs, the subtle intonations that distinguished the new service from its elders, the youthful "chip on its shoulder," the extraordinarily tight knot of dependence between those who did the flying and those who did the maintenance—such elements as these Lawrence could have woven into a coherent pattern as few others could. Yet he, too, had rejected as quickly as Baring the chance to write with genius about flying and the breed of men it produced. Trenchard often mused over the mystery.

Lawrence, he concluded, must have passionately wanted to shed his past and *live* the part, not identify himself vicariously with the R.A.F. in words alone. On the half-dozen occasions he visited the Trenchards at Dancer's Hill before his wish came true again, the troubled insecurity of the man showed through the habitual charm.

Trenchard, who had grown very attached to him, pitied his helplessness. There was something theatrical yet inevitable about the manner
in which Lawrence seemed to enjoy sticking pins in his own image.
Sometimes he carried the process too far and would speak quite
calmly and without self-pity of "ending it all." Yet the suicidal
frame of mind rarely lasted in Trenchard's presence. It became a
sort of private joke between them after the evening Lawrence
threatened to take his life and Trenchard said quietly:

" All right, but please go into the garden. I don't want my
carpets ruined." [6]

That pricked the bubble and brought a smile to Lawrence's
face; but jokes could not solve his deeper spiritual problem. He
needed, as he put it, "rules and rails" to guide him; so he went on
pining for a safe billet in the ranks as a religious man might have
pined for the seclusion of a monastery. The difference between
army and air, he had found, was that between earth and air; and
the Tank Corps was "an undiluted disease." Trenchard understood
why offers of commissions, either to serve or to write, were, for
Lawrence "refinements of cruelty." A man who could find no peace
in himself, and who therefore hated false independence all the more,
might yet discover a reason for living by subjugating his will entirely
to impersonal authority.

It was in July, 1925, after Churchill, Bernard Shaw and John
Buchan had interceded with Baldwin on Lawrence's behalf, that
Trenchard at last obtained official sanction to take him back. There
were strenuous objections from Hoare, whose prim sense of the
fitness of things was once more affronted; but largely through
Trenchard's wilful determination to make exceptions to all rules,
including his own, ministerial objections fell to the ground.

The R.A.F. had lost a potential historian, regaining instead a
tired, wayward eccentric overjoyed to be coming home to rest.
Trenchard put aside his hope of a book that would uplift and teach
outsiders. The air force would have to stamp itself by example on
the minds of ordinary people. Lawrence, in his perverse way, was
right: to go on living and learning in the shade seemed suddenly
more important than posing arrogantly for posterity.

Much happened in the next twelve months to convince Trenchard
that the R.A.F. needed no Boswell in any case. And since he still
drew wry amusement from the criticisms of ill-disposed Press lords
and hardly any from the adulation of well-wishers, a Boswell might
not have fared too well or lasted very long under his supervision.
As a result, the R.A.F.'s leanest years are still the least known; and

the Father who nursed and schooled and brought up the child has received less than his due from contemporary historians. But, in common fairness, it must be stressed that Trenchard partly brought this on his own head by his elected self-effacement.

On 1st January, 1925, a new command for the air defence of Britain came into being under Sir John Salmond. On 12th March, the estimates allotted Trenchard £15 millions, more than had been granted in any year since 1919; and Parliament learnt with mixed feelings that eighteen squadrons had been added in twelve months to the home defence force. Then Hoare took off with the Colonial Secretary, Amery, on a flying visit to the Middle East, emulating his Labour predecessor who had blazed that trail before him. A measure of continuity now pervaded official policy towards the service. Its stock had risen. Its morale, which had never fallen far, began to soar. Trenchard said one day to his wife when invitations to three separate and simultaneous functions were delivered by the postman: " It's a good sign. They're beginning to chase us socially now."

In London streets far removed from Hendon and the annual air display that summer, thousands of necks craned inquisitively upwards to glimpse the first mass formation flight of aircraft over the capital since the Gotha raids of 1917. Trenchard luxuriated in the pride of such moments. Only the present and future seemed important. What need had he of histories? By the end of October, 1925, the first four auxiliary squadrons were formed—No. 600 (City of London), No. 601 (County of London), No. 602 (City of Glasgow) and No. 603 (City of Edinburgh), giving the lie to repeated ministerial doubts expressed over the past five years about the aptitude of civilians for part-time instruction as pilots. He remembered in particular the incredulous scorn of Winston Churchill.

" Week-end fliers, Boom? Never."

The press of volunteers from all walks of life exceeded the number of vacancies; and the rapid crystallising of Trenchard's dream of a citizen air service set problems of improvisation in selection and training which might well have daunted a smaller man or caused a less flexible scheme to crumble.

Trenchard vetted the short-lists of adjutants and flying instructors himself, passing over regulation-bound applicants in favour of men whose ability to shift for themselves was personally known to him.

It was the same autocratic impulse which had once dragged him, line by line, through the first air force list ever published, like a breeder through a stud book, ticking off the names of junior officers whom he fancied as leaders of the future. That list has survived him, and the marginal ticks beside the names of then unknown junior officers now famous suggests that Trenchard's special brand of favouritism was guided by his almost unerring eye for potential strength of character. Portal, Tedder, and Slessor—all destined to rise in turn to his own eminence—were already being groomed for stardom in the early twenties. It was a small indication among many of Trenchard's faith in the living force that was being fashioned after his own image.

" Can't you do something, sir, to relax these Auxiliary Air Force regulations? " asked the new C.O. of the City of Edinburgh squadron on the telephone, soon after its formation. " I can't make head or tail of them."

He knew the man at the other end. The most gratifying feature of these local offshoots of the parent body, to Trenchard's mind, was the way in which they drew out of obscurity some of his finest wartime squadron commanders. Their chance to serve had come again; so had his to atone for the indiscriminate rejection of talents that had characterised so much of the demobilisation frenzy in 1919. He did not have to think twice on this occasion before replying:

"You're running your own show. If you don't like the regulations, rewrite them."

That was his own personal recipe for survival, one which honoured the principle that rules were made for men, not men for rules. Just as he thought it "foolish to give reasons," so he often lamented the rigidity of "people who will not understand that the regulation is only made for the fool to keep and the wise man to break." Such neat quotations for sermons on ideal behaviour related to daily life were, for Trenchard, maxims on which he always acted. The Edinburgh squadron did not abuse his trust; its growth, tended by local experts and enthusiasts familiar with the climate and the soil, was rapid and lasting. To squadron loyalty, a tenuous thing sometimes in a service that spanned the winds of heaven, was being added that stabilising element in all human concerns which matter —attachment to one place that men could cherish and would defend to the death because their human roots were there.

Hoare needed no conversion to the Auxiliary Air Force scheme. He was all for it. Under Bonar Law, he had run into unsympathetic opposition caused, as he suggests, by Sykes, the Prime Minister's son-in-law, who was sceptical whether part-time fliers would ever be of value as a reserve. Baldwin, however, was better disposed; Haldane proved anything but lukewarm, so that when Hoare returned to office the Auxiliary Air Force Bill had become law. Combining the roles of intermediary and travelling salesman, the Minister did much to break down the apathy of local authorities and local business interests and local citizens by his energy and sincerity.

" The experiment was successful from the very beginning," as Hoare testified. " The forebodings of the doubters and critics were soon proved groundless. So far from the non-regular units damaging the reputation of the regular squadrons, they actually added some of the most glorious pages to the history of the Royal Air Force during the Second World War."[7]

Characteristically, Trenchard stayed well in the background. Only two speeches of his during this quiet but vital period of development are on record. The more memorable was delivered at Cambridge one April evening in 1925; and his words to the University Aeronautical Society enshrined much of his experience and thought. The spontaneous cheering was not entirely ironic when he mentioned the various types of men he needed for an air reserve that would be healthy and well balanced.

" We want the mathematical genius—there is work for him. We want the literary genius—there is work for him, especially in my office. We want the scientific brain—there is more than enough work for him. We want the man of brains, and we want the man of common sense and little brain. We want the man of initiative and the man of action, the methodical man and even the crank. We open our ranks widely to all. . . .

" Remember that if we get the best and, in the future, if it is looked upon as much of an honour to belong to one of these Auxiliary Air Force squadrons as it is to belong to a good club or a good university, so will it be a great means of enabling the spirit of aviation to spread. . . . It will also give the brains of the country a chance of being used for aeronautical purposes which will be an important factor in home defence."

His purpose was to stimulate undergraduate interest in the special type of air unit devised for Cambridge, first among the older seats of learning, through the unflagging persistence of Hoare's Parliamentary private secretary, Geoffrey Butler, then one of the two M.P.s for the University. Here again Trenchard deferred to those who knew the ground, letting them draw up the regulations for membership; but nobody who heard him speak that night doubted where the master plan had originated. He was like the legendary sculptor releasing an image long asleep in a block of locally quarried stone; no flights of oratory were required to smooth or polish the rough, vigorous lines of it.

At one point a hint of something approaching gloom broke through. The Press seized upon the only puzzling novelty in a long, plain speech.

" I do not want you to think that I look upon the air as a blessing altogether," he said. " It may be more of a blessing for this Empire than for any other country in the world, but I feel that all the good it will do in civil life cannot balance the harm that may be done in war by it. If I had the casting vote, I would say 'Abolish the air.' I feel it is an infinitely more harmful weapon of war than any other. . . . The aeroplane is the most offensive weapon that has ever been invented. It is a shockingly bad weapon of defence, but it is the only one that has yet been discovered; and even in these days of great scientific improvements and inventions I have grave doubts that any other defensive weapon will take its place for a hundred years."

It is only once in a hundred years on average that a scientific discovery like radar is developed almost providentially in the nick of time to afford temporary shelter from the deluge. Trenchard was not budgeting on radar in 1925. That was why, though he regarded fighter aircraft as essential for the morale of city dwellers, his home defence plan allowed only one squadron for every three of bombers. It was the introduction of the strategic deterrent as an imponderable factor in the political art of keeping the so-called civilised nations at peace. In the last resort, the value of the air deterrent would depend on the wisdom of governments in maintaining R.A.F. strength; but that lay in the future. For the present it was enough that as many citizens as possible should understand in terms of an English parable the ultimate dilemma of air-power.

" I have sometimes been asked why we don't use only defensive aeroplanes. My answer is that if you play a game of football against an opposing team I take it your objective is to win. If the opposing team start to attack, and the members of your team are told only to defend their own goal, they could not possibly win the match and it is quite conceivable they would lose it. . . .

" Nothing is more annoying than to be attacked by a weapon which you have no means of hitting back at; but although it is necessary to have some defence to keep up the morale of your own people, it is infinitely more necessary to lower the morale of the people against you by *attacking* them wherever they may be.

" I will not call this the air peril. You could imagine for yourselves what would happen to this country if it was attacked from the air and we had no adequate means of defence. In one day more tons of bombs could be dropped on it than in the four years the Great War lasted."

The cumulative savagery of unrestricted bombing was an aspect on which he did not dwell. Its gradual inevitability was already clear to him; so were the limits of the average human being's extraordinary capacity for endurance. There could be no turning back now. Yet he had not been merely striving for histrionic effect in declaring that his casting vote would have been for the abolition of air-power. Other nations had begun to play with this two-edged weapon like children marvelling over a new toy. An assortment of prophets, like Douhet in Italy and Mitchell in America, had long foreseen as vividly as Trenchard himself the fatal trend towards wars of mass destruction, as fear and rivalry overshadowed understanding and scientific ingenuity leaped ahead of political means of containing it. There would never be a call for his casting vote; but Trenchard had compassion enough, in his enigmatic way, to groan aloud for the chance of one.

During the last months of his life, when he was reliving those days with an intensity given only to the very old and the very wise, he suffered no remorse, though the world had entered the age of the megaton bomb a decade before. Perhaps the one slight undertone of self-reproach was his failure to find an acceptable mouthpiece for his own dark but half-forgotten prophecies which, he maintained, were already implicit in the facts of the air fighting of 1917-18. But then, he grumbled, no writer he had heard of in any country had possessed insight or inspiration enough to set down the thoughts and feelings and spirits of high adventure animating the men who opened up the skies as pioneers in the nineteen twenties. I remember protesting: " What about St. Exupéry in France? Surely he got most of it down."

There were gaps in Trenchard's general knowledge. He admitted to having only recently encountered the writings of St. Exupéry, who was flying French mail to Africa and South America while R.A.F. pioneers were extending the first air routes to the Cape and across the Middle East. I promised to bring along the English translation of one of St. Exupéry's early works, *Wind, Sand and Stars*. I did so and read aloud a passage which enthralled him.

" That's it," he shouted.

It conveyed almost exactly what he had felt while his pilots were mapping new trails high over the face of the earth.

" It is not with the metal that the pilot is in contact. Contrary to the vulgar illusion, it is thanks to the metal, and by virtue of it,

that the pilot rediscovers nature. . . . The machine does not isola
man from the great problems of nature but plunges him more deep
into them. Numerous, nevertheless, are the moralists who ha
attacked the machine as the source of all the ills we bear. . . .
congeries of motives prevents us from blowing up our spinning mi
and reviving the distaff. Gandhi had a try at this sort of revolutio
he was as simple-minded as a child trying to empty the sea on to t
sand with a teacup. . . .

"We Europeans have become again young peoples, witho
tradition or language of our own. We shall have to age somewh
before we are able to write the folk songs of a new epoch. You
barbarians still marvelling at our new toys—that is what we a
Why else should we race our planes, give prizes to those who
highest or fastest? We take no heed to ask ourselves why we rac
the race itself is more important than the object. . . . So long as
were engaged in conquest our spirit was the spirit of conquero
The time has now come when we must be colonists, must make t
house habitable which is still without character."

The R.A.F. is the poorer for not having found a St. Exupéry
its own in its adolescence. For that Trenchard took and deserv
some of the blame. Yet the cloud of silence which for over thir
years has blotted out even the political arenas in which he foug
should no longer be allowed to obscure the clarity of his visic
He saw far beyond the present; but, surrounded, as he thought,
too many shortsighted enemies, he was equally to let his own lig
be pushed under the nearest official bushel.

Trenchard, being a man of few words, has been too free
maligned as a man of small intellect, immense conceit and lit
originality; or again as a stubborn, unapproachable dictator, whc
dynamic ambition was leavened only by organising ability a
elementary cunning. Such caricatures are scarcely credible
relation to his achievements as Chief of Air Staff, even allowing h
all the luck that was going. Many of the Ministers and milita
leaders who clashed or collaborated with him in his prime m
sometimes have wished that he had been cast in a more comm
mould. Maurice Baring, who knew him better than anyone, ne
ceased to wonder at the quite exceptional qualities of his friend a
former chief:

"When you said you doubted that even I realised how big
man 'the General' is, I don't think you are right," he wrote
Marson towards the end of 1925. "At least you cannot overestim
the pedestal I put him on . . . He was and is one of the few

nen of the world and incomparably finer and bigger than anyone I have met in my life in any one of the services, army, navy, air, or politics, in any country; and a big brain, lightening intuition as well as his obstreperous overwhelming character, personality, and drive . . . only it is not good to have this dinned into his ears—he knows *all too well that we think it.*"

It was an unpleasant revelation for the Sea Lords to be contradicted by an airman who knew that no major sea engagement for two centuries had been fought more than one hundred miles from shore, in other words well within striking distance of the land-based aircraft of the twenties. It was even more disconcerting to be told that Trenchard had discarded as useless all maps based on the Mercator Projection because they flattened and distorted the real shape of the world as it looked from the cockpit of a bomber.

" The study of aerial warfare," he said, " has made it necessary to alter completely wrong military impressions—as well as conventional ideas of the map of the globe."

In his room at Adastral House he had a different sort of chart with the American continent, not Britain, at its centre. It showed the true " land hemisphere," embracing Europe, Asia, Africa, North and much of South America as well as over 90 per cent of the world's population and most of its industrial wealth. Unfortunately for his opponents, Trenchard's mind was infinitely less conventional than outside critics often allowed.

On occasions the sheer unconventionality of his thinking enabled Beatty and Cavan to thwart him, as in July, 1923, when the Chief of Air Staff had pointed out the strategic value of Wrangel Island, a rocky, uninhabited place in the Arctic circle off the Siberian coast of Russia. It would one day prove an ideal base, he said, for air transport across the North Pole; and in an accompanying staff paper a table of mileages was appended to show the relative cutting down of time and distance. The suggestion was ridiculed and dropped nearly thirty years before the establishment of the U.S. Arctic bases or the inauguration of regular trans-Polar airline flights.

It is worth recalling these random facts. For one of the most baffling of Trenchard's traits, notably in the eyes of smaller men intent on belittling him, was his deplorable habit of being proved the only person in step—and of never troubling to remind the world of it in after days. Such indifference seemed to many almost too virtuous to be genuine.

18. The Anti-Climax

The childhood of the R.A.F. may be said to have ended early
1925. From then onwards Trenchard's purpose was to put flesh c
its small but well-formed bones. Perhaps it would be timely
recapitulate the stages of its precocious and victorious fight for li
against the apathy of political guardians and the enmity or spite
service rivals obtuse enough to see no harm in letting it die.

The campaign to kill the air force became Beatty's concern
1921, when Trenchard's right to control all aircraft, including tho
based on naval carriers, was first challenged. The Sea Lor
demanded no more than possession of the squadrons working wit
the fleet; but the records show that the R.A.F. would almost ce
tainly have withered away had their claim been granted. For, :
the straitened economic conditions of the early twenties, r
Government could have afforded and therefore permitted tw
independent air services to grow up side by side; and once tl
Admiralty regained its pound of flesh, the War Office would hav
stepped in to complete the logical process of mutilation.

The Governments were hardly neutral. Neither Lloyd Georg
nor Bonar Law believed in the value of the R.A.F.: indeed, bot
of them began by thoughtlessly countenancing steps to termina
its separate existence. As the author of the " Ten Year Rule ", Lloy
George was obsessed with twin delusions: that the peace impose
on Germany in 1919 would endure, and that therefore a third servi
would be a luxury. The Geddes Inquiry of 1921 was ordered wit
that at least partly in view, to the joy of the Sea Lords and tl
generals. Yet Trenchard convinced Geddes that the R.A.F., despi
its puniness and poverty, was already earning its keep. And wh;
was true on economic grounds was reaffirmed on strategic whe
Balfour, a former First Lord of the Admiralty, advised Lloyd Georg
after mature consideration that the air force must stay, whatev
the Admiralty and the War Office advised to the contrary.

New men brought new methods and old dangers in new shape

The principle of "thou shalt not kill but needst not strive officiously to keep alive" had been good enough for Lloyd George; it was not definite enough for Bonar Law. Fortunately, being a somewhat indefinite character when crossed, the first Conservative Prime Minister of the post-war years did not pursue his original intention of signing a summary death warrant. The Salisbury Tribunal was set up instead to investigate in depth the whole case for and against the retention of the R.A.F., while Balfour presided over a separate inquisition in response to the Admiralty's overt political campaign to win back the Fleet Air Arm. In the end it was Bonar Law's much defamed successor, Baldwin, who ensured justice, despite the efforts of the Sea Lords and their supporters to prevent it.

In spite of these repeated threats of dismemberment, the unwanted child was now almost double its original size, much of the growth having been put on in the eighteen months since Baldwin's announcement that fifty-two squadrons must be raised at home as an insurance against the strongest air force within range of Britain. In 1919 there had been only two; the bulk of the twenty-five complete squadrons salvaged from the wartime scrap-heap had been wisely posted overseas where they were needed. Under Ramsay MacDonald, who honoured his predecessor's policy, the number of squadrons had risen to forty-three, with eleven more forming; and by the spring of 1925, when Winston Churchill introduced his first Budget, there were fifty-four regular squadrons in being, including eighteen for Home Defence.

Trenchard's thrift, vigilance and singleminded foresight had triumphed: nothing that Beatty or Cavan could now contrive would fatally damage the foundations or the structure of the R.A.F. It seemed reasonable to hope that the next five years would be downhill nearly all the way, compared with the previous five. By 1930, if not before, Baldwin's target of fifty-two squadrons for Home Defence could be attained even at a decelerated rate of progress, while standards of training and quality of equipment could be so improved that the R.A.F. would become the *corps d'élite* of Trenchard's dreams, capable of quick expansion without loss of quality in any emergency. The outlook in 1925, then, had never been brighter.

Trenchard had no thought of retirement. The grey years of arrested development lay behind; a happier period stretched ahead. Others would complete the planned structure after he had gone, despite the continuing indifference or ill-disguised hostility of those who still denounced the air force as a parasite.

This review of the position half-way through the first post-w:
decade is vital. For during the five years of Baldwin's second ter:
as Prime Minister, Trenchard had to fight harder than ever to kee
what he had gained. His hopes of decisively altering the pattern (
strategic thinking through the Committee of Imperial Defence wei
doomed to frustration. The facts of air power were with him; bi
the tide of world affairs turned against him. And the men he relie
on most to assist him, Baldwin, the promoter of the 52-squadro
scheme, and Churchill, his earliest champion, chose to swim wit
the current. Towards the end of 1933, a full decade after Baldwi
introduced his air defence scheme, there were still only forty full
equipped squadrons, auxiliary and regular, based in Britain; an
by then Hitler had gained supreme power in Germany. In h
own account of this inglorious chapter, Churchill tends to lay th
blame for neglect at the door of others, discreetly passing over h
own omissions as Chancellor, which were not entirely irrelevar
or negligible.

Whether or not posterity will judge Britain's greatest wartim
Premier to have been its worst peacetime Chancellor, Churchi
must be counted among the least fortunate and the least successfu
Trenchard was pleased when Churchill staged his political come
back; but personal pleasure gradually turned to concern, concer,
to disillusionment and friction, as outside pressures led the Chan
cellor into the irresistible temptation of neglecting the true interest
of the R.A.F. The popular memory is short and selective. It tends ti
look at truth through the wrong end of the telescope. In Churchill'
case only the phenomenal war leader of the forties, and the un
popular prophet crying in the political wilderness of the thirties, ar
now remembered; the Chancellor of the late twenties is con
veniently forgotten. In Trenchard's view, Churchill, the prophet o
the thirties, had good cause to know what he was prophesying about
since the almost fatal weakness of the fighting services was largel
the fruit of his earlier exertions at the Exchequer: therefore, ii
rousing Government and people from slumber, Churchill, whethei
he ever fully recognised the fact or not, was merely performing
restitution for his own mistakes.[1]

In 1925, all started well enough. The manner of Churchill':
return to the summit of affairs hardly surprised Trenchard, whc
regarded his friend's impulsive action in deserting the Liberal
flagship and its feuding captains early in 1924 as entirely in character. Churchill dived overboard and struck out for a shore which
he knew to be populated by politicians with little reason to welcome

him. Instead of being eaten or, worse still, ostracised, Churchill was treated as a prize castaway. Six months before the first Labour Government was turned out, Churchill raised a banner of his own device, stood for Parliament as an "Independent Constitutionalist," and with strong Conservative support narrowly lost the Westminster by-election by forty-three votes. A safe seat was then found for him at Epping; and in the General Election at the end of 1924 Churchill was returned with a 10,000 majority.

The streak of the privateer in his friend's character did not scandalise Trenchard, who suspected that there was less behind the party labels than most politicians contended. The new Member for Epping would have been the first to understand had Baldwin left him to cool his heels on the Government back-benches for a while. He was half resigned to that fate, and not in the least prepared for the thrill of being sent for before the new Government was a week old and offered a position of power.

When the word "Chancellor" crossed the Prime Minister's lips, Churchill assumed that Baldwin was referring to the Duchy of Lancaster, a fair assumption for someone still very much on probation; but Baldwin corrected him.

"No," he said, "I mean Chancellor of the Exchequer."[2]

Churchill admits that he was dumbfounded to be offered the post which his father had held and then forfeited once and for all on a point of principle. Whatever happened, Winston would certainly be less forgetful of possible rivals than Lord Randolph: that lesson at least he had learnt from his father's misfortune.

Baldwin's choice was less quixotic than appeared. It was a time for reconciliations. The spectacle of the divided Liberals, and the knowledge that several leading Conservatives were still languishing in the political cold, persuaded the Prime Minister that he would be well advised to repair party unity which had been ruptured when the Lloyd George Coalition fell. His overtures were not unavailing. Austen Chamberlain, who responded favourably, was rewarded with the Foreign Office, though Curzon regarded that office almost as a personal incumbency. Birkenhead also signed his peace and received the India Office. As befitted the settled habit of the elder statesman, Balfour took his time before accepting the Lord Presidency of the Council. Even allowing for the abiding distrust with which Churchill was viewed by many Conservatives, Baldwin's offer of the Exchequer was defensible and opportune enough.

The Government had inherited one particular legacy of bitterness for which it had largely itself to thank. Labour, which had

maintained power through the dissensions of the Opposition, lo
it at last through the misplaced emphasis laid by its foes on tl
implications of the Zinoviev letter. MacDonald and his colleagu
felt that they had been cheated by a dishonest propaganda tricl
and the subsequent hardening of Labour hearts boded ill for an
inexperienced Chancellor who was both bent on reform and deepl
anti-Socialist by instinct.

As Joint Secretary for War and Air immediately after th
Armistice, Churchill had demonstrated to Trenchard's satisfactio
that his marvellous head for the wider strategic issues could be
veritable colander when financial expediency demanded. All woul
be well with the R.A.F. if his domestic policy worked; but if fo
any reason it did not, then the consequences of Churchill's mistake
or distractions would be off-loaded without a tremor on others. I
had happened before; it might happen again during a period c
unemployment and want when many thought it obscene to spen
money on defence. So Trenchard waited with fingers crossed. Th
Air Estimates for 1925 were well advanced before the change c
Government, and Churchill did not alter the generous provision
approved by Thomson and Haldane, and ratified by Hoare, th
returning Secretary of State for Air. An increase of nearl
£3 million for forming eight new Home Defence squadrons was no
questioned. The Chancellor already had his eye on bigger an
more sweeping savings beside which £3 million on or off the Ai
Estimates appeared an inconsiderable trifle. Whether the situatio
would remain easy for Trenchard depended on whether the pro
posals hidden in Churchill's battered red despatch box bore th
expected fruit.

2

On 28th April, introducing his first and fatal Budget, Churchil
announced a return to the gold standard that had been suspendec
during and since the First World War. It may be that he wa
merely acquiescing in a decision partly forced on him by the unanimous advice of the Bank of England and the majority of qualifiec
experts. Nevertheless, in shackling sterling to gold, the Chancello
gave an impression of sincerely believing that he was "shackling
Britain to reality." In the view of orthodox financiers, the returr
to gold was the final step in a logical process, that of strengthening
the pound by restoring it to parity. The Act under which payment

in bullion had been suspended was due to expire at the end of 1925, so the Cabinet had to choose between legislating to stay off gold for a while longer and going back to it at once.

The consequences are already a melancholy part of history. We have it on the authority of Sir P. J. Grigg, then one of Churchill's private secretaries, that "Winston has almost come to believe" in his later years that "the decision to go back to gold was the greatest mistake of his life." Trenchard agreed only to the point of believing that the "dear money" policy which inevitably followed the return to gold created as many difficulties as it solved.

The miners and coal owners were the first to suffer. The plight of an industry long in need of reorganisation, with its many uneconomic pits and its fluctuating standards of efficiency, was immediately exposed. The coal owners, averse to interference of any kind in the jungle of their affairs, were hard put to it to scrape a profit after paying the higher wages decreed by the Labour Government in 1924. When, as a result of Churchill's policy, production costs began to soar, and profits to drop, the owners retaliated by proposing a cut in wages, the largest item of expenditure. Not to be outdone, the miners dared them to try; the Trades Union Congress entered the ring in July, 1925, with the ultimatum of a General Strike; then Baldwin intervened by establishing a court of inquiry under the chairmanship of Lord Macmillan. Its conclusion was that the miners had every right to a living wage, but that the owners certainly could not afford to continue paying it at the level fixed by the Labour Government. One member of the tribunal, Sir Joshua Stamp, attached a long memorandum to the report in which he put the onus for the coal crisis fairly and squarely on Churchill. The threat of strike action could only be explained "by the immediate and necessary effects of the return to gold." An industry in dire straits clearly needed a substantial subsidy to tide it over. So the Government provided it. Nor was that all. A Royal Commission, headed by Sir Herbert Samuel, was empowered to investigate conditions and recommend reforms.

Stamp was not the only critic of Churchill's policy. The voice of J. M. (later Lord) Keynes was heard in the land, fulminating against "the economic consequences of Mr. Churchill." Nevertheless, at the obedient call of the Government, stood forces ready to applaud a measure commended by the City: the solidarity of a large parliamentary majority enabled Ministers to ignore the glum prognostications of dissenting experts like Keynes.

Churchill, whatever his private misgivings, could only persevere

in a part he did not understand. A strong pound might arguabl
set an example of good housekeeping to the world; but that implie
curbing public expenditure. The Chancellor therefore sought cu
that would not exacerbate industrial unrest. He had not far t
look. The service departments seemed ripe for a little judiciou
plucking. After all, they were costing the taxpayer abou
£100 millions a year; and nobody could say that the risks of wa
had grown.

3

On the contrary, the siren song of peace had been captivatin
Europe since the spring of 1925. There had been a welcome tha
in the international temperature, and the doves continued to co
encouragingly by the lakeside of Locarno, where presently th
peacemakers gathered to bury their ancient enmities. Thus wer
knotted together the two uneven strands of a single policy which
rightly or wrongly, Trenchard came increasingly to identify wit
Churchill rather than with Baldwin. For the Chancellor neede
stability abroad to secure a modicum of industrial harmony a
home; and his longing to see restored the historic unity of Europ
was deeply rooted. That would depend on healing the tradition
breach between France and Germany; and hopes of Franco
German understanding were reviving. When, early in 1925, th
German Government had declared its willingness to negotiate
non-aggression pact with France based on the existing Rhin
frontier, official reactions in Paris were reserved. It was only tw
years since the French occupation of the Ruhr had ruined th
German economy, virtually wiping out the German middle-clas
and creating the classic conditions for anarchy and civil war. Th
rot had been stopped just in time by wiser methods of extractin
reparations. Under the Dawes Plan, occupation troops wer
gradually withdrawn, an international loan raised, and the run
away mark revalued. American insistence on recovering her wa
loans, which Baldwin had pampered, somewhat over-generously
at the end of 1922 as Chancellor, meant that Germany could no
repay her creditors, including France, with borrowed dollars.

French doubts about German sincerity were relayed to Londo
It was agreed, after consultations, to hold a conference at Locarn
Though France now possessed in Aristide Briand a leader wh
believed as passionately as Churchill that a reunited Europe coul

be a bulwark of peace, the fears of Frenchmen were not easily placated; for, across the Rhine, Field-Marshal Hindenburg had meanwhile emerged as President of the German Republic, with a seven-year term of office before him. "Better a Zero than a Nero," rang the taunt of Hindenburg's extremist opponents; but Paris still wanted evidence of German goodwill before condescending to parley. It was quickly forthcoming. Germany agreed to join the League of Nations and to honour all her obligations. The stage was thus set for Locarno.

It is hard to explain the freshening breeze of optimism that blew everywhere as the delegates got down to business. Perhaps a yearning for security in the hearts of most Europeans found release in this concerted effort of their leaders to devise more tangible guarantees against war than the League of Nations had done. The superbly practical diplomacy of Austen Chamberlain was nowhere more evident than in the series of mutual assistance pacts arranged between Germany and her neighbours: France and Belgium in the west, Poland and Czechoslovakia in the east. The British Foreign Secretary, who later received the Nobel Peace Prize and the Garter for his efforts, had found a way, it seemed, of binding the Powers of Europe together as sworn guardians of peace.

Since Britain pledged herself to assist France or Germany, without discrimination, should either fall victim to an unprovoked attack by the other, the possibility of preventive war or of slithering into armed conflict by accident had ostensibly been ruled out.

Writing nearly a quarter of a century later, Churchill could still refer to Locarno as a " far-reaching military commitment . . . accepted by Parliament and endorsed warmly by the nations." And he could add, without fear of contradiction: "The histories may be searched in vain for a parallel to such an undertaking."

Thus, by a conjunction of oddly contrasted happenings, economic discontent at home and diplomatic success abroad, the then Chancellor was encouraged to pursue a financial policy which worked to the detriment of the fighting services. The foundations of the R.A.F. were secure; but the scaffolding which Trenchard had begun to erect with the consent of two successive Governments was destined to stay unfinished and gather rust. For Churchill's policy, so far as it affected the air force, was to cut costs by three per cent and still expect an increase in size of ten per cent per annum.

Hoare admitted to the Committee of Imperial Defence as early as February, 1925, at the time of Hindenburg's election, that "for the next ten or fifteen years France is as militarily secure as any

country could conceivably be . . . Militarily, Germany had ceased
to count in Europe." But British heart-searchings about French air
superiority were passing and would shortly vanish. The Chancellor, disregarding Trenchard's protests, ruled that R.A.F.
expansion must slow down.

Trenchard felt sufficiently strongly about the folly of being
penny-wise to draft a Cabinet paper in the autumn of 1925, which
Hoare obligingly endorsed:

"The relations between England and France are as friendly as
they could be," he stated. "Germany is altogether deprived of an
air force, yet France continues to maintain an air strength more
predominant than was ever her military strength under Napoleon
or Louis XIV. Are we justified in remaining for many years in a
position of such numerical inferiority in air strength? (With a total
of 960 front-line machines, the French then had nearly three times
as many bombers and fighters as the British for Home Defence.)
Ought we not in any case to seize the chance provided by the
Locarno Pact negotiations to bring pressure upon the French to
reduce their armaments? Is it not wiser to follow the successful
precedent of the Washington Conference and to approach them
with our programme of expansion definite and intact, rather than
with the public admission that on grounds of economy we are
anyhow going to postpone it? . . .

"Half the Expansion Scheme is now completed (26 squadrons
out of Baldwin's original 52); many commitments have been
entered into, contracts have been let, personnel engaged. The programme will not only be dislocated, but much public money wasted
if decisions are not quickly reached upon the main lines of our
future policy."

The Cabinet had already been flirting with the idea of calling
for an international halt in air armaments, despite the opposition
of France. In July, when the effects of Churchill's "dear money"
policy began to make themselves felt in the coalfields, and the
financial advantages of air disarmament seemed all the more alluring,
Trenchard was asked to weigh the problem and report back to the
Committee of Imperial Defence. He did so towards the end of
October:

"Only by the total abolition of all aircraft, civil and military,"
he advised, "can air disarmament be rendered effective." The
reasons which led him to this unpalatable but entirely sound conclusion were listed in detail, the most important being "the fact

that commercial aircraft, as at present constructed, can be very rapidly adapted for use in war." This fact, Trenchard recalled, had induced the Washington Conference in 1921 to abandon the search for a set of rules that would restrict the size and number of heavier-than-air machines. Airships could be so limited; aircraft could not.

"The requisite conditions for efficiency in civil and military aircraft are in some respects the same. . . . The conversion of [civil] aircraft for use as bombers, especially by night, presents no difficulty and is rapidly effected. . . . If all civil flying were to cease, an effective stage in the possible limitation of air armaments would have been reached."

But the dry implication that Governments might as well try to legislate against men thinking or eating or making love as against flying did not divert the swift flow of his thought.

" One of the principal difficulties in framing a scheme for international limitation of air armaments," Trenchard stressed, "is the fact that the air arm is a new arm, and its potentialities in relation to those of navies and armies are not yet established. The object of disarmament is to promote a feeling of security and to reduce expenditure. If, however, a nation elects to utilise her air forces in substitution for the older services, as we are doing in Iraq, it is clear that a corresponding increase in those air forces is involved, *though a reduction in total expenditure on armaments may concurrently have been obtained.*"[3]

The italics are Trenchard's, not the author's. Sometimes he could not resist underlining the obvious to jog the fickle memory of his political masters. No power on earth, in his opinion, could put the clock back now; manned flight could not be wished or decreed out of existence. For good or ill, aircraft would one day be used as the decisive weapon of war. And if in war the infinite expanses of the sky could not be securely guarded or patrolled by the biggest air force conceivable, how was it proposed to forbid, in peace, the stealthy development of air-power even in a vanquished land like Germany? However exhaustive the powers of inspection, however vigilant the Allied inspectors, evasion was simple enough for any modern industrial nation with an air tradition as solid as Germany's.

Trenchard's other contention that the R.A.F. could reduce defence spending by assuming more of the traditional duties of the army and the navy overseas was familiar enough to the Chancellor; but extending the Iraq experiment to Aden, to India, and

farther east again along the half-prospected air route from Chittagong to Singapore would involve curbing the expedition of the War
Office and Admiralty; and that would produce a vicious reaction
from the lobbies of the older services. Churchill therefore sat tight.
The "principle of air substitution" was not yet practical politics;
Churchill's instinct for self-preservation, the Cabinet's for half-
measures designed to give the least offence to the greatest number,
ruled it out as premature.

The Sea Lords and the Generals did not overlook Trenchard's
presumptuousness; and from October, 1925, when Churchill
decreed that the R.A.F. must continue to expand more slowly on
reduced funds and that all military spending must be reviewed,
friction became the permanent working practice of the Chiefs of
Staff in committee. Salisbury's simple rules were not exactly unworkable; but in the circumstances they were better suited to angels
or schizophrenics than to acquisitive mortals. While each service
chief had to fight, alone and blinkered, against a Chancellor who
could arbitrarily decide how much money should be allocated to
defence as a whole, there could be little room for constructive thinking or mutual trust. Scheming for the lion's share of whatever sum
might be going took precedence; and the Cabinet's advisers on
strategy consequently spoke not with one tongue but with three.

The tactics of Beatty and Milne that autumn had no place in
any "square ring." The law of the survival of the slickest replaced
the ideal system of collective responsibility laid down in 1923 by
Salisbury. Unnoticed by a Press and public uplifted by the new
Locarno spirit, the renewed campaign to do Trenchard down went
on for weeks behind the dignified façade of the building in
Whitehall Gardens where defence planning was supposed to be
formulated.

The Cabinet review of defence spending fell into two complementary parts. The first, undertaken by Lord Colwyn and a small
committee of financial experts, was an operation in good book-
keeping. Colwyn, a successful business man who had served on
similar tribunals before, was empowered to scrutinise all service
accounts and recommend cuts in expenditure. The second and
more critical task, which Birkenhead and Churchill jointly assumed,
was to reassess the 1923 programme for raising the number of Home
Defence squadrons in the R.A.F. to fifty-two. The proceedings of
the two committees often strayed far from the fixed terms of reference, leading as on earlier occasions to venomous and sometimes
aimless controversy.[4]

It shocked Trenchard to discover that Churchill could forget so much in his anxiety to compromise: the driving force of expediency, always an imponderable factor in the political equation, swung the Chancellor this way and that like a weather-cock in a hurricane.

Experience had taught him that Churchill was more amenable to flattery than to brow-beating. It was different when they were two individuals, dining *tête-à-tête* and swopping strong opinions. Years later, during the early part of the Second World War, when the Prime Minister and Trenchard on one occasion sat disputing till well past midnight the probable course of Japanese strategy, if and when the Mikado came in, it was Churchill who broke up the discussion by leaving the dinner table with the good-natured words:

"Well, good night, Boom. You and I can always get up an argument on any point—and at any distance from that point."[5]

On learning towards the end of October, 1925, that Churchill was so impressed by the Secretary for War's criticism of current R.A.F. spending that he had actually invited Worthington-Evans to submit alternative proposals for a separate army air wing, the Chief of Air Staff did not immediately explode. Instead, he appealed to Churchill's reason through his vanity:

"I am really seriously worried and alarmed," he wrote. "You know when you got me to come back and run the air force how very diffident I was, how I was doubtful whether I could do the job successfully, how I thought it would be too great a task for me, and how I was dubious of getting enough support to enable me to carry it through. And no one remembers better than I do your wonderful kindness and assistance, your constant assurance that I *should* carry it through and make a success of it. And now I ask you to look at the service that has been formed and is growing up. . . .

"Wherever you go, whether it is in a Punch-and-Judy show or in grand opera, in the highest circles or the lowest, you will hear the opinion that the air force do better than anyone else. Yet because a few people like Worthington-Evans state to you that they can save £4 or £5 millions by taking over the air and running it differently, you think we may have made a mistake.

"We have already saved £15 millions in one place alone—Iraq. . . .

"You know that the only true way of economy in the defensive services of this country is not to do away with the army or the navy but the substitution of the air in part of their duties and responsibilities."

Churchill's reply two days later was a mixture of the non-committal and the plaintive, an attitude very uncharacteristic of him when dealing with most issues and perhaps indicating a knowledge that he was not on very strong ground. He explained that as far as efficiency and leadership in the R.A.F. were concerned his views had remained the same, and he still believed it preferable that the air force should be independent of the other two services. He had also, however, to consider the cost of keeping it so, and he was not convinced that some form of compromise might not effect a considerable saving. The pressures to which he was being subjected at the Treasury were common knowledge, and he hoped that Trenchard, whose wise management of the R.A.F.'s finances had already made him many friends at the Treasury, would understand his difficulties.

It was the Chancellor's last word for the present; he had other concerns. Was not the decision to call in Colwyn a useful reminder to the public that he (Churchill) had the true interests of the taxpayer at heart? It was the Air Staff's business, not the Chancellor's, to prove that the Sea Lords and Generals were spendthrifts.

Experience had not fortified Trenchard's faith in the value of inquiries whose findings were seldom accepted as final; nevertheless, as he later reminded Baldwin, he left nothing undone to ensure that "the need for ecomony should not become a peg on which the older services could hang a fresh demand for our abolition. . . . I even asked Mr. Churchill and others whether you as Prime Minister could not say that this new battle over the air force should not take place. I was told that this was impossible, and the Admiralty and the War Office chose to reopen the issue before the Colwyn Committee on the pretext alike of efficiency and economy."

It was on 19th November that Baldwin announced officially, in reply to an Opposition questioner, that the case for or against a separate Air Ministry *did* come within the scope of Colwyn's inquiry. Beatty had reopened a book which Salisbury and Balfour were supposed to have shut for ever in 1923. Supported by a compliant C.I.G.S., the First Sea Lord once more exerted all his influence to undermine the R.A.F. in obedience to the immutable laws of self-preservation and Admiralty infallibility. Nest eggs were scarce; and far from regarding Trenchard as an eagle in his own right, the First Sea Lord still treated him as little better than a contemptible cuckoo.

4

"I am having a very strenuous time," Trenchard informed Ellington on 26th November, a week after Baldwin's public admission that the status of the R.A.F. was in question once more. "For the last few weeks we have been engaged with the Colwyn Committee on economy and with a Cabinet Committee, presided over by Lord Birkenhead, on air force expansion. . . .

"With regard to Colwyn, [he] has gone thoroughly into our finance and I have appeared before the Committee myself on three occasions . . . I think everything is satisfactory and that they will give us a good report as the Geddes Committee did.

"With regard to Birkenhead, two meetings have been held. . . . So far as I can see, they realise the importance to the country of a proper scheme of air defence—and also the fact that stopping or delaying our programme now that it has been launched is unlikely to bring about any substantial savings.

"I am afraid that possibly as a result of all this we shall have another fight with the Admiralty who still wish to go their own way, whether their way is reasonable or unreasonable or to the best interests of the country or not. The Admiralty have definitely put in to take back their Fleet Air Arm and the coastal reconnaissance machines and shore stations in addition. I counter-attacked and said I would take in the Fleet Air Arm entirely."

The C.I.G.S. had meanwhile been concentrating on what he mistakenly supposed to be Trenchard's weaker flank in Iraq, where the original eight squadrons and R.A.F. armoured car companies, supported by ground forces only six battalions strong, Indian, British and local levies, had propped up Feisal for three years. The facts spoke unerringly against Cavan; and on 29th December, relaxing at home after nearly a month under the Field-Marshal's ragged crossfire, Trenchard confided to Ellington with a rare whoop of jubilation that the General Staff had made even less impression on Birkenhead than the Naval Staff on Colwyn:

"I have kept my end up. We have *not* handed over the command of Iraq to the War Office, which they wanted and still want. Higgins [the Commander in Iraq] has *not* been superseded by an

army general as the War Office also wanted. We have *not* mobilised
divisions to fight Turkey; and we have *not* run the Empire into a
state of disaster. . . .

"I've had the toughest fight I've had for a long time over this
matter and have gained my finest victory. Beatty, of course, joined
forces with Cavan. . . . There is no doubt that economy is very necessary but—at the same time—I think they [the Colwyn Committee]
were impressed with the efforts we had made. At any rate they
ought to be as I'm doing all I can to cut down. . . ."

The cuts were not applied indiscriminately. Equality of sacrifice,
he knew, was a principle which did not always pay. When Higgins
sent a quietly-worded complaint about the inadequate entertainment allowance on which he was expected to keep up official
appearances in Baghdad, Trenchard promised to recommend it to
the Treasury:

"If you realise, as I dare say you do," he added as a cautious
rider, "what's going on at home with regard to economy, economy
and economy, you'll be aware of how difficult it's going to be to get
an increase."

What obsessed him most was the lot of the junior officer and the
regular airman serving abroad; and by some odd process of telepathy his solicitude somehow communicated itself to the lowliest
of his recruits on uncomfortable stations at the back of beyond. In
mess and barrack-room ballads, some of which originated in Iraq
at this period, there sometimes protrudes through the ribaldry
and macabre cynicism the hint of something akin to mocking
affection for "the man who *is* the R.A.F." Such a sentiment was
evoked in a popular refrain like this:

> "*Boom Trenchard loves us*
> *Boom Trenchard loves us*
> *Boom Trenchard loves us*
> *And so he —— well ought.*"[6]

The last line, had he ever heard it sung, would not have displeased him. Because he seldom paused to consider himself as an
image in others' eyes, he was seldom aware of the godlike devotion
often couched in the most blasphemous terms, paid him by the
obscurest of his men. Perhaps Lawrence, who knew both ends of
service life and whose least word Trenchard trusted, alone succeeded
in showing him the truth. For Lawrence had licence to speak out
whenever the spirit moved him to write a letter. Trenchard's replies
were equally frank and from the heart; indeed, the scavenger

school of criticism, which has tried to deface Lawrence's reputation by pecking to bits the contrary aspects of his character, would be well advised to study the hitherto unpublished correspondence between the two as a salutary corrective.

For the moment, it will be enough to quote one extract from a letter dated 1st May, 1928, in which "Aircraftsman Shaw" let himself go on the subject of the R.A.F. Obviously distressed at Trenchard's passing annoyance with him for having sent to his friend, David Garnett, the uncensored typescript of *The Mint*, that introspective and over-drawn account of his initiation to life as a recruit, Lawrence felt compelled to insist on "the essential privacy" of his gift to Garnett. He had already ensured that "nothing of it appears before 1950." The fact that Jonathan Cape, the publishers, had first refusal of his next book was immaterial since he intended in any case to make Cape refuse *The Mint*. Trenchard, for his part, understood Lawrence's queer sensibilities and violent antipathies without having to read the typescript, but objected to his advertising them in print:

"I am sad," Trenchard had stated. "What you have probably written is what is quite comprehensible to you and to me, as we both understand the position; but it would be seized upon immediately by the press if they got hold of it, and they would say what a hopeless air force it was, how badly it was run, what hopeless officers we had, etc., when I know that isn't what you mean at all, though I haven't seen what you have written. . . . And the air force is still young. It can't go on being abused by everybody. . . ."

Two months later, having read the manuscript, Trenchard was no less understanding:

"I know I shall not hurt your feelings; it was what I expected to read. I feel I understand everything put down at the time and your feelings, but I feel it would be unfair to let this loose on a world that likes to blind itself to the ordinary facts that go on day after day. Everything you have written—I can see it happening; the way you have written it is as if it was happening; but the majority of people will only say 'how awful! how horrible! how terrible! how bad!' . . .

"I read every word of it and I seemed to know what was coming in each line, and I feel no soreness, no sadness, about your writing; and yet again I feel all of a tremble in case it gets out and into the hands of people who don't know life as it is. But as the air force

gets more and more of the spirit I want it to get, so a lot of wha
you have written will automatically leave [it] without there seem
ingly being any alteration in the eyes of the public. What I like i
the book are the gaps. Where there are gaps, I feel you are conten
and happy."

Lawrence was inclined to agree. There were, he admitted
"too many fools in the street to broadcast it safely. They'd think
didn't like the R.A.F., whereas I'm as stoutly its lowest number a
you are its highest. You get a God's eye of it, I a worm's-eye view
The worm, let me assure you, hugs himself with happiness on hi
good days in it."

Of the R.A.F. and what it stood for, Lawrence wrote with a
transparent and moving sincerity:

"Please make no mistake here. I've enlisted twice in the ai
force. I've seen from the inside the Turkish and Arab armies an
something of the navy. The R.A.F. is streets finer in morale an
brains and eagerness than the lot of them. Agreed, it's not perfect
It never will be. We grumble—over trifles, mainly customs of dres
which you've inherited from the older services. If I was C.A.S. o
influential with him, they could be put right in one issue of Ai
Ministry Weekly Orders costing twopence. These silly detail
(regular Royal Oak apples) agitate our leisure accessory hours, bu
the actual *work* 99 per cent of the fellows enjoy. You have given u
something worth doing.

"Of course you have enlisted some duds. There are dud English
men, but the average of the R.A.F. is magnificent. As you know
I think the present other-ranks relatively too good for the officers
You must have some technical mastery to hold the respect of trades
men indefinitely. It's no use—or very little use—being just a
gentleman today. But the officers have seen that and are getting
down to it. They are better taught than we are, and will soon bea
us when they try.

"Do please credit your most experienced aircraftman, who ha
in his time been a man of action, and even made a tiny fighting
service out of nothing, when he assures you that the R.A.F. is the
finest individual effort in British history. As this is a private lette
I'm going to let myself go and tell you (what I'll never say in print
unless I survive you and write your life, which God forbid) that the
R.A.F. is your single work, that every one of us, in so far as he i
moulded to type, is moulded after your image, and that it's thank

to your being head and shoulders greater in character than ordinary men that your force even in its childhood surpasses the immemorial army and navy. No man in the three or four continents I know could have done what you've done.

"The R.A.F. is 30,000 strong, too huge for you to have personal contact with many of us; but there is not a barrack-room in which your trumpet does not regularly sound; and these thousands of your champions find no opponents. We grouse and grumble at everything and everybody, except you; and all but that one per cent of ignorant airmen know you as our exemplar and creator and try (does it frighten you? it would me) to be better copies. . . .

"Perhaps you've long guessed my feelings. I can let rip on paper; though they would never have got into words but for that fourth depressed page of this letter of yours saying you are weary, and wondering if the years had been a failure and the job too big for you. Not even you, who made it, shall call the R.A.F. a failure in my hearing. It's a masterpiece. But I do suspect that you've made something bigger than yourself, and in that sense the job has been too big for you. An overwhelming personality induces worship and the knowledge that the master is a great man doubles his servants' worth. You've been backed by the trusting wits of all these fellows who'd say Amen to the above summing up."

In asserting that airmen were relatively too good for their officers, Lawrence was partly right. Trenchard had long recognised a certain lack of balance between the mental and technical calibre of the average commissioned and non-commissioned men in the service. This was no doubt a vindication of his boy-apprentice training scheme, which had at last moved into its magnificently equipped home at Halton; but because it appeared to reflect on Cranwell standards and on the quality of his short-term pilots, Trenchard had striven hard to remedy it. The majority of his senior officers, he knew, blamed the short-term scheme itself. There he disagreed with them. The notion that the temporary pilot or observer was necessarily a cut or two below the permanent Cranwell product struck him as a delusion of snobbery. At Uxbridge, the setting for the rather muddy introspection of *The Mint*, Trenchard assembled several hundred of his permanent officers one January day in 1926 to describe how they as individuals could help to strengthen the R.A.F.

"When I started this job in 1919," he began, "there were exactly three officers—and not another single one—who had per-

manent commissions in the Royal Air Force. Everything else in it
was temporary, and frankly I thought my effort was likely to end
in failure. But, under pressure from Mr. Churchill, I undertook
the job."

There had not been money enough in the Exchequer to offer a
good career, with reasonably quick promotion, to all the officers
required by a young and highly technical service, however small.
So, thinking not of the next ten years but of the next quarter of a
century—"legislating not for the officers of the air force to-day
but for the day when all permanent officers will have been in from
their youth and have passed through Cranwell"—he had to hit on
the unprecedented expedient of engaging the bulk of R.A.F. officers
on a short-term basis:

"Well, gentlemen, I ask you to ask yourselves if it has not
worked out fairly well after seven years. . . . There is stability in
the permanent service, there *is* a reasonable chance of promotion,
and we shan't have a large half-pay list. Neither will officers be
chucked out too late in life to be able to take up any other profession.
The present age is what I may call an engineering or scientific age.
In the past the fighting services were largely drawn from and supported by what I may call the squires, who had the money, the
brains and the men. Now the centre of influence has shifted. . . .
Already we have an agreement that entry through the R.A.F. will
count towards short-term officers becoming Associates in the
Institution of Mechanical Engineers; their five years will be a
qualifying period. . . . Engineers have started to recognise that air
force education is going to be good. They've gone further in other
ranks and have agreed that after the course at Halton a pass mark
of 60 per cent will be equivalent to passing the studentship
examination. . . .

"We have tapped and are tapping—and it's up to you to continue tapping—the scientific brains of this nation, the intelligent
class who can learn and absorb quickly. . . . Remember also that
it's the short-service system which enables us to have a reserve of
officers young enough to fly, fight the enemy and hold the stick
themselves. . . . I want brains to be pooled in the R.A.F. I want
free discussion with the young officer as well as with the senior
officer to be encouraged, just as I encourage it in my own room. . . ."

Only towards the close of his speech did Trenchard touch upon
current controversies. The expanding role of the R.A.F., which
had brought about past collisions with the other services, was still,
he admitted, a source of rancour:

"In 1919, I said that as the air service developed there would be an arm for the navy and an arm for the army with a central body. Some have interpreted this to mean a separate arm. I have yet to learn that anybody could read that White Paper and interpret it in any other way than that I have two arms and they are not separate from my body."

Into the details of the latest quarrel with Beatty and Milne he did not enter; but he did explain why the repetitive Admiralty demand for a separate air arm was "a fallacy with two aspects":

"The first is the failure to realise that the functions of the naval air units are in essence no different from those working with the army and independently. This is true whether you think of the functions of fighting in the air, attacking objectives on the ground or ship at close range, high bombing or low bombing, spotting, launching torpedoes from aircraft—the principle is the same but applied to different objectives.

"The second is the belief that it is possible to fix a frontier in the air, and on that basis to divide responsibility. . . . Any of you who have applied themselves to this question will understand that this is impossible for a country so placed as Great Britain. We are unlike almost every other country in the world, and those of you who read [in] the papers . . . about the air controversy in America will see that it's quite a different problem. They have not got an Empire like ours with the possibilities of airports throughout the world. Don't think that America's is in any way similar to our problem—it's nothing like it."

Of recent tendentious reports in the press, only one detained him:

"You may have seen statements that the Home Defence Scheme is going to be deferred and reduced. Don't be under any misapprehension at all. The Air Force Expansion Scheme still exists, but the financial situation is such that it may be necessary to slow it up as much as possible. It will enable those squadrons forming—and there will be twenty-seven of them this coming year—to get perfect. If we can really make those twenty-seven perfect at a small cost, we may be able to add the others all the earlier. To tell me we have got to the end of cutting down the cost of running a squadron is to tell me what I don't believe."

Every squadron at home, he had decided, must manage from now on with only twelve machines instead of eighteen.

"I know there'll be a lot of criticism, but I'm certain it can be done. . . . By knocking down now the number of machines and engines that are necessary to keep the twelve machines in a squadron, I knock down the number of new machines we have to buy to keep up a given front-line strength."

It was an injunction to live on air; yet its effect would leave more capital for vital technical research and development. Half a million scraped off the bottom of the barrel now would pay enormous dividends in five years' time when existing types of aircraft were obsolescent. He was wiser in his generation than those critics who then or later condemned him as the blind slave of Government policy. Here was an instance of that flair for making the best of a bad bargain which induced a grateful and harassed Churchill to dub him "Thrifty Trenchard."

5

On 25th February, just five weeks after his Uxbridge address, Trenchard left his office after lunch and took a taxi to Westminster. Baldwin had an important statement to make; and Trenchard knew roughly what was in it. Colwyn had presented his report; the latest Grand Inquisitor had uncovered no evidence to support Admiralty and War Office charges of incompetence and extravagance at the Air Ministry. The Chief of Air Staff was eager to hear the verdict and to sample for himself the temper of the House.

The leading question was put by Ramsay MacDonald. Baldwin paused deliberately before replying:

"The Government have no intention," said the Prime Minister, "of reopening the question of a separate air arm and Air Minister. . . ."

The statement fell prosaically flat. It was as if Baldwin's off-hand manner was studiously calculated to exorcise passion and strangle interest. Only when the debate on the Air Estimates was joined did individual feelings come bubbling up. Trenchard stayed late listening to the speeches. Bread evidently meant more than air circuses like his to M.P.s from industrial areas where jobs were scarce and people knew the ache of hunger in their bellies. With the ink hardly dry on the Locarno treaties, could it be wondered that such speakers should press and harry the Government to drop air expansion altogether rather than slow it down?

A contribution of the sort came from Major Clement Attlee, whom Trenchard remembered as the late Under-Secretary at the War Office. Attlee's words were clothed with only a modest apprec-

iation of the strategic dilemmas; but a surprisingly acid wit
enlivened a reedily dull delivery, causing some noticeable squirming
on the Treasury Bench.

"There is no echo of the Locarno spirit in these estimates,"
said Attlee. "The Government's position is—'Someone else has
got an air force, therefore we must have one.' That is national
snobbery."

Attlee was not among those who would cheerfully have abolished
the R.A.F. He would have abolished instead an appropriations
system which vested too much power in the hands of the Chancellor.
That system was unfair to Parliament, the taxpayer and the service
chiefs, reducing these last to endlessly wrangling and jumping the
gun in their efforts to cheat each other of any cash that might be
going. A Minister of Defence would put paid to that. Attlee even
had a candidate in mind:

"The man for the job," he said amidst ironical laughter, "is
Mr. Churchill, who's had experience in the three forces—as a soldier,
sailor and airman, too. The Defence Minister ought to be in the
closest touch with the Secretary of State for Foreign Affairs, and the
League of Nations; and the co-ordination of the fighting services
ought to be dominated by a programme of disarmament."

Disarmament was being canvassed as a cure for all political ills.
Now that the smell of fear had been partly driven underground,
good Europeans, whatever their outlook, were drugging themselves
with lungfuls of the cleaner air of hope. Theoretically, a Defence
Ministry might have been useful to realign Britain's strategic needs
and rationalise military expenditure; in practice, no candidate but
Churchill would have wanted, or could have held, such a job for
long. Baldwin, of whom it has been said that he believed a nation's
happiness lay in "having no history," and who habitually acted in
the spirit of that belief, tactfully did nothing.

The Prime Minister's inertia was a poor consolation to the Sea
Lords, whose narrower hopes that Colwyn would take their part
had been unceremoniously dashed. Chatfield, the then Admiralty
Controller, dismissed the Colwyn Report in his memoirs as the con-
coction of "three civilians who had never been to sea."[7] The "three
civilians" had never flown either, so it was rather a pointless gibe.
Colwyn and his associates had simply done their job as conscientious
accountants; twice two might make twenty-two by Admiralty or
War Office reckoning, but not if the ordinary rules of arithmetic
were obeyed.

"We find no remedy," the inquisitor had declared, "in the

abolition of the Air Ministry urged by the two older departments. On the contrary we affirm the necessity for an independent Air Ministry. . . . We do not think that the estimates of administrative savings, which the other two departments claim would result from its dismemberment, would materialise. Nor would any such savings compensate for the greater savings which we hope will be secured by the extended substitution of air-power—a development which depends on the continued existence of a separate air authority, on improved co-ordination between the three services, and on the imposition of collective control."

Baldwin ignored Colwyn's recommendation that a Defence Minister should be appointed to impose "collective control" (and air substitution) on the Chiefs of Staff. The latter, he decided, must learn the gentle art of controlling themselves. If they failed once in a while he, as Prime Minister and *de jure* Chairman of the Committee of Imperial Defence, could always intervene. Beatty had reason to be grateful for Baldwin's easy-going indifference to problems that did not interest him. It encouraged the Admiralty, in preparing the 1926 naval estimates, to act as though Colwyn had never been thought of, forcing Trenchard to react vigorously in self-defence.

"I can see no shadow of justification," he complained to Churchill, "for putting £900,000 in Navy Votes for the Fleet Air Arm next year. . . . £700,000, as recommended on page 11 of the Colwyn Committee's Report, is ample. . . . We have agreed to postpone completion of the 1923 programme until 1935 and not a single new regular squadron is to be formed in 1926-7 or 1927-8. It is *ludicrous* to suggest that you *cannot* also postpone the new Fleet Air Arm units, particularly, if formed, they will only waste time and money kicking their heels ashore. . . .

"For heaven's sake let there be no more committees . . . to waste their time and ours on issues which have been tried and retried a dozen times during the last few years. . . .

"If there's to be any hope of substantial reductions in the cost of Imperial Defence as a whole, it's essential that a stop should be put to these frivolous actions which have frittered away so much of all our energies. . . . Please help me over the last stile, and forgive me if I have written strongly, but it's what I feel."

Churchill took the plaintiff's criticism well, passing it on to Baldwin with the suggestion that the Prime Minister should see the Chief of Air Staff in person. The interview was arranged. Down the Whitehall grapevine sped the whisper: "Someone's been sneaking to the Cabinet." With the contrariness of the guilty, blaming not themselves but the man who, they considered, had thwarted them, the Sea Lords unanimously decided to resist the Cabinet if necessary. It is recorded of George Bernard Shaw, that on being asked whether Frank Harris had a first-rate mind, promptly replied:

"He's neither first-rate nor second-rate nor tenth-rate. He's just his horrible, unique self."

Shaw's judgment on that dilettante of letters, expressed no doubt in saltier terms, fairly sums up the Admirals' opinion of Trenchard at this time. Beatty refused to let the Royal Navy suffer because this air maniac chose to misinterpret Colwyn, then mislead Churchill and the Prime Minister, for his own vain-glorious ends. The facts as Beatty saw them were damning: the Fleet Air Arm, despite the written agreement imposed by Haldane in 1924, had begun to languish; the R.A.F. had neither the money nor the interest to prevent this; so the Royal Navy had every right to forget Haldane and renew the old demand for a separate naval air force.

6

Before the end of March, 1926, Baldwin was forced to intervene. Any uncertainty as to which department exercised what powers over the Fleet Air Arm must be ended. But the Prime Minister did not hurry. The dispute was a minor affair indeed compared with the threatened General Strike then looming. The first could wait; the second could not.

When the Mining Subsidy expired in May, 1926, with no prospect of any compromise settlement of the disputed wage-cuts, the Trades Union Congress warned the Government that the miners' fight for social justice was theirs as well. "Not a shilling off the pay. Not a minute off the day." So ran the slogan of the miners' leaders, who had previously rejected the shorter hours and lower wages fixed by the owners. Strike notices were sent out; yet Baldwin still hoped to play the honest broker and find a peaceful way. He was defeated in the end by an ironic mischance. For the strike notices took effect almost literally at the eleventh hour in the printing shop of the *Daily Mail*, where several compositors expressed resentment at the tone of a leading article on the dispute by refusing to print it. This untimely attempt, on the night of 2nd May, to interfere with free speech was too much even for Baldwin, whose call for the withdrawal of the strike notices as a condition of further negotiations came too late.

The Cabinet was not unprepared for the emergency. Plans for maintaining essential services had been laid during the industrial unrest of 1919. Specific tasks were allotted to the service chiefs, Trenchard's being to organise daily communication flights between London and other cities and distribute the mail, as well as the spirited but boringly partisan Government newspaper, *The British Gazette*, which Churchill greatly enjoyed helping to write and edit. For several weeks the latest inter-service controversy was put aside. Beatty volunteered to let Trenchard borrow naval pilots as reliefs, a gracious offer that was politely declined. Partial at other times about their own prerogatives, the two adversaries were at one with Churchill in their inability to be anything but impartial when it came to a joint matter of extinguishing a dangerous fire.

The General Strike petered out quickly. The miners held out for six weeks, until their resources failed. Then Baldwin resumed his leisurely task of arbitration on the air-naval dispute. He reached a decision early in July. Once more it was a firm verdict against the Admiralty:

"The arguments which have been laid before me on the two sides of this great question of principle add practically nothing to those presented to the Earl of Balfour's Committee in 1923, and I see no reason to modify in any way the conclusions reached by that Committee."

It was a further jolt to Beatty's hopes, and an intimation that the Prime Minister was less gullible than such a master of compromise had any right to be. The man who presided at important C.I.D. meetings like a heavy still-life evidently had the knack of listening with his eyes shut and his ears wide open. Baldwin had not been hoodwinked. He could recognise a principle even when he appeared to be sound asleep; and the holier-than-thou attitude of the Sea Lords, who paid lip-service to the principles of air-power while promoting every conceivable legalistic quibble to subvert them, had roused his displeasure. This was Trenchard's reading of Baldwin's judgment and the three practical riders that followed from it.

The first denied to the Admiralty the administrative right to "pack" fleet squadrons with naval flying officers: since the Trenchard-Keyes agreement of Haldane's day the Sea Lords had exceeded the 70 per cent of pilots' vacancies then allowed, yet actually wanted Baldwin to increase their quota to 100 per cent. Having thus recovered *physical* possession of naval squadrons, they could then assert their quasi-moral right to strategic control. The claim did not deceive a Prime Minister allergic to Trojan Horses, with wings or without.

For that reason he had no hesitation in rejecting the Admiralty's second demand, a natural sequel to the first, ruling that the term "Fleet Air Arm" applied only to operational units embarked on carriers, not to shore bases and establishments. Beatty, who sought to infiltrate and swamp these too, in the proportion of two sailors to every airman, had appealed in vain to Balfour as witness that the Admiralty were obeying the letter and spirit of agreements already arrived at, whereas the Air Ministry were simply twisting these to suit their own ends.

Baldwin disagreed emphatically.

"My decision is," he wrote, "that the recommendation of the Balfour Committee should be interpreted as applying to the Fleet Air Arm afloat. . . . I have taken the precaution of consulting each member of the [original Balfour] Committee, and they all independently confirm that the ratio of seven to three (in terms of men) was intended to be restricted to the Fleet Air Arm in the narrow sense of those serving on board carriers."

The third ruling was the most shattering of all to the Sea Lords' aspirations. Baldwin rejected outright their demand for what is still R.A.F. Coastal Command, the land-based squadrons employed for tactical co-operation with the Home Fleet. The strategic arguments, he admitted, were finely balanced:

"The Admiralty maintain that these units, in wartime, will have the purely naval function of the protection of shipping from the attacks of submarines and surface craft . . . and that it is essential they should be embodied in a Naval Air Arm under Naval direction and control.

"The Air Ministry maintain that we cannot afford to maintain squadrons against every possible contingency, and that units must —as far as possible—be allocated more than one role, just as, for example, ten of the new Home Defence squadrons are organised on a mobile basis so as to be available under suitable conditions to accompany an expeditionary force abroad. They wish to extend this duality, and to increase the mobility of our air forces throughout the Empire.

"The air force are willing, however, that when the situation so requires, shore-based units may be placed under temporary naval *operational control* for the purpose of any specific operation or series of operations."

In Baldwin's judgment, the coastal squadrons must remain an integral part of the R.A.F. It was a matter for closer co-operation, not for strict and permanent subordination. He was not satisfied that the Admiralty and Air Ministry were showing the necessary mutual goodwill, and he bound over both to behave more tolerantly:

"The navy must utilise to the full the experience in regard to aerial matters accumulated by the air force as the result of research, experiment and flying in all parts of the world. The air force must regard it as an obligation of honour to give the navy a Fleet Air Arm of the highest attainable efficiency. I do not feel satisfied that this has been the case during the last two years. . . . It is impossible," Baldwin concluded, "to achieve progress if decisions of the Government are to be put in question at every opportunity."

7

Reluctant to complicate Cabinet business by drawing the old red herring of a Defence Ministry across its track, the Prime Minister decided that the special Chiefs of Staff sub-committee devised by Salisbury in 1923 must henceforth be permitted to work as its author had intended. From August, 1926, onwards it would function "under my direction. . . ." Its first chairman would be Beatty. Delighted as he was at Baldwin's initiative, Trenchard did not delude himself about the more obvious drawbacks. Discrepancies in outlook were too marked, the memory of past disputes too fresh, to produce anything better than collective evasions or agreements to suspend individual disagreements where questions of major strategic significance were concerned. The habit of special pleading, from narrow interests of service prestige, was too deeply ingrained to be altered quickly.

The recent Fleet Air Arm controversy had served only to darken counsel. The sting of defeat suffered by both army and navy as a result of the Colwyn Committee Enquiry would take time to remove.

It must be owned that Trenchard was correct in his surmise. And nowhere is the evidence more mournfully convincing than in the record of their deliberations on the Singapore project which Baldwin revived in 1925, reversing MacDonald's decision to postpone it. Trenchard's attempts to raise the issue above partisan level were foredoomed to failure.

With the exception of Churchill, there are few surviving witnesses more qualified to judge the Singapore fiasco from both ends, so to speak, than Sir James Grigg. A joint private secretary to Churchill at the Exchequer in 1925, when Singapore again became a bone of contention between the service chiefs, Grigg was Secretary of State for War in 1942, when the fortress fell. From the mid-twenties onwards he thus had inside knowledge of Trenchard's campaign to convince the Cabinet and his own professional rivals that Singapore needed aircraft rather than fixed siege guns for its security.

"I expect a good many people in 1942 thought it a pity that the Tories ever re-started this—in the event—quite futile enterprise," Grigg has written. " But this was a superficial judgment, for I have always considered that the real tragedy of the Singapore decisions was much more that Lord Beatty's view prevailed over that of Lord Trenchard in regard to the methods to be adopted for defending the base. The naval view meant fixed defences and big guns and forts, and these turned out to be useless. But it might have been a different story if Lord Trenchard's plan of entrusting the protection of the fortress predominantly to the air had carried the day."[8]

Churchill frankly admits in Volume IV of his memoirs why it was impossible during the Second World War to hold a Royal Commission of Inquiry into "the worst disaster and largest capitulation" in British history:

"We could not spare the men, the time or the energy," he said. "Parliament accepted this view."

It may rightly be pondered why no British Government since has seen fit to investigate the causes of the fiasco. As far as the public is concerned, it remains unexplained. It will be sufficient for the reader of this narrative to judge whether Grigg is broadly right or wrong in suggesting, long after the event, that the seeds of disaster were sown during the late twenties by the Chiefs of Staff sub-committee. To the extent that space permits, contemporary Air Staff records will be allowed here to speak for themselves. Their consistency is indeed startling. Whether particular papers were actually written by Trenchard or edited by his syndicate of "English merchants" hardly matters. The basic thought is unmistakably his, though style and details may well have been left to others in accordance with his usual practice.

"Singapore," Beatty wrote to his wife in January, 1924. "That infernal place's name will be engraved on my heart. The struggles I have had over it are to be repeated more bitterly than ever and with doubtful results."

The struggles and the bitterness returned in January, 1925, when Baldwin reintroduced the naval defence scheme and Trenchard again denounced the strategic assumptions of the Admiralty as ludicrously out-of-date. The special Cabinet sub-committee on Singapore then went through the familiar routine of inviting the Chiefs of Staff to reconsider the question and report back; and the renewed debate lasted eighteen more months.

In mid-July, 1925, Trenchard appeared before the sub-committee to elaborate his case against the cut-and-dried naval case for installing half a dozen huge 15-inch guns as the main armament of the future fortress:

"I feel that the defence of Singapore is a vital stage in the development of the air," he said. "In contemplating any change in such important questions as the defence of this Empire, there is always this great difficulty—the critics of such change say that the risk of experiment is too great and that therefore the well tried and old methods of the past must once more be used.

"They said so about Iraq, in 1921. . . . Now again they say in effect of Singapore—'We should put in old-style defences, all of them, and if after some years the air proves its case, it will be most interesting.'

"Meanwhile the money has been spent, and the success of the new (air) policy hindered by lack of development.

"The old-style at Singapore means an overlapping of expenditure, superimposing the cost of local air defence on to that of full-scale coastal defence. . . .

"I fail to see the necessity of taking a decision now as to spending a large sum in installing six 15-inch guns which may very conceivably be out of date when the future need arises. In a very few years' time the whole air situation in the East may have been transformed; any change that occurs will strengthen and not diminish the potentialities of air-power for the defence of Singapore and the Far East, and I would urge that no precipitate step be taken now which may involve the locking up of money in fixed defences whose function can be so admirably fulfilled at less cost by utilising the mobility of aircraft.

"The argument that since Singapore is vital therefore we can't risk any but a proved deterrent leaves me unmoved. . . . When we have a naval war, I feel even more certain that air will deter attacks by ships. I am not a visionary. I only try to look one step ahead on the basis of what I know aircraft can do."

Nobody in 1925, or even in 1935, could have foreseen the calam-

tous situation which would confront the outnumbered defenders
of Singapore in 1942. Pre-war appreciations took no account of
Japanese plans of aggrandisement, nor of Japanese means and
methods of total warfare. The Whitehall planners were reckoning
then in terms which events would wholly falsify; and the failure
was not only one of military logic. Diplomatic weakness, faulty
intelligence, and political sloth or complacency during the early
thirties, a period stigmatised by Churchill as "the locust years,"
must be set against the earlier blunders of the Chiefs of Staff. The
final odds were overwhelming for men, brought up on the orthodox
tactics and gentlemanly procedures of warfare as the British traditionally practised it.

Not even Trenchard was then fully prepared for the extremity
that came to pass, with land-based Japanese air units dominating
the coastal waters of Southern Siam, Indo-China and Malaya, and
having little to fear from the few R.A.F. squadrons which survived
the opening air assault on their forward bases. The R.A.F.'s first-
line strength in Malaya in early 1942 was only 158 machines, a
few of them bombers, many of them obsolete fighters, which barely
exceeded Trenchard's revised 1926 estimate of the minimum force
consistent with safety for checking a hypothetical seaborne invasion
from Japan. Alas, the money that might have provided the extra aircraft, the time and forethought that might have gone towards the
technical development of up-to-date machines, were squandered
instead, after further interludes for disarmament delays and strategic
evasions in the thirties, on a steel and concrete graveyard ringed
with huge fixed guns that never once opened fire in anger.

"I know the First Sea Lord, and I believe the C.I.G.S., regard
any delay as perilous," Trenchard's argument concluded. "They
think that the present is a most vital and dangerous time and that
the defences of Singapore should be completed in three or four
years' time. I freely admit that if putting Singapore into condition
to meet the maximum possible Japanese attack is a matter of red-
hot urgency, I cannot press for a scheme of defence by aircraft
instead of guns, [for] we cannot undertake that aircraft of the right
type would be available in sufficient numbers in the Middle East
and Far East, or that arrangements for ensuring their mobility
would be far enough developed.

"But if the Government decide that the problem is not of this
degree of urgency, then I claim that there is every reason for awaiting air development and for applying a scheme based upon the use
of aircraft in place of large fixed defences."

Baldwin took the chair at that meeting. He appeared almost a impressed by the cogency of Trenchard's thesis as was Churchill by it promise of comparative inexpensiveness. But the Cabinet, embroilec at that moment in a dispute over an Admiralty demand for fifteer large cruisers of the County Class, which the Chancellor hac struck off the naval estimates, were obliged to play cautiously. Indeed Beatty and Mr. Bridgeman, the First Lord, had already warned the Prime Minister (in the words of Beatty's biographer Rear-Admiral W. S. Chalmers) that "they would be compelled tc resign if the Government refused to act on the advice of the Board." Rather than antagonise the Sea Lords further by taking a contro- versial decision on this other remote and long-term problem o strategy, Baldwin chose the path of prudence and took no decision a all. And Churchill approved.

Again and again during the next few months, the Chief of Air Staff pleaded with Beatty and Milne for a fair chance. They countered by pressing for a detailed statement of the cost of *his* plan. They pressed at first in vain. Until the air route from Cairo to India was extended, and the R.A.F. grew stronger, Trenchard said that he could offer no precise estimates. The Cabinet alone could have extricated him from this dilemma; but the Cabinet, faced with a united War Office and Admiralty, were divided on the merits of his case. Baldwin hedged again by passing the problem back to the deadlocked service chiefs.

"The Air Staff are of the opinion," Trenchard declared, return- ing to the charge in a paper that typifies a dozen others, "that the presence of aeroplanes in sufficient quantity at Singapore would under present circumstances (a) prevent surprise as to the nature and locality of a Japanese landing or the formation of an advance base within 150 miles of Singapore; (b) act as a strong deterrent to the convoying and landing of an army within striking range of our base; (c) form a sufficiently powerful deterrent against bom- bardment of Singapore by capital ships as to make this form of attack so unlikely that the risk can be accepted."

Beatty and Milne would have none of it. Quite apart from their suspicion that Trenchard was "empire-building" again at their expense, they sincerely believed that he was exaggerating the accuracy and the hitting power of existing torpedo-carrying aircraft. They did not, indeed could not, deny that the air scheme would mean greater economy; but they emphasised that proved efficiency was worth paying more for every time. Besides, who could say how many squadrons, or of what type, would be ultimately necessary? Apparently not Trenchard. Who knew when the half-finished chain of airfields from Egypt to Singapore would be ready? Did Trenchard? Would he kindly descend from his cloudbank and submit even an outline of his requirements?

He put off committing himself as long as possible. Finally, however, the Committee of Imperial Defence insisted that Trenchard should substantiate his case by specifying how exactly he proposed to defend Singapore by air action.

On 12th May, 1926, he presented very tentative estimates of needs, based on his then meagre total force of thirty-seven regular and reserve squadrons. As he realised, this left him little, if any, margin for manœuvre; so he prefaced his argument with a plea for deferment.

"It has been accepted that war with Japan is improbable before 1935," he said. "I therefore maintain that if authority is given to the Air Ministry to proceed with the construction of the few remaining aerodromes (between Calcutta and Singapore) essential to the scheme, and which would amply repay the outlay quite apart from the defence of Singapore, the question of installing 15-inch guns would not become urgent until 1931. . . .

"The essence of the proposed plan lies in the ability to reinforce Singapore with air units employed in other theatres *before* the Japanese can possibly attack the base." The naval staff estimated "the period before relief," when the Singapore garrison would be left to fend for itself, as seventy days, assuming that the invading forces would set out from Japan. This was the whole basis of Beatty's demand for fixed guns to withstand siege conditions until British warships arrived, since the War Office ruled out as quite inconceivable any attempt by the Japanese to land troops in Malaya and to advance on the island fortress through the peninsula's "impenetrable jungle." Trenchard contended that, with aircraft, the "period before relief" postulated by the Admiralty would scarcely arise.

". . . It may even be possible during the strained relations period," he said, "to concentrate [air units] at Rangoon, in which case it would only take four days to reach Singapore."

But how many squadrons did he need? That was the crux. If he asked for too many, the Cabinet would refuse; if he asked for too few, Beatty and Milne would write off his alternative plan as fantastic. Trenchard pitched his demands deliberately low, allowing himself and the Cabinet four years to meet them. After the first stage of development, he urged, everyone could think again:

"My proposals for the air defence of Singapore may be summarised like this," he said.

"First, no 15-inch guns required. Torpedo-bomber aircraft (at least one squadron) to provide a deterrent against Japanese attack, in addition to the submarines, mines and fixed armament (including several 9.2 guns) already authorised.

"Second, two torpedo-bomber squadrons, possibly more, to reinforce Singapore from India when an emergency arises. . . .

"Third, one squadron of fighters to reinforce Singapore from India. . . .

"Four, two bomber squadrons could be sent from Iraq to India or Singapore during the period of strained relations. . . .

"Five, the development of the air-route Calcutta to Singapore to be started at once and continued during the next nine years. . . .

"Six, reconnaissance to be provided by one flight of aircraft whose type and peacetime location need not yet be decided. . . .

"Seven, in 1930, the question of permanent air units for Singapore to be reconsidered, the location of one flight or even one squadron of torpedo-bombers and of the reconnaissance flight to be then decided in the light of air development."

Considered as a modest beginning, the plan was sound enough. But its completion ultimately depended on the co-operation of the Government of India.

" I want an understanding with the Government of India," said Trenchard, "regarding the employment of air units for the reinforcement of Singapore. . . .

"I want two more bombing squadrons in India for reasons other than the defence of Singapore. I want the present type of bombing aircraft in India replaced by the new type capable of carrying bombs or torpedoes.

"I want authority to spend £200,000 during the next nine years on the development of aerodromes and landing-grounds between Calcutta and Singapore. It may be that all this money will not be required . . . owing to the development of Imperial Airways routes; on the other hand, the money may be spent in enabling Imperial Airways to develop their routes. The Dominions Governments may be able to contribute."

Even with the £200,000 necessary for completing the chain of Far East bases, the cost of Trenchard's five-year development plan was attractively low. According to conservative Air Ministry figures, which allowed for every military item already authorised except the

15-inch guns and their accessories, it would have knocked £7 million off the original £30 million bill.

Still the Cabinet hedged, unwilling to say yes or no. Churchill, who might otherwise have thrown his weight into the scales against Beatty and Cavan, had more immediate anxieties. The General Strike had begun when Trenchard submitted the above memorandum, a 5000-word document complete with detailed appendices and a map marking the sites of future landing-grounds from Chittagong to Port Victoria, from Alor Star to Kuala Lumpur and thence to Singapore itself. The memorandum failed to distract the Chancellor from his domestic preoccupations. Nor did it impinge deeply on the mind of Baldwin, who was more disturbed by the imminence of industrial anarchy than by an Air-Marshal's second opinion on an unreal military contingency in the Far East.

The plan lay undebated until Baldwin, having arbitrated against Beatty in the current Admiralty attempt to regain control of the fleet squadrons, informed the service heads that he, as Chairman of the C.I.D., would impose no decision regarding the finely balanced Singapore question. This was essentially one for them to settle between themselves. The spirit of appeasement, the breath of Baldwin's being, animated the homily accompanying the Prime Minister's ruling on the Fleet Air Arm. It has already been quoted, but it is relevant now as one of several possible explanations for a sudden, uncharacteristic and almost incomprehensible error of judgment on Trenchard's part. That at any rate is how he would always look back on the step he took at the beginning of July, 1926, to concede Beatty half his case on the Singapore dispute.

"It was," he told this author—not once but several times—"the worst blunder of my career. I was too trusting."

Beatty was ill when Baldwin announced his verdict on the Fleet Air Arm, but found strength enough to compose and send a personal note to Trenchard from his sick-bed. Its subject was Singapore; written in pencil and bearing all the marks of spontaneity, it was a begging letter. For the sake of the nation, not the navy, Beatty implored, could he not moderate his intransigent attitude to the present plan of defence? For a day or two Trenchard pondered over this unusual request. Then he replied, apparently surrendering in a few lines the substance of his case:

"I don't want to worry you and I hope you're getting better, but I don't know that this letter will make you better or worse. What I want to tell you is that I've thought over your appeal to me to try and come into line with my colleagues on the Chiefs of

Staff; and I've decided I ought to as I've at present failed to convince you of the practicality of my scheme—for which I'm sorry.

"I'm telling the P.M. this morning that I agree, subject to certain remarks, that a start should be made on the [first] three 15-inch guns for Singapore. . . ."

That morning, 6th July, 1926, Trenchard saw Baldwin and kept his word to Beatty. Two days later, an ecstatic note of thanks arrived from the First Sea Lord.

The official historian, in volume I of *The War Against Japan*, touches briefly and without comment on this early stage of the controversy:

"After many months of indecision," he writes, "the Committee of Imperial Defence recommended in 1926 that, as some four years would be necessary for the development of the air force, the Singapore defences should provide for the necessary close and medium-gun defences, plus three 15-inch heavy guns, and that the question of substituting aircraft for the remainder of the heavy guns should be re-examined later. In the meanwhile, however, action was to be taken to extend the air reinforcement route from Calcutta, where it then terminated, to Singapore."

Trenchard certainly erred in yielding to a conciliatory impulse. He erred doubly, while adhering firmly to the principle, in supposing that the debate would be reopened by his successor when the installing of the remaining 15-inch guns came up for discussion.

There would be further skirmishing, of course. Lieutenant-General Sir Henry Pownall, Chief of Staff to Wavell when Singapore fell, has noted that "it was not until 1933, after Japan had withdrawn from the League of Nations, that the Cabinet decided to take active steps."[10] Had Trenchard held firm to a scheme in which Sir John Salmond and Sir Edward Ellington, his successors, believed as staunchly as himself it is possible that the Singapore tragedy might have had a less catastrophic and ignominious ending. Pownall does not even mention the existence of an air scheme, nor the violent disagreements to which it gave rise in the twenties.

It is equally arguable, of course, that Trenchard, with only a half-grown force which was further stunted by Churchill's improvident extension of the "Ten Year Rule" in 1928, counted too much on the relative effectiveness of the torpedo-bomber as a defensive weapon. It may be that even in ideal conditions, with no "Ten Year Rule" to restrict him and his successors, and with all the financial and political assistance needed to build a balanced "mobile air reserve" in the Far East, Singapore would still have fallen. But his personal remorse, unmingled with self-pity, was enduring. For Trenchard lived to see the Japanese, admittedly with the tactical and numerical odds decisively in their favour owing to another decade of procrastination and of blunders more culpable than his, vindicate in reverse the strategy he had long advocated, using land-based bombers to immobilise airfields and to harass unseasoned troops in jungle terrain which the British General Staff had always deemed impassable. Undoubtedly the cruellest cut of all was the sinking for ever in 1942, in the shattered hulks of the *Prince of Wales* and *Repulse*, of that encrusted Admiralty legend which maintained that torpedoes could never harm ships of the line, while the duly completed battery of 15-inch siege guns stood pointing mutely out to sea.

8

"It is much better to have an objective, even if you fail." The speaker was Churchill, the year 1927, the subject finance. The Chancellor's objective had been a progressive reduction of £10 million a year in public spending. It had not come off. Opposition members were taunting him for persevering with policies which had long rubbed the pristine shine off his arithmetic. In trying to please some of the people some of the time, within the ever-shrinking limits prescribed by the gold standard, the Chancellor had succeeded in antagonising many others for most of the time. The noteworthy exceptions were his Cabinet colleagues and the City of London. Churchill had not in him that hard fixity of purpose about money that makes a good Shylock, or a safe Chancellor in an unsafe period.

Certainly the terms of luck as well as trade were against him; and nothing he tried could alter these in his favour, even the extra restrictions he imposed on the service departments. We find Trenchard informing Hoare, his Secretary of State, on 5th November, 1928:

"I consider it my duty to point out that we are in a lower state of preparedness in England, and to a certain extent abroad, than we have been for the last four or five years. I am sending this to you to place on record, in case emergencies develop in future after I have left office, and maybe after a change of Government, which would make it appear that the organisation of the air service was bad—and, it may be, expose it to public censure if it were not realised that it was done owing to great stringency of money."

Many enterprises were stillborn, others had to be abandoned. A few were mercifully kept alive, but only at the expense of others just as promising. How far was Trenchard guilty? One or two writers have censured him for gross neglect. In this section of a single chapter the charge must be examined.

The last two years of Baldwin's second administration were for Trenchard, as for many others, the most frustrating but not necessarily the most barren of the post-war decade.

Fear of over-spending a defence budget which had been scaled down in size, but apportioned in deference to the real or imagined wants of three Chiefs of Staff almost permanently in conflict, seemed to warp Churchill's normally balanced judgment. In private he would agree with Trenchard that new R.A.F. squadrons could well replace army garrisons or naval patrols in Middle East or Far East stations; officially, he would not press for such changes, though these would have saved millions. The Chancellor preferred not to let slip the dogs of war in Whitehall Gardens. There were too many curs yapping at his heels elsewhere.

At the Chancellor's bidding, the Air Ministry set an example to its rivals in 1927 and 1928 by living below its meagre net income of about £16½ million. This was worse than false economy. By 1929 the scale of R.A.F. working reserves, according to the annual review of the Chiefs of Staff Committee, was "only sufficient to meet normal peacetime requirements, and very minor emergencies." Trenchard's Home Defence scheme had all but ground to a standstill. The re-equipment of squadrons with up-to-date machines had halted. The return to a policy of making-do with obsolete and barely serviceable aircraft, while limited research and experiment continued on new machines which could never be ordered in quantity, was bad for an insolvent aircraft industry and for service morale. The effect on training, technical progress and forward planning was also grave and long-lasting.

On 11th February, 1927, while Hoare and his wife were on their way home after inaugurating the new Imperial Airways passenger service to India, Trenchard kept an appointment at No. 11 Downing Street. He wished to reinforce the following written reminder to Churchill of the consequences of cutting the R.A.F. to the bone:

"Our greatest trouble in this continuous effort at reductions is to keep the aircraft firms going only to such an extent that they are able to make the stuff *we* want. It is bad enough to tell them that we are only replacing one squadron of Bristol fighters this year. If we cut that out, we should have the utmost difficulty in replacing the equipment of one or two squadrons next year because the firms would have reduced their output and could not cope with the work."

Aircraft were the largest single item in the annual air budget; yet, as he told the Chancellor, the Bristol fighter of 1916 was still the standard machine of the army co-operation squadrons. A third of the bomber force at home and overseas consisted of patched-up D.H.9 A's: and "we are only replacing one squadron of those."

Trenchard then cast diplomacy aside:

" Everybody is saying that air ought to be increased, that it ought to be able to do a great deal of the work of the older services. We feel that everybody will say 'What is the good of the Chiefs of Staff Committee?' 'What is the good of the C.I.D.?' and 'What is the good of all this co-ordination,' which we have been working out for more than a year, if our estimates go down a much greater percentage, and on a much smaller tree, than the navy and the army. . . . ?

"Personally I feel I am put in such a position that anybody can say 'He doesn't mind how much it's whittled away so long as he draws his pay.' "

As Trenchard informed Hoare later in a long letter:

"Winston started, as usual, very difficult. Directly Sir Philip Sassoon (Hoare's Under-Secretary) asked what the navy and army votes were—to see if they'd come down their three per cent—he turned on him. He said this had nothing to do with us, that he would not allow it to become a subject of discussion. He would insist on going through our votes, as he had the army and navy votes, item by item, and would take us in front of the Economy Committee of the Cabinet, and would try to cut us down if necessary to £15 or £15¼ million. I then intervened and replied that I viewed the subject rather differently."

Churchill was not mollified by Trenchard's insistence that the R.A.F. could stand no further cuts, but finally offered a niggardly bonus of £100,000 for new aircraft and settled for an estimate of £15½ million. "He was more peaceable at the end," reported Trenchard, "but said he had his back to the wall and no money."

Critics have alleged that Trenchard misspent such pittances on the wrong objects. Had he been less intent on his air substitution policy abroad, they assert, more could have been done both to remedy the technical inferiority of his static force at home and to test his exaggerated strategic assumptions about bombing. Had he been readier to heed the best technical experts, the R.A.F. might not have remained for so long, comparatively well trained and manned, but armed with an outmoded fleet of wooden biplanes. The inference, usually left unstated, is that Trenchard stubbornly closed his mind to scientific advice and that only in the decade after his retirement was the leeway made up in the nick of time.

The truth is otherwise. Trenchard unquestionably had his prejudices, tending for instance to suspect the pure theorists as men working in private vacuums; his practice, nevertheless, was to discover ways of short-circuiting and applying their occasional brainwaves. This he did by adopting their inventions and then consulting test-pilots drawn as widely as possible from the squadrons about the value of the inventions. The highest common factor of their down-to-earth criticisms was, he found, usually worth volumes of expertise.

"His cross-examining of test pilots was always illuminating," commented Marshal of the Royal Air Force Lord Portal, who as a junior officer accompanied Trenchard on many such fact-finding missions in the late twenties. "His nose for sifting out technical defects was extremely sharp. He encouraged plain speaking and we'd come back from a day's outing with enough 'homework' to keep us busy for a week—and the designers for months. They never questioned the wisdom of modifying machines to his requirements."

By 1927 the doves of peace released by the statesmen at Locarno were still airborne but half forgotten. Discord between nations had ceased to be news. It was the discord between the haves and the have-nots within the nations, and between the political champions of both, which disturbed the social consciences of discerning onlookers. No democratic cure existed for unemployment or industrial contraction; and manipulating the gold standard had only multiplied Churchill's cares. Some looked enviously at Mussolini's "Corporate State" experiment in Italy, where even the trains were said to be running to time; others, pining for equality under monolithic Socialism, turned to the Kremlin as to a new Jerusalem. But for every extremist there were many who just endured, many more who did not care. It was not the ideal period for the master builder of an untried service. So Trenchard, in covering the hard bones of the new air force, had to confine himself to essentials.

He kept the goodwill and respect of leading aircraft manufacturers, whose stagnant businesses depended on contracts which

vere irregular and small, because he never dithered over what he
vanted. He was often playfully rebuked for "pawning the opinions"
of his test-pilots, subtracting them from the explanations of the
lesigners and, in the words of one world-famous maker, "pulling
out the square root as though it had been up his sleeve all along."

When, in 1925-6, the Fairey Aviation Company produced the
est-model of a new day bomber, the "Fox," under licence from the
American firm of Curtiss, Trenchard stirred up a political hornets'
est by placing a substantial contract after the machine's proving
ights. It seemed to him a marked improvement on the current
products of other makers.

" The industry needs a shot-in-the-arm," he told Hoare over
unch in a Cambridge hotel one Saturday morning in the spring of
925. "I've just administered one, and I want you to defend my
ction in Parliament."

Trenchard admitted that his had been a snap decision; there
vas no time to consult the Minister first. Hoare looked pained.
Vhy buy American when British aircraft workers were being laid
off, he asked? Trenchard's answer was that the Faireys deserved
ncouragement. They had set an example of enterprise that might
vell put fight into their competitors. Nobody would lose, even in
he short run, provided Hoare stood firm.

"Up to that point in our relationship," Trenchard told the
uthor, "I had kept him at arm's length. He still struck me as a
politician not given to risking his chances on an apparent gamble.
Here was an incidental way of testing whether he really had faith
n my judgment or was only posing. His courage under fire from
arliamentary and Press critics reassured me within a week. We
vere partners after that."

The Fairey "Fox" evokes no controversial memories to-day. It
vent into limited production, serving as the first of that last genera-
ion of wooden biplanes which saw the R.A.F. through its leanest
ears. As an air pageant model at Hendon in 1928 and 1929, it
elped to divert the vast concourse of spectators, few of whom
ould even then recall the anger kindled by Trenchard's adoption
f the machine in its infancy. The aircraft industry had not meanwhile succumbed to idle grievances. The evidence was written on
he cloudy ceiling of north-west London in the performances of
ew machines like the Siskin, the Grebe and the Gamecock.
Trenchard's "shot-in-the-arm" technique had worked.

What first attracted his interest in the "Fox" was its big, reliable
ngine. The American Curtiss Company had established a tem-

porary world lead as aero-engine designers in the mid-twenties, a
the results of the international Schneider Cup race testified
Believing that Rolls-Royce or Napier could do even better, Trenchard
set about inciting them to try. Funds at his disposal for subsidising
research were negligible, but by scraping here and saving there
enough cash was found, once Trenchard assured himself that
British incentive had been pricked awake again.

It was thus no accident that Britain recaptured the Schneider
trophy in 1927. The experimental Supermarine-Napier, in which
Flight-Lieutenant S. N. Webster won that year's Venice race
against strong Italian competition, was a by-product of revived
initiative. The teamwork between the R.A.F.'s picked high-speed
flight, the designers and the Air Ministry was precisely what
Trenchard had set his heart on. Being a two-yearly event, the next
Schneider Cup contest round the Solent course, between the Isle
of Wight and the Hampshire coast, enabled the British public as
well as the experts and the politicians to measure the success of
this small but remarkable joint undertaking.

Public interest in the 1929 race was intense, but even the Air
Staff could not have computed its historic importance. Flashing
round the seven laps of the circuit at an average speed of just over
328 miles per hour, Flying-Officer H. R. D. Waghorn in the "S.6"
experimental monoplane, complete with floats, retained the trophy
for Britain on a warm September afternoon.

The "S.6" bettered Trenchard's fondest hopes. A thoroughbred
not a freak, it embodied revolutionary innovations. The stream
lined fuselage, the low-slung, 30-feet metal wing, the tall rudder
above the fixed tailplane, presented a sleek appearance of power
which its specially built Rolls-Royce engine did nothing to belie
The result was a fitting end to the co-operation between F. R. Royce
and R. J. Mitchell; but the "S.6" was only an interim expression
of Mitchell's developing genius as a designer. Its final form would
be the Spitfire fighter; its final vindication that greater victory
above south-east England eleven years later, alongside the Hurricane

The Treasury tended to condemn enterprises of the kind as
ostentatious waste. Spendthrifts who blew their savings on experiments from which no visible return could be expected deserve
censure; and Trenchard was censured. Where was the consistency
in his wailing to Churchill about living conditions at Abu Dueis
in Egypt, for instance, where "married officers' quarters are still
made of canvas, petrol tins and boarding, with only one bathroom
between thirteen families"; or that "conditions at Biggin Hill are

so deplorable that we are obliged (for decency's sake) to start putting them right at once"; or that the very foundation stone at Cranwell had not yet been laid, "though seven years ago you (Churchill) wrote to me saying that building there was a 'crying necessity,'" when the Chief of Air Staff was so prodigal in other directions?

It was not easy to answer the pennywise. The effort of trying to justify and explain himself was an incidental trial; it was the summary sacrificing of equally sound ventures, each of considerable long-term value to national defence, which most upset Trenchard. Undoubtedly the most conspicuous instance was the discarding of the pilotless aircraft, an early and rudimentary "flying bomb," which had been undergoing intermittent development since the early twenties. Successfully tested at last in 1927, it had to be abandoned the following year.

In view of the tremendous psychological impact of Hitler's V.1 bombardment at a climactic moment of the Second World War, of the maximum effort required of Bomber Command to counter it, and of the unbroken silence that has since cloaked the existence of a similar though much cruder British prototype over fifteen years earlier, it would be as well to recount the evidence.

The weapon had the code-name "Larynx." It looked like a conventional aircraft and was fitted with a normal Armstrong-Siddeley Lynx aero-engine of 180 h.p. When first catapulted off a destroyer in Swansea Bay in the late spring of 1927, carrying half the explosive load of a day-bomber of the period, the missile was guided by its automatic pilot to a point within five miles of the pre-arranged target. The "Larynx" had a range of 200 miles; but this, for practical security reasons, was cut by half during the firing trials. Wireless signals emitted from the enclosed cockpit, every ten miles, enabled a chain of direction-finding stations along the coasts of Somerset, Devon and Cornwall to track its course. Trenchard and the Air Staff were delighted at the early promise of this deadly and relatively cheap form of a "catapulted bomb." Further experiments were carried out before the end of 1927. Then a slight complication arose when fragments of one missile were picked up by a French warship whose captain informed the Air Ministry with regret that no trace of the pilot could be found. Trenchard solemnly thanked him for searching, then ordered that the tests be transferred to the desert of southern Iraq, where there would be less risk of security leaks and no chance of such untoward incidents repeating themselves. The accuracy of the weapons was so improved that in 1928 the Chief of Air Staff applied to the Cabinet, through the Committee of Imperial Defence, for more money. Technical development, he pointed out, was lagging for lack of it.

"We looked on it as something of the utmost importance," Trenchard told the author. "In numerous secret memoranda the Air Staff argued that, on grounds of economy and simplicity alone, the "Larynx" had much to recommend it. If war ever came, a stockpile of these missiles would supplement or replace manned bombers during bad weather. The Air Staff also warned against neglecting such a weapon for others to develop. We were thinking, as usual, of an enemy in control of the coastline of Northern France."

The fearful prospect of batteries of catapults, fixed and mobile, deluging London and the large towns of Southern England with pilotless missiles, was thus roughly envisaged some fifteen years before the event. And how did the Cabinet react? They simply refused to authorise the extra spending necessary to allow experiments to continue, though this was currently estimated at less than £1 million. On the advice of a C.I.D. more influenced by dissent among the Chiefs of Staff than by the merits of the case, and again with Churchill's tacit approval, the "Larynx" project was discontinued.

Occasionally the shapeless pattern of defence planning did rouse the wrath of lay critics with sharp eyes and sharper pens. The editor of *The Observer*, J. L. Garvin, was one of several. Early in March, 1929, when Baldwin's Government was snoring its serene way towards the polls and a popular funeral, Garvin did some simple calculating aloud, remarking with some acidity that out of a total of nearly £600 million—"a stupendous sum"—spent on the fighting services in five years, the R.A.F.'s share had averaged a mere three shillings in the pound. Britain, he concluded, was "preparing hard for the last war" because the Cabinet had put its own political safety before elementary national security.

"We are relatively weaker," said Garvin, "than we ever were in our whole history since the Norman Conquest. Owing to the dense degree of our industrialisation, we are the nation in the whole world most vulnerable to air-power."

Militarily, France still held the lead in the air. Technically, the Italians under Mussolini were overtaking the British aircraft industry. In civil aviation, to which they were theoretically restricted, Germany was outpacing everyone; and, stressed Garvin, civil aviation "is the surest means towards ultimate war supremacy."

The popular Press avoided such facts and deductions presumably because they contained little of direct "human interest." The R.A.F. resembled the weather or the August Bank Holiday; it was good copy only when smashing speed or distance records, performing aerobatics at Hendon, locked in disputes with Admirals, or above all when counting its pilots killed and injured in action abroad or in accidents at home.

Largely owing to inadequate aircraft parks, to indifferent facilities for repairing and tuning up elderly machines and engines, and to a shortage of squadron technical officers, there was a run of fatal mishaps early in 1927. Trenchard regarded the ensuing public outcry as nine-tenths spurious.

Often the names and addresses of victims appeared in the Press before the next-of-kin could be informed. Trenchard did his utmost to put a stop to the practices of a few alert but unfeeling airmen who, profiting by the news value of tragedy, had taken to passing on the details to local journalists. Then Hoare was pressed by M.P.s to announce the full toll of recent casualties, and refused, thereby increasing suspicion that the Air Ministry had something to conceal. Criticism waxed fiercer, and so perceptible was its effect on service morale that Trenchard appealed personally to Baldwin. Would the Prime Minister visit one or two stations, form his own impressions, and perhaps allay ill-founded charges?

The Prime Minister readily complied. His statement to the Commons in due course was a masterpiece of its kind, blending sympathy with tact in a way that stilled farther clamour. He also authorised Trenchard to confer with the Newspaper Proprietors' Association on practical means of preventing unnecessary intrusions into private grief. This meeting, anything but a success, was the sole "Press conference" which Trenchard ever had a hand in summoning. His patience wore thin when Lord Burnham, the owner of the *Daily Telegraph*, in the course of explaining the mechanics of news-gathering, insisted that reporters also had a duty to fulfil and that editors had every right to print whatever was fit to be printed. There really were such things, he said, as Press principles.

This was too much for Trenchard:

"Don't talk to me about your precious Press principles. All you're interested in, the whole pack of you, is your miserable Press pence."

Then, glaring round the stricken company, he rose and swept out.[11]

Whether a Chief of Air Staff more tolerant towards the Press would have made fewer enemies in Fleet Street than Trenchard is a moot point. Old habits die hard, among journalists and military thinkers alike.

It is never easy, as Mr. Duncan Sandys has learnt in our own generation, for any Government, however convinced or determined, to favour unconventional weapons and techniques of defence at the expense of the conventional without running into trouble. This was as true of the crude R.A.F. bombers and unconventional Air Staff policies of thirty years ago, as it is of the V-Force, the guided missiles and the deterrent-strategy of to-day. What ruled out any informed public discussion then was the more widespread ignorance of the man-in-the-street, fostered as this was by the complacency or apathy of some Ministers, many politicians and most Press lords. On the other hand, it was asserted, notably by Brigadier P. C. R. Groves, a contributor to *The Times* on air matters during the twenties, that Trenchard must shoulder a good part of the blame for that false sense of security.

"The military mind enthroned at the Air Ministry," Groves wrote in chapter 4 of *Behind the Smoke Screen*, a rather diffuse and tendentious book on the R.A.F.'s declining fortunes published in 1934, when the vogue of seeking and hunting scapegoats was returning, "aquiesced in, even if it did not advise, the policy which during that decade (1919-29) brought us down to our present position in the air."

Another critic, Air-Commodore L. E. O. Charlton, who fell out with Trenchard over the bombing policy in Iraq, went further. In *War from the Air*, a book published in 1938, which was better calculated to make the reader's flesh creep than to satisfy his inquisitiveness about possibly mistaken policies, Charlton wrote of the R.A.F.:

"It needed a Nelson or a Marlborough, and it got neither. Resignation as a protest against the way its claims were slighted might have been expedient, but no one resigned. . . . Particularly it lacked a preacher; a preacher of the Solomon Eagle variety, who would first attract attention by his ranting and then be found to be talking common sense."

Any reader who has followed Trenchard's career so far may feel that resignation, or the threat of it, would not have added a squadron to the R.A.F. nor extracted another farthing from any British Government of the period. No doubt the root of secretiveness in Trenchard's nature, his intense dislike of personal publicity, and his total indifference to the opinions of men he despised, brought their toll of misunderstanding and denigration. Would a Solomon

Eagle have fared better? Might not a Nelson in a lounge suit have received a bowler hat from a Lloyd George in a tantrum, or even from a Bonar Law in a fix? Would a Marlborough have survived long enough to outmanœuvre a Churchill at the Exchequer? Is it not one of the oldest truths of history that prophets, whether they rant or no, usually go unhonoured and disregarded until the fire and brimstone begin to rain down? The words used by T. S. Eliot to describe the mission of Ezechiel might have been fashioned for Trenchard, the architect and engineer of the R.A.F. in the twenties:

> "And God said
> Prophesy to the wind, to the wind only,
> For only the wind will listen."

9

Beatty left the Admiralty in July, 1927. His successor, Sir Charles Madden, was less flamboyant and self-assured in manner, but no less dogmatic in outlook. This was proved conclusively the following year when, in spite of Trenchard's protests, the case for naval control of the Fleet Air Arm was tediously revived. The Cabinet examined once more a series of allegations that pivoted, as ever, on the naval staff's interpretation of the Balfour and Colwyn findings as well as the Trenchard-Keyes agreement. This time Salisbury was appointed arbitrator. Naval claims were again rejected: the relative positions of the two services remained unchanged.

Their relative attitudes were unchanged, too, when Trenchard vainly tried to broach again the question of the Singapore defences. In a letter to Hankey dated 21st November, 1927, he explained why, at the risk of embarrassing his colleagues, he wanted the issue debated afresh. Baldwin, he said, was "almost inviting us to reopen the subject." The Prime Minister had originally admitted, after Trenchard's capitulation to Beatty, that the Cabinet found it particularly hard to make up their minds when the military experts differed, and regarded "a fresh unprejudiced investigation" to determine whether aircraft should be substituted for the balance of the 15-inch guns as a reasonable idea.

But neither Hankey nor Madden nor Milne thought it reasonable of Trenchard to go back on his word to Beatty and propose that the number of 15-inch guns should be reduced to two; or, if that were rejected, that the installation of the big guns should be delayed "for two or three years." It really was not good enough; the jaws of the precedural trap into which Trenchard had heedlessly walked in 1926 could not be prised open so easily. The futility of academic argument soon became plain. The Chiefs of Staff Committee, in Trenchard's eyes, had grown fossilised in its thinking. The so-called "defence brain" was both anæmic and schizophrenic, yet the Cabinet behaved as though such acquired defects were normal. Since compromise was preferable to endless disputation and indecision, the more boneless the compromise the better Baldwin liked it.

Only on minor issues were concessions made to the R.A.F. Churchill, who would not side with Trenchard in recommending cheap aircraft rather than expensive guns as Singapore's main armament, seemed happier to support the gradual extension of R.A.F. "housework" in the Middle East. In February, 1928, a single squadron of machines replaced one of the two battalions of troops at Aden; and two weeks later the squadron went into action. Two sheikhs under British protection had been kidnapped by the Imam of Yemen, who had blatantly violated the frontier, despite repeated warnings from the Government. By 21st March the Imam had released the captives and was suing for a truce. In midsummer, the squadron was ordered out again. Leaflets were dropped from the air, offering the Imam four days' final grace to call off another "invasion." A few bombing attacks finally brought him to his senses.

"The operations were successfully carried out in less than six months by one squadron at a total cost of £8,567, with only one British casualty," Trenchard informed the Cabinet.

Air control in Iraq had saved the Exchequer many millions since 1922. This no doubt was why Churchill, who initiated the experiment, tended to be as open-handed to the R.A.F. in the Middle East as he was tight-fisted to it elsewhere. On 3rd November, 1928, Trenchard wrote to him privately:

"Yesterday the last battalion of the Indian Army cleared out of Iraq, and whilst I was thinking about it I could not help remembering the Cairo Conference. . . . Goodness knows how many battalions there were in Iraq in those days, but in less than eight years they have all gone. I grant there have been risks, and there still is a risk; but it was the first venture of the air force in carrying out a responsibility. Whatever the results in future may be, it has been a great success—and the air force should have this to their credit."

The following day Churchill replied:

" You have indeed made good all your undertakings. It is a great achievement, and no one but you could have made it possible."

The Turks no longer disputed Iraq's northern frontier. Peace reigned in Mosul. The artificial kingdom was outwardly stable, though Trenchard did not care to dwell too much on what might happen when the R.A.F. withdrew, leaving Feisal to the intrigues of corrupt politicians and treacherous courtiers. Would the Iraq Army, then being raised, stand firm in a crisis? The doubts of Ellington, the A.O.C., were not allayed by the inordinate ambitions of Nuri Said, who lived long enough by his wits to die an ugly death at the hands of the Baghdad mob in 1958:

" Nuri Said," wrote Ellington in 1928, " who is sometimes Deputy Commander-in-Chief and sometimes Minister of Defence and always a personal friend of King Feisal, is the most influential man in the army. He is first an intriguer for the love of it, second a politician and a prominent member of the Opposition in Parliament, and thirdly a soldier. He looks upon the army as a political instrument for the purpose of consolidating King Feisal's position in the country and incidentally his own power. He uses the officers of the army for political purposes and even some of them, known as the "army squad" for terrorising his political opponents. . . ."

To Trenchard, Iraq was only a means to a higher end: the "thin red lines" of his air routes were all this while being spun out across the sky. There were, in 1928 alone, Group-Captain Cave-Brown-Cave's flight to Singapore and Japan, Wing-Commander Stent's from Cairo to Kano, and Air Vice-Marshal Webb-Bowen's to the Cape and back. After several false starts, a service machine flew in April, 1929, from Cranwell to Karachi. Such undertakings had a purpose beyond the obvious one of blazing trails for Imperial Airways. Each served Trenchard as a new text for an old theme: that the R.A.F. should be given more say in overseas defence than the rival Chiefs of Staff would yet allow. The " Ten Year Rule" was altered on Churchill's initiative in 1928 to slide forward, as it were, on an endless moving belt, from one month to the next, so that the decade would run on indefinitely, subject to annual review by the Chiefs of Staff. This turning of the screw of expediency had many ill-effects; outmoded policies were conserved, new departures discouraged, the R.A.F. kept in its place, and objective discussion of Trenchard's strategic ideas deferred. His hopes of lifting the Home Defence scheme from stagnation, of reopening the Singapore issue, and of building up a mobile reserve for the greater security of the Middle East, India and the Far East gradually withered.[12]

Yet somehow morale was maintained, and with it that efficiency and adaptability for which the service was becoming renowned. Perhaps the crowning example was an improvised airlift—the first on this scale ever attempted—which rescued nearly 600 Europeans stranded in Kabul during the winter of 1928-9. Civil war was then raging in Afghanistan; the capital was invested with rebels intent on driving King Amanullah from the throne. The British Resident, Sir Francis Humphrys, a former R.F.C. pilot, still marvels at the whim which drew him into a West End shop, at the end of his leave the previous summer, to examine and buy the compact wireless transmitting set which he had seen in the window. His "toy" came in handy. He remembered it only when the stout Residency building, behind the walls of which the families of other diplomatic representatives sought refuge, was caught between the crossfire of the advancing insurgents and the palace guard defending Kabul. All communications with the outside world had by then been severed, so, slinging his aerial to a tree, Humphrys tapped out an experimental S O S on his set. To his astonishment, it worked. His message was acknowledged by an air force station in India. Humphrys knew that only the R.A.F. could intervene rapidly enough to forestall a possible massacre of Europeans, always providing that there were machines capable of flying over the snow-capped Hindu Kush in the depths of winter.

Hymphrys's call for help was passed on to Whitehall. Austen Chamberlain sent for Trenchard. The Foreign Secretary seemed nervous and hesitant, as though anything he suggested would invite the reply "No, it can't be done." His manner brightened when the Chief of Air Staff assured him that an airlift would be feasible. Troop transport machines were being combed out of the Middle East and sent to India. The operation entailed heavy risks, physical and political; but Geoffrey Salmond, his A.O.C., had measured these.

"Good," Chamberlain said to him. "Let's pray it comes off."

One serviceable Hinaidi carrier was diverted from Egypt to join the flight of Vickers Victoria biplanes from Iraq. On Christmas Eve, 1928, the air-lift began. It was completed nine weeks later, on 25th February, 1929. Twice a day, in good visibility, twice a week when blizzards blotted out the peaks, grounding the machines and heightening the agony of suspense on both sides of the moun-

tain barrier, the R.A.F. shuttled to and from the snowbound airfield
on the outskirts of beleaguered Kabul. Humphrys had arranged a
truce; but because of the intense cold, the engines were never
switched off after landing; and the sole civilian casualty during
these anxious and perilous weeks was a young German woman
whose head was sliced open by a propeller. She recovered.

Nearly 30,000 miles were flown before the last European civilians
from Kabul reached India. The episode momentarily thrilled the
British public; but the frank acknowledgement of the Indian Army's
Commander-in-Chief, in a Gazette Extraordinary, that the operation provided "a vivid illustration of the mobility of the R.A.F.,"
was not echoed in Whitehall, where the moral of the business was
played down.[13]

In once-backward India views were changing because enlightened C.-in-C.'s, Sir Henry Rawlinson and Sir Claude Jacob
among them, had persuaded a Government not noted for resilience
or alertness to accept the air weapon as a necessary evil at least.
Jacob was now at the India Office; partly through his advocacy,
the R.A.F. secured in 1928 two extra bombing squadrons. These
were to have formed the nucleus of Trenchard's proposed flying
reserve for defending Singapore. The windfall had dropped into
his lap two years too late.

"Who could tell how much, if we spent £4 million on the air,
we could take off the other forces?" Moore-Brabazon taunted his
own front-bench ministers during the 1929 Air Estimates debate.
Moore-Brabazon's scorn had an official outlet; Trenchard's
frustration had none. The multiple little cares, crowding on him
daily, consumed undue time and energy; too many capital problems
were deferred; too often he left the office late, feeling useless and
exhausted. Only the harmony of his home life and his ability to
relax with wife and children reconciled him to the strain.

He had no wish now to stay on. That would have been invidious
after turning out several reluctant colleagues who were blocking
the path of younger men up his carefully graded ladder of promotion:

"If the air force is going to remain a young service with young
ideas," he had recently advised Hoare, "the appointment of Chief
of Air Staff should not normally be held for more than five years."

It was not surprising that he offered his resignation to the Cabinet
more than twelve months before it was accepted. The news leaked
out in Christmas week, 1928; a few friends and colleagues had
known his intention for some time. One of these, the irrepressible

Lawrence, had been conducting from a fort in the Himalayan foothills a long-range dialogue with him on the subject. The letters of Aircraftman Shaw, the surname by which Trenchard addressed him on paper only, were always welcome for their underlying common sense.

"I have made up my mind to leave at the end of next year," Trenchard had written in the summer of 1928. "It is unfair to the service to go on stopping, and I am not sure that I haven't outstayed my usefulness."

After lengthy reflection, Lawrence agreed:

" You were lucky to have the chance for ten years," he commented. "No other man has been given a blank sheet and told to make a service from the ground up. Neither the army nor the navy have a father, in the sense of the R.A.F. Now you'll see the child tumbling down and hurting its knees and getting up again . . . Don't worry more than you need. It's a healthy and tolerably happy child. . . .

"There'll never be another king like you in the R.A.F. and I'll feel smaller under whoever takes your place. Allenby, Winston and you: that's my gallery of chiefs to date. Now there'll be a come-down. . . ."

The farewell was premature, the come-down rather different from what Lawrence had in mind. By the time his letter, dated 21st December, 1928, reached Trenchard at Dancers Hill, Lawrence had inadvertently backed into the limelight again. The discovery that he was serving as an aircraftman-clerk at an R.A.F. station not far from Afghanistan, where the rebellion against King Amanullah had recently broken out, provided one enterprising newspaper with a weapon against Baldwin. Pursuing the fancy that Lawrence must be a spy, the *Daily Herald* printed an unfounded report on 5th January, 1929, asserting that "the Afghan authorities have ordered the arrest of Colonel Lawrence on the ground that he is believed to be assisting the Afghan rebels to cross the frontier." It was preposterous nonsense; but official denials did not deflect the *Daily Herald* from honouring a duty to its readers, to its circulation department and to the cause of sensation.

Fleet Street could not resist joining in the hunt. Nor could the Cabinet ignore the immediate view-halloo from the Opposition benches at Westminster. Repercussions farther afield, particularly in Afghanistan, were more serious. Humphrys in his bullet-riddled Residency was then parleying with the rival military leaders for a truce and the safe-conduct to Kabul airfield of his fellow-diplomat

nd their families; his indignation at this absurd complication
new no bounds. He informed the Government of India that
Lawrence's presence anywhere near Afghanistan was intolerable
n the circumstances, and recommended that the miscreant be
moved forthwith.

Pressure was instantly brought to bear on Trenchard.[14] Austen
Chamberlain insisted that Lawrence, however innocent of the lurid
innuendos of Fleet Street, must return at once. Thus was "Aircraftman Shaw," who had gone east at his own request in 1926 to escape
unwelcome publicity, ironically recalled because he could not
scape it even there.

When the troopship on which Lawrence sailed put in at Plymouth, Trenchard at least had the satisfaction of foiling the Press.
Their quarry was lowered from a port-hole in civilian clothes and
whisked away in an air force launch from under the noses of
orrespondents who ventured out in boats to the place where the
essel lay at anchor, temporarily fogbound in the Sound.

Trenchard was determined to keep Lawrence from the jour-
alists by keeping the journalists from Lawrence, who spent his first
week-end with the Trenchards at Dancers Hill, rueful, bewildered,
nd contrite for having again become an unwitting source of
mbarrassment to the R.A.F. This "contented admirer and, when-
ver possible, obedient servant," as he had once described himself,
promised to lie low and do nothing that might add to the confusion,
 promise he fulfilled in typically contrary fashion. On the Monday
morning, the Trenchards drove him into London, dropping him
t Victoria. Lawrence was in civilian clothes. A few hours later,
n agitated Hoare rang up to inquire pointedly whether the Chief
f Air Staff realised that Lawrence was at the House of Commons,
wearing R.A.F. uniform and "holding court" with a group of
Labour M.P.s.

"I think you'll find he's instructing them in the error of their
ways," Trenchard answered shortly. "But I'll find out."

The irresistible urge to over-act when in trouble was a kink in
Lawrence's character which Trenchard understood and could for-
ive. How like Hoare, he reflected, to think only of the political
spect. Later Trenchard sent for Lawrence:

"Why must you be more of a damned nuisance than you need
e?" he asked.

"To stop Thurtle and his friends from asking any more foolish
uestions about me. I'm sorry if I upset the Minister. But I think
 succeeded."

(Mr. Ernest Thurtle, M.P., had been one of Lawrence's mos
active critics.)

Trenchard left it at that: Lawrence's troubles sprang fron
ineradicable contradictions in his character; the opportunitie
he offered to sensation-seekers and persecutors sprang from th
escapist paths he chose to follow.

There were more responsible positions in the R.A.F. which
man of his enormous talents could have filled with distinction
Someone so convinced that "the conquest of the last element, th
air," was the major task of his generation would have been a
asset, for example, at the new Imperial Defence College in London
which had opened its doors to staff officers from all three service
in 1927. Trenchard believed that Lawrence, turned loose there a
a lecturer, would have revelled in shattering the august certaintie
of naval and military colleagues whose concepts of warfare still le
air-power well out of the reckoning.

Trenchard was drawn only once into a dispute over funda
mentals with the first Commandant, Admiral Richmond, wh
suggested to the Chiefs of Staff that the principles of war should b
defined in identical terms in the manuals of all three services sinc
"the situation as regards aerial warfare is still indeterminate."

Trenchard could not let pass a misconception which merel
reflected "the unwillingness of the other services to accept the con
tentions of the Air Staff." So, in a reply which became the corner
stone of R.A.F. strategic thinking until "Bomber" Harris translate
theory into practice between 1942 and 1945, he set down the ai
doctrine of warfare:

"The object of all three services," he agreed, "is the same
to defeat the enemy nation, not merely its army, navy or ai
force. For an army to do this, it is almost always necessary as
preliminary step to defeat the enemy's army. . . . It is not, how
ever, necessary for an air force, in order to defeat the enem
nation, to defeat its armed forces first. . . .

"This does not mean that air fighting will not take place. O
the contrary, intense air fighting will be inevitable, but it will no
take the form of a series of battles between the opposing air force
to gain supremacy as a first step. . . . Nor does it mean that attack
on air bases will not take place. It will from time to time certainl
be found advantageous to turn to the attack on an enemy air base
but such attacks will not be the main operation. . . . The stronge
side, by developing the more powerful offensive, will provoke i

After his marriage to Katherine Boyle

With his family at Eton

At Scotland Yard on his first day as Metropolitan Police Commissioner

his weaker enemy increasingly insistent calls for the protective employment of aircraft. In this way he will throw the enemy on to the defensive; and it will be in this manner that air superiority will be obtained and not by direct destruction of his forces."

Conscious of the element of frightfulness inherent in bombing as an act of war, Trenchard next posed the question: Is an air offensive contrary to international law or the dictates of humanity? No international law, he noted, yet covered the subject, though a set of rules drafted at the Hague in 1922-3 by a commission of jurists admitted the legality of air attacks on military objectives.

"Such objectives," said Trenchard, "may be situated in centres of population in which their destruction from the air will result in casualties also to the neighbouring civilian population, in the same way as the long-range bombardment of a defended coastal town by a naval force results also in the incidental destruction of civilian life and property. The fact that air attacks may have that result is no reason for regarding the bombing as illegitimate, provided all reasonable care is taken to confine the scope of the bombing to the military objective. Otherwise a belligerent would be able to secure complete immunity for his war manufacturers by locating them in a large city which would in effect, become neutral territory— a position which the opposing belligerent would never accept. . . ."

Every kind of war material produced by an enemy, "from battleships to boots," would be fair game for the bomber, though "I do not wish for a moment to imply that the air by itself can finish the war. It will materially assist, and will be one of the many means of exercising pressure on the enemy, in conjunction with sea-power and blockade and the defeat of his armies."

Aircraft, operating with the army and navy, would have a necessary role in future land and sea battles, but "the weight of the air forces will be more effectively delivered against the targets above than against the enemy's armed forces. . . . In the course of a single day's attack upon the aerodromes of the enemy perhaps fifty aeroplanes could be destroyed—whereas a modern industrial state will produce 100 in a day, and production will far more than replace any destruction we can hope to do in the forward zone. . . . In the same way, instead of attacking the rifle and machine-guns in the trench where they can exact the highest price from us for the smallest gain, we shall attack direct the factory where these are made . . . and therefore more successfully assist the army in its direct attack on the enemy's army. . . ."

T.   T

There can be no doubt that Trenchard was broadly correct in predicting that a sustained bombing campaign would gradually undermine civilian morale. There can equally be no doubt that he over-estimated the power and accuracy of the bomber in inflicting vital damage. His bleak conclusion none would repudiate to-day, though his fellow Chiefs of Staff in the late twenties dismissed it as altogether too bleak for unqualified acceptance:

"There can be no question—whatever views we may hold in regard to it—that this form of warfare will be used. There may be many who, realising that this new form of warfare will extend to the whole community the horrors and sufferings hitherto confined to the battlefield, would urge that the air offensive should be restricted to the zone of the opposing armed forces. If this restriction were feasible, I should be the last to quarrel with it, but it is not feasible. We ourselves are particularly vulnerable to this form of attack: and foreign thinkers on war have already shown beyond all doubt that our enemies will exploit their advantage over us in this respect, and will thus force us to conform and counter their attacks in kind.

"Whatever we may wish or hope, and whatever course of action we may decide, whatever the views held as to the legality or the humanity of the military wisdom and expediency of such operations, there is not the slightest doubt that in the next war both sides will send their aircraft out without scruple to bomb those objectives which they consider the most suitable.

"I would, therefore, urge most strongly that we accept this fact and face it; that we do not bury our heads in the sand like ostriches, but that we train our officers and men, and organise our services, so that they may be prepared to meet and counter these inevitable air attacks."

Had the fact been accepted, the technical and tactical prepared-ness of the R.A.F. in 1939 would have been less backward than it was; yet the money Trenchard could spare for research on experi-mental aircraft, for developing the "Larynx", for the belated introduction of parachutes in 1929, for "aviation medicine" and for other carefully selected refinements which the Treasury deplored as so many wasteful frills, was not misused. He foresaw the worst and acted on it alone. This explained the circular concrete "mirrors," with directional microphones at the centre, the proto-types of which had sometimes puzzled inquisitive holidaymakers on the cliffs at Broadstairs in the early twenties. These strange-looking

objects even then provided early and accurate warning to trained
army and R.A.F. observers of approaching aircraft twenty miles
away over the sea. The mirrors increased in size and number with
the speed of machines; and by the late twenties a series of large
reflecting strips, each 200 feet in length, had been planned, one to
every twenty miles of the south coast of England, with vast rings of
concrete, some thirty feet in diameter, embedded in the cliffs at
intervals between.

"We weren't so fast asleep as people sometimes thought," was
Trenchard's comment on such experimental devices, among which
the secret "listening barrier" represented the last practical word in
direct eavesdropping on enemy air movements. Radar was a later
miracle. Without radar, Fighter Command's perilously small force
of Hurricanes and Spitfires could not have held the Luftwaffe in
1940; yet it should not be forgotten that without adequate money or
encouragement Trenchard and the Air Staff in the twenties had
vision enough to anticipate the problem with the paltry resources
at their disposal. There would have been no possibility of fighting
the Battle of Britain in 1940 had Trenchard lost the Battle of Whitehall in the twenties. He had reason indeed to be proud of progress
in almost every field of development, including even his highly
personal handling of public relations.

As a legacy to Salmond, he handed on an unfinished brief.
Towards the end of 1929, Trenchard's final statement of policy
was embodied in the form of a "last will and testament" to his
successor. The theme of this "swansong," as he called it, was familiar
enough, the effect explosive. To replace army and naval units
abroad with R.A.F. squadrons had long been proposed by Trenchard
on grounds of cheapness and efficiency. It had rarely been upheld;
in fact his alternative air scheme for Singapore had been rejected
mainly because it would have involved increasing the R.A.F. at the
expense of the others. The attitude of Baldwin and Churchill was
a classic example of the vicious circle: since, under the extended
" Ten Year Rule," there would be no war for an unending decade,
why encourage any novel scheme of defence which merely stirred
enmity and jealousy among the Chiefs of Staff?

The Labour Government, on its return to office in the summer
of 1929, was more sympathetic than its predecessor to Trenchard's
"last will and testament." It was printed and circulated as a Cabinet
paper, to the fury of C.I.G.S. and the First Sea Lord. Hankey was
beside himself with annoyance at what he regarded as a breach of
sacrosanct rules of procedure. Here was Trenchard, on the eve of

retirement, flinging down a gauntlet which committed Salmond to go on fighting unnecessarily controversial battles for him.[15] Yet Trenchard's proposals would certainly have left Britain better prepared for the Second World War had it been implemented. Involving an increase of up to fifteen squadrons in the R.A.F. overseas, with flying-boat patrols replacing naval units in the Red Sea and the Persian Gulf, torpedo-bombers instead of artillery for coastal defence, and extra squadrons to relieve army garrisons in India, East and West Africa, they were too contentious at the time to be examined on their merits.

"It was rather as though someone had suggested substituting a motor-cycle rally for the Derby," wrote Sir John Slessor, who helped to draft the offending paper. "Looking back on it, I have long thought he made a tactical error in doing so."

The entire British Press joined in a restrained chorus of praise when Trenchard said farewell to Adastral House for the last time in December, 1929. The honour of a peerage seemed no less than what was due to the "Father of the R.A.F.," a title he detested; yet few writers could understand the reasons for Trenchard's continuing anxiety about the strength of the service. He had deliberately drawn up his "last will and testament" as a means of adding to it without adding to the defence budget or tampering with the " Ten Year Rule " as amended by Churchill; but in doing so he undoubtedly over-called his hand. Prejudice against the R.A.F. died hard in Whitehall, and this on top of the economic problems weighing down the second Labour Government meant the indefinite postponement of any proposals for increased air reserves abroad.

"You'll feel exceedingly lonely and tired for a long time," Lawrence had written in his premature letter of farewell. "I wonder what you'll do. Perhaps you'll go and govern somewhere. That will be only the shadow of power after what you've had, but shadows are comfortable after too fierce a light. So possibly you'll be contented. You'll be shocked to find that three weeks after you've gone your past services haven't any interest or value in the Government's eyes. It's what we can do, yet, which makes us regarded."

Deep in his heart Trenchard knew that Lawrence was almost certainly right, as usual.

19. *Police Reformer*

Little enough was heard of Trenchard during the first eighteen months of his retirement. The "happy fate" as he termed it, of popular oblivion gradually overtook him. He was now a peer; and his special position as sole guardian and trustee of R.A.F. interests led him twice, in 1930 and 1931, to renew his unfinished argument with Beatty on the floor of the Upper House. Only the Press gallery appeared to relish the exchanges, for Trenchard's old idea of extending air control to the Far East had ceased to be a live issue of defence.

The two speeches, for that reason, caused displeasure at the Admiralty; dismay at Adastral House; in Whitehall, stern disapproval; in Downing Street, little response worth noting. MacDonald and his Cabinet associates had loftier business on hand than refurbishing Far Eastern strategy: arranging a world holiday from armaments appeared to them to be practical politics still.

That the "Father of the air force," with his inbred horror of publicity, should have become just another half-forgotten celebrity was not at all unnatural. He could not, of course, entirely escape the rounds of the social treadmill; but the banquets eaten, the functions attended, the stones unveiled and the school prizes distributed were no more to him than the tribute levied on the established; and this he accepted without a murmur. For every ten people who noticed him paying these tedious forfeits of the famous, there were tens of thousands beyond the linked circles of family, friends and service colleagues to whom Trenchard no longer counted, except as a name to which the tendrils of legend vaguely clung. Sceptics could still say of the R.A.F. with an effect of political wisdom: "To what end was all this waste?" Their delusion was fed by the common longing, two-thirds wish and one-third dread of the opposite consequences, that the nations would learn to live in peace, permanently disarmed by decree.

The pacifist indifference of the times was out of tune with the feelings of Trenchard, who in any case cherished oblivion for its own sake. He had earned the right to it; and he indeed found the shadows a comfort after a decade of exposure to too fierce a light.

A factor in his willingness to accept a peerage had been the platform it would afford him for defending the air force when the need arose. The honour itself, he genuinely believed, was more of a collective reward to the officers and men who had built the service with him than an accolade for anything personally achieved. The fulfilment of his boyhood dream of restoring the ancient lustre of the family name mattered less to him now as a man of fifty-eight. The drama of making the R.A.F. had been gloriously wilder than any dream. And because in the prolonged labour of creation he had fulfilled himself, Trenchard resolved characteristically never to stoop and "make a penny piece out of the thing that made me." Aircraft manufacturers who kept pestering him to join their boards could look elsewhere for recruits whose loyalty was less scrupulously adjusted than his. For this was a vow which Trenchard could never break, any more than he could bring himself to criticise in public the child he had reared and shielded and shaped to his own likeness.

Such private oaths were bound to limit the scope of any business activity he might take up. For the moment, his inquisitiveness was aroused by the perils of peace. The squabbles of the so-called victor nations seemed to him the greatest obstacle to understanding, its most depressing being form the bickering over unpaid war-debts. National pride and selfishness were evidently proof against treaty pledges; but the artificial blocking of trade channels against debtors, either as a precaution or as a reprisal, seemed a strange prescription for survival in a world of want. Tariff walls in such circumstances were simply asking to be knocked down. He was no economic expert, neither a free-trader nor a protectionist; the immutable principles worshipped by others were to him mere labels to be altered according to need.

To his more intimate associates, Trenchard's appointment as a director of the Goodyear Tyre and Rubber Company early in 1930 was a wise move on Goodyear's part. His name had been put forward, without his knowledge, by Sir Edward Peacock, a director of the Bank of England, at a time when this American firm was strengthening the board of its recently founded British subsidiary:

"They were looking not so much for seasoned business men," Peacock explained, "as men who knew their way around Government departments. I had no hesitation whatever in recommending

Trenchard and Leopold Amery, both of whom I knew and both of whom happened to be free."

Trenchard accepted the offer only after finding out all he could about Goodyear. He was chiefly impressed by the fact that the firm had sunk a good deal of capital into its new venture in the English Midlands. Despite the slump in the United States, and a decline in Anglo-American trade relations, Goodyear had branched out boldly, incidentally providing work for thousands of British employees who would otherwise have been on the dole. This was a challenging way of tackling industrial stagnation. If he could further the process, he would.

He had often heard Labour politicians assert that big business was at the root of nearly all the social misery in the post-war world. He disbelieved it, as he disbelieved most generalisations of the kind; but he wanted personal proof. Here was his chance. Later, as will be shown, he was able to broaden his quest as Chairman of the United Africa Company, an arm of the Unilever giant; but from the outset he could not see why any properly run concern, regardless of size, should fail to benefit people, regardless of nationality, by sinking money and goodwill overseas.

"There's no bank on earth that wouldn't have to shut its doors if all its customers withdrew their money," he told a North American audience after an extensive inspection of Goodyear plants in that continent. "It would be the same if there were only two men on this planet, one of whom produced food, the other clothes, with just sufficient surplus to go in for barter. If for any reason they lost confidence and stopped supplying one another, the first would die of cold, the second of hunger."

It was typical of his thinking. He enjoyed stripping such problems of the pompous jargon in which experts loved to clothe them. The Labour Government had run into heavy financial weather; but he could not stand the talk of Conservatives who blamed their opponents for failing to control the elements. No Government was wholly trouble-free or guiltless: so why condemn MacDonald alone? With his homely similes and non-partisan approach, Trenchard cut the figure of an eccentric individualist, especially at Chatham House. Many political, business and academic leaders of the day attended the informal discussions of the recently founded Royal Institute of International Affairs. There Trenchard learnt a little and taught a little, never fearing in his quest for plain facts to play the ignoramus and tease the experts.

On one occasion, he recalled, Keynes rounded on him for

having the effrontery to recount the history of the gold standard in terms of a modern parable, drawing the unfashionable moral that in a world short of freely transferrable gold there was much to be said for letting sterling find its natural level. Keynes later apologised, and agreed to join a semi-official study group under Trenchard's chairmanship.

There were two noteworthy results. The first was the production by the experts of a book of essays, analysing the disadvantages besetting any currency shackled to gold, and concluding that Britain should abandon the gold standard before it abandoned her. The second result was more personal: Trenchard came to the notice of the Prime Minister as someone whose simple talent for fundamentals merited a better outlet than among the lions of Chatham House.

In March, 1931, MacDonald approached him with an offer. Lord Byng, the Commissioner of the Metropolitan Police since 1928, was anxious to retire. Byng, he said, was in poor health and had never wanted the job, his reluctance being overborne only by appeals to his sense of public duty. The appointment, as Trenchard remembered, had been condemned at the time by Labour, in Opposition, as a retrograde step: and the Prime Minister now had the grace to admit that he and his colleagues had undoubtedly wronged this distinguished soldier and late Governor-General of Canada who, during the intervals of activity between his everlengthening absences from Scotland Yard, had succeeded in winning the confidence of the police. The Labour Cabinet, as if to atone for their previous error, agreed with Sir John Anderson, the permanent head of the Home Office, that another "militarist" in better health should follow Byng:

"The militarist we want, of course, is you," said MacDonald.

" The militarist you're not getting is me," retorted Trenchard.

The Prime Minister begged him not to rush his decision.

"Think it over carefully," he said. "I'm asking you because you're the best person for the job. Talk to Anderson, then let me know definitely."[1]

A few days later Trenchard had a long, confidential discussion with Anderson. Despite the latter's bloodless restraint, Trenchard gathered that the Government were concerned about the spirit of unrest in the Metropolitan Police. Despite appearances, Byng had failed to tackle two basic problems: reorganising the force and weeding out dissident elements. The men had responded well to the Commissioner's genial personal touch and recovered a measure of self-confidence. But, stressed Anderson, self-confidence without reform was not enough. Efficiency and discipline would deteriorate further unless a strong man took over the force.

"That's where you come in," Anderson said in effect.

He implied that the Home Office had long been alive to the dangers. So, in a more accidental and confused fashion, had the public. Disturbing symptoms had begun to betray themselves in 1927, within a year of the General Strike when the exemplary conduct of the London police had so edified people that the sum of a quarter of a million pounds was contributed to police funds by voluntary subscription.

A number of incidents, some of no great consequence in themselves, had caused the pendulum of popularity to swing violently the other way. The Press, admittedly, had helped to magnify the significance of these incidents in which individual policemen had overstepped the bounds of discretion.

Some of the evidence on which popular apprehension fastened was unsavoury enough. There was, for instance, the case of Sergeant Goddard, accused and convicted of accepting bribes from night-club owners. That had resulted in a first-class scandal. The temptation on the public's part to leap from the particular to the general, and to put an entire police force in the dock because of the delinquencies of one black sheep, had proved irresistible. It was doubly unfortunate that popular confidence received another hard knock while the memory of the Goddard affair was still fresh. For the repercussions of the Money-Savidge case rumbled on for months.

The two principals, Sir Leo Money and Miss Irene Savidge, were arrested and charged with indecent behaviour in Hyde Park. At the court hearing, both defendants disputed the allegations. The case was dismissed owing to a conflict of evidence; and, in dismissing it, the magistrate had commented unfavourably on the reliability of the police witnesses.[2]

The Press wrung the last drop of outraged indignation from the incident; and, as a result of parliamentary pressure, the Government instituted an inquiry by a Select Committee of the Commons to discover whether third degree methods had in fact been employed to extract a false statement from Miss Savidge. Relations between Scotland Yard and the public had seldom been so strained. Mistrust lingered even after the Select Committee sifted facts from rumours and declared that there had been much ado about little. Every subsequent disclosure of officiousness or petty dishonesty on the part of individual policemen was zealously reported in the Press.

Byng's arrival did not halt the denigration, which went on until the new Commissioner appealed personally to Fleet Street for fair play. The truce that followed was a rather uneasy one.

Such, according to Anderson, was the background for understanding how and why, in 1927, a Royal Commission was set up by Johnson-Hicks, the Home Secretary in Baldwin's second administration, to investigate existing police powers and procedures. Like most Royal Commissions, this one probed deep, by-passing the superficial symptoms of police unpopularity to explore the underlying causes. In their final report, published in 1928, the Commissioners drew attention to one particular point which successive Governments had either ignored or overlooked for many years. Strictly speaking, the question of recruiting and training policemen lay outside the Royal Commission's terms of reference; but members did not shirk it on that account, considering that the roots of the trouble could be detected in the character of the individual constable and in the way both he and his superiors were selected for promotion. Their verdict was that a system which had remained unchanged since the time of Peel no longer met modern needs:

"We wish to emphasise," they wrote, "that long experience and good service in the lower ranks of the force are not the only, nor even the most important qualifications for the higher posts, which ought to be filled in all cases by men who, besides being themselves upright and fair-minded, are capable of impressing their own standards on their subordinates. We should therefore regard as inimical to the public interest any system which limited appointments to the higher posts to those who had entered the police as constables; and we are of opinion that such posts should be filled by the best men available, irrespective of the source whence they are drawn. . . ."

Sir John Anderson, in his talk with Trenchard, dwelt on the far-reaching implications of the Royal Commission's conclusion. The Home Office, he said, were already at work on plans for a new Police College to change the traditional method of filling the higher ranks. It would require a strong Commissioner to carry through, given the uncertain temper of the force; and there was no better candidate for the post, in the Government's view, than Trenchard. Anderson seemed rather put out when Trenchard repeated that he had no inclination whatever to accept the post. His only wish was to be left in peace to pursue his private interests, and he intended to notify the Prime Minister that his decision was final.

The records suggest that the Home Office, in 1931, had only one other candidate in mind. Rather than approach Sir Walter Braithwaite, the man in question, Anderson chose to leave the matter open, presumably in the hope that Trenchard would relent if the domestic situation went from bad to worse. For the Labour Government was clearly in dire economic trouble. The harsh effects of the American slump were now being felt in Europe. Life-giving loans from the world's biggest creditor nation had dried up at source; and MacDonald's administration was living well beyond its means, trying to sustain, at minimum subsistence level, an army of unemployed that had risen to nearly three millions as the demand for exports fell away. Yet that could be done only by drawing heavily on shrinking State credit. How much longer the unequal conflict between the claims of social justice and the inexorable economic facts would last, nobody dared to predict. The opinion of the City was that a halt must be called forthwith to the rake's progress of over-spending, which was fast impairing the value of sterling.

There can be little doubt from the evidence that Anderson's appraisal of the general outlook influenced his judgment on the particular question of selecting the next Police Commissioner. A firm and utterly ruthless character would be needed; someone who would take difficulties in his stride and never be deflected by unpopularity from initiating sweeping reforms. Such a task would become doubly trying in the event of a national crisis; and in Anderson's view the only possible Commissioner in conditions of emergency was the half-forgotten Trenchard.

Time proved Anderson right, and much sooner than his unsuspecting candidate expected. Despite Labour accusations that the financial crisis of August, 1931, was nothing more than a "bankers' ramp," the evidence seemed to Trenchard to point the other way. Bankers, politicians, and ordinary people, whatever their nationality and political beliefs, were dragged down by a chain of apparently unconnected circumstances which left such a trail of economic disorder and distress, particularly in central Europe, that even dictators who moved in to master the chaos would be hailed at first as saviours.

In Britain, catastrophe was narrowly averted twice; and during the second phase of imminent collapse Trenchard changed his mind and went to Scotland Yard in conditions of unprecedented and almost melodramatic uncertainty.

The first portent of panic came in May, 1931, when the largest industrial bank in Austria, the Creditanstalt, had to close its doors.

Austria's post-war economy was propped up, like Germany's, by loans, chiefly of American dollars. After the slump hit the United States in 1929, the flow of dollar credits dried up and Austria grew steadily weaker. Now, with the failure of a bank, the nation faced bankruptcy. Nor could the blighting effects be confined to Austria; with three-quarters of the world's reserves of gold silting the bank vaults of Paris and Fort Knox, a mad scramble for the remaining quarter began, imperilling all currencies pegged to the gold standard, including Britain's.

President Hoover proposed towards the end of June, 1931, a year's moratorium on reparations and war debts; but by the time France had given her conditional consent to this palliative measure the German currency had collapsed as completely as the Austrian.

On 20th July, delegates of seven nations gathered in London for a financial conference in a vacuum.

"Seldom" wrote the late Lord Vansittart, "was so much eminence collected for such nullity. It remitted its impotence to a committee of experts."

The experts were as powerless as the Governments they represented. For the remedies suggested no longer fitted the facts. Britain's ordeal was at hand as the inevitable run on gold and sterling holdings in London increased. The disease of financial uncertainty had entered its malignant stage, and this at a time when the Labour Government had ceased to pay its way.

By one of those unnerving coincidences conceivable only in easy-going democracies, the unsoundness of the British economy was now announced to the world in damning detail. Earlier in the year, an independent committee, headed by Sir George May, had been invited to study Government spending; but the effect of the May Committee's Report at such a moment was to shatter the brittle faith in sterling of foreign investors.

The May Committee's most controversial proposals were that unemployment benefits, the largest and most unproductive item of State expenditure, should be heavily cut and the salaries and wages of public employees docked by $12\frac{1}{2}$ per cent. The Cabinet, suspended between anger, helplessness and its own internal divisions, did not move, although MacDonald and his colleagues were now, in effect, on trial before the world.

August, the traditional crisis month, had come again. The fall of the Government seemed only a matter of time. It was either that or national bankruptcy. The Bank of England raised £50 million from the Bank of France and the Federal Reserve Bank of New

York. The loan disappeared like water in sand. When, almost immediately, a further £80 million was sought abroad to offset the now alarming flow of gold from London, the bankers proved less obliging; the Americans, in particular, weighing the risks, wanted to know, before parting with their money, how the Labour Government proposed to use it.

The cry of "dictation" went up the Cabinet room; MacDonald, striving to hold his splintering team together, had to bow to the stronger dictation of the Trades Union Congress and find other ways of reducing expenditure than the obvious one of pruning the dole. The task was beyond him. On 23rd August he tendered his resignation to the King, who persuaded him that it was his duty to remain as Prime Minister of a new non-party Government.

"The greatest betrayal in the political history of this country," as Attlee described it, struck Trenchard rather as an unusual act of personal courage. MacDonald's example, in fact, influenced him in October, 1931, when the Metropolitan Police Commissionership was offered to him again. Trenchard did not refuse it a second time. His sense of public duty proved equal to the occasion, as Anderson had half expected; but neither Anderson nor anyone else could have foreseen the turn the crisis took before MacDonald's Coalition was a month old.

The new Cabinet announced that it "would not exist for a longer period than was necessary to dispose of the emergency." The King's reminder that there would be time to consider party advantage when the threat of bankruptcy had been staved off, was salutary. For MacDonald had inherited, in addition to a set of intractable problems, the malevolence of his former Labour colleagues, who expelled him from the Party along with Snowden, Thomas, Sankey and the few who had joined him in allegedly selling their souls for a mess of political pottage. It was in a mood of resolution chastened by uncertainty that Ministers met to prepare an emergency Budget.

By the standards of the day, Snowden's proposals were drastic. Income tax rose to five shillings in the pound, surtax by ten per cent. There were further cuts in defence. The price of petrol, tobacco, entertainments and beer went up; more significantly the pay of the armed forces, of civil servants, of teachers and of the police was reduced, as May had recommended. Then the ludicrously unexpected happened: a demonstration against pay cuts was staged by a few naval ratings and magnified, thanks to incredibly bad public relations and exaggerated Press reports, into a full-scale mutiny. Coming at a moment when the least sign of unrest in Britain was liable to panic investors and restart the pell-mell flight of gold from London, the Invergordon affair could not have been worse timed.

The fault was largely the Admiralty's, whose official letter to senior officers announcing the reduced scales of pay and allowances was unaccountably held back until 10th September, two days after units of the Home Fleet sailed from Portsmouth and other south coast ports for Scotland and the autumn manœuvres. The ships reached Invergordon on 11th September; the official letter, still on its way from London, was not delivered until the afternoon of 12th September. Not unnaturally, ratings were astounded on going ashore to read about the pay cuts in the newspapers. Minor disorders broke out among the men on shore next day, a Sunday; these were suppressed; but there were more serious developments when the battle squadron put to sea as scheduled. The men refused to obey orders, and the exercises had to be cancelled.

The news leaked out, and the Press made the most of it. The Admiralty, in tight-lipped embarrassment, recalled the ships to their home ports. The First Lord, Austen Chamberlain, put the calmest face he could on the Invergordon muddle in the Commons; but if many M.P.s and members of the British public were prepared to accept that the "mutiny had been the result of a regrettable misunderstanding," few foreign observers were immediately disposed to do so. The incredulity and passing dismay caused at home by the sensational Press reports were as nothing compared to the consternation caused abroad; if the Royal Navy could not be relied on to do its duty because its men disliked the Government's harsh financial policy, then Britain must surely be trembling on the brink of revolution. As if by reflex action, the run on gold began again. Foreign misgiving could almost be measured by the withdrawals. On 21st September, the Government was forced to suspend the gold standard.

Ministers were severely shaken. If a single outburst of feeling against the pay cuts could have such consequences, what if civil servants, teachers, and the police should decide on similar action too? This question seems to have dominated Cabinet thinking during the last ten days of September. According to Anderson, the Government had most to fear from the police. It was not merely that officials of the Police Federation, representing local forces throughout the country, strongly opposed the proposed ten per cent pay reduction: the new Home Secretary, Sir Herbert Samuel, had unwittingly given the

Government's case away by misinterpreting its intentions to them.
Both he and Sir Archibald Sinclair, the Secretary for Scotland,
apparently misunderstood the implications of a decision taken on
1st September, when the Cabinet discussed the pay cuts, and
had subsequently assured the police, to the perplexity of their
ministerial colleagues, that only half the proposed reduction would
be levied immediately on the men in blue. Unlike soldiers, sailors,
teachers and others, policemen would forfeit only five per cent of
their money, not ten per cent. The balance would be recovered in
the next twelve months by administrative savings.

Had it not been for the Invergordon incident, it is possible that
Samuel and Sinclair would have had to retract a mistaken and
invidious pledge; but rather than risk a Cabinet split, MacDonald
and Baldwin agreed to let the concession stand for the moment.
On 29th September Samuel told the Commons that the "Home
Office and Police Council have agreed that, instead of the whole
of these economies falling on the pay of the various ranks of the
force, as much as possible should be effected by administrative
economies." And there, provisionally, the matter was left. The
most disturbing aspect of the affair, which Samuel impressed on his
colleagues, was the uncompromising attitude of the Police Federation even to a five per cent cut in pay.

The possibility of a police strike, particularly in London, was
viewed with distinct apprehension by the Government. Quite
clearly, it would be unwise to provoke the Federation unnecessarily;
just as clearly, it was essential to recall the police to a sense of their
responsibilities. The salvaging of the economy depended on it. The
Metropolitan Force, which could inflict the most damage, needed
a resolute Commissioner, and the need was now extremely urgent.
Anderson advised the Cabinet that his opinion had not changed:
only Trenchard could handle the job. Samuel, according to his
own account, "took an opportunity of discussing it with the King,"
who "entirely concurred as to Trenchard; and I mentioned this
when I put the matter to him again and pressed it as a public
duty." Because Trenchard remained unmoved, Sir Warren Fisher,
the permanent head of the Treasury, thereupon agreed to act as
go-between.

Fisher spent many hours at Dancers Hill during the last week-
end of September. At first, Trenchard's response was discouraging.
He did not want the appointment and said so emphatically. Not
until Fisher fully explained the Government's predicament did he
gain a more attentive hearing. It startled Trenchard to be told, in

so many words, that the nation's economy was too weak to withstand
the strain of another shock of the kind that followed the Invergordon
affair and that the London police might well cause one.

"In my talks with him on Saturday and Sunday," Fisher wrote
in a confidential note to the Cabinet immediately afterwards, "I
made it clear that in my deliberate opinion his undoubted duty is
to accept the position; in fact that he had no alternative. I assured
him that it was the earnest wish of the King, the Prime Minister,
Mr. Baldwin and the Home Secretary that he would assent."
Fisher added that eventually Trenchard agreed, "though with the
utmost reluctance, partly based on modesty, partly on distaste,
partly because he would prefer to try, however humbly, to do
something constructive during the continuing period of unemployment and distress."

Fisher's note also indicated that the Cabinet gave him unusually
wide discretion to deal with Trenchard. There were only two conditions on which Trenchard insisted: first, that he should have the
unreserved right to leave Scotland Yard at the shortest notice if
"his life's work" at the Air Ministry were ever imperilled; and,
second, that if the prevailing unrest in India over the latest constitutional proposals grew worse, and it was felt that Trenchard
might be "more useful there," he should be released at once. This
is the only semi-official reference to one of his greatest, unfulfilled
ambitions—that of becoming Viceroy. His chances of being considered for so apparently incongruous a position were not perhaps
quite as slender as might be thought. For Hoare, who idolised
Trenchard, had moved to the India Office and was not unconscious
of this secret aspiration.

The practical details were settled easily. As regards salary,
Fisher felt that it would be wrong for a man with no private means
"who had accepted his title solely for the prestige of the R.A.F."
to suffer financial loss. When it came to the point, Trenchard
would not hear of taking a penny more than the statutory salary:

"You talk of equality of sacrifice as though it doesn't apply to
the boss," he said. "Tell the Prime Minister I don't like favours.
No don't, I'll tell him myself."[3]

MacDonald received him a day or two later with great affability. Trenchard thought that the Prime Minister looked "dread-
fully tired—a woolly-haired, sad old man, with watery eyes that
seemed to be giving him a lot of trouble, and a tongue that rambled
more than ever." When MacDonald mentioned the question of
salary Trenchard could not resist remarking that it ill-became any

Government in trouble to consider compensating a Police Commissioner whose men were clamouring to have their pay-cuts wiped
out. The Prime Minister nodded vaguely. He appeared to be only
half listening. He was glad that Trenchard had asked for time to
wind up his business affairs. When would he be returning from
America? Early in November? That would be soon enough. The
General Election would be over by then, and the Government
would be all the better for a solid mandate. He had no doubts
about the result.

Before the interview ended, Ramsay MacDonald suddenly
shook off his lethargy and displayed a flash of his old, remembered
vigour. He was busily assuring Trenchard of a free hand when his
visitor interrupted him:

"Even if it means turning the force upside down?"

"If that's necessary, we'll support you."

"Is this a good time for wholesale reforms?"

"If life has taught me one thing it's taught me that there's
never a good time for doing things that are unpleasant."

The Prime Minister said the words forcibly but without bitterness. And Trenchard left the room happier than he had entered
it.

2

He was on the high seas bound for Canada and the United
States when the news of his appointment was released on 7th
October. Momentarily beyond the reach of the British Press, he
could not avoid the friendly but occasionally naïve questions of
journalists in North America. His evasiveness was not resented at
Kitchener, Ontario, where he went to inspect the Royal Scots
Fusiliers of Canada as Colonel of the parent regiment; nor at Akron,
Ohio, where, as a temporarily retiring director, he watched the
maiden flight of a new airship built by Goodyears for the American
Navy; nor even in New York, where he paid a courtesy call on that
city's Police Commissioner.

"What are your plans for cleaning up London's underworld?"
an irrepressible reporter asked him shortly before his departure.

"What underworld?" he countered. "I didn't know London
had one. Next question please."[4]

The British Press greeted his appointment with the conventional
chorus of flattery. A thin period was predicted for enemies of the

law in general: Trenchard, with his reputation for getting difficult things done, would never allow them to thrive in peace. One or two of the more serious papers suggested that the Metropolitan police themselves would probably benefit from having a leader as noted for his sense of justice as for his sense of discipline. None so much as hinted at the true state of affairs or at ministerial fears of a police strike. The outside chance of one was discounted in Fleet Street partly because the National Government had consolidated its standing at the polls, partly because those ministerial fears were necessarily one of the best kept secrets of the hour.

On 19th December, when Trenchard was sizing up the more glaring defects of his own Headquarters' machinery and beginning to discern the magnitude of his reforming task in the four London police districts beyond, one of the sharpest and cleverest pens in the Labour Movement drew a quick, rough but not ungenerous character sketch of the new Police Commissioner. Without a sneer of condescension, Harold Laski, writing in the *Daily Herald*, commended Trenchard as "of the type whom you ask to do a piece of organisation in the knowledge that he will do it well. . . .

"His qualities are a good, ordinary intelligence and real moral power. You cannot be in his presence without the sense that he will drive directly to his goal. . . .

"Lord Trenchard is of the type of which the supreme example is the Duke of Wellington. Where other men talk of courage, he will talk of duty. His praise is economical and abrupt, but when you get it you feel as though you really had been singled out from other men. . . . He does not argue very well; he has no small-talk. But you cannot move him from the performance of his job. There goes into the doing of it a certain grim earnestness that has almost religious intensity about it. . . . He sets himself a limited task, but you cannot budge him from its accomplishment. He has little imagination and no nerves. He is slow but very sure, somewhat dour but just to the bottom of his being. . . ."

What Laski, in common with other critics, could not yet fathom was whether such a Commissioner had patience or insight enough to grasp the "psychological aspects" of the police problem in London:

"The cuts in police pay," said Laski, "have induced a good deal of intelligible unrest among the police. There are mutterings and grumblings. Lord Trenchard's type tends to meet this a little hardly. But he will not, I hope, lack the imagination to see that the way to meet grievances is not by repression but by the removal of its just causes. On another side, his stern sense of the need for obedience to orders need not prevent him from asking fundamental questions.

"He will not, I think, tend to assume that he must accept the present scope of police functions as a body of axiomatic principles. For it would be well worth inquiring whether, for example, the Goddard case did not arise from a tendency on our part to inflict upon the police duties the adequate fulfilment of which is hardly possible. . . .

"One wants to see a man at his job who insists on its limitations as well as possibilities, who gets ideas on the system of appointment and promotion as well as upon the duty of rigidly enforcing the existing regulations. A Police Commissioner determined to cultivate philosophy and imagination could make an epoch in the history of the force.

"I hope Lord Trenchard will remember that as he surveys his opportunity."

Standing upright again, in the glare of the public spotlight, Trenchard might not be Laski's "ideal man" for a thankless task. But the Cabinet could congratulate itself on having secured the services of the one man in Britain who, by acting as though the London police belonged to him alone, might succeed in outstaring the spotlight and bringing the force to reason. The King had touched Trenchard deeply by thanking him for acceding to the Royal wish that he should accept the post, by expressing every confidence in his judgment, and by inviting him to consult him privately whenever he wished; Baldwin had been as specific as MacDonald in promising support; many of his friends, including Maurice Baring and T. E. Lawrence, had written to say how happy they were that the Government had at last found something big enough for him to do.

There were other letters, too, short, scurrilous, threatening letters from anonymous writers.

"You have four days to live," one warned him in Morse dots and dashes, "so beware. . . ."

"Soon," another informed Lady Trenchard, "you will be a woman without a husband. If we do not get him in a certain time, your life will have to be taken."

A police guard was set to watch his home. Then one of his own children rapturously stumbled in trying to put a small tongue round a large word at the breakfast table one morning. When Trenchard came down early for a ceremonial parade, clad in his still unfamiliar dress uniform, he was greeted by his elder son, Hugh, as the "Metropolitan Police Commotioner?" The remark made his day; and the family learnt to treasure it as an unintended bull's eye.

3

It cannot be said that the Headquarters staff at Scotland Yard took kindly at first to their new master. From the day of his arrival, early in November, when the deputy Commissioner, Sir Trevor Bigham, led him round the congested building on the Embankment, introducing him to the heads of departments, Trenchard impressed them all as a disturbing personality utterly different from the gentle, self-effacing Byng. Senior officers quickly noticed, some to their discomfiture, that his eyes missed little; that his aggressive manner was no pose; that it was dangerous to keep him waiting and more dangerous still to fob off his questions with evasive answers. The optimists and pessimists alike acknowledged that the system of indirect rule favoured by Byng did not suit the style of his successor.

The machinery of Scotland Yard, the directing "brain" of the four districts into which the Metropolitan Police area was divided, had a suspiciously shaky look to Trenchard from the start. There were four main departments, each in charge of an Assistant Commissioner: one for crime, one for administration and discipline, and two for "civil business," a loose term embracing an extremely wide and expanding range of legal and statutory duties, from the licensing of pubs and pedlars to traffic control. It took Trenchard less than a week to decide that the work was badly distributed and that his four departmental chiefs were expected to discharge responsibilities beyond the capacities of all but supermen. He did not, at that stage, attempt to prejudge their individual worth. There would be time enough for that. The main fault lay in the system.

Introduced by Peel when London was still comparatively small, it had grown higgledy-piggledy over the years until the so-called "brain" could hardly be said to be in any fit condition to supervise the activities of the four outlying district chiefs and the main force of 20,000 men under them. The Yard's civilian secretariat constituted a smaller separate branch for handling correspondence and compiling staff records, accounts and statistics. As the normal channel of communication with the Home Office and the public, it also required a careful check; but Trenchard's first impressions of its reliability were on the whole good because in its head, H. M.

Howgrave-Graham, he recognised a man of integrity, intelligence and adaptability. He made an immediate mental note to use him if necessary as he had used Baring in France and Marson at Air Ministry; for Howgrave-Graham had the "feel" of a trusty mainspring in need, perhaps, of the oil of a little encouragement and the stimulus of tighter winding. His devotion to the late Commissioner was open and unqualified. Trenchard liked him for that, too, though he made no bones about his harsh view that Byng's habit of delegating important decisions to subordinates had thrown an extra strain on a system which groaned aloud for an overhaul. So Trenchard, within a matter of days, was ready to turn his own headquarters upside down.

"When he'd been at the Yard only a short time," Howgrave-Graham recalled, "he told me he proposed to go and sit in the rooms of each of the Assistant Commissioners for a day or two (sending them on leave) to see by personal experience exactly what they did. He asked if I saw any difficulty about this.

" 'None whatever,' I said. 'Provided you don't do the same to me.'

" 'And why not?' he asked rather fiercely.

" 'Because you'd spend half the day running in to the Commissioner's room and you'd always find it empty.' "

The riposte brought up Trenchard short. He was exceptionally busy at the time, browsing through files and documents which cluttered his office desk and his study at home, and rapidly absorbing an immense store of factual information which confirmed his view that Scotland Yard's growth had been a curiously casual affair. Nevertheless he greeted Howgrave-Graham's thrust with a laugh.

"All right. You'll just have to be trusted," he said.

The Assistant Commissioners submitted uneasily to Trenchard's personal method of weighing their exact responsibilities. Their relief was all the greater for his frankness at the finish. Calling them together, he told them what he thought was wrong. He paid them the compliment of listening, poker-faced, to their half-hearted suggestions for improvement, though all of them felt at a disadvantage in trying to follow his enthusiastic but somewhat incoherent manner of expounding his own ideas and exploding theirs:

"It is often said (and I had before those days always believed)," commented Howgrave-Graham, "that a man who cannot express himself clearly is unlikely to have any powers of clear or logical thought. This may be generally a sound proposition, but Lord

Trenchard was an exception to this rule—as to many others. . . .
He could drag the guts out of a complicated problem in a remarkably short time, and, when he had done it and held them up for
one to see, one realised at once that they were indeed the real and
only guts and that nothing else mattered much."[5]

However, it took everyone, including Howgrave-Graham, far
longer to appreciate Trenchard's eye for essentials than this retro-
spective judgment implies.   The new Commissioner's refusal to
stand on ceremony, his tendency to question rules and customs, his
reluctance to allow respect for persons or seniority to interfere with
his judgment of men and methods by the sole criterion of efficiency,
and a deliberately stern aloofness at other times which stimulated
uncertainty about his aims, such traits kept the four Assistant
Commissioners on edge.   None of them felt entirely safe or indis-
spensable any more.

The Criminal Investigation Department, Trenchard realised,
would be the hardest nut to crack, so he decided not to tamper with
it until later.   As the oldest and most specialised branch, the C.I.D.
had steadily detached itself since its foundation in 1874 from the
uniformed element of the force at every level, from headquarters
downwards to the beats.   It claimed for itself a degree of privileged
"independence" which Trenchard frowned upon as inadmissible in
principle and practice.   The second oldest department, Administration, which lent itself less readily to suspicion of abuses, was more
obviously ripe for quick reform.   Like the head of some primitive
monster, it seemed too small for the huge trunk below.   Yet this
was the branch concerned with the welfare and discipline of the
police.   It had been twice forced to cast off the new cells of separate
departments as fresh duties gradually over-burdened it: in 1884
such matters as the regulation of public carriages, licensed premises,
betting, charities, and hawkers were transferred *en bloc* to the
Assistant Commissioner of a third department empowered to handle
all this "Civil business"; then, just before 1914, the coming of the
internal combustion engine made it necessary to separate "Traffic"
from "Civil Business" under a further Assistant Commissioner. And
there the process of evolution had stopped.[6]

Trenchard's first problem was not as simple as might appear:
he wanted to undo the recent effects of fossilisation of the brain
without causing undue disturbance to the routine transaction of
Scotland Yard's business.   It was second nature for him to adopt the
method of "rushing my Assistant Commissioners off their feet"; and
the experiment was doubly productive. For it enabled him to uncover

n a remarkably short space of time a host of other deficiencies
hallowed by time and neglect.

One of his private secretaries has thus described his personal
method of approach:

" No matter what you were doing, and no matter who you were,
you came at the double when he called. In Lord Byng's time any
official, senior officer or secretary who entered the Commissioner's
room in a hurry would be quietly asked what the fuss was about and
invited to recover his or her breath. Trenchard was different. He
kept his finger pressed hard on the bell until the person he wanted
appeared. And he'd start dictating or questioning before you'd
time to collect your wits."

One day, during these early weeks of inspection, a Chief
Constable who had long cultivated the leisurely habit of arriving
at the office midway through the morning after exercising his horse
in Rotten Row, suddenly remembered, on arrival, that he had an
appointment with the Commissioner in less than five minutes.
The Chief Constable hastily changed his clothes and burst into the
corridor leading towards Trenchard's room, pulling on his jacket
with one hand and holding a file in the other. He did not get very
far. The statuesque figure of Trenchard was already standing outside the distant door of his own office, watching the distraught man's
every move:

"All right," Trenchard shouted. "I can see. Go back and dress
properly. I said 11 o'clock and it's two minutes past. I'll expect
you at 11 to-morrow morning."

There was a suffocating air of complacency about the place
which made it impossible for him to condone slackness or unpunctuality in individuals. Scotland Yard suffered from a chronic
shortage of space; this had led to overcrowding, lack of supervision,
carelessness and apathy. The atmosphere had an unpleasant whiff
of the old Hotel Cecil as he had known it at its worst, under
Rothermere.

The finger-print section of the C.I.D., for instance, did not exist
when the building was planned and erected in the 1880's. Its
growth in recent years had been rapid; that in itself was a fairly
good index of efficiency, to Trenchard's mind; but the resulting
overcrowding was serious. Certain corridors had been converted
into makeshift offices and efficiency was at the mercy of physically
cramped conditions. No better climate could have been sought
for the work-shy or the intriguer. And, in a critical period of
austerity, Scotland Yard could not be extended for several years.

This structure of solid granite, quarried and dressed by Dartmoor convicts in the name of short-sighted economy, lacked the interior spaciousness of the Grand Opera House which an enterprising but over-ambitious business man had once intended to erect on the site instead. The wry knowledge stiffened Trenchard's resolve to short-circuit the difficult conditions and the untidy habits these engendered by rearranging the duties of his headquarters' staff.

Before Christmas, 1931, the least useful of the four departments was abolished. The work of the "Legal and Civil Business" branch was divided between Howgrave-Graham's Secretariat and the Administrative Department; and a new department solely concerned with producing and developing ideas for toning up discipline and workaday procedure was established on a permanent footing. The concept of the "Ideas Branch," as it was familiarly called, had been introduced as an experiment by Byng towards the end of his period at the Yard, and Trenchard seized on it now as an instrument ideally suited to his purpose of internal reform.

There was work in abundance for it. Trenchard wanted to discover, for a start, how a force of 20,000 men, distributed over an area of 700 square miles, in four districts, twenty-three divisions and 180 police stations, actually spent its fifty million man-hours during a given year. He wanted to break down the indifferently filed statistics in the registry and test his "hunch" that too many constables had been pounding the same beats for too long. The research men in "Organisation" had been collecting and sifting a mountain of such facts for several months; now, with full authority, with every facility and with the Commissioner's unblinking eye upon them, the new department was set a major task of analysis and urged to complete it in record time.

Adjustments at Scotland Yard, without corresponding adjustments in the police districts beyond would, he knew, be futile; and Trenchard was conscious that these would be harder to enforce. Every Wednesday morning, according to custom, the Chief Constables of the four districts, accompanied by their divisional superintendents, gathered at the Yard for a meeting. The practice suited Trenchard admirably, so he extended it both to learn more about the problems of command "in the field" and to assess the characters and capabilities of the commanders. By and large, the latter disappointed him. Their complacency and evasiveness may have been partly due to his brusqueness in "grilling" them; he allowed for that, or tried to, but nothing could budge his fixed assumption that the District Officers were no longer vital links in the chain. Their position as intermediaries between the centre and the periphery was ill-defined, their grasp of what was happening either in their own districts or at the Yard weak and fumbling.

"Where is crime most prevalent in your district?" Trenchard asked one morning, stabbing a finger at a Chief Constable.

"Oh, it's pretty evenly spread."

"Show me how it's spread. On the map."

The District Officer hesitated, then admitted that he was "out of touch."[7]

The confession confirmed two points to Trenchard: first, that his surmise about the privileged "separateness" of the C.I.D. applied to the whole Metropolitan Police Area and not merely to headquarters, and, second, that unless he bolstered up or replaced his District Officers, any long-term reforms he attempted would fall to the ground.

His next move was entirely in character. At the end of November he approached the Home Secretary and demanded a personal assistant with exceptional powers. This right-hand man, he intimated, must be someone of his own choosing. Samuel inquired whether he had anyone in mind.

"Yes," said Trenchard. "Maurice Drummond."

Colonel the Hon. Maurice Drummond, who had served under him at the Air Ministry, was that rare mixture, the devoted, painstaking and completely trustworthy aide who could both anticipate and interpret the lightning workings of Trenchard's mind. The Home Secretary granted the request; and early in December Drummond joined his old master again as a Chief Constable freed from departmental duties. The appointment increased the feeling of uneasiness inside the Yard, and that in turn reinforced Trenchard's certainty that he had selected the right watchdog.

"The Commissioner's shadow," as these implacable critics thought of him, seemed to be no more than a pale but faithful extension of Trenchard's dynamic will. Few realised that Drummond also represented, apart from his status as a confidential aide, a recurring and indispensable personal need. Like Baring and Marson before him, though cast in a more prosaic mould than either, he would be relied on to echo his master's voice, to act as his *alter ego*, and thus to relieve him of excessive responsibility.

Before Drummond's arrival, Trenchard paid a series of unexpected visits at odd hours to nearly a dozen police stations in central and outer London. Once again, as at Scotland Yard, he created a distinctly unfavourable impression on the junior officers and the rank and file who crossed his path. The memory of Byng was still too fresh.

The late Commissioner had also been accustomed to visit stations or section-houses without warning, stopping men at random for friendly chats that invariably left a glow of fellow-feeling. Seldom, except in passing, did Byng discuss police work; he usually seemed far more interested in the families, the gardens, or the hobbies of the men he met. Trenchard's swoops were a different kettle of fish: his manner seemed impersonal, hard and domineering, his visits therefore were all the less welcome.

The questions he rapped out were about station routine or the oversights or ambiguities which leaped to his eye while inspecting books, documents, or notice-boards. It was remarked upon that Trenchard never paused. Nor did he solicit opinions on the one burning issue that consumed them all: the pay cuts. He would depart as he came with the abruptness of a man bound to an inflexible time-table, conscious of their grievances yet deliberately denying them a chance of airing them.

Their views on the pay cuts he knew all too well. He had read them till he was sick in the resolutions published on their behalf by the branch boards of the Police Federation. The tone of these was not to his taste, exceeding the limits of propriety in the worst tradition of militant trade union propaganda.[8]

Trenchard decided after several visits that his best course now was to assemble as many policemen of every rank as was practicable in order to "show himself" and "speak his mind," so that the Force should know what he thought and expected of *them*. Early in December, he hired the Queen's Hall, in Upper Regent Street, for the purpose; and Oxford Circus seemed suddenly to sprout policemen on the morning of the meeting as nearly 3000 officers and men from the four districts descended in groups on the rendezvous. When Trenchard entered, the babel of voices in the auditorium dropped to a whisper. Cigarettes and pipes were hastily stubbed out. He walked towards the platform, conscious of the rows of silent, stiff men, almost sensing their sullen hostility. The atmosphere was thick with smoke which obscured their faces and irritated his throat. Peering hard through the haze at one impassive face after another, he suddenly barked out:

"Clear the hall. Open all the windows. Be back in five minutes when I can breathe."

It was not too auspicious an opening. And his voice still sounded reproachful when his audience returned. He told them that, so far,

he had discovered several big flaws in the police system and many
smaller ones; practical reforms were being prepared; they would be
announced and enforced shortly. The major defects needed more
careful consideration, perhaps even a major operation. The force
had not a good name with the public. He did not necessarily blame
them for this; there were undoubtedly misconceptions on both
sides; but it was his business to wipe out all suspicion of police
dishonesty and so restore harmonious relations with the public. He
intended meanwhile to judge them by the willingness of their
response to his plans for their betterment.

Provided they did their duty, they would not find him too harsh
or unreasonable a person to deal with. But he could promise them,
there and then, that he would tolerate no further abuses of the
properly constituted channels for complaints. He regarded the
attitude of the Police Federation towards the Government's policy
on pay cuts as mischievous and uncalled for. Federation spokesmen
were doing the force a disservice by behaving as though regulations
could be infringed with impunity. The practice of ventilating their
views to the national Press must cease:

"If any unauthorised account of what I'm saying to you gets
into the papers," he warned, "the culprits will regret it."

He had already had drafted a short official statement on the
present meeting for publication, so that any potential culprits
present could save themselves trouble by holding their tongues
and hands.

The whole speech lasted less than fifteen minutes. Then
Trenchard invited questions from the floor, and had to rule nearly
every question out of order. Most of them betrayed an obsession
with three aspects of a single theme: the pay cuts, Samuel's pledge
to the Police Council, and doubts about the Government's "good
faith." Trenchard cut across their track by declaring that he knew
no more than they did. He had no assurances to offer; nor was he
holding anything back. But afterwards he saw Samuel and emphasised that "nothing interested the men except the cuts in pay."
The Home Secretary, he thought, took the news rather badly.

4

In the post-election Cabinet reshuffle, Snowden had been quietly
kicked upstairs to the Lords. His place at the Exchequer had gone
to Neville Chamberlain, a testier and more censorious minister,

who did not conceal his opinion that Samuel had been worse than rash in committing the Cabinet to treat the police more favourably than other public servants. Such discriminatory treatment was more than the Exchequer or the country could bear. Samuel, for his part, did not care for the critical attitude of the Chancellor whom he and his fellow Liberals in the Government had reasons of their own to distrust. Neville Chamberlain, the new broom, was evidently intent on sweeping some of their principles away. His idea of imposing a general tariff on imports, for instance, smacked of sacrilegious expediency to anyone reared on the pure Liberal doctrine of free trade. This early rift was patched up by a formal Cabinet "agreement to disagree"; but the personal antipathy between the Chancellor and the Samuelites remained. Chamberlain's relations with the Home Secretary worsened in the first half of 1932 when a special Cabinet sub-committee on Police Expenditure was weighing the practical consequences of Samuel's unfortunate pledge to relieve the police of half the cuts levied on all State officials, including Ministers of the Crown and judges.

The discussions of this high-powered sub-committee on which Chamberlain and Samuel, the two principals, continued their unedifying sparring, were attended by Trenchard. The Government, he could see, were neither as united as the public imagined, nor at all certain what to do for the best; and he tended to put the blame for this on Samuel's advisers rather than on Samuel himself. He greatly regretted that Sir John Anderson had allowed himself to be uprooted at such a delicate stage for the honour of governing Bengal. His own mainstay at the Home Office, the one man on whom he implicitly relied for sound guidance, had gone; and Anderson's successor, Sir R. Russell Scott, was, to Trenchard's mind, an inexperienced lightweight by comparison. Scott, Trenchard, and occasionally Warren Fisher, the head of the Treasury, were the only officials who regularly attended the sub-committee; and the records suggest that Scott rarely trusted himself to open his mouth.

The first meeting was held on 20th April, 1932, in the presence of the Service Ministers as well as the two protagonists-in-chief; and proceedings were immediately marred by a verbal duel between the pair. While the Home Secretary was repeating his tediously familiar account of how the original misunderstanding had arisen over the police pay cuts, the Chancellor interrupted:

"I must dissent," he snapped. "There was no question of departmental discretion."

There were far more important questions to be decided, Chamberlain implied; the sub-committee would have enough to do repairing the consequences of Samuel's blunder. Perhaps the Commissioner could tell them how the London police would react to an official admission that the concession to the police was all a mistake. Would it help if it were coupled with an appeal for restraint?

Trenchard replied that it would not help in the slightest.

Why? What, in his view, would the police do? Surely they would not strike?

"A certain number may strike," retorted Trenchard. "Ca'canny measures are also possible."

The Chancellor was inclined to pooh-pooh the plain warning. The notion of a police strike at this late stage appeared far-fetched to Chamberlain. What, he asked, was Trenchard's view of the ten per cent cut which the Cabinet intended to impose on the police as on everyone else? Was it justified or not?

"Yes," Trenchard replied. "The ten per cent cut is as justified for the police as for others but it was very wrong to have split it."

He was asked to explain why he held that opinion.

"I have avoided discussion as to whether the total cut would be hard on them or not, or what the position would have been had they never been told of the possibility that they would be let off the other five per cent. Since you ask me, I must say that there's the danger of a breach of faith both ways.

"I would like to refer to the fact that I am shortly putting up to H.M. Government, through the Home Secretary, a paper on certain abuses which I have found in the Metropolitan Police and which ought to be eliminated at the earliest possible date. The reforms which I believe to be necessary will in themselves lead to a good deal of dissatisfaction and unrest in the force."

Every member of the committee was eyeing him apprehensively, as if wondering what would come out next. Samuel said nothing. It was Chamberlain who steered the meeting single-handed. Evidently, he said, it would be inadvisable for the present to put out a statement, or reach any premature decision, about the pay cuts. Trenchard would have to quieten his men as best he could; the Government would let the problem rest until the end of the year in the hope that time would heal it.

"If there's a police strike this year," the Chancellor said finally, turning to the Commissioner again, "as a result of the Cabinet insisting on the further five per cent pay cut, would the strike take place in circumstances favourable or unfavourable to the Government?"

It seemed to Trenchard a fatuous question meriting an equally fatuous answer, but he restrained himself:

"I can't estimate whether a strike is really probable or how effective it would be. But if a strike broke out, we could deal with it."

Before the meeting broke up, Chamberlain suggested to Lord Hailsham, the Secretary for War, that it might be useful to sound the Chiefs of Staff on the question. What would be the reaction in the armed services if the Government compromised on its principle of "equality of sacrifice" and let the police off permanently with a five per cent cut?

The next session of the sub-committee took place three weeks later. The three Chiefs of Staff were called in to testify. Their evidence left the Chancellor with no further room for doubt.

Field, the First Sea Lord, said with all the emphasis at his command that if the Government discriminated, as suggested, in favour of the police their action would not please the Royal Navy.

"Would the effect be serious?" asked Chamberlain.

"Undoubtedly. It would be extremely serious."

Milne, the C.I.G.S., was even more specific.

"I must warn the Cabinet," he said, "that to differentiate in favour of the police in this matter would give rise to very grave trouble in the army." The Army Council were most anxious to make the position clear: they "would not and could not be held accountable for the consequences."

Salmond, the Chief of the Air Staff, was less pessimistic. He reminded the committee that "very few" in the R.A.F. (only about one in seven) had so far been affected by the economy cuts. The reason, in case the Government had forgotten, was that basic pay rates in the air force had been reduced in 1925 and pegged since.

A statement by E. H. Pelham, Secretary of the Board of Education, elicited another fact: the claims of the teachers could not be ignored either. The Chancellor must expect loud and indignant protests from them if he allowed this unfair concession to stand. Pelham's political master, Sir Donald Maclean, felt it only right to point the moral:

"The ultimate sanction for the preservation of law and order rests with the fighting services," he said. "I am more apprehensive of what might happen if serious trouble broke out in the services than if it broke out in the police force. It might not be a bad thing if the police were brought face to face with public opinion on a matter in which they would get little sympathy."

The discomfort of Samuel as he sat listening to these comments was only too clear to Trenchard. The Home Secretary intervened only once; that was to recommend that a final decision should be adjourned. His purpose all through, he said, had been to determine how much could be saved in administrative economies and passed on to the police; it was surely too early in the year to expect round figures. Trenchard had agreed to seek about £150,000 in savings by pruning overheads; the Commissioner was completing his arrangements for redistributing the force, its stations, and its beats. In the long term at least, these would yield greater efficiency at a lower cost. Samuel's plea had much to commend it.

The national purse might be better lined than in the previous September, when a few hundred British sailors, sublimely ignorant of the disproportionately vast damage they could do, had accidentally kicked over the gold standard; but the financial state of the country six months later was not yet sound enough for another Invergordon scandal, especially as disaffection seemed likely to spread to Aldershot and innumerable school teachers' staff-rooms as well. The police would have to lump their grievances; but Chamberlain and Samuel were agreed on one thing at least: Trenchard would be better able to handle a police strike in the autumn, when the pay cuts were reviewed, than now in the spring. So the question was deferred for another six months, and the Commissioner was glad of the extra time.

Trenchard could honestly feel sorry for Samuel. The Home Secretary was almost too eager to support a Commissioner who knew where he was going and what he wanted, and had promptly approved the scheme for placing the new "Organisers" in a department of their own, untrammelled by the administrative chores of old. And Samuel was duly gratified and astonished when, after two months of intensely concentrated effort, the "ideas merchants" at the Yard made good Trenchard's promise to revise the system of patrolling for the ordinary man on the beat. Byng, as the Home Secretary knew, had been contemplating such a step for over two years: Trenchard had arrived, instantly adopted Byng's draft proposals, briefed his experts, and driven them hard until they finished the job in record time and to his entire satisfaction. Some of the senior officers at Scotland Yard had spent a distracted Christmas, working against the clock; but at any rate an outline of the plan to redistribute stations, boundaries and beats was ready for the Press on 3rd January, 1931.

Newspapers in the capital extolled the practical advantages of "surprise," the new element which Trenchard, after Byng, meant to introduce into the business of pounding a beat. The changes would not be welcomed by criminals, who seemed to have adjusted themselves far better to the tempo of modern life than the stolid, slow policeman. Burglars and car-bandits, it was predicted, would have to move with more cunning. For, until now, these lawbreakers could tell the time from the measured tread of local constables passing on their unchanging rounds. Public opinion was gratified. Evidently Trenchard had decided to make the criminal's life a more risky and unrewarding affair by the practice of constantly switching his men about, using fast cars or motor-cycle combinations for that purpose. Londoners had long lacked a force capable of outwitting the new breed of criminals whose daring and ingenuity had increased with success.

The secondary aim of the scheme was missed by most commentators. Trenchard believed that by "shaking up" the force, imposing new duties in unfamiliar territory, he would reduce idleness and opportunities for mischief. It is only right to add that many officers and constables suspected and deplored this.

The feeling that the new Commissioner saw little right in anything waxed stronger: his notoriety as a tyrant, almost as impossible to please as to deceive, had not waned since his Queen's Hall address. In one way he welcomed their dislike: it had, he knew, a foundation of guilt.

Among the voluminous mass of Trenchard's "police papers," which he kept under lock and key until his death, seldom allowing anyone, even his biographer, to rummage freely through the large tin trunk which contained them, there is an *aide-memoire*, written at a later date, which lists the various deficiencies unearthed during these first six months at Scotland Yard. It is a telling indictment, and the salient points were points to which he repeatedly drew the attention of Samuel at the time. They deserve to be quoted:

"I found that the state of discipline in the force was not good. There was a great deal of discontent with the conditions of service.

"The Police Federation was holding 480 meetings a year and this had been going on for some twelve years. The Police Act of 1919 only sanctioned *twelve* meetings a year of one day each. . . .

"Many police constables were still patrolling the beats which

Trenchard mounted (*right*) during a rehearsal for the
Trooping of the Colour

In the Western Desert in 1943, on one of his many
visits to R.A.F establishments

were laid down by Sir Robert Peel a hundred years before. This
was in process of being examined when I took up the post of
Commissioner.

"The Statistical Branch, if it could be called such, did not
show where crime was most prevalent and was completely out of
date.

"There was no map-room.

"There was no scientific laboratory.

"There was no welfare officer.

"The facilities for sport and recreation were totally inadequate.

"The police section-houses, as they are called, were appalling—
the married quarters were even worse.

"There was a very large proportion of constables compared
with officers.

"There was too much corruption.

"There was too much tipping. . . ."

Samuel, to whom he showed the evidence, was distressed. To
remedy these imperfections would not result in the administrative
savings the Home Secretary hoped for; yet some could not wait
without incurring graver risks to morale on the one hand, and to
law and order on the other.

Specific allegations of corruption against officers and men frequently came in personal letters from members of the public.
Trenchard followed up every clue. He was scandalised to discover
that in most cases the allegations were not exaggerated. The taking
of bribes from street bookmakers, from publicans, and to a lesser
extent from prostitutes, seemed to be the commonest form of
"graft." And the records of previous inquiries, notably a Royal
Commission of 1906-8 and two Government committees which
covered the same ground in 1928 and 1929, suggested that the
temptation was one to which London policemen were particularly
prone.

Trenchard dealt mercilessly with all offenders; but he realised
that for every officer or man actually apprehended, there were
probably twelve who escaped scot-free. It seemed to him no argument to say that if the police accepted bribes it was usually because
people offered them bribes, and that the public were partly responsible. The unearthing of a moral evil only intensified his reforming
zeal. In his own down-to-earth fashion, he was all the more determined to answer the ancient riddle of Juvenal, "*Quis custodiet
ipsos custodes?*" by long-term preventive means. The London

T.   U police deserved better leaders: he resolved that they would get them.

It was largely the iron grip which Trenchard clamped on the force, notably during the first half of 1932, which discouraged any mass outbreaks of defiance. Because discipline, by his standard, was "appallingly slack," the code of conduct set down in the Regulations of the Secretary of State and in the General Orders of the Metropolitan Police became a weapon which he used unsparingly through his District Officers and divisional superintendents. There were nearly fifty ways in which policemen could commit an offence against the disciplinary rules, and Trenchard was in no mood to let them overlook the fact. This campaign, coupled with the transfers of staff involved in regrouping the force within the newly reorganised divisions, unquestionably gained him the breathing space he needed to prepare his major reforms.

He was aware of his growing unpopularity. In a sense he thrived on it. His ambition was to renovate the London police and he noticed on the visits he still paid to stations, unannounced, the depressingly high percentage of elderly constables with no prospects before them now except a pension. The observation was a reflection on the declining status of the police as a profession. For the records confirmed that the average London "bobby" was a member of a dull and ageing race. Then it gradually dawned on him that here lay one key to his basic problem; if he could only reanimate the force by transfusions of young and vigorous blood, much as he had reanimated the post-war R.A.F., the task would be worth all the unpopularity that was going.

Meanwhile, however, Trenchard was powerless to answer outside criticism of his repressive tactics. The Police Federation's attitude to him and all his works was one of unqualified antagonism and the popular newspapers, which branch officials kept supplied with the Federation's views, lost no opportunity of castigating the Commissioner for deliberately rubbing his men the wrong way.

The fact, for instance, that he employed constables in plain clothes as C.I.D. auxiliaries, yet deprived them of the small allowance drawn by established detectives, was played up as a genuine grievance. So was his attempt to put the "special police" to more effective use by letting them train side by side with regulars on the beat or at traffic points. Of all his innovations, this was the one which the Federation most keenly resented. But there were others just as deeply deplored. Proficiency pay, for instance, the extra

half crown per week which constables had always received as a
matter of course after so many months' service, ceased to be an
automatic increment. The policeman, so Trenchard decreed in
another of his bleak orders, would receive the rise now only if he
earned it. Was there any case in the hundred and two years'
existence of the Metropolitan Police of a Commissioner "putting
a premium on arrests"? The Federation doubted it.

Discontent boiled over in the late spring, when a list of complaints which Trenchard had refused to discuss with the Federation
appeared in the *Daily Express*. Fleet Street pounced at once on
something that had the ingredients of a juicy story. The Government became uneasy. The Home Secretary, whose standing with
the Chancellor and with the Cabinet sub-committee on Police
Expenditure was if anything weaker, begged the Commissioner not
to try his men too far. Trenchard assured Samuel that there was
no cause for alarm.

The newspapers, he said, were reflecting the frustration of the
Federation, whose leaders lacked the stomach for direct action.
He doubted indeed whether they would dare call a strike over
anything less than a reduction in pay. And since a five per cent cut
that brought them in line with other professions was quite justifiable, the police would forfeit all public sympathy if they were
foolish enough to take the law into their own hands. Even now, he
told Samuel, he was more or less ready to deal with them if they
did: his "specials" were up to strength and responding well to the
new training routine. By the end of the year, he would be prepared
for any eventuality, even a major stoppage.

5

One of Trenchard's most constructive and admiring critics, and the
most closely informed on his every move, was King George V. In
inviting the new Commissioner, during his first audience at Buckingham Palace, "not to hesitate to see me if there's anything you should
ever wish to consult me about," the King had not been talking
idly. Nor had Trenchard in promising to let him know, at every
stage, exactly what he was doing, and why. Both were plain-
spoken men; each kept his end of the bargain.

At eleven o'clock on the first Thursday in May, 1932, Trenchard
duly called at the Palace to report to the King on the improvements so far produced by altering the divisional boundaries south

of the Thames, and by overhauling the departmental machinery at
Scotland Yard. This, he emphasised, was only a beginning. There
had been some passive resistance and much ill-feeling in the force;
more could be expected; for he had more fundamental changes in
mind. He had prepared the first draft of a secret paper on the subject, and would be grateful if the King would read it and let him
have his observations.

Later on 5th May, the day of the interview at the Palace,
Trenchard sent on the document, with a covering note, to Sir Clive
Wigram, the King's private secretary:

"It does not put forward any scheme," he explained, "but shows
what are the chief matters that are wrong. It is a very hush-hush
paper, and nobody here has seen it, and only one or two Ministers
know of its existence. . . . I hope you will keep it very secret as it
would do untold harm if it became known."

Returning the paper two days afterwards, Wigram said that the
King had read it "with the greatest interest": he had impressed
upon His Majesty "how necessary it was to keep your observations
secret. . . . Doubtless you are up against an immense problem,"
the letter continued, "and it will be difficult to get Parliament to
face the facts of the situation. They would probably prefer to
blink. I cannot understand how any force can be efficient when it
has these Federation and Branch Boards. These seem to me mere
mechanisms for unscrupulous agitation."

The following week, the Press caught wind of the rising discontent in the force at Trenchard's steadfast refusal to discuss outstanding grievances with Federation officials. Trenchard wrote to
Wigram again:

"You may probably have seen a very bitter criticism against
me and mine in some illustrated paper last week, called, I think,
the *National Graphic*. And this morning I see there is very hot
criticism against me and all my works in the *Daily Express*. I hear
personally that there are one or two people behind the scenes who
are boiling up as much agitation as they can on this subject.
I thought, in case you had not seen this, that you might just like to
know about it."

A reply from the Palace came by return of post:

"We did indeed see the monstrous attack upon you in the
Daily Express and the King and everyone are more than disgusted.
Cannot you catch the agitators who are trying to stir up trouble?"

At heart, however, Trenchard, was not unduly perturbed by
"agitators" in the police or in Fleet Street. He said so in addressing

some 300 leading delegates of the Police Federation, who gathered in London towards the end of May, 1932, for their annual meeting. This opportunity of confronting his critics was too good to let slip. It enabled him to defend every disciplinary measure and practical reform he had imposed as essential to the only end that mattered: the rehabilitation of the force. He was heard in stony silence, as the *Daily Express* faithfully reported next morning.

Absorbed as he was with still bolder plans of a permanent nature, there were moments when Trenchard felt an acute sense of isolation. The friends in whom he might have chosen to confide were few; for cogent political reasons he dared not confide in any of them. To T. E. Lawrence, serving at home again in the ranks of the R.A.F., he wrote:

"You will hear of my iniquities if you come anywhere near London."

To Cunliffe Lister (later Lord Swinton) and other political acquaintances who occasionally stopped to congratulate or commiserate with him, he admitted quite openly:

"I've taken on something that's made me the loneliest man in Britain."[10]

Yet, on balance, the Press was not ill-disposed. He was a gift to the cartoonists, one of whom depicted him as a heavily moustached charlady spring-cleaning the dusty corners of the Yard with mop, pail and duster. He could even laugh a little with "Beachcomber" for suggesting dryly that the "monthly reorganisation of the Metropolitan Police will take place weekly in future." And he could always ignore the easy insinuations of the unsympathetic that the average policeman had forgotten more about the art of catching criminals than he would ever learn. He was in no position to answer back; and there was nobody in authority who could fully answer for him.

Samuel he liked; Samuel on the whole he trusted, despite the Home Secretary's disconcerting habit of trying to face both ways. But the proper time to discuss with him the details of the major reforms and the best method of putting these across to the public would come in the autumn, after the King had approved them in their final form. The *Police Book*, as he called the long treatise he was drafting on the evils of the existing system and the remedies for it, was not simple or consoling reading yet. Of the other members of the Government, only MacDonald might have been worth enlightening about progress; but the Prime Minister was so distracted that Trenchard thought better of it. Besides, as Trenchard more than once reminded Drummond and Howgrave-Graham in the privacy of his own office:

"The best way to get quick publicity for a secret is to tell it in confidence to a Cabinet Minister."

Hence his determination to hold back until the first flaws in his rough outline had been smoothed away in discussion or composition with Drummond, Howgrave-Graham and the half-dozen officials at Scotland Yard in whom he had no option but to confide; hence also the comfort he derived from the warm approval with which the King watched his ideas take systematic shape. Trenchard dispensed with a summer holiday in 1932 because he could not afford the time or the money for one. He was all the more touched when a parcel of grouse arrived in August from Balmoral with the royal compliments. He acknowledged to being "more than pleased at His Majesty remembering me in this way, especially as I have not been able to get away myself to shoot in the North—much to my regret." He had no need to add that there were a few larger yet more elusive targets on hand nearer home: the King understood already.

The Royal Family was still on Deeside when the second instalment of Trenchard's *Police Book* arrived by registered post:

"Would you tell the King," he urged Wigram, "that I realise too well the great changes I am proposing to make; but if we are going to have good work, I am confident we must introduce the well-educated class into the Police Force the same as in every other profession."

Unlike the introductory part which concentrated on the disruptive practices of the Federation, these central chapters diagnosed the defects which, by law and tradition, had gradually become an integral part of the Metropolitan Police system. The months of direct observation, of inspections, of meetings with senior officers, of interviews with delinquents and honest men of the force, of studying records and statistics, nothing of these had been wasted. Brooding over the lessons of the past and the ills of the present, Trenchard had looked for a simple, explanatory link—and found both it and the cure.

"I need hardly say," commented Wigram when he sent back the typescript about a week later, "that His Majesty was deeply interested in all the proposals in these chapters, and as far as I know the King entirely agrees with your views."

The pace that Trenchard set his small team of scribes and "devils" in compiling and composing those views had been phenomenal. "A ten-power man" was how the most fluent of them, Howgrave-Graham, had come to think of him at the office, though much of the work on a document as long as a novel was done outside office hours.

"It was as well that paper was cheap and plentiful in the thirties," commented Howgrave-Graham, looking back in after years on the tantalising excitements of those arduous days and nights. "The numbers of acres covered in the various drafts hardly bears thinking about."

As soon as a fresh instalment was ready, a fair copy would go off to the King. The substance of this "unauthorised version" was preserved to the end, only the construction and the immoderate language which Trenchard sometimes used for emphasis being altered when the original text came finally under Home Office and Cabinet scrutiny. Inevitably the freshness and vigour suffered in the process. The quotations that follow below are drawn from the uncensored typescript, before this was softened and flattened by the tired platitudes beloved of Whitehall officials, because it best illustrates Trenchard's stern approach to moral issues. These he saw and defined in uncompromising terms of black and white.

There is a striking example of this in a passage describing the misdemeanours of the Police Federation:

"Grievances are ventilated through this organisation rather than through the officers whose business it should be to prevent and remedy them. As a result, discontent and grumbling are widespread. *Esprit de corps* is almost entirely lacking. There is an atmosphere of suspicion and lack of confidence. Discipline is wooden, repressive and unintelligent. The standard of conduct is low and incidents of actual dishonesty occur at regular intervals. . . .

"Occasional incidents of individual policemen who use their positions for fraudulent or corrupt purposes need not cause any great anxiety in themselves; but when it is found that a group of officers have carried on a regular system for a long time, or that malpractices have been encouraged by gross laxity in supervision, the question naturally arises whether the detected cases are not merely symptoms of a much more widespread disease. . . ."

Trenchard's exacting logic and lofty personal code of behaviour were the yardsticks of his judgment. He was interested in cures, not palliatives. And since the system itself was tainted, it was the system which would first have to be renovated. To purge the force of its corrupt members at one swoop was not at all practicable.

For whom could he trust to investigate the investigators? He knew that the C.I.D., that specialist empire within an empire, was not above suspicion. The defects in the old unchanged methods of recruitment, training and promotion betrayed themselves. The police produced too few capable leaders fit for the highest posts. As Trenchard put it:

"Unlike any other comparable organisation, the personnel of the police, including the officers, are drawn solely from one stratum of society. . . . The present educational standard of the force as a whole is astoundingly low. Only eighteen per cent of the present strength have carried their education beyond the elementary school standard. The result is a noticeable narrowness of outlook and rigidity of mind even amongst those who reach the higher ranks. . . ."

Of the 759 officers on the Metropolitan Police establishment, only eleven belonged to what Trenchard thought of as "the educated classes," and every one of these was employed "indoors" on administrative work. Was it surprising, he asked himself, that only one constable since the time of Peel had attained the rank of Assistant Commissioner? What reason had the authorities to wonder that crime was on the increase, and to rack their brains for an answer which stared them full in the face? The most responsible positions had to be filled by outsiders because the police were still denied the chance of becoming members of a respectable profession capable of rearing its own natural leaders.

No Home Secretary for a hundred years had had the wisdom or courage to identify this fatal flaw in the system and correct it. Peel's rule that all appointments up to the rank of inspector must be filled by promotion from the ranks had been a necessary insurance against the jobbery so prevalent in the early nineteenth century, before the dawn of universal education and the introduction of competitive examinations for public posts. It seemed to Trenchard that Peel, in guarding against one evil, had unwittingly fostered another which had spread since like a weed through the negligence of his successors. From time to time there had been demands for "educated control" of the police; in 1869 the District Officers were brought in as a palliative, their numbers being increased as a further concession to public dissatisfaction in 1886.

Nearly half a century before, a committee of inquiry examining allegations of police misconduct during a Trafalgar Square riot found that "the number of officers of superior rank and education, or of experience in the habit of command, was insufficient." The

1928 Royal Commission, with wider terms of reference, had reached a similar conclusion, stressing that "long experience and good service in the lower ranks of the force are not the only nor the most important qualifications for the higher posts." Better pay and conditions had failed to attract a better type of recruit, even during the post-war years of unemployment.

More than half of Trenchard's 16,800 constables were men of "an ageing race." Having passed beyond the promotion zone, they had nothing left to look forward to but their pensions. One in every two of these plodding veterans had at least seventeen years' service: a dispiriting commentary indeed on the state of the force's arteries, and the *reductio ad absurdum* of the policy devised by Peel to obviate the evils and serve the simpler needs of a vanished age. Youth, initiative and incentive were at a discount; seniority, repetitive experience and cunning were at a premium as qualifications for advancement. Untrained themselves, and with too few exemplars to teach modern methods of fighting crime, the mass of his men were a poor match indeed for the modern criminal. The steadily rising crime rate, which had been worrying the public for several years, was inextricably bound up with the lax standards which the police had inherited.

Trenchard did not shrink from grasping the nettle which dozens of Home Secretaries and Police Commissioners before him had prudently shrunk from: if the only logical answer was to throw Peel's policy out of the window, then out of the window it must go:

"The proposal I wish to put forward is to introduce a short service system for a proportion of the constables taken into the force," he wrote. "The scheme I have worked out provides that there shall be eventually about 5000 constables serving for ten years, at the end of which time they will leave the force and receive a gratuity. Apart from the obvious effect of reducing considerably the average age of the constable grade, it will also have the advantage of improving the career of the long-service men by proportionately increasing the number of higher posts available to them. . . ."

Trenchard had to burn no midnight oil over this tried expedient. It had been the making of his air force, guaranteeing a steady career and rapid promotion to a minority by allowing three short-term commissions for every permanent one awarded at Cranwell. The device could be adopted to solve this more delicate problem, though he would probably be damned publicly for his pains. If the short-service R.A.F. scheme had been disliked by some of his own Air Ministry colleagues, he could expect no gratitude for applying that "militarist" formula to a civilian force. For Trenchard did not overlook the fact that there were now nearly three million unemployed in Britain; and had he done so, the Home Office would quickly have refreshed his memory.

"The first criticism that will probably be made of the scheme is that it is a form of blind-alley employment and that, unless vocational training is given, the men turned away from the Metropolitan Force at thirty to thirty-five years of age will tend to swell the ranks of the unemployed. The answer to this criticism is that there is a considerable field of employment as doorkeepers, watchmen, guardians, wardens and messengers, for which these men would be peculiarly suitable. They will have been specially selected for physique and good character, and trained to be watchful and resourceful.

"At present a considerable number of policemen secure employment after leaving the service although they are already middle-aged and have a pension which would enable them to live without further employment. Many of these openings should be available to the short-service police officers. . . . I propose to set up an Appointments Board . . . in order to secure that vacancies "may be reserved for [them] . . . if in spite of these arrangements a proportion have difficulty in finding employment, I suggest that this consideration is really unimportant in comparison with the increased efficiency of the force itself."

To what extent would the recruiting of young short-term constables without a secure future create incentive? Would a young man deprived of it be any better than an elderly man who had lost it? Again Trenchard tried to forestall his critics:

"The first answer to this argument is that enterprise and keenness are the natural attributes of youth, and it takes a healthy man a number of years to lapse into habits of slothfulness. With proper leadership and the stimulus of emulation I believe the young man on short-service terms will be much more likely to take an interest in his work and put energy into it than the man who has been at it for twenty years or more. . . .

"Police work of the ordinary kind is not conducive to activity. Slow and deliberate movements are intentionally cultivated. In some districts a constable may carry out his appointed task for weeks, months and even years without encountering a single incident which calls for rapid thought or action. The result is inevitably a tendency towards physical and mental lethargy. The force depends for its success on the keenness and initiative of

20,000 individuals acting more or less independently. Under the present system far too many of them are not only without real incentive to effort but even with a definite inducement to do as little as possible. Activity involves the risk of mistakes and the line of inaction is the line of safety.

"The men themselves can hardly be blamed. The fault is with the system. As it stands at present it is unfair to the men, and what is more important, it is unfair to the public to ask them to pay for a force which is carrying a deadweight of inertia and not giving full value in protection and service."

Trenchard's reasons for keeping his plans secret for as long as possible can be readily appreciated. Had any hint of such revolutionary ideas leaked out to the Police Federation and the Press, the consequences might well have put paid to his hopes. A garbled version, misconstruing his motives and lending itself to heated and unfair abuse, might have led the Cabinet to disown his reforms in advance. The risk was too great; so Trenchard followed his own path of security and surprise until the last week of September, 1932.

6

By then the original typescript was completed. The King alone had read it; but the moment was approaching when the Home Secretary must be allowed to review it in the light of practical politics. Samuel, of course, was aware in very general terms of Trenchard's diagnosis and proposed remedy. The two men had had several discussions on the "progress of the book." The Minister did not dispute the Commissioner's opinions as to the drastic treatment necessary; but Trenchard doubted whether Samuel, so reasonable and imperturbable in ordinary conversation, would support him through thick and thin if the Cabinet or even the Home Office experts were to challenge any of the proposals. The Home Secretary's rift with Chamberlain over the cut in police pay had undermined Samuel's authority and estranged him from the Conservative half of the Cabinet. The police reforms might conceivably deepen and widen the rift, with benefit to none. Hence Trenchard's mingled sense of astonishment and relief when, at the end of September, 1932, Samuel suddenly resigned on a totally different issue, making way for a successor whose tastes, outlook and temperament were perceptibly closer to the Commissioner's.

The break came over tariffs, an issue that had lain uneasily dormant between the Conservative majority and the breakaway Liberal minority since the formation of the emergency Government. As long as the economy stood in peril, both sides agreed to suspend open disagreement. But the partial recovery of sterling in the first half of 1932 encouraged Chamberlain to press harder for more Commonwealth trade and so speed the turn of the economic tide. The trade recession had left nearly thirty million people stranded and workless in various parts of the world; almost one in every ten of them was a Briton. What if the political price *were* the defection of the Liberals from the Government? It would be worth paying in the long run; and in the short run the Government was politically strong enough to rule without Liberal support.

The Ottawa Conference on tariff preferences within the Commonwealth took place in August, 1932, and proved, in the event, too much for the free-trade principles of Samuel and Sinclair, the figure-heads of Liberalism in the administration. It severed the frayed ends of an allegiance which had been worn thin by constant friction with the Chancellor over police pay. There was some sharp haggling in Ottawa before any tariff agreements were fixed; but the haggling did not deter the Samuelites from resigning in protest.

Trenchard liked the new Home Secretary, Sir John Gilmour, on sight. They had certain qualities in common. Gilmour, with his distinguished army record and something of a reputation as a blood sportsman, had won political promotion on merit by solid executive ability in the Ministry of Agriculture and Fisheries. Unlike Samuel, whose cast of mind seemed better attuned to abstractions than to facts, Gilmour laid claim to no intellectual pretensions. Nevertheless he possessed that down-to-earth logic which Trenchard had discovered in many Scotsmen, combining with it an enthusiasm for work and a taste for unpleasant decisions which seemed altogether rare. If Gilmour was overawed at first by the formidable personality of the Commissioner, he certainly did not show it. He was captivated by the thoroughness of Trenchard's researches and by a prescription for reforming the police which the facts manifestly justified even if the political situation did not.

Gilmour suffered from the disadvantage, politically speaking, of arriving on the scene too late to influence a work that was almost ready to be staged. As author and producer, Trenchard would not have welcomed either criticism or interference from a director who hardly knew his way yet about the theatre. Gilmour, however, was a willing learner. And there was nothing subservient or negative in his attitude. Neither the short-service scheme for the rank-and-file,

nor the complementary proposal to train a minority of selected
candidates as future leaders at a special Police College, struck him
as far-fetched or impracticable. He understood the reasons; he
accepted their soundness; and he was willing to defend them
before the Cabinet and the country.

Trenchard's spirits soared. The delays and obstructions which
he had feared might arise under Samuel were things of the past.
He took Gilmour fully into his confidence, gave him the completed
"book" to read, and begged him not to be misled by his own
officials who had apparently been nurtured in a tradition of
"humouring and spoiling" the police. Trenchard's proposals for a
Police College had not gone down too well with the Home Office
experts when he had explained them verbally. They fully agreed
in principle that a new and more highly qualified type of officer
was as urgently needed as a younger, more active class of constable
on the beat; but they deprecated the Commissioner's plans for
putting matters right. The public outcry that might ensue if he
got his way seemed to affect them more than the merits of the
reforms themselves:

"These people are afraid of their own shadows," he told Gilmour
contemptuously.

The Home Office experts, for their part, considered that
Trenchard was needlessly trailing his coat. They regretted the bad
blood which the Commissioner had already stirred up. They remembered, too, the fate that had overtaken their own recent scheme
for a National Police College. The details of this had been worked
out carefully to cause the least offence, and even a suspicious Police
Council had approved them at first as a just solution. It had been
agreed that only men with a minimum of five years' service should
be eligible for entry; and there had been good hopes of embarking
on the project without more ado when, suddenly and unaccountably,
in 1930, the views of police delegates veered the other way.

The Police Federation had denounced the National College
idea as "offering short cuts to promotion to a pampered few." The
local authorities, who were to have provided a large part of the
money, immediately took fright. The only group of policemen who
regretted the burial alive of a constructive plan were the superintendents; but the final decision whether to go ahead, in spite of
opposition, or to give up for lack of support, had rested with Byng.
Trenchard's predecessor, with more prudence than foresight, had
recommended that the college scheme be dropped. To Byng's mind,
it was doubtful whether such an institution could mould the

characters of grown men, an end that seemed to him infinitely more desirable than imparting a veneer of specialist knowledge and skill.

On this score at least, Trenchard applauded his predecessor's decision. He had informed the Home Office why he disliked their conception of what a Police College should be: it raised the average rate of entry far too high by insisting on five years' service as a condition of entry; it over-emphasised experience and took insufficient account of character training; and it made no provision for tapping the universities and other similar sources of recruitment. But the most cogent objection of all was the lukewarm attitude of the local authorities which were being asked to find the cash. This surely underlined the absurdity of seeking agreement on a national basis, Trenchard argued; the Metropolitan Police must have a college of their own, and the Government, through the Home Secretary, must foot the bill.

Gilmour was persuaded by Trenchard's devastating reasoning. His reading of the "book" demolished the last of his doubts:

"Any scheme for introducing officers of a different type into the force is going to meet with a great deal of opposition," began the relevant passage of the text. "It is this fact, no doubt, which has deterred the authorities in the past from attempting a reform so often advocated.

"There will be those who see in it an anti-democratic move, and others who will condemn it as an attempt to fly in the face of history. But I am convinced that until this problem is squarely faced, there can be no radical and lasting improvement and that— so far from flying in the face of history—it is accepting the lessons which a hundred years of history have taught. . . .

"The proposals I am making are intended to apply to the Metropolitan Police Force only. This is essential for a variety of reasons. In the first place there is the practical difficulty of devising a scheme applicable to 181 police forces [throughout Britain] varying in numerical strength from eleven to 2250, administered by 181 different authorities of all political complexions. The Metropolitan Force is a compact force under one authority, the Home Secretary, and comprises nearly one-third of the police strength of England and Wales. When the changes have been in operation for a period of years in London, it will be time enough to consider how far, if at all, they are applicable elsewhere."

The essence of Trenchard's plan was that it "picked men

young," regardless of length of service. Candidates would enter the inspector grade direct from two main sources:

"Some will come in by selection (with or without examination, according to circumstances) from candidates educated at secondary schools, public schools and universities. Others will be chosen from amongst those who have joined the force as constables. The men selected will be trained in a college somewhat similar to Sandhurst and will be subjected to various examinations and tests before they are posted as junior inspectors. From this rank they will be promoted to inspectorships after two or three years and will be eligible for promotion to higher posts on their merits.

"The normal age for reaching the superintendent grade will be about forty-five, and it is calculated that rather less than forty per cent of the entrants should reach this grade. Some people who have considered the problem have suggested that it would be sufficient to bring in a few educated men in the higher positions, as superintendents and perhaps chief inspectors, but I am fully satisfied that such a scheme would provide no real solution. Officers occupying such positions cannot possibly be in real day-to-day touch with their men, as their commands usually number something like 1000 of all ranks. An inspector has on average thirty to forty constables under him.

"He can, if he is of the right type, exercise a constant influence on every individual under him. . . . The officer that is wanted must be one who is prepared to be a guide, friend and philosopher to his men—ready to listen to their troubles, to watch their interest, to take part in their recreations and at the same time, by his own example, to maintain a high standard of duty and keenness. The point of introduction of the new men will therefore be at the inspector grade; but the number of inspectors will be reduced by about 200 and a new grade of sub-inspectors will be introduced. This will be the highest rank normally reached by those who join as constables and are not selected for special promotion. . . ."

To create more room at the top for younger men, Trenchard inserted another clause lowering the ages at which officers could be compulsorily retired. But to sugar the pill for those who might still wish to raise themselves from below, he guaranteed "a kind of backstairs route" up which they could still climb in the manner prescribed by Peel. As it usually took a constable "at least twelve or thirteen years" to reach the rank of inspector, Trenchard was really giving very little away; this led him to reserve in advance a

few of the higher vacancies for the ambitious few and to lay down
advantageous retirement terms for the rest.

Gilmour recognised that the Commissioner was driving in his
wedge at the weakest point, forcing open the seams where the wood
was thickest and most rotten. He thoroughly approved of a scheme
that balanced the best of the old with the new, offering careers that
were sufficiently attractive to coax in responsible outsiders, yet
holding open the door for any talented young man who through
misfortune or accident might have to start at the bottom. But what
would it all cost? The Home Secretary could find no figures, no
tables of extra expenditure and savings, in the typescript. Was it
just possible that Trenchard had overlooked what the Cabinet
would regard as one of the most important factors of all? He was
slightly incredulous at first when the Commissioner explained:

"When the scheme is in full operation, ten years from now, it'll
be no more expensive to run than the present creaking system. It's
for the Cabinet to decide whether it's worth spending £2 or £3
million now. My own view you know."

                                7

The Cabinet did not rise to the bait at once. A smaller but more
urgent question was clamouring for settlement; the size of the
policeman's weekly pay packet. The first year was almost up;
Samuel had departed; his concessionary pay cut still stood at five
per cent; and the Treasury, spurred on by Chamberlain, wanted to
wipe out an anomaly which could no longer be justified by vague
promises of "administrative economies." The arguments against
extending it were skilfully marshalled by Sir Warren Fisher:

"The people on the dole, most of whom would be only too glad
to work if they got a chance, would certainly claim that their
difficult lot should also be alleviated," he declared. "The public
at large would interpret it as a sign that the lean period was over.
In consequence, wage-earners throughout the country would treat
it as a ground for demanding improvements in their own conditions
and as an encouragement either to strike or, where, as in the case
of Lancashire, a fight has already started, to persist in it . . ."

The well-being of the community must be the supreme test of
State action, as in ancient Rome. With a Budget deficit probable,
and police costs likely to rise much higher yet, equity and merit
demanded that police pay be reduced to the standard level.

Trenchard again attended the sub-committee meetings and was glad that Ministers fully accepted Fisher's reasoning. In his own evidence, he dwelt on the paramount importance of correctly timing the Government's decision: retaliatory action by the police could not be entirely ruled out. Unless he, as Commissioner, were notified of the actual date, so that the case could be explained to the men beforehand, he would not answer for the consequences.

Trenchard was subsequently annoyed by the delay in arranging a definite day and hour for the announcement. After a week had gone by he asked the Home Secretary what was happening. Gilmour replied that the Cabinet, in its anxiety to ensure the utmost secrecy, would not disclose the date even to him.

"But that's utterly ridiculous," said Trenchard. " I must and shall be told."

The Commissioner's determination not to be defeated by excessive caution found expression in a letter to Sir Russell Scott in mid-October.

"I put great store by the way in which a Government decision of an unpalatable nature is communicated to the men as a whole," Trenchard wrote, adding that he did not care whether it was the Home Secretary's normal custom to break bad news to the Police Council first. These were not normal times. And if the procedure were observed on this occasion, "it is a practical certainty that the Federation will inform all the newspapers with such comments, criticisms and embellishments as they like and with no sense of responsibility for the accuracy of their statements. . . ."

The subservience of Ministers and senior civil servants to the letter of their own rules was not in the least amusing to Trenchard, and he had no inhibitions about saying so. Somewhat aggrieved, and with the air of a man forced into paying an irregular forfeit, Russell Scott consulted Warren Fisher at the Treasury and returned with the information that the announcement would be made on 20th October. Trenchard laid his plans accordingly: on the morning of that day, exactly two hours before the Police Council learnt from Gilmour's lips that the five per cent pay concession had been revoked, Trenchard assembled all his district and divisional officers at Scotland Yard to tell them the worst.

He sensed their shocked reactions and knew that he had been wise to forewarn his senior officers, so that the force could be informed by their own superiors, not misinformed by irresponsible Federation officials. There was no need to implement the emergency precautions which he had taken: the squads of "specials," secretly alerted for essential police duties in the event of strike action, were stood down. With a lighter heart, Trenchard braced himself for the next hurdle.

In November, 1932, the Cabinet was at last able to examine Trenchard's major proposals. A small working sub-committee, consisting of Home Office experts, Treasury officials, and representatives from Scotland Yard, was appointed to work under Gilmour. It was appropriately nicknamed the "Hush Hush." The Home Secretary laid down a meticulous time-table, and by the turn of the year committee members were dissecting the Commissioner's blueprint clause by clause, not without lively and sometimes heated exchanges. The most interesting point about the debate was the uncanny way in which the participants anticipated most of the objections that would be levelled against Trenchard's scheme five months later by Parliament, press and public. In the routine line of duty the Home Office experts played the role of Devil's Advocate, though they did so with something more than conventional sincerity. For Mr. A. L. (later Sir Arthur) Dixon, and his assistant Mr. (later Sir Frank) Newsam, strongly disapproved of Trenchard's scheme on several counts.

Dixon, the principal author of the abortive National Police College plan, questioned the democratic soundness of a new training system which laid too much emphasis for his taste on class distinctions. He also picked holes in the short-service recruitment scheme for constables, declaring that it was likely to defeat its own object. Far from eliminating corruption and efficiency, it might well increase the opportunities for both. Could it seriously be argued, he asked, that a dead-end job would attract a better type of recruit than at present? Would not the proposed ten-year engagement rather diminish a man's incentive and ultimately swell the army of unemployed?

Sir Russell Scott agreed with his subordinates that short-term recruitment must lead to "blind-alley employment." It would also tend to produce a less disciplined Force, not a better, by discarding men of long experience and reliability on grounds of age alone.

Trenchard stood up to this cross-fire of criticism without retreating an inch. There were, he pointed out, thousands of men and women already employed by the State in similar blind-alley jobs—" to add 500 or so in a year will be no great matter, and anyhow the ex-policeman won't find it hard to get work." The Receiver at Scotland Yard, Sir John Moylan, had detailed statistics which showed that "one in every four of the men who join now leave in any case before completing ten years." There was no escaping the figures. They were an oblique confirmation of the Commissioner's colloquial saying that "no amount of incentive will turn old men into young men."

There were repeated brushes of the sort. The atmosphere in the "Hush Hush" was charged at times with a thinly repressed tension which Gilmour, urbane and semi-apologetic, usually succeeded in lowering by moving the discussion to neutral ground. Rightly or wrongly, Trenchard suspected the Home Office advisers of being personally antagonistic to the scheme. He looked askance at Dixon and Newsam as fellow-conspirators who had prejudiced the issues and were intent on dragging the indecisive Russell Scott with them.

If this seems an unworthy construction for any Police Commissioner to put on the motives of men who were merely following standard practice in opposing him, it must also be said that relations between Scotland Yard and Home Office experts had perceptibly cooled since Anderson's departure about twelve months before. Trenchard thought that they carried caution to the limit of obstructiveness; they returned the compliment by deploring his strong-arm, secretive and often unconventional methods of procedure. His readiness to by-pass them and consult the Minister direct, then present them with some decision reached over their heads, was heavily frowned upon. Trenchard could not easily be reasoned with. They complained that his mind "resembled the jaws of a bulldog: once it closed on a solution he favoured, there was no moving him"—and this regardless of political hazards, precedents or the temper of public opinion. Like the bellman setting out to hunt the snark, he would merely repeat himself with greater emphasis as if to stress that what "I say three times is true."

Under a less adroit chairman than Gilmour, the "Hush Hush" proceedings might have ended in hopeless deadlock. But the Home Secretary's mind, as it happened, was made up; he accepted Trenchard's plans on their merits; and he was anxious to push on so that the Cabinet could ratify them and the necessary amending legislation be drafted. The need for speed was deemed as imperative as the need for secrecy. Before the end of March, the committee reported favourably to the Cabinet which formerly endorsed the proposals as they stood.

A "most secret memorandum," issued to each Minister as an easy guide to the Commissioner's detailed case for reform, served the Home Secretary well when he faced his colleagues. It provided him and them with an ingeniously balanced statement of the general reasons for and against the far-reaching changes contemplated. This had been drafted by Russell Scott, who set aside whatever private doubts he may still have harboured in the greater cause of public duty:

"It may be argued in some quarters not intimately acquainted with the facts that the Metropolitan Police are the pattern of what a police force should be, and that even if certain reforms are desirable the time is not opportune for the upheaval which Lord Trenchard's proposals will create. But I am satisfied that the application of these remedies cannot be safely postponed if we are to be able to rely on an efficient and loyal police force. . . .

"All these schemes of reform will be strenuously resisted by officials of the Metropolitan Branch Boards and the Police Federation as a whole. But it is equally certain that many members of the Metropolitan Police will welcome them, and their influence will tell in the final reckoning. There may be serious trouble, but I have little doubt that this can and will be avoided if only we are able to convince Parliament and public of the facts. . . ."

The objections previously raised by Dixon and Newsam in the "Hush Hush" sessions were not left out of the reckoning. Gilmour admitted that the college scheme for officers would probably be misrepresented as "a step in the direction of militarising the police service, and as an anti-democratic scheme based on class interests." The Cabinet, however, ought not be swayed by that. Sinister suspicions of the sort could easily be dispelled, "save from the minds of those so steeped in class prejudice that they see it everywhere, whether it exists or not."

In defending Trenchard's plan to recruit 5000 constables during the next decade on individual ten-year contracts, the Home Secretary appeared to be less at ease. Objections to this, he said, might be "more difficult to meet." What the Government and its supporters should reflect on, if tempted to reject the plan as socially unsound, was that "a wide field of employment would remain open to policemen who retired after ten years' service still active and young enough to earn their living." The Appointments Board which the Commissioner intended to set up would contribute to that end.

There was nothing defensive in Gilmour's attitude to the question of costs. Cash must not become a deterrent, he said, particularly at the beginning. Final estimates were being prepared by a joint group representing the Treasury, the Home Office, Scotland

Yard and the Government Actuary; but he could guarantee that there would be no extravagant expenditure: "even in existing conditions of economy," he argued, "no financial considerations should be allowed to stand in the way."

The Cabinet took only a perfunctory interest in most of these matters. They were more disturbed by the expressive language used by the Commissioner in various parts of his "book" to describe the shortcomings of the police; and they questioned the good sense of emphasising class distinctions in times of want, distress and unrest. Such terms as "the educated class" or "the officer class," of which he seemed unduly fond, should be pruned as far as possible. When the subject was debated in Parliament, similar restraint must be exercised by Government speakers. If it was necessary to show why the changes could not be delayed, it was equally necessary to avoid creating the impression that the London police had fallen from their high pedestal. Otherwise the confidence of the public might be undermined.

The Cabinet accepted Gilmour's suggestion that it would be opportune in the circumstances to let Trenchard hint at his difficulties and at the need for quick remedial action in his annual report for 1932. Then, if a condensed version of the police reforms were released as a White Paper a week after the Commissioner's report appeared, there would be every excuse for introducing the Bill and allowing time for its immediate passage through Parliament without having to answer Opposition charges of "panic legislation." Public interest would thus be held.

Gilmour was most insistent on the need for speed and faultless timing. He reminded his colleagues that successive Governments had shrunk from this problem for three-quarters of a century at least. "If it isn't undertaken by the National Government, it may be delayed indefinitely and fatally," he concluded.

Throughout the month of March, there was a renewed surge of clandestine activity among Trenchard's scribes at Scotland Yard. Finally, on 20th April, the cut and amended text of the "book" was delivered at the Home Office, along with the Commissioner's Annual Report. Trenchard sent two covering notes, one to Gilmour assuring him that all unnecessary uses of improper words like "class, officers and gentlemen" had been expunged, the other urging Russell Scott to "read the paper through and judge whether it is not really a brilliant effort, though you may think I ought not to say so."

The Commissioner was delighted with progress. Ramsay Mac-

Donald had honoured his pledge of a "free hand," his Cabinet colleagues jibbing only at the rough way in which Trenchard pushed his own beliefs and values. The impact on the public of the two documents, the Annual Report and the White Paper, descending one after the other with only a week's interval between, would probably be explosive, possibly dangerously so. Such was Gilmour's view; but Trenchard had fewer qualms. Otherwise it becomes difficult to account for his next move, an ingenious but quite uncharacteristic departure, which he took entirely on his own initiative and authority.

Trenchard may have sounded Gilmour before sending advance copies of his Report, with a set of gems collected from minutes of Police Federation meetings thrown in for good measure to illustrate what he understood by insubordination, to a select group of "the right people"; but there is not a scrap of evidence to suggest that he did this with the Home Secretary's consent.

For someone so mistrustful of publicity, he displayed resource and discretion in his approach. Perhaps an element of curiosity or even a dash of eleventh-hour uncertainty entered his calculations; but the impression conveyed by his action in imparting "hot" and heavily embargoed news to Barrington-Ward of *The Times*, Garvin of *The Observer*, Gwynne of the *Morning Post*, Camrose of the *Daily Telegraph*, John Buchan, then an outside contributor to the otherwise suspect *Daily Mail*, Sir Herbert Samuel, similarly engaged by the *News Chronicle*, and one or two other publicists of comparable standing, is an unmistakable impression of serene confidence in his own judgment. In giving these people virtually a ten-days' start on less favoured editors or proprietors, whose opinions were less worth sampling or whose appetite for pure sensationalism he had reason to deplore, Trenchard was taking no chances of a breach of trust.

The replies were much as he had hoped; nor was his extraordinary self-confidence misplaced; but his action would undoubtedly have caused collective heart-failure among senior civil servants at the Home Office had they had wind of it. One of them admitted to this writer that Trenchard's soundings in Fleet Street represented an "unprecedented" and "almost incredible" departure.

"The document will create a stir," commented Barrington-Ward. "The critics will find it hard to contest, and it points to inevitable action."

"You had to act," said Garvin. "I can see how this spirit of trade unionism (in the police) has risen to its present pitch. What-

ever else is done, amending legislation in this respect will become
a necessity."

"I am generally in full agreement," said Samuel.

"I congratulate you most warmly," said Gwynne. "You are
going to have a stormy passage." [11]

At least Trenchard knew how the orthodox journals would
react editorially, for the replies were without exception similar in
sentiment. Yet he eagerly devoured the extensive reports in the
Press as a whole on 3rd May, when his first annual report as Commissioner was released. With the exception of the *Daily Herald* and
the Communist *Daily Worker*, most of the national and provincial
dailies, as well as the leading weeklies, accepted the facts and
implications, some more reluctantly than others. Only the *Glasgow
Herald*, whose proprietor he briefed in person, put an unusually
shrewd finger on a tender spot, hinting at the underlying political
fears that had led first to Trenchard's appointment, and now to
these proposals for sweeping changes in the police system.

"It is not said in so many words that in a great emergency the
London police would act in such a way as to shatter public faith.
. . . But for the first time we have revelations which suggest a doubt.
. . . The only consoling reflection is that Lord Trenchard's fearless-
ness may save us from the actual experience."

In the spate of comment released by a very outspoken report,
the inspired hint of the *Glasgow Herald* passed almost unnoticed. It
was the unfriendly or uncomplimentary criticism which attracted
most attention. Herbert Morrison, for instance, writing in the
London *Star* as "an ex-policeman's son" well versed in the arts of
Government, central and local, advised the Cabinet to "think
again," and suggested that Trenchard would be doing himself and
the country a favour by getting rid of his "military complex." This
was mild stuff indeed compared with the bitter resentment expressed
in the House by Labour M.P.s. Under questioning, Gilmour stated
that a fuller version of the facts would be published at once as a
White Paper. The House, he promised, would have every opportunity to debate the issues. Legislation to alter the constitution of
the London Police would follow.

It was slightly too well timed for the taste of the Opposition.
A report, a White Paper, and now the threat of a Government Bill
rushed out, one after the other, in the space of a fortnight, could
scarcely fail to stir suspicions of "panic legislation." To what
sinister ulterior end? From 17th May, when the Metropolitan
Police Bill was presented, until 26th June when it secured its third

reading, speaker after speaker on the Labour benches pressed the Home Secretary to be less reticent about the underlying reasons for steam-rolling so controversial and revolutionary a measure through Parliament. Gilmour would not be drawn. With studied equanimity, he insisted that he had nothing to hide. The Bill was the thing. It must be discussed on its merits, clause by clause.

Those forty days of stormy debate were not without excitement or fitful anxiety for Trenchard. Prudently he gave the Distinguished Strangers' Gallery a wide berth. His name cropped up repeatedly in the House; despite repeated calls to order from the chair, it was usually taken in vain. The Opposition had no illusions about the author of this reactionary scheme which boded ill for British democracy; Trenchard was a diabolical figure who deserved to be impeached. There were certain aspects of the Bill which evidently disturbed even Government supporters; and once during the Committee Stage the Government narrowly averted defeat when the important short-term recruitment clause was passed by only eleven votes to eight. After that, the Conservative Whips were more assiduous, and any sceptics on the back benches were careful to leave their consciences behind them on the way to the division lobby.

The first two clauses of the Bill, empowering the Home Secretary to increase the number of assistant Commissioners at Scotland Yard from four to five and to lower the prescribed ages of compulsory retirement for senior officers, caused less commotion than the second two clauses barring membership of the Police Federation to the new ten-year recruits and to all officers from the rank of inspector upwards. A young Labour back-bencher called Aneurin Bevan was echoing the fiery but sincerely held sentiments of less eloquent colleagues in accusing Gilmour, " the least positive and most guileful" of Ministers, and therefore a suitable decoy for whatever nefarious plot the Cabinet had in mind, of giving the House inadequate information. Bevan was quite clear himself as to what the measure meant:

"It is entirely a Fascist development," he said. "It is to make the police force more amenable to the orders of the Carlton Club and Downing Street, if there is a disturbance. . . . I am not quarrelling with the Home Secretary or the Commissioner. I know that they want to do this and that they need to do it, but do let us recognise the reality of what they are doing and the reason why they are doing it. They want to militarise the upper hierarchy of the police force because they cannot trust the police force. . . .

[They] must have the janissaries of the State who can be relied upon to carry out the orders of the Government. . . ."

In less flamboyant language, misgivings of the same sort came from the Opposition front bench where Clement Attlee complained that "in not a single instance" had Gilmour "attempted to relate his remedy to an alleged defect" in the force. If the Home Secretary would not explain his purpose in curbing the Police Federation, Attlee could. It was "the desire to change the character of the force in the metropolis from a force that acts with the people and in sympathy with the people, and believes in the liberty of the people, to a force in the hands of the Home Secretary or the Government to use exactly as they please. It is not the danger from the higher types of criminals of which the right hon. gentleman is thinking, but the possibility of danger from the working class, and he wants a force to use against them."

The "hostility" of the Commissioner towards his men was mentioned by several critics. Others preferred to castigate the "rigidity" of the military mind. One Opposition member quoted from the King's Regulations of the R.A.F. to illustrate this last point:

"'A commanding officer will, by advice and kindly intervention, endeavour to promote a good understanding and to prevent disputes. He will discountenance any disposition in his officers to gamble or to indulge in extravagant expenditure—' And," interjected the commentator, "this is the best of all '—He will check any tendency among his officers to practical jokes.'

"That," he concluded, "is the world they live in, and the biggest practical joke that has ever been perpetrated upon Parliament is Clause 4." (The short-term scheme for constables.)

Re-reading the pages of *Hansard* to-day, one is left with an overwhelming sense of the cleavage of Parliamentary opinion along class rather than party lines. Whatever the need, the hour was ill-chosen for promoting new legislation which even appeared to create a special enclave of privileged and "superior people" in the one police force controlled by Parliament through the Home Secretary. Economic distress was still too widespread; mass unemployment and poverty had bred unrest, unrest this political rancour. It was the period of the hunger marches, of the dole, and of the hated "Means Test." The fear that a Government, National in name but now almost wholly Conservative in outlook and control, commanding an absolute majority of rare proportions, might go the way of Right Wing governments abroad, was as deeply embedded in the Opposition's subconscious mind as the fear of an unreliable police force was implanted in the Government's. Hitler had recently seized power in Germany. Mussolini had long consolidated his absolute authority over Italy. Oppression was rampant in Europe; and the shadows cast by the two dictators represented an intangible factor which should have been taken more into account when the Cabinet were considering a plan which seemed to touch, however indirectly, the freedom of individual citizens in times of great distress. It was a factor which Gilmour and other Government speakers unwisely chose to ignore as something beneath contempt, thus unintentionally helping to fix and harden the image of Trenchard as an "agent of reaction" rather than as a reformer to be judged in his own right.

One of the most thoughtful and dispassionate speeches at Westminster during the passage of the Bill was delivered by the late Home Secretary, Sir Herbert Samuel. In welcoming Trenchard's proposals, he offered Gilmour a line of defence which the Minister thought it better to disregard:

"The right honourable gentleman and others—I do not think he said it to-day—have spoken of a tendency in some countries in Europe to introduce Fascism as a substitute for Democracy. And it has even been suggested in connection with this measure that the police force might be perverted to be the instrument of some form of despotism. The real test of Democracy is in its efficiency. Even though measures may have to be taken from time to time which are unpopular with certain sections, unwelcome to certain classes, the real test of Democracy is whether a Democratic Parliament and a Democratic Government are willing to take those measures. . . .

"If we are ready to face some unpopularity now and then and here and there in order to secure efficient public service, our Democracy will be a success; if not, it will be a failure, and it is because Democracies have been a failure in their working that they have been superseded by other systems of government. . . ."

But Gilmour did not take up the cue that day or any other day. His efforts to narrow the field of debate were undoubtedly successful, but his success only aggravated the suspicion that the Government had something to conceal. It is right to add that many uncommitted onlookers with no political axes to grind took alarm; and the formation of the National Council for Civil Liberties in 1934 was a logical enough sequel. The view that Trenchard's reforms were part and parcel of a Right Wing policy of repression became fashionable with intellectuals and writers of the period as well as with Left Wing propagandists, and the Home Secretary's most glaring tactical omission was in letting that view gain ground unanswered. Gilmour foolishly tended to under-estimate its influence, even to despise it.

The one critic to strike a spark of responsive good humour in the Commissioner was George Lansbury, the pacifist Leader of the Opposition, who chose to concentrate on the alleged absurdities implicit in the reforms. He wanted a classless police force; and he could not see how it would help efficiency by bringing in a new officer *élite*:

". . . The Home Secretary talked about the methods of the modern criminal and said that in these days of science you have to deal with a more scientific type of criminal than ever before. Jack Shepherd was not a bad sort of cat burglar—at any rate he got away with it. . . . But nobody said it was the fault of the police force, and that it was necessary to call in the universities to redress the balance. To say that because criminals know a bit more to-day you must have 'varsity gentlemen to deal with them is too stupid for words."

The temptation to confront Lansbury and thank him for making a friendly speech was too strong for Trenchard. They met one evening at Westminster. The Leader of the Opposition stared at his visitor, puzzled and on his guard, when Trenchard congratulated him on a speech that had delighted him. It was not meant to be friendly, said Lansbury, only salutary. Would the Commissioner kindly explain what he was driving at?

"Certainly," said Trenchard. "You mentioned Jack Shepherd, didn't you?"

"Supposing I did?"

"Well that in itself was a great personal compliment."

"I'm afraid I don't follow you."

"It's quite simple. Jack Shepherd was an ancestor of mine. I always had a secret admiration for him, and I'm glad to see you sharing it in public."

Lansbury stared at him for a moment in astonishment. Then he burst out laughing. He was pleased at least, he said, that they had something in common after all.[12]

20. Police Administrator

While Press, politicians and public continued to argue the merits and implications of the changes at Scotland Yard, Trenchard moved about his domain with an easier mind. He believed that time would still the tumult outside; but there he was too optimistic. The Government had miscalculated badly in identifying the reforms as his. Controversial recommendations had appeared in the past over the names of experts; but for a Police Commissioner to receive carte-blanche to write his own and implement them at will was quite unheard of.

The Bill obtained its third reading in the Lords on 17th July, 1933, and almost at once Trenchard summoned delegates of the Police Federation to explain how the measure would affect them.

"You probably realise by now that I believe in frank speaking," he began. "I propose to speak quite frankly to-day. This is an official and confidential meeting." (He already had his eye on a man at the back of the room with a pencil and paper at the ready.) "What I say is not intended for publication in any newspaper." (Half-way through his speech he ordered the same man to cease scribbling and confiscated his notes.)

It was not his aim, he said, to block up "legitimate and ordinary channels for the ventilation of grievances"; but then "it was never intended that the Branch Boards themselves should do away with the usual channels through which grievances should be made known, that is through the men's officers to me. . . . I'm always ready to consider representations from you on matters that affect the welfare and efficiency of the force. If having made representations you are not satisfied, it is no part of your function to broadcast your views in opposition to those in authority."

He was aware, he said, that "men dislike being called upon for plain-clothes work." It was all very well for the Branch Board to let him know this, but not to "write and and dispute my decision."

There was another point: their use of language in wording

complaints was more appropriate to platform orators than to policemen. It could not be allowed:

"If you indulge in such cheap and disrespectful language— I MUST ASK YOU MEN AT THE BACK TO LISTEN—you lose the respect of those in authority and also the sensible and level-headed men in the force itself."

This being his first opportunity of addressing them since "the recasting of your constitution," and the last before officers withdrew from the Federation, he wished to rid their minds of certain misconceptions. There had been "wild and misleading" Press speculation about the compulsory early retirement of chief inspectors and superintendents, whose numbers fluctuated between a hundred and a thousand, according to the gullibility or hostility of the journals concerned. The vacancies, it was said, would be exclusively filled from graduates from the Police College. In case any of them had missed the official denial, he would repeat the true facts:

"Actually the number of vacancies at present is almost a dozen. And they will be filled by promotion within the force itself."

As to the additional higher posts sanctioned for the staff of the college, and for reinforcing the headquarters, districts and divisions:

"These, I hope, will all help promotion, and the resulting vacancies in the divisions will be filled from within the force. The senior men will not all come from within the force. . . . A little new blood will do us all good."

Trenchard gradually gained their interest as he explained how places in the new Police College at Hendon would be allotted. Not all were reserved for outsiders with the advantage of a good education.

"I mean to use up the latent talent amongst you. Ability and character will count as much as academic qualifications until then. But I must add, since I'm determined to hide nothing from you, that the number of outsiders will in the nature of things increase as time goes on."

Trenchard then mentioned two customs, each touching the pockets of his men, which he had abolished: private duties performed in public time at greyhound racing stadiums, football grounds and other places of amusement, and door-to-door ticket selling in aid of police charities, clubs and athletics:

"It is a remarkable thing about the police and the Press," he said, "that of all the letters of criticism I haven't had one on this subject of tipping policemen. The practice is non-existent in other forces. I don't blame you for it. It came into being here gradually.

It was fairly harmless on a small scale, but it is thoroughly bad when it reaches the gigantic proportions it has now. . . . I did not realise its size until I got the returns from the divisions. The change will have to be a gradual one."

He was grateful for the Federation's support in terminating the objectionable business of public ticket-selling. He respected their Joint Executive Committee for that. And he could promise them that the force would not suffer financially:

" Various friends of the force are helping to make good the loss of income, and the Government hope to lend a hand as regards capital expenditure when they can afford to."

He did not wish to rile them needlessly by dwelling on the almost inextricable financial muddle in which he had found most of their books. It was sufficient to tell them that he had assumed personal responsibility for reorganising their charities, canteens and athletic clubs. The so-called police "Provident Fund" was altogether more complicated. To this he did not even refer.

The shady accounts of the Provident Association had caused him deep anxiety while the threat of a police strike over the pay cuts had lasted. Aware that they lacked ready cash, he feared that the strike leaders might "borrow" from its funds, thereby exposing many innocent dependants to irreparable loss. Entirely on his own initiative, he had approached Sir Edward Peacock, a director of the Bank of England, for unofficial advice; Peacock gave him personal introductions to four leading businessmen in the City, including d'Arcy Cooper, the Chairman of Unilever; and each of these guaranteed him the sum of £30,000 to use as he thought fit. The danger that sent him cap-in-hand to Peacock in the first place had passed; but the credit was still available to draw upon; and Trenchard had every intention of letting the force benefit from this hidden windfall.

Business houses, banks and private individuals were meanwhile responding slowly to a "begging letter" which Trenchard had sent to the Press, inviting all who had formerly bought tickets or employed policemen to contribute just as generously in future to a new "Commissioner's Fund."

Unscrambling the ill-kept accounts of the "Provident" and one or two kindred funds had proved an unsavoury task. Trenchard was only incidentally concerned with the dishonesty of the bookkeepers; it was the innocent contributors he sought to protect, policemen and their relatives in tens of thousands, who had paid through the nose for inequitable benefits against death, ill-health or retirement instead of insuring themselves with established companies. Above all, he was determined to shield recruits from the pressure automatically brought to bear on them by officers to join a contributory scheme offering very dubious rewards.

A thorough examination of the fund since its inauguration in 1893 had confirmed Trenchard's suspicion that "if not actually dishonest, it was wide open to considerable abuse." The Home Secretary was promptly advised to act so that "present and future members of the force should be saved from the financial loss in which they would otherwise be involved," and Gilmour ordered an official inquiry by representatives of the Treasury, the Home Office and the Government Actuary's department. It would be many weeks before its work was done; but whether the Federation welcomed the intrusion or not, Trenchard felt certain that the average constable would one day thank him for it.

In shaking up men and institutions, Trenchard encountered passive resistance from dozens of senior officers, especially after uncovering substantial evidence of "graft" in high places.

"With regard to the attitude of the police," Trenchard informed the Home Secretary on 21st September, 1933, "the older men are still—as I said they would be—very sulky. Two of three superintendents who were told to go in six months' time have sent in their resignations to go in a month. So have one or two chief inspectors.

"It will be a good thing when they have gone, but it will be still better if I can only get in some chief inspectors who are gentlemen to keep an eye on what is happening. I have found out a good deal more since I saw you, and it is really most important that I should have some people I can trust in the districts."

Several C.I.D. officers had meanwhile over-reached themselves. They had been caught taking bribes. Trenchard referred to one of the more flagrant cases in his next letter to Gilmour, who was on holiday in Scotland:

"The superintendent I told you we were taking action against has been found guilty by the Discipline Board. Of course he has appealed to me. . . . It is a complicated case but at present, from what I have gathered, there is no doubt whatever about it. . . ."

He agreed with Gilmour that it was "difficult to get such a force clean after the last period of trouble and slackness." It would take time and luck to weed out all "wrong-uns," and the reconstruction of the force must not meanwhile be side-tracked.

"So many more things have just arisen," he wrote again early in October, "that I'm a little frightened that, owing to the fairly satisfactory steps we've taken in the C—— affair and the blackmail case, we shall have evidence coming forward in a torrent and we shall be overwhelmed with the amount of it. This I must try to check."

Less than a week later Trenchard returned to the same theme: "You may be interested to know of another piece of roguery. Norman Kendal, in charge of the C.I.D., says it's one of the worst cases he has known. The other night, at home, I was called up on the phone by a man called Watson who said he had been a notorious crook and that he was—to use his own language—being 'bled white' by certain senior officers of the C.I.D. In fact he was being blackmailed. My wife, who pretended to be the secretary, talked to him on the phone and we eventually fixed up a meeting between this man and Sir Francis Griffith, my new man here.

"With the information received, Kendal arranged a trap to be set for the senior officers whose names had now been given by Watson, and a few hours later we arrested a first-class detective-sergeant and a second-class detective-sergeant in company with this man who, after they'd had drinks together, handed over to the two detectives some money we had already marked and given to Watson. Watson vowed he had been paying money out like this for some six weeks.

"It is rather a horrible case because Watson is really, I fancy, living on money which is coming from unfortunate unemployed persons with very little means. The detectives must have known this. . . . I am now told by the Director of Public Prosecutions, and all my legal people that we cannot put the detectives in the dock. We can only dismiss them, as legally there is no offence we can convict them of in a civil court. . . . Though Kendal hopes there are no more like it, I feel there are more than we think. We just have not enough people to unearth them. . . ."

Conscious of the fact that Trenchard had not had a holiday for over two years, Gilmour suggested that the Commissioner should drop everything and join Weir and himself for some shooting in Scotland. It was an enticing idea, but Trenchard could not accept.

"I feel I ought not to go as I'm trying to race against time. Yet I get so bad-tempered unless I get away sometimes that I'm afraid I shall become impossible. I get rather disheartened never seeing anything finished, and I fear I shall not get finished for another year, if then. . . ."

He had, he admitted, begun to "poke about more actively" in

the closed shop of C.I.D. affairs; but the complications likely to accompany any drastic reform of that department deterred him.

"I rather agree with what was said on this subject by Moylan and Dixon before I came: namely, that nobody knew what anybody else did," Trenchard told the Home Secretary. "I think that was a fairly true criticism. I stopped the Moylan-Dixon inquiry [into the C.I.D.] because I found so many matters of greater urgency at the time, but when I wanted to find out anything about the C.I.D. I encountered the greatest difficulty in getting down to facts. . . . I still hope to make things right and I am putting Drummond on to help in the necessary reorganisation. I'm trying to carry the C.I.D. with me instead of superimposing new ideas on them, but it isn't easy. They've no experience of organisation of any sort or description."

The departmental machinery of Scotland Yard, which he had tightened up on arrival, was next on the Commissioner's list for a complete overhaul. Trenchard submitted his reasons to Gilmour in the same letter:

"This place has simply grown up with a lot of uneducated people doing really nothing to put it on a sound footing. Personally I am more than convinced that if I only had the courage to do so, I could safely knock off a thousand men, add 200 to the C.I.D. and have less crime. But the howl and the sulkiness would be awful if I did it like that. . . . I still get some amusing anonymous letters and even Christmas cards. These things are meant to be rude but are really amusing and keep the merriment going. . . ."

Scotland Yard itself, he freely admitted, "militated against good staff work." He had no space yet to spread wide his wings.

"Our accommodation, of course," he reminded the Home Secretary, "is beneath contempt compared with Berlin, Dresden, Vienna or New York. It is difficult to organise records properly if one only has a big room with all sorts of other business going on in it as well. . . ."

So firm yet discreet was Trenchard's method of exercising administrative control that few senior officers at headquarters realised the depths of his horror at the corrupt practices of individual members of the C.I.D. and uniformed branch. His gift for nosing out the facts and keeping them to himself, or, when disciplinary action had to be taken, confiding in only one or two close collaborators like Drummond or Kendal, proved an unmixed asset. Offenders were usually apprehended without warning. Yet his biographer has heard men

T.   X

who now hold some of the highest police posts question whethe
Trenchard did not exaggerate the amount of corruption prevalen
in the Metropolitan Force at a time when they themselves wer
novices. Allowing for his own lofty personal standards, and for hi
life-long belief that "nothing is worse than the corruption of th
best," these latter-day critics err in disallowing Trenchard credi
for being able to judge how far the rot had gone. He did not an
could not make an example of every delinquent; many did no
commit the unforgivable crime of being caught; and those wh
did represented only a fraction of the culprits.

"You can't measure corruption as exactly as you can measur
crime," he told his biographer. "But you can smell it, and you ca
prevent the occasions for it. I had time enough to deal only wit
the flagrant cases and to hope that the uncaught people woul
profit by the example I made of those to mend their ways."

It was probably just as well that Trenchard remained the targe
of Press criticism. He did not mind "helping to keep the cartoonist
in business." Nor did he care when M.P.s reproached or revile
him on petty issues, such as his alleged interference with the right
of Members to tip the policemen who served in the Commons
precincts. He would put out statements or corrections only when
truth or the public interest seemed to demand it; this he did, fo
instance, to refute an unfounded report in the *Daily Express* of a
plot to assassinate him outside Scotland Yard; or again when he
deemed it right to explain the circumstances in which a young
R.A.F. officer, Flying-Officer Fitzpatrick, had been wrongfully
arrested.

This case was unusual enough to provoke a storm of protest in
Parliament; being also a rare illustration of how erroneous suspicions
could arise on both sides, Trenchard felt that the public were fully
entitled to the facts. For the detectives who took Fitzpatrick into
custody genuinely believed that any man carrying a heavy bag
down a London street at half past three in the morning and refusing
either to account for his movements or to "come quietly" when
stopped, must be a thief, or worse. It was a sheer coincidence that
their suspect believed with equal conviction that he had fallen foul
of car bandits armed with forged police papers; so neither the
police nor their victim could be wholly blamed for the slight misunderstanding or the resulting violence. A handsome apology to
Fitzpatrick, and the simultaneous exoneration of the patrolling
plain-clothes man who apprehended him, stilled the clamour
quickly.

It would have been fatal for the force, and probably just as fatal for the Commissioner's plans, had any evidence of the squalor below the surface seeped into the light of day. Gilmour, who equally feared the consequences of disfiguring the public's absurdly romantic concept of a police force second to none in the world, solidly backed Trenchard in his campaign to clean it up quietly from within. The reforms were the best means to that end, their general unpopularity a reassuring sign that the average constable's integrity was unquestioned. The hoodwinking of Press, Parliament and the public seemed, in the circumstances, the lesser of two evils.

Opposition demands for a parliamentary inquiry into the condition of the force were refused; and the Government would not explain its refusal. Whether Gilmour did wisely to withhold information as completely as he did is debatable. His reticence certainly enabled the Commissioner to get on with his work; but, equally, it incited a critic like E. M. Forster, who was no respecter of reputations in his passion for personal rights, to declare that "our freedom to-day has more to fear from enlightened authoritarians like Lord Hailsham, Lord Lloyd or Lord Trenchard, than from Sir Oswald Mosley or Stafford Cripps."[1]

By drawing to himself the fire of such critics, Trenchard succeeded in drawing it off his men. Every reshuffle of senior officers he ordered, every list of new appointments he announced, was scrutinised and deplored as the latest example of his autocratic proclivities. He could count on fair treatment only from the few "responsible" papers; it had become almost too easy to anticipate the comments of the rest.

When in November, 1933, the rules for admission to the new Police College were published, those which excited most derision concerned "the dinner jacket suit, the four dress shirts and the patent leather shoes" which successful candidates would be required to bring. Trenchard took the ridicule in his stride. The lists for the entrance examination had to be closed early. Only a dozen vacancies were open to outsiders, yet 105 applied. Remembering how Peel's constables had been tricked out in blue swallow-tail coats, top hats and leather stocks, Trenchard could only suppose that aspirants for posts in the upper echelons of his reformed force were as immune as himself to inverted snobbery.

Lieutenant-Colonel Ramsay Halland, the Chief Constable of Lincoln, a man noted for his high sense of discipline and efficiency, was the Commissioner's choice for the post of Commandant. The instructors included a former member of the Indian Police Service, practical experts from both the C.I.D. and the uniformed branch of the force, and a civilian authority on law.

"Are you very sure about hydrostatics? Little things like Boyle's Law, and gaseous pressure, or the causes and effects of the Great War, or the broad features of the more important food plants? These things candidates must know and understand." So wrote one popular columnist of the day, possibly with tongue in cheek, about the un-policeman-like level of general knowledge expected of candidates competing for entry to Hendon in February, 1934.

The press bureau at Scotland Yard was encouraged by the Commissioner to feed Fleet Street generously with such titbits and to provide facilities for collecting its own. Yet because Trenchard's formal schooling had been so ragged, and he could still boast with only slight inaccuracy of "never having passed an exam in my life," he maintained a steady sense of proportion. Hendon would throw open a new career to talents of the most varied kind; it would mould character as well as develop brain-power. His promise to the Branch Board representatives that ambitious constables who took the trouble to apply would not be overlooked was fully honoured. In fact, of the thirty-two places in the first course at Hendon, twenty went to police applicants selected by panels of senior officers and exempted from the stiff entrance examination.

Three weeks before the Prince of Wales formally opened the college, on 10th May, 1934, the first cadets began their fifteen months' stint of intensive study and practical training (later extended to two years), which included six months on the beat as constables. The second intake was by then being slowly sifted from hundreds of fresh applicants; and the twenty-nine finally chosen entered the college in September, 1934. With an eye to his own conviction that education was a life-long process, never to be confused with cramming, erudition or mere precocity, the Commissioner again earmarked twenty of the twenty-nine college vacancies for his own rank-and-file.

The Times was being neither benignant nor condescending when it observed the day after the opening of the college in May:

"All will compete on equal terms for future promotion; and the prospects for the recruit are certainly improved by a system under which the necessity for bringing in distinguished military officers to fill the highest posts must soon disappear." The leader-writer was echoing the view of the Commissioner, as well as applauding his foresight. But Trenchard did not delude himself; "soon," he

new, was a relative term. Peering just a little way ahead, he could
admit to being more sanguine than would have been justifiable
only twelve months before. It might take twenty years for the
system to establish itself thoroughly. Provided it was left intact,
and graduates continued to leave Hendon as junior station inspectors
at the initial rate, the Metropolitan Police would have achieved the
status of a self-supporting profession, producing its own leaders, by
955.

As the present generation of senior officers retired, and they
were now being compulsorily retired far earlier than most of them
liked, there would be more room on upper rungs of the promotion
ladder. One day, a Hendon man would occupy Trenchard's chair
at Scotland Yard. That indeed had become a rational, thoroughly
feasible hope, the complement of Trenchard's older ambition of
surviving long enough to congratulate the first Cranwell cadet to
be appointed Chief of the Air Staff. Only political sabotage or
administrative cowardice could, in Trenchard's view, destroy the
rich promise of the scheme, now that it had been safely launched.
For he flattered himself also, wrongly as we shall see, that his short-
term system for constables, which appealed to the Cabinet in 1933
because it seemed to offer improved efficiency with inexpensiveness,
thus contributing towards Hendon's upkeep, would weather the
storm of early unpopularity and gradually consolidate itself.

Trenchard's mood, so stern and unyielding before, seemed to
mellow as the transition period grew more settled. He put himself
out, for instance, to persuade parliamentary critics that his reforms
deserved to be judged on their intrinsic merits. At his own expense
he lunched and dined "at least 200 M.P.s in small groups," according to his own calculations, during his last two years at Scotland
Yard. Again, through the hospitality and mediation of Lady Astor,
Trenchard met some of the most implacable in the informal atmosphere of her beautiful town house in St. James's Square. He could
almost bring himself to sympathise with their prejudices, rooted as
these mostly were in the economic hardship and social injustices of
the time. His candour won him respect, though he long remembered
the afternoon when Ellen Wilkinson stormed out of the room,
having argued with him for nearly two hours, shouting as she
slammed the door:

"You're the most dangerous man in England because you are
too just."[2]

What perhaps contributed most to Trenchard's mellowing outlook was the lightening of the immense physical and mental strain

which he had borne almost unaided for two long years. Among h
papers there is one which described the magnitude and complexit
of the Commissioner's job in such graphic terms that the Cabine
accepted his case for a substantial increase of senior staff withou
demur:

"Many a matter it is impossible for him to devolve even to hi
deputy," he wrote. "Apart from Ministers of the Crown, there ar
probably few, if any, servants of the Government who have to se
personally a greater number of important members of the public
often on difficult and delicate matters which they are unwilling t
discuss with anyone else. He has a large personal correspondence
he has to decide points of policy covering a wide range of statut
law; he has to hear all appeals against findings of Disciplin
Boards, interview senior officers at frequent intervals and take
personal part in the selection of men for higher promotions.

"Then there are nearly 200 police stations to be visited. Th
mere travelling to points fifteen miles from Scotland Yard occupie
a great deal of time and yet this is the only satisfactory way for hir
to see and understand police problems as they present themselve
to the constables and junior officers, and become familiar with th
men themselves and their point of view. Probably few except thos
who are directly concerned with the work of the Metropolitan o
some other large police force fully realise the scope which moder
conditions and the accumulation of legislation have imposed o
those responsible for administration."

From 12,000 officers and men in 1887, the force had expande
to 20,000; yet "the number of senior officers above the rank o
superintendent has only risen from ten in 1887 to thirteen to-day
This is the exact reverse of the process which may be noticed ir
well-conducted businesses. . . ."

Some fifty additional senior officers were authorised. The
included four deputy assistant commissioners, two chief con
stables, five superintendents and thirty-two chief inspectors. H
used them both to reinforce the weakened links between Scotland
Yard and the four police districts and to promote a more vigorou
campaign against crime with modern weapons.

Many of the newcomers had previously held commissions in th
services, a fact which was sourly noted by the critics. The new
comers, nevertheless, were only temporary keystones in the bridge
On them would fall the final duty of reorganising and stimulating
the force. When that was accomplished there would be no furthe
need for outsiders like themselves. The Commissioner interpose

these men as "safety valves" in positions where their influence and authority registered most quickly: in the districts, to steady the force; and at headquarters, to assist the four overworked heads of departments.

"Many matters have been neglected," he told Gilmour, "because of insufficient staff to deal with them. For instance, the introduction of wireless at headquarters, the organisation of transport, and the care of section-houses where policemen live." These section-houses were blots on the landscape, monuments to generations of official neglect. There was only one remedy: to reconvert some and gradually rebuild the rest.

"I would like to take you to see three or four of them when you return," he had written to the Home Secretary during the Christmas recess of 1933. "They really are a disgrace to civilisation, some of them. The canteens are in basements with practically no heating, and they are dark, smelly, dirty and worse almost than coal-cellars. Compared with the police quarters in most of the counties and small boroughs, they are amazing. In one case I came across six families with a communal bathroom. In another I came across a sub-divisional inspector in official quarters that had no bathroom at all. . . . It is hard to raise the status of the decent man if we do this sort of thing to them."

Public money was still the main obstacle to re-housing the police as it was to clearing the slums; but Trenchard's advice to Gilmour was simple:

"The Government will provide the funds if you dun them hard enough."

His well-worn axiom that "nice things make nice people" expressed a lifetime of experience. A man's physical environment could raise him to the heights or hasten his slide to the gutter; the squalor in which his policemen still had to spend most of their off-duty hours was a reproach which any self-respecting Government must wipe out, regardless of expense.

Trenchard won his point without argument. In threatening to devote half of the 1934 annual report to rehousing, Trenchard was not consciously issuing an ultimatum. He was merely underlining an unnecessary dilemma. Some Ministers appeared to resent his high-handedness; but the Cabinet let him have his way. Thus, the Commissioner's report for 1934, reviewing a year of change, looked also to the future. It was more or less evenly divided between an account of the new reforms and a survey of the wretched living conditions of the London police. And the warm response of the Press to his plans for erecting new section-houses confirmed his belief that the public cared as much as he did.

2

The Cabinet were taken aback early in 1934 when Trenchard began to show signs of restiveness. His understanding of the terms of service offered in 1931 was that his appointment would run for two years. Now that the two years were up, he had no desire to stay on longer than was absolutely necessary. Gilmour knew, as did Maurice Baring, T. E. Lawrence, and perhaps half a dozen friends in whom Trenchard occasionally confided, that the Commissioner took a grave view of the halt called on all forward defence planning and spending since 1931; but he refrained from saying so formally until 13th March, 1934, when he wrote to the Prime Minister:

"I have for some considerable time been thinking how and when I could resign the post I was asked to take in October, 1931. I do not want to comment on the work I have tried to do since I have been here. It will be for others to judge. . . . It will be remembered that when I became Commissioner the first cut in pay had been made, and the men were objecting to the imposition of the second cut (as well as objecting to the first). Further, at that time the state of discipline, in my opinion, could not be characterised in any other way than as extremely serious; also corruption was much too prevalent.

"Now I feel that my work is really completed, that is so far as it ever *could* be completed by me, let me summarise briefly what has been done:

"The second cut in pay was accepted, in spite of practically unanimous opposition from other police authorities as well as from the (London police).

"Better discipline and—in spite of the cuts—more contentment prevails.

"The extravagant activities of the Branch Boards of the Police Federation in the Metropolitan Police have been curbed, and the gross waste of official time stopped. Officers above the rank of inspector have been excluded from the Federation.

"The reconstruction of a wholly reorganised force with regard to divisional boundaries, stations, duties of officers, the system of

eats and patrols, etc., has been completed—and the way prepared
r completion of the telephone box system.

"The Police Act of 1933 has been passed, and the big reforms
authorised as regards recruitment to higher posts and the short-
rvice scheme have been put into operation. . . .

"The system under which police are employed and paid by
rivate persons in their own time is to cease in a month or
vo.

"My office has been entirely reorganised. A new Organisation
epartment has been set up, and matters such as wireless, transport
nd welfare placed under special officers. And—perhaps the most
volutionary of all—Scotland Yard is at last to have a scientific
boratory. More than fifteen officers have been brought in to
rengthen the headquarters and district staffs.

"A legal department is about to be introduced.

"The District Officers—introduced over sixty years ago—have
t last been given the status and the staff to enable them to act as
n effective link between Scotland Yard and the divisions.

"The state of jealous rivalry and non-co-operation which has so
ng existed between the C.I.D. and the uniform branch (somewhat
milar to the mutual ignoring of each other by the Prefecture and
ie Sûreté exposed by the Stavisky case in France) is gradually
eing put to an end, and the two branches integrated into one har-
ionious whole. Among the measures taken for this purpose is the
ppointment of crime chief inspectors in each division.

"Motor transport has been reorganised, and a new wireless
heme providing a system of continuous wireless control throughout
ie (London area) is about to be put into operation.

"The problem of police canteens has been dealt with, and a new
rganisation providing for proper responsibility and control will
iortly become effective.

"The Provident Fund, a most improvident arrangement which
as heading for financial disaster, is in process of being placed on a
roper footing.

"Drastic changes are required as regards conditions in section-
ouses. . . . These are well under way, but their realisation is a
uestion of money and new buildings, and therefore of time. A start
, however, being made this year.

"The Metropolitan Police Athletic Association has been put on
sounder basis and each of the four districts has now been provided
ith a good sports ground and buildings (two of them suitable for
ances and concerts).

"A reorganisation of the special constabulary on a mor
economical and efficient basis has been sanctioned.

"The Commissioner's Fund has been placed on a sound basis
and I hope it will have a capital of at least £35,000 and promise
of from £6,000 to £7,000 for the next two years. The latter sum
may not all be required as income and this, I hope, will enable th
capital to be increased."

It was an imposing list of changes, and Trenchard felt it righ
to disown any intention of claiming the credit.

"I don't want the above summary," he went on, "to be read a
meaning what a lot I think I have done because I know quite we.
how much was done by those who assisted me in the general wor
of reorganisation. . . . It seems to me that I shouldn't be letting th
Government or the Home Secretary down if I asked to be relieve
of my office at the end of this year.

"A large number of the changes will only achieve their full resul
in about twenty years' time, and as it is impossible for me to remai
here for much longer than another three or four years—even if th
Government wanted to keep me—it appears to me infinitely pre
ferable that I should retire at the end of 1934. There will have t
be a general election in 1935 at the latest. It would be impossib
for me to resign just before it, and probably very difficult to do s
just after.

"I feel also that my interests and my keenness now lie else
where. I am very interested in the question of Imperial Defence—
not that I want to make speeches, but I want to take a more activ
part than I can at present. I feel very strongly that this is a questio
of really national importance. . . ."

The Cabinet, however, were not in the least anxious to releas
him. And there were two reasons, or excuses, which enabled ther
to hold him. The first was the harder to rebut: the Cabinet coul
suggest nobody to succeed him. This might have flattered the vanit
of another man, but it did not move or impress Trenchard, wh
wondered in later years how far the Cabinet's calculations wer
affected by the second and more cogent reason for detaining hin
one which was never openly admitted to exist, namely the desire
Baldwin, Chamberlain and MacDonald to spare themselves th
trouble of having to answer his public criticisms of their neglect
the fighting services.

According to his biographer, Professor Keith Feiling, Chan
berlain, an exacting student of administrative competence, ha
nothing but admiration for the Commissioner's thoroughness i

cleaning the Augean stables of the Metropolitan Police"; but
Chamberlain was not yet interested in or concerned about national
defence. He would, so Feiling admits, have liked to turn Trenchard
loose in the distressed areas, where a planner of resourcefulness and
insight was needed. Had such a post been offered him, Trenchard
would certainly have rejected it. It was not offered him, as Chamberlain's biographer indirectly implies, because of the misplaced
odium surrounding the very name of Trenchard. This factor of
unpopularity, added to his known dissatisfaction with the Cabinet's
negative defence policy, stiffened their determination not to re-
employ him elsewhere.

Once again, as in 1931, when Ministers alone seemed unlikely
to convince him where his duty lay, King George V succeeded
effortlessly. Trenchard's respect for the sovereign's disinterested
judgment bordered on blind veneration. It was a thing apart from
allegiance to the throne as such. Both nature and training predisposed him to accept the least inclination of the royal will as a cate-
gorical command; and the King's express wish on this occasion for
the complete rehabilitation of "my police," as he habitually referred
to the Metropolitan Force, proved decisive. It is not improbable
that the Cabinet, recalling how promptly Trenchard had responded
to that earlier appeal from the King in 1931, readily fell back a
second time on the same slightly flattering manœuvre to retain his
services. The documents are not specific on the point. But,
prompted or not, the King did dissuade him, during an audience
at Buckingham Palace in the late spring of 1934, against leaving
Scotland Yard for at least another twelve months.

One consideration which weighed with the King was the Royal
Wedding which had already been arranged for the end of that
year. His Ministers, he said, were still rather nervous of crowds.
London would be full of them for the marriage of the Duke of Kent
to Princess Marina of Greece; and the security problem would
require delicate handling. Beyond that hung the unsettled question
of celebrating the Silver Jubilee of the Royal Accession. That would
not be until May, 1935; but the Cabinet appeared uncertain
about the propriety of ceremonial rejoicing in a period of economic
distress. Here again the hazards of assessing the popular mood and
of controlling street crowds in the capital would arise. The King
asked Trenchard to reflect carefully before finally making up his
mind. The clear indication of the royal will was compulsive:
Trenchard assented to stay.

The King and his household had learnt of late the value of the

Commissioner's guidance in curtailing visits or cancelling engage
ments whenever safety or common prudence demands this.

Trenchard's working rule was unpretentious; and nine time
out of ten it proved reassuringly effective: "It's better to appl
your sanctions or your force in advance than by way of suppressio
when it is too late."

His "intelligence reports" to the King were detailed yet succinc
And it is hardly surprising that the Sovereign had come to respec
the Commissioner as exceptionally adept at shepherding large an
potentially violent crowds.

"I do not want to be in any way an alarmist," ran a typical not
to Wigram, in February, 1934. "The Hunger Marchers are due t
arrive in London on either Thursday the 22nd, or Friday the 23r
February. . . . If I might make a suggestion I think it would b
best for the King and Queen to have no public or semi-publi
engagements during that week. . . ."

Apprehensive as Ministers undoubtedly were about maintainin
public order, Trenchard found the Cabinet extremely reluctar
to curb the activities of British Fascists. As early as October, 193
when he suggested to Gilmour that the "wearing of uniform
ought to be banned, the Home Secretary "took note" but di
nothing. Eight months later, Trenchard returned to the subject:

"The position," he stressed, "has become more serious. . .
There is no doubt that the wearing of uniform is in itself provocativ
and that this and other militaristic methods adopted by the Fascis
are a great stimulus to Communism. Since 1st May this yea
there have been many instances of Fascist meetings being interfere
with by Communists but none of Communists being interrupted b
Fascists. This will go on as long as the Fascists are allowed to g
about in uniform; and if it is not stopped, then I say that clash
between police and Communists are inevitable and may develo
into grave riots."

A Private Members' Bill, introduced by Commander Lock
Lampson, to prohibit the wearing of uniforms for political purpos
had recently been thrown out by the Government, to Trenchard
lasting regret. He now submitted to Gilmour the translation of
new Swedish decree which avoided the technical ambiguities o
Locker Lampson's approach by "making the organisation of an
thing in the nature of a private political army an offence again
the law." He also asked the Home Secretary for the necessar
power "to enter public meetings when necessary" and to "disban
processions of persons whose declared intention is to break up

political meeting." Almost a year after his original warning to the Government, Trenchard wrote bluntly that "if nothing can be done to stop the Fascists," he would have to ask for more policemen —and "this would entail considerable expense both to the rate-payers and the Exchequer."

He had to deploy nearly 7000 officers and men, more than a third of his entire force, to prevent the danger of large-scale dis-orders in Hyde Park on 9th September, 1934, when rival Fascist and Communist rallies were held within hailing distance of each other. Apart from this exceptional instance, he had been obliged, since 1st January that year, to employ nearly 3000 police at 570 Fascist meetings, relieving them of "their principal duties of pre-venting crime and street accidents," for the purpose. What Trenchard particularly resented was the unfortunate but unavoid-able impression created "among anti-Fascists that Sir Oswald Mosley's semi-military organisation is being permitted to develop under police protection." For the Communists did not miss this perfect opportunity of enhancing the respectability of their move-ment by acquiring the sympathy or allegiance of sensitive people who, but for the growth of anti-Fascist feeling, would probably have given neither.

The Government were unmoved by Trenchard's protestations. Not until several months after his departure, in 1936, was legis-lation brought in; and even then the Public Order Act did little to ease the difficulties of the police. Such sloth and drift did Trenchard's name little good. For it enabled the Left to persist in blackening him as a military reactionary of clandestine Fascist leanings.

In his dealings with the Palace, Trenchard avoided the error of smothering the Royal family in unwanted solicitude. The King, on the other hand, evidently did enjoy pelting him with comments and occasional suggestions, notably on smaller matters which occasionally escaped the Commissioner's attention in the press of bigger business.

Three examples out of many may serve to show that little escaped the Royal scrutiny, particularly where the least hint of lax or indecorous behaviour offended the Sovereign's somewhat stiff susceptibilities.

Drawing Trenchard's notice to an "appalling article" in the *Sunday Dispatch* of 24th July, 1932, with lurid descriptions of "the Gay Life, and Mad Car Races and Fox Hunting at 3 a.m.," Wigram passed on the message:

"His Majesty hopes that none of these foolish pranks are now the order of the day under your régime."

On another occasion, the King invited the Commissioner to explain what had induced one of the most respectable of British banks to permit a film company "to use their premises at Twicken-ham to make a film of a bank raid." This, in His Majesty's opinion, was an incomprehensible occurrence; any film produced in such authentic surroundings " might have a demoralising effect on the youth of the country." Trenchard at first disowned all knowledge of the circumstances; then, on further inquiry, he discovered to his annoyance that Scotland Yard had actually sanctioned the shoot-ing, though only indirectly. The Traffic Branch, after studying the film company's request "from the sole point of view of possible obstruction," had, he admitted, been "very stupid" to raise no further objection. It was too late to undo the mischief now, but he could assure the King at least that "I am doing what I can to prevent the film being publicly exhibited."

Then there was the extraordinary incident of the woman in the bathing dress. Queen Mary, so Wigram informed Trenchard, "was driving in the Park about opposite Knightsbridge Barracks when the apparition appeared." The King was aggrieved. He instructed Wigram to approach Scotland Yard at once and find out whether existing orders and regulations would enable the Com-missioner to deal firmly and promptly with ladies who walked public thoroughfares improperly, if not indecently, dressed.

"Would you tell His Majesty," Trenchard retorted with a touch of tartness, "that it is very difficult nowadays to say what kind of female dress is or is not indecent. It seems to me the best way to deal with the practice should it become extensive, would be to get the Office of Works to make a Parks Regulation saying that bathing costumes are not to be worn outside the [Serpentine] bathing enclosure."

3

Veneration of the King might lead the Commissioner to put away private ambition, but not to mistake royal officiousness with infallibility when such matters of taste were called to his attention. There was nothing subservient in Trenchard's attitude to a monarch whose stern feelings were so easily shocked, just as there was nothing lax in his approach to a Cabinet more concerned with what was expedient than with what was necessary to revitalise the Metropolitan Police. Trenchard's instincts were those of a latter-day Marcus Aurelius. Never at a loss for means to enforce standards which he deemed proper to public life, he served as keeper of the public conscience where the conduct of his own men was concerned.

It is disputable whether the Government would have offered Trenchard so free a hand in the first place had Ministers not feared for their own authority and for the maintenance of public order. The difficult circumstances of the day alone induced them to support him through thick and thin, whenever expediency dictated.

The corollary was perhaps just as inescapable. When the time came for Trenchard to hand over to a Commissioner less firm than himself and more amenable to organised grumbling from below, Ministers were readier to question the intrinsic value of his basic reforms and gradually to undo them. In a later section the technical excuses produced for undermining both the short-service system of recruitment and the Hendon College scheme will be briefly analysed.

There was little Trenchard could have done during his last two years as Commissioner to delay the reaction which gradually set in after his resignation. He could hardly have prevented it unless he had been prepared to spend the rest of his life at Scotland Yard. To that extent, the many subsidiary changes he introduced in 1934 and 1935 were robbed of their full effectiveness in his eyes. For Trenchard's primary aim as Commissioner was to renovate the spirit of the force. Only when that was accomplished did he seek to place the best technical weapons at its disposal so as to make life harder for the criminal. The main changes he introduced were referred to in his tentative letter of resignation to the Cabinet early in 1934, part of which has already been quoted; some of these must be studied more closely. Many of the technical deficiencies in the equipment of the force came to light during his first year of office; a few needed running repairs; but only in his last eighteen months as Commissioner could the rest be implemented.

When his two major reforms had become law, Trenchard completed his streamlining of the departmental work at headquarters. Recruiting was transferred to the administrative branch in 1933, and the new Organisation Department was further strengthened to handle a variety of schemes for the greater mobility and efficiency of the force.

The most outstanding were those concerned with wireless and

transport. What Scotland Yard lacked was not cars or drivers when Trenchard came but an organising brain to direct them Until 1931, control had been left almost entirely to the engineers and maintenance men, a drawback which Trenchard mentioned in his first annual report.

Nearly two years went by before he appointed an ex-army transport expert whom he attached to the Organisation Department with the rank of chief inspector. The jurisdiction of this specialist stopped short of buying, selling or repairing the police cars actually on the roads; these matters, Trenchard decided, were for the men who drove and used the cars.

From October, 1934 onwards, all motor vehicles were placed under the control of the new deputy assistant commissioners in charge of London's four police districts, each of whom had a transport specialist added to his staff. These four men and their controller at Scotland Yard became "the pivots" of a system which increased the mobility of the force to a spectacular degree. Not content with the views of his own transport experts, the Commissioner sometimes went outside for the best independent advice obtainable. For example, he consulted Sir Malcolm Campbell, the distinguished racing motorist and current holder of the world land speed record, who agreed to test every police driver individually before recommending practical methods of improving their skill at the wheel. Campbell reported in due course that "a properly equipped school for instructing drivers is overdue"; Trenchard at once acted on the recommendation. A training school was established in November, 1934, next door to the new Police College at Hendon. Tuition began the following January, and before the end of 1935, when the Commissioner retired, 378 officers and men had satisfied the examiners and could pride themselves on being among the finest drivers in the country.

Alongside the transport section at Scotland Yard, a wireless branch was formed during the same period.

On 31st January, 1934, Trenchard informed the Home Secretary:

"The flying squad cars have been fitted with wireless for a considerable time (about twelve years), and early in 1933 it was decided to extend the system to the Q cars and to a number of traffic patrol cars. The results achieved have made it perfectly clear that the employment of a number of cars fitted with wireless receivers and centrally controlled is the best—if not the only—answer to the activities of criminals who rely on motor cars, generally stolen, for reaching and escaping from the scenes of their crimes. . . ."

The telephone box system, inaugurated before Trenchard's time but greatly extended under him, had the same broad object of preventing crime by improving communications; but the Commissioner had no doubts whatever as to the superiority of wireless. "Obviously far more rapid results can be achieved by it," he told Gilmour.

Until 1934, the installation of sets was necessarily experimental; official backing and funds were necessary to cover a city as huge and congested as London. The Home Secretary watched the results of Trenchard's "pilot scheme" before committing himself. He was swayed by many such cases as the following:

"On the 15th January," Trenchard wrote, "a car reported stolen at Hyde Park Corner at 11.50 a.m. was seen at Hammersmith within fifteen minutes and reported. It was chased and stopped and four men were arrested. On 20th January, after a message sent out from Richmond had been intercepted, another car was stopped and the criminals were arrested in seven minutes."

The Commissioner stressed that "the actual number is not the important point. Once it is known among the criminal fraternity that movement on the roads in an identifiable car is a risky business, this type of crime will be checked."

Wireless development, like transport, had been languishing in the hands of a few technical specialists, "with no one on the police side to control its operation and study its application for the prevention and detection of crime." So, in December, 1933, Trenchard installed another Chief Inspector at Scotland Yard to advise the Organisation Department on the practical uses of wireless. Three months later the Commissioner's Office took over from the Receiver the routine business of training wireless operators. A school was prepared and opened next door to the driving centre at Hendon. Most important of all, steps were taken to create the permanent "Information Room" at Scotland Yard.

This world-famous institution, as originally conceived by Trenchard, was designed to serve "as a clearing house for the receipt of messages from all sources, principally relating to preventable crime." The entire Metropolitan district was carefully divided into fifty-two wireless areas by day, thirty by night, with a car on patrol in each throughout the twenty-four hours; and messages received in the Information Room could be transmitted to the cars in a matter of minutes. Simple in conception, the Information Room was one of Trenchard's most ingenious contributions to checking car thefts and smash-and-grab raiders.

Because he knew that ultimate success would depend on public co-operation, he strove from its inception in June, 1934, to rouse interest in it by issuing regular summaries of "victories obtained." Within six months he could assure Gilmour that "there's an increased feeling in the whole force, including the foot policeman on his beat, that wireless is helping us to prevent and detect crime, in a new way."

The misuse of men and man-hours had caused Trenchard in 1931 to speed up the inquiry then being carried out by Byng's rudimentary "Ideas Branch." The final evidence was invaluable. It enabled Trenchard to cut down the size of the force slightly by altering beats and local boundaries. His new rule that such questions should be systematically reviewed every two or three years was allowed to lapse after his departure in 1935.

The inquiry incidentally disclosed something else, namely Scotland Yard's "primitive methods" of compiling and using statistics. It was an axiom with Trenchard that statistics had a "vital part to play in the work of every department." He therefore decided that a new branch, equipped with all modern facilities, should be instituted to serve every other. An outside specialist was appointed early in 1932 to reorganise such records and equipment as existed.

The *Daily Crime Telegram*, providing all districts with the incidence of lawlessness throughout London, was an innovation, small but far-reaching, which followed the many visits Trenchard paid to police stations during his first six months as Commissioner. He often noticed how "out of touch" the majority of local officers were. The telegram seemed to him a simple method of keeping everyone abreast of criminal activities. It was started in April, 1932; and daily graphs showing the local fluctuations became the rule in all stations.

Again, on looking into existing crime statistics and discovering that "most of the figures didn't add up at all," he cross-examined individuals until he found the reason. It lay in the *Suspected Stolen Book*. For many years, it appeared, particulars of cases where it was presumed impossible to establish that a crime had been committed had been dutifully entered in this book. It was, to his mind, a source of muddle and a device which encouraged sloth by fostering the pretence that suspected crimes need never be followed up. Trenchard simply abolished the book in October, 1932, decreeing that *all* cases, however obscure, must henceforth be treated as crimes, and that missing goods should be regarded as "property lost." Inevitably the crime rate began to soar to its true height; and in explaining why this had happened, Trenchard drew a distinction in his annual report for 1933 between crimes which could be prevented by police action, such as breaking and entering or bag snatching, and crimes which could be dealt with only after the event, such as murder, fraud or embezzlement. From 1933 until his retirement, preventable crimes tended to decrease, detectable crimes to increase, another broad indication of rising police efficiency.*

A third innovation, deriving partly from his R.A.F. experience, was the decision to install a map-room at Scotland Yard early in 1933. The places where different types of crime occurred were marked with coloured flags and pins; his own staff and officers from the Districts and Divisions were encouraged to visit Headquarters to scrutinise, commit to memory, and reproduce in similar form, at local level, a complete picture of London's crime pattern at any given moment.

The C.I.D. was overlooked by Trenchard only in the sense that he under-estimated its inner powers of resistance to reform. Certainly, on paper, the changes he introduced were thorough-going enough. At headquarters, the chief constable in charge of crime was freed from administrative distractions by the appointment of a chief inspector to handle routine questions of discipline, promotion, etc. In the divisions a new type of officer, the chief inspector (crime), was brought in to co-ordinate the duties of the uniformed and plain-clothes men. With a single list of officers from which to draw, Trenchard hoped gradually to break down the "professional barrier of jealousy" that existed between the detectives and the rest. By increased interchangeability, there would be less friction and fewer opportunities for graft. It cannot be said that this hope was realised; for his reforms began to "take" only after his departure; and they did not touch the sublime faith of senior C.I.D. officers in their own exclusiveness as specialists. Beginners who entered the department under the new dispensation were not welcome. Some stayed; but none climbed easily or high. And it is instructive to note that few Hendon men, privileged as these were

---

* The official figures show that in the two years from mid-1933 to mid-1935 preventable crime in London fell by nearly 20 per cent. In the six months to June 30, 1933, 23,740 preventable crimes were committed.

"	"	"	Dec. 31, 1933, 22,335	"	"	"
"	"	"	June 30, 1934, 21,813	"	"	"
"	"	"	Dec. 31, 1934, 19,103	"	"	"
"	"	"	June 30, 1935, 18,400	"	"	"

in starting half-way up the promotion ladder, ever reached the top
of the C.I.D.

Trenchard's last step to modernise the machinery of his own
office was the introduction of a solicitors' branch, so ending the
quaint anachronism which had enabled an outside firm to transact
Scotland Yard's legal business since 1870. In May, 1934, one of
the Inland Revenue's legal advisers was permanently attached to
the Commissioner; eight months later the newcomer's take-over
proposals were approved first by Trenchard, then by the Home
Office.

"I've had a great meeting with Wontner's" (the outside legal
firm in question), Trenchard notified Gilmour in January, 1935.

"The three partners came to tell me how hardly they had been
used. . . . I pointed out to them what a lot they had got out of us
in the past, and that clients could choose their advisers or make
any changes without having to pay compensation. . . . I think they
left the room very surprised and feeling that they really had no
right to ask for anything."

The sixty-five-year partnership between the Yard and Messrs.
Wontner and Sons of Bedford Row was dissolved in April, 1935,
when an *ex gratia* payment of £3,500 was made and posts in the
legal branch were offered to all but two members of Wontner's
staff.

It was with the future clearly in mind that the Commissioner
promoted the scheme on which he set perhaps the greatest store for
"improving the scientific side of crime detection" in London.
Because he read widely and never let slip opportunities of "picking
the brains" of outside experts, Trenchard was determined not to
let Scotland Yard fall further behind equivalent Police Headquarters abroad in the forensic study of crime. In Paris, Berlin and
New York, the police were already equipped with their own medico-
legal laboratories and "some provincial forces in Britain were
already developing along the same lines"; yet the founding of a
similar laboratory in London had never before been seriously
considered. The Metropolitan Police depended entirely on the
services of Home Office or even on private pathologists, analysts and
chemists.

After consulting such eminent authorities as Lord Dawson of
Penn and Sir Bernard Spilsbury, Trenchard informed Gilmour
early in 1934 that he wanted to set up his own forensic laboratory
"as a definite part of the organisation of this force." The scientist
in charge would deal with actual cases, carry out research, lecture

at Hendon College and Peel House, and "educate the force as a whole to look at problems with a more scientific eye." He would therefore need the assistance of a junior doctor and a chemist.

The Home Secretary endorsed the request; but it proved hard to find suitable applicants. Forensic medicine was less well developed as a subject than Trenchard expected. When a highly qualified nominee of Lord Dawson's declined the appointment, Trenchard decided to start with a young scientist rather than risk not starting at all. In October, 1934, after being "vetted" on the Commissioner's behalf by the Deans of the principal London medical schools, Dr. James Davidson, of Edinburgh University's Pathological Department, became director of the new laboratory.

Trenchard's ulterior motive in sounding the best medical opinion was to stimulate the interest of the profession; his hope was that the study of medical jurisprudence would eventually be recognised, and that a central institute supported by leading doctors, by the universities and by the Government, would help Britain to overtake other countries in this specialist field.

At the formal opening of the police laboratory, on 10th April, 1935, Lord Atkin, one of a notable company of legal authorities present, insisted on the importance of a national medico-legal centre in London. Gilmour, who replied, took him up on the point. The Government, he said, had agreed to set up a permanent committee, such as Trenchard had been advocating, to advise on ways and means of putting the scientific study of crime on a proper footing.

It was a highly influential committee. Trenchard was its chairman, Atkin its vice-chairman, and its members included Lord Dawson of Penn, Sir Bernard Spilsbury, Sir Frank Smith of the Department of Scientific and Industrial Research, and Sir Russell Scott of the Home Office. Its subsequent fate remains a sad commentary on official lassitude. In 1936, the committee issued its first interim report and unanimously recommended the immediate founding of an Institute of Forensic Medicine. The Government was asked to decide forthwith on the principle of the scheme. The question of finance was not openly mentioned, though Trenchard told Sir John Simon, Gilmour's successor, that this was "the crux of the problem."

For twelve months more the Baldwin Government slept soundly on the report; and by December, 1937 (Sir Samuel Hoare having meanwhile taken over from Simon), Trenchard and his fellow-members of the advisory committee were growing short of patience:

"I have written to the Home Office, and called them up on the telephone several times lately to know what is going to be done about giving us an answer," Trenchard informed his colleagues. "When I told Hoare that it was not acceptable to us that no financial assistance could come from the Government he asked me to leave the answer over for a time. Well, I have left it over, and in spite of repeated warnings that we might really all feel it was not worth going on with, all I can get out of them is 'Oh, wait a little longer.' "

It was not the best moment to dun the Government for money. The rearmament programme had, by now, virtually extinguished any lingering hope of an official grant. Hoare was unable to commit a Cabinet still undecided on the principle of a forensic centre as a useful institution. In July, 1938, the committee adjourned *sine die*, a gesture which in theory at any rate left the door ajar for some future Government to reconsider the project. It is only fair to add, by way of epitaph, that no Government since has wasted any serious thought on it.

4

Trenchard's success in imposing a greater degree of organised control than ever before on the campaign against crime was the summit of his administrative achievement as Commissioner. Some policemen might acknowledge privately that "the Chief isn't as black as he's painted." Many thought of him as hard but just, inviting respect rather than affection. Yet none could deny the marked improvements he brought to their living and working conditions.

The Federation's distrust was only increased by the knowledge that Trenchard seldom put a foot wrong. His delving into the murky affairs of the "Provident Fund" has been mentioned previously. A simultaneous scrutiny of the accounts and management of police canteens, through a special committee he set up for the purpose in 1933, was equally systematic and led to objections from officials of the Joint Executive Committee of the Branch Boards, who disliked the reorganisation plan as too sharp a break with "tradition." That tradition, it should be said, left the Commissioner personally liable for any financial deficiency, and with no say whatever in the choice of representatives on the central body which ran the canteens in London. The Joint Executive Committee officially complained to Gilmour; the Home Secretary upheld the Commissioner.

The canteens badly needed attention. Many were in basements, few had facilities for cooking or serving hot food in comfort. When his own Board of Management took over in August, 1934, Trenchard obtained Gilmour's permission to include new canteens in his general rebuilding programme.

In November, 1934, the Commissioner was indignant on hearing that the question of rehousing the police would not be mentioned in the King's Speech at the opening of the new session of Parliament.

"I cannot understand this," he wrote to the Home Secretary. "I fear as a result that my position here will become impossible. . . . Could you get the Bill mentioned in the Speech, or a definite promise in the debate that the Police Bill will be introduced during this new session and soon after the New Year?

The original oversight was remedied. A measure authorising Moylan, the Receiver of Scotland Yard, to extend his borrowing powers by nearly £4 million over a ten-year period to construct or renovate section-houses, married quarters and police stations, was presented to Parliament early in 1935, receiving the Royal Assent the following April. The first two reconstructed section-houses were ready for occupation by the end of 1935, together with a new married block in Chelsea and a new station at Putney. Rearmament and the Second World War caused Trenchard's programme to be shelved indefinitely. To-day, over a quarter of a century later, it has still to be completed.

In point of time and significance, Trenchard's first intrusion into the financial affairs of the force occurred in 1932, when he banned the sale of tickets for bazaars, dances, raffles, concerts, athletics and dinners in aid of Police Charities. Between £15,000 and £20,000 was raised annually in this way; and if every penny had been used as intended, Trenchard would still have disapproved of a system which, as he told Gilmour, "lent itself to grave abuse."

In fact he found that substantial sums had unaccountably disappeared at various times because the funds were in the hands of "small and irresponsible bodies of police" who, to say the least of it, seemed to have been careful only in covering up their tracks.

To provide a permanent alternative source of revenue, he founded the Commissioner's Fund, which was registered as a Charity, with himself, Drummond and Howgrave-Graham as trustees. A group of anonymous financiers, bank directors and business men guaranteed him a minimum of £10,000 for three years: then in May, 1933, Trenchard formed a private committee of "friends of the Metropolitan Police" to raise contributions from London firms. Enough money was donated to provide well-equipped sports grounds and club-houses in each Police District. By 1935, the capital of the Commissioner's Fund stood at £42,000.

Though the force benefited from these amenities, Trenchard's aspersions on the old system "seemed to rub up Federation officials the wrong way," to quote one of his own staff. When a deputation protested that the police minstrel concerts, of which as many as 120 were organised in official time during the winter months, would not be a commercial proposition without door-to-door ticket-selling, the Commissioner retorted that this in itself argued a lack of genuine popular support, since those patrons who bought tickets probably did so under a sense of compulsion.

"Your minstrel concerts could be run at a profit if they were properly run," he told the deputation. "And there I can help you."

On his own initiative, Trenchard consulted Mr. Walter Payne, the chairman and managing director of a chain of variety theatres and companies, who offered to let the police minstrels have his halls without charge, guest artists without fees and free advertising. It was to no avail: the Federation had been slighted and would not co-operate.

"Notwithstanding all these efforts of mine, I've been unable to get any sign of support from any member of the force with the exception of one superintendent," Trenchard told Gilmour. "I must therefore regretfully allow the minstrels to cease."

Yet ticket-selling was less pernicious to Trenchard's mind than the employment of policemen on gratuity by private persons and companies. This distressed him because it had assumed the proportions of a "racket" in which many policemen, irrespective of rank, were involved.

"Since greyhound racing started," he had informed Sir John Anderson in February, 1932, "a very large number of both C.I.D. and uniformed policemen have been so employed and very large sums of money have been paid out in bulk. I see that before greyhound racing started in 1923, as much as £500 per week in emoluments was paid by private persons direct to police officers for work done in their spare time. I should think since then it must have increased considerably, if not doubled. . . . As far as I can gather this system has been in operation for 100 years. . . .

"I had a meeting of my senior officers (Chief Constables and upwards) the other day, and told them that this practice filled me with horror and that I wanted to inquire into it. The general feeling was, however, that it was a subject that should not be touched, as an investigation would probably cause unrest. . . . It seems to me appalling that an ordinary investigation should cause unrest, and it is something to which I am unaccustomed."

Anderson was then on the point of leaving the Home Office. The fact may have encouraged him to speak more freely than he otherwise might have done. What Trenchard told him about greyhound racing was, he admitted, "new" and "shocks me as it does you."

"The Home Office attitude," said Anderson, "has, I think, been clear and consistent throughout but quite frankly we have not been supported on your side of Whitehall. . . . It looks as if your predecessor quite deliberately flouted the Home Secretary's ruling."

Yet Anderson, while sympathising with Trenchard's views on the corrupting effects of the gratuity system, strongly advised him against precipitate action:

"This is not the moment to stir the matter up," he warned. "Whatever may be said against the system, the men can claim with truth that what has been done has had the sanction of the head of the force, and to alter things now with resulting loss to a number of men would be regarded, I fear, as evidence of want of sympathy with them in their present difficulties."

This plea for restraint went unheeded, though it was re-echoed by Anderson's successor, Russell Scott, who believed as sincerely as his advisers, particularly Dixon and Newsam, that any premature attempt to raise police standards of conduct would defeat its own object. Trenchard, for his part, had no time for tact, quite apart from suspecting that these Home Office experts opposed the principle as much as the method of his reforms, major as well as minor; hence his willingness to by-pass or even to ride roughshod over them as occasion seemed to demand. Such high-handed treatment was hardly calculated to sweeten relations between the two sides of Whitehall where it was commonly felt that Gilmour, the Home Secretary, had allowed himself to become so much putty in the Commissioner's powerful hands.

As a result, latent opposition to Trenchard's "New Order" at Scotland Yard was not entirely confined to the Police Federation. Experts at the Home Office had their own more sophisticated doubts about the Trenchard reforms; and these found bolder

expression after he left the Yard. Game, whom he recommended
to succeed him in November, 1935, on the clear understanding
that the major reforms would not be tampered with, grievously
disappointed him by departing from the spirit and the letter of that
undertaking.

Early in 1937, Game was reluctantly obliged to re-examine the
Hendon college system "not only because a number of difficulties
and criticisms were emerging"—to quote a contemporary memorandum on the subject—"but also because a decision was needed
as to the future of Peel House," the training centre for constables.

Trenchard had always intended that the police laboratory, the
College, Peel House, the driving centre and the athletic ground
of No. 2 district should be concentrated together on the one central
sixty-five-acre site at Hendon. This seemed to Game an impracticable arrangement and one which was already leading to congestion. He decided that Hendon should be converted into an
enlarged training centre for constables, and that future officer-
cadets should eventually be housed elsewhere. Before going further,
Game had to decide on the size of the new College, in terms of the
number of officers needed in the foreseeable future. This in turn
re-opened the whole discussion with the Home Office on whether
or not the rules of entry laid down by Trenchard were sound.

In fairness to Game it must be said that he did not conceal his
own uncertainties from Trenchard. The two commonest objections
to the original Hendon system were, in his view, the hardest to
explain away. He found it impossible to ignore the ill-will of the
Police Federation towards the Hendon scheme. Many policemen
who had grown up under the traditional system of rising through
the ranks were complaining that the chances of promotion had been
considerably reduced. Game agreed that this was an arguable
proposition; but he felt that there could be no argument about the
second objection to Hendon. Even members of the college staff
now agreed that selecting entrants by competitive examination
failed to "cream off" the best candidates from the public and
secondary schools. The reason was clear: the minimum age limit
(twenty) was far too high.

Then a more critical complication arose. It appeared to
strengthen the case for modifying Trenchard's master plan; and
its origins were part of recent history. Recruiting had ceased altogether during the First World War; and some 3000 constables
were enlisted in 1919 to bring the force up to establishment.
Almost simultaneously the qualifying period for full pension rights

was extended from twenty-six to thirty years. The Government
Actuary, whom Game consulted about the "future population" of
the new college, warned him, in effect, that before long there
would be too many policemen chasing too few posts at the top.
Between 1940 and 1950 there would be very few retirements;
vacancies in the higher ranks of the force would thus be abnormally low. It was inadvisable for that reason to train too many
Hendon officers at the then average rate of about forty a year. The
prospects of promotion for them or anyone else were bound to
become decreasingly good. The Commissioner took account of
these technical points in drafting a compromise plan for Hendon's
future.

"You will hate my recommendations," Game wrote to
Trenchard at the end of 1937. "I confess I am not over happy
about them myself. But the difficulties are real, whether we like
them or not."

One of his recommendations was that entry to the college by
competitive examination should be provisionally stopped, another
that all Hendon candidates should work for a year as constables
on the beat before entering, a third that the college itself should
be temporarily closed until the "promotion bulge" dispersed.

Trenchard was appalled. This was "the thin end of the wedge,"
as he put it. The idea of closing Hendon, even temporarily, staggered
him:

"Every effort must be made to induce some of the provincial
police forces to use the college," he counselled Game. "The
pressure for this can only come from the Secretary of State and the
Home Office. This could quite easily be done if Dixon was wholeheartedly in favour of it, but I feel he is not. . . .

"You have got to remember that all the chief constables of the
provincial forces were against it . . . [due] to the general feeling
that we were trying to rope all the police forces into one, and that
this was an insidious way of doing it."

The "pressure" which Trenchard vainly urged Game to call
into play was financial pressure:

"The Exchequer pays 50 per cent of the [provincial] police
forces, whose real efficiency would depend on getting these
[College] men," he reminded him. But Game was averse to using
such tactics.

Sir John Simon, Gilmour's successor, kept a judiciously open
mind. He was persuaded by the Commissioner and his own Home
Office advisers in 1938 that the competitive examination for Hendon

ought to be discontinued; that direct entrants selected on their academic qualifications should serve for one year as constables on the beat before entering the college; that the upper age limit for Hendon men drawn from the force should be raised from twenty-six to thirty; that the new ranks of station inspector and junior station inspector introduced by Trenchard should be scrapped; and that all inspectors, whether college-trained or not, should become eligible for further promotion.

The outbreak of war prevented the adoption of these and other measures which Trenchard angrily denounced as a perversion of his basic recipe for "keeping the force young." In 1939 the doors of the College were closed, never to be reopened; and the short-service recruitment of constables, which had not been working smoothly for quite different reasons, also came to an end.

Game was far from being alone in his distaste for the short-term scheme. Even Trenchard admitted to a meeting of superintendents in late 1935 that he had "failed to carry conviction" on it. The taunt of political critics that it was a "militarist conception" did not influence Game in the slightest; it was the discontent in the force which turned him finally against it. Few London policemen cared for it; the Federation loathed it. Trenchard's way of "choking off" agitators was not Game's, whose "sympathy with the underdog" predisposed him to pay more attention than his predecessor had ever done to the grouses of the reviving Federation.

Before 1933, all policemen in Britain were recruited on the same basis: that of serving for twenty-five years or longer, taking promotion if it came and then retiring on pension. The Federation wanted London to revert to the national pattern. Trenchard's new model had the alleged disadvantage of discarding good men just when their ten-years' training and accumulated experience were likely to be of the highest value. By dividing the force into "first and second class" constables, the scheme was also said to militate against true *esprit de corps*.

The advantages of periodically leavening the lump with alert young men were real enough; but the very terms of their engagements deprived these short-service recruits of a career as policemen unless they moved away from London. The records indicate that many of them did so.

In the opinion of Sir John Ferguson, the late chief constable of Kent, who served under both Trenchard and Game at Scotland Yard, and who was the last pre-war commandant of Hendon:

"An abnormally high percentage of short-term recruits were

bright young men—too bright by half to stay where they were. Hundreds resigned and joined provincial forces instead."

Howgrave-Graham, the secretary of Scotland Yard, shared Ferguson's verdict that "the system began to break down under Game because it became increasingly difficult to work."

Trenchard, on the other hand, held that the scheme became "difficult to work" mainly because his successor allowed himself to be overborne by the prejudices of Home Office experts and senior police advisers, and partly because of its unpopularity with the Federation which, he contended, should have been more firmly handled. The truth probably lies midway between the two conflicting standpoints.

Trenchard never wholly forgave Game for his "treachery" in undoing both major reforms after the Second World War.

By October, 1944, when the Churchill Government appointed a committee to consider the problem of reorganising the nation's police, Game had already convinced himself that there could be no return to the Hendon system. The question was not even put before the committee. The Commissioner had been working on a tentative plan of his own for a National Police College where sergeants, deemed suitable for promotion to the rank of inspector, would receive a six-months' course of instruction. A sub-committee was invited to work out the details; Ferguson, as one of its members, drew on his personal experience as the last commandant of Hendon to plead the case for reviving the quietly discarded College project, with slight modifications, on a national basis. Ferguson pleaded in vain. The main committee turned a deaf ear to his lone discordant voice.

The Labour Government buried Trenchard's key reforms in 1946. The compromise advanced by Game, with Home Office support, for a National Police College to train future inspectors, was adopted more or less intact. In Trenchard's view, it was foredoomed to failure. No policy of the kind could ever succeed in turning "middle-aged men into young men" or in "producing leaders of the necessary mental breadth" to hold their own against the criminal—or a candle to the past products of Hendon. Time has still to prove his verdict wrong, as the records unmistakably suggest.

The College system was in operation for only five full years, from 1935 to 1939. The total number of students admitted was gradually restricted, as we have seen, by the capacity of the Metropolitan Force to absorb them; yet the results achieved in those five

years can be described as truly remarkable. Of 197 graduates
nearly a third have since risen to the highest posts in police forces
both here and in the Commonwealth. They include Sir Joseph
Simpson, the present Metropolitan Commissioner, the Chief
Constables of twenty English counties and of at least three important
cities and boroughs, as well as scores of senior officers in slightly
lower positions. Hendon College seems to have amply justified its
founder's claims for it as a forcing house of future police leaders.
And the authorities, local and national, are likely to be at a distinct
loss for trained replacements when this single generation of
"Trenchard's young men" passes away. For with the aboliton of
Hendon, the career of the London policeman ceased to be a career
open to talent.[4]

5

In the weeks before the wedding of the Duke of Kent in November,
1934, police precautions in London were intensified. King Alexander
of Jugoslavia had recently been assassinated in Marseilles, and the
memory lingered uncomfortably in the various Whitehall Departments responsible for pageantry and security.

"Seventy royalties," in Trenchard's words, were expected to
attend. A watch had to be kept on British ports for undesirable
visitors from abroad, an extra duty for the "Special Branch,"
which prompted the Commissioner to write rather sharply to
Gilmour:

"I am much exercised over the extraordinary system regarding
the admittance of foreigners to British ports, some of whom have
what purport to be British passports that may be forged. We have
no proper means of surveillance, except to scrutinise persons and
stand behind the immigration officers who examine their passports,
and we do not take much part in the interrogation."

It hardly mattered. The Royal marriage, which added two years
to Trenchard's term at Scotland Yard, passed without a hitch;
and the personal congratulations of King George V were a balm
to the regrets he still harboured. The crowds were well behaved
and good humoured. The manifestations of affection for the Royal
family were unforced and deeply felt. The popular acclamation
was greater still during the Silver Jubilee celebrations in May,
1935, when Trenchard's proudest and most vivid experiences were
the three private royal drives through south, east and north-west

London which the King asked him to arrange, entirely on the spur of the moment, on 10th, 12th and 26th May. These outings caused acute agitation in the Home Office. After the first, Gilmour, who at the particular request of the King had not been informed, sent for the Commissioner and reprimanded him mildly. Trenchard expressed contrition for failing to refer the matter to the Home Secretary first. It was only after the third that Gilmour thought of asking:

"Are any more planned?" to which Trenchard answered quite truthfully:

"No."

In the narrow streets of Poplar, gay with flags and choked with wildly cheering multitudes, Nott-Bower, one of Trenchard's small retinue, had to "pull people bodily off the bonnet of the royal car," while the King waved and the Queen bowed at the throng hemming them in. It was then that Trenchard overheard the King saying again and again in happy bewilderment:

"I didn't realise they felt like this for us."[5]

The new Highway Laws of this period were among Trenchard's final preoccupations. The increase in motor traffic and the rising toll of road casualties, though far less grave than to-day, had begun to rouse public concern and to call for official action. The Government were fortunate in having a Minister of Transport as energetic and resourceful as Hore-Belisha, and a Commissioner as quick off the mark as Trenchard. It seemed reasonable to hope, for a while at any rate, that London would master its traffic jams and reduce the hazards besetting drivers and pedestrians alike.

The new thirty miles an hour speed limit had to be enforced in built-up areas; special police cars were employed to that end with only partial success; and pedestrians did not take kindly or easily to the practice of crossing thoroughfares at the new Belisha beacons since no sanctions were applied. Co-operation between the traffic department at Scotland Yard and the Ministry of Transport was close and mainly cordial. On occasion Trenchard found himself embroiled in disputes over trivialities with members of his own or of Hore-Belisha's staff:

"As I've said before," he wrote to the Home Secretary one day, "I don't care in the least *how* the pedestrian crossings are marked— with an image of Belisha or a skull and crossbones or anything else —so long as they *are* marked. No two people will ever agree as to the best sort of sign, and whatever is settled will be laughed at by the so-called artistic people."

And later, reporting progress, he wrote again:

"I've had three long meetings with Belisha, also many letters and talks on the telephone. People are beginning to use the pedestrian crossing places a little bit more—not very much more, but still just a little."

There had been a slight decrease in the incidence of serious crime since his arrival, though the aggregate showed, as he expected, a rise in the number of "detectable" offences. Being a realist, Trenchard was only relatively pleased. Crime, like disease and dirt, would never be wholly eliminated; the search for the best men and the most up-to-date means of containing it had to go on ceaselessly. By mechanising his force; by increasing the number of radio cars and providing even a helicopter; by opening the new laboratory at Hendon, the map-rooms, and the statistical branch; by insisting on the *Daily Crime Telegram*; by revising the duties, and generally by trying to broaden the general outlook of the men on the beat, Trenchard did more in four years to mobilise the Metropolitan Police for crime-fighting purposes than any Commissioner for a century.

He lived long enough to mourn the passing of his two major reforms for elevating the policeman's job to the status of a true profession; he insisted to the last that, in time, some Government uninhibited by fear or prejudice would discover that the only sure way of raising leaders from the police ranks was to reintroduce a modified version of his Hendon scheme. He prided himself on the fact that before his resignation in November, 1935, many members of the Metropolitan Force knew in their bones that he was leaving Scotland Yard a cleaner and healthier place than he found it.

One of his final engagements as Commissioner took him to the Garrick Club in London in October, 1935, for a dinner in his honour. The speech he prepared was light and slightly self-deprecating.

"When I started my career, too many years ago, the last thing I thought possible was that I should ever be a policeman," he said. "I might be a victim of crime, or I might be a criminal—a painfully easy thing to be nowadays—but to be a policeman never entered my head. And now, after four years of it, I still feel an amateur at the game. Which is perhaps not a bad thing. The amateur is liable to look at crime and such matters from a broader and possibly a more tolerant and charitable point of view than the professional."

His life at Scotland Yard, he admitted, had not been entirely heavy and without laughter:

"There is a certain grim humour in opening a letter which

With Tedder in the Western Desert, 1943

Trenchard and Dowding (*right*), both retired, watching a
Battle of Britain fly-past in 1954

With one of his grandchildren

tarts: 'Last Sunday my wife called my mother a barmy cow, and
. threw her over Hungerford Bridge near Charing Cross.' Another
rom a youth in Belfast asked me to put him in touch with a reliable
acing man who would supply him with a few winners every day,
romising in return a commission on his winnings. Then, of course,
here are the numerous people who want advice on how to evade
he law, or who, having broken it, are anxious to avoid the conse-
uences. I'm not sure that the best type of person to have as Com-
nissioner might not be a thorough-going rake. If the Home Secre-
ary were also a thorough rake, what a happy place London would
e. At any rate for the rakes."

He could not resist ending with an anecdote which gave to his
udience the distinct impression that a man big enough to tell such
tale against himself must be congenitally incapable of developing
swollen head. Trenchard described how in the previous June, after
irtually four years as Commissioner, he had to attend another
inner such as this on the very day of his predecessor's death. The
dy seated next to him at table had only just heard the news; she
st little time and no composure in imparting its melancholy
gnificance to him in loud and affected tones that carried further
cross the room than he liked.

"Oh, Lord Trenchard," she said finally. "Isn't it too sad that
ear Lord Byng has passed on? Whoever do you think they'll find
o take his place at Scotland Yard?"

21. *The Oracle*

When an outstanding man of action is relegated prematurely ¹
the shadows, the slow death of oblivion will usually overtake hi
long before the natural end of his days. So, in part, it proved :
Trenchard's case.

At the time of his departure from Scotland Yard in Novembe
1935, he was sixty-three years old and at the very peak of h
administrative powers. Renowned, if somewhat feared, for tl
dynamic thrust of his personality as much as for his proven adapt
bility as an organiser, it seemed that no Government could affor
to pass Trenchard over. For Ministers were growing more unea
at last about the international situation and the appallingly wea
condition of the nation's armed forces; and leaders of Trenchard
calibre were not so common that his claims, quite apart from h
private desires, could be lightly discounted. Yet discounted the
were, then and for the next twenty years.

The final duty of his biographer must, therefore, be to sho
how and why such a fate almost inevitably befell a man who cou
not help remaining as true to his own lights as Trenchard, so th
until his dying day he was left apparently to flounder in the shoa
of public life.

It may well be asked why this happened, especially in the la
thirties and early forties, while creatures of milder disposition ar
smaller talents mishandled or avoided burdens which Trenchar
was better qualified to shoulder. Can it be said that the fault la
only on one side? Or was it true, as some of his self-confesse
admirers have claimed, that Trenchard, eternally true to forr
proved to be "his own worst enemy"? Must these years be reckone
a tragic waste, a blessed deliverance for him and others, or mere
the predictable destiny of one whose opinions were too uncon
promising, his character too strong, for politicians to tolerate?

The answers to such questions shed more light on the mind
Trenchard, on the pitfalls he encountered or dug for himself, ar
on the inscrutable public figure he cut from 1935 onwards, than a

ιe anthologies that could be compiled of his sayings and doings
ν a business man, a Member of the House of Lords, a husband and
.ther, or even as the oracle of the air force, none of whose leaders
εserted him but some of whom evidently thought it prudent not
ɔ consult him. References to Trenchard's professional and private
ιterests and to his self-appointed role as an adviser, will occur in
ιe following pages, but only episodically. Such tasks were not
ithout their influence or importance; but they cannot be compared
ith the greater tasks which were denied him.

This closing chapter records the gradual decline of a giant whom
ιany lesser men had written off already as redundant. The morals
ιrtually write themselves. They are, in this writer's belief, of lasting
ʒlevance to the story of our time.

2

.t the start, all went as well as could be expected. Trenchard, as
ιas been stated, intervened only twice in defence questions between
ƍ30 and 1933. Sir John Salmond proved an admirable Chief of
ιir Staff in a dismal period when military affairs were neglected
ιd service morale touched rock bottom. The economic depression,
ιlmost universal in its impact, encouraged Governments as well as
ɛoples to withdraw from the world and think mainly of themselves.

Trenchard was wise enough to leave Salmond alone. Not that
ɛ would have been thanked for interfering. Relations between the
ιir had always tended to be distant. Closer in age and standing
ιan any other two senior air force officers, both had commanded
ιe R.A.F. in war, and each had been of immense assistance to the
ther when the service was earning its permanent wings in Iraq.
. slight undercurrent of rivalry, not to say of jealousy, still held
ιem apart, despite the strong bond of esteem between them.

The mistakes that Salmond could have perpetrated in the early
ιirties were few. This was not a time for enterprise. Churchill's
ιodified " Ten Year Rule " was rigorously applied. The air vote
ɔod frozen at an average of £20 million a year. The Chief of Air
ιaff was just able to hold his own; and the controversial plan
εqueathed to him by Trenchard, under which the R.A.F. would
ιaγe systematically enlarged its strategic role overseas, withered
ιvay, unlamented.

Because Britain was not alone in misfortune, it is hardly astonish-
ιg, in retrospect, that these economically stagnant years hastened

the drift towards international anarchy by making the world safe
for bandits. In September, 1931, at the height of the financia
crisis in Britain, Japan fired the first shot. Seeking thereby t
relieve her own plight, she picked a bogus quarrel with China an
invaded Manchuria. The following January, fortified by the spoil
of conquest and undeterred by the impotent indignation of th
League of Nations, Japan went further, landing an expeditionar
force at Shanghai, routing the Chinese again, accepting Wester
arbitration only after she had achieved her immediate objectiv
and thoroughly scaring the British Foreign Office into the bargair
For unimpeachable information had meanwhile reached Londor
pointing to the probability of an attack on Singapore should th
Japanese encounter Western resistance at Shanghai. Trenchar
learnt of the threat. And overwhelmed as he was by his earl
difficulties at Scotland Yard, he offered the Government som
unsolicited advice.

    The Chiefs of Staff, to their credit, reacted at once by demandin
the abandonment of the "Ten Year Rule." In March, 1932, th
Cabinet complied. But the service chiefs were warned that whil
Britain's economic troubles lasted, defence needs must wait. Since
however, Japanese covetous designs on Singapore could not b
ignored, the plans for constructing and defending a new naval bas
there, which had been on the shelf since Trenchard's day, wer
taken down and dusted by a special Cabinet sub-committee unde
the chairmanship of Baldwin.

    Trenchard at once submitted a paper to the Air Staff whic
lucidly summarised the arguments for air control of the base. I
infuriated Hankey, and did not wholly please Salmond, wh
naturally preferred to conduct his own case in his own way.[1] Partl
as a result of Trenchard's intrusion the flames of inter-service cor
troversy leaped high again. With Hankey's help, Baldwin manage
to damp them down. In May, 1932, the air plan for Singapore wa
finally rejected. Its relative inexpensiveness and strategic sounc
ness were not denied; but in the interests of inter-service harmony
Baldwin favoured the customary path of compromise. To quote th
words of the official historian of *The War Against Japan*:

    "The Baldwin Committee, having heard all the evidence avai
able, recommended that coast defences should be organised on
basis of co-operation between the three services, the gun retainin
its place as the main deterrent against naval attack. . . ."

    The first of Trenchard's sallies into the arena he had lately le
thus came to nothing. The second, a few months later, was mor

effective. The Government's desire for peace predisposed its Ministers to treat the disarmament negotiations at Geneva with an earnestness which seemed thoroughly hypocritical to Trenchard, in view of the aggressive attitude of the Japanese. He needed no encouragement to contribute, again as an outside expert, to the preparatory discussions of the Committee of Imperial Defence. Trenchard confined himself to one general question only: the proposal to abolish all bomber aircraft by international decree. This was due to be debated by the Geneva delegates in August, 1932. Side-stepping the legal difficulties of enforcement, he invited the Cabinet, point-blank, to reflect on the consequences for Britain of endorsing it.

"Were we to abandon the aeroplane as a weapon of defence against invasion, I see only two alternatives for the future. . . . Either we must be content with a very low degree of security, or else we must face the enormous cost of providing the old methods of defence on an adequate scale. . . . We have twenty-five thousand miles of coastline to protect at home and abroad, our navy is relatively weaker than ever before. Any hostile power that attacks us can, to some extent, choose the time and place; it has always seemed to me that our main chance of successful defence lies in the development of the air routes. Along these our air forces can move with almost the same freedom as the navy and with four or five times the speed."

He considered it grimly ironic that past neglect in developing air routes, particularly east of Suez, had provided Baldwin and Hankey with a plausible excuse for turning down his air scheme for defending Singapore. There was something unhealthy, to Trenchard's mind, in the influence exerted by Hankey on defence affairs. As secretary to the Cabinet, he had the confidence of every Minister; as secretary to the Chiefs of Staff, he was the sole official empowered to interpret or misinterpret strategic needs to suit the convenience of his political masters. For no Minister pretended to be interested in these secondary problems. A scrupulously careful functionary, who abhorred dissension, Hankey had succeeded only too well since Trenchard's departure in investing with a bogus harmony all exchanges between the Chiefs of Staff.

The service leaders were no longer expected to think for themselves; "unanimity" was Hankey's golden rule; any plan which gave rise to disagreement was deferred; and so the number of questions left unresolved multiplied. In Trenchard's opinion, Hankey was a liability; he had taught the service leaders the

negative ways of conformity by applying the polite rules of a parlour
game to issues of life and death.

The compliance of the Chiefs of Staff struck Trenchard as
doubly dangerous because of the secrecy surrounding defence
affairs: both Cabinet and country were being misled about the
true state of unpreparedness; yet, being a public servant himself,
Trenchard could not openly protest. Besides, his preoccupations
at Scotland Yard were such that he had little leisure to do so until
the end of 1933. The friends to whom he confided his fears wondered whether he was not being too hard on Hankey. None of
them, not even Churchill, would believe at first that this outstanding civil servant could be as obstructive as Trenchard alleged or
should be blamed for ministerial sins of omission.

It might be true that not a single R.A.F. squadron had yet been
formed for overseas bases such as Malta, Hong Kong, Trincomalee
and Freetown; that only one squadron of torpedo bombers existed
for the defence of Singapore; that, at home, the fifty-two squadrons
programme, announced by Baldwin in 1923 as necessary to deter
the largest air force within striking distance of Britain, was still
ten short of its target. But surely he was going too far in condemning
Sir Maurice for these deficiencies as well?

Unable to influence his friends, Trenchard had to reconcile
himself to the distasteful knowledge that he was equally powerless
to influence even minor Air Staff decisions. Early in 1933, for
instance, he learnt of Sir John Salmond's impending resignation
when it was too late to intervene. The Chief of Air Staff had at
least another year before him; and had Trenchard been consulted, he
would certainly have striven hard to dissuade him against leaving
just then. For the Cabinet was being driven by the pressure of
events in Europe to turn its mind reluctantly to defence. Salmond's
retirement, in fact, almost coincided with Hitler's rise to power in
Germany.

Trenchard's annoyance was all the keener on discovering the
reason for Salmond's reticence. Sentiment more than anything else
had evidently moved Sir John to step aside for his younger brother,
Sir Geoffrey, who took over from him in March, 1933, suffering
from incurable cancer, only to die within six weeks. Thus, at one
improvident stroke, the line of succession prepared by Trenchard
before his departure in 1930 was irretrievably broken. The older
and more experienced of the Salmond brothers, and the best fitted
to steer the R.A.F. through the rapids of change ahead, became
overnight just another onlooker. The tiller was handed on to Sir

Edward Ellington, a staff officer of ability but one without the necessary training or self-confidence to assert himself quickly.

Having vowed never to criticise his own service in public or in private, Trenchard said nothing. All that he could hope was that Ellington would be more responsive to his advice than Salmond. Again he was disappointed. For though Ellington listened to his counsel, he did not always heed it. Had the Air Ministry possessed a more forceful Secretary of State than Lord Londonderry, whose unfailing amiability did not, in Trenchard's view, compensate for a lack of tenacity which increased the worries of an untried Chief of Air Staff, he might have minded less. But during the twelve months immediately after Hitler emerged as the absolute ruler of Nazi Germany, while Trenchard himself was grappling with his hardest problems at Scotland Yard, the bargaining position of the R.A.F. grew weaker instead of stronger. Ellington appeared to know no better than to knuckle under and obey the self-denying rules of what Trenchard thought of as "Hankey's Parlour Game."

3

The Cabinet kept its word. The reversal of the " Ten Year Rule " did not open the Treasury coffers to the fighting services. The Chancellor, Neville Chamberlain, deferred the secondary claims of military expenditure until the last quarter of 1933. By then events had begun to overtake the Government and the Chiefs of Staff. Hitler had recently served notice of his intentions by withdrawing from the Disarmament Conference and the League of Nations, thus tearing up the Locarno Treaty and disturbing the peace-loving men who ruled the chancelleries of Europe.

The Führer's potential capacity for mischief could not be dismissed as lightly as that of the Japanese war-lords; for Germany was uncomfortably closer, her past misdeeds too fresh in popular memory.

A special defence sub-committee was therefore set up in haste towards the end of 1933. Its members were Fisher of the Treasury, Vansittart of the Foreign Office, the Chiefs of Staff and Hankey. They were authorised to recommend specific measures of "positive action." Information about the exchanges filtered through to Trenchard only by degrees; and Ellington's aloofness more than ever upset him. He suspected, not without reason, that the Chief of Air Staff had been warned off him as a "disruptive influence."

That Trenchard was in bad odour with Hankey had become clear enough to the Chiefs of Staff and to others with inside knowledge. That Trenchard had unwittingly begun to impair his standing with the Government by associating with its most merciless critic, Churchill, was less apparent at the time. Any friend of this former Chancellor, who, having fallen out with his colleagues on the issue of constitutional reforms for India, now seemed intent on widening this comparatively narrow area of disagreement into an impassable wilderness, was almost bound to be viewed with disfavour. Yet Trenchard, political innocent that he was, would have been astonished at the thought. For while broadly agreeing with Churchill's reasons for denouncing the Government's inadequate defence policy, he disagreed with his line of attack and repeatedly implored him to be less destructive.

It was too easy, in Trenchard's opinion, to indict any Cabinet for idleness; and, as he was fond of reminding Churchill, such indictments ill became the author of the modified " Ten Year Rule." Trenchard tried to focus his attention instead on the deplorable state into which the existing defence machinery had sunk under Hankey's control. Here lay the key to the situation: for until the Cabinet appreciated the fact that the Chiefs of Staff were virtually forbidden to think for themselves, no amount of resolution on high would rectify the muddle below. The backlog of deferred defence projects would overwhelm everyone when the decision to rearm eventually came.

Vansittart was Churchill's main source of information about the proceedings of the Cabinet sub-committee; Warren Fisher was Trenchard's, largely because of Ellington's reluctance to confide in him. The private strictures of both these officials on the excessive caution displayed by the Chiefs of Staff in their desire for unanimity hardened Trenchard's misgivings. Vansittart, in his posthumously published memoirs, *The Mist Procession*, has disclosed a small but not insignificant example which is worth repeating because it tallies with the contemporary account given by Fisher to Trenchard:

"We touched the nadir of our defence estimates, and after Hitler's advent an effort had clearly to be made. Warren Fisher, Maurice Hankey and I formed a committee with the three Chiefs of Staff. I asked for twenty-five extra air squadrons, but the amenable trio would not go beyond the five for which they were sure of sanction. Gratifying support came from Fisher; it was heartening to find the head of the Treasury ready to face the immensity of our need, but the experts remained immovable. . . . So started the tug-of-war in which the British never pulled their weight. Within two years we were in irretrievable arrears. . . ."[2]

Those twenty extra squadrons would certainly have saved the Air Staff much recrimination a year later, when Hitler confounded the Government with his boastful assertion that the German Air Force had achieved parity with the R.A.F. Though this happened to be a premature claim, it caused considerable heart-searching in Whitehall without uncovering the one question of substance that went unchallenged: the collective unwillingness of the Chiefs of Staff to decide which of the many neglected defence problems facing them should be tackled first. That, in Trenchard's judgment, was the inevitable result of Hankey's inhibiting power over them.

A copy of the interim report of the Defence Requirements Committee was sent to him by Warren Fisher, in strict confidence, for his comments. The document was a fairly exhaustive "shopping list." As he waded through it, in the spring of 1934, Trenchard immediately recognised that it would take a nation far richer than Britain longer than the five years laid down by the Cabinet to meet the deficiencies listed. Yet the Chiefs of Staff still refused either to whittle them down or to fix a definite order of priority, as though resigned to abdicating their responsibilities in the interests of continuing harmony. So Trenchard drew up for Fisher a quick short list of essentials. It was, he admitted, "a very disjointed amateur effort which omits a good deal." It could obviously be improved on; but having no staff, nor access to official files, he could do no better:

"First in order of priority I would put:

Anti-aircraft guns and search-lights for England and south of the Wash (army).

Increase of Home Defence Air Force up to 100 squadrons, two-thirds being offensive bombers (air).

Coastal Defence Batteries, guns of six inches or less for Home Ports (army).

Completion of Singapore Defences (army, navy, air).

Submarines and fast destroyers for Singapore (navy).

Oil reserves for ports east of Suez (navy).

The 'spearhead' expeditionary force for securing continental air bases (army).

"Second in order of priority, though if the country's resources permitted some of them could be dove-tailed with items on the first list, would come the following:

Completion of army-air co-operation squadrons (army).

Anti-aircraft guns and search-lights for England north of the Wash.

War stocks and equipment at ports east of Suez to be brought up to date (navy).

Defence (including aircraft) for Hong Kong, Penang, Colombo.

Provision of oil fuel at ports west of Suez (navy).

Increase of Fleet Air Arm (but I don't agree that the number need, as suggested, conform to Japanese strength).

Simultaneously with the first list steps should be taken to remove the establishments at Woolwich, Kidbrook, Chatham and other such places to areas in the north and west of England."

The service chiefs, he complained, had no right to soft-pedal "the overriding consideration, namely, the order of magnitude and imminence of the various dangers . . . and, as a corollary, the order of priority of the various steps necessary." Common sense demanded that this should be settled first, "regardless of the particular service concerned." The fact that he was an airman had no direct bearing on the placing of items in his tentative short list. Military necessity alone dictated it:

"Unquestionably the greatest danger is from Germany," he wrote. "Japan may be perhaps almost equally important, but not as a separate factor—rather as a threat on our flank if we become involved with Hitler . . . I therefore regard the provision of anti-aircraft guns and searchlights for the South of England, and the increase in the Home Defence Air Force as the most urgent needs. In the early stages at any rate, the real danger from Germany will be in the air. Her aircraft can reach London and other industrial centres with ease, whereas her own vulnerable areas are far less accessible from England. . . . We could only strike at her extremities, she could strike at our vitals. . . ."

Trenchard's proposals, timely as they appear to-day, were not welcomed then. Because of the vast expenditure entailed, and because the Chiefs of Staff remained as warily non-committal as before, the Chancellor of the Exchequer became the reluctant arbiter of defence planning.

"Unhappily," Neville Chamberlain noted in his diary on 12th May, 1934, "it is part of my nature that I cannot contemplate any problem without trying to find a solution for it. And so I have practically taken charge of the defence requirements of this country. . . ."

And again, on 6th June, that year:

"In accordance with my suggestion it was decided to examine the Defence Requirements Committee's proposals on their merits in the first instance. . . . I have now completed a paper making revised proposals, which bring the five-year expenditure down from seventy-six to fifty million, excluding ship-building."

It was not altogether surprising that Trenchard's frustration induced him, in March, 1934, to ask the Government to relieve him of his duties at Scotland Yard. It was a rash, perhaps even a fatal, move in the circumstances; yet, given his insight into the troubles which the Chiefs of Staff were hoarding up for themselves and the nation, it is impossible to see what else he could have done. What happened was this.

Early in the month, Trenchard wrote to Gilmour for permission to address the House of Lords during the forthcoming debates on service estimates. He was inviting a snub, for his private view of defence policy was well known; and as a public official he was bound by the customary obligation of loyalty to desist from openly criticising the Government. The Home Secretary told him verbally that MacDonald and Baldwin were against breaking with precedent. Why was he so anxious to speak? Surely he could inform them confidentially?

Trenchard's immediate retort was that they had better start looking for another Police Commissioner. His "interest and keenness" already lay elsewhere, he wrote, since his main reforming work lay behind him. This letter, part of which has been quoted in the previous chapter, was tactfully worded: it summarised what Trenchard had already achieved at Scotland Yard, and stressed that "twenty years" might elapse before his remedies bore full fruit. For that reason he wanted to go as soon as possible, and by the end of 1934 at latest.

The Cabinet, however, did not want to part with him. Sorry as they might be to lose so efficient an administrator, they would have been sorrier still to see him emulating Churchill as an informed critic of defence policy. For, with astonishing lack of finesse, Trenchard had meanwhile obliged MacDonald with the draft speech which he intended to deliver in the Upper House. The Cabinet studied it and learnt the worst. They could congratulate themselves for a start on having forbidden him to deliver it.

"War appears to be a certainty in the future," ran its key passage. "How near or how far it may be away, it's not for me to say. . . . Apparently it is an accepted fact that a war in which

Germany will be the chief magnate (though Japan must not be forgotten) is almost a certainty. . . . If that is so, I feel no time must be lost in dealing with what, to my mind, is still one of the most important questions. This is to obtain unanimity on what are the right defensive measures to take—both publicly on the broad principles and secretly in the Committee of Imperial Defence. . . .

"Some may think that I have in the past exaggerated the importance of the air. But I have never gone so far in stressing its importance as the Lord President of the Council [Baldwin] on at least two recent occasions. . . . The prospect held out to us [by him] is that in the next war civilisation itself is in danger of destruction from the air. . . . During the years of peace, when there was no war or even any thought of it for a long time to come, the controversies between the services in regard to taking over peace responsibilities became very acute. Seldom, however, except in regard to the formation of the R.A.F., were these acute differences allowed to come to a head and be decided by the considered view of the Cabinet in favour of one or another. We, the Chiefs of Staff, agreed on many points, but all points of disagreement were left for future consideration.

"Why am I in favour of what may be called an arming debate? I am in favour for this very important reason: I dread to think of the day coming when we shall find ourselves at war and, instead of being a united nation, going into it steadily and calmly with full confidence in the Government and the heads of the fighting services, we should be rent from top to bottom with our differences and there would be endless arguments and confusion such as appear to be inevitable at the end of a war but should be avoided at all costs at the beginning. With the dropping of the first bomb on this country we shall become a nation of men fighting and arguing among ourselves on how best to defend ourselves. . . .

"What is needed, it seems to me, is the immediate appointment of a Minister without portfolio to preside at the meetings of the Chiefs of Staff when the Prime Minister cannot be there or even when he is [for] the Prime Minister can only find time to attend occasionally and cannot immerse himself in all the questions.

"It would be the duty of this Minister to see that our defensive policy is threshed out as a whole, to expound it and the views of the Chiefs of Staff to the Cabinet, and also in the House of Commons . . . in the same way as the Foreign Secretary expounds foreign policy. . . . He must not be a Minister of Defence dealing with questions of administration and of detail but a guide and adviser on general policy. . . ."

Whether Hankey read this thinly veiled onslaught on his own prerogatives is uncertain. It hardly mattered. The speech would only have confirmed an unfavourable opinion of which he had long been aware. The suppressed speech sealed Trenchard's immediate future. Any ministerial doubts about the wisdom or unwisdom of holding him down in indefinite silence were removed. Through the personal persuasions of the King, the Police Commissioner was induced to stay on at Scotland Yard for nearly two more frustrating years, while Neville Chamberlain, a competent accountant but little more, lorded it over the irresolute proceedings of the Chiefs of Staff.

4

Trenchard's was a household name in Britain long before he walked out of Scotland Yard for the last time in November, 1935. Acclaim and notoriety were his in roughly equal proportions; and it was virtually impossible to read a newspaper without finding some praising or damning reference to his work. For whether men hated or admired what he did, none could ignore it. Rumours of his impending retirement began to circulate from mid-1934 onwards; only towards the end, when his artificially prolonged term of office became wearisome, did Trenchard foster their growth by quietly briefing two or three well-disposed M.P.s to question the Home Secretary in the Commons on his behalf.

It was generally assumed that a grateful Government would next offer Trenchard some new post connected with national defence; and Left Wing critics could not restrain a cynical cheer or two at the prospective transfer of this capable autocrat to a sphere where his military brand of efficiency would no longer be out of place.

Such critics deceived themselves. Grateful the Government might be, but it was equally chary of re-employing him, above all in the field of defence planning. With Ministers as individuals Trenchard appeared to be on excellent terms. The attitude of the leading trio of MacDonald, Baldwin and Chamberlain was guardedly friendly. Sir John Simon, first at the Foreign, then at the Home Office, stood in immense awe of this "tremendous fellow" who, as Chief of the Flying Corps, had taken him down a

peg or two nearly twenty years before. Hoare's devotion was jus
as deep. And of Gilmour's regard for Trenchard the reader wil
probably have formed an accurate impression already. Only th
Service Ministers, with the solitary exception of Londonderry
tended to be mistrustful, though it should be borne in min(
that until 1936 their opinions carried little weight.

It was because they knew him too well that Ministers collectivel
suspected him of suffering from the defects of his virtues. He wa
too outspoken for comfort, too overpoweringly efficient himself t(
brook inconsistency or inefficiency in others, and too obsessed witl
the weaknesses of the armed forces to be entrusted with an immediat(
hand in strengthening them. As a defence administrator, Trenchar(
would not be easily muzzled or controlled; yet unless he wer(
restrained, the Chiefs of Staff would resume their quarrelsome way
and co-ordinated planning would become impossible. Better a saf(
politician than an unmanageable expert, especially one with s(
definite a bias in favour of his own service.

Trenchard's candour, not perhaps his most disarming or endear-
ing quality, was increasingly frowned upon as a sign of incurabl(
political naïveté. The pace he maintained as Police Commissioner
afforded him little leisure for crusading or conspiring; nevertheless
it was noted that he continued to associate with Churchill, whose
views were slowly winning adherents at Westminster. These were
counted as black marks against Trenchard when a reconstructed
Cabinet, headed by Baldwin, decided in March, 1936, that it could
procrastinate no longer—and the reform which he had advocated
as essential for national defence planning was introduced nearly
three years too late.

The record of Trenchard's activities outside Scotland Yard
from April, 1934, to November, 1935, discloses no evidence of disloyalty to the Government. His propaganda, though indiscreet,
was almost invariably conversational. He did not believe in
plots or plotters: wherever his social and official engagements took
place, he simply regaled anyone who would listen with his startling
opinions which reached the distressed ears of Ministers in due course.

Occasionally he would deliberately make a dead set at a person
wielding potentially great influence. One such meeting with
Geoffrey Dawson, the editor of The Times, must do service for a
dozen that could be cited. The two had a meal together on 1st
June, 1934. That night Dawson wrote in his private diary that
Trenchard was "very voluble and interesting about the police, his
new College (opened yesterday), his idea of retirement, his anxiety

or the new section-houses: and then Imperial Defence, co-ordinat-
ng Chiefs of Staff, etc. (He believes now for the first time in a
var within five years and ascribes it to the new spirit in Germany.)
. ."

Dawson's biographer, Sir Evelyn Wrench, describes this as
'the most significant entry of the year in Geoffrey's diary," adding
rather sententiously that "had Geoffrey been endowed with the
are gift of second sight and realised what an amazing prophecy
he had just listened to, and promptly acted upon it, British preparedness for the Second World War . . . would have undoubtedly
been more advanced than it was five years later."[3]

Trenchard's impression of Dawson on that occasion was less
flattering. "A complacent man," he called him, "who believed
that everything the Government did was for the best, and who smiled
rather condescendingly at me when I got going on defence."
Nothing came of that brave attempt to disturb the smugness of
the editor of The Times.

Between Trenchard and Churchill, the near-certainty of an
eventual conflict with Hitler's Germany was common ground. It
should, they felt, have been common ground between them and the
Cabinet because—and here lay a grotesque irony worthy of Swift—
the alarming details of Germany's air preparations had been
pieced together in 1934 not by military intelligence but by the
Ministerial Committee on Disarmament. Its report, pleading for
"positive action," had led to the appointment of that other committee headed by Vansittart, Fisher and Hankey, whose proposals
had been robbed of urgency by the meek irresoluteness of the Chiefs
of Staff, Chatfield, the First Sea Lord, Montgomery-Massingberd,
the C.I.G.S., and Ellington.

The disarmament delegates had not suppressed anything. The
facts indicated that as early as spring, 1934, the German aircraft
industry was capable of producing at least 100 contraband military
machines a month and that Germany already had about 400 of
these, as well as four times that number of civil and training planes.
It was thus reasonable to estimate that within eighteen months the
German Air Force, which had no legal existence yet, would comprise roughly 1000 machines. So, concluded the disarmament
delegates, "the mere announcement of a substantial increase" in
the R.A.F.'s front-line strength might be expected to "act as a
deterrent to Germany."

The Air Ministry, with its own sources of intelligence, ridiculed
the suggestion that a collection of aircraft, however quickly mustered,

could be construed as an air force: the unofficial Luftwaffe still
had to be formed into battle-worthy squadrons with cadres and
reserves. Churchill's warnings that it would overhaul the R.A.F
unless the British Government bestirred itself were resented by the
Air Staff, on grounds which Trenchard could not wholly accept in
view of ministerial complacency. In March, 1934, Baldwin assured
the Commons that if the Disarmament Conference failed, then
steps would be taken to secure an Air Disarmament agreement. If
that failed, then steps would be taken to increase the R.A.F. until
its strength equalled that of the most powerful air force within
striking distance of Britain. Almost exactly twelve months later,
in announcing the complete breakdown of disarmament negotiations,
Ramsay MacDonald commented with slovenly vagueness that "the
deliberate retardation of our armaments as part of our peace policy
has brought them below the level required for the fulfilment of these
objects."

The weeks passed. Then came an announcement by Baldwin
that taxed Trenchard's credulity to the utmost: by March, 1937,
the strength of the R.A.F. at home would have risen to 1500 front-
line machines. This was an unattainable target, as Trenchard well
knew, without the ruthless driving force of a Defence Minister
behind Hankey and the service chiefs. The reason for Baldwin's
inexcusably wild promise was only too plain: the Government had
been bowled over by Hitler's recent boast to Simon and Mr.
Anthony Eden in Berlin that the German Air Force, whose formal
existence had been admitted only a matter of days before, was
already equal in size to the R.A.F.

With a masterly display of that "appalling frankness" which
he reserved for moments of embarrassment, Baldwin went on to
blame the Air Ministry for deceiving everyone, including itself,
about the rate of German air expansion:

"We were completely misled on that subject," he confessed on
22nd May, 1935. "I will not say we had not rumours. There was
a good deal of hearsay, but we could get no facts, and the only
facts I have—are those I have from Herr Hitler himself."

Lord Londonderry was forthwith replaced as Air Minister by
Sir Philip Cunliffe-Lister on the pretext that the Secretary of State
for Air should be a member of the Lower House, a pretext whose
hollowness was exposed within seven months when Sir Philip for-
getfully accepted a peerage without immediately forfeiting office
on that account. Such symptoms of panic worried Trenchard less
than the reactions of Ellington.

The Chief of Air Staff, realising how vain were the chances of more than doubling the front-line strength of the R.A.F. by March, 1937, pleaded that the period of development should be extended to 1939. Baldwin might promise, Churchill complain, but neither promises nor complaints would enable new aircraft and spares to sprout conveniently from factories which had been producing few or none for years. An expansion programme had been hastily drawn up without reference to the capacity of the British aircraft industry, and foisted on an Air Staff fearful that the machines would be out-of-date when delivered, and that the men needed to fly and maintain them would not be properly trained, even if they could be recruited in time.

Somewhat to his surprise, Trenchard was at last asked for his advice. Early in May, 1935, Charles Evans the longest established of the senior civil servants at the Air Ministry, revealed something of Ellington's bewilderment in a confidential letter.

"At the present moment it looks . . . as if a sub-committee of Ministers, Cunliffe-Lister, Ormsby-Gore and Runciman, are likely to commit the Air Ministry openly to a hurried scheme of expansion. Their line seems to be . . . that our S. of S. [Londonderry] has not got sufficient drive, that the department is lacking in imagination, and that Cunliffe-Lister and company can show how things ought to be done. . . . You may think that [this] has some justification, but whether that is so or not, we shall not mend matters by panic and impracticable programmes."

Evans enclosed with the letter "a purely personal" appreciation of the effects of Hitler's lying propaganda. The appreciation faithfully reflected the current views of the Air Staff:

"It is unfortunate that we should ever have been driven into these purely arithmetical comparisons of strength between Germany and ourselves. They are a legacy of Disarmament Conference discussions but the Government and Foreign Office are becoming slaves to them."

As for the accelerated programme, about to be published, by which "something in the order of seventy *new* squadrons are to be built in less than two years," Evans denounced this as "*impossible* under peace-time conditions of voluntary recruitment and purchase of land and material in the open market. . . . All that would be produced by March, 1937, would be the façade of a large and inefficient force. . . ."

Trenchard replied by return, on 8th May, 1935:

"I'm afraid I don't altogether agree with you. I think you are looking at the problem from the wrong angle. It is most unfortunate that you have got drawn into a battle on the question of whether your estimates or those of the Foreign Office as to the strength of Germany are correct. It may be that the Germans are cute in claiming to be stronger than they really are. Anyhow I feel the answer is publicly to proclaim that the gap has got to be filled— with a margin—AT ONCE. This is required by the people of this country and by the Government. . . .

"You are not going to wreck the efficiency of the air force by doubling it. There are many necessary brakes on, and you won't do any good being like Canute and saying to the tide—'Thus far and no farther.' It will only overwhelm you. . . . I feel strongly that we are getting into deep waters at Air Ministry by setting our faces against a quick expansion. I would not talk about squadrons. I would frankly say that I am going to order 1000 bombing machines for the first line, up to 500 fighting machines and reconnaissance machines, half of which would be of the best type available now and the other half to be the best type that designers have in their brains for the next year. . . ."

Because Ellington preferred not to compromise himself by openly consulting him, Trenchard talked freely to the more accessible Newall, who was already being groomed as the next Chief of Air Staff. The R.A.F., Trenchard warned, must not let slip this chance to expand; the plan was badly conceived, no doubt; it would fall behind schedule for want of a planner with ministerial powers; but it was not Ellington's job to teach the Government its business. That was the Opposition's duty, though it was being left almost exclusively to the dictators in Europe.

Early in June, 1935, Baldwin became Prime Minister again. One of his first acts, as already explained, was to send for Londonderry, and "kick him upstairs" to the leadership of the Lords. Trenchard sympathised with the victim to whom the R.A.F. owed much both for his moral and material support in its earliest and leanest years of the early twenties and for his later courage in resisting attempts to outlaw the bomber and in pushing through contracts for the multi-gunned Hurricane and Spitfire fighters, despite Treasury discouragement, Londonderry's misfortune was that he had failed to see in time that he could not demand too much.

For the rest of 1935, by private lobbying that was usually the reverse of judicious, Trenchard sought to play the elder statesman in securing the removal of Hankey. This, in his view, had become a matter which impinged on the nation's ultimate safety.

Captain B. H. Liddell Hart, the military analyst, was one publicist for whose support Trenchard was grateful. Over lunch at Brook's in London, on the third last day of June, 1935, they discussed the military dilemmas facing Britain. Liddell Hart took notes at the time. Trenchard expressed himself, according to his guest, "fervently if rather incoherently":

"His dominating idea was that the British Empire should go on. If trouble was coming, one should try and put it off as long as possible. He had sons at school and wanted to give them a breathing space. . . .

"The prestige of the British Navy was, Trenchard, thought, still an immense factor in world opinion (I suggested, when I could get in a word, that it was nothing like it used to be); and that even though he and I might realise that its technical value was much over-rated, we wanted to prevent foreign countries discovering this for certain as long as possible. To move the battle fleet, or even five battleships, to Singapore (in an emergency) was to invite its destruction by the Japanese . . . just as it would be in the North Sea. Let us send as many submarines and light craft as possible—and they would have far more effect in deterring the Japanese without the same risk of exposure. . . ."

On the specific problem of Germany, Trenchard's ideas were no less definite: "The Germans," he was sure, "did not want war, but were mentally ready for it—that was the difference compared with us. When combined with the tilting of the sexual balance, the development of physical fitness and the scale of warlike preparations, it promised a very dangerous development. He was more frightened than many people in Whitehall appeared to be. He thought Londonderry, etc., had paid too much attention to the minor question of whether Germany actually had at the present time the strength that was ascribed to her—the real point was that she would have it before very long. . . .

"Speaking of the 'big man,' Trenchard said he thought it was mainly that such a man was not really much more than one who gauged the tide correctly and interpreted the current of ideas. . . . Nothing was more fatal for the country than " 'a contented old man at the head of affairs.' . . ."

"The contented old man" had recently passed over Churchill in reshuffling his Cabinet. Baldwin's reasons for doing so are outlined in Geoffrey Dawson's memorandum of a private talk he had with the Prime Minister beforehand, on 6th May, 1935. In answer to the question 'Should Winston be included?' Baldwin stated that he had "no personal objection," but that "Winston would be a disruptive force, especially since foreign relations and defence would be uppermost."[4]

Trenchard's apprehensions here, too, were confirmed by the event. His repeated reminders to Churchill that "if you'd only use facts constructively they might pay more attention," were never welcomed. At lunch or dinner in the Other Club or the Grillon, as the Trenchard papers attest, Churchill often retaliated by baiting the Police Commissioner for wasting his substance in a job that was far too small for him. Why did Trenchard persist in hanging on? Was his aim to make the London "bobby" as incorruptible as himself? Surely he must know that every man, even the London "bobby," had his price? It was not a happy time for well-informed outsiders. They were still too few and too prone to bickering among themselves.

Less than a month before Trenchard left Scotland Yard, Mussolini invaded Abyssinia; less than a week afterwards, the League of Nations imposed economic "sanctions," scrupulously drawing the line at the oil required by the Italians for modern war-making in East Africa. The militant reactions of certain British Labour leaders, who abjured armed violence except such as might be blessed by the League, indicated to Trenchard that nearly half the nation must be unaware of Britain's inability to defend herself except by bluff. Baldwin hardly reacted at all; his reward was a renewed mandate from voters in November, 1935, to carry on in office for five more years.

By now, Trenchard was free to say what he wished without hindrance. The new Government contained no Churchill; Hankey still controlled the service chiefs; evidently the Cabinet would not move until the pressure of informed opinion forced Baldwin's hand. Trenchard decided to organise that pressure forthwith. He was immediately helped by Liddell Hart and, more surprisingly, by Geoffrey Dawson; on 2nd December, 1935, The Times published a leading article advising Baldwin to reconsider the archaic structure of his defence machinery. The Committee of Imperial Defence cried out for improvement. It needed a full-time controller, since no Prime Minister could give it the attention it deserved. Then the newspaper advanced a novel suggestion: Baldwin's nominee for so responsible a post should preferably be someone "who was not, or who had ceased to be, an active politician."

For the next month, the correspondence columns of The Times were filled with expert comment. Lord Salisbury, who probably knew more than anyone about the subject, agreed that reform was overdue but declared that only a Minister of Cabinet rank would carry the necessary authority to act decisively. Other letters followed with a weight of knowledge and a depth of concern which no Government could disregard. Trenchard's appeared on 16th December. It went straight to the point:

"You suggest that the position might be more suitably filled by a man 'who was not, or who had ceased to be, an active politician.' This would have some advantages but I fear that difficulties would arise as to ministerial responsibility, and for this reason I incline to Lord Salisbury's view that the man at the top must be a Minister."

His "English merchant" on this occasion, a high Air Ministry official, camouflaged Trenchard's scorn for the evasions of the Chiefs of Staff:

"I fear that, under pressure of work and from other causes, unanimity has been too often reached by tacit agreement to exclude vital differences of opinion. . . . What is wanted in the higher examination of the defence policy is not that the Government should get unanimous reports. We want to promote free discussion and not to drive differences of opinion underground."

For that reason, the new Minister, as permanent Chairman of the C.I.D., "should regularly preside at meetings of the Chiefs of Staff. . . . This would indeed be his most important function. His staff should also be enlarged and most carefully chosen since Ministers were "apt to be tumbled out at General Elections and five continuous years in one appointment is reckoned longevity!" As it would be hard to improve on Hankey as Permanent Secretary, that position filled itself; but, "when a successor has to be found, it would, I suggest, be desirable that the post of Secretary to the Committee of Imperial Defence should cease to be combined with that of Secretary to the Cabinet."

The compelling need for speed found expression in the closing paragraph:

"Lastly, I would most earnestly urge that the next step forward be taken *before* the Government come to any major decision as to what is necessary to repair 'the serious deficiencies' which at present exist in all three services."

Hankey was exceedingly annoyed. He accused Trenchard, to his face, of "trying to stab me in the back," spurning the explanation that personalities did not enter into it. They parted on bad terms, with Trenchard convinced that any influence Hankey pos-

sessed would be used, as never before, to dissuade Baldwin against
any "premature" reform.[5]

The Times refused to let the matter drop. In a further lead
ing article on 2nd January, the newspaper renewed its call for
Cabinet action. More letters followed, including one from Field
Marshal Lord Milne, the former C.I.G.S., which adopted the same
line as Trenchard's. The death and burial of King George V
merely postponed a decision. It had become plain before the
reassembly of Parliament that Baldwin would have some explaining
to do.

On 2nd February, the new Secretary of State for War, Duff
Cooper, invited to dinner at Buck's Club a party of known "mal
contents." They were Churchill, Trenchard, Major-General J. F. C
Fuller, the tank pioneer and military analyst, and Liddell Hart
who recorded the gist of the exchanges. On the question of co
ordination, "Winston spoke of the great effect of *The Times* leader
Trenchard insisted on the importance of the C.I.D., not merely
listening to official opinion (Baldwin's practice) but calling in out
siders, people like Richmond, Fuller, etc., as had been done pre
war. Winston strongly agreed.

"Winston expressed great admiration for Hankey's past service
but considered he was now holding up necessary progress. Trenchard
said he (Hankey) was not fitted for chairmanship. . . ." Then
Trenchard raised a second reason for reform. This was:

"The dominating attitude and influence of the Admiralty and
its refusal to admit any discussion of its claims. Duff Cooper
agreed . . .

"Winston was clearly dubious of the value of the battle fleet
although inclined to think that laying down one or two battleship
would act as a sort of bluff. . . .

"They spoke of the raising and equipping of a British Expedi
tionary Force, and of sending it to the Low Countries 'to secur
air bases.' . . . Duff Cooper said that the mobilisation plan now
was to get it there in fourteen days although there was only one
mobile division. I questioned whether this would be in time. . .
Our field force could not be re-equipped until 1939 and by that
time the range of aircraft which would be just coming into use
would be so large as to make these intermediate positions super
fluous. D.C. and Winston showed great concern at the possibility
that the Germans might move in 1937.

"D.C. chided Winston as being the author of the rule of 'no war
for ten years' which we had only abandoned since 1932. Winston

argued that he had introduced this simply as a working rule to be reconsidered each year. . . ."

Liddell Hart added this personal reflection:

"Very stimulating, yet it had a rather depressing effect. For here one had several of the outstanding men in the realm of defence for the past generation—much bigger minds certainly than the present heads of the services—yet much of the discussion was chaotic, sometimes rhetorical rather than reasoned, and often marked by an obvious failure to grasp the point. . . ."

It was a war council with a period flavour, earnest but devoid of that intolerant bellicosity of which men like Trenchard and Churchill were so often accused by ill-informed contemporaries. On one topic only was there unanimity and clarity: the importance of putting teeth into the Committee of Imperial Defence. This had become so contentious yet fashionable a topic among Government supporters that Baldwin could ignore it no longer. The Whips had to be withdrawn at Westminster when Parliament reassembled to permit the luxury of free discussion.

"Wonderful private members' day," one Conservative M.P., Wing-Commander (now Sir Archibald) James, scribbled in his diary of 14th February. "We've got the Government on the run."

Dissatisfaction was the keynote in both Houses. The level of debate in the Lords was less acrimonious, as became a forum which then included, apart from two service Ministers, five ex-service Ministers and at least the same number of past and present members of the Committee of Imperial Defence. Not all of them spoke. Salisbury did, however; he was followed by Trenchard, who elaborated on the arguments which he had been sharpening in private for two years. A curious fact to which more than one parliamentary correspondent drew attention was that both these speakers stuck manfully to their prepared scripts, advocating the adoption of measures which the Prime Minister had announced in the Commons a quarter of an hour before Salisbury rose to his feet. Baldwin, on that afternoon of 27th February, 1936, was not allowed to steal all the thunder from the place next door.

The Cabinet had yielded. A Minister to co-ordinate "the whole of the Government administrative machinery" necessary for running a war was shortly to be appointed. He would supervise man-power, trade, war risks insurance, food and oil supplies, censorship, emergency legislation, and "orders for action in every Government department—what we call the "War Book."

Trenchard's first thought was that the Cabinet would need a modern Hercules; the range of duties was too wide and vague to be practicable for any ordinary Minister. And, by accident or design, strategy had been left off the list.

There were few obvious candidates in sight. Press columnists were hard pressed to name more than half a dozen "probables." Churchill's claims were not discounted; Trenchard's were canvassed more openly; those of Sir Edward Grigg, of Weir, and even of Hoare (who had recently left the Foreign Office in disgrace when news of the proposed Hoare-Laval "Pact" for appeasing Mussolini in Abyssinia leaked out) were also mentioned. Nobody considered the name of Sir Thomas Inskip.

Baldwin's announcement came on 9th March, two days after the Führer's troops moved, virtually unarmed, into the demilitarised Rhineland. The political world was still reeling. But the *coup* shocked Trenchard far less than the Prime Minister's choice. The limitations of Inskip as Britain's new defence co-ordinator were well known to him. After all, this former Attorney-General was his brother-in-law by marriage.

5

The appointment was dictated, as we now know, by the Cabinet's obsession with political tactics. Inskip, in Churchill's mordant phrase, "had the advantage of being little known himself and knowing nothing about military subjects." Churchill possessed all the qualifications necessary but one: he was politically unacceptable, at home and abroad. Trenchard appeared to have been turned down for slightly different reasons: he lacked political subtlety; he was a member of the Upper House; and he shared Churchill's pugnacious outlook. The antagonism of the Chiefs of Staff, of the Opposition, and of the dictators in Europe would be ensured by appointing another Pitt or another Kitchener too soon. So the claims of Churchill and of Trenchard were ignored.

It is instructive to recall that Dawson of *The Times*, virtually alone among serious commentators, experienced no difficulty whatsoever in following "the process of thought which has led the Prime Minister to promote Sir Thomas Inskip." Baldwin, he wrote, had been wise to ignore other claimants, on the grounds "that they were Peers, or otherwise without a seat in the House of Commons, that they were ill-adapted to teamwork or (what was equally important) to work with their particular team . . . above all, that their appointment at this particular moment in the world's affairs might be misunderstood and misrepresented. . . ." [6]

Trenchard, who had not expected to be considered, suffered none of the personal frustration which made him feel so keenly for Churchill: he had only just resumed a business career that attracted him in several ways, not least financially. To his directorship with Goodyear had recently been added, through his Scotland Yard association with D'Arcy Cooper of Unilever, the chairmanship of the new and expanding United Africa Company: its interests in Nigeria, a colony which once he had helped to pacify, irresistibly drew him. "I can do more good from outside," he assured his friends. And he meant it.

With access to the highest political circles, he believed that he could still bring some indirect influence to bear on policy-making. As a member of the Lords, a forum whose importance he consistently over-rated to the end, he would not lack a platform. His attitude owed not a little to domestic considerations. The salary of a Police Commissioner, augmented by the half-pay of a Marshal of the R.A.F., had forced him to live frugally for four years. The school fees of two sons at Eton, provision for three step-children about to go into the world, and the many club meals incidental to his intensely personal methods of trying to mould others' opinions, had eaten away his modest savings. He simply had to earn more money; and he was glad of his freedom to do so.

Had Baldwin offered him a seat in the Cabinet, it is nevertheless extremely doubtful whether he would have declined it. And had he imagined that Inskip was in the running for a key post, on which the recovery of national security would largely turn, he might not have been so reticent about his own claims. Any doubts he felt, he swallowed. In a congratulatory letter he begged the new Minister not to hesitate about approaching him for advice. Inskip, he noted, made a studiously vague reply.

The Admiralty rejoiced in the appointment. The embers of the old Fleet Air Arm controversy still smouldered, though the efforts of Chatfield, the First Sea Lord, to blow them into flame had been hitherto thwarted by Hankey's ban on inter-service disputes of any sort. The expansion of the R.A.F. had revived the charge, virtually unheard since Beatty's day, that naval interests were being neglected. Both MacDonald and Baldwin received formal demands, in 1935, for the training of naval ratings as pilots and for drastic changes in the terms of service of R.A.F. pilots with the fleet. These issues were referred for settlement to the departmental Ministers. No agreement had yet been reached.

Until November, 1936, Inskip confined himself to examining the alleged causes of friction. Then Chatfield grew bolder. The First Sea Lord warned Hoare, who had been appointed to the Admiralty the previous summer and had so far steered clear of a controversy he found distasteful, that Inskip's inquiry and report to the Prime Minister could not be regarded as final since it provided "no adequate solution." It left untouched a system of divided control which would never withstand the test of war, for the work of aircraft with the fleet was "second only in importance to the firing of its guns." Realising that the Admirals were bidding for Coastal Command as well as control of all carrier-borne aircraft, Hoare dutifully informed Baldwin but took the precaution of simultaneously informing Swinton at the Air Ministry. Within twenty-four hours, Trenchard, in his self-appointed role as the R.A.F.'s watchdog, was forearmed for the fray.

In the Lords, on 18th November, 1936, he delivered what the sedate *Morning Post* described next day as "an astonishingly vehement" speech. . . . "A few months ago, he was difficult to hear. To-day his voice rose to parade-ground pitch." Trenchard recalled that he had addressed their Lordships only once before on this subject, in the previous March, when he had received official assurances that, in spite of rumours, no change in the control of the Fleet Air Arm was contemplated.

"This is not a question of the air force versus the Admiralty," he said. "It is a question of the Government versus the Admiralty . . . I have seen in letters and in reminiscences threats of resignation from the Board of Admiralty. I feel it impossible to carry on an argument on that footing. . . . Surely each of the services has its hands full of work at the present time. The menace of the air is surely more immediate than any conceivable naval war."

Sea Lords in the Upper House naturally disagreed. The veteran Salisbury, an arbitrator in past battles, sprang to Trenchard's aid. Gathering his immense dignity about him, he implored the Government not to tamper with R.A.F. control:

"Why should we, on account of certain professional feeling among sailors, which I dare say is very good in its way, interfere with all that is being done in the development of aeronautics and of fighting in the air? To deprive one large division of the air service of the experience obtained in the other branches would be the most uneconomical method you could pursue. . . ."

Realising that the Admirals, once roused, were not likely to let go, and fearing that Ellington might not fight them off, Trenchard sounded a louder warning in a letter to *The Times*.

He was leaving the country, he explained; he would be away on business "for many weeks." He therefore felt it right to state why the Government ought to stand fast and "not allow the country to be committed to what would be, I firmly believe, a disastrous dualism in the organisation of our air resources."

"The resources of the country in men, personnel, material and money," he declared, "are not inexhaustible; and there is no chance of our being able to maintain two wholly separate air organisations on a scale adequate, one, to ensure defence against air attack on this country; the other, to provide for all possible needs of air co-operation with the navy. . . . The views put forward by naval partisans obstinately ignore the inescapable consequences of the fact that the operations of aircraft know no frontier between the air over the sea and the air over the land."

By March, 1937, when Trenchard returned to London, the Sea Lords had gained ground. One of their most powerful converts was, of all unexpected people, Winston Churchill.

"I was rather sad on reading your speeches lately in regard to the Fleet Air Arm," Trenchard wrote to him, "partly because I remember the time when you enabled the air force to show what it could do in Iraq, and when you did so much to preserve its very existence in the days the War Office and Admiralty were both set on destroying it. Therefore when *you* attack the present policy about the Fleet Air Arm I feel very differently about it from what I do when the naval diehards attack it. . . .

"From what you have said in conversation I feel that you think we are playing a sort of dog-in-the-manger game; that the Fleet Air Arm is a small part of the air resources of the country; that it means very little to the air force but a great deal to the Admiralty; and that it is only through *amour-propre* that the Air Ministry hold on to it. I beg you to believe that this is not so."

The senior service had been outmanoeuvring the Air Staff, just as he feared. In January, it appeared, Chatfield had informed Hoare that he would resign unless Admiralty claims were met. Trenchard, who had still to see an Admiral resign, did not mind that so much. Nor did he mind being stigmatised by Sir Roger Keyes, in a House of Commons speech of rare ferocity, as the "evil genius" mainly responsible for arresting the development of naval aviation; indeed, sitting in the Peers' Gallery overhead, he was observed to "smile broadly" at his relative's unfriendly references to himself. What he did deplore was the Cabinet's decision to let the three Chiefs of Staff hold another inquiry under the chairman ship of that other relative, Inskip. For Trenchard doubted whether, this time, he would be consulted at any stage of the hearing.

There were only two logical solutions that he could see. He put both to Churchill, hoping that his friend might also see—and recant:

"It seems to me," he wrote, "that there are two ways of defending these islands. . . . One is by a self-contained navy with shore-based aircraft, as well as a Fleet Air Arm sufficient to deal with all attacks that may be made on commercial ships, on their own fleet in the narrow seas around Britain, and on the docks. . . . The other way is for the air force as at present constituted and the navy and army all to work in close co-operation as equals . . . so that the entire resources of one service can, if necessary, be used for the other service. I am convinced that the first alternative, apart from its cost, would mean operational chaos under war conditions—and that, I think, is the root of the matter.

"In your speech of 11th March you seem to suggest that the line of division should be at 'the aeroplanes . . . which start from ships of war or aircraft-carriers.' The naval case, as put forward by the Admirals, includes much more than that, and I don't believe you could stop—or that if you're going to have two air services at all it would be right or proper to stop—at that line of division. You will have to give them not only a Fleet Air Arm, but a large number of shore-based aircraft if the Admiralty are to do what they claim to be their essential job."

Churchill was kind but unmoved. He sent Trenchard some notes he had prepared, adding:

"It would be a great pleasure to me if I could feel that, to some extent, they met your views. I am just as ardent a supporter of the independent air force and Air Ministry as I was in those years when we worked together. I propose to publish these notes some time or other in the near future, but of course they represent nobody's views but my own."

Churchill had no thought then of submitting them to Inskip. He did so only when the Minister approached him rather than Trenchard for help. The inquiry was now deadlocked. Both sides had produced virtually unanswerable cases; and neither would yield an inch. The public yawned, bored with the whole affair. There were more wholesome and exciting events in store. The abdication drama of the winter was about to be rounded off happily and in accordance with tradition by the solemn enthronement of another King. The Coronation interlude assisted Inskip; so, indirectly, did Baldwin, whose resignation immediately afterwards left Chamberlain, his successor, with some clearing up to do. Other Ministerial changes lengthened the delay; by mid-June there was still no sign that Inskip had come to any final decision about the Fleet Air Arm.

Chatfield, fearing that Parliament would rise for the summer before the Government acted, waylaid Duff Cooper, the new First Lord, and handed him a fresh ultimatum. Unless the issue was forced at once, he, Chatfield, would go. The threat of resignation was enough; Inskip, according to Chatfield, "undertook to make an immediate report to the Cabinet on his own responsibility," which, of course, had been the whole idea from the beginning.

Trenchard had no direct wind of what was happening. Inskip had taken to avoiding him, in and out of the family circle; yet it was reliably whispered that other outsiders had been, or were being, consulted; and there was one extraordinary and persistent rumour that Churchill had actually been invited to draft the verdict.[7] This proved true. An authority whose views harmonised with the political needs of the moment had been discovered; and the Cabinet was content to swallow the Churchillian verdict as if it were Inskip's own.

Towards the end of July, Trenchard and his wife met the Chief of Air Staff at a Buckingham Palace garden party. Ellington admitted to being quite unperturbed; he knew and suspected nothing untoward. The inquiry had been hanging fire, and that was regrettable; but the Air Staff had every hope that their case, on its merits, would convince the Cabinet. Trenchard cut him short:

"Do you never leave your office, Ellington? The thing's over. It's been decided over your head, which is well buried in the sand as usual."[8]

The rebuke stung hard, coming as it did from a man whom Ellington, for all his distant veneration, blamed, and would go on blaming, for having failed "to make sufficient allowance for what was given away to the Admiralty, in your own and Hoare's time." Nearly a decade later, in 1946, Trenchard was still capable of rubbing in a little salt:

"You say you don't know what 'maintaining a battle' means," he wrote in answer to Ellington's dry criticism of the phrase in a recent pamphlet on air strategy, "but may I say, and I am hitting hard, that if you had maintained the fight for the Fleet Air Arm, we should never have lost it."

A sense of his own powerlessness oppressed him in July, 1937, when he realised what Inskip had done with Churchill's help. A letter to Hoare, now at the Home Office, conveyed an almost desperate sense of loss:

"I gave over twelve years of my life to help establish . . . an air force, and now we are going to have the Fleet Air Arm broken completely adrift from us. I do feel sad that I have not been consulted once. After all I had a good deal to say. Tom Inskip has not discussed the question with me, and from what you say he has not discussed it with you. . . ."

Could Hoare, even at the twelfth hour, reopen the question? Alas, Hoare could promise nothing. His surprise at Trenchard's dejection was quite unfeigned. The position now, said Hoare, was "so entirely different from what it was when the R.A.F. was small and struggling for its life" that he considered the Air Staff would "be well rid of the sea-borne units." There was no risk that he knew of a separate naval air force emerging. It seemed to Trenchard a slender straw for a strong man to clutch, but Hoare was right. For the Cabinet, in trying to marry two irreconcilable viewpoints, fell back on a characteristic compromise.

Chamberlain, who felt, in his own words, that "this departmental war had been allowed to go on much too long," decreed that shore-based aircraft should remain part of the R.A.F.; only those embarked with the fleet should be controlled by the Admiralty. It seemed to Trenchard a thoroughly illogical and unsound solution that stopped short of strategic reality. The Air Staff were aggrieved, the Admiralty dissatisfied:

"The failure to obtain the control of shore-based aircraft," said Chatfield, "reduced my satisfaction at winning back the Fleet Air Arm for the navy. But . . . it was only by a supreme effort that summer I had obtained a decision at all."[9]

Operationally, the Fleet Air Arm under R.A.F. management had undoubtedly maintained a standard of efficiency higher than the Admiralty ever allowed, higher certainly than could feasibly be reached again before the outbreak of war. That was the heart of Trenchard's fear; time proved it well founded; and the subsequent cost to Britain in blood and gold has never been calculated.

Even Churchill would admit in 1940, as First Lord of the Admiralty, that he "had not conceived how enormous was the charge involved." The duplication of depots, shore establishments and training centres added untold millions to the taxpayers' burdens, subtracting greatly from the Royal Navy's fighting efficiency. Late in the race for aircraft orders, the Sea Lords had themselves largely to blame, though they chose to blame the Air Staff instead, for the ill-equipped force which was theirs when the conflict came. Only experience could teach them the stragetic lessons which Trenchard's dogmatism had made so unacceptable, namely that in narrow waters "an aircraft-carrier is just a very vulnerable and a very expensive aerodrome."

6

Half of Inskip's difficulties as defence co-ordinator sprang from his own lack of knowledge and initiative, the other half from the ill-defined nature of the office he held.

"In his place, I'd have sorted it out or resigned," said Trenchard. "Inskip, unfortunately, wasn't the resigning sort."

The Minister had nominal power without final responsibility; in 1938, as in 1930, the Committee of Imperial Defence still jogged along at half speed. Inskip, lacking all sense of direction himself, seemed relieved to take instructions from Chamberlain who, in Trenchard's view, displayed most of the bad qualities of the back-seat driver.

On the few occasions Inskip appealed for outside help, this was given with alacrity. In the Fleet Air Arm dispute Churchill obliged willingly enough. And so did Trenchard on the solitary occasion his advice was sought. This happened in 1936; and the result was the all-important "Shadow Factory" scheme without which the Luftwaffe might well have triumphed in 1940. Remembering the aero-engine shortages which had cramped his tactical style in France from 1916 until the 1918 Armistice, and foreseeing the industrial havoc that would be caused by the eventual bombing of British cities, Trenchard put the project to Swinton, imploring him to bring in Weir, whom he considered the ideal man to carry it out.

Inskip responded gratefully; Weir was agreeable; and before the end of 1936 work had begun on six Government-owned plants for mass-producing aero-engines. The Austin, Daimler, Rootes, Rover and Standard Motor firms, together with the Bristol Aeroplane Company, took over a factory each; two separate assembly plants, managed by the Bristol and Austin concerns, were then erected. It was, according to Weir, "a very arduous and round-about way of doing business." It nevertheless served a vital purpose which, left to himself, Inskip would probably have neglected until the eleventh hour.

The relative pace of British and German rearmament still worried the Government far less than its critics. Trenchard, like Churchill, would have welcomed a debate in secret session; but this request was scouted. Instead, Baldwin received the protestations of eighteen Privy Counsellors and others at the Commons on 20th July, 1936. Neither the Labour nor the Liberal Party would associate themselves with the move; the delegates, including Trenchard and Salisbury from the Lords, were, without exception, dissatisfied Conservatives. Baldwin, Inskip and Defence Staff officials listened to their complaints. A full reply was not offered until 23rd November, 1936, when Inskip put a cheerful face on production prospects, chiding Trenchard and other speakers for taking altogether too despondent a view of the position. The Government, said the Minister, had no intention of introducing premature emergency measures. The voice was certainly Inskip's; the brief was just as clearly the absent Chamberlain's:

"If we were now to follow Winston's advice," the Chancellor wrote in his diary on 25th October, 1936, "and sacrifice our commerce to the manufacture of arms, we should inflict a certain injury on our trade from which it would take generations to recover. ... The one criticism which has, I think, something to be said for it is that Tom [Inskip] is so occupied with supply that he has no time to attend to strategy. This is not quite true, and moreover is founded on the belief of Winston that the Minister should himself be a strategist. ...."

A defence co-ordinator better versed in the business of strategy could have forced up military production by making and sticking to a short list of priorities, as Trenchard had suggested in 1934. But Inskip, as obedient to the rules of Hankey as to the prompting of Chamberlain, went his own way. And rearmament staggered forward at a snail's pace.

So Germany's lead in the air race lengthened. The chance of closing the gap was lost. Estimates might soar, as paper plans were progressively revised; but industry, like Inskip, followed at the pace set by a cautious Chancellor. The air planners produced nearly a dozen improved versions of the 1934 expansion programme

Talking to Queen Elizabeth at a garden party
in 1950

The Prime Minister, Harold Macmillan, unveils the
Trenchard statue

before 1939; but the effect of each revision on an industry short of tools, men and incentive was one of increasing confusion.

"It would have been easy," wrote Swinton, the Secretary for Air, "to produce large quantities of aircraft of the type then in production. Firms would have been only too happy to do so. We could have produced a fine balance sheet of numbers; and we should have lost the Battle of Britain."

Weir was the expert on whom Swinton leaned the hardest; and Weir persevered, without pay or position or anything but his technical ability and patience to sustain him. He insisted on the highest standards of quality production, an aim with the double disadvantage of consuming still more time and money; but Weir appreciated to the full Trenchard's old axiom that the pilot, being the soul of the machine, must have unqualified confidence in it. Morale, as both men knew, was more important even than quantity production.

Weir's reaction on inspecting the Spitfire in 1936, before farming out orders to sub-contractors, typified the painstaking nature of his approach. He had the machine stripped down.

"I wanted to see every detachable part laid out," he told this writer, "to decide which could be eliminated without loss. There was no other short-cut to quantity production. The Spitfire proved in the end the finest fighter ever designed; it was a sheer delight to fly; but it was an engineer's nightmare to build. It's small wonder the Hurricane came into the line long before the Spitfire and bore the main brunt of the German onslaught in the Battle of Britain."

By 1938 the Luftwaffe had twice as many medium bombers and fighters as the R.A.F.; but the R.A.F. held and never relinquished the lead it held in excellence of quality. The technical "bugs" in the Spitfire were gradually eliminated. To it and the Hurricane were fitted eight machine-guns, a variable pitch propeller and a new retractable undercarriage, the final refinement being a V.H.F. radio link between the pilot and the ground controller. These "extras" represented a triumph of team management under exceptionally adverse conditions; and Weir has still to receive his share of the credit. Without his quiet guidance in the late thirties, the aircraft industry would not have supplied, either in quality or in quantity, the fighters needed in 1940, whatever may be canvassed in favour of Beaverbrook's claims as a twelfth-hour miracle-worker.

7

The policy of appeasement which the Government followed from 1936 onwards seemed consistent to Trenchard. There was no alternative, in his opinion, but to play hard for time. Those who condemned Chamberlain for betraying British honour at Munich excited his contempt:

"To me," he told the Lords, "their attitude is quite incomprehensible. . . . They think of nothing but defence . . . yet they would have gone to war in the hope of saving Czechoslovakia! How could all these dug-outs, anti-aircraft defences, and fighters they are clamouring for ever have prevented the Sudeten Germans from being incorporated in Germany? . . . The only thing that will stop war-makers is the knowledge that if they attack they will be hit harder than they themselves can hit. . . ." His strategic views had the hallmark of simplicity. He did not change them merely to curry favour with a Cabinet which contradicted itself at times as pathetically as did its critics.

Trenchard went into the division lobby with Addison and other Opposition peers shortly after the Munich settlement to vote for the immediate establishment of a Ministry of Supply. It was already twilight; and he saw the madness of waiting with Chamberlain until German bombs began to fall on London.

His services were still unwanted; but he was buoyed up by the hope that his chance would come. Commercial life had its consolations. He had no ambition whatever to grow rich and leave a fortune, having left it too late to "build a Harrods" of his own. He preferred to spend what he earned and to earn no more than he judged sufficient for his family's need and his own frugal tastes; his sons would enjoy battling to the top, after his example, with the one notable difference of a better start. He therefore settled his own Chairman's fee of £2000 a year with the Unilever Board, and would not hear of having it raised by as much as a pound until his death, despite the steady slide in the value of money from 1939 onwards.

Travelling, a pleasure that had been denied him in middle age, was as great a consolation to Trenchard as writing proved to Churchill. He spent practically one week in every four of the last two years of peace touring abroad on behalf of Goodyear, of the United Africa Company, or of Rhodesian Railways, the third company to seek and obtain his services as a director. Twice he visited

Africa; and the transformation of Nigeria, where he spent half the winter of 1936-7, almost took his breath away. Remembering how he had helped to pacify an unmapped wilderness in the first decade of the century, he could rejoice that the campaigns he led as a soldier had not been in vain; civilisation had taken firmer root than he would have dreamed possible in so short a span. A later and more extensive tour of South, Central and West Africa deepened his admiration for British colonial achievements still further: here was a field in which he would have quite happily invested all his energies and interests, had Hitler permitted.

Lady Trenchard remembered her husband's second African journey for a different reason. He returned to London practically blind in one eye. Characteristically, he said little to the family until his sons remarked on the deterioration of his form at tennis and—what was odder still—the suddenly erratic quality of his once deadly aim with a sporting gun. Resting the specially altered stock against his right shoulder so as to take aim with his good left eye was less easy now; for the doctors had been summoned too late to restore his sight. It appeared that the tiny blood vessel which burst one day on the steamer sailing down the Congo River was in the centre of the retina, and no amount of medical treatment afterwards removed the clotted film that distorted his vision.

Of his repeated trips to Germany, one in particular filled him with foreboding. This was in the summer of 1937, when he had a violent argument with Goering, and discovered from Dutch, American and German business associates the extent to which Hitler had mobilised industry for war. Accompanied by two Unilever directors, Trenchard met the Luftwaffe chief at the Air Ministry in Berlin. The notes of their conversation are on record; a copy was forwarded later to Lord Halifax, the Foreign Secretary. The original transcript is among Trenchard's papers.

The visitors were nominally interested in more trade with Germany. Goering, who welcomed Trenchard not as a business man but as the creator of the Royal Air Force, for which he professed a marked respect, proved rather off-hand on the subject of commerce. Germany might have, perhaps, fifty million pounds a year to spend on imported oils and fats if arms production were cut. He could offer no assurance of any change in policy, however; the German people were doing without butter and soap because these were less necessary for the moment than guns and aircraft.

Through an interpreter, Goering answered Trenchard's questions with a deference which impressed D'Arcy Cooper and Rykens, his

fellow-directors. The Reichsmarshal put himself out to be pleasant
to a fellow-airman whose name, he said, was respected and admired
in Germany. Once, in the late twenties, when the ban on civil
flying was lifted, Trenchard had exchanged a few letters with
Goering, whose skill and bravery as a young air leader in France
he had not forgotten.

A banquet was arranged by Goering in Trenchard's honour. It
took place on the night of 1st July, 1937, at the Charlottenburg
Palace. The truth began to flow with the wine, and increasingly
disagreeable it sounded to the guest, despite the interpreters'
evident anxiety to soften the menacing words of his loquacious host,
resplendent in a white uniform festooned with innumerable medals,
orders and decorations. Next to Goering sat Milch and Udet, two
senior Luftwaffe officers whom Trenchard had entertained the
previous winter when they visited Britain as guests of the Air
Ministry. To judge by Goering's jovial indiscretions, the pair had
formed a fairly high opinion of the R.A.F.'s spirit and training, and
a correspondingly low one of its size and equipment.

"It will be a pity if our two nations ever have to fight," Goering
said at one point. "Your airmen are very good. We have you to
blame for that. It's a pity they haven't the machines that we have."
He then rattled out a mass of facts and figures which Trenchard
saw no point in disputing. His observations had already confirmed
indirect evidence gathered from various confidential sources over
the past three years that British manufacturers were lagging far
behind. Compared with the monolithic programme under which
German designers, engineers and makers were furnished with all
the funds, raw materials and priorities they needed, the R.A.F.
expansion scheme was an amateurish and muddled affair. No
wonder Goering was so full of grimly genial bluster; no wonder
Udet, the Luftwaffe's head of research and development, was so
eager to show Trenchard round in order to convince him that the
German lead in the air could never be challenged.

The toasts over, Goering led his guests out of doors. A magnificent fireworks display followed, and for an hour rockets and
multi-coloured stars lit up the sky between the palace terrace and
the island across the lake. When Trenchard remarked that the
night air was chilly after the warmth of the banqueting hall,
a servant in knee-breeches stepped forward with a German general's
greatcoat and Goering helped to sling it loosely over Trenchard's
shoulders. Then came a noisy diversion which drained the last drop
of pleasure out of a strange evening. The crackling of the fireworks

was suddenly swallowed up in a more sinister welter of sound. In Trenchard's words, "someone seemed to switch on an amplified recording of a modern artillery barrage mixed with the whine of formations of dive-bombers swooping and dropping their loads." The din was deafening. The garden was cold, the atmosphere eerie. Trenchard suddenly shuddered, and as he did so Goering turned on him a face wreathed in a knowing grin:

"That's German might for you," he shouted. "I see you trembled. One day German might will make the whole world tremble."

"You must be off your head," said Trenchard. "You said earlier that you hoped we wouldn't have to fight each other. I hope so, too, for your sake. I warn you, Goering, don't under-estimate the R.A.F."[10]

Goering seemed put out of countenance by the outburst. Even if the translators softened the harsh edges of it, nothing could disguise the blazing anger of Trenchard, who made an excuse and left soon afterwards with his two startled and silent friends.

He never set eyes on Goering again, but that single encounter persuaded Trenchard, as nothing else could, that men of such twisted mentality still thought of war not as an ugly threat, not even as an old-fashioned instrument of policy brought up-to-date, but as a glorious end in itself.

In the small hours of the following morning Trenchard spoke on the telephone to Halifax in London, having shaken off the hesitant efforts of the Berlin British Embassy staff to discourage him. The Foreign Secretary listened to his plea for a stiffening of the British Government's attitude to Germany, then suggested that it would be better if he called with a fuller report on his return. Trenchard did so gladly, but without effect.

The Government, said Halifax, saw no reason to alter its policy. To introduce industrial controls at home would only unsettle the public by implying that peace was past saving; to provoke Hitler would help nobody but Hitler, even supposing that Trenchard's interpretation were correct.

At the height of the Munich crisis, nearly three months later, Trenchard wrote to Chamberlain, offering his services to the Government. "The P.M. told me of your letter," Inskip replied by return. "I don't think you will have many more days to wait. There are so many posts . . . that we shall most certainly want anyone with your experience."

No summons came, however. The crisis passed, and official

reservations about employing a strategic dogmatist returned. Even the Air Staff were secretly relieved. Newall, who had succeeded Ellington in late 1937, had often to endure the lash of Trenchard's tongue; for the latest revision in the air expansion programme laid too little stress, to his mind, on bombers. Sir John Slessor has summarised in his book, *The Central Blue*, the reasons for that belated shift of emphasis:

"The setbacks experienced in the Hurricane and Spitfire programme, our growing awareness of the miserable inadequacy of our counter-offensive resources . . . and the glaring deficiencies in A.A. guns, searchlights and balloons which had weighed so heavily upon us in the recent Czechoslovak crisis—all these conspired to justify beyond all argument the allocation of first priority to the defensive fighter to which . . . we had hitherto attached insufficient importance."

Trenchard, however, was still more concerned about the potential weakness of our bomber strength. He feared, mistakenly, that the Air Staff planners were letting panic dictate policy. This, of course, did less than justice to men with a more detailed knowledge of defence shortages than he could have; and his friend wished that he would curb his tongue. They suspected, with reason, that Trenchard had once again "talked himself out of a job."

"The one real disagreement I had with Trenchard," said Liddell Hart, " was over his refusal to see that fighters might prove to be a greater need."

"On the long view," said Swinton, "Trenchard was right. But he was, I think, almost too far-seeing, so that he would not admit there were limits to what the bomber alone could do."

The only concrete offer yet had come from Hore-Belisha, who, at the suggestion of Weir, invited Trenchard to become his unofficial War Office adviser at the end of 1937, when members of the Army Council were obstructing the new Minister and "asking to be purged." But while approving Hore-Belisha's plans for a small, heavily mechanised army, Trenchard pleaded "business reasons" for declining to serve a Minister who, however forthright and enterprising, was benighted enough to favour a separate air arm for the land forces.

"The whole question," Trenchard wrote to the Cabinet in July, 1938, "resolves itself into what proportion of our forces should be utilised for the protection of England against bombing, and what proportion should be used for the bombing of Germany. Let me say at once that I personally am in favour of doing everything that is possible adequately to protect London and these islands so as to keep up our morale to its maximum. . . . If this were the only consideration it would be easy enough to obtain by building a large number of small machines that are a fifth of the cost, or less, and that only take a fifth as long to manufacture—in other words, to build nothing or practically nothing but single-seater fighters. . . . This would have an enormous effect by enabling the Government to claim equality or even superiority with Germany, but I maintain with all the power at my command that it might well lose us the war. . . ."

He wanted bombers as well as fighters; although he feared, at a time when radar was still unproven, that the war might be won or lost by a knock-out blow from the air, he also pointed out that while fighters might provide a good defence they could never win the war.

The four-engined Manchesters, Stirlings and Halifaxes ordered "off the drawing-board" in 1938 would not be available until 1942 at the earliest; he therefore deplored diverting materials and manpower from the unfinished medium bomber programme. "The old man is a bit out of date," fairly summarised the common verdict at Adastral House.

Newall, who was wounded by Trenchard's constant carping, implored him to exercise more discretion:

"I'll go down on my bended knees," he said, "if that will stop you talking."

Early in 1939, Inskip was transferred to the Dominions Office. The groove he had dug as Defence Co-ordinator proved too deep for his successor to turn in; no Ministry of Supply yet existed; and presently Chatfield became, like Inskip before him, a mere overburdened middle man between the Treasury and the Service Departments. At the end of August, 1939, Trenchard sent from his holiday address in Scotland a pre-paid telegram to Kingsley Wood:

"Am I wanted now by you or the Government?" it said.

"Will wire if I hear of suitable appointment," came the reply.

8

When Trenchard returned to London a cyclostyled form from the Ministry of Labour was awaiting him. It invited him to register for specialist duties and to state his qualifications; but as he could not decide what his were, he threw the form into the waste-paper basket.

On 1st October, the Prime Minister at last sent for him, but only to offer him the task of organising an advanced training scheme for R.A.F. pilots in Canada. Trenchard turned it down for reasons which he confirmed in writing:

"I am not the man for this job. It requires a young man up-to-date in training. My experience and qualifications are more for the shaping of the broad policy of how to use air-power. I still feel that one day I may be of more use at home in England than I should be if I went to Canada. . . ."

Chamberlain returned the short answer that he did not feel "it would be right for me to press you further." According to Hoare, certain members of the Cabinet, including the Prime Minister, regretted that Trenchard, whose strictures on their "wait-and-see" policy upset them, did not even nibble at the bait.[11]

The following note, written at the time, and found among the Trenchard papers, indicates why the Cabinet would have been glad to see the back of their most unsparing critic.

"I wrote a memorandum for the Cabinet advocating strongly hitting at German communications from the air as we had every geographical advantage. I never stopped arguing this. . . . Different members of the Government at different times gave me four different reasons against it.

"First, the humanitarian side—killing civilians and women and children: the answer I gave to the Archbishop of Canterbury among others, was to the effect that I objected to those people who were 'protecting their so-called reputation as guardians of humanity.' For by it we should prolong the war, kill millions of young men, and make untold misery among whole populations. The second reason they gave was that America would dislike it. I said that, politically, America might be giving lip service against it, but the majority of Americans were wondering if we were really seriously going to try to knock Germany out as we'd done nothing.

"The third reason given was that we were not ready: my answer was that numbers don't count in the air, efficiency does. The Germans were not ready to hit at us, we could hit at them from France, and every bomb we dropped would be in Germany. The German position was such that it increased the strength of the R.A.F. ten times.

"The fourth reason was that France would not agree: and to this I said you'd never convince the French of the necessity if you were not convinced yourselves. . . .

"Churchill was against me, except once, some time in December,

1939, when he said: 'Are you still of that opinion?' I said 'Yes.'
He put his hand on my shoulder and said 'I'm coming round to
your opinion. Keep going at it!' A fortnight later, he changed his
again. . . ."*

Business life had ceased to console him, a fact recognised by the
authorities. But they found him even harder to accommodate than
to placate. Early in 1940, Newall was prompted to approach him
with another offer: to start "camouflaging the whole of England."
Trenchard again rejected the proposition out of hand.

"I answered at once that nothing would induce me to do it,
that I did not believe in defensive warfare, nor did I put the value
on it that he did owing to the inaccuracy of bombing."[12]

That spring, Trenchard visited scores of R.A.F. units. In March
he paid his first and last visit to squadrons of the Advanced Striking
Force, on their forward airfields in France. Air-Marshal Sir Arthur
Barratt, the Air Officer Commanding, was impressed by the
passionate force of his denunciations. Trenchard seemed already
to have "some premonition" of the ordeal to come. Britain would
have to pay for immobilising the one weapon that might have upset
Hitler's plans. Instead, time as well as strategic opportunities had
been misused by timid men. The half-dozen daylight raids from
Britain against enemy warships were, in his view, senseless diversions,
very properly dealt with by the enemy. He would have attacked
German cities by night from forward bases in France, defying the
political odds and the self-styled military experts to pick up the
gauntlet where he had dropped it—over twenty years before at
Nancy. The Allies, he complained, were still prisoners of 1914 land
strategy; by refusing to use air-power until Germany did so, they
were wasting their best asset in the absurd hope of overtaking the
Luftwaffe on the production front.

The R.A.F. leaflet raids were, to Trenchard's mind, a mon-
strously ineffective means to a useless end. To suppose that propaganda would influence the Germans at that stage was a fallacy as
pathetic as the Air Staff belief that the crews derived invaluable
operational experience from the missions. This was "playing at
war," not waging it to win; and the continued Anglo-French ban
on bombing prompted him to warn the Cabinet privately that

* This personal memorandum plainly indicates how far Trenchard was out
of touch with the actual state of readiness of the R.A.F. for any sustained bombing
offensive even in the static conditions of 1939-40. Bomber Command's shortcomings at this time in weapons, tactical and technical training etc., are considered
at length in " *The Strategic Air Offensive Against Germany* ", Sir Charles Webster and
Noble Frankland, Vol. I pps. 107-143.

Hitler would demolish this legal fiction once his bombers were ready to strike at the West.

And so it proved in April, 1940, when the Norwegian campaign began. Chamberlain's inopportune remark that Hitler had "missed the bus" stupefied Trenchard. Even the metaphor rang with pedestrian falsehood.

In the Upper House, on 8th May, Trenchard finally let himself go:

"Why did we wait? What prevented us at once bombing the assembled transports or the growing and practised troop formations? I want to put all the emphasis I can on this. Why did we not attack them at their bases? We should no longer have had to await a summons to help that came too late and base our plans on guesses as to objectives which were unknown to us. . . . I cannot believe that any staff paper written since 1920 by any staff officer, senior or junior, would ever have concluded that such an operation (as landing in Norway) was practicable. It was bound to end disastrously if we could not secure air bases first, and even if we could obtain all the air bases that are in Norway, the much greater proximity of the land air bases in Denmark and Germany would have made our task very severe. . . .

"We have had eight months to watch the Germans, and does it not look as if their one intention at present was to prevent . . . the war being carried into Germany? . . . Can anything be more satisfactory to the Germans than to see both sides bombing a harmless, civilised neutral country—except perhaps when the time comes to bomb this island? Make no mistake about it; when the time comes, and it suits Germany's book, she will hit us by air—open towns and military objectives alike—mercilessly and thoroughly. Why should we await her convenience before striking at her military might in Germany?"

The strategic implications of the Norwegian débâcle were forgotten during the post-mortem in Parliament. Chamberlain had to pay the political price of failure; but his overthrow left Trenchard with the unpleasant feeling that the Commons, in transferring their confidence to Churchill, were purging the real or imaginary guilt of Munich rather than anything else. Churchill's hour had come almost by acclamation; the strategic awakening, perhaps a terrible awakening, would swiftly follow unless the new Prime Minister succeeded in rousing the people from slumber first.

On 11th May, the day after the Germans launched their assault on France through Belgium, Holland and Luxembourg, Sir John

Salmond sent a belated letter congratulating Trenchard on his recent speech.

"So much has happened since I saw you," he wrote, "but what I now want to know is this: will the new Government make up its mind that it is essential to bomb the sources of supply of German aircraft *in Germany*? . . . If and when Hitler succeeds in over-running Belgium and Holland with its aerodromes, he will use every machine he has to bring this country to its knees. . . . That must be his plan, and if we don't bomb his sources of supply now, when we are in a favourable position to do so and he is not, being immersed in operations in Belgium and Holland, then it may be too late.

"Have you any means of impressing the new Government with this point of view, if you agree with it? My great hope is that you may be Secretary of State yourself."

There was no chance whatever of that; Sir Archibald Sinclair's appointment had been fixed by the time Salmond's letter arrived. Barratt and his squadrons of the Advanced Striking Force were by now fully extended; but the initiative had passed to the enemy. The Battle and Blenheim bombers were outclassed as well as out-numbered. Their losses during the early and decisive stage of the enemy advance rose alarmingly. The fact, in the circumstances, was hardly surprising:

"On 10th May," records the official air historian, "there had been 135 bombers serviceable. . . . By the close of 12th May the number had dwindled to seventy-two."

Most of the bombers were sacrificed in unescorted, low-level daylight raids on enemy columns and communications; such sorties were of their nature suicidal, since the attackers were sitting targets for swarms of virtually unopposed enemy fighters. Urgent calls for intervention in the land battle continued to pour in on Barratt, who, still denied the right to strike at military targets on German soil, had no option but to continue sending out machines and men to litter the battlefield with burning wreckage and bones. The alter-native—to await passive destruction on the ground—was unthink-able.

The Chiefs of Bomber and Fighter Commands were openly critical of Air Staff policy. Portal, recently promoted to Chief of Bomber Command, objected as strenuously as Dowding to frittering his force away in a land battle that had cut already in Barratt's effectives by half a week. These dissensions sapped Trenchard's dwindling faith in Newall and impelled him to propagate his own uninformed views of what should be done. First, he insisted, British bombers should concentrate on military targets in Germany; second, all available fighters should be disgorged at once "to help maintain the battle in France and Belgium."

On 14th May, the Luftwaffe carried out a savage air attack on Rotterdam, extinguishing the last sparks of organised Dutch resistance and justifying Trenchard's renewed personal warning to Churchill that this was only a foretaste of what unrestricted bombing would mean if the enemy knocked France out of the war and then turned on Britain.

The Prime Minister lifted the ban on German objectives; and the first R.A.F. raid took place over the Ruhr the following night. It was not successful. Few of the ninety-six machines managed to reach the allotted oil targets; but at least the bombing of enemy homeland had started, after nearly a year of war. Inevitably, however, in response to French pressure, bombers were still diverted to the confused battlefield; and the unwilling Dowding had to part with four more squadrons of fighters, despite his dramatic plea to the War Cabinet on 15th May against denuding Fighter Command of reserves at a time when Bomber Command was inciting the Germans to counter-attack. In France, the reckoning came with catastrophic swiftness. Split from the French, the British fell back, blocked to the north and south by encircling enemy armour. The Belgians capitulated, and Gort, the Commander of the British Expeditionary Force, confronted with alternatives bleaker by far than those confronting Haig in March, 1918, ordered a withdrawal from Lille towards Dunkirk, his only remaining avenue of escape.

Every ship, big and small, was mustered by the Admiralty to lift survivors from the beachhead. It was hardly expected that more than 30,000 could be rescued. Friendly aircraft were rarely seen or recognised by the exhausted columns of men patiently awaiting their moment of deliverance; but miles behind, over and beyond the shrinking pocket, daylight attacks on ground targets by British bombers with scratch fighter escorts went on almost incessantly:

"For the first time," General Halder noted on 24th May, "enemy air superiority has been reported by von Kleist. . . ." "Dunkirk," says the air historian, "was for the R.A.F. a battle of all arms—not, as is sometimes imagined, an affair of fighters alone."

The Chiefs of Staff, instructed to advice on "British Strategy in a Certain Eventuality," reported back to the Prime Minister that though Hitler "has most of the cards," the final test would be whether "the morale of our fighting personnel and civil population will counter-balance the numerical and material advantages which Germany enjoys." They added their own unreserved belief that it would. . . .

The new Government team was broadly representative and united behind a Prime Minister magnanimously aware of the special claims of men who had endured with him the years of privation in the wilderness. Churchill had not forgotten Trenchard; and on 20th May he put out a feeler through Beaverbrook, the recently appointed Minister of Aircraft Production. Sir Samuel Hoare, who had vainly tried to lure Trenchard back as his Chief of the Air Staff at the end of April, agreed to play the role of intermediary.

"Beaverbrook needs someone to organise the defence of aircraft factories," Hoare told Trenchard. "He'd like you."

Very reluctantly, Trenchard accompanied Hoare to Weybridge. The meeting with Beaverbrook was brief. Trenchard came to the point abruptly:

" Isn't some general supposed to be doing this? "

Beaverbrook agreed, and mentioned the general's name.

"In that case either the man's doing his job properly or he isn't. If he is, keep him. If he isn't sack him. I'm not interested in helping to do someone else's work."

Beaverbrook prevailed on him to inspect existing defence arrangements at the factories in Weybridge and Langley, and next day they met again. Trenchard agreed that the defences at both plants were "very badly organised—but a child could put them right."

The Minister drew him aside. Churchill, he said conspiratorially, had something else in mind for Trenchard. The Prime Minister would be getting in touch with him personally. This gratuitous information was slightly displeasing, coming at second hand almost as a last-minute sop to console him. That evening Trenchard wrote to Churchill:

"Beaverbrook tells me that you are writing to me. Before you do so, will you see me, overwhelmed as you are. If you can't I shall understand. 'Too many cooks spoil the broth' and I don't want to be the unnecessary one."

The summons came late on 23rd May. The telephone rang in Trenchard's South Kensington flat. The Prime Minister invited him to "come round now for dinner and a chat." Assuming that nobody else would be present, Trenchard was dismayed on reaching the lift below Admiralty House to find the Secretary of State for War, Mr. Eden, waiting to ascend. He had little opinion of Eden, and could have wished him elsewhere, for he had several questions of significance to ask. He feared that Churchill's weakness for play-acting before an audience would render frank discussion difficult. He was right. The evening was a disaster. And Trenchard's version of it, recorded immediately afterwards, must be quoted:

"Winston began by attacking me for not having supported him when he was attacking Baldwin, conveniently forgetting that I had attacked Baldwin though not on Winston's lines. I replied rather angrily that he had succeeded—whether he meant it or not—in attacking the R.A.F. and the pilots. He had done worse than that by wanting only fighters and not bombers. The withdrawal towards Dunkirk was in progress, and I was more than horrified when Winston and Eden broke off three times to answer the telephone and proceeded to discuss with someone, presumably at the War Office, whether a brigadier in charge of the defences of Boulogne nearly 100 miles away was doing the right thing in resisting the Germans at one end of a quay or another.

"I heard him give instructions on how the brigadier should fight his battle. It seemed to me that Churchill was acting like a com-manding officer instead of a Prime Minister, and I said so. Churchill next made me more annoyed by suggesting that he and I together were responsible for reducing the R.A.F. after the Great War. This amazed me since he had borne as much responsibility as any-one for enforcing the 'Ten Year Rule.'"

At one point, Trenchard turned and apologised to Churchill's wife and her daughter, Mary, who had been listening in silence to these exchanges.

"Don't worry about me. I'm enjoying myself," said Mrs. Churchill. "I like to hear you two arguing. I want to see which of you will get the better of it."

"Oh, Winston will get the better of the argument, as usual, but that won't alter the case," Trenchard replied.

After dinner, when the ladies left the room, Churchill came to the point.

"He turned to me," Trenchard's narrative continues, " and said, 'Now what about this job of General Officer Commanding that I want you to take?'"

Churchill was explaining the scope of the appointment, which would have placed Trenchard in control of all land, sea and air forces at home in the event of invasion, when the latter cut him short:

"Let me tell you first what I think ought to be done. The only proper way to run the defences of this country in preparation for an invasion is to appoint a Deputy Minister of Defence to yourself, someone who'd be that and a generalissimo combined and who'd be acting with the Prime Minister's authority. A nominal G.O.C. would be powerless. He'd be for ever appealing to the various Service Ministers, to the Chiefs of Staff, and to the Cabinet. Whereas a generalissimo, who was at the same time the Prime Minister's deputy for defence, would be able to make decisions without holding numerous conferences. . . ."

Anger was not the best advocate for what Trenchard had to say. As he subsequently admitted, "I feel I said it badly." By saying it at all in an atmosphere already super-charged with discord, he reduced Churchill almost to the verge of apoplexy:

"Winston completely lost his temper and became almost as incoherent as myself, muttering something about not having a dictator or a Mussolini at the top, something else about unwarranted attacks on politicians, and something else about making sure of his own powers to curb the stupid generals.

"He then got up and said, 'We had better join the ladies,' so I said, 'If we are to join the ladies I think I will leave.' I said goodbye and left."

Late that night, Trenchard sat down and wrote to Churchill, apologising for "making you cross."

"I did think when you began 'What do you feel about becoming G.O.C.?' that I must explain what I felt was the best way I could help. You of all men know that I am very bad at putting my case, and you probably quite rightly resented the way I said it. Had our discussion continued, I feel you would have agreed that whoever is appointed must be given as free a hand as possible and more power than has ever been carried in that post, owing to the speed and rapid changes in this war which must be met at the same speed or faster. Believe me, I did not want to be a dictator."

Churchill did not reply; but his version of the argument, supplied over ten years later, broadly coincides with Trenchard's:

"This was a very bad moment in the war. I offered Lord Trenchard the post of Commander-in-Chief, Home Forces, after dinner, when the ladies had retired to the drawing-room. He started making all kinds of conditions, and I dropped the matter abruptly. Mr. Eden was with me. We neither of us liked Lord Trenchard's attitude at this time. He seemed to think we had called him in to help us out of a plight. Going up in the lift, he said to Mr. Eden: 'So this is the time when they call me in,' or words to that effect. He demanded enormous powers which would have rendered him virtually independent of my and the Cabinet's authority."[13]

As Minister of Defence and Premier, Churchill was rightly determined to exercise full control over the Chiefs of Staff as well as the Cabinet: whatever happened, there must be no repetition of the unseemly struggles between generals and "frocks" which had bedevilled the conduct of the First World War. Friction there might be; military blunders there inevitably would be. Disclosures such as Alanbrooke's, in his edited diary of the war years, exposing as these do the limitations of Churchill as a strategist, scandalise only the sentimentalists who imagine that war leaders must somehow be credited with infallibility. On the whole it was arguably safer and saner, even in 1940, that supreme power (including that of making mistakes) should be vested in the head of the Government.

Churchill's pride of office was immense: men served him on his terms or not at all; Trenchard certainly blundered in refusing to offer himself blindly, on trust; yet he knew Churchill too well of old not to demand cut-and-dried terms.

The argument was soon over. Trenchard had lost it, together with his last chance of playing a leading part in military affairs.

9

It was not his war, so he watched it. He hankered after something better than a ringside seat but never found it. He had cut himself off by a few angry words spoken out of turn; and he knew it. The knowledge haunted him continually between 1940 and 1945. It caused him less anguish later, in the evening of his life. For though his pride was hard and great, his gratitude for the privilege of living to see many of his prophecies fulfilled was greater still and more ennobling.

There were incidental compensations, of course, even for an onlooker. As the R.A.F.'s unofficial "Inspector General," flying tens of thousands of miles to visit squadrons behind the battlefields of Africa and Europe, Trenchard rediscovered his powers as a morale-raiser; as the unsleeping champion of his own service in the Lords, in the columns of the Press, and in his private dealings with the Air Staff, he was conscious of his privileged responsibility and discharged it vigorously; and as a quarrelsome friend of Churchill's, he did not care how often or how much he was baited so long as he could ventilate at will his personal views on the strategic mistakes of the war.

It says much for the generosity and resilience of both men that they were at table together, arguing as though nothing had ever come between them, within two weeks of the clash at Admiralty House. Their debate continued intermittently for the next five years. Only once, and then in the strictest confidence, did Churchill make Trenchard a further straight offer of employment. That was on 30th November, 1940, the Prime Minister's birthday, when they lunched tête-à-tête at Chequers. Both were in nostalgic mood. They discussed in general terms the negative policies that had led, step by step, to the recent testing and proving of the R.A.F. in the Battle of Britain. Churchill was full of praise for the pre-war handiwork of his guest. The air force had made history; Trenchard, who had made the air force, could not stand aside when there was still so much to be done. The approach was all the more flattering for its spontaneity. In that cordial mood of Churchill's, it was, to quote Trenchard, "all the harder to disappoint him by refusing his latest offer."

The Prime Minister wanted "a big man" to reorganise Military Intelligence. He was dissatisfied with it as it was. He had been casting about for candidates but could think of nobody better qualified than Trenchard. Would he think about it?

"I know you could do it," he said. "You did wonders with less backing than you'll get from me, when you ran the police. If you'd rather not, say so. I shan't be vexed, Boom."

In a personal letter dated 2nd December, Trenchard gave his answer:

"I spent two nights thinking over it . . . three points struck me. First, there might be a lot of feeling in the services on what they'll think is interference . . . [with] their operational work, and my presentation of all the combined intelligence may run counter to their interpretation of the facts, however much I try to keep only to facts. . . .

"Second, whether you consider it is the best organisation to do what you suggest and though, I think, it's necessary to try to bring the departments closer together, I frankly am doubtful whether this is the best way. . . .

"Third—this is really the most important point—the work would require very delicate and tactful handling and I feel I am not the right type of man to carry it out enthusiastically and satisfactorily. . . .

"I more than appreciate your saying you would not be vexed with me if I were to say 'No, I'd rather not.' I hope I may be able to help you one day in some position I feel I could do, and I would sincerely ask you to believe that I do want to help."

After that, there were no further moves on either side. A note among Trenchard's papers registers the one exciting rumour of useful work that reached his ears at a later date:

"I was told, probably with no truth, that when they made a change at the War Office and Mr. Anthony Eden left, he and the Chief of the Imperial General Staff recommended me as Secretary of State for War. I doubt if this could be, but anyhow nothing came of it. . . ."

Trenchard's faith in the service he had built never wavered. It sustained him until the end. He did not doubt the outcome of the Battle of Britain. He knew the temper and morale of the pilots too well. For him as for no other man, it was among the most decisive and the most unnecessary battles ever fought—"the only battle," as he said during it, "which will mean the loss of the war and of all we cherish, yet a conflict against odds which could have been considerably reduced by the proper use of air-power in the early months of war."

At the height of the crisis, and only at the express request of the Prime Minister, did Trenchard extract permission from a reluctant Dowding to visit the hard-pressed squadrons. His report was reassuring. Without descending to personalities, he declared that "the pilots and junior commanders are less tired or rattled than some of their senior officers." And he left it at that. There were lonely moments when, remembering the young Dowding who had protested at the high casualty rate among R.F.C. pilots on the Somme, Trenchard entertained qualms about his leadership. He was glad to be proved wrong, gladder still to tell Dowding that he had gravely underestimated him.[14] By his careful tactical handling of an outnumbered force, the Chief of Fighter Command secured temporary air ascendancy over the home base, though Bomber Command contributed as much to that result as Trenchard had predicted, and far more than the contemporary military analysts have yet acknowledged. The threat of a German invasion receded; instead the people of London and other cities settled down to weather the nightly terror of the blitz.

Of all Trenchard's keepsakes, the most treasured arrived by registered post from Windsor Castle. He remembered the day well. It was 7th September, 1940, the fateful day when the Luftwaffe, retaliating on direct orders from Hitler against R.A.F. token raids on Berlin, switched its onslaught from Fighter Command's semi-immobilised sector airfields to the docks and bricks and mortar of London. From then onwards, the tide slowly turned in Dowding's favour. There could have been no more appropriate date for the letter from the King:

"Having served in the Royal Air Force on your staff in France in the Great War," it began, "and having followed with much interest the growth of the service in the last twenty years, I feel I must tell you how much the wonderful spirit and efficiency of the air force which we see daily at this moment is due to your leadership and foresight in laying well and truly the foundations in the early days. You must feel proud of them, and that all your hard work has borne such good fruit.

"I have seen a great deal of the fighter and bomber squadrons and I am always amazed at their modesty when talking to them of their achievements. . . . But that is their training, and that is what counts so much in this battle against the vast numbers of enemy aircraft they have to meet and fight. . ... I am certain that is due to your having fought all those battles for them in the early days."

"You give me credit for much more than I deserve . . ." Trenchard wrote in reply. "I have also been round nearly every squadron. . . . The spirit they are all imbued with is wonderful. . . . They are what I had not thought possible—better than in the last war. On the R.A.F. I feel will fall the heavy burden of fighting all through the winter in very hard conditions, but I know their spirit will pull us through whatever happens. . . ."

10·

History will certainly say of Trenchard that without ·him there would have been no R.A.F., and therefore no possibility of even fighting the Battle of Britain. The knock-out blow would have fallen on a stricken and defenceless realm: invasion and occupation would sooner or later have followed. What history will say of him as an indirect oracular influence from 1940 onwards is a more debatable question. Ministers and senior staff officers of the older services ridiculed and opposed his large claims on behalf of air-power. The Press, for the most part, ignored them. "Boom," said Churchill on more than one occasion. "It's not very apt as a nickname. You should change it to Bomb." The Prime Minister felt that Trenchard too often spoiled a reasonable case by over-stating it, or turned a good into a bad by proposing unconstitutional remedies.

In the spring of 1941, for instance, when squadrons were being withdrawn from Bomber Command to assist in the Battle of the Atlantic, and the British public were being misled as to the effective-ness of R.A.F. night raids on German industry, Trenchard sub-mitted to Churchill a memorandum intended for publication. It advocated a more resolute offensive, regardless of technical diffi-culties and losses. The Air Staff did not like it; and Sir Archibald Sinclair subsequently informed him that Churchill would not per-mit such views to appear in print. "It would not," he said, "be in the national interest to do so."

Trenchard was upset. He protested to Churchill that "a memorandum such as mine would have done a tremendous lot of good. While the majority of the country would undoubtedly welcome it, its appearance would have helped—not hindered—you in your task of convincing the minority who would be opposed to it.

"There are certainly a number of people, as you must un-doubtedly have heard, who say that [increased] bombing will lead us nowhere. Such comment is to my mind very dangerous. There are others who bid us wait until our resources are more ample. That, too, to my mind, is a most dangerous view to take. We have got to hit now, with what we have got, continuously, and so try to shorten the war. . . .

"But another important reason . . . is to squash the notion, which many constantly press, that a large number of machines must be built for use in purely army operations at home. This force cannot be used offensively . . . until Germany begins to crumble and so it will sit idle and constitute a big diminution from the country's offensive power against Germany. . . .

"Pressure is brought to bear on me on the grounds that an article published over my name as a Marshal of the Royal Air Force would have too great an effect on the country. I do not admit that my position as a Marshal of the Royal Air Force does carry that weight; but if it does, surely it also carries the duty of expressing publicly my convinced and considered view as to what I regard as a vital issue in these tremendous days. . . ."

He could not change the habit of a lifetime. He had to pro-claim the truth even if it was unpalatable to some of his own disciples. Creating publicity for a controversial cause had become his main *raison d'être*; but Trenchard drew the line at defying Churchill or adding needlessly to the burdens of Portal, his "favourite disciple," who had succeeded Newall as Chief of the Air Staff in the autumn of 1940.

Of the hundreds of personal letters Trenchard received and answered each week, many came from airmen or the relatives of airmen; on his frequent visits to R.A.F. units, he made a point of soliciting the views of all ranks. By the following spring, when the air force numbered over a million men, adverse criticism in the Press and in Parliament began to weigh so heavily on the morale of the service that he begged Churchill to do something:

"All this has been accentuated by the collapse of Singapore, the setback in North Africa to our tanks, and the escape through the Channel of the battleships from Brest, and the failure to destroy them.

"The morale of an air force is a delicate weapon easily blunted, not by casualties but by the feeling that they are unjustified and fruitless. Air warfare is an individual business—the air-crew out in their bomber or fighter or torpedo-bomber are working on their own. . . . They do not want to be told they are heroes. But they do want to feel—they *must* feel—that they are not being mishandled and that their efforts are not in vain. . . . In my many talks to the flying crews, the air-crews and the maintenance personnel, I have done my best to instil that spirit. On the other hand their daily reading of articles and letters in the newspapers tends steadily to undermine that confidence. This criticism is also voiced very openly by a large number of naval and army officers.

"All the disasters we have suffered in the very recent past are put down by the 'popular' Press and by speakers in Parliament to the organisation of the Royal Air Force and the bombing policy, and seldom are they attributed to the actual causes, such as shortage of shipping, or the necessity of a powerful gun in the tanks.

"I think it will be disastrous to the nation and the war if these continuous criticism of organisation are not stopped by an authoritative statement by the Government."

He was reassured when Churchill replied on 30th March, 1942:

"I am in sympathy and agreement with almost all you say.

"I consider the unrestricted bombing offensive against Germany is our major way of striking at them in the present year. I do all I can to protect the Bomber Command from the demands made upon them for other services. These demands are, however, sometimes backed by overwhelming reasons. I shall try to say something about the bombing offensive the next time I broadcast.

"I also agree with all you say about the recklessness of unin structed criticism. Much harm has been done to the country this winter by writers and speakers who have dwelt only on our 15 per cent shortcomings so that people have forgotten the 85 per cent solid achievement.

"I have always been a supporter of the independent air force, but it is the duty of the Air Ministry to satisfy the army and give them every comfort and aid, and of course the liaison between the Admiralty and Coastal Command must be so close as to be practically a merger."

The relationship between Coastal Command and the R.A.F. was never easy. The Sea Lords recruited unlikely allies at times in their intrigues to recover operational control of land-based aircraft serving the fleet. Perhaps the unlikeliest of all was Lord Beaver-brook, who, towards the end of 1940, when he was still Minister of Aircraft Production, joined forces with Sir Roger Keyes to help Mr. A. V. Alexander, the First Lord, and the Admirals in their untimely campaign. Trenchard, who considered that Beaverbrook had damaged the air force enough in his ministerial capacity without doing more as a Press lord, decided to frustrate his activities. Leaving the Air Staff to win their own battles with the Admiralty, he set about compiling evidence to prove that, far from being the hero who in the nick of time provided Fighter Command with the Spitfires which Air Staff incompetence had denied them, Beaver-brook had reaped where men like Sir Wilfrid Freeman had sown and seized all the credit for the harvest. But Trenchard was still more determined to prove that aircraft reserves had since fallen off through the misdirected zeal of this sorcerer's apprentice.

"I hear you're after the Beaver," Churchill said to him one evening at the Other Club. "Why can't you leave him alone?"

Trenchard replied that he had no intention of doing that. He did not care so much about Beaverbrook's efforts to glorify himself as a national saviour; he was not even concerned with his belittling of the "bloody Air Marshals," as he usually referred to them. The harmful effect of his disruptive policy on future air strategy was, however, a different matter, especially as Beaverbrook was apparently seeking to rob the R.A.F. of Coastal Command at the same time.

In July, 1940, Beaverbrook had ordered the recasting of the air expansion production on receipt from the United States of a tentative promise that, by the New Year, Britain could expect the first deliveries of American aircraft, including four-engined bombers built to Air Ministry design, which would steadily rise to the tune of 3000 a month. The records show that in the last week of April, 1941, after the Minister of Aircraft Production had personally called at his flat one morning to beg him not to attack him in public, Trenchard moved the House of Lords into secret session to debate the true state of affairs in the British aircraft industry. He was able to expose, to his own satisfaction at least, the pretensions of Beaverbrook that output gave no cause for disquiet, though Beaverbrook told this author that Trenchard's speech was on the whole "good and constructive." Afterwards the antagonists had a private word together; and Trenchard could not resist handing the Minister a copy of his latest S O S to British aircraft manufacturers, urging "a supreme effort" on them since "casualties last week once more exceeded production."

"I could have quoted that against you, too," said Trenchard. "I didn't stoop to that because my methods are not your methods."

In August, 1942, Trenchard inveighed against the idea of a Second Front in Europe in a forcefully argued paper which Churchill circulated to the Cabinet. Its tenor can be judged from these extracts:

"If we are to win the war in a reasonable time we must avoid entanglement in land campaigns on the mainland of Europe and instead put everything into air-power (British and American) against the enemy's vital spots. If we can put such force into attack from the air German morale and ability to continue the war will be broken. . . . At present very considerable air resources are being employed on two-dimensional operations in the Atlantic which are purely defensive. . . . The place to hit the submarines is where they are made and to mine the seas where they emerge instead only of hunting them over the illimitable area. . . . To-day air-power decides the issue in every field. Only by means of it was the situation saved in Libya and Egypt. Malta can only be held if we can hold or defeat the attack from the air on our essential convoys. The raid at Dieppe was only possible by the fullest use of air-power. Its success or otherwise can be judged by what we achieved in the air. . . .

"Air, the new dimension, the new power in military science, has given the Allied Nations the great alternative. If we decide to use it with determination and concentration we can not only save millions of lives but we can shorten the war by months, perhaps by years. . . .

"As the enemy conquered Poland and France by their 'tank blitz,' so can we smash the German machine by the 'bomber blitz.' . . .

"Finally, the carrying out of this policy requires that there should be one brain responsible for the purely military (in its widest sense) strategical conception of the war in Europe, supported of course by a staff representative of all three services. It would be essential that this commander should be one who believes in his weapon, the power of the air, and should have had experience of command in this war—there are many such. . . ."

The Prime Minister bridled at the constitutional implications of that closing paragraph:

"It is very difficult," he retorted, "to divorce the Head of the Executive in any country from the chief responsibility for the conduct of the war. . . . To pick an airman, give him plenary powers, and tell him to win the war is certainly a policy, but I wonder whether you have thought it out in all its implications. He would certainly have great difficulty with the other two services. He would also have difficulty with the Allies, who adopt quite different systems, and particularly with the United States, who hold rigidly to a subordinate air force. There might also be trouble with the House of Commons, the Cabinet, and all those sort of things. Should the right man be found, however, many of these difficulties would be overcome by his becoming, at the same time, Prime Minister. If I were convinced that this solution would bring about a speedy victory, I should be very glad to make way for him. Would it be too much to inquire whom you have in mind? . . ."

Trenchard replied:

"I was not suggesting that the Head of the Executive should be divorced from the chief responsibility of the war. I have never expressed or held such a view. What I was trying to say was this. In many newspapers and discussions it has been suggested that there should be one commander-in-chief appointed for Europe— a man like Marshall or Wavell, and I wanted to combat the idea that it must necessarily be an army man. If air is the dominant force, the force that can give us victory, why *must* the commander be a military man? Why is our strategy to be based on the 'ground' view when we know now that it is the Air which decides? . . ."

The Americans, in fact, were more sympathetic to this point of view than the British War Cabinet; but Churchill's attitude grew more favourable with time, and nobody was more pleased than Trenchard when Tedder was appointed deputy Supreme Commander to Eisenhower before the Allied invasion of Europe in 1944.

Throughout these years, Trenchard and his wife lived in a flat overlooking the south side of Hyde Park. The family had dispersed; Dancer's Hill, the home where they had known so much happiness together, had to be given up. One morning, during the blitz, he took a taxi to his office in the City. There was a hold-up in the Strand. A section of the road was roped off, and the police were directing vehicles and pedestrians down a side-street. Trenchard paid off the driver. He had an urgent appointment and thought it would be quicker to continue on foot. Ignoring the barrier, he walked straight on towards a group of men standing beyond the far end of the roped-off area. He recognised one of them immediately as a former colleague at Scotland Yard:

"You know, Lord Trenchard, you shouldn't have done that. You've just walked over two time-bombs. They may go off at any moment."

"In that case why did the constable at the other end let me come through?"

"I don't know, sir, but I think he may have recognised you."

The Trenchards' flat was a lonely place. Only Tom the youngest saw much of his parents, and he would soon be going overseas like the others. Three of Trenchard's boys were already dead: John, his elder stepson, had been killed in action serving with the Royal Scots Fusiliers in Italy, Eddie in a flying accident, and Hugh, his first-born, with the Guards Brigade in North Africa. The loss of Hugh, the apple of his eye and a young man who bore a remarkable resemblance to himself in outlook and temperament, cut Trenchard to the heart. Yet grief was not allowed to interrupt the strict routine which he laid down and religiously followed. Apart from his business commitments and his attendance at Westminster, the regular tours of R.A.F. stations at home and overseas left him little time to himself. The value of these sometimes exhausting journeys by air he rated higher than his spasmodic attempts as an outside critic to influence the shaping of Allied strategy. And there he did not err.

He thought of the air-crews and ground-crews as his own, irrespective of the gulf in age and rank between them and him. He seldom failed to quicken their blood. Senior officers who knew him of old, and perhaps still dreaded his comings a little, were constantly amazed at his virtuosity. He had no talent for the rolling period. The "first principles" which he never tired of drumming into the heads of war leaders, American as well as British, had no place in these informal discourses. It was the human warmth he radiated which touched them all.

"Lord Trenchard," noted Hector Bolitho in *A Penguin in the Eyrie*, "has a talent for saying the right word with such sincerity that his anecdotes are always fresh. Perhaps his greatest flash of imagination came in Egypt, when he was talking to airmen working in the vast caves dug by the Pharaohs and converted into engineering workshops for the R.A.F. He said to them, 'The Pharaohs would be pleased that they dug these caves if they could come back and see a generation as fine as yours working in them '."[15]

Being with such men helped to assuage his grief for his own dead sons. To the end, he loved the spirit of youth for its infinite promise.

His impressions of North Africa in 1943 confirmed convictions that he had held unrepentantly for over a quarter of a century: "We won the battle of the air," he wrote, "before El Alamein and Tunisia could be won." It was the same in Sicily and Italy; the same again before the landings in Normandy could be attempted. And the pattern was as predictable and as inevitable in the Atlantic, the Bay of Biscay or the far-off Pacific as anywhere on land.

Almost exactly eight years after his unpleasant encounter with Goering, he saw Berlin again, a broken bastion where civilians walked the ruined streets with the dazed look of people raised from the dead. It was July, 1945. The founder of Hitlerism was rumoured to have died by his own hand in an underground bunker before the banners of the victors were hoisted above the rubble. The intervening period of agony, confusion and personal tragedy for millions of men and women had also witnessed the awesome vindication of Trenchard's lifework.

A young squadron-leader who had joined the R.A.F. as a boy-apprentice in the twenties stood beside Trenchard on that overcast summer's morning. From a platform of littered masonry they stared across towards the distant lakeside palace, Trenchard recalling the boastful words of Goering which had roused him to warn the Luftwaffe leader not to play with fire.

"He made one mistake," said Trenchard. "He thought too much of numbers, too little of men. I wish he could be here to count the cost of his folly."

Epilogue

They buried him in Westminster Abbey, in the Battle of Britain Chapel he had helped to provide as a memorial for "The Few." He needed none for himself. The sky was his monument. Death took him, not without a struggle, a week after his 83rd birthday, on 10th February, 1956. None of the mourners, not even Churchill or the six marshals of the R.A.F. who acted as pall-bearers, knew that he should have died nearly sixty years before and that he had lived since with only one whole lung and gleeful memories of having cheated the undertaker largely by luck and phenomenal will-power. None but his family and a few friends knew.

The sombre dignity of other men's funerals had sometimes moved him to tears in the past; he would have laughed at his own, and possibly did. His reverence for human life, the gratitude he always felt for the gift of his own, did not exclude self-mockery. Trenchard was a considerable stoic. His reticence was as proverbial as his endurance. He did not prize fame for its own sake. The thrill of striving and of succeeding was recompense enough. Men might say that he had added a third dimension to the art of warfare if they pleased. He had never felt any compulsion to tell them of the ambush into which he had once walked in a nameless South African valley, of the bullet that left him temporarily paralysed and permanently devoid of a lung, of the Australian doctor breathing into his face and pronouncing him as good as dead already. The circumstances of his recovery, like the humiliations of childhood, were strictly his own affair: he was one of fate's aptest and most silent pupils.

He had lived long enough to witness the logical culmination of his efforts to promote air-power in the scientific development of thermo-nuclear bombs and ballistic missiles, insisting to the last that these were essentially airmen's tools but doubting whether mankind would ever be mad enough to use them in anger. He left much unfinished business, little money, and a mass of papers which

731

proved that as his years increased so did his appetite and capacity for work. In our age of anxiety, his mental vitality was proof against an infirmity of body which would have carried off many a younger man sooner. In 1953, on Coronation Day, he lost the sight of his good remaining eye. After that, he had readers in to keep him abreast of the news of the day; after that, too, there is a marked duplication in the voluminous records of his meetings, speeches, lectures, memoranda and personal correspondence.

Of the projects nearest to his heart, some failed. He tried to interest scholars and influential leaders on both sides of the Atlantic in an Anglo-American history of the Second World War. He was unsuccessful. He declaimed vigorously against the abolition of his major police reforms, in vain. He protested just as loudly against the abolition of his "week-end pilots"; and the decision to wind up Auxiliary Air Force squadrons was deferred, as a kindness, until he was in his grave. He was rightly proud of being asked by Generals Arnold and Spaatz, who, like the great Doolittle and other American air leaders, paid him the unaccustomed homage due, as they put it, "to the patron saint of air-power," to brief them for the bitter debate which preceded the formation of an independent United States Air Force shortly after the Second World War. He also succeeded in gathering about him on his 80th birthday a remarkable cross-section of men who had, in his own phrase, "either helped or hindered me in my career." He was unsuccessful, too, on that occasion in preventing Churchill from preaching a panegyric which ended:

"And now I've only one word to add—Boom."

The Battle of Britain Chapel, where Trenchard found his last resting-place, was the first of two such undertakings. The other was the Anglo-American Memorial, in St. Paul's, which was not completed in his lifetime. It was General Spaatz again who inspired him to promote its construction one day in 1945, with the remark that he (Spaatz) would not rest until a fitting monument to the dead airmen of both nations rose on American soil.

"No," said Trenchard, "this is where we must have it. England was their base."

In raising funds, in organising the early plans, Trenchard enjoyed himself hugely until the venture reached the formal and rather chilling committee stage. He walked out after encountering opposition from the Archbishop of Canterbury, who cast a mildly disapproving eye over the first designs drawn to Trenchard's general instructions. Dr. Fisher was not enamoured of their secular flavour. They were, he intimated, somewhat out of keeping with "our traditional concepts of ecclesiastical symbolism."

"Fine words, Archbishop," Trenchard thundered in reply, "but what do they mean?"

Then, raising an admonitory finger, he said:

"The trouble with you, and prelates who think like you, is that you imagine all religion stopped when Christ was crucified." And with that he strode out of the room.

Trenchard was what orthodox theologians would call an "*anima naturaliter Christiana*." He went to church but it is questionable whether he believed in a personal God. The approach of death puzzled rather than daunted him. "How," inquired Alexander the Great of the Jain holy man whose life hung on the wisdom of his answer, "How long is it good for a man to live?" The disarming reply—"As long as he does not prefer death to life"—would have been Trenchard's nearly twenty-two hundred years later. He did not want to leave his little world of distinguished obscurity because his zest for living remained inordinately huge until the last. Besides, there was always so much still to do.

Whether man was a being whose unique but undeveloped faculties postulated a Creator, Trenchard never paused to inquire. His curiosity was confined to people. He was concerned only for mankind. If nothing else survived, the memory of human endeavours, noble or infamous, certainly would. He was a remarkably good man by the highest Christian standards; wholly incorruptible by his own. His life was sternly regulated by a will of tempered steel which a Greek philosopher might have been happy to possess.

Major events in the outside world upset him less in these declining years than during or before the Second World War. The perils of peace were for the valiant and the far-sighted to master; such landmarks as the Berlin airlift, the confining to a limited battlefield of the Korean conflict, and the steady consolidation of the Atlantic Alliance under a common air shield, demonstrated that there were still valiant and far-sighted men in the service of the West. Trenchard continued to look out on a world that had largely forgotten his existence with sympathy and a detached sense of humour. He read widely and deeply; when his sight failed, he hired the eyes of daily readers. He was fond of reminding the influential, notably in the political sphere, that nothing on this earth was entirely new or strange. The self-important seldom appreciated the elaborate care he expended on the actual form and shape of these reminders, fearing that Trenchard was becoming something of an eccentric in his dotage.

"The following," began a typical broadside, "is a quotation from a gentleman called Isocrates, who lived five hundred years before Christ and witnessed the beginning of the decay and breakdown of the ancient Greek civilisation.

" 'When I was a boy,' declared Isocrates, 'to be rich was considered so safe and so respectable that almost everyone pretended to be wealthier than he actually was, so as to have his share of this respectability. But to-day one has to disclaim in self-defence any wealth as though that were an utter violation of the moral law. And to watch his step if he is going to get away with it. For it has become a more scandalous thing to seem to prosper than to be an open malefactor.' "

Trenchard had a thousand copies of this quotation printed and distributed for well-wishers and critics, including a few Socialists, to keep and ponder.

Having long ago put away ambition, he did not succumb to it now. Nor did he seek to impose his will on Life, that nearer mystery which still baffled him on the brink of the grave more than all the high-flown speculations about its Author. If there were a personal God, he could take Trenchard as he found him, with his many scars and his few but well used talents. Organised religion was acceptable largely as a pillar of the social order; the competitive zeal of rival church leaders, he felt, could hardly fail to make the Almighty shudder, particularly in times of chaos and human stress.

The biting lines of Sir John Squire were lines which exactly fitted Trenchard's view of that oddest of all signs of contradiction:
"God heard the nations shout:
'Gott strafe England.'
'God Save the King.'
'God this, God that, and God the other thing.'
　'Good God! ' said God,
'I'll have my work cut out . . .' "

To the end he sympathised with God, the unknowable, not least on national Days of Prayer; but he was content with what lay within his experience, a blinkered visionary who had contributed his own apocalyptic footnote to the history of this tortured and frenzied age. A giant in his own right, he kept faith with his high and lonely destiny.

Bibliography

Notes on Sources

Bibliography

ALDINGTON, Richard, *Lawrence of Arabia*, Collins, 1955.
AMERY, L. S., *My Political Life*, Hutchinson, 1953.
ASPINALL-OGLANDER, Cecil, *Roger Keyes*, Hogarth Press, 1951.

BALDWIN, A. W., *My Father the True Story*, Allen & Unwin, 1955.
BARING, Maurice, *Flying Corps Headquarters, 1914–1918*, Heinemann, 1930.
BEAVERBROOK, Lord, *Politicians and the Press*, Hutchinson, 1926.
Politicians and the War, Oldbourne, 1932.
BAIRD, H. C., *Wings*, Hurst & Blackett.
BLAKE, Robert, *The Private Papers of Douglas Haig, 1914–1919*, Eyre & Spottiswoode, 1952.
The Unknown Prime Minister, Eyre & Spottiswoode, 1955.
BORASTON, J. H., *Sir Douglas Haig's Command*, Dent, 1922.
BOLITHO, Hector, *A Penguin in the Eyrie*, Hutchinson, 1955.
BRABAZON, Lord, *The Brabazon Story*, Heinemann, 1956.
BRYANT, Sir Arthur, *The Turn of the Tide*, Collins, 1957.
BUCHAN, John, *History of the Royal Scots Fusiliers, 1678–1918*, Thomas Nelson, 1925.
BURLINGAME, Roger, *General Billy Mitchell*, McGraw-Hill Book Co. Ltd., 1952.

CALDWELL, Major-Gen. Sir C. E., *Field-Marshal Sir Henry Wilson: His Life and Diaries* (2 vols.).
CHALMERS, Rear Admiral W. S., *The Life and Letters of David, Earl Beatty*, Hodder & Stoughton, 1951.
CHAMBERLAIN, Sir Austen, *Down the Years*, Cassell, 1935.
Politics from Inside, Cassell, 1936.
CHARLTON, Air Commodore, L. E. C., *War From the Air*, Faber, 1931.
CHARTERIS, Brig.-Gen. John, *At G.H.Q.*, Cassell, 1931.
CHATFIELD, Lord, *It Might Happen Again*, Heinemann, 1947.
CHURCHILL, Sir Winston S., *The World Crisis* (VI) vols., 1911–1918, Odhams, 1932.
Thoughts and Adventures, Butterworth, 1933.
Great Contemporaries, Butterworth, 1938.
The Second World War (IV) vols., Cassell.

COOPER, Duff, *Haig*, Faber, 1936.
    British Prime Ministers, Wingate, 1953.
COLLIER, Basil, *Leader of the Few*, Jarrolds, 1957.
    Heavenly Adventurer, Secker & Warburg, 1959.

DAVIDSON, Maj.-Gen. Sir John, *Haig, Master of the Field*, P. Nevill, 1953.
DICTIONARY OF NATIONAL BIOGRAPHY
DUGDALE, Blanche, *Arthur James Balfour*, Hutchinson, 1938.

EDMONDS, Sir James E., *History of the Great War*, H.M.S.O., 1949.
EMBRY, Air Chief Marshal Sir Basil, *Mission Completed*, Landsborough
    Pubns, 1958.
ELIOT, T. S., *Collected Poems*, Faber, 1936.

FEILDING, Keith, *Neville Chamberlain*, Macmillan, 1946.
FOKKER and GOULD, *Flying Dutchman: The Life of Anthony Fokker*,
    Routledge, 1931.
FULLER, Gen. J. F. C., *Last of the Gentlemen's Wars*, Faber, 1937.

GARNETT, David, *The Letters of T. E. Lawrence*, Jonathan Cape,
    1938.
GIBBONS, Floyd, *The Red Knight of Germany: Baron von Richthofen*, Cassell,
    1930.
GRIGG, P. J., *Prejudice and Judgment*, Jonathan Cape, 1948.
GRINNELL-MILNE, Duncan, *Wind in the Wires*, Hurst & Blackett.
GROVES, Brig. P. C. R., *Behind the Smoke Screen*, Faber, 1934.

HARINGTON, Gen. Sir Charles, *Tim Harington Looks Back*, Murray,
    1940.
HARRIS, Sir Arthur, *Bomber Offensive*, Collins, 1947.
HOWE, Ronald, *The Pursuit of Crime*, Arthur Barker, 1961.
HOWGRAVE-GRAHAM, H. W., *Light and Shade at Scotland Yard*, Murray,
    1947.

ISMAY, Lord, *The Memoirs of Lord Ismay*, Heinemann, 1960.

JONES, N. A., *War in the Air*, Vols. 2, 3, 4, 5, 6 and Appendices, Clarendon
    Press, 1928–37 (for Vol. 1, see Raleigh).

KEYNES, J. M., *Economic Consequences of the Peace*, Macmillan, 1921.
KINGSTON-MCCLOUGHRY, E. J., *The Direction of War*, Jonathan Cape,
    1955.
KRUGER, Rayne, *Good Bye Dolly Gray*, Cassell, 1959.

LAWRENCE, T. E., *Seven Pillars of Wisdom; The Mint*, Jonathan Cape, 1955.

LIDDELL HART, Capt. B. H., *The Other Side of the Hill*, Cassell, 1951.

LLOYD-GEORGE, David, *War Memoirs*, (IV) vols., Nicholson and Watson.

LUDENDORFF, *My War Memories, 1914–18*, Hutchinson, 1919.

MCCUDDEN, James Thomas Byford, *Five Years in the Royal Flying Corps*, The Aeroplane and General Publishing Co. Ltd., 1918.

MACMILLAN, Capt. Norman, *The Royal Air Force in the World War* (4 vols.), Harrap, 1950.

Sefton Brancker, Heinemann, 1935.

MINNEY, R. J., *The Private Papers of Hore-Belisha*, Collins, 1960.

MOYLAN, Sir John, *Scotland Yard*, Putnam, 1929.

MAURICE, Maj.-Gen. Sir Frederick, and Capt. Maurice Harold Grant, *The History of the War in South Africa, 1899–1902* (4 vols.), Hurst & Blackett, 1906-1910.

NICOLSON, Harold, *Curzon*, Constable, 1937.

Peacemaking, Constable, 1945.

King George V, Constable, 1952.

OWEN, Frank, *Tempestuous Journey*, Hutchinson, 1954.

PETRIE, Sir Charles, *Life and Letters of Sir Austen Chamberlain*, Cassell, 1940.

RALEIGH, Sir Walter, *War in the Air*, The Clarendon Press, 1922.

RICHARDS, Denis & Saunders, Hilary, *Royal Air Force, 1939–45*, H.M.S.O., 1953.

REITH, Charles, *The Blind Eye of History*, Faber, 1952.

REPINGTON, Lt.-Col., C. A., *The First World War*, Constable, 1920.

REYNOLDS, Quentin, *They Fought for the Sky*, Cassell, 1958.

RIDDELL, Lord, *Intimate Diary of the Peace Conference and After, 1918–1923*, Gollancz, 1933.

ROBERTSON, Field-Marshal Sir William, *Soldiers and Statesmen, 1914–18*, Cassell, 1926.

RYAN, A. P., *Mutiny at the Curragh*, Macmillan, 1956.

SAMUEL, Viscount, *Memoirs*, Cresset Press, 1955.

SAINT-EXUPERY, A. de, *Wind, Sand and Stars*, Heinemann, 1954.

SEVERESKY, Alexander, P. de, *Air Power: Key to Survival*, Jenkins, 1952.

SIMON, The Rt. Hon. Viscount, *Retrospect*, Hutchinson, 1952.

SLESSOR, Sir John, *The Central Blue*, Cassell, 1956.

The Great Deterrent, Cassell, 1957.

SMUTS, J. C., *Jan Christian Smuts*, Cassell, 1952.

SMITH, Maxwell, A., *Knights of the Air*, Cassell, 1959.

SMITH, Cecil Woodham, *The Reason Why*, Constable, 1953.

STEEL, Col. J. P., *A Memoir of Lt.-Col. A. E. Steel*, Hamilton, 1921.

SUETER, Murray, F., *Airmen or Noahs*, Sir Francis Pitman, 1928.

SWINNERTON, Frank, *The Journals of Arnold Bennett*, Penguin Books, 1954.

SWINTON, Lord, *I Remember*, Hutchinson, 1948.

SYKES, Sir Frederick, *From Many Angles*, Harrap, 1942.

THOMSON, Malcolm, *David Lloyd George*, 1948.
    Life and Times of Winston Churchill, Odhams, 1955.

TEMPLEWOOD, Viscount, *Empire of the Air*, Collins, 1957.

VAN ZANDT, *The Geography of World Air Transport*, Washington, 1944.

VANSITTART, Lord, *Lessons of My Life*, 1943.
    The Mist Procession, Hutchinson, 1958.

WALLACE, Graham, *R.A.F. Biggin Hill*, Putnam, 1957.

WEIR, L. MacNeill, *The Tragedy of Ramsay MacDonald*, Secker & Warburg, 1938.

WILMOT, Chester, *The Struggle for Europe*, Collins, 1952.

WRIGHT, Peter, *At the Supreme War Council*, E. Nash, 1921.

WRENCH, John Evelyn, *Struggle, 1914–1920*, Ivor Nicholson & Watson, 1935.
    Geoffrey Dawson and our Times, Hutchinson, 1955.

WOODBURN, Kirby S., *War Against Japan*, H.M.S.O., 1957.

WEBSTER, Sir Charles and FRANKLAND, N., *The Strategic Air Offensive Against Germany, 1939–45*, H.M.S.O., 1961.

YOUNG, George Malcolm, *Stanley Baldwin*, Hart-Davis, 1952.

Notes on Sources

There are five principal sources on which I have drawn for Trenchard's version of the events in this biography.

1 His *Autobiographical Notes*: some 130 pages of manuscript which appear to have been dictated by Trenchard in the early 1920s. They are more reliable, in my judgment, for expressions of opinion than for detailed facts such as dates, names of places and people, etc.

2 The *Trenchard Papers*: the voluminous official papers which Trenchard kept from 1914 onwards.

3 The *Trenchard Correspondence*: scores of letters between Trenchard and the political and military leaders over many years.

4 *Trenchard conversations*: during the last ten months of his life in 1955, I visited him almost daily and filled six bulky notebooks with his reminiscences and reflections. It was usually possible to check this personal information subsequently against official records; in doing so I found Trenchard's memory to be remarkably accurate, even at the end of his life.

5 I interviewed over 600 of Trenchard's colleagues and contemporaries, both famous and little-known. Their evidence also served to expand and corroborate Trenchard's own records.

In the course of the narrative I have often included quotations of direct speech. Scholarly historians tend to object to this practice, but I consider it perfectly justifiable where the spoken words are clearly remembered by reliable witnesses.

CHAPTER 1: A VICTORIAN CHILD
The main evidence for the facts of Trenchard's family and childhood come from two original sources: the two volumes of the Trenchard family annals and the conversations of the author with Trenchard himself.

CHAPTER 2: THE SOLDIER
1–3 Autobiographical Notes and conversations.

CHAPTER 3: THE PHOENIX
1   Autobiographical Notes.
2, 3 Buchan, *History of the Royal Scots Fusiliers*, p. 217.
4   Major-General E. A. Beck.

5   Autobiographical Notes, confirmed, by Sergeant Lewis in a letter home.

CHAPTER 4: THE LEADER
1, 2 Autobiographical Notes.
3   Trenchard conversations, and Group Captain J. R. W. Smyth Pigott.
4   Edward Steel, *A Memoir*.

CHAPTER 5: AIR APPRENTICE
1   Marshal of the R.A.F. Sir E. Ellington.
2   *War in the Air*, Vol. 1.
3   Air Commodore E. L. Gerrard and information given privately to the author.
4   Autobiographical Notes, corroborated by Group Captain J. R. W. Smyth Pigott.
5   Lieutenant-General Sir B. Fisher.
6   Biard, *Wings*, p. 47.
7   Information given privately to the author.
8   See Ryan, *Mutiny at the Curragh*, pp. 95–7, 106–7, 202–3.
9   Blake, *The Unknown Prime Minister*, pp. 121–6.
10 Ryan, *Mutiny at the Curragh*, p. 99.

CHAPTER 6: THE IMPROVISER
1   MacMillan, *Brancker*.
2   Churchill, *The World Crisis*, Vol. 1, p. 265.
3   *War in the Air*, Vol. 2, pp. 88–9.
4   Autobiographical Notes, corroborated by Air Chief Marshal Sir John Salmond, T. E. Bates and others.
5   Autobiographical Notes.
6   *War in the Air*, Vol. 2, p. 124.

CHAPTER 7: THE AGGRESSOR
1. Baring, *H.Q., R.F.C*, pp. 105–7.
2   Lord Brabazon.
3   Wing-Commander Sir Archibald James.
4   Autobiographical Notes.
5   Churchill, *The World Crisis*, Vol. 1, p. 266.
6   Quoted in *The Private Papers of Douglas Haig*, p. 126.

CHAPTER 8: THE PROPHET
1   Baring, *H.Q., R.F.C.*, p. 130.
2   Air Chief Marshal Sir Philip Game; also Baring, *H.Q., R.F.C.*, p. 134, and Autobiographical Notes.
3   Autobiographical Notes.

CHAPTER 9: THE ROCK

1 Ballaiche Air Enquiry Report, Nov. 1916.
2 Autobiographical Notes.
3 Euan Gilchrist.
4 The late Viscount Weir's private papers.
5 Autobiographical Notes.
6 *War in the Air*, Vol. 3, p. 323.
7 *The Private Papers of Douglas Haig.*
8 Trenchard conversations; see also *War in the Air*, Vol. 5, p. 29.
9 *War in the Air*, Vol. 6, pp. 2–3; also Henderson private papers.
10 Edmonds, *History of the Great War*, Vol. 12, p. 371.

CHAPTER 10: THE HOSTAGE

1 Trenchard Papers, corroborated by Weir personally and by the Trenchard-Brancker correspondence.
2 The Smuts Report. See also Churchill's memorandum on this subject, dated 21st Oct. 1917, and quoted in *The World Crisis*, Vol. IV, Appendix N.
3, 4 The late Viscount Weir.
5 Autobiographical Notes and conversations.
6 The late Viscount Weir.
7 Lloyd George, *War Memoirs*, Vol. 4, p, 2228.
8 Autobiographical Notes.
9 Baring, *H.Q. R.F.C.*, p. 259.
10 Autobiographical Notes.
11 Air Chief Marshal Sir Arthur Longcroft, corroborated by Trenchard Papers.
12 Angus Hambro and Lord Hugh Cecil.
13 Autobiographical Notes.

CHAPTER 11: BOMBER BARON

1, 2 Autobiographical Notes.
3 Beaverbrook, *Men and Power*, p. 222.
4 Trenchard conversations.
5 The late Viscount Weir's private papers.
6 Angus Hambro, Marshal of the R.A.F. Sir Edward Ellington and others; see also *Repington's Diary*, Vol. 2, p. 283.
7 Trenchard's "Operational Diary" (Nancy) consists of four small notebooks and covers the six months from May to Nov. 1918.
8 Baring, *H.Q., R.F.C.*, p. 296.
9 Autobiographical Notes, confirmed by Salmond.

CHAPTER 12: THE COMEBACK

1 Group Captain J. R. W. Smyth Pigott's notes and oral testimony

(The substance of the narrative from p. 317 to p. 325 is drawn from two principal sources: Trenchard's own written account and his official report to the War Office on the Southampton mutiny.)

2 The late Viscount Weir.

3 Trenchard conversations and Autobiographical Notes.

4 Trenchard-Weir correspondence.

5–8 Trenchard conversations and evidence supplied by Lady Trenchard.

9 General Seeley (later Lord Mottistone) as reported in Trenchard conversations.

10 Trenchard conversations, confirmed by Lord Hankey.

11 Trenchard conversations, confirmed by the late Captain Marson.

CHAPTER 13: POOR RELATIONS

1 Trenchard conversations, corroborated by Maurice Baring's private papers.

2 Trenchard Papers (Air Staff); also Marshals of the R.S.F. Sir Arthur Harris and Sir John Salmond, and Trenchard conversations.

3 Trenchard Papers corroborated by conversations.

4 Trenchard Papers (Air Staff), confirmed by the late Captain Marson.

5 Caldwell: *Field-Marshal Sir Henry Wilson: His life and diary*, p.216.

6 Churchill: *The Aftermath*, Appendix, p. 461.

7 Trenchard conversations corroborated by the late Captain Marson and others.

8 Trenchard papers (Air Staff) corroborated by conversations.

9 Though Trenchard, as shown, recovered the use of his paralyzed legs after being gravely wounded in South Africa, he never fully regained control of his hands. This so affected his ability to write that he would hold his right wrist in his left hand to steady it when signing his name.

10 Trenchard Papers and conversations.

CHAPTER 14: THE HERETIC

1 Trenchard Papers (Air Staff) and conversations.

2 Trenchard conversations corroborated by the late Captain Marson.

3 Trenchard conversations, the late Captain Marson and Charles Evans, and Sir Christopher Bullock.

4, 5 Trenchard Papers (Air Staff).

CHAPTER 15: THE UNWANTED

1 Frank Owen, *Tempestuous Journey*, p. 631.

2 Trenchard–Brooke-Popham correspondence.

3   Marshal of the R.A.F. Lord Portal, and A. Gordon Bond. Corroborated by Captain Marson.

4   Maurice Baring.

5   Trenchard-Lawrence correspondence, conversations; see also Churchill, *Great Contemporaries*, p. 125 (Odhams Edition).

6   Trenchard conversations.

7   Trenchard conversations, also Lady Trenchard.

8   Air Commodore the Hon. J. D. Boyle.

9   Blake, *The Unknown Prime Minister*, p. 446.

10   Templewood, *Empire of the Air*, pp. 36 and 42.

CHAPTER 16: THE UNDEFEATED

The great mass of written evidence in the Admiralty-Air Ministry controversy is contained in six bulky files among the Trenchard Papers (Air Staff).

1   Templewood, *Empire of the Air*, p. 60.

2   Autobiographical Notes.

3   Trenchard Papers (Air Staff).

4   Salmond's Operational Diary (1922–23).

5   Blake, *The Unknown Prime Minister*, p. 488.

6   Curzon, *The Last Phase*, p. 324.

7   Hoare Memorandum (among the Trenchard Papers).

8   Trenchard Papers (Air Staff) and conversations.

9   This was the opinion of the late Charles Evans, also Sir Christopher Bullock and the Air Staff generally.

10   Templewood, *Empire of the Air*, p. 61.

11   Trenchard Papers (Admiralty); the Naval side of the case is more than adequately given in these, the aim of the Air Staff and of Trenchard in particular being to examine the Naval arguments systematically one by one.

12   Templewood, *Empire of the Air*, p. 61.

13   Harris, *Bomber Offensive*, p. 22.

14, 15 Trenchard Papers (Admiralty); also Lord Hankey and the late Viscount Weir. A comparison between Balfour's amendments and Weir's first draft indicates that the elder statesman was more concerned about style and presentation than about substance.

16   Templewood, *Empire of the Air*, p. 65.

17   Amery, *My Political Life*, pp. 264–5.

CHAPTER 17: THE MASTER-BUILDER

1   Chalmers, *The Life and Letters of David, Earl Beatty*, p. 344.

2   It must be said that Wilson and Cavan, with the respective staffs, were primarily responsible for underwriting the Admiralty plan to defend Singapore mainly with fixed naval guns. It was the War

Office contention from 1921 onwards that no enemy could land and occupy the impassable jungle terrain of the hinterland. The Admiralty, for various reasons, accepted the contention: The Air Staff held to its reservations.

3   Trenchard Papers (Air Staff).
4   Haldane as quoted by Trenchard in conversations.
5   Trenchard Papers (Air Staff).
6   Trenchard conversations.
7   Templewood, *Empire of the Air*, p. 193.

CHAPTER 18: THE ANTI-CLIMAX

1   Though this is the common verdict of all Chiefs of Staff at any period on the reigning Chancellor of the Exchequer, Trenchard held that Churchill's rare strategic acumen made him somewhat exceptional to the normal rule of criticism.
2   Churchill, *The Aftermath*.
3   Trenchard Papers (Air Staff).
4   Colwyn Committee Enquiry, as contained in Trenchard Papers (Air Staff). Proceedings of the separate Churchill-Birkenhead investigation of the Air Expansion Scheme are grouped in separate folders.
5   Trenchard conversations.
6   From *Airman's Song Book*, Ed. C. H. Ward Jackson (1945), Sylvan Press, London.
7   Chatfield, *It Might Happen Again*, p. 11.
8   Grigg, *Prejudice and Judgment*, p. 133.
9   Sir P. J. Grigg and Sir Christopher Bullock.
10 Churchill, *Second World War*, Vol. 4, Appendix D, by Pownall, p. 764-7.
11 The late Captain Marson.
12 Trenchard Papers (Air Staff).
13 Trenchard Papers (Air Staff), corroborated by Sir Francis Humphrys.
14 Trenchard Papers (Air Staff).
15 Trenchard Papers (Air Staff): " Last Will and Testament."

CHAPTER 19: POLICE REFORMER

1   Trenchard conversations confirmed by Maurice Baring.
2   Moylan, *Scotland Yard*, p. 328. Goddard "secured for himself a sum more than sufficient to bribe a whole Division."
3   Warren Fisher's confidential note: a copy of this is in the Trenchard Papers. See also Viscount Samuel *Memoirs*, pp. 219-20.
4   Trenchard Papers (Press).
5   Howgrave Graham, *Light and Shade at Scotland Yard*, pp. 22-4.
6 *et seq.* The Trenchard Police papers are a large collection, ranging

from the highly confidential to the scurrilous type of anonymous letter already quoted in the text. They include not only copies of all important reforms, from the draft stage to the finished "plan for the Cabinet," but the Buckingham Palace correspondence, the voluminous private correspondence between Trenchard and the Home Secretary, and confidential reports on many of the activities —good and bad—of the various Scotland Yard Departments, Police districts and so forth. These records have still to be catalogued and classified.

7   Trenchard conversations, confirmed by Sir John Ferguson.
8   Testimony given to the author by Police Officers who wish to remain anonymous.
9   Trenchard conversations and papers (Police Reform).
10 Lord Swinton.
11 Trenchard correspondence.
12 Autobiographical Notes. It is also worth recording that Lansbury never again attacked Trenchard in public.

CHAPTER 20: POLICE ADMINISTRATOR

1   *The Spectator*, November 23rd, 1934.
2   Trenchard conversations confirmed by Lady Astor.
3   Trenchard-Gilmour correspondence.
4   Trenchard papers confirmed by Sir John Ferguson. The latest figures indicate that virtually fifty per cent of all Hendon graduates who persevered in their careers as policemen reached the rank of Chief Constables
5   Trenchard-Nott Bower correspondence.

CHAPTER 21: THE ORACLE

1   Trenchard Papers (Air Staff).
2   Vansittart, *The Mist Procession*, pp. 443-4.
3   Wrench, *Geoffrey Dawson*, p. 310.
4, 5 Trenchard conversations, confirmed by Captain Liddell Hart.
6   Wrench, *Geoffrey Dawson*.
7   Confirmed by Churchill in *The Second World War*, Vol. 1, Appendix B, p. 536. See also Chatfield, *It Might Happen Again*, p. 108.
8   Trenchard conversations.
9   Chatfield, *It Might Happen Again*, p. 109.
10 Trenchard conversations, partly confirmed by his Papers.
11 Trenchard-Chamberlain correspondence. Also Lord Templewood.
12 Trenchard Papers.
13 Churchill note on the meeting with Trenchard.
14 The late Viscount Weir and Captain Marson.
15 Bolitho, *Penguin in the Eyrie*, p. 219.

Index

749